SOURCEBOOK

The Dream of Steam, 1854–1873

Other Santa Cruz Trains books
by Derek R. Whaley

Santa Cruz Trains: Railroads of the Santa Cruz Mountains
Santa Cruz Trains: Reflections on the Mountain Route
SIDETRACKED: Laurel & Glenwood
SIDETRACKED: The Santa Cruz Beach to 1903

Other books by Zayante Publishing
The History of Rancho Soquel Augmentation
by Ronald G. Powell
Part 1: *The Tragedy of Martina Castro*
Part 2: *The Reign of the Lumber Barons*
Part 3: *The Shadow of Loma Prieta*

Our Old Santa Cruz... Volumes 1–2
by Ernest Otto

SOURCEBOOK

The Dream of Steam, 1854–1873

Compiled by
Derek R. Whaley

First edition, April 2025

Published by Zayante Publishing
Santa Cruz, California

www.ZayantePublishing.com
www.SantaCruzTrains.com

ISBN 978-1-953609-07-6

Library of Congress Control Number: 2025905892

Copyright © 2025 Derek R. Whaley
The moral right of the author has been asserted.

All rights reserved. Without limiting the rights under copyright reserved above, no part of this publication may be reproduced, stored or introduced into a retrieval system, or transmitted, in any form or by any means (electronic, mechanical, photocopying, recording, or otherwise), without the prior written permission of the copyright owner.

Publisher's Cataloging-in-Publication data
Santa Cruz Trains Sourcebook : The Dream of Steam,
1854–1873 / compiled by Derek R. Whaley.—1st ed.
Santa Cruz Trains
xiv, 774 p. ; 21 cm
ISBN 978-1-953609-07-6
1. Santa Cruz County (Calif.)—History. 2. Santa Cruz (Calif.)—History. 3, Watsonville (Calif.)—History. 4. Southern Pacific Railroad Company—History. 5. Railroads—California—Santa Cruz County—History. 7. California—History, Local. I. Whaley, Derek R. 1983–. II. Title. III. Series.
F868 .S3 W43 2025
979.471   2025905892

Contents

Introduction vii

Sources 1

Appendix 747

Introduction

By Derek R. Whaley

The people of Santa Cruz County, California, love to debate railroads. Indeed, it may be one of the county's oldest pastimes. The first published debate on the topic occurred in January 1864, only fourteen years after statehood and over five years before the completion of the transcontinental railroad. The earliest surviving reference to a train to Santa Cruz County was made in the *San Jose Telegraph* in May 1854 as the aspirational goal of a still conceptual San Francisco and San Jose Railroad. The earliest editorial on the topic was published in the *Santa Cruz Sentinel* on December 13, 1862. And discussion has continued ever since, ebbing and flowing with the tides of popular discourse, political interest, and economic realities.

This sourcebook memorializes these early discussions relating to railroads to and within Santa Cruz County in the years prior to the incorporation of the county's first successful railroad, the Santa Cruz Railroad, in May 1873. A sourcebook such as this is an academic tool, often used in teaching. It gathers together quotes from a variety of sources and organizes them in a logical manner and theme. This book is arranged chronologically around the theme of local railroading news, discussions, analyses, debates, and opinions. In total, there are over 500 articles that together form a record of the motivations and difficulties of building railroads in Santa Cruz County around the time of the American Civil War.

The sources included in this book are almost entirely from local newspapers because that is where the idea of railroads was first widely discussed and debated. Around thirty newspapers and publications from throughout California are quoted, some directly, others via an intermediary source. In addition, an appendix includes transcriptions of articles of incorporation of nine companies that intended to build a railroad to or through Santa Cruz County prior to 1873. All but one of these were transcribed from the originals or certified copies held at the California State Library and the Santa Cruz Museum of Art & History.

The vast majority of the newspaper articles come from two four-page weekly newspapers: the *Santa Cruz Sentinel* and Watsonville's *Pajaronian*. The *Sentinel*'s origins date to the 1855 *Monterey Sentinel*, which became *The Pacific Sentinel* when its owner, John McElroy, moved to Santa Cruz in 1856. The name settled on *Santa Cruz Sentinel* in June 1862, at which time it was owned by several men, most notably Charles Osgood Cummings. Duncan

McPherson came on in 1864 and eventually became majority shareholder of the company in 1879. Around the same time, Benjamin Parke Kooser became part owner and served as editor-in-chief until 1876.

A companion to the *Sentinel* arose in Watsonville in April 1863 under the name *The Pajaro Times*, which altered its name several times over the following eight years, although most other newspapers simply called it the *Times*. Following almost annual changes in ownership and a general lack of direction, the *Times* was incorporated into the *Sentinel* in July 1871. Throughout its brief existence, the *Times* exchanged letters and editorials with the *Sentinel* and provided occasional counterpoints, but relations were generally cordial between the two papers.

The same could not be said about the *Sentinel*'s more prominent rival in Watsonville, the uniquely named *The Pajaronian*. Founded by Joseph A. Cottle on March 5, 1868, the *Pajaronian* focused its attention on both sides of the Pajaro Valley, as well as Corralitos and sometimes Aptos, leaving the rest of Santa Cruz County to the *Sentinel*. Charles O. Cummings, previously of the *Sentinel*, took over the *Pajaronian* in October 1868 and brought a fiercely combative spirit to the local newspaper arena.

These newspapers differentiated themselves both in geographic focus and in political inclination. The *Sentinel* was a hardline Republican Party-oriented newspaper and the *Pajaronian* a Democratic stalwart. This situated the two papers against each other on many issues and allowed for heated exchanges in the editorial columns between Kooser and Cummings, some of which are featured in this sourcebook. While the two editors generally remained on friendly terms in life, their discourses often became impassioned. Nonetheless, these papers were first and foremost meant for advertisements and the editors had to maintain a strict balance between advertisements, news, sports and society, weekly serials, letters to the editor, editorials, and government notices.

This sourcebook follows a format similar to that developed by Christopher Tolkien for his collection, *The Letters of J. R. R. Tolkien*. Each transcribed article is given an article number and citation information, including the publication name, page number, and column numbers (in parentheses); for example: 19. *Santa Cruz Sentinel*, March 26, 1864 (2:1). Anyone wishing to cite an article in this book can either use the provided source information—most of the original articles are available on the California Digital Newspapers Collection (CDNC) or Newspapers.com—or cite this book and the article number rather than the page numbers.

Collecting the material for this volume was a time-consuming process. It was gathered primarily by searching issue-by-issue, page-by-page through the *Sentinel*, *Pajaronian*, and *Times* between their foundings and May 1873. However, some issues are missing from the microfilm and digital records, and others were captured so poorly as to render them unreadable. Thus, there are a few instances where one source will reference an article in another source but that other source is unavailable. Where these three newspapers quote from or reference other newspapers, the original articles are included, when possible, but their sources have not been researched with the same degree of thoroughness as the *Sentinel*, *Pajaronian*, and *Times*.

In the age of type-set printing, there was much room for error and newspapers were more prone to this due to the speed at which they had to be assembled and printed. Thus, newspapers in general had a high number of typographical errors, often in the form of spelling and punctuation errors. In this sourcebook, these types of errors have been corrected when obviously made in error, but stylistic spellings and punctuation have been retained. American English was also less standardized in the nineteenth century, so spellings of words may differ from those today, but these have been retained to remain faithful to the original source material. Nonetheless, some transcription errors have doubtless made it into this book and will hopefully be corrected in future editions through user feedback.

A sourcebook concerning the development of railroads in and around Santa Cruz County is a new approach to an old topic and one that will hopefully provide clarity regarding why a railroad was sought in those early days. This book was designed first and foremost to assist me in my own research for my next major book, *Santa Cruz Trains: The Road to San Francisco*, and other books I have planned. However, I hope it also proves informative and even entertaining to everyone who reads it. The history of railroads in Santa Cruz County is long and complicated—this sourcebook provides the first deep look into the origins of that history.

SOURCEBOOK

The Dream of Steam, 1854–1873

Sources

1. *San Jose Telegraph* **via the** *Shasta Courier*, **May 13, 1854 (4:1)**

Railroad.—We learn that there is in contemplation a survey of a route for a continuation of the San Francisco and San Jose Railroad, as far as the Rio Pajaro. Doubtless the people of our valley, and those below us, will be glad to hear of this. The project is a laudable one, and all feel interested in its success. We are pleased to learn, also, that the road from San Francisco to this place will be commenced soon.

2. *Pacific Sentinel*, **June 1, 1860 (2:3)**

Railroad near Santa Cruz.—The enterprising proprietors of one of the lime kilns, one mile from town, have built a railroad, on which they transport their rock, and the wood with which they burn it. The road extends in the direction of the redwoods, and when completed will be two or three miles in length. These gentlemen employ their capital beneficially to the county, and are of that class of men before whom obstacles to improvement recede as shadows before the sun, as it ascends to its meridian.

3. *Santa Cruz Sentinel*, July 4, 1862 (2:2)

There are thousands of people living in the mountains who are looking to the valleys for permanent homes; and no greater kindness can be done them than to show them the right place. Every year the facilities for reaching this place will be likely to improve. The railroad to San Jose, in effect, shortens the distance from San Francisco to this place; and it will yet be for the interest of some enterprising party to increase the facilities by water.

4. *Santa Cruz Sentinel*, September 13, 1862 (2:3)

It may be well, also, to keep in mind the fact that, before another summer comes round, the railroad will be completed to San Jose. It will then be little more than half day's ride from San Francisco to Santa Cruz—and with just the right proportion between rail and stage to make the trip interesting.

5. *Santa Cruz Sentinel*, December 13, 1862 (2:1)

The Pacific Railroad Terminus.

The *Sentinel* having listened quietly to the Railroad discussion of all the other papers in the State, now claims its put in. More modest than the San Francisco press, it will not require the Pacific Railroad to terminate at the seaport of Santa Cruz before the work is begun. A long-headed old codger from New York once said: "No matter where the Pacific Railroad is located, it will run to New York." The wise men of San Francisco do not feel equally easy in reference to their city, as well they may not; for the Pacific Railroad, after arriving at San Jose, can reach the ocean at Santa Cruz in thirty-five miles—a shorter distance by ten miles than it will require to go to the rival port of San Francisco. Ten miles, at $50,000 a mile, is precisely half a million dollars—a larger sum than San Francisco, with all her boasted wealth and shrewdness in business, will subscribe towards any Railroad outside of her corporation limits. The comparative advantages of Santa Cruz and San Francisco as a terminus will eventually receive the attention of those who ride on railroads. In the meantime, it is earnestly hoped that this rivalry between the two principal seaports of the Pacific coast will not deter the gentlemen named in the act of Congress from prosecuting their great work from any point on the interior waters of the State towards the city of New York, as fast as possible. We assure those gentlemen, that the difficulties between Santa Cruz and San Francisco will be solved in good time. If we cannot convince them that ours is the best point to reach the ocean, we will not complain, though the magnificent benefits of their enterprise be poured into the lap of our rival.

We acknowledge to a little chagrin that neither place will subscribe to the great undertaking till the question of terminus is definitely settled between us. But then neither of these two ports, nor yet both of them together, contain all the available capital of the country; nor is the entire business capacity of all the United States and Europe concentrated (we mean no offence) in San Francisco. It seems to us at this distance, that the California Company will be able to go ahead independently of our arrival at the Bay. Forty-eight thousand dollars to the mile, virtually donated by the Government, is a great deal better than subscriptions to that extent in San Francisco, Santa Cruz, or anywhere else, and then it is said the Company have munificent land and timber grants. It will be noted that we, unlike our brethren of San Francisco, encourage the great scheme of linking the West to the East, and our generosity in this regard ought not to be overlooked when finally the question of reaching a seaport is debated.

But there is a rumor afloat which, so far as the California Company is concerned, required an explanation. It is said they are constructing a turnpike road over the Sierra Nevadas, nearly on a line of their proposed Railroad, which toll road will be immensely profitable as soon as a small portion of the Railroad is completed, and continue to pay enormously till the rails are laid quite to Washoe. In fact, we have the authority of the Alta, Call, Bulletin, *et id omne genus* of papers in Stockton, Oroville, Marysville and Placerville, that the said toll and Railroads will take all the trade and travel to and from Washoe and Humboldt. And this is precisely the complaint—that the California Company should, in addition to their magnificent Government franchise, also monopolize the rich transmountain trade to Nevada Territory. It would afford immense relief to some, if the Legislature about to meet, would further amend the State Constitution so as to prohibit the said Company from transporting any freight or passengers over their line till completed entirely to Washoe. Such a provision would eliminate the chief opposition to the enterprise, and leave newspapers in general free to advocate the taking of stock.

It cannot be counted otherwise than unfair, that this new Railroad and turnpike should be made, or be permitted to become, richly paying concerns almost from the start, to the detriment of existing toll roads, neither of which has paid for itself more than half-a-dozen times over as yet; and to the prejudice, likewise, if not ruin, of one real and seventeen other imaginary Railroads. The California Company, in order to relieve itself from this charge of bad faith, should immediately disclaim any intention of making their end of the Pacific Railroad a paying institution.

That our remarks may have their due weight in fixing destinies of the great Atlantic and Pacific Railway, it is proper that we should make known in this connection, that we own no stock in any other Railroad, nor in any toll road over the mountains. As to whether we ought not to possess a few shares in the California Pacific Railroad, in consideration of our disinterestedness, is a question which we confidently submit to the Directors of that Company.

6. *Santa Cruz Sentinel*, March 28, 1863 (2:1)

Watsonville is the trading place for the inhabitants many miles beyond the valley; teams can be seen constantly coming and going from and to the country; this taken in connection with the fact that there are prospects of connecting that place with San Francisco by Railroad sooner or later, and what may we not prophetically say of her future.

7. *California Wine, Wool, and Stock Journal,* July 1863 (129)

Watsonville

This town has improved wonderfully, during the past year. Many new buildings and stores have been erected, streets laid out, and at present, I am told, there are one hundred licensed business houses of various kinds in town, of which over thirty are devoted to merchandise and supplies for the whole country around, including the great Pajaro Valley to San Juan and the Salinas, who depend upon this place for their supplies. With the impetus given to it from the facilities of ocean navigation, and the steamer which plies between here and San Francisco, together with the prospect of increased communication and trade by the railroad to San Jose, it bids fair to become a commercial town of some importance in the future. Notwithstanding the dry weather, the Pajaro Valley, with its extensive grain fields, looks prolific indeed, and no cause for complaint at present exists as to any possible injury to the grain crops.

8. *Santa Cruz Sentinel,* September 26, 1863 (2:1)

SANTA CRUZ—FUTURE PROSPECTS.

The San Francisco and San Jose Rail Road has been completed as far as Belmont, 20 miles. In one month it will be completed to Redwood city. Some time next Winter the cars will be running to San Jose. There are now, at least, one hundred persons traveling daily between San Francisco and San Jose, by the Sophie McLane and the stage routes on either side of the bay. It is reasonable to assert that at least 25,000 persons, other than the regular business travel, will go Southward on the new rail road, next summer.

San Jose has no attraction to retain a stranger more than a day beyond his business engagements. A man of ordinary capacity can *do* San Jose in twenty-four hours. There is nothing there to invite a longer state.—No mountains—no beautiful scenery—no ocean—no sea beach. Now every one must have noticed the instinct in humanity, to push beyond any prescribed limit. No one was ever satisfied to stop at the terminus of a rail road, unless that terminus was in a great metropolis. Each one longs for the *ultima thule*, he wants to go beyond. Of the 25,000 reaching San Jose, each with this instinct in his breast, one half will be deterred by reason of expenses or urgency of business, from proceeding further and return home. The other half, 12,500, will conclude to go elsewhere. Where will they go? They will not go back to the Warm Springs, because they have all been at the springs. They will not go to Gilroy, that is no place. Where can they go but to Santa Cruz? especially, as it is becoming famous all over the State, for its attractions and watering place. By that time we shall be able to offer the inducement,—which is irresistible to a man seeking pleasure, of elegant and luxurious hotels. It is mathematically certain therefore, that we may expect 12,500 strangers here next summer. Of these, one half, or 6,250 will be looking out for a safe, healthy, flourishing business place, in which to invest. Where, in the State of California, can they find a more promising field for investment than Santa Cruz County, with its rich uncultivated lands, capable of supporting a population of 100,000,—with its mountains as favorable for the cultivation of the grape as the hills of France,—with its harbor, a safe haven for ships during three quarters of the year, and which can be rendered, with a small outlay, perpetually safe,—with its inexhaustible supply of timber,—with its mineral wealth, still undeveloped,—with the water power of the San Lorenzo. One half of the 6,750, or 3,375 will be induced by these attractions to locate in this vicinity. This reasoning is by no means chimerical, it is reasonable and logical. We must therefore be prepared for a great increase of population and business. The *Sentinel* will always be on the *qui vive* to give them all desired information.

9. *Santa Cruz Sentinel,* November 28, 1863 (2:2)

General Prospects.

Many improvements are on the tapis which only require time and capital to develop, Buildings are rapidly going up in Santa Cruz and Watsonville. A rail road from Santa Cruz to the interior of the County for the purpose of bringing more easily to the coast the lumber and minerals of the interior, is contemplated. In a few years a rail road will be constructed to meet the extension of the San Francisco and San Jose railroad southward. Santa Cruz is already very much visited as a watering place for which it has attractions that will eventually make it *the* great centre of fashionable resort in the summer. Labor is at all times in demand and well paid. There are therefore in this County a variety of channels and fields for a remunerative investment of capital or a lucrative return for labor which is rarely found elsewhere in the same compass of territory.

10. *Pajaro Times*, January 1864, republished on February 10, 1866 (2:4)

This question so carefully asked by doubting men, will bear a most favorable calculation. Without multiplying words, we will multiply figures; and in so doing, earnestly request the attention of our readers to the result. We have within our valley—that is to say the McDougal, Va[squez], Ximanos, Rodriguez, Amesti, and Castro ranches—sixty-thousand acres under cultivation, one third of which was in wheat the past year. Twenty thousand acres in barley equaling fifty bushels per acre, weighing fifty pounds to the bushel, gives twenty-five thousand tons. Ten thousand acres in potatoes, at one hundred and fifty bushels per acre, at sixty pounds to the bushel, will equal forty-five thousand tons. Ten thousand acres in beans and other products, giving fifteen hundred pounds to the acre, will equal seven thousand two hundred tons. Allowing one-tenth of the whole crop for home consumption, amounting to nine thousand five hundred and twenty tons, leaves eight-five thousand six hundred and eighty tons. Add to this two thousand tons of back freight, making eighty-seven thousand six hundred and eighty tons for Pajaro Valley. Allowing $4 per ton, will amount to $350,720. San Juan and Pacheco valleys could give but little freight, unless the road should pass through Flint & Bixby's, Colonel Hollister's, and Crane's ranches—at the same time making it convenient for the Pacheco, San Philepa, and Santa Anna ranches. This route will throw about fifty thousand acres into cultivation, which would give, at the least calculation, thirty-five thousand tons of freight. The freight that has been brought from San Francisco and San Jose to San Juan, Pacheco, San Joaquin and Visalia, was about fifteen hundred tons the past year. The amount of wool freight from San Juan and Salinas was about four hundred tons the past year. The New Idria quicksilver mines, which, without doubt, will be at work before long, produces one thousand flasks per month, weighing one hundred pounds per flask, equal to six hundred pounds per annum, and back freight forty tons per month, equal to four hundred and eighty tons per annum—in all making thirty-seven thousand nine hundred and eighty tons for San Juan. This, at $3.50, would give $132,930. Add to this twenty thousand head of beef cattle at one dollar per head, and twenty thousand head of sheep at twenty-five cents per head, making in all $152,930. This added to Pajaro freight amounts to $503,650. Should the Burra Burra mines prove to be rich—and there are but little doubts of that—with other leads in the same district, which will probably pay well, would give to this road an immense amount of freight. The freight would be brought down the San Benito. An excellent road can be made, with but little cost; the distance would not exceed thirty-eight miles in length to where it would strike the proposed railroad route. From Gilroy to San Jose there are about one hundred and ten thousand acres of valley land, and, about one half of this is under cultivation. Allowing fifteen hundred pounds to the acre, would give forty-one thousand two hundred and fifty tons of produce, which, at $2.50 per ton, would amount to $123,750. Add to this the two million feet of sawed lumber, at $5 per thousand, and five thousand cords of wood at $2 per cord, beside posts and rails, stock, butter, cheese, etc., say $5,000, making in all for the entire freight, $661,400. Allowing thirty-three and one-third per cent. for the privilege of running over the San Francisco road, which will leave $440,033. Now, let us see what the expenses of the road will probably be. Every eight miles of the road between San Jose and Watsonville requires five men—seven sections thirty-men and freight men. Six men to make repairs at each end of the road, and eight freight-men at each end of the road; also, two engineers, two firemen, and five brakemen—in all, seventy-five men—fifty of whom, at $50 per month, would be $30,000 per annum; twenty-five men at $100 per month, would be $25,000; and officers $30,000; three thousand five hundred cords of wood, at $250 per cord, $8.750; and $30,000 for general expenses— making in all $128,750 expenses per annum. This taken from $444,033, would leave $312,183. The road will cost $20,000 per mile stocked, (the distance being sixty miles,) or $1,200,000. $312,183 would give an interest of twenty-five per cent. on $1,200,000. This is a flattering showing, without adding the enormous traffic in passenger and incidental freight. We are all interested in this project, and let the work commence. Let meetings be called in the different towns, that the question may be thoroughly canvassed, and the proper statements set forth capable of inducing immediate action. We must have a railroad; and it is silly to indulge a doubt whether the enterprise will pay. Let our San Jose and San Francisco capitalists consider upon the question. It will be a safe investment.

11. *Santa Cruz Sentinel,* January 23, 1864 (2:1-2)
THE RAILROAD.

Our friends in Watsonville will never cease to build "castles in Spain." At one time their little hamlet will be the metropolis of a great agricultural county; at another time they will have a railroad at their doors and the steam-car shelf wheel them and their produce to distant places and bountiful markets. How they dispose of the somewhat weighty considerations, that in the one case the lands of Santa Cruz and Monterey lie on the top of their broad, fanciful acres, and in the other, that it will require some smart legerdemain to call into existence a couple of millions, we are not advised; but as these questions belong to practice, and they are theorists, it is likely they do not trouble themselves about them. Well, they have precedent for the chimeras. Sir Thomas More dreamed of Utopia three hundred years ago. Now in saying this, we certainly are not affected by any feeling of puerile rivalry which by some persons is supposed to exist between the citizens of Santa Cruz and Watsonville. We should still rejoice in the prosperity of Watsonville, if the Fates should so revolve that Santa Cruz returned to

The Dream of Steam, 1854–1873   13

chaos. But we would willingly, of, friends, aid you to dismount from your airy Pegasus which seems inclined to fly away with you. Suppose a railroad could be built from San Jose to Watsonville—a distance somewhat over fifty miles—for one million of dollars—and the probability is that it would cost over two millions—from what secret coffer would you get the first ten per cent.? After the railroad was built, what would you do with it? You would have a white elephant on your hands. If some genie should build for you in a single night a complete railroad from Watsonville to San Jose, and you should offer it free of charge to the San Francisco and San Jose Rail Road Company, it is very doubtful whether they would accept it, upon the conditions that they should run cars upon it more than half the year. The Pajaro valley is very fertile; but, two trains of cars a day would in less than thirty days wheel away its entire annual agricultural product. After that time, the travel between Watsonville and San Jose would not warrant the running of a train of cars a day, or even every other day. Your main, avowed object of a railroad is, that you may get your produce to market. Have you not observed that Nature has spread out between you and the principal market on this coast a broad highway, upon which she asks no toll? As if to invite you to use this highway, she extends from it towards you for several miles a byway; you call it a slough. But what's in a name? The simplest, cheapest and most natural mode of transportation is by water; the most intricate, expensive and artificial is by railroad. Before you can be said to have tried the natural, you talk of the artificial. Do you wonder that we smile because you talk of a railroad, when we know that for years you have permitted one enterprising man to govern and monopolize this, your simple and natural channel for transit and transportation? Do you wonder that we smile, because you talk of expending millions for a railroad, when you do not seem inclined to lay out mere thousands for what would at present be better than a railroad? Cease your vagaries, your chimeras and your romancing, and enter upon what is practical, practicable and possible, you have in the Assembly a representative from your own town, a capable and energetic man. The able Senator from your District is also very friendly to your interests. You will have no difficulty in obtaining from the Legislature such a franchise as may be necessary for the improvement of the Pajaro river, so as to render it permanently navigable, and for the construction of wharves on it. Less than $100,000 judiciously expended would render the Pajaro river permanently navigable, would build the necessary wharves upon it and would place upon the route between Watsonville and San Francisco two substantial propellers, which could run regularly, at a stated hour, from Watsonville four times a week. The passage from Watsonville to San Francisco would then be safe, quick, pleasant and certain, and the steamers would carry all or nearly all the passengers. These steamers could do all the carrying business that is done from Watsonville; or if more vessels were necessary at the freighting season, they could tow sailing crafts up and down the river. Do you say that it would not pay to run such a line of steamers from Watsonville? Then we answer, how supremely ridiculous it is, for you to talk of a railroad, to establish which would cost twenty times as much as to establish such a line of steamers, and the daily expense of which will be at least twice as much. If such a line of steamers were established, and the people of the Pajaro valley could find business for them, they could afford to transport grain and other freight to San Francisco for $3.00 per ton, which is cheaper than any railroad that can be constructed within the next ten years could afford to do it.

Nevertheless, it needs no ghost from the grave to tell any intelligent man who has looked over Santa Cruz County, that in the course of human events there will be a railroad to Watsonville. However, the first railroad to that town is, in our opinion, likely to be west and not east of the line of hills that separates Santa Cruz from Santa Clara. We have heard no one here talk of a railroad, but whenever we have wandered out, we have seen "railroad, railroad" written on the mighty redwoods, on the rich minerals and on the fertile valleys; the soft zephyr has whispered it, the landscape has reflected it, and old Ocean has caught up the refrain and echoed "railroad." A railroad could be built from Santa Cruz directly to San Jose [via Watsonville] with an easy and inexpensive grade; but it is doubtful if such a railroad would pay, because it would run through but a small portion of the wooded district of Santa Cruz. A railroad however could be built along the valley of the San Lorenzo to its head waters, thence by an easy passage into the plain eastward of the mountains, thence to San Francisco. Such a railroad would pay immediately; first, because in its whole distance through Santa Cruz county it would pass through a district fertile as the delta of the Nile, beautiful as the vale of Tempe, and covered with a forest of pine and redwood the most magnificent upon this planet; second, because it would have passengers to sustain it. The consumption of lumber in the city of San Francisco alone is about 10,000,000 feet per month. And yet there is almost no valuable lumber accessible to the great water arteries that empty into the Bay. There is plenty of valuable timber in the forests of the Sierras and in the wilds of the Northern and Southern Coast Ranges, but it is not accessible. The market of San Francisco is now mostly supplied from the vicinity of Puget Sound and the Columbia River. There is lumber enough in the county of Santa Cruz to supply the whole state of California for an age. The Santa Cruz lumber is preferred before any other in the California market. This lumber must now be hauled from the forest to the point of shipment. The cost of hauling is often equal to the cost of transportation from the place of shipment to market. If a railroad were constructed to San Francisco through the timber district of Santa Cruz, the lumber trade alone would give it perpetual business. No railroad not even the least expensive, can pay expenses with mere freight alone without charging more freightage upon staple articles of freight than the producers can afford to pay. To carry passengers is the main paying support of railroads, a man of 150 pounds will pay as much for passage as will be received for a ton of freight, and it costs nothing to load or unload the cars with passengers. There were as many as fifty persons a day who traveled from Santa Cruz to San Francisco and *vice versa* some days last Summer. This travel is likely to be increased at least 100 per cent. another season even with the inconveniences of the stage route. Santa Cruz with a railroad to San Francisco would be the most popular place of Summer resort on the Pacific coast. Not less than a thousand persons a day would travel on the railroad for pleasure alone. Our manufactories and mines would also offer to such a road a continual business—not remitting, as the business of a purely agricultural district must necessarily be.

After this railroad was established, it might finally be extended to Watsonville. It probably would be. Believe us, friends of Watsonville, the railroad we have described, or one similarly situated will be the first one that will reach your town.

12. *Santa Cruz Sentinel*, February 6, 1864 (2:2-3)
THE RAILROAD.

Sometimes indulge the mind in extravagant thoughts, but do not always give them expression. It is the misfortune of some men, not to be able to discriminate between what is only wild and impossible, and what is truly progressive. The boy who cried for the moon, and said "the moon is nice I will have it," was progressive, but he was wildly so. No less foolish than the boy, are the people of Watsonville, if they expect a railroad upon the statements of the *Pajaro Times*. The several articles concerning a railroad from Watsonville to San Jose, which have appeared in that journal, even now, seem very much like a canard. Is it that the wags of Watsonville are playing with the credulity of those editors, or are certain extraordinary columns of figures really abstracts from the "valuable statistics" of which said editors "are in the habit of making memoranda'? If the former, we hereby censure the Watsonville wags. If the latter, the fact helps to disclose the *forte* of these editors. They should confine themselves to fancy, for hyperbole with poetry is sometimes sublime; with mathematics it is always ridiculous. In the region of the imagination such as copper, Joaquin meetings, moonlight, Burra Burra and kindred themes, the *Times* is really strong; in the exact sciences, such as Law and mathematics, it is really weak.

To go over the whole array of figures furnished by the *Times* on the railroad subject, would make our article too cumbersome. It will suffice to notice only those concerning the Pajaro valley and vicinity, places with which it ought to be best acquainted, and concerning which the figures in question ought to have least exaggeration.

The annual surplus of wheat, barley, potatoes and beans, in the Pajaro valley, after deducting a tithe for home consumption, is, according to the *Times'* statement, 85,680 tons.... The weight of the annual surplus of wheat, barley, potatoes and beans in the Pajaro Valley, which the *Times* calculates would be freight for the railroad, is about three times as great as the whole weight of the entire product of these articles in 1863, in both Santa Cruz and Monterey Counties, as given in the Surveyor General's report. But the area of the Pajaro Valley is less than one-thirtieth of the area of these two Counties, and the southern boundary of Monterey is over 100 miles from the centre of the valley. Throughout the whole of the *Times'* statements, is the same unmeaning hyperbole. Does it knowingly exaggerate, or is it ignorant of its theme? Since it is engaged in collecting valuable statistics, we are willing to send it a copy of the annual report of the Surveyor General, to the end that it may never again shock its friends with such a display of nonsense.

A railroad from Watsonville to San Jose, would by no means have as freight, the entire surplus product of the Pajaro Valley. Vessels can well afford to carry freight from Watsonville to San Francisco, for $300 a ton. This is less than half what a railroad would be forced to charge. Certainly one sixth of the freight which now goes out of the slough, comes from its southern side. The hauling distance of this freight to Watsonville, would average about fifteen miles. The distance to Cooper's, or to other landings on the southern side of the slough, would be one half less. This freight would therefore be shipped, as it now is. All the produce near Gilkey's landing, on the slough, and Brennan's landing on the coast, would still be shipped to save the expense of hauling. The produce of the San Andreas ranch has an excellent shipping place at Miller's landing and would never be hauled from seven to ten miles to Watsonville. Anywhere along the coast from Castro's to Santa Cruz, are good shipping points. It is unreasonable, therefore to think that produce would be hauled from Castro's, 14 miles to Watsonville.

Because our former article on the railroad was too simple and truthful to admit of a refuting answer, the *Times* termed it ingenious. The unequivocal statement that the method of transportation most beneficial to the people of the Pajaro Valley would be by certain and regular passages to

San Francisco by water, which could be effected by the necessary improvement of the slough, was met by the quibble, that a duck could not swim in the Pajaro river. The Salinas has been making trips from the Slough, this winter, during a time when most of the rivers of California were lower than they had been for many years.

We could have no object in decrying any proposed improvement for Watsonville. The truth will remain truth, whether it be said or unsaid. There is now, and there will be for the next ten years, only *one* feasible and financially practicable route for a railroad from Watsonville to San Francisco. That route is from Watsonville through Santa Cruz, thence up the valley of the San Lorenzo into the plain eastward of the mountains, and connecting with the San Francisco and San Jose railroad, at or near the Seventeen-Mile House. This whole route is level and would require but little grading. It traverses a district unparalleled upon this planet for the beauty of its scenery, the salubrity of its climate, the fertility of its soil and the value and magnificence of its forest. The distance from Santa Cruz to the Seventeen-Mile House, by this route, is about forty miles. A railroad from Watsonville to the same point, would be about the same length as a road from Watsonville to San Jose by the way of Gilroy, and would be much less expensive, because all the wood for the railroad would be already upon the ground. We have given substantial reasons, in a former article, why such a railroad would pay. Such reasons have not been, and cannot be given, concerning the road from Watsonville to San Jose.

13. *Santa Cruz Sentinel,* February 6, 1864 (2:3)
Santa Cruz Road Project.

"There will soon be presented a bill to grant certain parties the franchise for a toll road from Santa Cruz to some point on the San Jose railroad near Redwood City, by a route that would enable travelers to make the trip comfortably in 4 hours from Santa Cruz to San Francisco. The present route crosses the Coast Range between Santa Cruz and San Jose by a heavily graded, tedious road, consuming six hours, and travelers do not reach San Francisco till the next day, having to stay over night at San Jose. The new road would follow up the San Lorenzo river on the east side of the mountains to the northern corner of Santa Cruz county, where it would cross the Coast Range through a low Pass, intersecting the San Jose railroad at or near Fairfield. The distance to the last named point, it is claimed, would be made in three hours, or in half the time now consumed in crossing the mountains to San Jose, and another hour's ride on the cars would land the passenger at the metropolis."— Sac. Cor. S. F. *Bulletin.*

It seems by the above that certain parties have discovered that a toll road will pay upon the very route on which we have been trying to prove that it would be feasible to build a railroad. The whole route presents the appearance of design by Nature to have a road there. How it could have been overlooked, when the expensive and tedious road over the mountains to San Jose was constructed, is a wonder. That there will be a railroad on this route in the progressive course of this country, is as certain as that the year of Grace '65 will follow '64. But in the mean time a good stage road will be a great benefit to us. We speak within bounds when we say that 5000 persons, last year, were deterred from coming to Santa Cruz on account of the tediousness of the road hither.

14. *Santa Cruz Sentinel,* February 13, 1864 (2:2)

Rain.—The people of Monterey have—the *Gazette* says so—received rain in answer to their prayers for it. We advise them now to put in prayers for a road to the Salinas, or an extension to Monterey of the Watsonville and San Jose Railroad. The faithful of Monterey ought to know, what faith like a grain of mustard seed can do. *En passant*, it really strikes us with surprise that the Pajaro *Times*, which is always on the alert to propose improvements, has not thought of extending the new railroad to Monterey. The extension would very greatly add to the business of the road. We venture to say, that, according to the *Times*' method of calculation, Monterey would furnish for the railroad at least 5,000,000,000 barrels of whale oil, 1,000,000,000 tons of mackerel, besides innumerable tons of soles, sturgeon, smelts, muscles, cockles, crabs, abalones and soft shell clams.

15. *Santa Cruz Sentinel,* February 13, 1864 (2:3)

The Railroad.—We must continue to advise people of Watsonville to improve those means of transit and transportation which Nature has given them. Namely: to effect regular and certain passages by water from Watsonville to San Francisco. But if they still hanker after a railroad, now is the time for action. "There is a tide in the affairs of men which taken at the flood"—they know the rest. A company is about to construct a toll road from Santa Cruz to Redwood City. With a little pecuniary persuasion they could be induced to build a railroad instead of a toll road. If the people of Watsonville should now raise $200,000 for the purpose, a railroad would be commenced at once. It might be called the Watsonville and San Francisco Railroad. Santa Cruz wouldn't come in at all, it would only be a small station by the way.

16. *Santa Cruz Sentinel,* February 13, 1864 (2:4)

[Watsonville] is healthy, and wants nothing,—unless it is a railroad.

17. *San Mateo County Gazette,* February 26, 1864 (2:1)
New Franchise.

An application is now pending before the Legislature, for a Toll Road, to connect Santa Cruz with the Railroad, which is well worthy the attention of our citizens. The applicants are not very specific in their request, but want a kind of running charter, authorizing them to tap the Railroad at any point between San Francisco and San Jose. The Legislature are unwilling to give them so much latitude, and prefer to confine them to one or two given points.

There is no doubt but that a toll road from Santa

Cruz to the Railroad would meet with universal favor with the traveling public, would be a blessing to the country through which it passed, and a splendid investment for the owners. But the degree of these benefits must depend very much upon the route selected, and the terminus on this side of the mountains. The true policy both for those who invest their money in these works, and those who advocate their construction, is to have them so established, as to make the distance between the two points desired ultimately to be reached, the shortest possible, and at the same time, secure the greatest amount of travel, and accommodate the greatest number of people. A little reflection on the part of any one familiar with the country, cannot fail to satisfy him as to the route for this road, possessing all these advantages in the highest degree. The people of Santa Cruz desire to reach San Francisco by the shortest route. To strike the Railroad at Redwood City makes that trip thirteen miles shorter than to strike it at Mountain View. Our opinion is, that the road could be more easily constructed, running to the former than to the latter place, and we are confident that no route could be selected which would insure so much of the general travel, and so large an amount of heavy teaming as the one terminating at this point. It must necessarily traverse the best portion of the lumber regions of the coast range—it passes through the flourishing village of Searsville, and the district of Woodside, each of which, furnishes a very considerable amount of travel—and it would open up a way to market for the products of the rich agricultural region of Pescadero, than which, few can be found more productive in the country. These are matters which will tell largely upon the projectors of this work, if any effort is made to call their attention to them. And it does seem to us, that the citizens of this place overlook their own interest, if they do not use every honorable means to secure the selection of this route. No one thing has ever been done, or projected, which would add so much to the local business of Redwood City, as the opening of such a road, terminating at this point. All the business of the western slope, would then necessarily centre here, and it could not in the nature of things go directly through, but must make this a resting point on the road to the commercial metropolis, and thus add to the traffic, and to the business of every industrial pursuit in our place. The time is not far hence, when, with the facilities now opened up to us, Redwood City will become a suburb of San Francisco, and if our citizens are not blind to their own interests, she may as easily become the market place for the products of all the surrounding country, as to remain as she has been, in all past, a simple way station, through which these products pass, almost without notice by, or profit to ourselves.

18. *Santa Cruz Sentinel,* February 27, 1864 (2:4)

The people of this place [Soquel] may be considered sound on the Rail Road question. We are all in favor of a Rail Road to Watsonville, but we prefer to have it come by the way of your town [Santa Cruz], you see. Soquel might become a small station by the way as well as Santa Cruz.

19. *Santa Cruz Sentinel*, March 26, 1864 (2:1)

Four gentlemen, C. Brown, W. W. Broughton, Adolphus Brown and Walter Rice started Tuesday morning on their *caballos* for an exploring expedition to the sources of the San Lorenzo. On their return they will probably be able to give correct information concerning the feasibility of a railroad up the valley of San Lorenzo, and also concerning the pass through the mountain divide.

20. *San Jose Courier* via the *Santa Cruz Sentinel*, August 12, 1865 (3:1)

Santa Cruz Railroad.—We understand that a party of surveyors started this morning for a preliminary survey of the valley as far as Watsonville. A railroad line south will benefit San Jose and all the country though which it may pass. We hope to hear the car whistle from the south on the ensuing year.

21. *San Jose Courier* via the *Santa Cruz Sentinel*, August 19, 1865 (2:2)

San Jose and Watsonville Railroad.—From one of the surveying party who assisted in the preliminary survey of the railroad route from here to Watsonville, we learn that the ground is much more favorable for a railroad track than was at first supposed, no cutting or filling of any account being necessary until the route reaches within about four miles of Watsonville, where there is a pass of about four or five hundred feet through which the cutting will be about fifty feet deep. From the Twenty-one Mile house to San Jose, the road to the eye appears a perfect level, still the instruments show a descent of about 231 feet. The inhabitants along the route express much satisfaction at the prospect of hearing the shrill whistle and seeing the cars rush down the valley, in which we gladly join.

22. *Santa Cruz Sentinel*, January 6, 1866 (2:2)

The Necessity of a Railroad.—
How and where can it be built?

Editors Sentinel.—Many of the leading men of Watsonville and Santa Cruz have, for some time, tried to devise means to connect various points of our county by a railroad to San Francisco, but, up to the present time, nothing has been accomplished. Three different routes have been spoken of, but, owing to the many difficulties which would have to be encountered to build a road across the mountains in the northern and middle portion of our county, the route from San Jose up the valley to Gilroy, and thence along the Pajaro river to Watsonville, seems to be the most feasible and the most likely to pay, because it would run nearly all the way through fertile land where no good shipping facilities can be had. The road might be extended to the town of Santa Cruz, but, although desirable, it is very doubtful whether that portion of the road could be made to pay even running expenses. We have a large amount of freight, but can ship much cheaper by water than by rail. To the Pajaro valley this road has become a necessity.

While the people in our neighborhood have no immediate, direct interest in a railroad ending at Watsonville, no one will deny that it would be very convenient to be even within nineteen miles from the terminus. Feeling interested in the enterprise I propose to start the ball a rolling by suggesting a plan:

Let the interested parties raise a sufficient amount of money to pay for grading the road and to purchase the necessary ties, the iron to be bought on credit, giving mortgage bonds as security; the road, when finished, to be delivered to the San Jose Railroad Company, they agreeing to carry freight and passengers at a stipulated price, using their own rolling stock, to keep the road in repair, to pay the interest on the mortgage bonds, and after the first or second year, to set aside five or ten per cent, of the gross receipts for the gradual redemption of the mortgage bonds.

So far as I can ascertain, it has cost for grading, ties, depots and laying down the track on the San Jose railroad from $10,00 to $14,000 per mile. The distance from San Jose to Watsonville is said not to be more than forty-five miles, and as the road would run nearly all the way through level land, with the exception of say five miles of steep hillsides between Gilroy and Watsonville, the expense of grading, etc., would not be more, perhaps even less than on the San Jose road.—The necessary timber for ties would also be at a convenient distance. But, taking the highest estimate the road would cost, exclusive of iron and rolling stock, $600,000. This amount would be raised as follows:

The Dream of Steam, 1854–1873

San Jose Railroad Company	$150,000
Citizens of Santa Clara County	$250,000
" Monterey County	$100,000
" Santa Cruz County	$100,000
Total	$600,000

But the people of this county could raise $200,000 if needed, particularly as the money would be payable in installments within a term of three years, and even that sum would not be one-third of the amount of the direct benefit to be derived by the building of the road. There are 10,000 acres of land in Pajaro valley which would increase in value,

$30, per acre, making	$300,000
10,000 acres, $15, " "	150,000
10,000 " ....$5, " "	50,000
The remainder of the county would surely be benefited	100,000
Total,	$650,000

The people of Pajaro valley, and of the county generally, should act at once. Let there be a railroad meeting at Watsonville.   F. A. HIHN

23. *Santa Cruz Sentinel,* January 13, 1866 (2:5)

In the last *Sentinel*, Santa Cruz, January 6th, 1866, I observed an article, written by F. A. Hihn, advocating a Railroad to Watsonville and showing by an exhibit of facts and figures, a plan by which it may be built. With all due deference to Mr. Hihn's statements and admitting there is a feasibility in the plan, I beg leave to differ with him and show that if a railroad is a necessity to this county (which many will admit) the route should be a different one from that mapped out in the article referred to. The railroad should enter the county at the north-east line, and cross the divide near the head waters of the San Lorenzo, coursing through the dense and valuable timber-belt of the mountain slopes east and west of the Santa Cruz range, thus affording an outlet for the great lumbering interests and numerous saw-mills on the San Lorenzo and its branches.

Being somewhat posted in railroad matters, I propose to give, briefly, a detailed argument in favor of the route named, pointing out the general course the road would be likely to take. From Santa Cruz to Mountain View, or Redwood City the distance is probably thirty-two miles, by the line of the contemplated survey, which by adopting a maximum grade of ninety feet to the mile and possibly a tunnel of one-half mile at the divide or summit west of McCartysville, the road is practicable and can be built, in view of the facilities afforded; such as convenience of timber for ties, truss, trestle and grillage work, but more particularly on account of the favorable condition of the soil, than on any other mountain route in California. The best of granite for foundations, bulkheads, coping, abutments, etc., can also be procured at convenient distances, all along the route. The most of the ground on the western slope, is a dense chalk-rock, easily excavated, yet sufficiently firm to make a secure natural embankment, impervious to rain and not liable to slide or sag by percolation in wet weather; this is quite a consideration, where heavy embankments much be made, with short curvatures or radii, in a ninety-foot grade.

Following the wake of Mr. Hihn's proposition, for Watsonville, I will in part adopt his plan to raise the means

The Dream of Steam, 1854–1873

to build the road, but will not agree to give the San Jose railroad Company the absolute control of the road, for the privilege of using their old, worthless, worn-out rolling-stock; but will, in the place of that, point out the means by which the equipment may be secured by the Company building the road. In the first place take a glance at the great natural resources and prospective wealth so lavishly displayed on the route proposed; at the immense and inexhaustible bodies of redwood timber, for lumber—such as is usually made from that valuable California requisite; the immense ledges of granite, fire-rock, limestone, and varieties of tree-stone useful for building purposes; another great source of way-trade will be the fire wood, tan-bark, powder-wood (alder and willow), and the madrona—the very best of hard-wood, equal to boxwood for engraver's use also for making planes, buttons and in fact all articles where a flint-hard wood of fine, solid texture is required; hoop-poles, staves, shingles, shakes, pickets, fence-rails, telegraph-poles, and a hundred other different articles of traffic would find an outlet and a market, by this route, which without a railroad will remain buried in the forest for years to come. Another great advantage of this route is, it runs mostly through wild or government land, and it would cost nothing for the right-of-way or timber to build the road, as sufficient "stumpage" would be found in clearing the track to build the road its entire length. Twenty miles of the route is wild land—fifteen of which is unsurveyed—all heavily timbered with the most valuable timber known on the coast, divide this up into 160 acre lots, and see the amount of taxable property it would give, and its value in the aggregate: say twenty miles long and five miles wide on each side of the road—the lots being one-half mile square—and we find that eight hundred lots are added to the Assessor's books; some of them would be completely worthless, yet others we are credibly assured would be worth three thousand dollars for the timber alone, and after clearing would be as good grain farms as any in the State. We are assured that they would average from $500 to $5,000 per lot—say $1,000 per lot and we have a showing of $800,000 in the increased value of land alone, without referring to the impulse given to commerce, labor and all the requirements of demand and supply, in the production and consumption of a large, healthy and industrious community. I will in a future article make a showing of the way-trade and the manufacturing resources which will enable the road to be fully occupied the year round, as also the income from passengers, mails and express, with lime, leather, paper, powder, petroleum and whale oils, glue, fruits, building materials, cordwood, hay, grain, live stock, butter, cheese, eggs, poultry and a hundred other different articles of way-freight, not taken into account by the proposed Watsonville route, where but a limited amount of wheat, barley, potatoes, mustard-seed, wool and hides are autumnly shipped.

Time is money—Time and space will overcome all difficulties—are truisms, and railroads are no exception to the rule. Then why build one hundred and thirty miles of railroad (for the road would eventually come to Santa Cruz even if built to Watsonville) to reach the Santa Clara road at San Jose, when thirty miles of road will connect at

The Dream of Steam, 1854–1873

or near Mountain View, fifteen or twenty miles nearer San Francisco? The greatest item of expense is the railroad iron ⊥ pattern, costing $55 to $65 per ton—say, with superstructure, $8,365 per mile, which includes sidings, chairs, frogs, switch-irons, water fixtures, turn-tables, spikes, nails, ties, etc., and the laying down of the track. This expense is just as much on level plain as on mountain or hill-side; a prudent man can easily see the difference between thirty and one hundred and thirty, not computing the cost of grading. So much for space, or distance. Now as to time: The passenger and freight trains would reach San Francisco, by the San Lorenzo route, in less than four hours, while it would take full eight hours by the serpentine or tape-worm route (forming an immense geographical letter S,) around and through the hills from Pajaro to Gilroy, and thence to San Jose. Why it is preposterous, in this telegraphic age of steam, to think of it! In a word, Mr. Editor, the route up the San Lorenzo, is the *only practicable* one and it is useless to discuss the matter further, as when a railroad is built by Santa Cruz County, or for her interests it will be on that route. The San Jose railroad in time, no doubt, will be built to Gilroy, the valley of St. Johns, and will cross by a short tunnel, the spur of mountain through Dr. Stoke's ranch, near the residence of W. S. Johnson, and thence course up the Salinas Plains to the Mission of San Miguel. Probably, the Santa Cruz road may, in time, extend to Watsonville, but not by the route proposed by Mr. Hihn. In my next, I will give a summary of estimates of the cost of thirty miles of railroad, on the San Lorenzo route, in three division and eighteen sections, predicated on actual survey and estimates over ground of a similar formation. Excuse this as it is hastily written and not carefully digested. Yours, etc. SEYANTE

24. *Santa Cruz Sentinel,* January 20, 1866 (2:5)

And now to "Sayante." He is a noble fellow. While warmly advocating his cause, he does not stoop to use low, ungentlemanly language towards his adversary. His motives being pure, he would spur the low creature who being corrupt himself, interprets the actions of others to suit his own way of thinking. But unfortunately for "Sayante," he is a little ahead of his time. Railroads are still a luxury in this county. Before resorting to rugged mountains let us embrace our fertile valleys. Build up first, the farmer, so as to enable him to buy the products of the forest.

But it would be unjust to prejudge the case of "Sayante," let us have his facts and figures. H.

25. *Santa Cruz Sentinel,* January 27, 1866, reprinted November 21, 1868 (1:6-7)

MR. EDITOR:—In a former article I promised to give an estimate of the probable cost of a Railroad *via* the San Lorenzo Gap—near the Tin Can Ranch—to connect Santa Cruz with the San Jose railroad, at or near Mountain View. The distance is a little over thirty-one miles; but the estimate is based, for the convenience of calculation, at the even figures and for the same reason the estimates were predicated on the grading of two divisions, instead of three, as proposed. The arguments produced in my first article, are admitted to be sound; and the necessity of the road, its practicability and utility, is admitted by all who have given the subject any attention. It is only necessary, at this time, to glance to the route proposed, and contemplate the vast resources, undeveloped, waiting the impulse of enterprise and capital, to provide a market. The lumbering interests; the great amount of fire-wood, building materials, such as granite, free-stone, lime-rock, fire-rock, and we might add minerals—as iron, cinnabar, gold and silver ore, coal, etc., all of which will be developed and carried to a market through this channel. The amount of way-trade would more than pay ten per cent. per annum on the total expense, not taking the through freight into consideration, such as manufactured articles and natural products of the farm, orchard, field and garden, so bountifully grown in the rich valleys along the sea coast, adjacent to Santa Cruz. The passenger list would also be large, in view of the fact that Santa Cruz is the Newport of the Pacific coast, and that as a watering place will always take the lead, on account of the facilities of mountain streams and ocean beach—affording the angler and hunter the best field for recreation and pleasure in the State.

Estimating each division at about 15½ miles, and allowing at least two-thirds of the distance for the western slope of the Santa Cruz mountains, including the divide on the summit, the skillful engineer will readily admit that the remaining or second division of the road is the least difficult to survey and grade; the incline is less precipitous, and the curves will not be so short and the bridges, embankments, etc., less expensive, especially after striking the level plain. Dividing the expense in sections of one mile each, the distance can be approximated to almost within a thousand dollars of the actual cost.

The first division would commence within the environs of Santa Cruz—West End—where the first station house would be built (allowing the depot, turn-tables, machine shop, etc., to be erected on the vacant lands near the sea), the alignment would run north-east, parallel with the divide and the San Lorenzo river, inclining east with the curves of the stream, adopting such deviation in the general direction, location and grade as the nature of the country would admit, or facilities of trade and freight might require—the greatest advantage being the lumber, wood and lime interests on the route. This traffic would more than repay the first ten miles of grading, in Santa Cruz trade alone. The grading, masonry and bridging would cost about $582,086.37, or $18,776.97 per mile. The first part of second division would be more difficult to grade, as the country is more rugged and the surface irregular from deep gulches and the mountain streams flowing into the head waters of the San Lorenzo; yet as the soil is of a loose, porous nature, and but little hard rock to be blasted away, the route is practicable and the grading can be done at less cost, even at California rate of wages, than any part of the Baltimore and Ohio railroad from Cumberland, Maryland, to Wheeling, Virginia. For this division $432,317.18 is allowed for grading, or about $28.821.14 per mile, which is

The Dream of Steam, 1854–1873

within bounds, when averaged with some six or seven miles of level plain in the Santa Clara valley, south-west of the junction. Allowance is made in the estimate for a half mile tunnel—which might be necessary, to carry the road over, at a 90-foot grade—on the divide, and a permanent and durable bridge over the north fork of the San Lorenzo. This division, especially the first five sections, will be the most difficult to grade of any on the proposed route. The soil is entirely different on the Santa Clara slope, presenting many difficulties and natural obstacles not found on the Santa Cruz side, all of which must be surmounted at enhanced expense. A largely increased amount of curvatures, with much shorter radii, will be necessary, with changeable grades, at different points of 85 to 90 feet per mile; heavy embankments will be required, granite and other hard rock occurs, and costly copings, truss and trestle work, with grillage timbers for laying foundations, will be, no doubt, required as well as bridging over the abrupt gulches, would make the grading difficult and expensive, taxing the best of engineering ability to its utmost capacity.

No preliminary survey has yet been made, over the route, but at different times surveyors and engineers have crossed the mountains, at the point indicated, and from such information it is predicted that a 90-foot grade would carry the road over. The amount of grading required, is mere conjecture, but a knowledge in such matters might be useful. The Pacific Railroad has done much, similar work, both at the Pass above Vallejo's Mills and near Colfax. It costs about 24 cents per cubic yard to excavate and build embankment, allowing 8 per cent. for shrinkage; excavation in solid earth or gravel, when the debris must be removed some distance costs a trifle more, in proportion to the distance hauled. Log-drains and culverts cost $4 per foot—this road would cost much less on account of the convenience of timber. The average cost of simple gradation, where no excavation or embankment, more than ordinary, is required, is about 24 cents per cubic foot. The following estimates would probably cover the entire expense of building the road:

ESTIMATES—FIRST DIVISION.

Gradation, Masonry and Bridging Superstructure	$258,324.16
1,946 tons of ⊥ iron, @$55 per ton	85,030.00
34,785 ties at 30 cents each	10,435.50
7,791 wrought iron chairs at .35	2,736.85
61,840lbs spikes at .5	3,092.00
Laying track 15-46-100 m's @$600	9,276.00
Four stations and station buildings	8,605.51
Equipment—rolling stock, etc.	39,269.60
Superintendence and contingencies	15,962.29
Total cost of first division	$330,725.91

Average per mile about $22,018.39

ESTIMATES—SECOND DIVISION.

Gradation, masonry and bridging Superstructure	$323,762.21
1,772 tons of ⊥ iron, @$55 per ton	97,460.00
7,800 C. I. Chairs, 16lbs $60 per ton	3,744.00
311 8 10 tons spikes @$100	3,118.00
35,077 ties @.30 each	10,522.10
Laying track, 15-59-100 m's @$600	9,354.00

The Dream of Steam, 1854–1873

Four stations and station buildings....................... 8,605.51
Equipments, rolling stock, etc. 9,598.60
Superintendence and contingencies.................. 47,752.76
Total cost of second division............................$432.317.18
Average per mile about $28,821.14.
Add first division $330,725.91
Total cost of 31 m's railroad compl'td.........$763,043.09
Total average per mile about $24,646.56

Now, let the reader glance at our natural resources, keeping in view the increased wealth and trade that the road would open to the world and a market. We have already shown that the building of this road would open a scope of country, now comparatively idle and waste, which might add eight hundred farms to the assessor's books, estimated to be worth from $500 to $5,000 per farm, in lumber, fire-wood, tan-bark, hoop-poles, fencing, shingles, etc., and that the land after cleared of this wealth, (or obstacles if you prefer to say so,) would be valuable for orchards, vineyards and farms. Here is shown an increase of $800,000 added to the county assessment roll, with a productive population sufficient to work and manage this new wealth. Last year the total valuation of poetry in this county was $1,284,379, paying a tax of $37,244—showing an increased assessment over the previous year of $274,790, now add to the first figures $800,000 for new farms opened and half as much for increased value of real estate, and additional personal property, and the intelligent reader will find our assessment increased to $2,484,379 by this one enterprise alone. But lest some captious cynic might think this is romance, I will enumerate a few of the productions of Santa Cruz county, the past year, all of which would be increased more than ten fold, by this cheap, speedy, ready and convenient transportation to market:

Lumber, number of feet	10,500,000
Shingles, bundles	1,000,000
Tanbark, cords	5,000
Hoop-poles, number	1,000,000
Fence rails, pickets, shakes, staves	100,000,000
Blasting powder—kegs 25 lbs each	48,000
Sporting powder, pounds	20,000
Lime, barrels	84,000
Leather, pounds	720,000
Paper, printing, pounds	288,000
Paper, straw, bales	21,800
Cheese, pounds	250,000
Butter, pounds	100,000
Wool, pounds	3,000
Wheat, bushels	168,000
Barley, ''	246,000
Oats, ''	92,000
Rye, ''	4,000
Corn, ''	14,400
Potatoes, ''	135,000
Beans, ''	14,600
Hay, tons of	8,550
Fruit, boxes of (estimated)	20,000
Strawberries, quart boxes	20,000
Value of animals slaughtered	$50,000
Value of fruit shipped	20,000

A thousand other articles might be enumerated, not now taken into consideration, for the want of a market, such as

The Dream of Steam, 1854–1873

small fruit, vegetables, fish (fresh-water speckled-trout and the fine barracoota, etc., caught in the Monterey Bay) hides, tallow, glue, soap, whale-oil, petroleum—now being extensively manufactured in this county—eggs, poultry, game, etc., all of which would go to make up a constant and heavy freight and passenger list.

The necessary equipment of the road, which is included in the table of estimates, would be about as follows:

Five locomotives and tenders, at $9,000	$45,000
Six passenger cars at $2,550	15,300
Three baggage cars at $1,000	3,000
Twenty-four freight cars at $800	19,200
Thirty-six box freight cars at $900	32,400
Eighteen wood and granite cars at $450	$8,100
Five hand cars	750
Total cost of equipment	$123,000
Superintendence and contingencies	50,000

This showing may be considered as the cost of the road, if paid in cash, as the work progresses, allowing three year's time to complete the job. Now, Mr. Editor, can Mr. Hihn make a better showing for the Watsonville railroad? I think not. The route up the San Lorenzo has the advantage of time and space in its favor, and also a larger proportion of trade. In my next, I will endeavor to show how the money can be raised to build the road. SEYANTE.

26. *Santa Cruz Sentinel,* February 3, 1866 (2:1)

Railroad Meeting.

There is to be a mass meeting, held at Watsonville this evening, to devise ways and means for building a Railroad from that town to San Jose, by the S route, to connect with the San Jose Railroad.... We are in favor of railroads, all the time, and if "Seyante" can't "cook" a railroad *via* the San Lorenzo, let it come into the county *via* Watsonville. The farmers in that vicinity are suffering for want of transportation; the Salinas is laid up, and no good or safe shipping point is offered, consequently the large amount of grain, at Paul's Island, the Landing, and other places, cannot be shipped at the present time. The farmers are at a heavy expense, and must raise money to put in their crops now, to take advantage of the present favorable rains, yet they cannot borrow money, even with warehouse receipts for collateral security, at less than 2 per cent. per month, which is a ruinous rate of interest. The Railroad, eventually will be built, then why not proceed and build it now? It will not interfere with a railroad to this town *via* the San Lorenzo route, as the timber, and manufacturing interests of this section, would alone pay to build our road.

27. *Santa Cruz Sentinel*, February 10, 1866 (2:3)

The Railroad Meeting at Watsonville.

Notwithstanding the bad weather the railroad meeting at Watsonville, on last Saturday afternoon, was well attended. The people of Pajaro valley have become aware, that it requires action on their part to bring a railroad to them, and if they only persist in their efforts, they will finally succeed. Judge Bockius acted as Chairman. Mr. Hihn being called upon, gave an estimate of the cost of the road, as follows:

Estimates of Cost of Railroad from San Jose via Gilroy to Watsonville.

Length of Road Forty-Eight Miles:

10,000 cubic yards embankment and excavations, per mile, on average, at 30 cents per yard—per mile	$3,000
Or for forty-eight miles	$144,000
120,000 Railroad ties at 60 cents each	72,000
Bridge across Los Gatos, 160 feet long at $30 per foot	6,400
Bridge across—, 120 feet long at $40 per foot	4,800
4,5000 perches masonry at $8 per perch,	3,600
Laying 48 miles of track at $750 per mile	36,000
Station buildings, side tracks, etc,	50,000
Superintendence, etc.,	50,000
Total	$399,200
5,280 tons of Track Iron, @70 p ton	369,600
60,000lbs Spikes, @7c	4,200
2,700 Wrought Iron Chairs @ 9 cents	2,430
Iron spikes and chairs for Side Track	15,000
Total	$391.230

ROLLING STOCK.

Three Locomotives and Tenders, at $12,000	$36,000
Three Passenger Cars at $2,500	7,500
Two Baggage Cars at $1,00	2,000
Twenty-five Freight Cars, at $1,000	25,000
Total cost of Equipment	$70,500

SUMMARY.

Cost of gradation, Station Buildings, and Bridging	$399,200
Cost of Iron,	391,230
Cost of Rolling Stock	70,500
Total cost	$861,930

A motion was then made by Mr. Hihn that a Committee of three be appointed, and that it shall be the duty of said Committee to ascertain—

1st, The cost of the Railroad.

2nd, On what terms Railroad men will interest themselves in the road.

3d, The amount of stock or money required to be subscribed by the people and property holders in this county.

4th, To prepare a list of parties interested in the construction of the road in this County and to make an equitable adjustment as to the amount of subscription required from each.

5th, To invite the co-operation of the influential men in Santa Clara and Monterey Counties to assist in the enterprise.

6th, To make a report of their doings.

Mr. I. C. Wilson was in favor of raising the necessary means by issuing the Bonds of the County.

Mr. Stearns and others were opposed to the issue of County Bonds, and Mr. Hihn's motion being carried, the meeting selected as the members of said Committee, F. A. Hihn, Henry Jackson and Matthew Tarpy. Judge Bockius was afterwards added to the Committee.

D. Tuttle and B. A. Barney were chosen to solicit subscriptions to defray the expenses of the Committee.

The Committee are going ahead and are receiving much encouragement from capitalists in this county and San Francisco. We think, in all probability, the road will be built by the plan and route proposed.

28. *Pajaro Times*, February 10, 1866 (2:2)
Santa Cruz County Affairs.

The Railroad question is the topic of general conversation. The best informed tax-payers regard the present movement in the most favorable light, and strong minds are energetic in the work. A large meeting will be held in Watsonville in a few weeks to hear the report of the committee appointed Saturday last. Due notice will be given.

29. *Pajaro Times*, February 10, 1866 (2:2)

Can't Publish It.—The communication from Santa Cruz, signed "Greenhorn," referring to Messrs. Hihn, Drennan, Stephens and Willson, in connection with the Railroad project, we must decline publishing, as no responsible name accompanies it. We do not vary from this rule at any time, and no confidence is betrayed by the proprietors under any circumstances.

30. *Pajaro Times*, February 10, 1866 (2:3)
The Railroad Meeting in Watsonville.

Notwithstanding the inclemency of the weather, a large number of the tax-paying citizens of Santa Cruz and Monterey counties assembled at Independence Hall, Watsonville, Saturday afternoon last, February 3d, to discuss the merits of the railroad extension from San Jose, via Gilroy, to Watsonville. G. M. Bockius was elected Chairman and Patrick J. Kelly Secretary.

Mr. F. A. Hihn, of Santa Cruz, being called upon, addressed the meeting in an earnest, matter of fact manner, evidencing that he thoroughly understood the question under discussion—introducing to the audience figures and facts resulting from a careful study of the subject. He estimates the length of the road at forty-eight miles, and the total cost of construction $861,930. The general impression prevails here that his estimate is correct. Mr. Hihn spoke of the great advantages which would arise from the consummation of the project to this section of country; and expressed it as his opinion that the proper way to proceed would be by subscription—and, in furtherance of his understanding of the whole subject, proposed that a committee of three be appointed whose duty it shall be to ascertain: 1st. The cost of building a Railroad; 2d. On what terms Railroad men will interest themselves in the construction of the road; 3d. The amount of money or stock required to be subscribed by the people and property-holders of Santa Cruz county; 4th. To prepare a list of parties interested in the construction of a Railroad in Santa Cruz county, and to make an equitable adjustment as to amount of subscription required from each; 5th. To invite the co-operation of the influential men in Monterey and Santa Clara Counties to assist in the enterprise; 6th. To report at a future meeting the result of their labors.

The motion of Mr. Hihn's being seconded and unanimously agreed to, the meeting selected as said committee: F. A. Hihn, M. Tarpy and Hy. Jackson; the Chairman, Judge Bockius, was added to the committee.

Mr. I. C. Wilson, of Santa Cruz, being present, was

The Dream of Steam, 1854–1873

called upon to express his views upon the subject. He held the regular I. C. Wilson attitude—eloquently setting forth the necessities and advantages of a Railroad to Santa Cruz County, but proposing the only method by which the movement could be smothered. He held that a Railroad would benefit the whole county and that the county should be made to foot the bill, and proposed that the county donate $100,000 towards its construction. Mr. Wilson knowns little of the "internal feeling" of the northern end of the county, or he is a very large anti-railroad man in small railroad disguise—for he cannot help knowing that should such a question be presented before the people, one half of Soquel would vote against the measure, and Santa Cruz town and Pescadero would be almost unanimously opposed, and vote the whole subject a residence in a tomb as secure as that of the Capulets.

Mr. J. P. Stearns then addressed the meeting, showing the groundless position assumed by Mr. Willson, and advocating in forcible language the views of Mr. Hihn. The gentlemen well informed himself in the premises, and his remarks relative to the question under consideration were animated and to the point.

Mr. Stearns then moved that when the meeting adjourn it adjourn subject to the call of the above mentioned committee. The motion was seconded and agreed to.

Mr. Stearns suggested that the above committee be authorized to collect funds from the people to defray the expenses of its duties; but, in the form of a motion, it was resolved that a committee be appointed for that purpose, and Messrs. Tuttle, Roberts and B. A. Barney were selected. The meeting then adjourned.

We will take occasion here to direct the attention of our readers to an article, in another column, entitled: "Will a Railroad to Watsonville Pay?" It seems to us that actual stupidity and vulgar selfishness breed in the minds of many an indifference to this important measure—the rich fearing it will benefit the poor and the poor fearing it will benefit the rich; both are correct; all grades and classes must prosper under its influence, and the funds invested by capitalists must return with big interest. Let the "heavy" and the "light" railroad men of San Francisco, and other portions of the State, acquaint themselves with the sleeping resources of this section, awaiting only the presence of the iron-horse to spring into active light, and our word for it their discernment and judgment will extend the necessary aid. We also desire to warn our people against the chilling skepticism of a few in our midst whose self interests or lack of intelligence debar them from grasping the merits of so gigantic a scheme. They are the leaden colored clouds that obscure the bright sun now struggling to shed life-giving ray upon the future of Pajaro Valley. A Railroad we want; a Railroad we must have.

31. *Pajaro Times*, February 10, 1866 (2:4)
Will a Railroad to Watsonville Pay?

Now that the railroad question is again attracting considerable attention among capitalists, and surveyors have gone over the ground, and made favorable reports to their employers, it may not be uninteresting to our readers to glance over the following facts and figures, which were published in the *Times* in the month of January, 1864. [*See* Article 10 above.]

32. *Santa Cruz Sentinel,* February 17, 1866 (2:1)

What's Up?—The last Pajaro *Times* comes out in favor of F. A. Hihn's railroad plan, to build the Watsonville Railroad, and commends that gentleman, personally, in very decided terms. Is it possible that Mr. Hihn has purchased an interest in the *Times*, or that they have buried the hatchet! We knew that the *Times* was for sale, but did not think they were hungry enough to bite at this Railroad bait. The editor of the *Times* expresses himself convinced a railroad can be built, on the plan proposed by Mr. Hihn. "Seyante," thinks differently. "No hab got how can do?" This is to help out "posterity."

33. *Santa Cruz Sentinel,* February 17, 1866 (2:3)

We must not suffer our minor troubles to overbalance our greater ones. I will stop moralizing, as it don't pay, and will not build a Railroad, which is at the present a subject of deep importance and the propriety in, or rather the feasibility of building one to this place has been, of late, freely discussed. All unite in deeming it necessary; the only drawback is "can it be did?" Have we the means and will we come down with the needful? Whenever we answer that question in the affirmative, we may expect to hear the "iron horse" snorting, and may look out for the engine, when the bell rings.

34. *Santa Cruz Sentinel*, February 24, 1866 (2:2)

The Watsonville Railroad.—We learn from San Francisco, that considerable interest is taken, in that city, in the proposed Railroad from Watsonville to San Jose. Heavy capitalists have taken the matter in hand, and deputized one of their number (the leading banker of the city), to proceed to New York and contract for the iron and rolling stock. It is generally conceded that the road will be built. In the meantime home capitalists should subscribe liberally, and show San Francisco men that they are in earnest and have confidence in the road. Every one should subscribe, if only $50, it will help, in the aggregate to make up the amount. Let us have the Railroad—two of them, if possible.

35. *Santa Cruz Sentinel*, March 3, 1866 (3:1)

"Pine Grove."—This correspondent, has an article on fourth page, in reference to Railroads, worthy of perusal. The letter is the experience and views of an old mountaineer who has spent the past six years in the region of which he writes. In due time "Seyante" will give his estimates. It is easier, sometimes, to show that a railroad is required and will pay—yes even to build one—than to show how the money can be raised to do the work, purchase the iron, etc.

36. *Santa Cruz Sentinel*, March 3, 1866 (4:1)

Railroad Up the San Lorenzo.
Santa Cruz, March 1st, 1866.

Editor Sentinel:—The plan proposed by "Seyante," to

The Dream of Steam, 1854–1873

build a railroad from Santa Cruz, via the San Lorenzo Divide, across the mountains to Santa Clara valley is practicable and would, no doubt, pay a handsome return, on the investment. The Railroad will and must be built, within a few years, to supply the necessities of the lumber and wood market of Santa Clara valley and San Francisco. Look at the disasters in our coast trade, the past year, and see the many lumber-vessels lost or wrecked on the north-west coast. Carefully scan the many difficulties, from breaking of booms "on the Noyo" and other rivers, also the loss of logs and lumber be freshets and it will be at once ascertained why so many extensive lumber-dealers, in San Francisco, have recently failed for such large sums—one failure alone amounting to near half a million dollars.

I propose to give a slight sketch of the vast lumber-region, on the tributaries of the San Lorenzo, at this time, leaving the Soquel and other streams, up the coast, for future reference. The San Lorenzo valley is about twenty miles long, and ten to fifteen wide, embracing the country from the head of the Pescadero to Santa Cruz; it is located between the Santa Clara mountains and the mountains that runs from Santa Cruz to Pescadero. The general direction of the San Lorenzo is from north-west to south-east; the main river is capable of furnishing water-power for twenty-five mills or factories, and it has six tributaries, viz: Seyante, Fall Creek, Big Creek, Rock Creek, Lion Creek and Bean Creek, which can furnish water-power for twenty-five more mills—say water-power for fifty mills in the valley—besides smaller streams, useful for steam-power, almost without number. The San Lorenzo, and its tributaries drain a country densely covered with a vigorous growth of redwood, fir, pine, chestnut-oak (and other varieties) sycamore, laurel, alder, madrona, poplar, box-elder, willow, (for powder wood) balm-of-gilead, silver-maple, pepper-tree, etc., all of the best quality, and as is well known, unsurpassed in usefulness for the various arts and manufactures for which they are adapted. There is besides, a large quantity of arable farming land in the valley, also oil-springs besides lime-rock, iron-ore, cinnabar, silver and gold, with an inexhaustible supply of the finest sand in the world for making flint-glass. But a part of the many natural resources of this favored region have been enumerated, and as you can come and see the balance, your readers will then soon be informed if not convinced that I have done feeble justice in this description.

A railroad can be built cheaper, through this valley, to connect with the San Jose road at Redwood City or Belmont (from Santa Cruz), than any other line of the same length in the State, for many reasons, viz: Along the line of the proposed route, almost the entire distance, in clearing for the track, sufficient timber would be secured to supply the road with ties, grillage and trussel-work—which is cheaper than grading and more safe. Now as to the route: An easy grade can be obtained, from Santa Cruz to the divide, between the head waters of the Pescadero and the San Lorenzo; then follow this divide easterly to a gap in the Santa Clara or main mountain; from this point a good grade can be had to Redwood City or Belmont; the distance to either of the above named placed, from Santa Cruz, is not more than thirty-eight miles.

Nearly all the redwood timber in the State, south of San Francisco, is in this section of the country and the supply is almost unlimited, at least for generations to come, millions of railroad ties, telegraph poles, with lumber beyond computation, could be annually sent to market, by the proposed road, at less rates than it now costs to haul the lumber to the Santa Cruz harbor. A railroad through this part of the country, would pay for its cost, in three years by carrying lumber and ties for other roads exclusively, without taking into account the way-freight, passenger trade, farm products, manufactured articles, etc., which go to make up the commerce of this flourishing section. Build the railroad and there will be a factory or mill on every half-mile of the San Lorenzo and tributaries for over twenty miles distance. What a change would such an improvement work? What a numerous, hardy, healthy and thrifty population would it introduce—tax-payers, who with sturdy strokes and mechanical skill, would open out new homes and additional sources of wealth. Our Alpine scenery would soon be the abode of the rich as well as the poor; the country mansions of retired merchants would soon fill the pleasant places in every nook and corner on the route, while the palaces of the capitalist and manufacturer would grace the charming terraces which look out on the sea, while the innumerable cottages of the lumberman, mechanic and laborer, like the lesser stars would sparkle on hill-side and in glen, a joyous throng of happy homes, merry with the gladdened voices of gleeful children. Each head of a family would have his own tenement and nearly every section of land would boast of its own village and school house. All this, and may be, more, would naturally follow, in a few years after the opening of the proposed road.

You may think I am enthusiastic, but the subject warms me up, so that I can't help it. It seems impossible that this section should have remained so long unnoticed, with its great wealth and abundant natural resources, and within such a short distance of San Francisco too, on a direct line to the bay of Monterey. This is the shortest and best route for a railroad to Watsonville and the Salinas Plains for Los Angeles. I have no time, at present, to enumerate the resources of the country, this road is destined to pass through, but may at some future time do so. PINE GROVE.

P. S. This is written for the benefit of your railroad correspondent "Seyante." P. G.

37. *Santa Cruz Sentinel,* April 7, 1866 (4:1)

Considering all these circumstances we believe there is no county in the State offering so many inducements for the location [of an agricultural, mechanical and mining college] as Santa Cruz County. Its unrivaled fertility, salubrious climate, abundance of natural resources, such as timber, stone and metal, magnificent mountains, whose mineral wealth is still almost untouched, but which are known to contain silver, gold, copper, quicksilver, iron, lead, coal and doubtless other products, make it exactly the spot for such an institution. It is very near the centre of the State as to latitude, besides being in a far better climate than those situations lying east of the Coast Range. It is accessible by sea without difficulty, and will probably very soon be visited regularly by a line of passenger steamers, having already one for freight. The railroad will shortly connect it with San Jose and San Francisco, while in time it will be extended to the more southern counties. The buildings necessary can be constructed at less expense probably than anywhere else, off account of the abundance of materials.

38. *Santa Cruz Sentinel*, May 12, 1866 (2:5)

Editorial Visit.—Mr. William Biven, editor of the Stockton *Herald*, visited Santa Cruz county last week, and spent several days in this village, enjoying the splendid scenery and balmy atmosphere of this region. We had the pleasure of accompanying Mr. Biven on a "trip up" the San Lorenzo, to Harry Love's mountain home—the Pine Grove Ranch. The weather was fine, the scenery grand, and our hosts very hospitable and agreeable, so that we were highly delighted with the excursion. We shall say but little of the superb flowers and fruits, growing naturally in great abundance in that section, nor describe the numerous mountain deer, squirrels and quail inhabiting the region, nor even revert to the bee-trees, and bee-gives, on the farm, as we intend soon to visit the place and examine and describe in detail, including the Railroad route over the San Lorenzo divide. Mr. Biven will probably "do" our trip ample justice. We fished some, hunted some, and drank "some" of Harry's splendid lager, (the ambrosial nectar which Mr. Diesing and our host delighteth to honor,) and had a free run over the hills, through the tall grass and wild flowers, on the charming slopes of the clearing. Went up Spring Creek to the Falls, and caught a few fish; Biven caught one trout, and a "hook," and we caught—Harry Love, pulling out the fish which Biven claimed, as his, after we had prepared the line and baited the hook—it was a line trout and professional courtesy prevented an exposure, *at the time*, but the truth of history compels us to say Biven "hooked" the fish, before taken from the "hook" (Love Hook) of its capturer—a slight-of-hand trick that would do credit to an expert "crib" player, not distracted by a peeled nose.... After a lunch, and a superb cup of coffee, with sweet butter and cream, we returned.... Those desiring a nice drive through grand old woods, rich vallies and towering mountains, should go up the San Lorenzo to King's Farm, about six miles above Harry Love's. They would see all that is desirable in nature, for the senses to enjoy, or that heart could crave.

39. *Santa Cruz Sentinel,* June 16, 1866 (2:1-3)

Railroad Interests in California.

The Chief Engineer of the Stockton and Copperopolis Railroad—Wm. S. Watson—has kindly furnished us a copy of his Report to the President and Board of Directors, recently published. The Report is most able and complete, establishing a satisfactory manner that the road is not only feasible, but that it will pay; and giving a fair exhibit of the resources of that section, and a close calculation as to the cost of the road, and running expenses, all of which we shall refer to at some future time. Our present purpose is to direct attention of our citizens to the great necessity of a railroad from Santa Cruz, or Watsonville, (or both places,) connecting with the San Jose road to San Francisco. We have heretofore published several articles on the subject, proving that it was practicable, and would pay, to build the road *via* the San Lorenzo Divide, keeping the dividing ridge on the north bank of that stream from the Tin Can Ranch to Santa Cruz. The statistics of our resources and manufacturers, furnished at that time, were compiled from actual accounts, and were believed to be correct, but some of our Rip Van Winkles thought the enterprise in advance of the age, and beyond the means of this small county to accomplish such an undertaking; but we argued that San Francisco would furnish the capital, if it could be shown that there was money in the investment. We estimated the cost of thirty-one miles of railroad, from tide water, at Santa Cruz, to the nearest point connecting with the San Francisco road, at about $28,000 per mile, which would amount to $868,000 for building the road, besides rolling stock and equipments. From the published Report before us we extract the following, which gives a fair showing that our figures were not underestimated:

Comparative Cost of Railroads.

For your information on this head I will call your attention to the annexed table of the cost of all the roads in the United States, showing the average cost per mile of the twenty-four Northern States, $41,368, and of the Southern States per mile, $26,151; the Stockton and Copperopolis per mile, $31,250.

Cost of Railroads.

STATES.	MILEAGE.		Cost of Road and Equipment.	Cost per Mile.
	Total.	Compl'd.		
Maine,	1,140.59	509.37	18,297,635	35,948
N. Hampshire,	687.43	659.22	23,572,830	34,201
Vermont,	586.17	586.17	23,841,120	40,619
Massachusetts,	1,348.55	1,280.93	58,979,200	46,041
Rhode Island,	151.74	119.25	4,572,496	38,445
Connecticut,	715.07	635.07	22,497,496	35,744
New York,	3,570.94	2,896.49	135,623,240	46,875
Pennsylvania,	4,323.01	3,610.26	169,180,691	46,608
New Jersey,	1,001.25	836.27	38,964,372	46,608
Delaware,	182.50	124.90	4,548,850	35,817
Maryland,	699.40	467.30	23,847,113	51,662
West Virginia,	361.00	361.00	22,126,393	61,122
Kentucky,	898.40	564.20	20,877,180	37,016
Ohio,	3,954.38	3,388.65	131,147,588	35,747
Michigan,	1,614.50	876.22	34,130,367	41,244
Indiana,	2,482.50	2,199.40	71,318,673	32,417
Illinois,	3,660.70	3,119.40	217,375,523	37,620
Wisconsin,	1,449.70	1,045.20	41,880,302	49,076
Minnesota,	1,584.00	161.00	7,709,000	46,385
Iowa,	2,037.10	801.80	27,715,052	34,428
Missouri,	1,412.30	925.75	51,187,255	55,277
Kansas,	360.00	40.00	1,400,000	35,000
California,	628.98	147.30	7,870,000	52,175
Oregon,	19.50	19.50	500,000	25,000
S. and C. R. R.	40			
Total,	34,310.61	25,372.25	1050,354,406	41,868
Total, South,	14,927.50	9,069.40	237,054,548	26,151
	49,237.82	34,441.71	1287,310,993	

The greatest obstacles feared by those who had not given the matter attention, was that a one hundred foot grade to the mile would not carry the road over the Divide,

and was impracticable. From the Report we extract:
Grades.

While on the subject of grades I will call your attention to some of the leading railroads of the United States, whose operations are daily carried on over grades much higher than any that will be found necessary to establish on the Stockton and Copperopolis Railroad, on the Central Pacific Railroad of California, located by the late Theo. D. Judah, Esq., Chief Engineer, and now under successful operation nearly sixty miles eastwardly from Sacramento. We find planes of from one to eight miles in succession, of 105 feet per mile grade, operated daily with engines of thirty tons and under, at the rate of twenty-five miles per hour.

The Hon. Leland Stanford, President of that road, in his report to the President of the United States, dated October 10th, 1865, days:

"The highest grade used on the Central Pacific Railroad is 105 feet per mile, of which there are thirteen and one-half miles on the present completed line. (Sacramento to Clipper Gap—forty-five miles.) We find no difficulty in operating this portion of the road, running our regular passenger trains thereon at twenty-five miles per hour, and freight trains twelve miles per hour. A greater speed could be obtained, but so far it has been found unnecessary."

The freight trains mentioned here are, of course, freight going east, or ascending. On the Pennsylvania Central Railroad are gradients of ninety-five feet, for nine and three-fourths miles in succession, over which passenger and freight trains pass at the rate of twenty-four miles per hour. Many other instances of operations over high grades might be produced; one or two, however, will suffice. The most interesting instance in the United States is that of the Baltimore and Ohio Railroad, connecting the seaboard with the Mississippi Valley, across the Alleghany Mountains. In the year 1850 there was transported 447,000 tons of merchandise, and 180,000 passengers, over this road; and in the year 1860 the large amount of 2,362,893 tons of freight, and 1,182,640 passengers. On this road, some of the heaviest gradients that have yet been adopted by American engineers, have been successfully used. Near the summit of the Alleghanies is a grade of 116 feet per mile, for eleven and a half consecutive miles—ascending, going west; and again, on descending, we find gradients of 116 feet per mile, for eight and a half consecutive miles. These gradients, together with curves of 400 feet radius, in many instances, have been successfully operated on one of the great thoroughfares of the country for sixteen years. Again, on the Virginia Central Railroad, also crossing the Alleghanies, are gradients of 296 feet per mile, and the road was successfully operated for five years.

Reference is here made to the report of the late General Charles Ellet, the Chief Engineer of the road, who says:

"The length of descent from summit to foot of grade, on the eastern side, is two and thirty-seven-one-hundredths miles; the road descends, in this distance, 610 feet, with an average grade of 237 feet, and a maximum grade of 296 feet per mile."

And on the western side:

"The length of the descent is two and two-one-hundredths miles.

"Road descends, in this distance, 450 feet.

"Average grade, 223 feet per mile.

"Maximum grade, 280 feet per mile.

"On both sides of the mountains, the ruling curves are described with a radius of 300 feet; on which, gradients of 238 feet per mile occur.

"The locomotives relied on, to perform this extraordinary service, of 55,000 pounds, or twenty-seven and a half tons, have failed *but once*, in two and a half years, to make their regular trips."

He further says:

"The mountains have been covered with snow for weeks in succession; the cuts have been filled for long periods, many feet in depth, with drifted snow; the ground has been covered with sleet and ice; and every impediment due to bad weather and inclement seasons, has been encountered and successfully surmounted in working the tracks. The total weight of engines if 55,000 pounds, or twenty-seven and a half tons, when both boiler and tanks are supplied with fuel and water enough for eight miles."

He also says:

"Ascending, the engines stop daily on a grade of 280 feet per mile, and are held by the brakes while the tanks are filled, and started again, at the signal, without difficulty."

Again, says the captious cynic, "it will not pay." Let us again glance at the Report, and see what railroads have done for the Eastern States, and what effect their building has had on property in other places. Read the following:

The following table will show the operations of eleven of the great thoroughfares of the Northern States, for the years ending 1861 and 1865:

ROADS.	Rev. in 1861 DOLLARS.	Rev. in 1865 DOLLARS.
Atlantic and Great Western,.......	Not Built.	6,938,611
Chicago and Alton,........................	1,098,464	3,840,092
Chicago and Rhode Island,..........	1,261,056	3,222,692
Chicago and North Western,.....	2,811,544	7,958,980
Chicago and Great Eastern,.........	211,077	1,103,821
New York and Erie,......................	6,214,182	15,295,915
Illinois Central,.............................	2,899,612	7,181,208
Michigan Central,.........................	2,025,142	4,504,549
New York Central,........................	6,303,703	13,357,703
Pittsburg, Ft. Waye & Chicago, .	3,031,787	8,489,062
Philadelphia and Reading,............	3,315,501	6,324,083

And while we see that the traffic on our railroads has increased to such an extent as to tax their full capacity, the financial condition of the companies was never so prosperous.

Value of Railroad Securities in April, 1866.

Value of Stock.

Baltimore and Ohio Railroad 112½
New York and Central Railroad, ... 91¾
New York and Erie Railroad, ... 108¼
Little Miami Railroad—Ohio 140
Boston and Worcester Railroad—Massachusetts 134
Camden and Amboy Railroad—New Jersey 120
New Jersey Central Railroad 135
Delaware, Lackawanna, and Western Railroad 132
Philadelphia and Trenton Railroad 114
Cleveland, Columbus and Cincinnati Railroad 115
Cincinnati, Hamilton and Dayton Railroad 123
Hudson River Railroad—New York 107½

Before closing this report, I take the liberty to lay before you some general conclusions on the

RAILROADS OF THE UNITED STATES

Apparent to all who have watched the progress of this commercial and social necessity, equally as applicable to the railroads of California, which are as yet in their infancy, as to those of the Western States from which they are drawn.

The value of every species of property must depend upon the degree of necessity for its general use. The instrumentality that supplies society with food, and with other articles, always equally indispensable, and that is the sole medium for the movement of its members from place to place, must rank vastly higher, as an investment, than such as depend upon the faith of individuals, or even on political organization; or of enterprises which, while engaged in supplying human wants, are often injudiciously prosecuted, and are liable to be pushed far beyond the public consumption.

Such an agent, of prime necessity, is a railroad. And, although only about thirty years have elapsed since its first introduction, it has now become so much of a necessity as to be included in, and became a part of, all the operations of society.

The railroads of the United States have created by far the greatest part of our national wealth; and without them there could be neither domestic nor foreign commerce carried on to any considerable extent. By their instrumentalities the producer and customer are brought in contact. Every day increases their usefulness and power. So much are railroads interwoven into our well being as a nation that society cannot put forth a single great effort in which a railroad is not the chief agent and actor.

The universal necessity of their use measures and establishes their value as an investment. In the United States such use is not only universal, touching every industrial operation, but of its extent there can hardly be a limit, because no limit can be placed to the production and commerce which demand their construction. These productions, whether agricultural, mineral, or mechanical, are necessary in proportion to the new influences that are continually being brought to use. This fact should be constantly borne in mind. The commerce, for example, between New York and Chicago, is four fold in volume and value what it was six years ago, when Chicago numbered 85,000 inhabitants, against 185,000 at present time. The traffic now exceeds the capacity of all the lines opened for its accommodation; and it is well known that if the capacity of railroads between New York and Chicago were doubled, there would be more freight offering than all of them could move. The same result is also apparent, but not so great an extent, on our roads in California. The operations of the Central Pacific Railroad, for the month ending October, 1863, amounted to about $76,000, through a section of the State that, in 1861, was mostly unoccupied mountain lands. The San Francisco and San Jose Railroad has fully doubled its business since the commencement of its operations. The Sacramento Valley Railroad increased its business, from one state line in 1864, to a business of nearly $270,000, in 1864.

The railroads of the United States were, almost without exception, undertaken, not as an investment, but as means for the creation of capital, by the development of resources.

It has been for the purpose of opening new outlets, alike for the benefit of the producer and the customer, that almost all the railroads in America have been undertaken; all involved great pecuniary sacrifices to those employed in their early construction; they were to create, in a great measure, a trafic, and years were required to do it; the country along most of our leading railroads, then nearly uninhabited, is now teeming with population, supplied with all the appliances of productive labor, so that the chief concern of those early projectors and pioneers of railroad lines is not how to develop a trafic, but how to accommodate all that offers.

There can, in fact, be no contingencies in which the trafic of our railroads should not increase in the future as it has done in the past. The return of peace has not diminished it, as we find that the leading railroads in the United States have, in many cases, doubled their business in the last three years.

They are nearly all relieved from the pressing liabilities that weighed them down eight years ago, and consumed their earnings. Their increased receipts have enabled nearly every company to secure any money accommodation necessary for conducting their business, in the most expeditious and economical manner, and most of them, instead of being borrowers, and always in the market with their securities, are now mostly all large capitalists, and investing in the National loans.

The effect of building railroads upon the prosperity and wealth of this State cannot be better illustrated than by the rapid enhancement in value of all property brought within their influence. As examples we will take the States of Pennsylvania and Iowa.

Within the railroad era of Western States, or the last ten years, the rate of increase of real and personal wealth in Iowa has been more than nine hundred per cent.; the absolute increase of wealth has been two hundred forty-seven million dollars. While Pennsylvania has increased at the rate of ninety-six per cent.

The wealth per capita of Iowa, in 1850, was $132, while in 1860 it amounted to $366, or 277 per cent.

The wealth in Pennsylvania, in 1850, per capita, was $312; in 1860 the per capita wealth was $487, a rate of increase of fifty-six per cent.

No one acquainted with California will deny that there are more causes to produce the same, or even greater results, from the building of railroads in this State than existed in Iowa previous to the building of her railroads.

For these reasons, which all can easily understand, I believe no property of any kind or nature is so well worthy the attention of capital as the railroad securities of the United States. They underlie the whole of our social and commercial fabric. They must be built and used just so long as men eat, drink, and move. Indeed, it is impossible to find any interest, or investment, of which so much can be said in its favor, or against which so little can be urged.

It is believed that of the 34,441 miles of railroads now running in the United States, which have been built within the last thirty years, at a cost of $1,287,310,9993—yielding a revenue of not less than $269,427,276—that there is no forty miles thereof that can offer better inducements for profitable investment than the Stockton and Copperopolis Railroad; and it is certain that no forty miles of road in the United States, was ever undertaken with such an assurance of business, already developed, as that waiting for the construction of your road.

The Copperopolis road is now under contract, and will be completed within three years, at an expense of over one-half more than it would cost to build the Santa Cruz road, while their resources in timber and manufactured articles would not equal ours, and they have not the advantages of this section, resulting from travel, etc., direct from San Francisco to the Newport of the Pacific Coast. We think the general reader, after perusing these extracts, will admit that the contemplated road, *via* the San Lorenzo, is not only practicable and feasible, but would be a paying investment, at its completion and would increase in value, yearly, as new avenues of trade and wealth might be opened, especially, when the water-power of that splendid stream comes into extensive use, manufacturing every article which the trade of the Pacific Coast demands.

40. *Sacramento Bee*, June 21, 1866 (3:6)

Santa Cruz Railroad.—The Santa Cruz Sentinel urges the building of a railroad from that place to connect with the San Jose and San Francisco Railroad. The cost of thirty-one miles of railroad, from tide-water at Santa Cruz, to the nearest point connecting with the San Francisco road, at about $28,000 per mile, would amount to $868,000 for building the road, besides rolling stock and equipments.

41. *Santa Cruz Sentinel,* November 3, 1866 (2:2)

As the mail is now carried, we are behind every P.O. in the Country from 24 to 36 hours, whereas, if the mails were brought direct from San Jose, as per contract, we would be in advancer of *all* other places in getting telegraphic dispatches in the daily city papers as much as the time occupied by the stage in going from Soquel to Santa Cruz, without any detriment to the last named place, as it is conceded by all that better time can be made on the Soquel route than on the turnpike or Mountain Charlie road as it is called; furthermore, there is no P.O. on the turnpike from Lexington to Santa Cruz. There is *one* quite respectable *little* settlement at Scott's Valley, the remaining portion of the intermediate country being sparsely populated, while on the Soquel route, it is one continuous succession of mills above, and cultivated farms below Soquel to the town of Santa Cruz; we think capitalists in traveling the Soquel route would form a more favorable opinion of the resources of the County, than in traveling over the comparatively uninhabited route now used, over which the timid pleasure seekers now ride, in many places with eyes dilated, fingers distended and hair erect, on account of the giddy heights of some of the precipices necessarily incurred, thereby lessening the summer resort to Santa Cruz, while no such dangers will be encountered by the proposed change. The county on the headwaters of the Soquel Creek is of easy grade,—and a safe and expeditious trip—making it incomparably the better route of the two, as well as the quickest from S.F. to Santa Cruz, until the iron horse comes thundering down the San Lorenzo Valley, laden with the almost inexhaustible timber, making the city of "The Holy Cross" the Bangor or Chicago of California for her lumber exports. VOX POPULI.

42. *Santa Cruz Sentinel,* November 17, 1866 (2:3)

The railroad from San Jose will soon be graded through to Gilroy and San Juan; from thence Watsonville will bring it into Santa Cruz county to open to the thrifty farmers a market for their surplus grain and produce. This county already has great influence upon the destinies of California, and will soon be the manufacturing county of the State.

43. *Santa Cruz Sentinel,* November 24, 1866 (2:1)

Railroad to Watsonville.

We have reliable information, of a positive nature, which induces as to say that within two years' time a railroad, from San Jose *via* Gilroy to Watsonville, will be under contract, and in part completed. All that is necessary, according to the plan proposed, is for the people of Watsonville and Pajaro Valley to subscribe liberally, to have the alignment of the road surveyed and located along the Pajaro river so as to strike the Salinas Valley near their town. Already the engineers are at work in making the preliminary survey, and the county—consisting of a large number of heavy capitalists and influential men—have determined on the route, and adopted a programme, but we are assured a hearty and earnest effort on the part of the Pajaronians will bring the road through the centre of their beautiful valley, and thus afford an outlet for their purpose.

44. *Santa Cruz Sentinel,* November 24, 1866 (2:4)

A railroad is the only thing that will relieve farmers of their present drawbacks in the way of shipping produce.

45. *Santa Cruz Sentinel,* December 15, 1866 (2:1)
The Southern Pacific Railroad.

We learn that the Surveyors are now in the field, making the alignment survey (the preliminary survey having been made some time since) of this great National enterprise. Mr. Wm J. Lewis is the Chief Engineer, and the road will be located, ready for grading, from San Jose to Gilroy the present season. It is the intention of the Company to petition Congress for an appropriation the present session, and should they get the required amount the road will be built the coming year, but any rate it will be built as soon as the iron and rolling stock can be manufactured, as the grading and ties are of little consequence, over an almost dead level plain and in such close proximity to the vast forests of redwood timber. The people of Watsonville and Monterey should take up and at once proceed to secure the advantages of the road. A liberal subscription would lead the road into Pajaro Valley thence south in the center of the Salinas Plains to the Mission San Miguel. Unless some prompt and united action is taken by the farming and mercantile interest of the route indicated the road may go up the San Benito or Peach Tree valleys and never touch on the Salinas. The Stockton *Independent*, of a recent date in noticing the proposed road says:

'The proposed route of the Southern Pacific Railroad, starting at San Jose, is along Santa Clara Valley, between the Santa Cruz and the Monte Diablo ranges to Gilroy, thence to San Juan and along the valleys between the Santa Lucia mountains on the west and the coast range of mountains on the east, to San Luis Obispo; thence through Santa Barbara, and along a comparatively rough route near the sea coast, through Los Angeles to San Diego. The vast valley of the San Joaquin is wholly ignored—totally left out in the cold. Let the Southern Pacific Railroad be constructed along the route at present contemplated, and it might be half a century before capitalists would engage in the work of constructing a road from Los Angeles into the head of Tulare Valley, and coursing through the entire extent of San Joaquin Valley, connecting with the Western Pacific road at or near Stockton. We perceive that at a recent meeting held at San Jose, it was stated that the Southern Pacific road would be begun and cars running during the coming Summer or Autumn. Speaking of the meeting, the San Jose *Patriot* says that Peckham made a short, clear and forcible speech, which called up Phelps, who gave a satisfactory answer to some inquiries

Peckham had made.... Phelps, in the course of his remarks, distinctly made this statement: That the company wished to commence the work on the road at San Jose soon by preliminary surveys, and that without further legislation by Congress the company had the means to complete the road as far as Gilroy, and hoped to be able to finish it and have the cars running thereon as far as that town some time during the nest Summer or Autumn months. What is the legislation already done by Congress for the encouragement of this enterprise? What positive measures have been adopted? It appears to us that along the route they propose from San Francisco to Lower California, a railroad will be much more difficult to construct, and equally as along, as it would be to follow the Western Pacific road into San Joaquin Valley, and traverse said valley its entire length. The newly projected road from San Francisco to Salt Lake would form a junction with the Southern Pacific at some point probably in Tulare county, east of Tulare Lake. To be sure, it has been proposed to run the Southern Pacific road, from San Juan, across the coast range of mountains at Pacheco Pass, thence through Merced and Fresno counties to Visalia, at or near which point the connection with the proposed road to Salt Lake would probably be formed; but, from present appearances, there is but little reason to expect that the Pacheco Pass route will be chosen by those who have the business of the Southern Pacific Railroad in hand. In fact, it is almost certain that choice will be made of the route west of the coast range of mountains; and as energetic efforts are apparently being made to push the work of construction ahead, it becomes men who have the interest of San Joaquin Valley at heart to be up and active in devising means and preparing the way for a railroad through the richest and most extensive agricultural section of California. No time should be lost in urging the necessity of a railroad along the valley east of the coast range of mountains, upon the attention of the Senators and Representatives from the Pacific States. Remote as much of the very best land in the country is from centres of commerce, the development of its resources can only be accomplished by affording speedy and cheap means of transit, such as only railroad communication can afford. The notice of the Representatives from California should be particularly and immediately drawn to the urgent necessity of securing all the Government aid possible for the accomplishment of so necessary a work. Should Government subsidies be granted the Southern Pacific Railroad Company to build a road along the proposed route near the coast of the Pacific, subsidy for another road, traversing the San Joaquin and Tulare Valleys from Stockton to Visalia, might possibly be granted with some reluctance.

About a year ago, a company of gentlemen formed an incorporation for the purpose of constructing a railroad from Stockton, through San Joaquin Valley, and to extend to Fort Yuma. The bill necessary to secure the right of way and receive Government aid, it is expected, will be passed during the approaching session of Congress. The measure should be strenuously urged; for unless the needed aid is afforded by the Government, a vast area of territory, rich in both mineral and agricultural wealth, must remain, in a measure, a vast unpeopled solitude for many years to come. The welfare of the State demands that railroads should first be built along routes where the most extensive industrial developments are likely to be made and the interests of the people, at large, most thoroughly subserved by the means of cheap transit and speedy communication. By glancing at the map, our Representatives at Washington will perceive the superior claims for Government aid in a railroad through a section of country of vast extent and rich in resources, to that of a road which would comparatively have the effect of only making a few people rich.

46. *Los Angeles News*, December 18, 1866 (2:3)

There is no immediate steps being taken to extend the road to Gilroy, San Juan, Watsonville and Santa Cruz, although it would pay richly. Rival companies have the franchise, and perhaps no money, which is too often the case.

47. *Santa Cruz Sentinel*, December 22, 1866 (2:2)

Congressional Election.

The telegraph is silent, as to the probabilities of the New Congress being called to meet on the fourth of March, by the provisions of the Bill now pending. Since our last publication, we have heard of several new names proposed, as Congressional candidates, in this district. Besides Mr. C. T. Ryland, the names of Harvey Brown, Alfred Barstow and J. M. McShafter, have been mentioned. The political elements are agitated, and what questionable shape they may assume—whether Conness or anti-Conness—it is hard to discover, from the crude materials to work. Some have expressed surprise at our suggesting the name of Mr. C. T. Ryland, for Congress, in last week's *Sentinel*. We done so through the influence of his friends who appear to take an active interest in the matter, believing him amply competent and worthy to fill the position. Mr. Ryland is a quiet unassuming gentleman, and may have not made such a political record as some of the lawyers named, but we are assured that he is a firm and unyielding Union man—not one of the peanut stripe—but on the broad and National basis of the Constitution and laws, detesting the whole coterie, backed by Felton's monied interests and the corrupt bargain-and-sale cabal who are now in every city, town and village, making and breaking political "slates," to suit the whims of the Conness clique. We also knew Mr. Ryland was in favor of the Southern Pacific Railroad, *via* Gilroy, and the Salinas, to Los Angeles, an enterprise that is absolutely required to aid the farmers and stock-raisers of this section of the state, in securing a market for their produce, and which may not be built for years if allowed to be controlled by the Conness faction who are so largely interested in the Sacramento roads and Eldorado and Placer county property. For the same reasons last year we have Mr. Cole, our cordial support, and the people, through their representatives, endorsed him by the handsome Senatorial vote he received, notwithstanding the efforts of "Honest John"—the intensely sobered—who, with his hired crew done all they could to defeat Mr. Cole. We say this much for the few in this vicinity, who are now endeavoring to sustain political vitality by hanging on to the skirts of the successful Senator—Cornelius Cole—while covertly obeying the behests of his unscrupulous enemy. The Santa Cruz and Watsonville *Times* can make a note of it for future reference.

48. *Santa Cruz Sentinel,* January 5, 1867 (4:1)

The initial survey of the first thirty miles of the Southern Pacific Railroad from San Jose to Gilroy, has been completed this week, and the work of construction will commence early in the spring. The probable route from Gilroy to the Colorado river, it is thought, will lie through the Coast Range at the southern end of Tulare Valley; thence through a new pass in Santa Barbara to the Santa Clara river; thence by the mission of San Fernando to Los Angeles, and east from Los Angeles to Fort Mohave or La Paz, in Arizona. This is the most fertile and best populated route. We are informed that a large amount of the stock of the Southern Pacific Railroad has been disposed of, and that the company are confident of their ability to keep the work going after it is once begun.

49. *Santa Cruz Sentinel,* February 16, 1867 (2:3)

The contemplated Railroad from San Jose to Gilroy, thence to San Juan and Watsonville, will bring us in the front market, and it is now reduced to a certainty that the road will be built at an early day. This certainly is no "dead" one, like the Vallejo and Marysville Railroad. Few persons know the true value of the land from San Juan to the Colorado. There are many rich and genial spots where laughing grain will soon take the place of unbroken wilds. Tanneries and flouring mills are upon either hand, and laboring men find ready and lucrative employment. The powder mill is now daily exporting hundreds of kegs of powder, thus supplying both the mining and farming regions of the Pacific Coast. The paper mill is in active operation and is doing a good business. The lime company is shipping vast quantities of lime to San Francisco and find a ready market. The health of the country is good, although the recent visits of the diphtheria has sent many a thrill of horror to the mothers of this region. Not many cases have proved fatal, however, and we hope that fair weather will soon dispel the infection from our midst.

50. *Santa Cruz Sentinel*, March 2, 1867 (2:6)

To give an outlet to this immense wealth [from Rancho Soquel Augmentation], a wharf will be erected near the mouth of Tannery Gulch, from which a railroad will be built, at an easy grade, four miles long, to the point where the sawmill will be erected on the Aptos creek. The road will eventually be extended still further, into the heart of the forest, as the timber may be cleared off along the proposed route.

51. *Santa Cruz Sentinel*, March 16, 1867 (3:1)

Internal Improvements.

Santa Cruz has been in a perfect fever of improvement during the past week. Early Monday morning gatherings of the *substantial* men of the town were seen in earnest discussion of some important enterprise. "On Change was all bustle and excitement, and casual observers from an occasional remark, would have imagined that the San Lorenzo was to have been bridges towards Soquel, and also towards George Anthony's; or mayhap a railroad up the valley of Bean Creek, tunneling the mountain under "Charley," and run down again on the other side in the valley of "Los Gatos" to San José; and surmises even ran down the San Lorenzo, and pictured a splendid "Liverpool Dock," just inside of the sea, capable of holding not half the navies of the world. The town was alive with rumors and with men.

52. *Santa Cruz Sentinel*, March 30, 1867 (2:1)

Scenery Around Santa Cruz.—The weather during the past week has been delightful; as soft and sunny as June days in our old homes. The hills and plains are all covered green with the richest verdure of spring, and the woods and shrubbery are just donning their earliest leaves. The wild flowers are springing in myriads. in a thousand colors and forms, and giving nature its sweetest adornment. The bay and the ocean spread their blue and shining fields, undiminished by fog, and the mountains rise in sublime majesty clothed with the darkest forest, and rifted with deep glens. Sea, earth and sky, this glorious spring weather, strive which shall do most to wake up the magnificent panorama, that surrounds Santa Cruz on every side. There is no eye so dull, no soul so tame in this beautiful valley, as not to feast with delight upon the riches of a scenery that needs the pen of a poet, and the genius of a painter to delineate. We do not believe that in any part of California can there be found a spot that contains so much to attract the eye, and enchant the heart of man as lies in the valley of Santa Cruz. No stranger ever visits our town without expressing his surprise and admiration, and his wonder that so few know of the rare magnificence of landscape which we here possess and enjoy.

53. *Santa Cruz Sentinel,* April 13, 1867 (2:1)

As a manufacturing region, it is unequalled by any part of California. The San Lorenzo and its tributaries will supply power in the length of twelve miles, yet unoccupied by any permanent business, equal to six hundred horse power, and adapted by location and access to almost any kind of manufacturing business; and when capital can be induced to look out of San Francisco for advantageous investments, we shall have a railroad up this stream, crossing the mountains at its source, and joining the San José road at Bay View Park or San Mateo. Such a road would open a beautiful mountain country; and the resources are sufficient, right along the line of the road, in lumber, wood, bark, posts, rails, shingles, and passengers, to make it at once a paying institution. The extensive forests all along the lines of the San Lorenzo and its tributaries condense a great deal of moisture from the fog clouds of the ocean, so that the stream is very permanent.

54. *Santa Cruz Sentinel,* June 1, 1867 (3:1)

Watsonville is destined at some future time, not many years hence, to be one of the most flourishing towns in the State. The railroad will be built and a market at the very doors of the farmers afforded for all they can raise, and then this land, now selling at from $100 to $300 per acre, will be worth three times as much. At present money is scarce and business slack, so we were informed, on account of a want of market facilities. The railroad to Gilroy will be 21 miles distant, at the nearest point, but that is too far to haul butter, eggs, fruit, etc., over a mountain.

55. *Santa Cruz Sentinel,* June 22, 1867 (2:1)

Railroad Meeting at Watsonville.

A joint stock company was formed in Watsonville last week, for the purpose of building a railroad from or near the above named town, to extend near the town of Gilroy, or to the nearest practicable point of junction with the Southern Pacific Railroad. The capital stock of said company has been placed at four hundred thousand dollars, in four thousand shares of one hundred dollars each. Twenty thousand dollars of said stock has already been taken, and ten per cent, of the same paid in. The following gentlemen have subscribed towards the road: N. W. Chittenden, Chas. Ford, L. Sanborn, A. W. Blair, T. D. Alexander, F. A. Hihn, B. A. Barney, A. Mendia, R. Pinto, Hy. Jackson, P. J. Kelly, D. McCusker, T. Sheehy, Jas. Lyman, J, Sheehy, Robt. Johnson, R. Struve, J. D. Ordish, G. M. Bockius,

Thos. Snodgrass, Jas. W. Thrift, Jas. P. Sargent. The company has been incorporated under the general railway law of 1861, and will be known by the name of the "California Coast Road Company." A meeting of stockholders was held, and the following persons were elected Directors: N. W. Chittenden, F. A. Hihn, Chas. Ford, A. Mendia and B. A. Barney. The Directors held a meeting and elected N. W. Chittenden, President of the Board, and B. A. Barney, Secretary and Treasurer.

It is contemplated to have a survey of the route made as soon as possible, and the books of the company will be open in a few weeks for further subscriptions. The President is now in San Francisco, and will endeavor to secure the services of some good practical engineer to make preliminary survey, etc. Very little grading will be required, and the distance being short, (not more than sixteen miles,) it is presumed that the proposed line can be built without a great deal of expense; and we trust before long to be on the "lookout for the locomotive when the bell rings."

56. *Santa Cruz Sentinel*, June 29, 1867 (2:4)

Watsonville Items—From an Occasional Correspondent.
Watsonville, June 20th, 1867.

Editor Sentinel:—Watsonville is happy—supremely happy; and why shouldn't it be? Don't we see in the near future those thousand dollar-a-foot corner lots? Don't we look upon those imposing blocks of brick that are soon to rise all along Main street—aye, even upon side streets? Don't we perceive that our town is going to be one of the smartest little city-ettes in the State of California? And best of all, don't our palms begin to itch with the prospect of those hard shiners that are to fall into them for rents? But you say, what is all this pother about? Simple soul! Havn't you heard of the railroad—railroad, Sir? Havn't you heard of the wharf that Capt. Lemon is building? Why, Sir, Watsonville is going up like a rocket, (Heaven forefend that it may not come down like a stick.) Look out now, Santa Cruz; we shall out-vote you before you know it. The fact is that we have forgotten to talk politics; even "Observer" didn't say a word about Ed. Williams for twenty-four hours. Ah, me! I have dropped from the sublime (railroad) to the ridiculous (politics.)... RAILROAD.

57. *Santa Cruz Sentinel,* July 13, 1867 (2:5)

Railroad.—We learn that an enterprise is on foot to build a railroad up the San Lorenzo, to King's farm, from the Santa Cruz landing. The directors are S. A. Bartlett, Horace Gushee, Dr. Peabody, Edmund Jones, Samuel Brown and others.

58. *Santa Cruz Sentinel,* July 20, 1867 (2:1)

Accident.—On Tuesday last, one of the engineers of the San Lorenzo railroad surveying party lost his foot-hold and precipitated some hundred feet. Fortunately no serious injury was received. A valuable instrument was badly crushed in the fall.

59. *Santa Cruz Sentinel*, July 20, 1867 (3:1)

California Coast Railroad.—The directors of this enterprise have been in session the past week and went out to view the route and find it practicable. A contract has been made with Mr. Blake, a Civil Engineer of high standing to make preliminary and final surveys, after which books will be opened for the subscription of stock, and as the Company do not expect to get any State or County aid every person should subscribe as much stock as his interest in the completion of the road will justify.

60. *San Francisco Examiner*, July 30, 1867 (3:2)

New Enterprise.—Parties in San Francisco, Benicia, and this place, says the *Santa Cruz Times*, have organized a company for the purpose of building a railroad from Santa Cruz to the head waters of the San Lorenzo. The officers are: Horace Gushee, President; S. A. Bartlett, Treasurer; Edmund Jones, Secretary, and the capital stock is $100,000. The route up the river is being surveyed and will be completed in a few weeks, when the company will commence building the road. This road will open a large tract of country to settlers, at present of no great value, and will give employment to many laborers, besides affording easy access to this port for the large quantities of lumber, lime, and other resources of our county, produced on the San Lorenzo and its tributaries.

61. *Daily Alta California*, September 23, 1867 (2:3)

[Regarding building a breakwater at the Santa Cruz Harbor.]

The contemplated improvements could be built at a small cost, comparatively, as we have the best of facilities and material to erect them. Our granite quarries are unsurpassed for durability and extent, within a few miles of the proposed location of the work. A railroad is already surveyed and will soon be built to several granite and limestone ledges on the San Lorenzo, and to the timber regions, where redwood, fir, oak, laurel, madroña and other hard wood grow in dense forests, affording unsurpassed facilities. We commend the enterprise to thinking and speculative minds.

62. *Santa Cruz Sentinel*, October 5, 1867 (2:1)

A railroad is about to be constructed, running up the San Lorenzo river, which will make this stream available for ten or twelve miles above here, on every mile of which there is at least half a dozen good privileges. The manufacturing interests already established here, requires steady and uninterrupted communication with the outside world, and that can only be made safe and certain by the erection of a breakwater like the one mentioned. What will be the need then, when for ten miles above here the whole power of our beautiful river shall be devoted to manufacturing purposes, the raw material of which must be brought here by vessels, and the manufactured article sent away by the same means of conveyance?

63. *Santa Cruz Sentinel,* October 12, 1867 (2:4)

The preliminary steps for the construction of the Pajaro and Gilroy railroad, such as surveying and locating, are being taken, and so soon as they are completed, books will be opened to receive subscriptions for its final completion. Success to the enterprise, and when its completion is consummated it will add materially to the amount of taxable county property, its continuation to Santa Cruz remaining but a problem of time. Who is sufficiently advanced in mathematics to solve it?

64. *Santa Cruz Sentinel,* November 16, 1867 (2:3)

The San Jose and Gilroy Railroad.—We learn from the San Jose *Mercury* that there is a prospect that this road will soon be put under contract and immediately built. The enterprise is of great importance to Santa Cruz county, also to Monterey and all the great agricultural, manufacturing, stock-raising and timber interests of this section. It is contemplated to make a connection with Watsonville as soon as the road is completed to Gilroy; in fact, the road would be extended, in due time to Hilltown, and further south on the Salinas, as well as north to the timber belt, and manufacturing interests of Santa Cruz. The plan proposed by Peter Donahue, for the S.F. and S.J.R.R. Co., to the Supervisors of Santa Clara county, is to surrender to the county $100,000 of the county Bonds and agree to construct a railroad from San Jose to Gilroy within two years from the date of their obligation. This proposition also has a condition that the suit now pending against the Road shall be withdrawn. We hope that Santa Cruz county will agree to the proposition.

65. *Santa Cruz Sentinel,* December 7, 1867 (2:3)

The San Lorenzo Railroad.—This public improvement is progressing, we are informed, as fast as the weather and the nature of the work will admit. The route has been surveyed and found practicable, and the work will be commenced as soon as the right of way is secured. The enterprise is of great importance to Santa Cruz, as it will give from 500 to 1,000 men constant employment for many years to come in constructing the road and getting out lumber, shingles, hoop-poles, tan bark and firewood, granite and a hundred other natural resources, so bountifully supplied in that favored region in and around the head-waters of the San Lorenzo.

66. *Sacramento Daily Union,* December 11, 1867 (2:4)

The San Lorenzo Railroad project is progressing as fast as the weather and the nature of the work will admit. The route has been surveyed and found practicable, and the work will be commenced as soon as the right of way is secured.

67. *Santa Cruz Sentinel,* January 4, 1868 (2:5)
RAILROAD NOTICE.

NOTICE IS HEREBY GIVEN THAT THE FIRST Annual Meeting of the Stockholders of the San Lorenzo Railroad Company, for the election of Directors to serve for the ensuing year; will be held on MONDAY, JANUARY 27th, 1868, at two o'clock, P. M., at the office of Dr. W. F. Peabody, in the town of Santa Cruz, in the county of Santa Cruz, and State of California. By order of the Board of Directors.

HORACE GUSHEE, *President*
EDMUND JONES, *Secretary*
Santa Cruz, January 4th, 1868.

68. *Santa Cruz Sentinel,* January 4, 1868 (4:1)

Railroad to Gilroy.—On Tuesday, Dec. 24th, the Board of Supervisors of Santa Clara, says the *Argus*, passed an order accepting the proposition of the San Francisco and San Jose Railroad Co., and have thereby insured the early connection to Gilroy and this city by a railroad. By this arrangement the county has discontinued her suit against the Co. for the recovery of $209,000 advanced in bonds and surrenders the stock held as security therefor; the company has paid $100,000 in currency into the treasury, has paid the costs of the suit and all interest due the county, and binds itself to complete the road to Gilroy within eighteen months—pledging the stock surrendered by the county as security for its doing so. We are assured by Maj. Hammond, the Company's Chief Engineer and Superintendent, that the road will be completed far within the time agreed upon, in all probability, in time for freighting the next harvest to market. We congratulate the people of the county, and especially our friends at Gilroy, on this wise action of the Supervisors, for we feel confident that the $100,000 in bonds given by the county in aid of this enterprise is the merest trifle in comparison with the immense benefits that are sure to flow from it in the immediate future.

69. *Santa Cruz Sentinel,* January 11, 1868 (2:3)

Board of Supervisors—Adjourned Meeting.
Tuesday, January 7th, 1868.
Present—Hihn, Moore and Parsons.

On petition of C. D. Stillman and others for a new school district to be formed out of "Carlton District;" said district was established and named "Railroad School District"—line bounding on Pajaro river and thence through lands of Sillman, Wiley, Driscoll, Fining, Carleton, Jr., Folgey, Casserly, to the east line of Santa Cruz county, and thence to the Pajaro river and down said river to the place of beginning.

70. *Santa Cruz Sentinel,* January 11, 1868 (4:1)

Certificates of Incorporation.—The Sacramento *Union* says: There were filed in the office of the Secretary of State, Thursday, certificates of incorporation of the following companies:... "Santa Clara and Pajaro Valley Railroad Company"—for the purpose of owning, constructing and maintaining a railroad from a point at or near the city of San Jose, in the county of Santa Clara, connecting at such point with the San Francisco and San Jose Road, and to pass to a point at or near the town of New Gilroy, in said county, a distance of thirty miles. Capital stock, $1,000,000, in 10,000 shares of $100 each. The Directors chosen to act until others are elected in their places are Charles Mayne, Peter Donahue, Richard P. Hammond, Henry M. Newhall and Myles D. Sweeney.

71. *Santa Cruz Sentinel,* February 1, 1868 (2:1)

Election.—On Monday, Jan. 27th, the San Lorenzo Rail Road Co. elected five trustees: Joseph Boston, S. A. Bartlett, H. Gushee, E. Jones and W. F. Peabody. On Wednesday, Jan. 30th, the above named trustees elected W. F. Peabody, President; E. Jones, Secretary; Jos. Boston, Treasurer.

72. *Santa Cruz Times* via the *Daily Alta California,* February 5, 1868 (1:7)

Last Monday, pursuant to notice, a railroad meeting was held at the office of W. F. Peabody for the purpose of perfecting measures for the constructing of a railroad from King's Ranch (14 miles up the San Lorenzo) to the landing on the opposite side of the river, and just below Santa Cruz. It will be a horse railroad, and used for a more ready transportation of the fine lumber, etc., along the San Lorenzo, to market. It will open an immense lumber country, and will prove of great benefit to this county. The following officers were elected: President, Dr. W. F. Peabody; Secretary, E. Jones; Treasurer, Joseph Boston; Directors, A. Gushee, S. A. Bartlett, Joseph Boston, E. Jones and Dr. W. F. Peabody.

73. *Santa Cruz Sentinel,* February 8, 1868 (2:1)
Railroad to Watsonville.

We learn from private information, and from the Santa Clara papers, that the railroad from San Jose to Gilroy is now under contract and will be completed within two years. The well known energy of the parties building the road, and the heavy interests involved, are sufficient guarantee of prompt work and early completion of the road. The people of this county, especially in the southern portion, are deeply interested in the work. There is not an individual or an interest in Santa Cruz County but would be benefited by having the proposed road continued to Watsonville, and even to the County Seat, at the earliest day possible. Already the preliminary survey has been made, and estimates furnished for alignment survey, grading, cost of laying track, rolling stock and equipments for eighteen miles of track, sufficient to bring the road, with turn-outs, down the centre of the valley, 0on the north side of the Pajaro river, to the Watsonville Depot. All admit the necessity of this road, and a large sum has been subscribed or promised, in this county, Monterey and Santa Clara, to aid in the building of the road; the balance, it is believed, can be readily secured in San Francisco. Experience has proved that during winter, freighting to San Francisco by sea, is not safe and very uncertain. The long continued storms, lasting for months, almost isolates this portion of the county from the outside world, consequently every mechanical branch and productive enterprise suffers.

Our grain merchants want the road, but more especially is it the farmer who would be enriched by having a safe, speedy and cheap transportation to market for his produce; the dairymen desires it to send his butter and cheese promptly to market, when good prices rule and a demand exists; the lumberman requires it to send forth the products of his mills and the yields of the forest in wood, staves, shingles, lath, hoop-poles, etc. The mechanic must have it to receive his supplies, and the manufacturer to send his leather, lime, powder, paper, soap, glue, starch and other articles to a metropolitan market. Our dry-goods merchants and grocers, want it to enable them to take advantage of the markets at all times, to receive their goods when the coast is stormy and dangerous; and that they may be enabled to ship country produce at all seasons of the year, and thus be able to compete with other localities. Our manufacturers want it for the same reason that they can be constantly supplied with the raw material. Our wood-men and teamsters want it to ensure them constant employment during the entire year, instead of one-half the time. Our blacksmiths, wagon-makers, tinners, saddlers, shoe-makers, tailors, etc., want it to increase their business and enable their customers to pay cash down for their work. Our land-holders want it that the price of real estate may advance, and farmers must absolutely have it that they may be justified in cultivating and improving their farms to greater extent than heretofore, as it will secure them a daily market for their products and double the value of their farms. The different localities—Watsonville, Corralitos, Aptos, Soquel and Santa Cruz—want it, to enable capitalists who are looking for a location, to visit their towns and let them know we have an easy communication at all times, with all the world and the "rest of mankind." In a word, we all want it, in order that we may go and come at pleasure, and what is more important to every individual that we receive our mails at the proper time, and not be dependent on the whims of contractors or the delays consequent to bad roads. And to sum up, every man, woman and child, who desires to make a semi-annual visit to Frisco, want it to go and see the fashions and return without being, possibly, subject to a week's delay and corresponding expense. For all these, and ten thousand other reasons, the road should be speedily built, and our citizens should as promptly put their shoulders to the wheels and subscribe liberally for the stock.

74. *Santa Cruz Sentinel,* February 22, 1868 (2:1)

The San Jose and Gilroy Railroad.—The work, says the *Call* of Feb. 16th, on this line is to be prosecuted without delay. Ties for the entire distance of thirty miles were contracted for in this city, on Friday, at forty cents apiece. Yesterday afternoon a batch of Chinese laborers, with tools and supplies, were forwarded from here, and with no unforeseen interruption, San Jose will before many months be in railroad communication with Gilroy.

75. *State Capital Reporter*, February 19, via the *Santa Cruz Sentinel*, February 29, 1868 (3:2)

San Lorenzo Railroad Company.—The annual report of this company for the year ending December 31, 1867, was filed in the office of the Secretary of State yesterday. The following is the exhibit of the condition of the company: Capital stock, $150,000; amount subscribed, $15,000; amount actually paid up, $2,300; amount due on unpaid assessments, $700; expended in incidental expenses and surveying road, $2,231; amount in hands of Treasurer unappropriated December 13, 1867, $69. The company has been completed and maps and profiles returned. The report is subscribed and attested by Horace Gushee, President; S. A. Bartlett, Treasurer, and Edmund Jones, Secretary.

76. *Santa Cruz Sentinel*, March 28, 1868 (4:1)

Letter From Santa Cruz.

Mr. Holman, a traveling book agent, who has been canvassing the past winter in this County and Monterey, and occasionally contributing his observations to the Yolo *Democrat*, writes under date of March 1st 1868, as follows:

Santa Cruz, March 1, 1868.

"... In regard to the bay of Monterey, a prevailing error should be corrected. In the little that I have known heretofore, I had supposed—and indeed it is the prevailing opinion that Monterey was little better than an open roadstead; but the truth is, it is a safe harbor both from a nor'-wester and southeaster; the only points from which heavy weather is ever expected. Under pressure of the former, shipping can and does take refuge and lay quietly in Santa Cruz, and in case of the latter, the town of Monterey furnishes safe anchorage, and in ordinary weather, either, and both are good; and hence the Summer breezes, always from the north or northwest, rendering the Santa Cruz side especially placid and desirable for a Summer resort; and soon when beautiful little Santa Cruz shall be in railroad connection with San Francisco, and hence with all parts of the State, and United States, and indeed the world's commerce centering in the harbor of San Francisco, as a consequence attendant upon the completion of the great international railroad, and the already inaugurated commercial relations with Asia, a consummation realizing our happy situation to the world, necessarily eventuating in the most rapid influx of population, most intensely quickening every interest of our entire Pacific slope and none more than Santa Cruz with its gentle climate, its rich and variated resources, including the unprecedented watering privileges. In conversation I learn much of interest regarding the harbor of Monterey, as well also of the immense water-power yet unimproved upon the San Lorenzo and its tributaries, which only awaits capital—sure to find its way here so soon as all the advantages of manufacturing in this place, rather than in San Francisco, is realized.... W."

77. *Santa Cruz Sentinel,* May 2, 1868 (2:2)

After repeated calls, Mr. T. Seeley [Seelye] Farmer responded, by disclaiming any merit as a speaker, but would say that we had got a thoroughfare that is not only a credit to Santa Cruz, but to the whole State. But we must not stop here—we must go on and complete the good work; the road must go on until it reaches the top of the Santa Cruz range of mountains, and goes over it. He could safely predict that within ninety days the iron horse would be at our doors, and once start the railroad, it will not stop until it connects Santa Cruz with San Francisco, and the rest of mankind.

78. *Santa Cruz Sentinel,* May 16, 1868 (2:1)

The San Lorenzo Railroad.—On last Monday, May 11, the first work, of grading, was commenced on the new railroad, now building up the San Lorenzo river. On that day the surveyor and engineer, Mr. T. W. Wright, and the Superintendent, in company with one of the Directors and several citizens, initiated the work by breaking ground near the school-house at the terminus of the newly graded wagon road. The work was commenced with a small force, which will be gradually increased as facilities and demand may offer, but an effort will be made to complete this section of the road, during the summer and fall, and we are assured that the road will probably be completed and in running order before the next season, as far as the school-house station, and judging from the means and energy at command, and the interest manifested, we think the superintendent will be able to carry out the intentions of the Company. At present, the ties used will be redwood with oak rails, so laid as to be plated with bar-iron, as no rails of the T pattern can be had at this time. The entire length of the road when completed to King's farm will be 15 miles, where surveyor's stake 162 is located at a point near the mouth of King's creek, where a madrona tree 18 inches in diameter is marked B.M. The scale of the map is 400 feet to the inch, and shows no tunnelling, but that the road will cross the creek several times, keeping principally on the north-west side; two crossings are made in the first section. The lower one opposite Davis & Cowell's mill, where the road crosses to the south-east side, and thence down the canyon, to Santa Cruz, on the opposite side from the powder and paper-mills. The terminus of the present survey is 549 above tide water, and 516 feet above the initial point. When this road is completed a new era will dawn on the enterprise and business resources of Santa Cruz. Then the wealth of these grand old hills, in wood, lumber, lime, granite &c., will roll into our town without intermission, at all seasons, regardless of muddy roads or rain, and we foresee the day when a speedy connection will be made with the San Jose railroad to San Francisco. Before another summer season, a railroad will be built from Alviso to Saratoga Springs, through Santa Clara, which will only leave a gap of some ten or fifteen miles between King's farm and Saratoga, which will no doubt be connected b a good stage road, so as to enable passengers to make the distance from the Bay City in much less time than at present, without any of the "unpleasantness" of dust and delay now experienced. We shall not cease advocating these improvements until they are completed. In the meantime let every citizen aid the enterprise in a liberal manner.

79. *Santa Clara Union* via the *Santa Cruz Sentinel*, May 16, 1868 (2:5)

Right of Way Granted.—By reference to another column it will be seen that the Two Council has granted the right of way through the town to the Saratoga, Santa Clara and Alviso Railroad. We congratulate the company upon the good spirit shown by the Council and hope that they will be able to secure the right of way along the entire line without delay.

80. *Santa Cruz County Times*, May 16, 1868 (3:1)

San Lorenzo Railroad.—The work upon this road was commenced last Monday, and will be vigorously prosecuted until we shall have direct communication with San Francisco via Menlo Park. The Railroad Company moved in this undertaking quietly, and without any flourish of trumpets. They have been fortunate in securing the services of Mr. W. W. Waddell, as Superintendent, and will soon have a large gang of hands at work clearing the line of the road, and making ready for the grading. The first section will be completed this season. Mr. Stanley is laying out an embryo city near the school house in Sayante Valley, which will be on the line of the road, and will probably be the first depot between this place and San Francisco. The energy of the Superintendent and the gentlemen who own the road is too well known to this community to require from us a word of comment, and assures the early completion of the road to Menlo Park.

Santa Cruz should extend to this enterprising Company, all sympathy and active aid. The completion of the Railroad is now a fixed fact, and we must now make terms with the Company, so as to secure the route through town to the beach. We understand that the Company desire to run the road upon the present bulk-head or levee, and extend the same to below the Blackburn estate, and to raise the grade about two feet and widen, so that a street will run by the side of the railroad, this improvement would bring a large amount of land that is now worthless into market, but it will cost $25,000 more than to build the road on the other side of the river. We think the owners of the property reclaimed from water would be benefited ten times the amount of the additional cost between the two routes. While if we have railroad community with San Francisco, the passenger depot should be on this side of the San Lorenzo. Will our citizens not take this into serious consideration and move in the matter promptly?

81. *Santa Cruz Sentinel,* May 23, 1868 (3:1)

Felton.—This is the name of a new town recently located and surveyed, at the schoolhouse on the San Lorenzo, near the terminus of the newly graded road and the railroad. Lots are already much sought after. Mr. Horace Gushee, will give all necessary information and sell lots to those desiring to purchase.

82. *Santa Cruz Sentinel*, May 30, 1868 (2:1)

Considering that Felton is to be the terminus of the first section of the San Lorenzo Railroad, we know of no better investment for parties of limited capital than is offered here.

83. *Santa Cruz Sentinel*, June 6, 1868 (2:1)

The sand-hills on the San Lorenzo, are inexhaustible, located near the eastern side of the stream, and within half a mile of the new railroad now being constructed.

84. *Santa Cruz Sentinel*, June 13, 1868 (2:4)

At Felton, everything was life and bustle, new lots are being laid off and improved. The fine new building of W. J. Cooper and J. M. Merrill is nearly completed, and will be fitted up for a hotel and store. Already refreshments are furnished, and the weary tourist can find all the appetite craves either in the eating, drinking or resting, so necessary after a successful day's fishing. We wish them success in the new enterprise, being satisfied that they are gentlemen well versed in the wants of the public, and will do all that can be done to make their guests comfortable. In a short time will be open for the accommodation of the public. The new road is in fine condition, and a more pleasant one, to travel at this season, cannot be found in the State. It is the favorite drive in the vicinity of Santa Cruz, and no visitor should fail to make the trip. Workmen are engaged in widening the road, and no fear need be entertained in passing the many large teams, now traveling the road, heavily loaded with all kinds of lumber, bark, wood, lime, etc. Workmen are engaged on the railroad, clearing the way, and the new sawmill is nearly finished. We advise all who wish a pleasant day of recreation, to start early, and spend the day along the classic banks of the San Lorenzo and Zayanta.

85. *Sacramento Bee*, July 10, 1868 (3:1)

Filed.—There have been filed in the office of the Secretary of State...the certificate of incorporation of the San Jose and Santa Clara Railroad Company.

86. *Santa Cruz Sentinel*, July 18, 1868 (2:3)

Lime, Etc.—Davis & Cowell, we are informed by Henry Jordan, are burning and shipping an average of one thousand barrels of lime per week. Who says Santa Cruz is about to "peg out?" The "individual" we would like to see, if one so crazy there should be. The resources of this county are in an undeveloped infancy, and he who cannot see the prosperous future that is opening for her, is blind indeed. But such scrawny sluggards there are; men who supinely hug the delusive hope that they are foreseeing undeveloped financial giants, and all they need to make their mark, is a "show." They are the "wooden men" you hear about; the "fellers" who stand on street-corners or whittle fence-posts; the "know-alls" who can minutely describe other men's business; can instruct you how to do yours; can tell you how completely impracticable the building of a railroad up the San Lorenzo is, how it will never pay, how visionary the minds who conceived, planned and are now executing it, and how dead the town will be when it is completed.

87. *Santa Cruz Sentinel*, July 25, 1868 (2:2)

The Santa Cruz people are already constructing a wooden railroad some fifteen miles up the San Lorenzo creek, and if we are correctly informed in regard to the topography of the country, it is not more than ten or twelve miles from Page's Mill to the terminus of the San Lorenzo Railroad. The distance from Redwood City to Page's Mill is about twenty miles, which would make the distance from Santa Cruz to this place by this route, forty-five or fifty miles. A road running to Santa Cruz by this route would afford one of the most delightful and romantic drives to be found in the world. For twenty miles at least, the road would pass through the boundless forest of redwood timber, which is just beginning to be penetrated by the industrious and fearless lumberman.

88. *Daily Alta California*, July 28, 1868 (2:2)

Twelfth District Court.—Sexton, J.

Isaac E. Davis et al. vs. San Lorenzo Railroad Company.—Order for injunction upon defendants.

89. *Santa Cruz Sentinel,* August 1, 1868 (2:3)

INJUNCTION.—We learn that on Wednesday last, Davis & Cowell served an injunction on the San Lorenzo Railroad Company, forbidding further progress of the work, consequently indemnifying bonds were given.

90. *Santa Cruz Sentinel,* August 15, 1868 (2:3)

An Important Case.—An important decision, interesting to most of the inhabitants of Santa Cruz, was rendered on last Monday, August 10th, by Judge Sexton, of the Second Judicial District, now holding Court in San Francisco, for Judge Pratt of the Twelfth Judicial District. Judge Sexton, in a suit brought in that District by Isaac Davis and Henry Cowell against the San Lorenzo Railroad Company, had ordered an injunction to issue against the Company, forbidding them to proceed with the railroad on the lands of Davis & Cowell. A motion to dissolve the injunction had been pending for about ten days or two weeks, and was, after a full argument, sustained by the Court. The Company, as a condition of dissolving the injunction, were ordered to file a bond to plaintiffs in the sum of $10,000, conditional to pay the compensation which might be adjudged due them in the proceedings for condemnation of lands, now pending in the County Court of said county. The order also stayed all proceedings against the Company in the action in the District Court of San Francisco. Messrs. Wilson & Crittenden, of San Francisco, appeared for Davis & Cowell, and Charles N. Fox, Esq., of Redwood City, for the Company.

91. *Daily Alta California*, August 11, via the *Santa Cruz Sentinel,* August 15, 1868 (3:1)

INJUNCTION.—Isaac E. Davis et als. vs. the San Lorenzo Railroad Company. Ordered that the injunction be dissolved upon defendant filing a bond to plaintiffs in the sum of $10,000, to be approved by the Clerk in accordance with law.

This decision, rendered in the Twelfth District Court, Sexton, Judge, enabled the San Lorenzo Railroad Company to push forward their praiseworthy enterprise, and we understand that it is now the intention to enlarge the working-force to one hundred men, thereby enabling the iron horse to go puffing and snorting over the track before Christmas. May fortune speed the enterprise.

92. *Santa Cruz Sentinel,* September 19, 1868 (2:5)

The Southern Pacific Railroad Co. are building a depot 40 by 300 feet at Gilroy, and will put up a large hotel opposite.

93. *Daily Alta California*, September 28, 1868 (2:2)

The people of Santa Clara County are agitating a project for a railroad from Alviso to San José and Santa Clara. A Company has been formed and surveys have been made for the road. The cost is estimated at $170,000, the main items being $96,000 for eight miles of track, $14,000 for rolling stock, and $60,000 for two steamers to connect with the cars. It is presumed that such a line could deliver grain on the wharf in San Francisco at $1.50 per ton from

San José, whereas now it is necessary to pay $3 to the railroad and $1 for cartage from the station to the wharf. There is also talk about a railroad from Alviso, through Santa Clara, to McCartysville and Saratoga, which is to be connected by a turnpike road with King's Ranch, the northeastern terminus of the San Lorenzo Railroad.

94. *Santa Cruz Sentinel,* November 14, 1868 (2:3)

The last mile of the railroad from San Jose to Gilroy is graded.

95. *Santa Cruz Sentinel,* November 21, 1868 (2:1)
Santa Cruz Railroad

We republish an article on the first page of this issue which we prepared and published in the *Sentinel* of January 13th, 1866, under the caption "Railroad to Santa Cruz;" and as that affords ample data, going to prove the necessity for the construction of a railroad, we will not recapitulate, but take the liberty of further comment, and give the facts connected with the railroad which some of our enterprising townsmen have undertaken, and which, if God is willing, they will sooner or later complete from Santa Cruz to the headwaters of the San Lorenzo river, and thence to some point on the line of the railroad along the Bay. That this enterprise deserves well of every citizen in the county, and especially of this immediate region, need not be stated; all are willing to acknowledge the necessity for the road, the practicability of its construction, and the certain great benefit to be derived therefrom. Every day, more and more shows us how much the growth of prosperity of Santa Cruz and the country along the projected route, suffer for the want of this road. The timber of 250 square miles must be either brought out over this road, or hauled with the more expensive and slower means of transportation now in use. Read the article in full referred to, and then judge whether we conclude rightly or not.

The community are aware that the company of gentlemen who started in so energetically to prosecute this road to completion some few months since, were, from the very outset, beset with hindrances interposed at the instance of Messrs. Davis & Cowell, the wealthy lime monopolists of this coast, of the most perplexing kind. First, an injunction was sworn out; the affidavits of Mr. Davis showing that the company were insolvent, when the facts are, that the company promptly and honorably discharged every liability against them, and have always had money in their treasury, while some of the stockholders are worth hundreds of thousands. This injunction was dissolved as soon as the company could obtain a hearing. Then commenced a long and tedious investigation in the County Court of this county, at the instance of the same parties, to show if possible, grounds for denying the appointment of the Commissioners as directed by law, thus attempting, after the expenditure of many thousands dollars in grading, to block and kill this truly laudable and needed enterprise. The Court, after many days of patient hearing, finally decided the undertaking worthy the Commissioners, and proceeded to appoint as directed by law. Some two weeks have now been spent by the Commissioners in taking testimony, pro and con, whereupon they might predicate a decision that will be just to all parties, and we doubt not that such will be the final action of the Commission, for it is composed of gentlemen of probity and ability. We must say, in justice to those gentlemen interested in obtaining the right of way for their railroad, that they have offered everything fair and in reason, that falls without the lines of unjust demands and extortion, that any honorable man or men could or should require; and still this investigation is relentlessly prosecuted in the vain hope of finally killing the enterprise; and it remains to be seen whether the citizen of this county, so greatly interested in the construction of this road, will sit passively by and see it sworn out, bought out, and forced out of existence, to their eternal shame and disgrace; or whether they will come up like men and make common cause with their respected fellow citizens, and see that this road does go on unto final completion. We have heard men who never before give utterance to opinions, express their utter indignation and disgust of the unfair means employed in attempting to extort damages for this right of way.

It is the duty of every community to foster every laudable enterprise which is manifestly for the general good of all; and it is equally the duty of the community to see that the opponents of every good undertaking which does not afford some Shylock a base monopoly, are not petted and pampered for such opposition. It is unfortunate for this project that it had not been put forth prior to the establishment of Bennett and Bull in the lime business; then we opine Messrs. Davis & Cowell would have considered the road of infinite advantage to them, by the increased facilities offered for transportation their lumber, wood, tan bark and other products which abound in their immense possessions. The road would have been graded by this time, and ready in early Spring for transporting, had not the obstacles interposed been so relentlessly adhered to. We have never had any doubts as to the ultimate result of this issue, but those interested in the road will see the end, let come what will; law must make an end to this matter sooner or later, then we will have a road that will make Santa Cruz the greatest lumber emporium on this coast.

96. *San Francisco Chronicle*, November 26, 1868 (3:4)

The San Lorenzo Railroad Company have suspended work on the road for the present.

97. *Santa Cruz County Times*, December 26, 1868 (3:2)

San Lorenzo Railroad.—Now that the long contest with Davis & Cowell about the right of way is at an end, this railroad will soon be completed. The character of the soil along the route forbidding work to any extent during the rainy season, not much progress can be made until spring, when the road will be pushed along with vigor, and it will be entirely completed late in the spring. This R. R. although short, (some eighteen miles in length,) will open up to trade with this town a valuable territory of about two hundred and fifty square miles in extent.—By means of its valuable quarries of lime stone of vast extent and capacity for supply will be opened out, and besides that, immense supplies of timber, lumber, tan-bark, cord-wood, etc., that without this R. R. could not be brought to market. It will facilitate transportation to and from the lime kilns, the paper and powder mills, and saw mills, and become an incentive to the erection of other works of an industrial character that will add population and wealth to the county, and cause a degree of activity among our people that will be highly encouraging to all business men among us.

Hitherto the lime market of this State has been almost at the mercy of the firm of Davis & Cowell, they having supplied as near as we can ascertain about 80,000 barrels per annum of the best lime sent to market.—Santa Cruz County possessing, as it does the most extensive quarries of the best kind of lime stone in the State, it has long been an object of interest to our citizens to have them opened out and made accessible to market. The San Lorenzo R. R. will be the means of opening these quarries, and it will expedite and cheapen the transportation and delivery of lime, as well as other articles of commerce to the shipping of this port.

To Dr. W. F. Peabody, the President of the R. R. Co., and as well to all the Directors, this community is much indebted for the energy and perseverance that they have displayed thus far in the management of this enterprise. We are also under obligations to the faithfulness and tireless energy of Joseph Boston, Esq., the Secretary of the Company, and not forgetting J. H. Skirm, Esq., the Attorney of the Company, for the skill displayed in his management of the legal difficulties attendant upon this work. We look for a good time now for Santa Cruz.

98. *Daily Alta California,* January 3, 1869 (2:1)

Work has also been commenced on the San Lorenzo Railroad, to run fifteen miles northward from Santa Cruz.... The Petaluma, the San Lorenzo and the Los Angeles roads will have no connection with any other roads, but the first two are so situated that they can readily have branches to other roads.

99. *Santa Cruz Sentinel,* February 6, 1869 (2:1)

Railroad from Santa Cruz to the Salinas Valley.

We learn that a number of our leading business men and capitalists, have taken the initiatory step to build a railroad from the heavy timber belt south and east of Santa Cruz, to the rich and extensive agricultural district known as the Salinas Plains. The present line of the proposed road will follow, nearly, the route of the stage road to Watsonville, making such changes as alignment or interest may require. We are informed that a preliminary survey, by competent engineers, will be made as soon as the weather will warrant the undertaking of field operations. The amount of funds required for the surveys, has already been tendered by parties interested.

Over three years ago we urged the building of the San

Lorenzo railroad, and published several articles showing the practicability, necessity and probable expense of the undertaking, demonstrating plainly that it was not only feasible, but would be a profitable investment. The result was that we have now a live company of enterprising capitalists, who have surveyed the route described, commenced the grading, and would have the road, in part, ready for use by early Spring, had it not been delayed by a vexatious lawsuit, founded on a captious quibble, by interested parties of the old fogy school. The San Lorenzo Railroad, however, is a fixed fact, and soon the iron horse will be making semi-daily trips from Santa Cruz to San Francisco, affording a certain and speedy travel the year round, to our now weather-beleaguered trade and citizens.

We propose to show the advantages of a railroad from Soquel to Salinas, in order to afford an outlet for the immense supply of timber, firewood, bark, etc., so easily and cheaply procured in the hills east and south of the village. In fact the belt of redwood timber, as also fir, various kinds of oak, and other hard woods, extends near the line of the road proposed, for one-fourth of its distance. This inducement, of itself, is enough to effect its completion. Let us glance for a moment at a few facts in furtherance of the object in view: Freight to and from San Francisco to Santa Cruz, is $1 35 per ton, without wharfage, while freight from Watsonville to San Francisco, including hauling, is $6 50 per ton. At Castroville the price of good redwood lumber has been from $22 to $28 per M, all this season, and dealers were unable to half supply the demand. The freight on lumber from here to Castroville is $5 50 per M. The amount of grain shipped by vessels here and to San Francisco from the Pajaro valley this season has been 15,000 tons, and the back freight near half that amount. Is not this exhibit encouraging? Therefore we hope and trust that every citizen of the county will aid, to the whole extent of his ability, in the erection of this railroad enterprise. Nearly every man is interested in it, as the whole country would be benefited by its completion. We honestly believe that the stock will be a paying investment almost from the beginning. With the immense lumber, wood and grain trade that must pass over this road the stock cannot fail to be highly remunerative; but even if this were not so, every property holder within miles of the road would be amply repaid for his stock, were he to subscribe and pay to the extent of at least one-fourth of the value of his property. Every acre of land within five miles of the road will be enhanced in value more than double by the completion of the road. The people in all other sections of our country are becoming awake to the importance and advantage of railroad improvements, and are acting accordingly. They are sowing their fifties that they may reap hundreds therefrom. Why will we not follow their example?

Our manufacturers are also largely interested, as is also dairymen, stock-raisers, fruit-growers and gardeners. In a hundred ways the proposed road will be of very great importance to the best interests of the country through which it will pass, and far beyond the terminus of the route. We all know the prosperity of the farmer depends much on being convenient to a good market for the surplus produce he may have to dispose of. This road will supply that convenience. In many cases it will afford a market at the farmer's very door. Farmers very frequently put up buildings and in various ways expend money to improve and add to the value of their property; but the road when completed will be of more value to the farmers near it than any improvement they have ever made, or can make. Even supposing the money we are about to invest in this great public improvement should never yield any of us a cent of dividends, still it will in other ways be by far the most profitable investment we have ever made. Merchants and artisans of every description will be greatly benefitted by the construction and use of this road. Our schools, colleges, seminaries, and all our institutions of learning will also have their prosperity greatly enhanced by it. It is therefore, of the highest importance to the best interests of our country, that this improvement be speedily completed.

The parties who contemplate building this road have taken hold of its earnestly and in good faith, and will furnish the bulk of the capital to complete the work. All they ask is a limited assistance and a general support from the owners of land on the route, who will be the most materially benefitted by the road. If stock is freely subscribed the work will be completed at once, as the necessary iron and rolling stock is secured and can be at once diverted for the purpose. There is no doubt that the San Lorenzo railroad will be built or finished as far as the redwoods, this season, to be eventually extended to the line of the San Jose railroad. Connecting with this route is the only way a railroad from San Francisco will ever reach the Pajaro and the Salinas valleys, for it is not only practicable, but every mile of the road will pay.

100. *Santa Cruz Sentinel,* February 13, 1869 (2:4)
Letter from Watsonville.
Pajaro, Feb. 9th, 1869.

Editors Sentinel:—If acceptable to you, I will pen you a brief letter for publication. You seldom have anything in the paper from these parts, unless taken from our valuable *Pajaronian*, and doubtless will not object to an occasional letter, if containing anything of general interest. It has been said, and many may believe it, that there exists a prejudice of purely a local character, among us, against the people and prosperity of Santa Cruz. This I do not believe, for our interests are in no degree adverse, as no considerable amount of good can be bestowed on any part of the county without resulting in a corresponding benefit to every other portion.

In the last issue of the Sentinel you presented a subject of more than passing interest to every citizen of this county, and which, so far as my observation reaches, meets with warm approval. What other county in the State would have delayed the construction of a railroad that promises so greatly to augment the value of all property, and build up enterprise within its borders, as does a railroad from Santa Cruz to Watsonville? It clashes with the interests of no man; but seems to point directly to a prosperity desires, needed, and which if not fostered, will cause a long regret. This railroad will do more to promote our mutual interest in all that bares on the material progress and prosperity of the county, than all other enterprises combined; and when once properly understood and appreciated, will have no opponents among those interested in the future welfare of the two sections. Were this road in operation, our population would double in two years; our product quadruple, and every one of these magnificent ranches and grants would be made to produce to their full capacity. There is not a farmer in the valley, or along the line of the road, would not consider his farm worth double the present amount, because of the road; and would he not consider wisely? Will any sane man pretend to say, or believe, that the enhanced value of property, would not more than exceed the cost of such a road? And if this is a fact, it is a matter for our serious consideration; for the road cannot be constructed unless it is through the aid, enterprise and united efforts of all concerned. The farmer may feel to poor to render immediate assistance, but could we not render our aid during a term of years, in small payments that would not embarrass us, yet forward the deserving project? There are many farmers who will willingly donate to any company, $1,000, if allowed to pay in yearly payments of 4250, and will give ample security for its faithful payment.

One of the greatest items for our consideration is the facility and cheapness with which we can send our grain and produce to market. We have long borne the heavy tax of freight and inconvenience attending a shipment at the Salinas Slough, which at best is bad, and now that there is a sure and certain remedy offered, let us recount the advantages to us in case a railroad is put in operation from Santa Cruz into these valleys. Our present freight amounts to about $6 per ton, for every ton of produce landed in San Francisco; this includes the expense of hauling to warehouse; while at Santa Cruz shipments are made at $1 35 per ton, and $2 would be about the freight from this valley to Santa Cruz, by railroad, making an aggregate cost of $3 35 per ton, a saving of $2 65 per ton on every item of saleable produce. If this be so, and our farmers will scarce deny it, how long would it take for this small item saved in freight alone, to pay the amount required to build the road?

With this means of speedy concentration why may we not expect, as soon as our produce demands, that ships will come to Santa Cruz from San Francisco, and make shipments direct to any part of the world; thus saving freight, wharfage, commission, etc., from which we will willingly be relieved. This is a possibility that we may realize soon, as our shipments warrant. Again, we will be greatly in need, at no distant day, of the wood and lumber so abundant in your section, which if freighted by teams, will make it rather expensive living in these parts, when added to our excessive freight to and from Salinas.

This road, being so much needed by all sections of the county, could be materially assisted by the county's asking a law to enable it to loan its bonds for thirty years, for an amount sufficient to construct one-third of the road, and have that loan the first on the road. We believe that the increase of population, enhanced value of property, and the increase, consequently, of taxable property, would justify the county in assisting the road to a much greater extent. No county can thrive unless it lends its aid to enterprises that will advance the general public good, become an abiding source of revenue to itself, and profit to its citizens. Is this road not an enterprise which offers all this, and even more? It promises to be of incalculable benefit to Monterey county, by affording cheap and easy means of transporting the product of her vast Salinas Plains to a ready market.

If this road is built, and we sincerely believe it will be, within two years, there will be a daily communication between Santa Cruz and San Francisco, by water, that will enable farmers of every class to ship their produce at all times to suit the market and their own convenience. That this matter may be something more than talk, can you not be instrumental in calling the people of the county together, either here or at Santa Cruz, and let us interchange ideas and opinions, and get up an enthusiasm that will set us thinking rightly on this all-important subject; in this way we will soon find cut the off ox who never pulls, but always eats corn.

…We are again afflicted with a few cases of small-pox among us, none I believe of the type that caused the death of so many of our good citizens. Business is consequently dull, and will be until Spring opens, in fact we may expect to have dull times until the completion of the railroad from Santa Cruz to Watsonville.

The idea of a railroad from Gilroy to Watsonville has been abandoned, as the road would not reduce the freight sufficient to compete with the conveniences at Salinas Slough; besides, it is doubtful whether such a road would add much to our prosperity. There must be some other object beyond that of travel and transporting the product of our broad acres to make the undertaking successful. It might pay one way part of the year, but what would it do the balance? Yours, C. R.

101. *Santa Cruz Sentinel,* February 20, 1869 (2:2)
Railroads Again.

The *Pajaronian* gets excited over a railroad article which appeared in the *Sentinel* some two weeks ago. The emotional editor—nothing but a railroad article or a treatise on chewing gum, ever gets up an emotion in his torpid brain—sallies out with an array of figures to show that a railroad is *contemplated* "from Watsonville to connect with the Southern Pacific near Gilroy, a distance of only fourteen miles." We admit that the route is surveyed, as Santa Cruz capitalists aided in the work, and it is quite probably that $1,200 has been expended, and $30,000 subscribed to build the road, and $20,000 more is sought, to commence grading. We want to see the work promptly commenced, and speedily completed, but as to average expense of building and stocking a railroad is about $40,000 per mile, we would like the sapient editor to tell us how many miles of road, their funds, on hand would build, and also to show the way—trade and travel that is to pay a profit on the investment? We admit the road *can* be built, and so stated, but *will it be built?* That depends upon the energy and liberality of the citizens of Watsonville and Pajaro valley, and if our articles—in absence of any *home production* on the subject—prompts them to immediate action, we are content. The Santa Cruz and Salinas Valley Railroad will certainly be built, and we cannot see how it will interfere with Watsonville or Pajaro interest, in the least. We are not opposed to the Watsonville-Gilroy railroad, and the editor of the *Pajaronian* knew he was falsifying our record, and misquoting us when he allowed his interests or prejudices to make a different statement on the subject.

102. *Santa Cruz Sentinel,* February 20, 1869 (2:6)

Real Estate Sales.—We learn that several large sales of real estate were made in Santa Cruz during the past few weeks.... Another party is negotiating for a large body of timber land east of Soquel, at a round figure. Capitalists from up country appear to be investing freely in Santa Cruz property at this time. The prospect of an early completion of the Santa Cruz and Salinas Railroad, has no doubt created a demand for real estate near the line of the proposed road.

103. *Santa Cruz County Times,* February 20, 1869 (2:3)

Watsonville, Feb. 17th, 1869.
Ed. Times:—...The *Sentinel* of last week seems to have been afflicted by some one who was troubled with an eruption, and had to give vent to his feelings. We trust he feels relieved, and hope may soon get well.

"Afflictions sore
Long time we've bore."

But his is the worst of all; we have no objections to a railroad to Santa Cruz or any other place, but do object to his assertion that the road from Watsonville to Gilroy has been abandoned. We are of the opinion that this "See-R" lives at Santa Cruz and dates his letter from this place to create the idea that he was setting forth the sentiments of the people here. I hope his letter will have a good effect in arousing the people on the railroad question, and hear they will make up the balance of the subscriptions. Thirty thousand dollars have already been subscribed, and the rest will be added shortly, and the locomotive will be here from Gilroy before long. Then Santa Cruz can have the track extended to that place at any time by coming down with the means. We are, no doubt, liable to the charge of dullness of comprehension—of being blind to our own interest; but we are not quite so stupid as to commence laying the track the wrong way—that is, toward Santa Cruz—and have it end there. It might suit Santa Cruz, but not our purpose. If the astute correspondent of the *Sentinel* will have patience he will have the pleasure of reaching San Francisco by rail from here, before a year rolls around, and we can assure him that we will have freight and travel enough to make it an object. We do not know what else is needed besides "travel and transportation" to make a railroad successful; if there is enough of that, surely we can ask no more.

The benefits to be derived from a railroad are so apparent, have been set forth and shown so often through the press, that it is unnecessary to particularize.

People are slow to invest their money unless a fair compensation is to be had from the outlay. Many objections are urged by parties who would prefer to keep their money buried, and allow their more enterprising neighbors to invest in an undertaking that will ultimately benefit all. While we may have some of the selfish class referred to, we trust we have enough of a more liberal class who are willing to help enhance the prosperity of the county, thereby enriching themselves and benefitting others. A railroad will infuse new life into the Valley— will tend to throw off the sluggishness that surrounds us and drive away the slow and easy way we have fallen into.

We trust that those who have not subscribed, will do so liberally. NEMO.

104. *Santa Cruz Sentinel,* February 27, 1869 (2:3)
Letter from Watsonville.
Pajaro, Feb. 25th, 1869.

Editors Sentinel:—Writhing under the poignant thrusts of "Nemo's" letter to the *Times*, and the *Pajaronian*'s editorial remarks concerning my letter published in the *Sentinel* some two weeks since, which spoke approvingly of the projected railroad communication between this valley and Santa Cruz, we, in vindication of what was then stated as facts, see nothing in either Nemo's epistle, or "Clearquill on familiar texts," that induces a different opinion; but, on the contrary, their own showing is against them.

It would be my greatest pleasure to know, or even believe, that there ever would be a railroad in operation between Gilroy and Watsonville. We all know that such a road is feasible, but who knows that the investment would ever prove valuable? Certainly the people of Watsonville do not, or the sum of thirty thousand dollars subscribed to the stock in one year, would have been eclipsed by a subscription of two hundred and fifty thousand in three months, the probably cost of the road. I don't believe that there is a person in this valley who would not gladly see such a road completed; but the proper subscriptions could not be obtained, because the Company owning the road would not agree to carry freight from this valley for less than five dollars per ton, and this price seems no exorbitant one for freighting a distance of nearly one hundred miles. We are all aware, and cannot disguise the fact, that the produce of this valley can be as cheaply shipped by way of Salinas, as Gilroy, in any event. The freight must be reduced to four dollars at least, and no such reduction can be hoped for unless these valleys are connected with Santa Cruz by railroad. If freight can or will be taken as cheap by way of Gilroy, then it is to the interest of all of us to aid in the construction of the road, and we will, when the Company bind themselves to those prices. I venture to say, that with the present feeling respecting the two roads, that, excepting the immediate town of Watsonville, two dollars would be subscribed to the Santa Cruz road, to one of Gilroy, were subscriptions sought for both. I have never understood that it was disguised to carry the freight from this valley by rail, farther than Santa Cruz, and there shipped by water. The idea of Santa Cruz ever being connected with San Francisco by rail, seems most absurd. I can conceive of nothing that would so greatly impair her prospects of building up a good and profitable shipping. To take the lumber from the upper San Lorenzo over the mountains by cars, would be suicidal in the extreme. Santa Cruz must concentrate every energy and enterprise at its beach, and make it profitable to establish a daily steam communication with the great city. We of Watsonville need not be jealous of Santa

Cruz for this idea of progress; whatever tends to its advancement—if a railroad is constructed—will most assuredly promote and build up our best interests. If any one would discourage this project, he must show the people that some other road will be of greater benefit to them; and the most that concerns our farmers is the reduction of freight. I stated in my former letter, that the saving in freight alone, would justify the immediate construction of the road from Santa Cruz to Watsonville. I may add to this, that the increased production because of a road, would in two years pay for it.

Perhaps some one may say that if freight can be taken so cheaply by way of Santa Cruz, there will be an opposition in time that will take it as cheap by some other route. Very well, if nothing short of the road to Sant Cruz can stimulate a competition and break monopolies, let us have the road; we win in any event; all is our gain, nothing can we lose.... C. R.

105. *Santa Cruz Sentinel,* February 27, 1869 (2:4)
Benefit of Railroads to Farmers.

As the construction of the Salinas and Santa Cruz Railroad is just now a subject much mooted in this community, we append an extract from a late number of the *Agriculturalist*, showing what Railroads do for a community. Its suggestions will doubtless be of special interest at this time to our readers:

"To haul forty bushels of grain 50 miles on a wagon costs, says the *Agriculturalist*, at least $12 dollars for team, driver, and expenses. A railroad would transport it for $4 at most. Allowing an average of forty bushels per acre, the crop would be worth $8 more per acre, or 8 per cent. $100. As the relative advantage is about the same for other crops, it is clear that a railroad passing through a township would add $100 per acre to the value of the farm. A township ten miles square contains 64,000 acres. An increase of $100 per acre is equal to $6,400,000, or enough to build two hundred miles of railroad, even if it cost $12,000 per mile. But two hundred miles of railroad would extend through twenty townships ten miles square and cost but $10 per acre if taxed upon the land. These figures are given merely as an illustration. If the farmers had taxed themselves to build all the railroads in this State, and given them away to any companies that would stock and run them , the present increased value of their land would have well repaid all the outlay.

106. *Santa Cruz Sentinel,* February 27, 1869 (2:5)

We are out of all patience with the editors of the *Pajaronian*, on the subject of railroads. Last week we pinned him in a falsehood, but no sooner had the insect been impaled than he "wriggled" out of it by asserting another, equally as false and more gross, by misquoting us. There is no use holding a discussion unless truth is adhered to, and the free use of CAPITALS and *italics* will not remedy the matter. We stated that the "average expense of building and stocking a railroad is about $40,000 per mile," and the editor misconstrued by making the sentence read "it costs $40,000 per mile to build railroads."

Thus are we falsified by the editor leaving out the words "stocking," "average" and "about." Shame on you. A tethered calf chewing his own rope for want of hay or seeking to regain its liberty, is comfortable and independent, compared to a victim of such unfortunate prevarication. But for the sake of argument let us examine into the merits of the case, superficially, lest anything of depth should fail to be comprehended. The *Pajaronian* says it would cost, according to our estimates, $1,600,000 to construct the forty miles of railroad from Santa Cruz to the Salinas. Now for the truth: The distance from Santa Cruz to depot near Castroville, via Watsonville, or on an air line, near the bay, would be about 28 miles, and as it costs about as much to equip a road with rolling-stock, build relays, turnouts, turn-tables, water-tanks and depots, as to construct the road, it will be found that no such a sum as $40,000 per mile is required. Our estimates of the Gilroy and Watsonville railroad, was predicated on fourteen miles of road, and it is inferred that the equipment, rolling-stock, etc., of that distance will cost as much as 28 miles,—just twice the distance—consequently the pro rata of equipment should be reduced just one-half. We again assert that in advocating the Salinas and Santa Cruz road, we are not opposing, either directly or by inference, the Watsonville and Gilroy road, but rather aiding it by spurring up the citizens of Watsonville to prompt action, and a liberal subscription. If the editor of the *Pajaronian* cannot see this, he is as blind to the interests of Watsonville, as he is selfish to his own interest when he tries to array our Watsonville friends against the Sentinel, that he may thereby profit on his own subscription list, which is evident from the special pleading in his "New Prospectus."

107. *Santa Cruz Sentinel*, March 6, 1869 (2:1)
Watsonville and Gilroy Railroad.

A meeting of the Stockholders of this railroad was held in San Francisco, the past week. Messrs. Chittenden, Barney and Hihn were present. The meeting was full and enthusiastic. Good progress was reported and favorable arrangements made, to complete the road at an early day, and secure cheap freight. right of way and other advantages not heretofore enjoyed. We now entertain the idea that the road will be built, and promptly put in running order. The liberal subscriptions by citizens of Watsonville and Gilroy and on the route shows that they appreciate the advantages of the road and will make an earnest effort to obtain a controlling interest in the road. The counties of Santa Cruz, Santa Clara and Monterey, through their Boards of Supervisors, should aid the enterprise. We are assured that this county will give her quota in the way of subscriptions. The completion of the road will not in the least interfere with the Santa Cruz and Salinas railroad but rather benefit it. A branch railroad is now being surveyed up Soquel creek—east of the town, to connect the timber district at that point, with the wharf and the main line.

108. *Santa Cruz Sentinel*, March 6, 1869 (4:1)

Not satisfied with common roads and not to be behind the rest of mankind, the San Lorenzo railroad is intended to still further develop the treasures of your mountains, and deliver to the port, the lumber, lime and bark of the immense forests covering the course it traverses. A projected railroad to Watsonville, will still add to your neighborly intercourse and consequent prosperity. But still another railroad or turnpike should be stretched out west or northerly along the beach or the beach skirting the shore. Having traveled that course on leaving your beautiful town, I can write the want there is in that quarter.

109. *Santa Cruz Sentinel*, March 13, 1869 (2:1)

Mountain District.

This District was formerly comprised in that of Soquel, but set off to itself during June of 1867. The body of the land in this District is heavily timbered, while the balance is of the richest and most productive in the State, it being pastured or cultivated, and watered by innumerable springs and brooks. The pasture land is on and along the foot-hills, while the farming land is on either side of the Soquel creek and its tributaries. Two or three new sawmills are soon to be erected, and as a railroad has been surveyed through a large portion of its territory from the Soquel wharf, and a large addition of taxable property being made, as well as a material increase of population, it is reasonable to conclude that within one year the school census will enumerate two hundred children. The manufacturing interest of the District is represented by three saw-mills and one tannery. They are run by water. The creek is one continuous waterpower, and if the proposed railroad along its banks become a reality, its manufacturers will employ and support a large population.

110. *Santa Cruz Sentinel*, March 13, 1869 (2:2)

The San Lorenzo Railroad.—This laudable enterprise, which for the last four months has lain dormant, is about to be entered upon with renewed vigor. Under the new officers it will be pushed ahead rapidly, and completed so far as Felton within the next five months or less. There is no lack of purchasers of stock since the President returned from the city. The only fear is, that there will be a desire, with some, to get control of more stock than the interest of small stockholders will warrant. Cheap freight will soon create a large and extended business, which must prove a source of great wealth to the owners of the road. Every citizen interested in the development of Santa Cruz and her resources should take stock to the amount of his ability, and not allow capitalists of San Francisco to own the majority, which will give them control of its interests and management. We have been informed that the parties who purchased the Stanley property are ready and desirous of taking a hundred shares of the stock. A few more of our wealthy citizens might render material aid to this enterprise.

111. *San Francisco Chronicle*, March 17, 1869 (1:2)

A railroad is projected from the town of Santa Cruz to the Salinas valley, with a branch up Soquel creek.

112. *Santa Cruz Sentinel*, April 10, 1869 (2:5)

Railroad Celebration at Gilroy.—A correspondent of the *Bulletin* writes:

On Thursday April 8th, the people of this county celebrated the opening of railroad communication by a grand barbecue, speechification and dance at Gilroy. All the folks of the surrounding country were invited. A special train was sent from San Francisco to bring invited guests. John B. Felton, W. H. L. Barnes and George Barstow said a few congratulatory words to the Gilroy people on the occasion. Visitors were welcomed by Colonel Hatch and Sawyer Wilson of Gilroy. The dinner (barbecue), was served in the railroad depot, at half-past two o'clock. Toasts and volunteer speeches followed, and the young people had a dance in the evening, which passed off pleasantly.

113. *Santa Cruz Sentinel*, April 17, 1869 (2:1)

Davis and Cowell own 68 acres of tide land, near the beach and close to the Powder Co's wharf, which is held for speculation, and it is said as a bar against public improvements, in preventing a railroad connecting with the bay. It is very valuable on this account, probably worth $20,000, yet it is only assessed at $100. Was this assessment just and fair to the poor taxpayer? We think not.

114. *Santa Cruz Sentinel*, May 1, 1869 (2:4)

Davis & Cowell vs. The San Lorenzo R. R. Co.—The lawsuit that has been pending between the above named parties, was decided in favor of defendants in the April term of the Supreme Court, J. Crockett being the only dissenting Judge. We congratulate the company on the successful *finale* obtained, and join with the people in feeling thankful that the rich can not, regardless of right, law or justice, impose upon the poor by trampling under foot public enterprises that furnish employment for the working masses. The Railroad Company offered all that appeared to be just and equitable—far more than the land was worth for any other purpose than the privilege of a railway. But this was not, though it was made to appear so, the object of controversy, for had it been, arbitration would soon have settled it. Was not the objection raised to protect a lime monopoly, and every advantage of the law's delay, crook and turn, pettyfogging, resorted to? Men of wealth who are wielding influence in a community, become enemies or friends to the extent of their power, and assume the characters of benefactors or obstructionists, and it stands in hand for the people to deal with such powers as if working for a selfish purpose, and one buried by a mistified surface. Down with monopoly; down with centralization. Let every thing be done that will aid and assist the furtherance of the San Lorenzo railroad. The vexatious lawsuit is at an end, and we hope and expect to be able soon to inform our readers that the railroad company is preparing to move immediately upon the works, and stick to it till the track is laid and the iron horse, with lungs of steel and breath of fire, going screeching through our town.

115. *Santa Cruz Sentinel*, May 1, 1869 (3:1)

The railroad question was at one time freely agitated. Subscription-books were opened, and a large number of shares taken, but at present, *all* is quiet. I am anxiously waiting to see which of two routes the Southern Pacific will take from Gilroy if it follows the more northerly through or near the Pacheco Pass, crossing into the San Joaquin Valley. Our road must be about fourteen miles in length, but if it is follows the more southerly, and passes through the upper portion of Salinas Valley, it will be much shorter and built sooner. Very few here doubt but that sooner or later it will be built.

116. *Santa Cruz County Times*, May 1, 1869 (3:2)

The San Lorenzo Railroad.—These gentlemen, Davis & Cowell, who have been fighting the progress of this railroad almost from its very incipiency have been beaten again in the matter of their appeal from the decision of one of our District Courts, which was rendered against them. These men claimed enormous damages for condemnations of their lands for the use of this railroad and made every effort possible to defeat the road. Yet they are among the lowest tax-payers per acre in the county and we presume that they would sink the whole county of

Santa Cruz, except their special property, of they had the power.—We hope that the County Assessor will look after all such men in future as value their land at low rates for taxes, but at high rates, when needed for public improvements that will tend to the general welfare of the community. We give the decision of the Supreme Court of the State in the case from the Sacramento *Union*:

Davis & Cowell vs. The San Lorenzo R. R. Co. [No. 1,828].—This is an appeal from an order of the District Court dissolving a preliminary injunction, which had been issued to restrain the defendant from cutting trees and doing other acts in the nature of waste upon the lands of the plaintiff. The defendant, upon the hearing of the motion, justified the acts complained of under the provisions of the statute in relation to the condemnation of lands for railroad purposes (Statutes 1861, p. 607; 1863, p. 610; 1867-8, p. 705), by showing that they had instituted proceedings under that Act, in the County Court of the proper county, to condemn the lands in question, and had obtained an order from that Court allowing them to enter and proceed with the construction of their road while the proceedings were pending.

The applicant claims that the injunction ought not to have been dissolved, for the following reasons:

First—The provisions of the Railroad Act, by which the defendant is authorized to enter upon the lands of the plaintiffs and construct its road before the compensation is ascertained and actually paid, are repugnant to that clause of the Eighth Section of the First Article of the Constitution, which provides that private property shall not be taken for public use without just compensation.

Second—The County Courts have no jurisdiction over the proceedings to condemn lands.

Third—The bond taken by the County Court as security for the payment of such compensation as might be awarded does not satisfy the statute, because it is a penal bond, and not a general undertaking to pay whatever may be awarded.

1. The first point has been fully considered and determined by this Court against the views of counsel for the appellants in the case of Fox vs. Western Pacific Railroad Company (31 Cal., 538.) The learned counsel for the appellants have combated the conclusion reached by us in that case in a very able and ingenious manner, but we fail to perceive any substantial reason for not adhering to our opinion.

2. The statute which was passed prior to the amendments of 11863 to the Constitution confers jurisdiction over proceedings to condemn lands for railroad purposes upon both County Courts and District Courts (Sec. 24), but it is claimed that the statute has become unconstitutional, so far as it confers jurisdiction upon County Courts by reason of the aforesaid amendments to the Constitution.

Before the amendments of 1863, the Constitution provided that County Courts should have "such jurisdiction, in cases arising in Justices' Courts and in special cases, as the Legislature may prescribe, but shall have no original civil jurisdiction except in such special cases." (Art. VI., Sec. 9.) This section was copied from the Constitution of New York, and there seems to have been some difference of opinion among the Judges of the Court of Appeals of that State as to the true meaning of the words, "special cases," some holding that the cases were such as ware in their nature special and peculiar cases, for which Courts of general common law jurisdiction do not afford a remedy—others holding that it meant such cases as the Legislature might see proper to assign to the County Court by special designation. (Rudolph vs. Tolheimer, 12 N. Y., 593; Doubleday vs. Heath, 16 id., 80; Arnold vs. Rees, 18 id., 57.) Yet that Court held that the foreclosure of mortgaged and partition of lands were "special cases." A like contrariety of opinion seems to have existed in this Court. Parsons vs. Tuolumne Water Company (5 Cal., 43), was an action to abate a nuisance. It was brought in the County Court, and it was held that the statute which conferred jurisdiction in such cases upon the County Courts was unconstitutional—the Court declaring that "special cases" meant such new cases as are created by statute, and the proceedings under which are unknown to the general framework of Courts of common law and equity. This construction was adhered to in the subsequent cases of Brock vs. Herrick, 5 Cal., 279, and Sanders vs. Haynes, 13 id. 145. But in Jacks vs. Day, 15 id., 91, after a more thorough examination than had been previously given to the question, it was declared that, aside from previous decisions of the Court, "special cases" meant such cases as the Legislature, in its discretion, should assign to the County Courts by special enumeration and definition; and again, in McNeil vs. Borland (23 Cal., 144), the Court leaned the same way, but finally held that the jurisdiction of the County Court could be sustained in that case upon either theory. There is no doubt in our minds but that the one suggests in the last two cases was the true construction. Jurisdiction in civil cases had been previously conferred upon the District Courts in general terms. It was then provided that the County Courts should have jurisdiction in such civil cases as the Legislature might specially designate.

The Legislature of the present Constitution is quite different, however. It is that the "County Courts shall have original jurisdiction of actions of forcible entry and detainer, of proceedings in insolvency, of actions to prevent or abate a nuisance, and of all such special cases and proceedings as are not otherwise provided for." * * * We think the special cases here contemplated are such as the "special cases" of the old Constitution had been declared to be by this Court prior to the amendments of 1863; that is to say, cases of special statutory creation and regulation, or for which some special remedy and mode of procedure is provided, the intention being that in such cases the County Court should take jurisdiction, unless the Legislature should provide expressly that they should go to some other forum. Under it the County Court could have taken jurisdiction of the proceedings in question had the statute been passed since the change in the Constitution and had been silent as to the forum in which the proceedings should be prosecuted. Under the rule in Courtright vs R. R. and A. W. and M. Co. (30 Cal., 573), it lies in the discretion of the Legislature to send such proceedings to another forum, and it has done so, so far as to leave the forum, as between the District and County Courts, to the election of the parties concerned. Under the rule of construction adopted in that case, which was to the effect that a grant of jurisdiction in the Constitution to a particular Court, without words of exclusion, does not of itself deny a concurrent jurisdiction to other Courts, the Legislature is at liberty to send proceedings of this character to either the District Courts or the County Courts, or both. The statute does the latter, and did not, therefore, become repugnant to the Constitution upon its amendment in 1863.

Third—We see no objection to the bond on account of its form; but if there was any valid objection to it, the County Court has full power in the premises, and it is the proper tribunal to apply to for its correction.

    Order affirmed.   SANDERSON, J.
    We Concur: SPRAGUE, J.
                                        SAWYER, C. J.
    I dissent: CROCKETT, J.

117. *Marin Journal*, May 8, 1869 (2:3)
Condemnation of Land for Railroad Purposes.

Davis & Cowell, of Santa Cruz county, says the *Santa Cruz Times*, who have been fighting the progress of the San Lorenzo railroad, have been beaten in the matter of their appeal from one of the District Courts for the condemnation of certain of their lands for railroad purposes. They claimed enormous damages, but didn't get them. Like some we wot of in this place they don't want to "go a-riding on the railroad keers."

118. *Santa Cruz Sentinel,* June 26, 1869 (3:1)

Timber.—A few years ago hard-wood was a drug in the market at five dollars per cord. Now it is scarce at five. Those having timber should save it from unnecessary waste, It is wealth at interest; that can be converted into coin and give remunerative employment to man and beast when other sources of revenue are monopolized. All that is necessary are roads—railroads; iron and steam instead of muscle and bone. We are bold to say that not a cord of wood which reaches San Francisco from Santa Cruz nets one cent stumpage, yet how much has been cut and squandered.

119. *Santa Cruz Sentinel,* July 3, 1869 (2:4)

Railroad Survey.—On Saturday, June 26th, a surveying party left Santa Cruz for Monterey, per Steamer *Senator*, to survey a railroad route from Monterey to Oakland, *via* the Salinas, Pajaro, Gilroy, Santa Clara and Alameda vallies. The distance is about 100 miles, over a level country, easy to grade and densely settled. The land in these vallies is the richest and most valuable for agricultural purposes of any in California.

120. *Monterey Democrat* via the *Santa Cruz Sentinel,* July 31, 1869 (1:7)

The Railroad Survey.—We understand from the engineers that they had encountered little difficulty in running their line and that the grades to the river will be light.

The line selected will cross the river somewhere below Estrada's crossing, the stream at that point being easier to approach, and, there meeting the tide, having at seasons of flood no velocity to speak of. We have no doubt the report of the survey will favor the undertaking of the work.

121. *Santa Cruz Sentinel,* October 2, 1869 (2:2)
Railroads.

We wish to export the abundant yield of this and a large portion of Monterey county, and to furnish the inhabitant thereof and of the whole lower country, by land, with lumber, lime, powder, leather, paper, glue, soap, piles, fencing, etc., and in order to do this we must have a railroad tapping the San Lorenzo to its headwaters and another, penetrating, feeding and accommodating the country designated. This has got to be done. It is a work of ten years, but should be accomplished, in this age of machinery and improvement, in three. The initiatory step is the San Lorenzo railroad or the railroad from Gilroy to Watsonville. The steam-horse once in Watsonville and steam will not be allowed to go down till he comes snorting and screeching into Santa Cruz. Real estate and business men of this town and county, you have your choice, to either set sucking your thumbs, complaining about scarcity of money, dull times, want of enterprise and energy, or go to work, right away, and build these roads. Better do it as a business enterprise, rather than as a financial necessity, in the latter instance resembling the beast that pulls against the "grain" with ears thrown forward and tail erect, or, better still, for the love you bear your children, don't leave it for your children to do. This is the necessity of to-day. If you don't meet it, not by walking up the hill and then down again, but by actually accomplishing it, your successors must. Just think of it. The lumbermen of San Lorenzo, Soquel and Corralitos, and other points, loading their lumber at the various mills, hauling it to different landings; then unloading; then loading on to a snail-speed sailing vessel; then unloading at Santa Barbara, San Luis, San Diego, and, worst of all, (right at home) at Moss & Beadle's or landings on the Salinas Slough; then unloading; then re-loading wagons, and, after all this labor, waste of time and expense, for the smallest compensation, delivering it at from $25 to $40 per thousand feet, at exactly the place the railroad would deliver it in twenty-four hours after it left the saw-mill, at reduced prices for the purchaser, and at advanced profit for the manufacturer. The way lumber is being exported at the present time, we doubt whether there is any clear profit in the business, yet the timber is falling before the study stroke of the ruthless axeman, to give him and others a chance to toil hard and live sparingly. Can you see it; see the immediate and pressing necessity of a cheaper and quicker mode of transportation? We hope you can, and as the Watsonville people are soon to hold a meeting in relation to the Gilroy and Watsonville railroad, we hope they will not let the grass grow under their feet before they commence digging up ground and laying down iron.

122. *Santa Cruz County Times*, October 2, 1869 (2:1)
The New Railroad.

In this age of improvement, when "Forward" is the constant watchword, the people of Santa Cruz County should not be behind the other portions of the State in public enterprise; and the prospects of having a new railroad, bringing us in direct communication with San Francisco and other prominent points in the State, should be heralded with delight by every intelligent and wide awake citizen. The feasibility of such a road has never been questioned, and the people have only been waiting for our most prominent and influential business men to set the ball rolling. That is now being done, and we have no doubt but that the people of the county will take hold with hearty good will, and do their full share towards helping on the noble enterprise. The new road will start from a point where the western road crosses San Francisco bay, at or near Redwood City, thence down through the immense redwood forests, along the line of the San Lorenzo river to Santa Cruz; thence to Watsonville which will be the terminus. The entire length of the road will be about 50 miles, and the cos for completion and stocking will be about $25,000 per mile, amounting in total to about $1,250,000. Of that amount Santa Cruz county will be called upon, (and she can afford it, when we taking into consideration the great benefits which she will derive from the building of the road,) to vote her bonds for $300,000. That $300,00 would be a nucleus around which we would soon gather a sufficient capital to build the road. Neither will the building of the road depend on home capital alone, for just as soon as the project can be shown to be feasible, outside capital can be drawn in, and in fact men of large capital are only waiting to see what steps the people are willing to take in the matter, before putting their capital into the road.

The great advantage which we as a county will derive from the new railroad cannot be estimated by dollars and cents. It will develop the resources of the county, and increase the valuation of property 100 per cent. in less than five years. It will bring to us enterprising business men, who will use their capital in building up the manufacturing interests of the county. It will bring to us a large class of industrious farmers who will cut up our large ranches, now comparatively worthless, into small productive farms. Large vineyards will cover our mountain sides. Tasteful and elegant villas which give tone and character to a town, will grace our beautiful hills, and Santa Cruz, for whom nature has done so much, will become the most attractive summer resort on the Pacific Coast. Population, enterprise and wealth always follow along the line of railways. The large population which is now finding its way into the southern portion of our State by railroad, would come to us if the way was open. People will not travel by the old state coach. That mode of getting round the world is fast becoming played out. There are some that will tell you that heavy taxation will result from the building of this road. What great enterprise was ever projected and successfully carried through without taxation. They will tell you that the county is already in debt $85,000.

Well, what have you got in return? You have one of the finest court-houses in the State, that will always be an ornament to the town. You have fine bridges over which you can drive without danger of breaking your necks, and you have excellent roads which enable you to get about to attend to your business. Bear in mind one thing, all the monies voted for enterprises of this character will return to you four fold. Let us therefore be wide awake and keep pace with the other portions of the State in the great march of improvement; and ;et it not be said that Santa Cruz county is the Rip Van Winkle of California.

123. *Santa Cruz Sentinel,* October 9, 1869 (2:2)

Railroads.—By a singular coincidence our sick sister, granny *Times*, contained an article on railroads, as the *Sentinel* did. From posters we observe that a railroad meeting is called for to-night. Every tax-payer should attend, as it is a subject of vast importance to the county—one that ere long you will be forced on to vote "Yes" or "No." We favor railroads, as we do every other general improvement, let them come over the mountains, through the mountains or around the mountains, by the way of Watsonville or Felton, or by both.

124. *Santa Cruz Sentinel,* October 16, 1869 (2:1)

Railroad Meeting.

In according with notice given by posters, a meeting was convened at the Courthouse on last Saturday evening for the purpose of canvassing the feasibility and practicability of constructing railroads in this county; also, to ascertain if it was the wish of the people to loan county bonds for such purposes. All present, who addressed the meeting, favored the construction of a railroad or railroads. They differed as to the location and amount of road to be built, the amount of bonds to be issued by the county per mile, when payable and as to amount of taxation. The meeting was addressed by F. A. Hihn, Col. Heath, C. E. Burrows, R. C. Kirby, E. L. Williams, G. M. Jarvis, F. Adams, Lucien Heath and Prof. Tuthill. F. A. Hihn and E. L. Williams favored a trunk and branch roads, the truck road to extend from the town of Santa Cruz to Gilroy, and the branch roads from Soquel ten miles up the Soquel creek, and from Santa Cruz fifteen miles up the San Lorenzo river. R. C. Kirby and others favored none but the main trunk road, affirming that if too big a project was undertaken, the people would vote all to the ground. Prof. Tuthill advocated the construction of railroads as something actually necessary to keep up the with financial, social, civil progress of the age. The feeling manifested was harmonious and earnest, healthy and encouraging to those who favor internal improvements. Read proceedings.

125. *Santa Cruz Sentinel,* October 16, 1869 (2:2-3)
RAILROAD.

From the proceedings published in today's paper it will be seen that a Railroad Meeting was held on last Saturday evening in the Court-house, for the purpose of taking into consideration, the ways and means to build a railroad from Santa Cruz connecting with the San Jose road. The meeting was full and interesting, many speakers advocating their peculiar views, in an earnest and intelligent manner. All agreed that a railroad was almost an absolute necessity to keep up the town and advance our local interests. The only disagreement was as to routes, and the way to raise means to build the road. The majority of the meeting, advocated the building of a main trunk road from Santa Cruz to Gilroy, *via* Soquel and Watsonville, while the minority, with equal zeal, favored the San Lorenzo route *via* Felton, to Belmont or Redwood City, and a few were prepared with facts and figures to establish the fact (from actual estimates and surveys) that the road could be built to San Jose, up the Soquel creek, at a less expense and in a shorter distance than either of the proposed routes. All these propositions were entertained and discussed pro and con, in a manner that manifested a sound and healthy sentiment. After the discussion a Committee was appointed to act in the matter and report at a future meeting to be held at the same place.

Since the meeting, the Committee have met and organized by electing E. Bennett, Chairman, whereupon it was moved that engineers be employed to view out the various routes, and report at the regular meeting. The question was discussed by the Committee in a full and interesting manner. To-day, Dr. Spencer and Alexander McPherson, Sr., will examine the Felton route, as far as the Tin Can Rancho, and over the divide. The Soquel route has been examined and a preliminary survey made by T. W. Wright and others; while the railroad engineer, Mr. Black, will report on the Watsonville route from Santa Cruz *via* Soquel, Aptos, &c., to Gilroy. From reports predicated on surveys heretofore made, it is estimated that the San Lorenzo route, on the divide at the Tin Can Rancho, would be about 2,000 feet, on the Blackburn Gulch (where two divides occur) some 1,400 feet, and on the Soquel route, to Santa Clara, *via* Los Gatos, 1,430 feet, or 1,340 at the lowest point. But the grade on the latter route could be materially reduced by running a tunnel one mile (5,000 feet) through soft chalk rock. By the Soquel route the distance from Santa Cruz to the connection with the San Jose road would be about 31 miles, while on the other routes it would be much greater.

At this time we do not propose to go into details, or make an exhibit of facts and figures, to show the advantages of disadvantages of either route, leaving that for the engineers appointed, to report on next Saturday evening. But we would briefly advert to the arguments used by different individuals, on the various routes, and submit them for the benefit of our readers. The friends of the San Lorenzo route, (which we claim to be superior in many respects to either of the other routes proposed) advance the argument that it would open up a larger scope of undeveloped country than any other, and that it would place us within four hours of San Francisco at all seasons, and be the means of affording a constant and ready communication direct to San Francisco, the year around, to ship our manufactured articles, lumber, fire-wood, hoop-poles, etc., at a cheaper rate than by the other routes advocated. The Soquel people claim similar advantages, with only 31 miles of road to build (while they say the San Lorenzo route is 80 miles) and that by tunnelling, this divide can be crossed at an elevation of 600 feet, while the divide at the Tin Can Ranch is, (after tunnelling) about 1,700 feet. The people of Watsonville, Aptos, and on that route claim that in building the road and connecting with the San Jose road at Gilroy, a way trade of greater extent and importance than either of the other routes under consideration. It would also tap the Salinas valley and soon Santa Cruz would become the shipping point for the immense grain, wool and dairy products of that granary of the State; furthermore, the completion of the Watsonville road would soon force the San Lorenzo through the mountains, direct to San Francisco, and then the freighting and passenger business of the lower counties, from Santa Cruz and Monterey, South to Los Angeles, would take this route instead of through Santa Clara or the Tulare plains, *via* the Tejon or other passes southeast of the tule lakes. If this latter view were practicable, it would be the grandest and most profitable road on the continent. The Salinas plains are from sixty to ninety miles long, and they hinge on to an interminable series of smaller vallies reaching clear to Los Angeles, or the plains of San Gabriel. We might mention the rich vallies of Santa Margarita, Arroyo Grande, Santa Maria plains, Santa Barbara, Santa Clara, six miles south of San Buenaventura, all rich and prolific in every kind of grain, vegetables and fruit grown on the coast. In this section, oranges, limes, lemons, figs, olives, English walnuts and soft-shelled almonds, are always grown in luxuriance and abundance, for the San Francisco market. The Santa Clara valley, not the largest of the series, has an immense area, extending in various directions, with all its windings and ramifications, embracing, as we are informed, a body of three hundred thousand acres of completely level land, of the finest quality. It extends as far as the eye can reach, with only a distant view of the hills on either side. On every hand a dense growth of wild mustard attests the extreme fertility of the soil. If the coast road, from Santa Cruz to Watsonville and thence south, through these rich valleys, would eventually bring this trade through our town, and afford a market for our lime, lumber, leather and other products, as claimed by the friends of the southern route, then we say by all means let us vote our subscription to build the Watsonville road, especially if its completion would force the road through the hills north-east of us, into Santa Clara valley and direct, on an air line, (or as near to it as possible) to San Francisco.

But the main object of the meeting seems to be, not whether we should build any or either road but, whether the county is willing to subscribe a sufficient sum to prompt capitalists to take hold and build the road. The meeting seemed to be almost unanimous in favor of subscribing a bonus of $150,000 or $200,000 to build a main trunk road, by either of the proposed routes to connect with the Santa Clara Valley road, but were opposed to subscribing anything to build branch roads. Some contend, however, that branch roads, should be first built, to open up a trade of sufficient importance to prompt capitalists to build a main road; in this a majority seemed to differ. Before next meeting the surveys will be made, and the Committee will then be able to report intelligently, and the meeting can then discuss the subject in a practical and satisfactory manner. In the meantime we hope the subject will be agitated, and all the possible information obtained.

126. *Santa Cruz Sentinel,* October 16, 1869 (2:4)
Railroad Meeting.
Santa Cruz, October 2d, 1869, Court-room.

Meeting called to order at seven and a half o'clock; Jacob Parsons, of Soquel, Chairman. The following paper was introduced by F. A. Hihn:
TO BE SUBMITTED TO THE VOTE OF THE PEOPLE.

Proposition for the county of Santa Cruz to aid the construction of a Railroad from the town of Santa Cruz, up the San Lorenzo river for fifteen miles, and from the town of Santa Cruz through Soquel and Watsonville to the southern boundary of the county, with a branch up the Soquel creek for ten miles, by the issuance of county bonds, bearing eight per cent. interest per annum, and payable within twenty years, to the amount of six thousand dollars per mile, upon the construction of each five miles of such road, with a good iron tee rail; such bonds to constitute a first-mortgage on such road. The interest on said bonds to be paid by the county for the first ten years. Such road to be taxed the same as other property, but not to be assessed at less than eight thousand dollars per mile, and all taxes collected therefrom to be used towards the payment of the interest on said bonds. At the expiration of ten years such additional sum shall be annually collected from said road, which added to said taxes will be sufficient to pay the interest, and one-tenth part of the principal of said bonds.

Mr. Hihn then stating that while the above proposition had been drawn up for the purpose of bringing the subject of railroads before the people, with the view of obtaining county aid, for the benefit of every part of the county, as far as practicable, read the following statement for the purpose of showing that a railroad, even if built in one end of the county, only would result to the benefit of the whole county, and therefore deserved county aid.

Pajaro township, including town of Watsonville, has a territory of 10 square miles, or, in acres 64,000
Deduct for waste land, acres 14,000
Total 50,000

Present assessable value, $4 per acre, making a total of $200,000, which at two per cent. yields now a County tax of $4,000.

It is generally admitted that the value of this land would be double, if connected by railroad with Gilroy, yielding thus an additional tax of $4,000.

The interest on bonds for ten miles of railroad from Watsonville to the center of county at the rate of $6,000 bonds per mile, would amount annually to $4,8000.

Deduct tax derived from railroad $2,400
Balance int. to be paid by county $2,400
Increased of county tax on real estate in Pajaro township by construction of railroad $4,000
Annual net gain by county $1,600

Without counting the increase of personal property and improvement in real estate, or the increase of value of property in all other parts of the county.

Col. Heath moved an amendment. Discussion pro and con and paper laid on the table. R. C. Kirby moved that a Committee of seven be appointed, to report two weeks from to-night on this house, on the plans of constructing a railroad, and that the Chair appoint such Committee. The motion was carried, and the following named gentlemen placed on said Committee:

S. L. Bennett, San Lorenzo; A. Pray, Sr., L. Heath, Santa Cruz; B. Porter, Dr. Fagan, Soquel; Dr. Ford, B. A. Barney, Watsonville. By motion F. A. Hihn added to Committee.

Adjourned to meet in the Court-room, Saturday evening, seven o'clock, October 23d, 1869.

DUNCAN MCPHERSON, Secretary.

127. *Santa Cruz Sentinel,* October 16, 1869 (3:1)

A preliminary examination of the head-waters of San Lorenzo river is to be made for railroad purposes.

128. *Santa Cruz Sentinel,* October 23, 1869 (2:1)

Mountain Trip.

In accordance with our announcement last week, Dr. Spencer and Alexander McPherson visited the mountain range from near the "Tin Can Ranch," down near to Taylor's Gap. The level was taken from the streets of Santa Cruz, which are 12 feet above ocean level. The second measurement was taken at the watering-place, Parson's ranch, which was found to be 400 feet; the third, Ed.

Scott's house, 610; the fourth, Bean Creek crossing, 640; the fifth, "Mountain Charlie's," 1,800; the sixth, going northward, head of Zeyante gulch, Doherty's mill, 1,900; the seventh, Conley's gulch, 2,075; the eighth, head of Newell creek, or, branch of Bear creek, Bauer's farm (Mountain Hope Ranch) 2,300; the ninth, branch of the San Lorenzo, near the "Shingle House," 2,500; the tenth, "Tin Can Ranch," 2,700; the eleventh, going southward from "Mountain Charlie's," Sheltie's, 1,440; the twelfth, Taylor's Gap, 1,420; the thirteenth, Burrell's house, 1,350. These altitudes were taken in the lowest possible depressions in the mountains, and as will be seen, with increased elevation from the south to the north; the first, taking the ridge of the mountains, Burrell's house, being but 1,350 feet, while the last, near the "Tin Can Ranch," some eighteen miles further up the range, was 2,700.

In taking these heights, it being for the purpose of ascertaining the feasibility of constructing a railroad to connect this town with some point on the S. F. and S. J. railroad, in the Santa Clara valley, by going over or tunneling through the mountains, especial attention was paid to the slope of the mountains towards Santa Clara and Santa Cruz, and the width of the ridge through which a tunnel would have to be dug if built at all. The best place to cross the mountains is believed to be at the head of Bear creek, the ascent being more gradual on the Santa Cruz side, and up an open and unobstructed canyon, timbered nearly to the head, with a narrow ridge to tunnel through, estimated at half a mile, with an easy descent into the Santa Clara valley, either by the way of McCartysville, or to the right of it. The distance by this route would be thirty-seven miles, with a rise of 2,000 feet. It is seventeen miles from the top of the mountains at this point to Santa Clara, and at a rough guess it was calculated to be twenty to Santa Cruz.

In passing along the ridge the traveler is stuck with the marked difference in appearance of the foot-hills. On the Santa Clara side they are abrupt, jagged, barren and desolate, save here and there a patch of sage brush, while at their feet away as far as the eye can reach is the rich and fertile valley of the Santa Clara. On the Santa Cruz side the hills taper, apparently, gradually to the sea, presenting an unbroken forest of redwoods.

There are several valuable farms on the mountains, composed of loose and porous soil, suitable for raising the smaller grains and orchards and vineyards, two of the latter which are heavily laden with grapes, California variety. Springs are abundant. No timber is found along the ridge save hazel and oak, the former growing on the Santa Clara side in great abundance.

The Santa Clara people are after our redwood, and they are at the present time getting shakes, shingles, pickets, posts, etc., out of the canyon but a short distance above Charlie Martin's house, and through every sag in the mountains for six miles above "Mountain Charlie's."

At the head of the Zeyante, one mile below the pass in the ridge, Doherty's sawmill is cutting from ten to fifteen thousand feet of lumber per day. The lumber is "snaked" from the mill to what is styled the landing, some three-quarters of a mile, and sold at $19 per M. Teams here double to the top of the ridge, then haul to Santa Clara or San Jose, making the trip in one day, delivering the lumber at a cost of from $28 to $30 per M. All the goods consumed at the mill houses, and by farmers in the neighborhood, are purchased at Lexington or San Jose, there being no roads down any of the canyons to Santa Cruz.

The "Tin Can Ranch" is noted more for its name than for any farming or timber value. As near as can be learned it never had a name, properly speaking, or a proprietor, save a herder of sheep or cattle. When the first known American visited it, they found near a spring a number of empty oyster and sardine cans, which they supposed to have been left by a band of robbers, cattle or horse thieves, and from this discovery originated the name "Tin Can Ranch."

The settlers from "Mountain Charlie's" up to the boundary of the county, complain and we think justly, of the burdensome task of voting, all of them having to go to Scott's Valley, some of them having to travel a distance of fifteen miles. They wish the Board of Supervisors to establish a precinct at Doherty's mill, and to do something in the way of opening roads to the headwaters of the San Lorenzo and Zeyante, enabling them to come to Santa Cruz without going way round by "Mountain Charlie's." They pay their taxes in this county, do their voting here, but their isolated condition sends them to San Jose, to make their purchases.

129. *Santa Cruz Sentinel,* October 23, 1869 (2:2)

Estimate of Traffic on Felton Road.—The following is an estimate of the traffic on the Felton road per day for eight months in the year:

Lumber, feet, 50,000; lime, barrels, 150; tan bark, cords, 10; shingles, quarter bunches, 30; wood, cords, 6; shakes, posts, etc., 300.

The amount paid out annually for freight on the above articles, is more than would pay the interest on a first-class railroad, thrice over, and leave a handsome margin for repairs besides.

130. *Santa Cruz Sentinel,* October 23, 1869 (3:1)

Don't forget the adjourned railroad meeting for to-night. The Committee appointed two weeks ago will report the result of its deliberations. The altitudes of the different depressions in the mountains from "Mountain Charlie's" to near the Tin Can ranch has been taken, and among other business will be submitted to the meeting.

131. *Daily Alta California*, October 27, 1869 (2:2)

A Railroad to Santa Cruz.

Santa Cruz needs a railroad. It has a thrifty industry and a large area of land that could make a profit of five hundred per cent. by building a road. There are 100,000 acres of good redwood timber, some of the best in the State, and as much more of valuable pasture. The fogs are abundant and the grasses succulent. The average yield of wheat per acre, in 1868, according to the Assessor, was 26 bushels: Of barley, 37; and of oats, 35. There are 36,000 apple trees, 240,000 grape vines, 5,200 near cattle, 7,800 chickens, 2,000 registered voters, 10,000 inhabitants, 15,000 acres under cultivation, and $2,434,522 of taxable property as ascertained by official valuation. The Gabilan Ridge, the summit of which forms the eastern boundary, is about 2,000 feet high, on average, and seems to corral the clouds so that the rainfall is considerably greater than in the Santa Clara Valley a few miles to the eastward, or in San Francisco, and the consequence is that the Santa Cruz streams, though not long, have relatively large bodies of water. The forests contain large quantities of oak timber, there are considerable deposits of lime, and the abundance of the redwood, oak, lime and fresh water, near a good roadstead and not far from the metropolis, have led to the establishment of factories. Last year the country produced 19,000,000 feet of lumber, 10,000,000 shingles, 1,700,000 pounds of powder, 1,600,000 pounds of leather, 13,000 pounds of glue, 125,000 barrels of lime, 20,000 barrels of flour, and some paper, fuse, soap, and other articles of less note.

Besides the lumbering, manufacturing and real estate interests, there is a pleasure resort interest which demands a railroad. The town of Santa Cruz is fitted by nature to be a favorite watering place. The scenery in the neighborhood is romantic, the foliage remains green until late in the summer, the beach is beautiful and there are good places for bathing. It attracted less attention last season than in previous years because other places were more accessible. While roads have been made to the Geysers and Yosemite, there has been no improvement in the means of reaching Santa Cruz. Pleasure-seekers must be accommodated, if

The Dream of Steam, 1854–1873

their custom is to be obtained. People submitted to be smothered in dust so long as they could not get out of the city in any direction without going through it, but now they are released from the necessity.

Santa Cruz can be reached by water, but the roadstead is insecure in winter, the trade is not large enough to pay for daily trips of a steamer, the voyage on sailing vessels is slow, and the wagon road over the mountains is steep and dusty in summer and muddy in winter, and expensive at all times. It would certainly pay to build a railroad, but those who would derive the most profit—that is, the land-owners generally—are not disposed to do anything, Some of them do not believe in railroads, and others think they can by waiting a year or two get all the benefit without bearing any of the expense.

Three routes for reaching Santa Cruz by rail are proposed. A road is projected to run southward from Redwood City, and after crossing the Summit descending the valley of the San Lorenzo. By this route, fifty miles of new road would have to be built. Half the distance is in San Mateo County, nearly all the way in valuable timber, where there are few people. The highest elevation is about 2,000 feet, and can be reduced by a tunnel to 1,700. It is generally conceded that the road cannot be built without county aid, and Santa Cruz would not pay for making a road in San Mateo. If the owners of the redwood would pay what they could well afford, the work would be done; but the majority of the people in both counties have no interest in the district that would receive the most benefit from this road. The second route proposed is thirty miles long, to run from Santa Clara, and cross the Gabilan Ridge near the head of Soquel Creek. The elevation could be reduced by tunnelling to six hundred feet. Soquel is near the centre of population of Santa Cruz County, and this route would probably accommodate the people generally better than any other. The distance from Santa Cruz to San Francisco by either of these two routes is 80 miles. The third route is 30 miles long, starts from Gilroy, and makes the distance from San Francisco 110 miles. It is claimed that this road will bring the produce of Gilroy and northern Monterey to Santa Cruz, to be sent thence by schooners to San Francisco, in preference to going 80 miles by rail from Gilroy. At a meeting held in Santa Cruz Mr. Hihn, Assemblyman elect, submitted the following proposition: [*see* Article 125 above.]

No final action was taken, but the matter was referred to a subsequent meeting. The course of Mr. Hihn in taking the opinion of his constituents on a question of this kind in advance, instead of keeping silent till near the end of the session, and then rushing a bill through before its character is understood, or perhaps even before its existence is known, is deserving of all praise.

132. *Santa Cruz Sentinel,* October 30, 1869 (2:1)
Railroad Meeting.

In accordance with the adjournment, a second railroad meeting was convened at the court-house in this place on Saturday evening last. The Committee on Railroads reported the result of their labors, Dr. Fagan, Secretary, reading the same. R. C. Kirby moved, and it was seconded, that the report be accepted and the Committee discharged, which was accordingly done. Dr Spencer reported the result of observations made on and along the ridge of mountains at the head of the Zeyante and San Lorenzo rivers, the altitudes being as published in last week's Sentinel. Oral statements were offered by E. L. Wiliams and Alex. McPherson as to the proper place to cross the mountains with the San Lorenzo railroad. F. A. Hihn spoke as to the object of the meeting, stating that the altitudes of the different depressions, as reported by Dr. Spencer, were taken to ascertain the practicability of constructing the San Lorenzo road into the Santa Clara valley, that the road had been surveyed for seventeen miles, and at the upper end the elevation attained was seven hundred and forty feet. R. C. Kirby said he did not suppose the meeting was called to *oppose* a railroad; that he was in favor of a railway—the Watsonville route; that he was of the opinion that the road by the way of Gilroy was the only practical one; that it was all nonsense to talk about branch roads, for the people wouldn't stand it, and that they ought not to; that the meeting should be addressed by all tax paying, thinking men; that he was in favor of the county issuing bonds and loaning its credit, even to the amount of $12,000 per mile. E. L. Williams said that the proposed road up the San Lorenzo was to run as near as practicable along the bed of the stream, and at a grade of forty feet to the mile; that while he did not oppose other routes he earnestly favored that of the San Lorenzo. Wm. Moore favored the road that could be built for the smallest amount of money; said $6,000 bonds per mile was enough for the county to issue; that those interested in private roads should build them;

that the San Lorenzo company had a good thing, and they knew it, and that if they didn't like it there were parties to buy them out, and all they had to do was to throw up their franchise; that Hihn would build the Soquel road himself; that it would be very well to have a railroad running up the coast to his house, but that when he wanted it he would build it without calling on the county. F. A Hihn said he favored the issuing of $8,000 in bonds per mile, as he thought many of the taxpayers wished, but that a majority of the Committee favored $10,000, and that he had signed the report submitted on that ground. E. Bennett said the same. Hy Jackson, of Watsonville, said he was on the Committee for Messrs. Ford and Barney, who, for indisposition, were unable to attend in person; that the Watsonvillans would have a railroad to Gilroy; that they wished the assistance of the Santa Cruzans in the construction of the Watsonville and Gilroy road, and that they would assist in the construction of the Santa Cruz and Watsonville road; that they did not ask aid for the entire distance from Watsonville to Gilroy, nineteen miles, but only for ten miles, the distance the road is to run in this county. George Anthony said that the building of the San Lorenzo road over the mountains was impracticable, and the only road to be thought of was by the way of Watsonville; that the tax-payers and voters had a word to say as in what direction the public funds should be expended; to benefit the greatest number and represent the greatest amount was the larger good; the most of the taxable property is below, not above. Prof. Tuthill expatiated at some length on the necessity and advantages of a railroad; said he had quite recently traveled over a considerable of the territory of the State, especially the Sacramento country, and while doing so had conversed with many gentlemen who proposed spending a brief season, with their families, in Santa Cruz, but delayed doing so from the fact that if they came by water they would be seasick, while if they traveled by land they would have to go the circuitous rout of "around the horn" or cross on a narrow mountain road somewhat notorious for its accidents and hairbreadth escapes; that roads must not be looked at alone from the net profits they would yield the first year; that it was for this people to say whether we should prosper like Chicago, the queen depot of railroads and mother of progressive men, or, like Providence, with all her natural and unimproved advantages, stand unchanged for seventy years. Elihu Anthony said he realized the necessity of a railway, and his heart and hand was in the good work.

The meeting was at attended by a goodly number of earnest, solid business men, who wished to see the project a thing of reality, and all bids fair that it will be.

133. *Santa Cruz Sentinel,* October 30, 1869 (2:2)
Proceedings of Railroad Meeting.

Pursuant to appointment of previous meeting, an adjourned Railroad meeting was convened at the Courthouse on Saturday evening, Oct. 23d, 1869, Jacob Parsons, of Soquel, Chairman. The report of the surveying party, as to the altitudes of the different depressions or sags in the mountains on the head-waters of the San Lorenzo and Zayante, were reported the same as published in the Sentinel of 23d. The report of the Committee, who were appointed to examine and report as to the most feasible and practicable route of connecting the town of Santa Cruz with San Francisco by a railway, and the aid Santa Cruz county should render in the construction of said road, reported as follows:

Report of Committee.

Your Committee, appointed to take into consideration the expediency of the county of Santa Cruz making an appropriation to aid in the construction of a railroad, leading from the town of Santa Cruz to the town of Watsonville, and from the town of Watsonville to the line of said county, on the line of railroad running from Watsonville to the town of Gilroy, in the county of Santa Clara, beg leave to submit the following report: That they recommend that the county of Santa Cruz aid in the construction of said railroad from the town of Santa Cruz, by the way of Watsonville, to the south-east line of said county, to the amount of $10,000 per mile, in the bonds of said county, bearing interest at the rate of *eight* per cent. per annum, and payable within *twenty years* from the issuance thereof. Said bonds to be issued upon the construction and completion of each five miles of said railroad,

Provided, That $4,000 per mile, in bonds, shall be withheld on the road from the eastern line of county to Watsonville, until the railroad is constructed to a point at least *ten miles* westerly from the said town of Watsonville, when the said $4,000 per mile shall be paid to the Company who shall have constructed said last mentioned ten miles of railroad. Such bonds to constitute a first-mortgage on such road,

Provided, That on the road from the south-eastern line of the county to Watsonville, and additional amount of $4,000 per mile may be borrowed by the company owning said road, and to be secured jointly with the amount received from the county, as first-mortgage bonds, in said road. The interest on said bonds to be paid by the county for the first *ten years*. All taxes assessed on, and collected from said road, to be used toward the payment of the interest on such bonds. At the expiration of ten years, such additional sum shall be annually collected, by the county, from said road, which added to the taxes, will be sufficient to pay the interest and one-tenth part of the principal of said bonds. And your Committee further report on the construction of the San Lorenzo and Soquel branches of said road, as contemplated in the original document; That they consider them as highly expedient and advantageous, and would greatly conduce to the final completion and business of the main road; that they would open up a region on country rich in natural resources, and full of the elements of future prosperity, but *inexpedient* at this time, to submit so broad a proposition to the people, for fear of defeating the whole.

Committee:
    E. Bennett, Chairman,
    P. B. Fagen, Sec.,
    Lucien Heath,
    Amasa Pray,
    F. A. Hihn,
    Hy Jackson.

In compliance with an inquiry of Prof. Tuthill as to the

cost and profit per annum, of the road proposed by the Committee, F. A. Hihn submitted the following:

Estimates of cost of construction of a railroad from Santa Cruz to Watsonville, 19 miles:

Grading, earthwork between Santa Cruz and Soquel, 3¾ miles, $2,000 per mile, average $7,500
Between Soquel and Aptos, 3¼ miles, $2,000 per mile 6,500
Between Aptos and Watsonville, 12 miles, $2,500 per mile............ 30,000
Total $44,000
Culverts and trestle work, 5,650 lineal feet, at $8 per foot, average............ $44,200
Bridges, 400 feet, lineal measurement............ 16,000
40,000 ties, at 40 cents apiece 16,000
2,000 tons iron, at $70 per ton 140,000
Laying track, $600 per mile 12,000
Ballasting road, $1,000 per mile 20,000
Depots 10,000
Total $302,200
Fencing and right of way 20,000
20 per cent. margin 64,000
Final total $386,200

Business of the road from Santa Cruz to Watsonville:

20,000 tons grain, at $2 per ton $40,000
10,000,000 feet of timber, (lumber sawed and split) at $3 per M 30,000
All other freight, both ways, 10,000 tons 20,000
Average of 50 passengers per day, at $1.25 23,000
Mail and Express 1,500
Total, per annum $114,500

The meeting, as was the previous one, was called to obtain the sense of the taxpayers and citizens of this county, as to what amount the county should loan, at what interest and for what length of time, toward the construction of a railroad within its boundaries, and in what direction such road should be located, and a Committee was appointed to investigate as to said route and amount of bonds to be loaned by Santa Cruz county; and the report, as published above, was offered as the result of deliberations of the Committee, and by unanimous vote, was accepted and endorsed by said meeting, the same instructing the Representative elect, F. A. Hihn, to submit a bill to the next Legislature in accordance with the provisions thereof. There being no more business for consideration, the meeting adjourned *sine die*. Duncan McPherson, Secretary, *pro tem*.

134. *Santa Cruz Sentinel,* October 30, 1869 (2:3)
Railroads.

Under the head of "A Railroad in Santa Cruz," we publish an article from the *Alta* and another from the Monterey *Democrat*, which we submit to the perusal and serious consideration of every man in the county. There is no use of dodging the issue. The progress and prosperity of the county, comparatively, has come to a stand-still, and will remain so for years to come unless she keeps pace with her sister counties of San Mateo and Santa Clara in the construction of internal improvements, first among which are railroads. Without railroad connection with the demand and production of the State, we can not expect our extensive water-power to be occupied by machinery, and without the establishment of manufactories, one of our great natural resources will remain unimproved. As for thinking this place will remain a leading watering-place (if it now is?) with an open sea on one side and mountain barriers on all others, or a tedious stage ridge of eighty miles, with railroads leading to and from every mart in the State, is the height of folly, showing a childish ignorance of the improvement of the age. Railroads accommodate all by the employment they give, by the taxable property they add, and by the accommodations they afford, while they especially benefit the taxpayers by doubling, and, in many instances, quadrupling the value of property. Were there a railroad leading from the town of Santa Cruz to San Francisco and the Salinas Valley, millions of dollars that are now employed in other parts of the State, or on the Atlantic side, would find investment here, while our population would be increased ten-fold, making this a city in five years of third importance in the State.

San Francisco is becoming one of the busy hives of humanity—a leading commercial mart,—and she must have outlets and country residences, the same as New York has her Hudson river, and as the country, water, climate and future prospects of the mining counties fail to furnish inducements or accommodations for these, they must necessarily flow to the country along the coast, but not till cheap, easy, safe and rapid communication is established. Our geographical position, with our mild, pleasant and healthy atmosphere, varied and beautiful scenery and mountains, hill and dale, sea-coast and rivers, pleasant drives and shady groves, fields and forests, desirable locations for the erection of houses, commands a large share of this population.

We are isolated without railroads, and will be without railroads, until we construct them. There is no inducement for the investment of outside capital in our midst, while we oppose, directly or indirectly, the advancement of public or internal improvement. Neither is it right that individual citizens should make the necessary outlay alone, for the county, as a body corporate, is mainly to be benefitted, by the increase of property and population, and she should contribute liberally towards such construction, not by actual gift, but by loan of her bonds.

We hope the next sessions of the Legislature will not be allowed to go unimproved, but that a bill will be introduced and passed that will enable us to move in this much-needed work, and that the people, as a man, will take it up and construct a railroad in the shortest possible time. Let there be no drawbacks—men going around and howling "Taxation!" "Taxation!" who know as little of railroads as they do of heaven, but who, to be heard and felt, are willing to howl, doing nothing themselves but to destroy the labor of others. No man of enterprise, energy and progressive views, will, if he justly realizes the advantages of a railroad, oppose its construction. He may, and should, if any, oppose its objectionable features, demanding a just and judicial expenditure of public moneys.

135. *Daily Alta California* via the *Santa Cruz Sentinel*, October 30, 1869 (2:4)

A Railroad to Santa Cruz.

Santa Cruz needs a railroad. It has a thrifty industry and a large area of land that could make a profit of five hundred per cent. by building a road. There are 100,000 acres of good redwood timber, some of the best in the State, and as much more of valuable pasture. The fogs are abundant and the grasses succulent. The average yield of wheat per acre, in 1868, according to the Assessor, was 26 bushels; of barley, 37; and of oats, 35. There are 36,000 apple trees, 2400,000 grape vines, 5,200 neat cattle, 7,800 chickens, 2,000 registered voters, 10,000 inhabitants, 15,000 acres under cultivation, and $2,434,522 of taxable property as ascertained by official valuation. The Gabilan Range, the summit of which forms the eastern boundary, is about 2,000 feet high, on an average, and seems to corral the clouds so that the rainfall is considerably greater than in the Santa Clara Valley a few miles to the eastward, or in San Francisco, and the consequence is that the Santa Cruz streams, though not long, have relatively large bodies of water. The forests contain large quantities of oak timber, there are considerable deposits of lime, and the abundance of the redwood, oak, lime and fresh water, near a good roadstead and not far from the metropolis, have led to the establishment of factories. Last year the county produced 19,000,000 feet of lumber, 10,000,000 shingles, 1,700,000 pounds of powder, 1,6000,000 pounds leather, 13,000 lbs. glue, 125,000 barrels of lime,

20,000 barrels of flour, and some paper, fuse, soap, and other articles of less note.

Besides the lumbering, manufacturing and real estate interests, there is a pleasure resort interest which demands a railroad. The town of Santa Cruz is fitted by nature to be a favorable watering place. The scenery in the neighborhood is romantic, the foliage remains green until late in the summer, the beach is beautiful and there are good places for bathing. It attracted less attention last season than in previous years because other places were more accessible. While roads have been made to the Geysers and Yosemite, there has been no improvement in the means of reaching Santa Cruz. Pleasure-seekers must be accommodated, if their custom is to be obtained. People submitted to be smothered in dust so long as they could not get out of the city in any direction without going through it, but now they are released from the necessity.

Santa Cruz can be reached by water, but the roadstead is insecure in winter, the trade is not large enough to pay for daily trips of a steamer, the voyage on sailing vessels is slow, and the wagon road over the mountains is steep and dusty in summer and muddy in winter, and expensive at all times. It would certainly pay to build a railroad, but those who would derive the most profit—that is, the landowners generally—are not disposed to do anything. Some of them do not believe in railroads, and others think they can by waiting a year or two get all the benefit without bearing any of the expenses.

Three routes for reaching Santa Cruz by rail are proposed. A road is projected to run southward from Redwood City, and after crossing the Summit descending the valley of the San Lorenzo. By this route, fifty miles of new road would have to be built. Half the distance is in San Mateo county, nearly all the way in valuable timber, where there are few people. The highest elevation is about 2,000 feet, and can be reduced by a tunnel to 1,700. It is generally conceded that the road cannot be built without county aid, and Santa Cruz would not pay for making a road in San Mateo. If the owners of the redwood would pay what they could well afford, the work would be done; but the majority of the people in both counties have no interest in the district that would receive the most benefit from this road. The second route proposed is thirty miles long, to run from Santa Clara, and cross the Gabilan Ridge near the head of Soquel Creek. The elevation could be reduced by tunnelling, too six hundred feet. Soquel is near the centre of population of Santa Cruz county, and this route would probably accommodate the people generally better than any other. The distance from Santa Cruz to San Francisco by either of these routes is 80 miles. The third route is 30 miles long, starts from Gilroy, and makes the distance from San Francisco 110 miles. It is claimed that this road will bring the produce of Gilroy and northern Monterey to Santa Cruz, to be sent thence by schooners to San Francisco, in preference to going 80 miles by rail from Gilroy.

136. *Monterey Democrat* via the *Santa Cruz Sentinel*, October 30, 1869 (2:4)

In the State, north of San Francisco Bay, railroad enterprises are numerous, and the time does not seem far off when their number will meet the requirements of business.

The Santa Cruz people are moving to the same end; their object being to build, or assist the construction of, three railroads—to the San Lorenzo redwoods, to Watsonville and thence to Gilroy. They propose that the county shall contribute in the shape of interest bearing bonds.

A gentleman, who is in a position to know what is a fact, told us some little while since that the Southern Pacific is actively perfecting its organization. He added that the programme is now to come from Gilroy down the Pajaro river to the Salinas Plain, then to the head of the latter, and so on southward to the Gila, through our coast counties. The Louisville Commercial Convention lately in session, endorsed this route, and the people on the Memphis side, that being the eastern terminus resolved upon, are now giving through and action, zealously, to the realization of the scheme.

We are well aware that there is little capital in this county to be employed in such enterprises as an investment, but at the same time it is expected and it is just that populations so much benefitted by such improvements should do something toward the expenses of their construction. The ultimate benefits of a railroad are manifested most in the appreciation of property and growth of population along the lines of road and those benefits, where the counties receive no dividends from the road itself, would far more than compensate for the aid lent. It is a very simple problem. Say a county guarantees $300,000 bonds bearing a moderate interest, and obtains therefrom an improvement, which builds towns, fills the adjoining country with settlers and creates hundreds of thousands of dollars of taxable property—she has got *quid pro co*, certainly made a capital investment, however long the bonds are to run.

A railroad is a very good thing, no doubt of it; and in the present age such transportation as is employed on the Salinas Plain appears terribly slow. The people in question generally take the same view of the matter we feel assured, nor is the time inopportune to debate it. If the Southern Pacific is to pass through this county, very well; it will be useful. We submit, however, that the original scheme of a railroad to Monterey be carefully cherished; for by such a road, reaching sea transport in so short a distance, freight can be conveyed more cheaply than by a continuous railroad to San Francisco. This is demonstrated by what is taking place at Stockton now—wheat from the western bank of the San Joaquin, being brought by the Western Pacific road to that place to be shipped by steamer and schooner to the city, instead of going on by rail to Oakland.

137. *The Pajaronian*, November 4, 1869 (2:2)
Railroad Matters.

Last week we gave a report of the railroad meeting, held

in Santa Cruz, Oct. 23, composed of many of the first citizens of the county. We did not have time to comment on the action of the meeting, but propose to say a few words this week.

The proposed railroad, as stated in the report, will commence at Santa Cruz, go to Watsonville, via Soquel, and from Watsonville to the county line, ten miles toward Gilroy. The estimates made by Mr. Hihn, in regard to the cost of the road, amount of freight, travel, etc., are very fair, and show more than a passing knowledge of railroad matters. The report of the railroad Committee, however, is open to a great deal of criticism. Here is the principal part of the Committee's Report:

"That they recommend that the county of Santa Cruz aid the construction of said railroad from the town of Santa Cruz by the way of Watsonville to the southwestern line of said county, to the amount of $10,000 per mile, in the bonds of said county, bearing interest at the rate of eight per cent per annum and payable within ten years from the issuance thereof. Said bonds to be issued upon the construction and completion of each five miles of said railroad.

"*Provided*. That four thousand dollars ($4,000) per mile, in bonds, shall be withheld on the road from the eastern line of the county to Watsonville until the railroad is constructed to a point at least ten miles westerly from the said town of Watsonville, when the said four thousand dollars per mile shall be paid to the company who shall have constructed said last mentioned ten miles of railroad. Such bonds to constitute a first-mortgage on said road.

"*Provided*. That on the road from the southeastern

line of the county to Watsonville an additional amount of four thousand dollars per mile may be borrowed by the company owning said road, and to be secured jointly with the amount received from the county as first-mortgage bonds on said road.

"The interest on said bonds to be paid by the county for the first ten years. All taxes assessed on, and collected from said road, to be used toward the payment of the interest on such bonds. At the expiration of ten years such additional sum shall be annually collected by the county, from said road, which, added to the taxes, will be sufficient to pay the interest and one-tenth part of the principal of said bonds."

From the above report, it will be seen that the 20 miles of road from this place to Santa Cruz, will receive $10,000 per mile, while from here to the county line, $4,000 of the bonds are to be withheld, leaving us only $6,000 per mile for the 10 miles! What is that for? No one with any idea of justice will vote in favor of such a proposition. It looks to us as though a touch of coercion is to be tried on at this end of the county. We will not charge any man in Santa Cruz with enmity to the interests of Watsonville, but will say that the Committee have doubtless made a mistake in regard to the proposed appropriation of county bonds, and before further action is taken in the matter we would advise them to make proper corrections. After the ten miles of road are completed, however, from Watsonville to the county line, the $4,000 withheld shall be paid to the Company who constructs the aforesaid ten miles of road, the county taking a mortgage thereon. What good, we would like to know, would $4,000 per mile do us after ten miles of road is completed. There would still be ten miles more to construct before we reached Gilroy. To sum up this question of county aid, it stands thus: The citizens of the Pajaro Valley desire a road to Gilroy, twenty miles in length. To aid us in this venture certain astute individuals at the County Seat propose that the county give us for the first ten miles the sum of $60,000 to start with, then take a mortgage on the road for $40,000! This operation will effectually knock the remaining ten miles of road to Gilroy higher than Gilroy's kite; for moneyed men, of whom we expect aid, will not touch a road on which there is a prior mortgage.

At the same time the citizens of Santa Cruz desire a road from Watsonville to Santa Cruz, and the aforesaid astute individuals propose to obtain aid from the county to the amount of $200,000, but say nothing about withholding two-thirds of the amount until the road is completed. They take the turkey and give us the crow, or give us the crow, and they take the turkey. The least that could be done under the circumstances would be to give us the full $10,000 per mile withholding nothing.

The proper way for the county to act in the matter is to take stock in the 30 miles of road to the amount of $300,000, the same as Los Angeles, Santa Clara, San Joaquin and other counties have done. If the county intends to aid in the construction of a road let it do it in a businesslike way. Take stock in the road or loan its credit to each mile alike, or do nothing. By taking stock as we propose the county would have a controlling interest in the road and would be amply secured.

138. *Santa Cruz Sentinel,* November 6, 1869 (2:2)

It seems to be settled that the coast line railroad will be built. The probable route will be from Gilroy down the Pajaro river, to the Salinas Plains, then to the head of the Salinas Valley, passing through Estrella pass and continuing down through the tier of Coast counties, connecting with a transcontinental road.

139. *Santa Cruz Sentinel,* November 6, 1869 (2:3)
Railroads.
San Lorenzo, Nov. 3d, 1869.

Eds. Sentinel:—Our people in this section have heard with surprise and regret of the action of your Railroad Committee. We can't see with what reason of justice they have ignored this section of the county, in this proposed railroad scheme. If, as they say in their report, they consider a railroad up the San Lorenzo "as highly expedient and advantageous," and "would open up a country, rich in material resources," why did they not recommend it being built, when they well know that upon the development of these resources depends, in a great degree, the prosperity of their town? We think it can be demonstrated beyond the shadow of a doubt that a railroad communication with this portion of the county would enhance the value of the taxable property in the county to such an extent, that there would be no necessity for the rates of taxation to be increased, even if the county loaned her bonds to assist in the building of the road. And Eds.

Sentinel, a road up the San Lorenzo would be a *paying investment*, which is more than can be said of a road to Watsonville. We do not believe in the right or justice of taxing the people of this section to build a railroad from Santa Cruz to Watsonville, unless we, also, are placed in railroad connection with your town. But we are good-natured, and are willing to compromise matters. You assist us in building our road so as to enable us to get our millions of feet of lumber and redwoods of all description to your market, and we will assist you in building your road to Watsonville, so that pleasure-seekers may visit your town during the summer months, and avoid the circuitous route by sea and the perilous passage of the mountains. Unless your citizens take the sober second thought and act fairly in this matter, we intend to oppose your proposed scheme by every legitimate means. Our county is small, our population few in number, and we are already overburdened with debt. Our small proprietors are taxed for *every dollar they are worth*, while our *larger proprietors* go comparatively scotfree. Our rates of taxation are now over three per cent., and we do not intend to stand any greater pressure upon our industry, unless we are to be benefitted. SAN LORENZO.

140. *Santa Cruz Sentinel,* November 13, 1869 (2:2-3)
RAILROADS.
San Lorenzo, Nov. 9th, 1869.

Messrs. Editors:—Your committee in their report on the construction of the proposed Railroad, from Santa

Cruz to Watsonville, has assumed the cost of said road, to be in round numbers $386,000; and the total receipts per annum, to be $114,500, about thirty per cent., or 2 1-2 per cent. per month profit, a pretty good investment; and if their figures are correct it would be an excellent idea for the county in their corporate capacity, (if the expression may be allowed) to build the said road entire, without aid and assistance of outsiders; so as to pay off our county indebtedness. Just think of it, Messrs. Editors, a little investment of only $386,000, the interest thirty per cent. per annum, and in three and a half years the road paid for, and a regular income thereafter of $114,500 per year. Who wouldn't build a railroad to Watsonville? Why! Messrs. Editors, if their figures are correct, (and it is said that figures never lie,) it would indeed by a splendid county speculation, and our *small landed proprietors* would only be compelled to hear the *outrageous taxation* now *imposed upon them* about *five years longer*. After that period had elapsed, they would really feel that the morning of the millennium had at last dawned upon Santa Cruz county, and that each and ever man, woman and child, could sit under their own vine and fig-tree, and no assessor or tax-gather to molest them, or make them afraid. But, Messrs. Editors, with all the due respect to your committee, and we up here in the "redwoods," know them to be gentlemen of great moral worth, and who have the best interests of the county at heart, do you not think that they acted with a *little* inconsistency when (as it is said) they with but few dissenting voices were willing to concede that a railroad in this direction would be, not only a feasible, but a profitable route, and at the same time admitted that the Watsonville route would not pay as an investment for capitalists? If it be true that they entertained and expressed their opinions, is it not strange that they should recommend that our county should subscribe bonds to the amount $10,000, per mile, thereby increasing out county indebtedness to an immense amount, and overburdening our people with increased taxation, and *benefitting nobody except a few large landed proprietors?* "Oh! consistency, thou art a jewel." But Messrs. Editors, again, with all due respect to your committee, we can't figure out this $114,500 profits, and *defy your committee* to do it. We can't understand why the farmers in the vicinity of the proposed railroad route, would send their 20,000 tons of grain to Santa Cruz, and from thence to San Francisco; the destination of nearly all the grain raised in California, when a very small line of road would enable them to find equally as good a point of shipment at Pajaro Landing, or a line placing them in communication with Gilroy would give them facilities for shipment to San Francisco, without breaking bulk.

As the object of your citizens is to build a road that would develop the immense resources of the county, enhance the value of the real estate, pour the accumulated wealth into your own, and place your people in communication with the outside world. A railroad up the San Lorenzo, for ten miles, and eventually on toward San Francisco, connecting with the San Francisco and San Jose road at Menlo Park, making the entire distance sixty-five miles, will prove the most desirable route; the route by Watsonville to San Francisco would be about one hundred and thirty miles; the *time and distance and freight* being *one-half in favor of the San Lorenzo* route. As in investment for capitalists, this is one of the best in California. Let facts demonstrate the truth of this assertion. Our people in this section have only two hundred and twenty working days in the year to get their products to your market, and notwithstanding we are few in number, we now pay over $120,000 per year for freight per wagons to your town. We know that one hundred acres of our heavily-timbered land will give as much employment in one year to a railroad, as 3.875 acres of land producing grain will in the same length of time. Now for the figures. We have many thousands of acres in this region that will yield 50,000 feet of lumber to the acre, or five millions of feet to one hundred acres; give millions feet of lumber at $1.25 (now costing $3.50 to $4.00) per thousand freight, will give 6,250 dollars; three thousand cords wood, (and this is a small estimate) at fifty cents per cord (now costing two dollars per cord) freight, will give $1,5000; in all $7,750. Assuming that your grain land will yield an average of thirty-three bushels of wheat, or a ton of 2,000 pounds to the acre, which is a very large average, (and much larger than it will be a few years hence, as they lands in this state are deteriorating very rapidly under the present system of cultivation) it would require the entire crop of 3.875 acres, or 3,875 tons of wheat, at two dollars per ton, freight, to give the same employment to a railroad as one hundred acres of timbered land; and we have a strip of land ten miles wide, and twenty miles long, seven-tenths or over 100,000 acres of which are covered with a heavy growth of timber. By far the greater portion of this land is now valueless for want of railroad facilities. It is a well established fact, that facilities for railroad transportation will increase it many fold, and we are all well convinced that *without any increase in the quality of our productions, or to the number of our population in this section*, that a *railroad up the San Lorenzo would now be a paying investment*. We know that the increase in the value of the land in this portion of the county would more than pay the entire cost of the road. We have lime quarries, turning out 40,000 barrels of lime per year. This lime is sent to your town for shipment at the freight of (now costing twenty-five cents) ten cents per barrel is $4,000 per year; as much freight as two thousand acres of grain land in the vicinity of your *favored* Watsonville route, would give at two dollars per ton, taking the foregoing estimate of thirty-three bushels, or one ton to the acre as the maximum yield. We have also sufficient manufacturing facilities, unequalled in California. With these few simple, plain facts, patent to every man living in this section, and well known to many of your leading citizens, we were astonished, I might say, confounded, when we saw in the columns of your paper that we were ignored in favor of the Watsonville route, upon the ground that if our railroad project were submitted to the people, tacked on to the Watsonville bill, the people wouldn't stand it. Why, Messrs. Editors, your citizens are not blind to their own interests. They are not to be hoodwinked in this manner. They will not swallow the Watsonville railroad bill. They all know that such a road would not benefit them in the least, and would not enhance the value of their real estate one farthing. They well know that their prosperity depends, in a great degree, upon the construction of a railroad through this section, the richest in internal resources, and the most beautiful in California. It has been said by some who object to our railroad, that when the timber is cut off, the land will then be valueless. The answer to this objection is: The people have been cutting timber here for eighteen years, and have not *yet made a hole in the landscape, and from the tops of our loftiest peaks there is nothing but forests to be seen;* and the child is not born in Santa Cruz county, who will live long enough to see this portion of the county denuded of its redwoods. And even in the event of our forest growth disappearing, our lands will then be very valuable for raising of cereals, and for the cultivation of fruit. We have as many acres of timbers lands as there are prairie or cleared lands, and of equal fertility of soil. We are not prepared to say what a railroad up the San Lorenzo would cost; but we are of the opinion that there is no mountain country in California where a railroad could be built at as little expense; and to us it looks as though Nature intended railroad enterprise. We need a railroad, Messrs. Editors. Talk to your people; show them the great importance of opening up a county (to quote the language of your committee) "rich in natural resources, and full of elements of future prosperity." We would like to see your people prosper; your town become a great center of wealth, refinement and learning; your business marts full of animated life; your spacious stores and warehouses filled to bursting; your wharves piled with products, and your harbor dotted with fleets of white winged messengers of commerce; and *WE*, also, wish to prosper; we wish to hear our mountain-sides re-echo the shrill whistle of the iron horse; we wish to see the stream of immigration pouring over our hills and operating in our valleys; we wish to see our manufacturing facilities developed, and our San Lorenzo that now goes roaring, sparkling and laughing in mimic cataracts on its way to the ocean, to be made to contribute to the wants and profits of our increasing population. SAN LORENZO.

141. *Santa Cruz Sentinel,* November 13, 1869 (3:2)
San Francisco Letter.
San Francisco, Nov.—, 1869.

Eds. Sentinel: ...Your people seem to be thoroughly awakened to the importance of railroad facilities; and there are some new ideas and plans of railroad building now being matured here, which will be applicable to the country you wish to line with road. As soon as fully matured I will lay it before your railroad men, and believe that the facilities your county needs can be built for much less than your estimates; and so much less, as to bring it within the immediate possibilities. Knowing somewhat of the topography of Santa Cruz county, I can speak with confidence as to the adaptability of these plans, and hope to yet have a run around your noble bay on the iron rail, connecting with Gilroy, Watsonville, Salinas, and other noted places, not forgetting the home of our friend, Daubenbiss. YOUR STROLLER.

142. *San Francisco Examiner*, November 17, 1869 (2:4)
A Coast Railroad Needed.

The *San Mateo Gazette* argues that a railroad is needed down the coast from the metropolis, between the mountains and the ocean. It says: The country with its increasing business demands it, and it's only a question of time, and the short time too, probably. The attention of business men and capitalists should be called to the arguments in favor of taking Redwood City as the starting point of such a road. Connecting here with the present road, the most favorable location for the route presents itself. The approach to the mountains by the way of Woodside or Searsville is the easiest to be found. The rise to the summit offers no serious obstacle to engineers. There the valuable forests of timber are reached at their beginnings in the range. Thence the road could keep the top of the ridge, or descend to the rich agricultural country at the base, and by either route make easy the shipment of the vast productions of lumber and produce. Such a road would open up a vast amount of wealth, which otherwise must be of slow growth, and this town is certainly one of the most favorable points for connections with the trunk road.

143. *Santa Cruz Sentinel,* November 20, 1869 (2:3)
Railroad Bill.

Eds. Sentinel:—As it is time to go to press, I send you only the three first Sections of a proposed railroad act. The remainder will be furnished for next week's issue. I drawing said bill I followed mainly the instructions adopted by the Mass meeting held on the 23d day of October last, with the following exceptions: Instead of $6,000 County Bonds to be issued per mile for the first ten miles, and $14,000 County Bonds per mile for the next ten miles, the bill provides for the issue of $5,000 for the first ten miles and $12,000 for the next ten miles, and authorizes the issue of $12,000 first-mortgage bonds by the railroad companies on each mile, instead of $10,000 and $14,000, as provided in the resolution. These alterations are offered by the advice of a number of leading citizens of the county, and with the concurrence of a majority of the members of the Committee who offered the resolutions. For the purpose of further discussion on this subject, and also on other matters, I would request the citizens to meet at the Court-house next Saturday the 27th inst., at 2 o'clock P.M. F. A. Hihn.

AN ACT

To Authorize the County of Santa Cruz to aid the Construction of Railroads in said County, and other matters pertaining thereto.

Section 1. The Board of Supervisors of Santa Cruz County are hereby directed to order an election to be held in said County within ninety days from the date of the passage of this Act, at the several election districts, for the purpose of submitting to the qualified electors of said County the question whether the County of Santa Cruz shall aid the construction of a railroad from the eastern line of said County, to the town of Santa Cruz.

Sec. 2. It shall be the duty of the Board of Supervisors to cause notice of at least twenty days, to be published in one or more newspapers printed and published in said County, stating the propositions to be submitted to said electors, and the time and manner of voting thereon. The ballots to be used shall have written or printed thereon the following words: "Railroad aid, Yes," or "Railroad aid, No." Said election shall be conducted in the same manner as is provided by law for the election of School Trustees in the County of Santa Cruz. Returns of the votes cast at such election shall be made in the same manner as provided in the case of election of County officers, which returns shall, within one week from the date of such election, be canvassed by the said Board of Supervisors.

Sec. 3. If at the election a greater number of the electors of said County voting upon said proposition shall vote "Railroad Yes" than shall vote "Railroad No," then and in that event aid shall be granted for the construction of a railroad from the eastern line of said County to the Town of Santa Cruz, in the following manner: Whenever any Railroad company now organized, or which may hereafter be organized under the laws of this State, shall have completed five consecutive miles of said railroad, ready for the conveyance and transportation of passengers and freight, supplied with good T rails and with all necessary bridges, culverts, crossings and turn-outs, the Board of Supervisors, on demand by such company, shall cause to be exchanged bonds of Santa Cruz County for an equal amount of the bonds of such railroad company, secured by a first mortgage on the portion of railroad thus constructed to the following amounts: "On the first ten miles of railroad from the eastern line of said County towards the Town of Santa Cruz, to the amount eight thousand dollars per mile; on the second ten miles on said route, to the amount of twelve thousand dollars per mile; on the remainder of such route to the town of Santa Cruz, to the amount of ten thousand dollars per mile; *Provided*, that the whole amount of first-mortgage bonds issued by such company or c companies shall not exceed twelve thousand dollars per mile of the road actually constructed. Said County bonds shall be made payable in gold coin within twenty years from the date of their issue, and shall bear interest at the rate of eight per cent. per annum, payable semi-annually in gold coin; said bonds shall be signed by the Chairman of the Board of Supervisors, and by the County Auditor and shall have the seal of the County affixed thereto. Coupons far the interest shall be attached to each bond signed by said Chairman. Such bonds shall thereupon be delivered by the County Auditor to the County Treasurer who shall receipt for the same.

144. *Santa Cruz Sentinel,* November 27, 1869 (2:4)
Railroads vs. Hard Times.

Editors Sentinel :—Give me leave to say a word in your valuable paper on the subject of Railroads in this county. A

Committee, appointed by a meeting of citizens, has reported in favor of giving aid to Railroads from Santa Cruz to Watsonville, and thence to Gilroy; and it has decided not to report in favor of giving aid to Railroads up the San Lorenzo and Soquel creeks.

Am I not right in supposing the purpose in granting County aid to Railroads is to develop the resources of the county and add to its taxable property and wealth? Now, I am prepared to assert and maintain that the two short Railroads above referred to, up the San Lorenzo [and?] Soquel creeks, will develop the wealth of the county twenty times more than the road from Santa Cruz to Watsonville. They will open up the [fruit?] and almost the entire wealth of this part of the county. The Railroad to Watsonville would be a convenience, and desirable no doubt; the others are necessities, urgent, undeniable, pressing necessities. I hope the roads already reported in favor of will be built; but if they are, it must be in conjunction with these other roads. Our people, in Santa Cruz and up the San Lorenzo and Soquel creeks, are not so verdant as to assist in [subsiding?] a debt of $300,000 on their own shoulders while not one dollar of it is given to aid their interests. A Railroad, fifteen miles up the San Lorenzo river, will do more for this county, bring more money and men into it, and more to taxable in one year, then times,—yes, twenty times—over than will the Railroad from Santa Cruz to Watsonville.

The true plan, as I think, is to aid all; but if not, then the aid by the county should e rendered to a Railroad from Watsonville towards Gilroy; a Railroad from Soquel, five miles up that creek; and a Railroad from Santa Cruz, ten or fifteen miles up the San Lorenzo.

I hear it is said by some, these roads are good investments, and will be built themselves. Experience does not sustain this statement. A Company has been organized more than two years to build a railroad up the San Lorenzo; some work has been done—but the road is not built. Facts are stubborn things, and the above statements are facts. Again, if this road is so fine an investment, it is evidence the county would lose nothing by aiding it. And if it risks nothing, it would assuredly be unwise to refuse aid.

Our beautiful town, our merchants and mechanics,—every enterprise—languishes, for the lack of this road. Build this road and within eighteen months you will double your population, quadruple your business and where now all is dull and lifeless you would present the appearance of a prosperous and thriving mart. I do not think, either, that the money necessary to build the latter Railroads would be one half what would be required for the road hence to Watsonville.

In short, Messrs. Editors, there is no sound argument against my proposition, can be none, and every argument and every interest is in its favor.

Let us then help each other, and not like the jug-handle, be entirely one-sided.

For a moment let us glance at the resources of the San Lorenzo valley: Lumber of unsurpassed quality and in quantity sufficient to make rich a larger county than ours. Fire wood of first-rate quality and which, with a Railroad could be cut and transported at a handsome profit, now being destroyed annually by fires, by thousands of cords, injuring other and more valuable timber, and helping nobody. Lime of such excellence and in such quantity as only requires means of exit, to wit: a Railroad, to enable it to compete with and put down all monopoly. Water privileges that will, when accessible by Railroad, be sought after and used for extensive manufacturing purposes. In short, if this part of our county has wealth it is up these creeks, and if it is up these creeks, only Railroads can bring it out profitably. Surely nobody here will be so blind as to oppose these Railroads. They open the fountains whence must flow our wealth. Obstruct them and such hard times as we have never yet seen will soon be upon us. PUSH.

145. *Santa Cruz Sentinel,* November 27, 1869 (3:2)

A Coast Railroad Needed.—The San Mateo *Gazette* argues that a railroad is needed down the coast from the metropolis, between the mountains the ocean. It says: The country with its increasing business demands it, and it's only a question of time, and short time too, probably. The attention of business men and capitalists should be called to the arguments in favor of taking Redwood City as the starting point of such a road. Connecting here with the present road, the most favorable location for the route presents itself. The approach to the mountains by the way of Woodside or Searsville is the easiest to be found. The rise to the summit offers no serious obstacle to the engineers. There the valuable forests of timber are reached at their beginning in the range. Thence the road could keep the top of the ridge, or descend to the rich agricultural country at the base, and by either route make easy the shipment of the vast productions of lumber and produce. Such a road would open up a vast amount of wealth, which otherwise must be of slow growth, and this town is certainly one of the most favorable points for connection with the trunk road.

146. *Santa Cruz Sentinel,* December 4, 1869 (2:1)
Legislative Meeting.

A meeting was called to convene at the Court-house of this place at two o'clock on Saturday afternoon last. At the hour appointed a large number were present, Felton being largely represented. Albert Hagan, as Chairman, called the meeting to order. Mr. Hihn addressed the assemblage, stating that the meeting had been called for the discussion of "Legislative matters," he wishing to know the desires of the people that he, as Representative, might act in accordance therewith; that the railroad subject was commanding considerable attention from all men, no matter of what complexion of sentiment; that some residents of the county favored only the road from Gilroy to Watsonville; that others favored the continuance of the road to Santa Cruz; that others favored the construction of the road through to Felton, making that point the terminus; that a number of the residents of this portion of the county favored and warmly advocated the construction of a road from Santa Cruz to Felton only; that others advocated the building of a road up the Soquel creek, while many favored the construction of all the roads named, and were willing that the county should assist in the construction of the same, but that there were those with whom he had conversed who were opposed to railroads in any form, shape or manner, permanently stopping public improvement. Mr. Hihn then showed in what condition this county would be if the wishes of the men who were opposed to public improvement should prevail; that, practically speaking, everything would be stagnated, no immigration encouraged, no buildings erected, no timber exported, or lime, or paper, or powder, or leather,—no wagon roads opened or railroads built, or, in other words, he asked what would be the result if we should come to the conclusion that we had reached perfection and were satisfied to stand still. The speaker he was in favor of progress, energy, enterprise and go-aheaditiveness; that there was no such thing as standing still, for the world moves and the people around us act, and that we must either advance or go back; that he was in favor of railroads and awaited the action of the meeting. Joseph Boston stated that he endorsed the sentiments and declarations of Mr. Hihn; that he had been to Sacramento, Vallejo, and other terminuses or points touched by railroads, and that he was astonished at the amount of energy, industry, improvement and prosperity there displayed; that Santa Cruz was the second largest point of exports on the coast, and what we wanted to make this county one of the most prosperous in the State, was railroads—then manufacturing would follow on every one of our unlimited waterpowers, and our lime would find purchasers in every locality of the State; that the time was coming when a bulkhead would be constructed in this harbor, and that the granite for its construction could be found along the line of the San Lorenzo Railroad.

A committee was appointed to draw up a bill, and the same is published as a portion of the Secretary's report, in today's issue, T. S. Farmer was loudly called for. After some hesitancy on his part, he arose, stating that he did not come prepared to make a speech, but that he was a Felton man, and could show by facts and figures that it would be a paying investment to any company to build a railroad up the San Lorenzo, and that it would pay the county to aid in the construction of railroads within her borders; that the history of the attempt to get the county of Santa Clara to lend or donate her bonds towards the construction of railroads, was about the same as that being experienced here; but that seven years ago the people of Santa Clara did pass a bill to aid in the construction of a railroad to the amount of $200,000; that five years ago the taxable property of that county was $4,300,000, and that last year, mainly owing to the railroad, it had increased to rising of $11,000,000; that the railroad had been continued to Gilroy, and that another railroad entered the county by the way of Oakland, and that instead of making the tax-payers poor, it had actually made them rich; that the freight paid, during the first eight months on hauling from the San Lorenzo averaged *six hundred and fifty dollars* per day, and that if a railroad was built the amount of freight would be doubled. Mr. Farmer was repeatedly cheered, taking his seat amid thunders of applause. Mr. Hihn spoke of the provisions of skeleton laws published in the Sentinel, and although the meeting had been called for their consideration, nothing short of railroads could be treated of to attentive listeners.

Whatever may be the result of the meeting as to any bill Mr. Hihn may have passed by the Legislature, it is evident that the people are in favor of railroads, differing only as to the part the county shall take in their construction.

147. *Santa Cruz Sentinel,* December 4, 1869 (2:4)
Railroad Meeting.
Santa Cruz, Nov. 27th, 1869

Meeting called to order by Judge Albert Hagan in the Chair. On motion, a Committee was appointed to consider the feasibility of the county of Santa Cruz aiding by loan or donation the construction of branch Railroads up the Soquel Creek and San Lorenzo River, and the following named gentlemen were appointed on said Committee: J. N. Besse, Albert Hagan, Santa Cruz; Lucius Sanborn, Watsonville; Jonathan Havens, San Lorenzo; Dr. Fagen, Soquel. The Committee retired, and after an hour's deliberation submitted the following as the result of its deliberations:

AN ACT

To Authorize the County of Santa Cruz to aid in the Construction of Railroads in said County, and other matters pertaining thereto.

Section 1. The Board of Supervisors of Santa Cruz County are hereby directed to order an election to be held in said County within ninety days from the date of the passage of this Act, for the purpose of submitting to the qualified electors of said County the question whether the County of Santa Cruz shall aid the construction of a railroad from the eastern line of said County, to the town of Santa Cruz, and branch lines of said Railroad, to wit: One from the town of Santa Cruz to a point ten miles up the San Lorenzo river, and one from the town of Soquel to a point five miles up the Soquel creek, said branches beginning at the tide-water, at each of said towns of Soquel and Santa Cruz.

Sec. 2. It shall be the duty of the Board of Supervisors to cause notice, of at least twenty days, to be published in one or more newspapers, printed and published in said County, stating the propositions to be submitted to said electors, and the time and manner of voting thereon. The ballots to be used shall have written or printed thereon the following words: "Railroad aid, Yes," or "Railroad aid, No." Said election shall be conducted in the same manner as is provided by law for the election of School Trustees in the County of Santa Cruz. Returns of the votes cast at such election shall be made in the same manner as provided in the case of election of County officers, which returns shall, within one week from the date of such election, be canvassed by the said Board of Supervisors.

Sec. 3. If, at the election a greater number of the electors of said County voting upon said proposition shall vote "Railroad and the branches aforesaid, Yes," than shall vote "Railroad, No," then, and in that event, aid shall be granted for the construction of a railroad from the eastern line of said County to the town of Santa Cruz, in the following manner:

Whenever any Railroad company now organized, or which may hereafter be organized under the laws of this

State, shall have completed five consecutive miles of said railroad from the eastern line of said County to the town of Santa Cruz, ready for the conveyance and transportation of passengers and freight, supplied with good T rails and with all necessary bridges, culverts, crossings and turn-outs, the Board of Supervisors, on demand by such company, shall cause to be exchanged bonds of Santa Cruz County for an equal amount of the bonds of such Railroad company, secured by a first-mortgage on the portion of Railroad thus constructed to the following amounts: "On the first ten miles of railroad from the eastern line of said County towards the town of Santa Cruz, to the amount of eight thousand dollars per mile; on the second ten miles of said route, to the amount of twelve thousand dollars per mile; on the remainder of such route to the town of Santa Cruz, to the amount of ten thousand dollars per mile; *Provided*,

That the whole amount of first-mortgage bonds issued by such company or companies, shall not exceed twelve thousand dollars per mile of the road actually constructed. Said County bonds shall be made payable in gold coin within twenty years from the date of their issue, and shall bear interest at the rate of eight per cent. per annum, payable semi-annually in gold coin. Said bonds shall be signed by the Chairman of the Board of Supervisors, and by the County Auditor, and shall have the seal of the County affixed thereto. Coupons for the interest shall be attached to each bond signed by said Chairman. Such bonds shall thereupon be delivered by the County Auditor to the County Treasurer, who shall receipt for the same.

Sec. 4. Whenever any Railroad company, now organized, or which may be hereafter organized, under the laws of this State, shall have completed two consecutive miles of either of the branch Railroads from the tide-water at the town of Santa Cruz, up the San Lorenzo river, and from the tide-water at or near Soquel up the Soquel creek, ready for the conveyance and transportation of passengers and freight, supplied with good T rails and with all necessary bridges, culverts, crossings and turn-outs, the Board of Supervisors, on demand of such company, shall cause to be exchanged bonds of Santa Cruz County for an equal amount of the bonds of such Railroad company, secured by a first-mortgage on the portion of Railroad thus constructed to the following amounts:

On the first two miles of Railroad from tide-waters aforesaid, at said towns of Soquel and Santa Cruz, up said Soquel creek and San Lorenzo river, to the amount of six thousand dollars per mile; on the remainder of each of said routes, to the amount of six thousand dollars per mile, to be paid at the completion of each two miles thereof; *Provided*,

That each of said Railroad companies shall pay to the County of Santa Cruz *all the interest* on said bonds, at the rate of eight per cent. per annum, payable semi-annually, less the amount of taxes that either of said Railroad companies shall be assessed for during any year after the issuance of said bonds.

All of which is respectfully submitted by your Committee.

A. Hagan, Chairman,
P. B. Fagen, Sec'ty,

J. N. Besse,
Jonathan Havens.

The report was accepted without discussion. On motion, the Representative elect, F. A. Hihn, was instructed to draft a bill, the same giving the voters the alternative of voting whether the County of Santa Cruz should or should not aid in the construction of said Railroad or Railroads by loan or donation; and if by loan, the amount specified in said report, and if by donation, two-thirds of the amount specified in said report. No further business coming before the House for consideration, the meeting adjourned *sine die*.

ALBERT HAGAN, Chairman.

P. B. Fagen, Secretary *pro tem*.

148. *Santa Cruz Sentinel,* December 4, 1869 (3:1)

Marine Intelligence.—Eleven schooners and two steamers were in port on Monday last. More evidence of the necessity of a railroad.

149. *Santa Cruz Sentinel,* December 18, 1869 (2:2)

In the Senate, Hon. Chas. Maclay has introduced several important bills. The following, published in the Sacramento *Union*, reads:

"Mr. Maclay gave notice of a bill for a railroad from deep water, San Francisco Bay, in San Mateo county, through San Mateo, Santa Clara and Santa Cruz counties, to Monterey."...

This looks like business, and our members should

promptly respond and assist the measures. We need a railroad, and the county will no doubt liberally aid the measure. The road we require is the one that can be built on the most direct route to San Francisco. Mr. Maclay's bill, as we understand it, is to build the road on as direct line from Santa Cruz to Redwood City as practicable. The route, surveyed by citizens of Redwood City, which is practicable, crosses the divide at or near the head of Bear creek, and thence down the creek to its junction with the San Lorenzo, at Sylvar's saw-mill dam. The route *via* King's farm, further north, is deemed impracticable. From Sylvar's mill the road would follow the San Lorenzo valley to Santa Cruz town, thence to Soquel, Aptos, Watsonville, Castroville, Salinas City, and south of that point. We believe this is the road that would be the most beneficial to the farmers and settlers, generally, on the route, and that more especially would it advance the interest of Santa Cruz county. From the first this is the route we advocated, and we believe, if there ever is a road built, it will be on the route proposed. Tax-payers will be called on to aid this road, and we hope they will at once petition our Representatives, to give the Maclay bill their cordial support. We want no branch railroads—build the main trunk, and branch roads will soon be built, by private enterprise, whenever required. At Waddell's, already a railroad has been built, by the proprietor, some six miles from the mill to the landing. This road was built some five or six years ago without county or State aid, and similar roads up Zayante, Soquel, Aptos and other creeks would soon be built by local enterprise and capital. Let us drop all personal interest and work for the county in uniting on a main road, by the shortest route from Santa Cruz town to San Francisco. There is a novelty in being united. Let us try it.

150. *Santa Cruz Sentinel,* December 18, 1869 (2:2)
Letter from Hon. F. A. Hihn.
Sacramento, December 14th, 1869.

Editors Sentinel:—...In Railroad matters I have yet done nothing; that is to say I have not introduced any bill, nor shall I before next month, for the following reasons: It is proposed to have the State aid the construction of Railroads to the extent of, say $5,000 per mile, survey and location to be approved by a Board of Commissioners. Furthermore, Mr. C. Maclay, Senator from Santa Clara, has introduced a bill, of which, I have not got the insight yet, proposing the granting of a franchise for a Railroad through the counties of San Mateo, Santa Clara, Santa Cruz and Monterey. Besides this it is proposed to extend the road from Gilroy, south, via Salinas, by the San Jose and San Francisco Railroad Company, if sufficient aid is granted. All these projects will develop themselves within a few weeks; and by that time it may also be possible that the conflicting interests of our county will come to some better understanding. I get all kinds of letters on this subject. Every writer seems to be sure, unless his views are adopted, we will have no Railroad at all.

151. *Santa Cruz Sentinel,* December 18, 1869 (2:3)

Railroad.—A railroad meeting is called to be held in Watsonville to-night.

152. *The Pajaronian,* December 30, 1869 (2:1)

It is proposed in the new plan that the county aid in the construction of a main trunk road from the eastern line of the county to Santa Cruz, to the amount of $7,000 per mile. The Soquel branch is ignored, entirely, but the county shall aid the construction of a road ten miles long up the San Lorenzo river, to the extent of $2,000 per mile. The amount of aid by the county, according to the above plan, is not large—hardly more than one-half by the former plan. We shall probably see a copy of the bill before our next issue, when we can speak more at length on the subject.

153. *Santa Cruz Sentinel,* January 1, 1870 (2:1)

Hon. F. A. Hihn was in Watsonville on last Wednesday, and conferred with leading railroad men of that section in regard to getting up a railroad bill which would be more just to the county at large, than the last bill as published in the Sentinel. A new plan is proposed to the effect that the county aid, in the construction of a main trunk road from the eastern line of the county to the town of Santa Cruz, to the amount of $7,000 per mile. The Soquel branch is ignored entirely, but the county to aid the construction of a road ten miles along the San Lorenzo river, to the extent of

$2,000 per mile. The amount of aid by the county, according to the above plan, is not large—hardly more than one-half by the former plan. We shall probably see a copy of the bill before our next issue.

154. *Santa Cruz Sentinel,* January 1, 1870 (3:1)

Protest.—The Legislature has received a protest from the citizens, or a number of them, against this county aiding in the construction of branch railroads. They favor and are willing that the county should aid in the construction of the main trunk—from Gilroy to Santa Cruz.

155. *Stockton Independent,* January 6, 1870 (2:3)

Santa Cruz Railroad.—The *Pajaronian* says Mr. Hihn, member of the Legislature from that county, has conferred with the people concerning a railroad, and a bill has been decided upon which will greatly decrease the amount of county aid first proposed. The new bill provides for a main trunk road from the eastern line of the county to Santa Cruz, and the county is to aid in its construction to the amount of $7,000 per mile. The Soquel branch is ignored entirely, but the county shall aid the construction of a road ten miles long, up the San Lorenzo river, to the extent of $2,000 per mile.

156. *Santa Cruz Sentinel,* January 8, 1870 (2:2)

Stockholder's Meeting.—An election for Directors of the

San Lorenzo Railroad Company, will be held at the office of Dr. Peabody, in Santa Cruz, Monday, January 31st, 1870, between the hours of 2 and 4 o'clock, P. M. Stockholders are duly notified to attend.

157. *Santa Cruz Sentinel,* January 15, 1870 (2:3)
Farmers' Club Meeting

The second regular meeting of the Farmers' Club of Santa Cruz, was held in the Court-house at 1 o'clock P.M., January 8, 1870. J. S. Mattison, President, in the Chair; John W. Morgan, Secretary....

County Aid to Railroads.

The subject appointed for discussion was then taken up.

Moved and carried that if any one present was in favor of the proposed railroad, he should give his reasons.

Mr. Humphrey—Was in favor of postponing the question to the next regular meeting, to be held next Saturday, January 15th. Several members asked a postponement, as they were not then prepared to express an opinion and defend their positions for or against the proposed.

Mr. Alex. Russell—Was in favor of the railroad from Santa Cruz to Watsonville, thence to Gilroy—in fact, into the Tulare valley.

Mr. J. S. Morgan—Was opposed to the railroad, until some one would demonstrate its benefit to the farmers of our county; show where it was to go and where the terminus; the route should be made known and the most direct route to San Francisco adopted.

Mr. Alex. Russell—Explained that he meant, by advocating an extension into Tulare valley, that the road should be built by some other company. The Santa Cruz, Watsonville and Gilroy is the one I am in favor of now,—tell us what you think of it?

Mr. M. J. Leonard—Inferred that there was to be several railroads introduced in the bill—one to Watsonville, to Gilroy, one up Soquel creek, another up the San Lorenzo, besides the main trunk from Santa Cruz to Watsonville. The county is already from eighty to ninety thousand dollars in debt (that's so, responded the Chairman), and now are we going to bind ourselves to pay ten per cent. per annum on five or six hundred thousand dollars more to build a road that would not, in the least, increase the value of our produce, or raise the price at home? This is a serious matter to farmers, and one of vital importance to every tax-payer. A break-water in our harbor, if practicable, would be of more immediate benefit to tax-payers, (especially shippers of produce) than a railroad. Was not opposed to the proposed road; on the contrary, was in favor of it whenever sufficient evidence was produced proving that it would be a paying investment, and beneficial to a majority of the farmers and tax-payers of the county.

Mr. Alex. Russell—Replied that the proposed road, when finished, would double the price of property, our population and the facilities of our market. The redwood lands were eventually to be our best earning lands. The lands can easily be cleared of stumps. A redwood stump of large size, could be removed at a cost of fifty cents, by simply boring a hole at the base, near the ground, through the stump or tree, and pouring a pint of crude coal oil into the hole and setting fire to it. The fire will soon turn the stump down three feet below the ground. When a railroad is once built, it is perpetual, and the trade established; no rival company can take it away or divert it; the company will retain it, ever afterwards in spite of any and every opposition. He would ask what is going to keep up the town of Santa Cruz? Why railroads and steamboats. No city has ever prospered without these adjuncts. The fact is we are now getting just San Francisco prices for our produce, less the cost of freight and commission to the city. (He might have added wharfage, storage, drayage, shrinkage, ratage and leakage, besides charges for mending sacks, weighing and handling them, now charged by some consignees.)

Mr. M. J. Leonard—Thought the San Joaquin railroad would be of no relative benefit to the Santa Cruz road, even if they connected. If there is money in our railroad, why is it that local capitalists hold back and don't invest in the stock? They are sharp and shrewd business men, and have ample means; but they prefer to loan their money at one per cent. per month, to subscribing for railroad stock. (Mr. Russell—interrupting—Said that it was a mistake that railroads pay, generally, on first opening. There are but three in the world that paid from the start. One in Russia, one in England and one in America.)

Mr. V. Humphrey—As I understand the question, it is not to give $5,000 or $6,000 per mile, of first bonds, as a bonus to build the road, but for the purpose of *exchanging* that amount of bonds for railroad stock, which is quite a different thing from a donation. Railroads are taxed about

$6,000 per mile, and if assessed at full value, $10,000 would be the minimum tax. Good lands within one or five miles of Santa Cruz are now held at an average of $30 to $50 per acre. The lands in Pajaro valley, although richer and yielding better crops, are held at a lower price. All these lands would be very materially enhanced in value by the building of the proposed railroad, and much new property would be brought on the assessor's book; more than enough, (including the taxes paid by the railroad company) to pay the increased taxes on the bonds would incur. Santa Cruz lands were quite high enough at present, and it would be necessary to build a railroad to keep up the present price or increase the value of real estate.

On motion, the subject was then postponed for one week, to be discussed at the regular meeting, to be held on Saturday, January 15th, at 1 o'clock, P.M. Adjourned.

158. *Santa Cruz Sentinel,* January 22, 1870 (2:2-3)

Farmers' Club Meeting.

On Saturday, January 15th, 1870, at 2 o'clock P.M., the Farmers' Club, met, pursuant to adjournment. All the officers and a full meeting present. Minutes read and approved....

Railroads.

The subject of discussion being railroads—are they advantageous to farmers generally, and especially the one proposed in Santa Cruz county?—was then declared in order.

Mr. V. Humphrey—Was not prepared to discuss the subject, at present, in all its bearings, relatively. Did not have a proper understanding of its merits. In considering

The Dream of Steam, 1854–1873

this important question, we had first to view it from the stand-points—do we want a railroad? What is its cost and are we prepared to pay for it? Some of the advocates say we want the road to bring the grain from Pajaro valley to Santa Cruz for shipment to San Francisco and to a foreign market, but it is evident that they will have another route to ship their produce to market as soon as the Gilroy railroad is extended to the Pajaro and Salinas plains. In the State of New York, farmers ship grain in bulk, by having wheat cars constructed. This plan could not be adopted in Pajaro. Farmers on the Salinas could not afford to send their grain to Santa Cruz, by railroad, unless we could afford to pay as good a price as San Francisco; that being the case, (shipping produce cheaper *via* Gilroy,) there would be no inducement to this town. We don't want a railroad to ship produce from here to Watsonville. Our farmers are not interested in sending lumber to the Salinas plains. We have now a good lumber market in San Francisco, and down the coast by sea-going vessels. It is not the interest of farmers to cut off the redwood forests any faster in the future than in the past. Our foreign market is not for refuse lumber, or such timber as is only fit for firewood, pickets, &c. Will some advocate of the proposed railroad tell us what we want it for? Our harbor is quite sufficient at present, for all commercial purposes. We can never make a San Francisco of our town, until we have as good a harbor as that city. As to the cost of a railroad—say 25 miles: it is proposed to give $6,000 per mile for bonds to draw interest (the Chairman, interrupting—Said the last plan adopted was to subscribe the stock, amounting to $7,000 per mile, and take a second mortgage on the road; the interest on the bonds to be 7 per cent. per annum. Now, 25 miles of railroad would be $150,000; this sum would draw interest some time before the road would be completed. Did not think the railroad bonds would be worth as much as county bonds; the interest on them would be nearly $10,000 per year). Very well, said Mr. H., this sum would be better invested to expend it on our county roads, and farmers would receive more immediate and substantial benefit. "Could not see" the benefit to be derived from railroads, to the farmers. The railroad might cheapen the price of lumber to the southern counties, which would inure to their benefit—not ours. Don't "see it." Another advantage—and he did "see it"—the railroad would enable the town people of Santa Cruz to live a little cheaper, and at the expense of the producers and farmers, outside of the town.

Mr. Elihu Anthony—Viewed the subject only from a small farmer's stand point, otherwise, he should speak differently, being decidedly in favor of railroads. In view of our interests, as a Farmers' Club, extending only as far as Aptos—that being the southern boundary of our district—his views were limited—but we, of course, should look after the interests of the southern portion of the county.

Had a small farm and cultivated it. Always expected to do so. Believed that railroads would rebound to our benefit. No farmer, this side of the Aptos, but would be materially benefitted by the proposed railroad. Hay was our most profitable crop—we could not raise grain for the San Francisco or foreign markets, and make it profitable. The southern portion of the county had larger farms and would be more generally benefitted. A railroad would bring us consumers; if farmers only had a home market, to consume their little produce, they would be all right. "Very well"—the railroad would make the market by introducing new manufacturing interests and giving renewed impulse to those already established. We have the natural resources in abundance, such as water-power, wood, granite, lime, etc., with a vast belt of mountain range, affording almost anything needed by the manufacturing interest of the coast. A railroad would develop these resources, prompt the building of woolen mills, &c., and bring a large population of consumers into the county, to purchase our grain, vegetables, fruit, butter, cheese, eggs, poultry, and surplus productions, and also increase our population a hundred-fold. Look at the towns in the Eastern and Western States, and see what railroads have done for the farmers! We may expect the same advantageous results. The town of Santa Cruz will be the terminus of the railroad, inevitably, which will naturally accrue to the benefit of us all—especially the small farmers, the gardeners and the fruit-growers. It is a foregone conclusion that Pajaro valley and Salinas grain can be shipped from 50 cents to $1.25 per ton, cheaper, from Santa Cruz harbor than by the way of Gilroy and San Jose, on the railroad. To gain this advantage, suppose we do have to pay $1.00 on the $100 taxes, more than we are worth; for one year, we could stand it. Contended that the tax would only have to be paid one year, as the enhanced value of property and the increased amount entered on the Assessor's books would pay the tax the second year. The taxable wealth of the county would be more than doubled by the fact that a safe, speedy, and reliable railroad was to be built, especially when completed, and farmers had a constant and certain market for their produce. We *must* build the road as a business protection and a matter of necessity. We *must* aid capitalists to build the road. Had better vote to donate $7,000 per mile in 20 years, (for 30 miles,) and then lose the principal, than not to be brought into contract with the manufacturing world. Go to places where they find cheap and ready facilities to carry on manufactures and see the results: progress is the order of the day, and all is life and bustle. We have the facilities; this is demonstrated by the factories already here and in successful operation (powder, paper, lime, leather, glue, soap, starch, etc). Heavy freight goes by water, generally, and light freight and passengers by railroads. Build the road and all the wool of the Southern coast would come here to be manufactured. We live in a railroad age, and it is inevitable that business, trade, population, capital, manufactures and real wealth will follow the track or line of railroads, where the natural resources, like ours, are undeveloped.

Mr. Alex. Russell—The position to take is that all railroads enhance the value of lands; was especially in favor of the Watsonville railroad, at a cost of $170,000—say $7,000 per mile—for the main trunk to Santa Cruz, and $2,000 per mile for the Felton or San Lorenzo road. The reason, the county had to take second-mortgage bonds for security, was, that the railroad company or contractors could go into England or Wales, with the money realized on the county bonds, added to that raised by first-mortgage bonds, and purchase sufficient iron to build the road, and stock it. Look at our situation now! About one-half of the county don't pay taxes at all. Our lumber lands are not sufficiently taxed, and large quantities of real and personal property is not on the Assessor's books, because so scattered and worthless, for want of roads and markets. Take, for instances, the lands up the San Lorenzo, three miles from the valley, on each side of the stream, and they are entirely worthless for the want of a railroad, although heavily timbered and valuable for stock raising and farming. Build this railroad and a new town would spring up at every depot, or intersected valley, and all the towns now laid out, on the line of the road from one end to the other, would be increased in value from hundreds to thousands. The poorest men we have, now, are the lumbermen; their business is lagging for want of roads, and cheaper freight to the landing. The Southern lumber trade may be good, but how, in the name of sense, are we to get the lumber to market without a railroad? Where will the great Tulare valley get lumber to supply her thousands of farmers now settling on the plains? By railroad! And if we don't supply the demand from this side, the people of Santa Clara will come over and cut the timber and supply the people of San Joaquin from their side. They already have an active and constant market for lumber cut in Santa Cruz county, this side of the divide, and hauled for miles, up hill, in small lots to stations, and then sent by large teams to their line of railroad. As to grain, the producer could not afford to ship it by railroad, and we could not ship by sea-going vessels, in bulk. No grain can be profitably shipped, from California, in bulk. Bins have to be constructed in the hold of the ship, at an expense of say $1,000, which have to be removed at the end of every voyage, before again used, consequently the cost won't pay the whistle.

Mr. V. Humphrey—Thought we had railroad on the brain; confessed that he had it. It was a humbug to build a railroad *via* Gilroy, predicated on the belief that it would assist the farmer. The speaker got excited and denounced the plan, contending that the railroad was advocated by the town people because it would inure to their individual benefit, by making subsistent supplies cheaper, and affording a more ready market for staple goods.

Mr. Elihu Anthony—Then I understand you to be in favor of a railroad *direct* to San Francisco, by the nearest and most practicable route? "I am," said Mr. Humphrey, "but willy you please name any one article or some production our farmers have to send to market over either of the three proposed direct routes—*via* the coast, San Lorenzo or Soquel—that will pay a more remunerative price, after the roads are built, than at present. Railroads cannot compete with water transportation when heavy freight is to be sent to market. Admitted that light freight and passengers would take the railroad, in preference to any other route. Mountain travel, by railroad, costs 5 cents per mile more than on the level plain, and freight charges were higher. Admitted that the most profitable crop was not barley, but hay, and the proceeds of the dairy, orchard and garden. The lower end of the county was willing to pay its portion of the railroad tax.

On motion, the whole subject was deferred to next regular meeting, to be held on Saturday, January 29th, at 1 o'clock, P.M. Adjourned.

159. *Santa Cruz Sentinel,* January 22, 1870 (2:3)
Legislative.

The Legislature, during the past week, has made but little progress in the right direction….

The following Bills were introduced into the House, Tuesday last:

By Mr. Blankenship—An Act to authorize the citizens of Monterey county to aid the Santa Clara and Pajaro Valley Railroad Company, and to authorize a railroad from the town of Gilroy, Santa Clara county, through Pajaro valley to some point in Salinas valley at or near Salinas City.

By Mr. Hihn—An Act to authorize the county of Santa Cruz to aid in the construction of a railroad in said county.

160. *Santa Cruz Sentinel,* January 22, 1870 (2:4)
Santa Cruz County.

We copy the following statement from the report, for 1869, of the Surveyor-General and Register of State lands for California:

Assessor's Office, Santa Cruz, October 16th, 1869.

Hon. John W. Boat, Surveyor-General: Sir:—In compliance with law, I hereby transmit my annual report and statistics of this county for the years eighteen hundred and sixty-eight and eighteen hundred and sixty-nine... Railroads don't prosper much in this county. The one commence last year remains in *statu quo*. The people of Pajaro Valley need a railroad very much to get their grain to market, their shipping points being very rough in the winter months. It was estimated that the actual loss to the farmers last fall in consequence of not being able to get their produce to market in season, was from seventy-five thousand to one hundred thousand dollars, surely quite an item in a farming community. The matter has been *talked* of and a survey been made for a railroad from Watsonville to Gilroy, but not quite enough stock taken to put it through. The people are beginning to see the importance of it so much that they will move in the matter....

N. TAYLOR, Assessor of Santa Cruz County.

161. *Santa Cruz Sentinel,* January 29, 1870 (4:1)

Gilroy and Salinas Railroad.—There was filed in the Secretary of State's office last week articles of association of the California Southern Railroad Company, formed for the purpose of constructing a road from some point near the town of Gilroy to or near Salinas City, Monterey county. Stock has been subscribed equal to $1,000 per mile of said road, and ten percent. in cash actually paid in. The length of the proposed road is forty-five miles; capital stock $1,500,000. Directors, Charles Mayne, Peter Donohue, Richard P. Hammond, H. M. Newhall, and N. S. Sweeny.

162. *The Pajaronian*, February 3, 1870 (2:1)

Railroad Bill.—We present this week, Mr. Hihn's railroad bill, which, we consider is highly important for all to thoroughly understand. We have not time this week, to comment upon the bill. We will give Mr. Hihn credit, however, for such skill in drawing up the document, inasmuch as provisions are made to benefit all parts of the county alike. We would also call attention to Mr. Hihn's letter, written to District Attorney Lee, of this place.

163. *The Pajaronian*, February 3, 1870 (2:2)

Letter from Assemblyman Hihn
Sacramento, Jan. 31st, 1870,

Julius Lee, Esq.—*Dear Sir:* Enclosed I send you my railroad bill, with the request to have it published in this week's *Pajaronian* and have proof sheets furnished to both the Santa Cruz papers as early as Thursday morning. The bill will be introduced this morning and I shall push it along as fast as possible, but it will take several weeks before I can get it into the Senate and there it can lay long enough, so that any amendment can be made which may seem proper. I am well aware that this bill will not give general satisfaction and I suggest that to draw a bill to suit everybody, would be an utter impossibility. The interests of the citizens of our country are so conflicting, or I may rather say so distinct in the different sections, that any bill must be objected to which ignores the interests and claims of any section. In advocating the granting of aid for branch roads to the amount of two thousand dollars, but not exceeding in all thirty thousand dollars, I take into consideration that the county could not possibly make any better investment, because if with this and these roads should be constructed, the annual saving in construction and repairs of the [pah-lie] roads running up the valleys where these branch roads are proposed to be built, would be more than sufficient to pay the interest and gradually the principal on the these bonds, while the taxes on the roads and the increase of values of taxable property in the neighborhood of these roads would add vastly to the revenues of the county.

As to the $5,000 coast road appropriation, I will say that justice demands of us to have a reasonable amount of money expended whether railroads are built or not.

But in order to enable the people to grant just such aid as they may desire, I have inserted into the bill the fifteenth and sixteenth Sections. No such provisions are to be found in any other railroad bill, but I deem them highly proper, in order to carry out the intention of these Sections. I would suggest that on the second Saturday in April, Railroad mass meetings be held in every precinct in the County and that at such meetings Committees be appointed to attend a Railroad convention on the Tuesday following and this convention to be the final arbiter of all questions at issue. Representation to be on the basis of one delegate from every precinct and one additional for every hundred votes cast at the last election. Yours. F.A. HIHN.

164. *The Pajaronian*, February 3, 1870 (3:2-3)

Railroad Bill. An Act to Authorize the County of Santa Cruz to aid in the construction of Railroads and Other Roads in said County and for other purposes pertaining thereto.

The People of the State of California Represented in Senate and Assembly do enact as follows.

Section 1. The Board of Supervisors of the county of Santa Cruz, are hereby directed to order a special election to be held in said county at the several election districts, on the fourth Saturday of May next, for the purpose of submitting to the qualified electors of said county the proposition, whether the county of Santa Cruz shall aid in the construction of a railroad from the eastern line of said county to the town of Santa Cruz, and branches connecting therewith, as in this act specified.

Sec. 2. It shall be the duty of the Board of Supervisor to cause notice of at least twenty days to be published in one or more newspapers printed and published in said county, stating the proposition to be submitted to said electors, and the time and manner of voting thereon. It shall be the further duty of said Board of Supervisors to cause ballots to be prepared with the words, Railroad Aid Yes and Railroad Aid No, written or printed thereon. Every ballot in favor of the said proposition shall have the word yes written or printed thereon, and every ballot against said proposition shall have the word No written or printed thereon. Said election shall be conducted in the same manner as elections for school officers are now held in said county, and sealed returned shall be made of the vote cast on said proposition within five days after the said election, to the Clerk of said county, of the number of voters voting Yes, and of the number voting No, which returns shall be the said fifth day or on the second day of June A. D. one thousand eight hundred and seventy, opened and counted in the same manner as the returns of the votes for county officers, and when so opened and counted, the result thereof shall be declared officially by the Board of Supervisors who shall at the time prescribed for the opening and counting of the returns of said election, meet as a Board for that purpose.

Sec. 3. If at the said election a greater number of the electors of said county voting upon said position shall vote Yes than shall vote No, then and in that event the county of Santa Cruz shall be deemed to have agreed and contracted to grant, and there shall be granted aid for the construction and maintenance of a railroad from the eastern line of said county to the town of Santa Cruz, and branches connecting therewith in the following manner:

Whenever any railroad company now organized, or which may hereafter be organized under the laws of this state, shall have completed on the route from the eastern line of the county to the town of Santa Cruz, five consecutive miles of a railroad supplied with iron T rails, so as to be enabled to pass over the same the engines and cars of the construction trains, the said board of Supervisors on demand by such company, shall order that there shall be issued, signed, executed and delivered to said company by its representative the bonds of said county of Santa Cruz to the amount of seven thousand dollars for each mile so constructed, provided that, if on the completion of the railroad to the town of Santa Cruz, the last section of such road should be less than five miles, then and in that case the said Board of Supervisors shall order that there shall be signed, executed and delivered to such company the bonds of said county to the amount of seven thousand dollars per mile for such last section; and whenever any railroad company now organized or which may hereafter be organized under the laws of this State, shall have completed three consecutive miles of any branch railroad, connecting or to connect with a railroad from the eastern line of said county to the town of Santa Cruz, ready for the conveyance of freight and supplied with iron rails, the said Board of Supervisors on demand of such company shall order that there shall be issued, signed, executed and delivered to such company or its representative, the said bonds of Santa Cruz county to the amount of two thousand dollars for each mile so constructed; *provided*, that the whole amount of such bonds to be issued for such branch roads shall not exceed thirty thousand dollars, and *provided*, further, that eighteen thousand dollars of the county bonds to be issued for such branch roads shall be reserved for the term of one year from the first day of June, A. D. one thousand eight hundred and seventy, to and in the construction of a railroad from tide-water at the town of Santa Cruz, and running thence on or near the present survey of the San Lorenzo Railroad Company along the San Lorenzo river to the town of Felton; and, *provided*, further, that the Board of Supervisors shall have the power to designate the location and general route of such branch roads, subject to the reservation herein last named, on the first Monday of May, A. D. one thousand eight hundred and seventy, and if not so designated, it shall be deemed that six miles of such branch road shall be located commencing from the tide water near the town of Soquel, and running thence up the valley of the Soquel creek.

Sec. 4. For the purpose of this Act, and for none other, the Chairman of the Board of Supervisors of Santa Cruz county, the Treasurer and Auditor of said county, in addition to their other duties as such officers and their successors in office, shall constitute a Board of Commissioners, to be styled the Railroad Aid Fund Commissioners of Santa Cruz county, whose duty it shall be to issue bonds in the sums of five hundred and one thousand dollars, in equal proportions, and for such an amount as the Board of Supervisors may from time to time direct, and assist in this act provided.

Sec. 5. It shall be the duty of the Board of Supervisors and they are hereby authorized, empowered and required to cause to be prepared bonds of Santa Cruz county, to be known as and styled "Santa Cruz County Railroad Aid Bonds," in sums of five hundred and one thousand dollars each in equal proportions and not exceeding in the aggregate, the sum of two hundred and forty thousand dollars, and shall cause the said bonds to be issued by the Railroad Aid Fund Commissioners to the railroad company or companies entitled to receive the same, according to the provision of this Act. Said bonds shall draw interest at the rate of eight per cent. per annum from the date of their issue, principal and interest payable in gold coin of the United States; and principal thereof shall be made payable on a specified day, to be named in the bonds, which shall be twenty years after the date of their issue at the office of the Treasurer of said county, the interest accruing on said bonds shall be due and payable semi-annually so long as such bonds are outstanding and unpaid, and shall be made payable on a specified day, to be named in the coupons at said Treasurer's office, provided the first interest due on said bonds shall be paid one year from the date of the issue of the same, and the faith of the said county shall be pledged to the payment of the principal and interest as herein provided. The said bonds shall be signed by the Chairman of the Board of Supervisors, the Treasurer and Auditor of said county, as such officers as the Board of Railroad Aid Fund Commissioners, and when so signed shall be presented by the Chairman of the Board of Supervisors to the Clerk of said county, who shall counter-sign the same as such Clerk in the presence of a quorum of such Board at a meeting thereof, and it shall be the duty of the Board of Supervisors to cause the fact of such countersigning of said bonds to be entered upon their journal, together with the number, date and amount of each bond so countersigned by such Clerk, and upon the countersigning of said bonds, it shall be the duty of the Board of Supervisors to cause the seal of the county to be affixed to each bond, and appoint a committee of two of their number to deliver said bonds to said railroad company to which the same may be issued as herein provided for, and it shall be the duty of said Committee to take a receipt for the same from the Treasurer of said railroad company or other officer of said company duly authorized and empowered to receive and receipt for the same, setting forth in said receipt the number, date and amount of each bond so delivered, and report the same to the Board of Supervisors at their next meeting.

Sec. 6. Coupons for the interest shall be attached to said bonds so that the coupons may be removed without mutilation. Said coupons shall be signed by said Railroad Aid Fund Commissioners. Upon the payment of any of the said coupons, the County Treasurer shall cancel the same and on the first day of the next regular meeting of the Board of Supervisors, such cancelled coupons shall be destroyed, after having been inspected by the Board of Supervisors.

Sec. 7. It shall be the duty of said Board of Supervisors previous to the making out of the duplicate of the general assessment list for said county in each year after the issuance of any bonds under the provisions of this Act, to levy a tax on the taxable property of said county to by styled a "Railroad Aid Interest Tax," at a sufficient rate to raise the amount of interest required to be paid each year on said bonds issued hereunder, and previous to the making out of the duplicate of the general assessment list of said county after the expiration of ten years from the date of the issue of any bonds under the provisions of this Act, the said Board of Supervisors shall levy annually and until all the bonds so issued shall have been paid and liquidated, a tax on the taxable property of said county at a sufficient rate for the purpose of raising a fund for the annual liquidation of at least ten per cent. of all the bonds which shall have been issued under the provisions of this Act, ten years prior to the date of the levy of such tax. Such fund shall be styled a "Railroad Aid Fund." The said taxes for the "Railroad Aid Interest Fund," and the "Railroad Aid Fund" shall be levied and collected in the same manner as the general taxes for county purposes, and when collected shall be paid unto the County Treasurer, who shall account for the same to the said Railroad Aid Fund Commissioners to be by them applied—*first*, the Railroad Aid Interest tax to the payment of the interest falling due on said bonds; *second*, the Railroad Aid Fund to the redemption of said bonds as hereinafter provided.

Sec. 8. If there shall be collected as such interest tax in any one year, a sum greater than is required to pay the annual interest on said bonds issued hereunder, then the said Treasurer shall transfer such surplus to the general county or current expense fund as he may be directed by the Board of Supervisors.

Sec. 9. It shall be the duty of said Railroad Aid Fund Commissioners to make arrangements for the payment of the interest on said bonds when the same falls due, at least thirty days before the time of payment; and in the event said interest is insufficient, the said Treasurer shall draw on the common or general fund of the said county for such purpose, and deliver the same to said Commissioners, and in the vent that those funds prove inadequate, the said Commissioners are authorized and required to make such contracts and arrangements as may be necessary for the payment of said interest and the protection of the faith of said country.

Sec. 10. Whenever at any time there shall be in such Railroad Aid Fund a sum of money amounting to one thousand dollars or upwards, the said Commissioners shall advertise in a public newspaper printed and published in said county, and in a public newspaper printed and published in the city of San Francisco, for a space of four weeks, for sealed proposals for the redemption of said bonds; and ten days from the expiration of the time for such publication, the said Commissioners shall open the sealed proposals, and pay and liquidate as far as the Railroad Aid Fund then on hand shall extend. Such bonds presented under said proposals shall have the lowest value proposed at which they may be liquidated—*provided*, the same shall not be for more than the par value thereof; and, *provided*, should there be no proposals made for less than par value—then the payment of said Railroad Aid Fund on hand shall be made on said bonds according to the number of their issue, of which the said Commissioners shall give four weeks' notice of the number of bonds to be paid, after which time such bonds shall cease to draw interest; and, *provided*, whenever there may be sufficient money in such Railroad Aid Fund for the extinguishment of the bonds issued under this Act, it shall be the duty of the said Commissioners to advertise in a like manner for the space of four weeks, for the redemption of all outstanding bonds issued under this Act, after which time such bonds shall cease to draw interest. Any moneys remaining in said Railroad Aid Fund, after the redemption of said bonds, shall be transferred by the County Treasurer to the general county or current expense fund, as he may be directed by the Board of Supervisors.

Sec. 11. Whenever any bonds shall have been paid, and redeemed by the County Treasurer he shall mark the same "cancelled" over his signature, as County Treasurer and Commissioner, and immediately deliver the same to the County Clerk, taking his receipt therefor and the said Clerk upon receipt of such cancelled bonds shall file the same in his office.

Sec. 12. The County Clerk shall open with the said Commissioners an "Interest Tax account," and a "Railroad aid fund account," and shall balance and settle the same quarterly on the first Mondays of April, July, October and January of each year.

Sec. 13. The said Commissioners and all other officers herein specified, for the performance of their duties, under the provisions of this Act, shall in all things herein required of them, be subject to all the liabilities and penalties to which they are subjected on the performance of any other of the duties of their respective offices, and the Board of Supervisors shall, and they are hereby fully authorized so to do, require of each of said Commissioners such bonds and security for the performance of their duties herein required of them, as they, the said Board of Supervisors, shall deem proper. The said Commissioners shall, when so required, execute the said bonds, in the same manner as other official bonds are executed, and to be approved by said Board of Supervisors and filed in the office of the County Clerk.

Sec. 14. The proceeds of all taxes except taxes for State purposes, levied, assessed and collected to and on Railroad Companies for and on all railroads for the construction of which bonds have been issued under the provision of this Act, and for and on the rolling stock, used on such railroads shall be set apart by the County Treasurer to the credit of the Railroad Aid Interest Fund while any of such bonds are unpaid and outstanding, and shall be applied to the payment of the interest on such bonds.

Sec. 15. If at the election provided for in this Act a majority of the electors voting shall vote, Railroad aid Yes then and in that event it shall be the duty of the Board of Supervisors to cause to be surveyed and relocated the road running from the town of Santa Cruz along the coast to the northern line of the county, and to establish the same as a public highway and to cause to be made plans and specifications of all improvements required on such road, and shall contract for any and all if said improvements in the same manner as is now provided by law in case of contracts for the erection of public buildings, provided that no construct shall be let until the right of way on the routes as relocated for a public highway has been obtained without expense to the county and provided further that the county shall not become liable by such contracts for more than five thousand dollars, which amount the Board of Supervisors are hereby authorized to pay in the bonds of Santa Cruz county, which bonds shall bear the same rate of interests and the principal and interest shall be paid as the same time and out of the same funds, as the bonds of Santa Cruz county issued under the Act, entitled an Act to authorize the Board of Supervisors of Santa Cruz county to issue and sell bonds of said county and to provide for the payment of the same. Approved March 24th, 1868.

Sec. 16. The Board of Supervisors shall have the power to establish the point of commencement and the terminus of the railroad from the eastern line of the county to the town of Santa Cruz, for the construction of which, aid is to be granted under the provision of this Act.

Sec. 17. Upon the written application signed by the owners of the major part of the taxable property of the county according to its valuation on the last preceding assessment roll and filed with the Clerk of the Board of Supervisors prior to the first day of May, A. D. one thousand eight hundred and seventy, the said Board of Supervisors shall have the power, and it shall be their duty on the first day of their regular meeting in the month of May in said year, after having caused such application to be spread upon the minutes, to amend the proposition provided to be submitted to the electors of said county and all things or matters depending or appertaining thereto in such manner as shall be directed in such application, and the proposition so amended shall have the same force as the original proposition, provided that the whole amount of bonds authorized to be issued shall not be increased by such amendments.

Sec. 18. Upon the written application, signed by the owners of two-third parts of the taxable property of the county, according to its valuation on the assessment roll last preceding the date of such application and filed with the Clerk of the Board of Supervisors at any time after the first day of June, A. D. one thousand eight hundred and seventy, the Board of Supervisors shall have the power and it shall be their duty, after having caused such application to be spread upon their minutes to take, substantially such action in regard to the granting of county aid for the construction of railroads as may be directed in such application, and to annul either totally or in part as may be directed by such application, any obligation which the said county may have incurred by the provisions of this Act or by the result of the election authorized to be held by the provisions of this Act; provided that the county by such action or in any other manner shall not become liable to aid in the construction of railroads in a greater amount than two hundred and forty thousand dollars; and provided further that the Board of Supervisors shall have no power to annul or amend any obligations or liability of the said county to and with any railroad company who shall in good faith have actually commenced the construction of their road, one month prior to the filing of such application with the Clerk of the Board of Supervisors and who shall complete their road within two years from the date of the filing of such application.

Sec. 19. This Act shall take effect from and after its passage.

165. *Santa Cruz Sentinel,* February 5, 1870 (2:5)

The railroad bill introduced into the Assembly by F. A. Hihn, is a ponderous document and will be found in today's issue. It is the duty of each tax-payer in the county to closely examine it, and if any of its provisions are found objectionable, to make the same manifest before it becomes a law. All admit that railroads are for the general good.

166. *Santa Cruz Sentinel,* February 12, 1870 (2:2)
THE NEW RAILROAD BILL.

We have given Mr. Hihn's Railroad Bill as recently introduced, a casual examination, and while we are desirous that a railroad should be built upon the routes indicated, evan at some sacrifice to the county interested, still we must enter our protest against some of its most important provisions. By opposition to those, we trust that the people will be induced to agitate the question until a fair bill is introduced and passed. It is by and through this very opposition that we desire to make sure the fact of a railroad in our midst. In Section 3 of the bill now before the Legislature, we find the following words:

"Whenever a railroad company now organized or which may hereafter be organized under the laws of the State, shall have completed on the route from the eastern line of the county to the town of Santa Cruz, five consecutive miles of a railroad supplied with iron T rails, so as to be enabled to pass over the same with the engines, &c."

It is easier for the law-makers to so shape a statute that the real object may be apparent, than to hide what might be the real law of the case when the statute is passed. Now the object of the bill should be that the railroad company should commence building the road, either at the Eastern line of the county, or at the town of Santa Cruz, the two termini of the road. Under the clause above quoted, what prevents the company from commencing at Soquel, for our readers will see that those five must simply be built "on the route of said road?" Now, in view of the doubtful construction of the above provisions, we would suggest an amendment which will obviate any bad result from its ambiguity. It is this:

Whenever any railroad company now organized or which may hereafter be organized under the laws of this State, shall have completed five consecutive miles of a railroad from the eastern line of the county of Santa Cruz to the town of Santa Cruz, the construction of which railroad shall be commenced, either at said eastern line, or at the town of Santa Cruz, to be determined by said company, &c.

With this amendment, or some change fixing the point of commencement of the road, we can also strike out the unwise and dangerous provision of Section 16, which is as follows:

"Sec. 16. The board of Supervisors shall have the power to establish the point of commencement and the terminus of the railroad from the eastern line of the county to the town of Santa Cruz, for the construction of which, aid is to be granted under the provision of this Act."

We do not see what inducements would be held out for capitalists to invest in a road so fixed, and so materially interfered with by a Board of Supervisors. This we consider due the most dangerous provision of the bill, and looks like strangling the thing at its birth. Let the company control its own road, and locate the terminus at any point it chooses; *provided*, that they shall construct a road from the eastern line of the county to the town of Santa Cruz. The same system can be urged against the following provision in Section 3:

"*Provided*, further, that the Board of Supervisors shall have the power to designate the location and general route of such branch roads, subject to, etc."

Unwise legislation is often destructive to the wisest measures. By telling a railroad company that an irresponsible Board might control with friendly or unfriendly designs, the entire road in which they propose to invest so much, would doubtless impair the stock and weaken the enterprise of the same. Don't hamper the very men we propose to assist. Don't say you will give $20,000, but reserve the right and power to injure more than is given. This is no assistance. Again, we come to Sections 17 and 18, which should be expunged entirely, for reasons we cannot now give for want of space.

167. *The Pajaronian*, March 3, 1870 (2:3)
RAILROAD ACT.

Amend Section 1, so as to read as follows;

Section 1. The Board of Supervisors of the county of Santa Cruz, is hereby directed to order a special election to be held in said county at the several election districts, on the fourth Saturday of May next ,for the purpose of submitting to the qualified electors of said county the proposition, whether the county of Santa Cruz shall aid in the construction of a a railroad within the limits of said county, from some point on the Pajaro river *via* the town of Watsonville to the town of Santa Cruz; and in the construction of a railroad from tide water at the town of Santa Cruz, and running thence for a distance of ten mils up the valley of the San Lorenzo river *via* the town of Felton.

Amend Section 3 so as to read as follows:

Sec. 3. If, at the said election, a greater number of the electors of said county voting upon said proposition, shall vote "yes," than shall vote "no," then, and in that event, the county of Santa Cruz shall be deemed to have agreed and contracted to grant, and there shall be granted, aid for the construction and maintenance of the railroads specified in section 1 of this Act in the following manner:

Whenever any railroad company now organized under the laws of this State, shall have completed within the said county, on the route from a point on the Pajaro river to the town of Santa Cruz, five consecutive miles of a railroad, connected by railroad with the town of Gilroy, in the county of Santa Clara, supplied with iron T rails, so as to be enabled to pass over the same with the engines and cars of the construction trains, the Board of Supervisors, on demand of such company, shall order that there shall be issued, signed, executed and delivered to said company, or its representative, the bands of the county of Santa Cruz, to the amount of seven thousand dollars for each mile so constructed; *provided*, that if on the completion of the railroad to the town of Santa Cruz, the last section of said road should be less than five miles, then, and if that case, the said Board of Supervisors shall order that there shall be signed, executed and delivered to such company, the bonds of said county, to the amount of seven thousand dollars per mile for such last section. And whenever the San Lorenzo Railroad Company shall have completed two consecutive miles of railroad, on or near the present survey of the route of the said company, and connecting by railroad with tide-water, at the town of

Santa Cruz, ready for the conveyance of freight, and supplied with iron rails, the Board of Supervisors, on demand of such company, shall order that there shall be issued, signed, executed and delivered to such company, or its representative, the bonds of Santa Cruz county, to the amount of two thousand dollars for each mile so constructed; *provided*, that if the said San Lorenzo Railroad Company shall fail to construct six miles of its railroad connecting with tide-water, at the town of Santa Cruz, during the year 1870, or shall fail to construct ten miles of its railroad, prior to the first of June, 1871, then, and in that event, the said San Lorenzo railroad company shall forfeit all right to county aid in the construction of its railroad, and the Board of Supervisors shall have the power, and it shall be its duty to grant aid in the construction of a railroad to the extent of two thousand dollars per mile, commencing at tide-water, near the town of Soquel, and running thence up the valley of the Soquel creek, in the same manner and to the same extent, as is provided in this section for the granting of aid in the construction of a railroad of the San Lorenzo railroad company; and *provided*, further, that the whole amount of bonds to be issued in aid of the construction of the railroad from the Pajaro river to the town of Santa Cruz, shall not exceed two hundred and ten thousand dollars, and the whole amount of bonds to be issued, in aid of the construction of the other railroad or railroads, in this section specified, shall not exceed the sum of twenty thousands dollars.

Strike out Section 16, 17, and 18.

168. *Santa Cruz Sentinel*, March 5, 1870 (1:5)

Letter from Hon. F. A. Hihn.

Sacramento, February 23d, 1870.

Mr. ——:—I send you, herewith, my amendment to the Railroad Bill, a Road Law, and an Estray Law, which I request you to have published in both Santa Cruz and Watsonville papers. I have left off the Soquel Railroad branch, except under certain contingencies; not because I think the people living there are not entitled to it, but BECAUSE I have some interests there myself. The time within which the San Lorenzo Railroad is to be built, has been limited, because I believe the people demand that, if built at all, it shall be built within that time. Yet I shall be very glad to provide for an extension of time, if it is thought desirable. Please canvass the subjects: and let me know, soon. The Railroad Committee of the House was very much opposed to Section 17 and 18, authorizing the taxpayers to amend or annul the proposition to grant railroad aid and as these Sections did not seem to have many friends in our county, I consented to have them stricken out, as well as Section 16.

169. *Santa Cruz Sentinel*, March 12, 1870 (2:2)

Another Railroad.

We herewith publish the line of a railroad that proposes to connect this county with San Francisco by way of Half Moon Bay. Mr. Hihn's bill, as amended by amendment published last week, is more acceptable than the original, but the time provided for the construction of the San Lorenzo portion is inadequate for the completion of the work, it being but one year. We are reliably informed by responsible parties that if the time is extended to two years, and the bill becomes a law, that its construction is a certainty. The new bill was introduced by Assemblyman Ryan, and grants to A. J. Bowie, Samuel Purdy, James Regan, Theodore Le Roy and James Johnson, the right to construct a railroad over a route described as follows: Commencing at the corner of Illinois and Sixteenth streets, in the city and county of San Francisco, thence along and upon Sixteenth street to Seventh street; thence along Seventh to Market; across Market to McAllister; along McAllister to Masonic avenue; along Masonic avenue to Oak street; along Oak street to Stanyan street; thence southerly by the most convenient route through the city and county of San Francisco and the county of San Mateo to Spanishtown; thence southerly by the most convenient route through the counties of San Mateo and Santa Cruz to Santa Cruz and Watsonville, and thence back through the city and county of San Francisco, along and upon Oak street to Market, across Market to Eleventh; along and upon Eleventh to Channel; along Channel to the water front, and along the water front to the place of commencement. The Company is authorized to construct a double track, upon which they can use steam, except east of Larkin street, where the motive power shall be designated by the Supervisors. The bill further provides that upon the completion of the road in San Francisco, the city shall issue to the Company $300,000 of bonds bearing seven per cent. interest, and upon the completion of the road in San Mateo and Santa Cruz, respectively, they shall issue $100,000 of bonds each to the Company.

170. *Central Californian* via the *Santa Cruz Sentinel*, March 12, 1870 (2:3)

No Cause for Alarm.

Some people may be startled at the idea of this county's investing $500,000 in a railroad, the bonds bearing seven per cent. annual interest, and due in twenty years. "Penny wise and pound foolish" may be written as the history of many a county, when the golden opportunity came and was suffered to pass forever out of reach, from the undue weight given to narrow and short-sighted notions of economy. Men forget their liability to take one-sided views of great questions. In just this way they deceive themselves. Come, now, to the case in hand. Howe many of our readers, at the first thought of the proposition to issue the bonds of the county for half a million dollars, at once saw that the tax along on this immense property would go a long way towards paying the interest on the bonds? This fact no one will fail to see when it is once named.

But we will be a little more specific, and take a closer view of the case. Consider this one fact, that a railroad running through this county, by the way of the coast, would be at least 150 miles long. The taxable value of such road, including its depots, rolling stock and equipments, would be not less than $10,000 per mile. Here then, are $1,500,000 of taxable property added to the county, the county tax being say, two per cent., the amount to be paid into the county treasury by the railroad, would be annually, at least $30,000. The interest on $500,00 in bonds, at 7 per cent. per annum would be $35,000, so it is manifest that the county would be paying only $5,000 per annum for the railroad.

Consider another point. Any farm hand in the county can point out, after he has studied this grand problem, that such a coast railroad as the one proposed, would at once double the value of the taxable property of the county. He will tell you that some parts of the county will be worth, cash in hand, five or six times their present value as soon as the road is done, and when the tax is to be paid the property will pay it and not feel it.

Finally, this is not a donation of $500,000. It is nothing of the kind. The county simply exchanges its bonds for the stock of the company, and certainly such stock would be worth in the market, quite as much as county bonds. Where then is the risk? There is none, while the benefit to the county is beyond calculation.

As the railroad when built, would more than double the value of all property in this County, would it not be easy to pay, $5,000 more than tax-payers are now paying, without the road.

171. *Santa Cruz Sentinel*, March 19, 1870 (2:4)

The bill authorizing Santa Cruz county to aid railroads [A. B. No. 264], therein, has passed the Assembly.

172. *Sacramento Daily Union*, March 22, 1870 (3:3)

California Legislature.
Eighteenth Session.
Assembly.
Saturday, March 19th.
Bills Introduced.

By Mr. Finney—An Act providing for the construction of a tram-road in the counties of San Mateo and Santa Cruz. [Allows the Menlo Park Turnpike and the San Lorenzo Railroad Companies to consolidate and construct a tram-road, with a wooden or iron rail, from Redwood City to Santa Cruz, with a branch or two to Canada Mundo, etc.; also, authorizing those counties to subscribe $3,000 per mile aid.] Rules suspended and passed.

173. *The Pajaronian*, March 24, 1870 (2:3)

Legislation.

Ed. *Pajaronian.*—I have just been asked by a friend if I had noticed the number of bills introduced by F. A. Hihn at the present session of the Legislature.

"Why," said he, "they are as numerous as the locusts of Egypt and just about as useful. He has been voluminous to a most ridiculous extent; he goes about two cents on *quality*, and the balance of the dollar on *quantity* in fact, quantity is his strong suit. He appears to wish to become celebrated for something, and that of Statesmanship is suggested by his inordinate vanity, of which material he has more than a brigade of drunken peacocks, and as to brass, why, bless your soul, he has more in fee simple than Charley Delong and the

Vanderbilt statue combined."

But you voted for and supported Mr. Hihn, why did you do so?

"Why you see," replied my friend," we knew we could not elect a Democrat, so the next best thing was to elect a man not a Republican; but I am afraid we have played h— on our watch, for he having gone into the Democratic caucus at the first session, thereby becoming identified with our party, his sins, which are enough to sink a ship, will be put upon our shoulders, and may sink us, which he observing will take a pliant hour to rejoin the party he has just deserted."

"... Have you time to look at this, his eighteen-section railroad bill? eighteen long sections to provide that the County of Santa Cruz shall aid to the amount of $7,000 a mile, in the construction of a railroad, from the eastern line of the County to the town of Santa Cruz, when the entire meaning, spirit and intention of the bill could have been contained in *one* of its shortest sections"

I remarked that, probably it was Mr. Hihn's intention to conceal rather than to explain his thoughts, in such cases it requires a prodigious amount of language.

"True," said my friend "to *conceal* was his intention, but did it require *seventeen* extra sections to conceal the fact from his constituents that he was providing for $20,000 to be given of their money, for the construction of a branch road on his own land and almost entirely for his own benefit?"

I again remarked that the "laborer was worthy of his hire."

"Granted, but Hihn's labor is much higher than it is worth, especially when done in such a bungling manner."

"I love and respect a good mechanic, he is modest, is not puffed up, needs no putty to cover up defects, but with a few skillful licks he executes his work nearly and well, and looks and acts as if such was expected of him; but I have the most gigantic contempt for a bungling blustering, butchering botch who wonders why it took more than a day to build Rome, and who would attempt, without apprenticeship or means of art, to haggle it up in half that time."

It being late and having more important matters to attend to, I bade my friend as I now do you.   GOOD BYE.

174. *Santa Cruz Times* via *The Pajaronian*, March 24, 1870 (2:3)

[Amendment first published in the *Santa Cruz Sentinel* March 19, 1870 (2:2), without commentary.]

Aid to the San Lorenzo Railroad.

Amendment to an Amendment, supplementary to and amendatory of an Act to provide for the construction of the San Lorenzo Railroad:

Section 3: Amend it by striking out all from the word "provided," in the 55th line, to and including the word "Company," in the 80th line, and insert as follows:

Provided. That if the said San Lorenzo Railroad Company shall fail to construct six miles of the railroad, connecting with tidewater at the town of Santa Cruz, prior to the first day of September, one thousand eight hundred and seventy-one, or shall fail to construct ten miles of its railroad prior to the first day of September, one thousand eight hundred and seventy-two, then the right of the said San Lorenzo Railroad Company to county aid, shall cease and determine, and no more county bonds shall be issued and delivered to the last named company, and it shall then, and at any time within two years thereafter, be the duty of the Board of Supervisors, and they shall have the power to grant county aid in the construction of an iron [tracked] railroad to the extent of $2,000 a mile, commencing at tide-water, near the town of Soquel creek in the same manner and to the same extent as is provided in this section for the granting of aid in the construction of the San Lorenzo Railroad Company.

We feel authorized in stating that beyond question the conditions of the proposed amendments will be compiled with by the S. L. R. R. Co. The restriction imposed, although to some extent ... will only stimulate the Company's renewed exertions. The completion of the railroad and the connection of Santa Cruz with the metropolis by an air line road is only a question of time, and that is no distant future.

175. *Sacramento Bee*, March 23, 1870 (3:2)

Southern Coast Railroad Company.—A new corporation under this name, filed its certificate of incorporation to-day in the Secretary of State's office. The Company contemplates the construction of a railroad from San Francisco to San Diego, running through the counties of San Mateo, Santa Clara, Santa Cruz, Monterey, San Luis Obispo, Santa Barbara, Los Angeles and San Diego, with such branch roads through the counties of Los Angeles, San Bernardino and San Diego, as m[a]y be deemed advisable in order to connect with the Southern Pacific Railroad at some point near the Colorado river. The length of the road is to be 620 miles, including branches. Capital stock, $20,000,000, divided into 200,000 shares of $100 each. Directors—John Forster, M. J. O'Connor, William H. Sharp, A. F. Hinchman, J. B. Shaw, W. S. Rosecrans, L. C. Gunn, C. B. Polhemus, Benjamin Dreyfes, Edward J. Pringle and Edward Martin.

176. *Santa Cruz Sentinel,* March 26, 1870 (2:2)
San Mateo and Santa Cruz Railroad.

On the 21st of March, a bill was introduced into the Assembly, by Mr. Finney—"Provided for the construction of a tram railroad in the counties of San Mateo and Santa Cruz." [The bill allows the Menlo Park and Santa Cruz Turnpike Company and the San Lorenzo Railroad Company to consolidate, and construct a tram railroad, with either wooden or iron track, from Redwood City to Santa Cruz, with a branch from San Mateo to Half Moon Bay, connecting with the main line through the Cañada Mundo. The said counties to issue bonds to the amount of $3,000 per mile, running from five to fifteen year, bearing interest at the rate of six per cent. per annum: *provided*, the citizens so decide by a majority vote at an election to be duly called.] Passed.

Cost of Railways.—In this connection we have been to some trouble to get a true estimate of the probable cost of an iron and wooden tramway track. The following is a comparative estimate of the cost of each system of wooden rail and of iron T-rail, fifty-six pounds to the yard. The calculation is based on a five feet six inch gauge, and the cross ties are included:

 Iron rail (56lbs.) .... $5,000 per mile
 Block-wood rail .... 2,100 ''
 Single wood rail, No. 1 .... 1,290 ''
 Double wood rail, No. 2 .... 1,420 ''

An iron railway, of say 56 pounds to the yard, should last, with a fair traffic, about ten years, and the best hard wood rail, with a similar traffic, could not last over two years. Engineers state also that a well-constructed hard wood rail, if properly maintained, would probably last five years with a small traffic and light engines, not running over a speed of from ten to twelve miles an hour.

It is proposed to build a road, with turnouts, side-tracks, station-tables, etc., sixty miles long, and capable of carrying 200 tons daily; whereupon an experienced engineer rendered the following bill of materials and cash expenses for a wooden track road in Pennsylvania, namely:

Three locomotives, ($7,600 each, in gold,) $22,800; sixty four-wheeled platform cars, $225,) $13,500; three eight-wheeled box-cars ($800,) $2,400; three passenger cars, ($1,500,), $4,500; ten gravel and repair cars, ($200,) $2,000; ten rubble cars, ($60,) $600; four hand cards, ($125), $500; total $46,000. To run two trains per day, of one hundred tons each, leaving an extra locomotive for repairs, etc. Cost of running 100 tons the round trip: One engineer $3, one fireman $1.50; two brakemen, ($1,) $2; four cords 3-foot wood, ($1.50,) $5.00; oil, $1; total, $12.50. Running expenses, per ton, 12½ cents. Cost of building a road on a fair route, timber at medium price, no large bridges $4,000 per mile. Rolling stock and incidentals, $1,000. Say, road complete with rolling stock, $5,000 per mile. The above is a fair, and he considers a safe estimate for the general run of the country and prices of timber in Canada. He also states that the highest grade on the Gosford line is 50 feet per mile against the load.

In comparing the advantages of a light iron track with a wooden one, on a railway for use in opening up a new district, the following estimate of cost and maintenance of rails for fifteen years will furnish a fair idea of the expense, presuming that the traffic would be of such a light nature that the road laid with iron rails of fifty-six pounds to the yard would stand fifteen years without renewal; and allowing three years for the period of renewal for the wooden rail:

Iron rails for one mile, 56 pounds, or 88 tons, at $50 per ton, ...$4,400.00
Fish-plates, at $1 per pair, ... 550.00
Spikes, ... 200.00
Ties, 2,112, at 20 cents,... 422.40
Track-laying,.. 250.00
Total cost, per mile, ...$5,772.40

The following estimate was submitted by another engineer, touching the construction of a wooden railway per mile, viz:

2,640 ties, notched, at 20 cents, ... $528.00
25,000 feet B. M. hard-wood rails @10c 250.00
1,510 wedges,... 50.00
Track-laying,.. 250.00
Total cost, per mile, ...$1,078.00

It will be seen that the difference in cost of renewal is in favor of wooden rails. The difference in first cost in favor of wooden rail amounts to $4895.40, or say, $4,600.00 the interest on which, at six per cent., amounts to $276 per annum, or $4,140.00 in the period of fifteen years, for which the renewals of each rail are given. There can be no doubt that, taking these facts into consideration, the wooden railway supplies a desirable means of opening up the resources of a new district, with a light traffic, which would not yield a proper return for the more costly iron. But in building such a railway, through fertile districts, the work should be constructed with a view to the wooden rail being replaced by an iron one at a future period, when the increased traffic should render such a change desirable. The San Lorenzo and San Mateo Railroad Company might find it necessary and advantageous to first lay wooden rails, to be replaced by T-iron.

177. *Santa Cruz Sentinel*, March 26, 1870 (2:2)

The Assembly passed Ryan's bill for a railroad from San Francisco to San Mateo and Santa Cruz.

178. *The Pajaronian*, March 31, 1870 (2:1)

Important Railroad Rumor.—We were told by one who ought to know—whether he does or not—that the surveyors who started from Gilroy the other day are surveying a railroad from that place to run across the San Benito, thence to Watsonville, on the Monterey side, following the toll road to within half a mile of Castroville, and so on down through the Salinas Valley.

179. *San Francisco Examiner*, April 1, 1870 (2:1)
A NEW BILL.

We see by a dispatch that, in view of the failure of the bill to aid in the construction of the Southern Pacific Railroad, a new bill was introduced by Senator Wand which, it is said, will receive the Executive sanction. This bill, says a telegram to the *Oakland Transcript*, passed both houses under a suspension of the rules, and went immediately to the Governor. It authorizes the issuance by San Francisco of $1,000,000 in bonds of $1,000 each, $250,000 to be issued after each fifty miles of road south of Gilroy is completed. The bonds are payable in twenty years, at 7 per cent. per annum, the question to be submitted to the people, and the terminus to be in San Francisco.

We sincerely hope that this bill will become a law. It is one in which not only the people of this city are deeply interested, but also of the counties south of us. The great want of the southern coast counties is railroads. They have boundless resources, but are so completely cut off from market that they add little to the productive wealth of the State. A railroad through Monterey and San Luis Obispo would add immensely to the assessable value of these counties, and in a few years would greatly increase their population. The prejudice that exists in some quarters against railroads is little better than barbarism.

The large ranch owners, who have their cattle roaming

over thousands of acres of splendid lands, oppose them as a matter of course. The settler and cultivator of the soil are looked upon by them as intruders. They know that railroads will bring these, and the solitudes of their splendid domains will be encroached upon. They have a good thing now, and care not for bettering it. They pay taxes on an assessed value of some twenty cents per acre where they would not sell their lands for twenty dollars per acre. Of course they do not wish the people to have any voice in the matter of railroads. They argue that, sooner or later, the railroads must be built without any expense to them. Such selfish policy should not be encouraged. These lords of the soil have been the curse of the Southern counties. The Commissioners of Equalization will have it in their power to break up this state of things. Let their lands and cattle be assessed at some approximate figure to their real value, and we will soon find those counties dotted over with prosperous farms and farm houses. They can not stand the Equalizers and the railroads.

But it was not our purpose to discuss these. We simply meant to give our emphatic endorsement to the compromise bill of Mr. Ward. It is one the property owners of San Francisco—the real estate men, the bankers, capitalists and merchants will endorse. It will carry before the people by a very large majority.

180. *San Francisco Examiner*, April 1, 1870 (2:3)

Sacramento, March 31, 1870.

Editor Examiner:—The particular sensation in this city is the Governor's veto of the Railroad bills. The veto message did not confine itself to a simple murder of the railroad bills, but carried the war into Africa, and strongly criticized the general policy of railroad subsidies. Although the opposition to the Governor's veto has been very bitter, there is still a general disposition to sustain it. The general observation of the Governor in his veto message are eminently sound and sensible, and cannot be successfully controverted.

The bill to authorize San Francisco aid to a coast line railroad has just passed both Houses.

The railroad dispute, as it now stands, involves a sort of general inconsistency. Certainly it is to the interest of counties and State to encourage a general railroad system; but a legitimate encouragement does not require of counties to mortgage their entire taxable property to assist to build roads. As far as this view of the matter is concerned, the Governor's message is notably appropriate and correct.

181. *Santa Cruz Sentinel*, April 2, 1870 (2:3)

New Railroad Company.—There was filed in the Secretary of State's office Saturday the certificate of incorporation of the San Francisco, Santa Cruz and Watsonville Railroad Company. The corporation contemplates the construction of a railroad from a point at or near the city of San Francisco to the town of Watsonville, in Santa Cruz county, running through San Francisco, San Mateo and Santa Cruz counties. The length of said road is to be eighty miles. Capital stock, $3,000,000; divided into 30,000 shares of $100 each. Directors—Samuel Purdy, James Regan, Frank McCoppin, Thomas W. Brennan, A.

J. Bowie, C. D. O'Sullivan and Thomas W. Moore. Principal place of business, San Francisco.

182. *Santa Cruz Sentinel*, April 2, 1870 (2:4)

We are told by one who ought to know—whether he does or not—that the surveyors who stated from Gilroy the other day are surveying a railroad from that place to run across the San Benito, thence to Watsonville, on the Monterey side, following the toll road to within one half mile of Castroville, and then onward through the Salinas valley.

From a gentleman who lately went to San Juan, we learn that the Surveyors who lately left Gilroy, are at work near the former place, surveying the Southern Pacific Railroad. And it is supposed the road will run within eight or nine miles of Watsonville, and within half a mile of San Juan.

183. *Santa Cruz Sentinel*, April 2, 1870 (4:4)

Railroad Survey.—A party of railroad engineers, says the Gilroy *Advocate*, of the 26th of March, said to be in the employ of the Southern Pacific Railroad Company, arrived here on Tuesday evening. We were unable to find out anything about what route they intended surveying on. Those best informed say that there is little danger of the terminus leaving Gilroy for years, even then it will, because of its position, be the principal shipping point from this end of the Valley, and will not at all retard the growth or business of our city.

184. *Santa Barbara Times*, April 9, 1870 (1:4-5)
THE SOUTHERN COAST RAILROAD COMPANY.

We take the following from the San Diego *Union* of the 31st ultimo:

We publish below the articles of incorporation of the California Southern Coast Railroad Company, as filed in the office of the Secretary of the State, at Sacramento, on Wednesday, March 23d. The names of the incorporators are a sufficient guarantee that this is as strong a company as has ever been formed in the State. Dr. J. B. Shaw, of Santa Barbara, is one of the largest real estate owners, and one of the wealthiest men in that county. Mr. B. Dreyfus is of the firm of Landenberger & Co., of Anaheim, and is both wealthy and influential. Don Juan Forster, San Diego county, is well known as one of the wealthiest and most substantial citizens of Southern California. Chas. B. Polhemus, of Santa Clara, has large landed interests in Los Angeles. He was one of the builders of the railroad from San Francisco to San Jose. Edward Martin, cashier of the Hibernia Savings Bank, of San Francisco, is known as one of the best financiers in that city. He is a brother-in-law of Governor Downey, and has large interests in Los Angeles. A. F. Hinchman, formerly of Santa Barbara, who ably and honestly represented that county in the Senate in '52, has considerable property in each of the counties of Santa Barbara, Los Angeles and San Diego. Edward J. Pringle, Esq., is the law partner of Hon. John B. Felton, and is one of the heavy company who own the lands at San Buenaventura, which made so much stir in 1865 on account of the coal oil which is there found. Wm. H. Sharp,

The Dream of Steam, 1854–1873

lawyer, and M. J. O'Connor, of the firm of Conroy and O'Connor, wholesale dealers in iron and hardware, San Francisco, are both well known as possessing capital and influence. General W. S. Rosecrans has not only a local but a national reputation, with no tarnish on his name. L. C. Gunn is well known to the press of California, and though not himself among the capitalists of the State, has influence with those who wield capital.

This company *means business* and if the people in the coast counties want a road built, and are prepared to aid the company, it will not be long till the cars are running over the whole line. But the work is great, and it cannot be accomplished without liberal subscription of money and donations of land. We trust that the people of the Southern counties will awake to the brilliant future which is so near at hand. There is no doubt now that the Thirty-second Parallel road will be built at least from El Paso to the Pacific; for El Paso is made the point at which several railroads from the East converge; and we know that the Eastern portion of that line is already in course of construction, operations in Texas and Louisiana being actively prosecuted. With a transcontinental railroad, connecting Norfolk on the Atlantic, with San Diego on the Pacific, and a coast line road with its branches—connecting San Diego with San Francisco, and traversing the counties of San Diego, Los Angeles, Santa Barbara, San Luis Obispo, Monterey, Santa Cruz, Santa Clara and San Mateo, a new era of prosperity will dawn upon Southern California. It needs but enterprise on the part of our people to hasten the day.

[For Articles of Incorporation, *see* Appendix Item E.]

185. *Santa Cruz Sentinel*, April 9, 1870 (2:2)

The bill authorizing Santa Cruz county to vote on a proposition to aid a railroad from Pajaro river to Santa Cruz, $210,000; also, from Santa Cruz to San Lorenzo river, $20,00, was defeated.

186. *Santa Cruz Sentinel*, April 16, 1870 (3:1)

The San Francisco Board of Supervisors has issued an order granting to the San Francisco, Santa Cruz and Watsonville Railroad Company, the use of the required streets in San Francisco for twenty-five years, for the laying down of a single or double track railway with switches, turn-outs, etc. What this railroad will amount to or how far it will be constructed, is more than can be judged at present. But if built at all it will be on a line to Santa Cruz by the way of Half Moon Bay and Pescadero. It is certain that the time is not far distant when this place will have a railroad connection with San Francisco, either by the way of the Coast, the San Lorenzo or Watsonville, and it remains for the people in the county and capitalists out of it to say which route shall be adopted.

187. *Santa Cruz Sentinel*, April 23, 1870 (2:1)
Railroads.

The Supervisors of San Francisco have ordered an election to take place on the 7th June next, at which time will be submitted the proposition to donate $1,000,000 to the Southern Pacific Railroad Company. This order is

The Dream of Steam, 1854–1873

in conformity to an Act of the late Legislature, and there is no doubt that it will meet with popular endorsement. Another ordinance, passed to print, provides for submitting, on the same day, a proposition to issue the same amount of bonds to the San Francisco, Santa Cruz and Watsonville Railroad Company. The last mentioned road is intended to run from San Francisco to Pescadero along the coast, "thence through the Santa Cruz mountains through the depression formed by the Butano and San Lorenzo creeks to Santa Cruz, a distance of 75 miles; and thence to Watsonville, in Pajaro Valley, a distance of 20 miles further. A railroad by this route would traverse a fertile, though narrow, agricultural belt on the outer line of the Coast Range, until it entered the Santa Cruz mountains, when it would traverse a splendid redwood region, where fine quarries of building rock and limestone exist, emerging again into a fine agricultural valley contiguous to the bay of Monterey. Several coast towns would be directly connected with San Francisco, and considerable way of traffic would be created." It is a matter of grave doubt whether the people of San Francisco are, at the present time, ready to appropriate $1,000,000 towards establishing a connection of the character proposed with this county. Although, probably, a little ahead of the times, it is exactly what we need and eventually must have. A railroad down the coast would make this town one of the most thriving cities in the State, doubling, if not tripling the population within three months of the completion of the road. A few hours' ride from the metropolis would make this county the home of many of the merchant princes, and the lumber, lime, granite, grain and passenger travel that would have to pass through our burg, would put the wheels in motion of a thriving and prosperous community. It is stated that Stanford and his company are thinking seriously of running what is known as the Southern Pacific Railroad by the way of Santa Cruz, tapping the coast counties down to the Mexican line. We assume no responsibility for this statement, there being nothing in relation to it as yet definitely determined, but can see nothing unreasonable or improbable in the proposition. There is one thing certain, our redwood is the best on the coast, and the railroad kings are bound to have it. Who knows but that our miniature town of to-day may not, ere another decade, be a mighty entrepot, and a city that will number its population by tens of thousands? It is an age of wonders; a time in which cities rise and fall like bubbles upon the water. Hoary antiquity and the unborn future will stand aghast at the mighty changes in the ages, as grey-headed men do to-day who trace the steps of progress made during the period of their short existence. Light, Steam and Electricity, are made the servants of man, while the iron-horse, with arms of steel and nostrils of fire, fys with the speed of the wind and a tail as long as that of a comet, over the land from ocean to ocean.

188. *The Pajaronian*, April 28, 1870 (2:1)

Railroad matters are quiet, with the exception of vague rumors, like echoes, passing over the land. Santa Cruz is still somewhat excited at the prospect of a railroad from San Francisco through Pescadero to Watsonville. The route may be practicable, but before any action is taken in that direction it would be well to know first, in which direction the railroad will go when it leaves Gilroy. If it comes within three or four miles of Watsonville there will be no need of the Pescadero road. We do not know who in Santa Cruz are advocating the Pescadero project, but from specimens of railroad maneuvering in that section heretofore, we think nothing will be accomplished.

189. *Monitor* via the *Santa Cruz Sentinel*, April 30, 1870 (1:7)

San Francisco and Santa Cruz R. R.

Under the general law empowering the Boards of County Supervisors to submit to a vote of the people whether or not they are willing to aid railroads within their borders to an amount *not exceeding* five per cent, of the assessed property valuation, a company has been formed to construct a railroad from *some suitable point* near the water from of San Francisco, thence along certain streets to the cemeteries, and thence by the most practicable route [which means along the Fulton street toll road, or convenient thereto, to the vicinity of the Ocean House, thence south to the San Pedro Rancho] to Half-Moon Bay, in San Mateo county, thence to Santa Cruz and Watsonville. Application has been duly made to the Supervisors for the necessary authorization to submit the question to the people on the 8th of June, the appropriation asked being $1,000,000, would be a little less than one per cent. on the assessed value of the property. No doubt the supervisors will make the necessary order, and the people can say yes or no, as they believe their interests will be affected. We are firm advocates of internal improvements of every kind, and believe that railroads do more than any other to develop the resources of a country. The road immediately under consideration will be a direct benefit to San Mateo and Santa Cruz; and of course whatever benefits the interior will, although in a reduced ratio, also benefit the commercial centers. But would it not seem more reasonable for those places that are benefitted most to contribute most? The road will run through the whole length of San Mateo and Santa Cruz counties, hugging the seashore in its course—a portion of country now practically valueless to the husbandman and the trader, because of the difficulties and expense of bringing the produce to market. The land along its route will be enhanced from one hundred to three hundred per cent. on present valuations, and thus the assessable property materially increased. These are the impressions that strike us at first glance. We shall ponder the matter more fully and advise our readers how to act before the question comes to a vote.

190. *Santa Cruz Sentinel*, April 30, 1870 (2:2)

The books for subscription to the capital stock of the San Francisco, Santa Cruz and Watsonville Railroad Company, will be opened to day in San Francisco.

191. *Santa Cruz Sentinel,* June 11, 1870 (2:5)

The election held in San Francisco to appropriate $1,000,000 for the Southern Pacific Railroad, resulted in defeating the measure by 124 votes. So much for workingmen being led by political demagogues.

192. *Santa Cruz Sentinel,* June 18, 1870 (2:3)

The Railroad Subsidy.—At the recent election, held in San Francisco, the election canvassers declared the one million dollar appropriation defeated by 124 votes. The railroad company demanded a recount of the votes, when it was found that a majority of 62 votes was in favor of the appropriation. We are glad of it, as the road will now be at once pushed forward from Gilroy to the southern line of California.

193. *Santa Cruz Sentinel,* June 18, 1870 (2:4)

Railroads.—Now that an appropriation has been made, of one million dollars in aid of the Southern Pacific Railroad, another proposition for a similar amount will soon be voted on to aid the San Francisco, Pescadero, Santa Cruz and Watsonville road. This railroad will eventually divide the patronage of the Southern Pacific, from the Salinas valley, north, and afford a market for our vast timber resources, and also lime, powder, &c., manufactured in this county. The route will be from the San Gregorio valley, crossing the divide near the head-waters of the Pescadero, Butano and San Lorenzo creeks, coming down the latter valley, through

Felton to Santa Cruz, and thence to Soquel, Aptos, Watsonville and Salinas City; thence south to the missions of Soledad, San Miguel, and to the warm springs of D. D. Blackburn. On Monday evening, June 13th, the Board of Supervisors of San Francisco, as reported in the *Bulletin*, acted on the contemplated road as follows:

The ordinance granting to the San Francisco, Santa Cruz and Watsonville Railroad Company the right to lay a railroad track on certain streets in the city was read.

The original ordinance contemplated an ordinary railroad track with the privilege of running locomotives. The route commences at Sixteenth and Illinois streets, and comes to the city front, near Rincon Hill, by way of McAllister, Seventh and Brannan streets.

Mr. Ashbury proposed an amendment, the provisions of which would convert the track to a city railroad.

Mr. Story objected to the route, on the ground that it would pass the new City Hall, on McAllister street, and must cross Yerba Buena Park to reach Seventh street.

Mr. Badlam said the railroad company was a myth. It was not yet incorporated. He moved to postpone the ordinance one week. The applicants asked for a steam railroad franchise, and had entirely abandoned the idea of getting it. It was not worth while to force a city railroad franchise on them when they had not asked for it. Give them a week's time to ascertain whether they wanted it or not.

Mr. Ashbury said he had submitted his amendment to the gentlemen interested, and they were contented with it.

Mr. Story moved the indefinite postponement of the

ordinance.

Mr. Badlam thought it wrong to grant these franchises to parties who did not expect to build the roads. The franchise extended through a term of 25 years. It could be held and sold on speculation.

Mr. McCarthey said the gentlemen asking for a franchise intended to construct the road.

The motion to indefinitely postpone was lost, *Ayes*—Badlam, Riug, Story. *Noes*—Winkle, Harrold, McCarthy, Ashbury, Shrader, Canavan, Kelly. *Excused*—Flaherty, Adams.

The ordinance was then, on motion, laid over one week.

194. *Santa Cruz Sentinel*, August 20, 1870 (2:2)

San Francisco, Santa Cruz and Watsonville Railroad.

Order No. 945, granting to the above railroad, certain rights, passed by the Board of Supervisors of San Francisco county, August 1st, and has been approved by Mayor Selby. A vote granting a loan to build the road will be taken by the people of San Francisco at the next general election. The franchise granted the road, is to continue for twenty-five years, provided, the work on the road shall be commenced within one year, and the entire work completed within three years. After leaving the city, it will pass through Half Moon Bay, crossing the headwaters of the Butano and Pescadero creeks, and come down the San Lorenzo to Santa Cruz and Watsonville. There is a prospect of our having a railroad after all.

195. *San Francisco Bulletin,* August 26, via the *Santa Cruz Sentinel,* September 3, 1870 (4:1)

The New Alviso Route.

The electors of Santa Clara county yesterday voted on the question of granting a subsidy to the Santa Clara Valley railroad and Transportation Company. There is some doubt about an affirmative vote. The railroad which it is proposed to build will extend for the present, from the town of Santa Clara to deep water beyond Alviso, a distance not exceeding twelve miles. If the subsidy fails, a road which would have so many advantages could well be built by the residents of that county who are interested in this enterprise.

The projectors of this line, we believe, have entertained the project of extending this road from Santa Clara, or to the foot of the Coast Range of mountains beyond. From this point the upper valley of the San Lorenzo could be reached by crossing the ridge, a distance of say six miles. For a part of the way a good turnpike road has already been constructed, and the whole way is passable, we believe, for buggies, certainly for people on horse back, to King's Ranch in the San Lorenzo Valley. A railroad company is organized at Santa Cruz for the construction of a road from that town to the head of this valley, say a distance of fifteen miles. Considerable work in the way of grading has already been done; and the company expect to push on the work as means may be obtained until it is completed. Premising that it is feasible to extend these roads to the foot of the mountain on either side, until the gap requiring heavy work, would be only six or eight miles, and that this was filled for the present by a good turnpike road on an easy grade, it is reasonably certain that the bulk of the trade between Santa Cruz and Santa Clara would be transferred to the new route.

Two lines of stages with extras, have been running full all summer upon the present stage route, between these towns. A large number of passengers in the summer time bound for Santa Cruz, take the sea route by steamer, to avoid the dust and tediousness of the long drive over the mountains which, by the way, is a very pleasant one in the early part of the season, but becomes irksome later in the summer when the heat increases and the dust is very deep. The time consumed by the stages on this route averages about six hours in the summer, and about eight hours in the winter season. To add two and a half hours on the railroad, and the time required to make the journey overland between this city and Santa Cruz is about nine hours in summer and ten in winter, averaging probably nine and a half hours all the year round.

Were the railroads completed to the foot-hills by the way of Saratoga on one side of the San Lorenzo, on the other to the foot-hills, the time between Santa Clara and Santa Cruz, including staging, could be reduced to three hours.

Besides the passenger traffic, a very large amount of lime, lumber, wood and tanbark now hauled by teams down through the valley of the San Lorenzo, would be transported over the railroad. A considerable amount of the same kind of freight, including that required for the paper mills at Saratoga, would be brought from the western slope of the Coast Range to Santa Clara, or to tide water. Between Santa Clara and Santa Cruz there would be no competition with existing railroads. From Santa Clara by way of Alviso and the bay to the city, there would be a sharp competition, there being already railroad communication on both sides of the bay.

The people of the town of Santa Cruz, particularly, desire a direct railroad connection with this city. But this is not needed so much for any new facilities which might be gained in sending freight to this city, as for the advantage of an easy and rapid passenger transit. In a close competition, the sailing vessels and steamers would transport freight either way between Santa Cruz and this city for $2 per ton, or even less. In fact, contracts for freight by sailing vessels can even now be made at these rates. With a railroad, lumber, lime and wood would still be transported by water, because sailing vessels would furnish the cheapest freight transportation in the world. The railroad, as outlined, would take a large amount of freight from the valley of the San Lorenzo to tide water; and this would be of great advantage to the town. It would secure like results on this side of the Coast Range, bringing in from the mountains and the intermediate plains freights cheaper than they can be transported by ox or horse teams. Such a route established, would not only take all the passengers between Santa Clara and Santa Cruz, but passenger traffic would be largely increased by this rapid and comparatively easy transit.

In this view, the Alviso route, would become a very important one; but much more so from this southern extension than because it would be a competing route between this city and Santa Clara. A narrow gauge road with light rails and light locomotives is all that is needed for this traffic.

Such a road can be constructed and stocked where only the ordinary difficulties of grading are presented, at not more than half the cost of railroads of the common gauge and weight of rails and locomotives. If ever there is direct railroad communication between this city and Santa Cruz, on a paying basis, the enterprise will probably assume pretty nearly the shape which has been here outlined.

196. *The Pajaronian*, September 22, 1870 (2:1)
Railroad Rumors.

Rumor has it that the Central Pacific Railroad Company will take possession of the San Jose and Pajaro Railroad—commonly called the Gilroy Road—on the 1st of January. It is also stated that by the 1st of July next, the above road is to be extended 20 miles, according to contract of the requirements of Government. Now the question will be asked: "what direction will this twenty miles of road take?" Rumor says—and very emphatically for Rumor—that the extension will follow down the Pajaro river to a point at or near Watsonville, thence the Company will run a branch to Santa Cruz, in order to tap the magnificent forests of lumber stretching from Watsonville to the latter place. This view of the route above mentioned, is reasonable and eminently practicable. Eminent surveyors have decided that the route down the Pajaro is by all odds the best, and if the Company propose to continue their road southward—and of this there is no doubt—lumber in immense quantities must be had, and the best place to procure this lumber, at cheapest rates and with the least trouble, is in Santa Cruz county.

Thus all things seem to *drive* the road this way. Each end of the county is now threatened, and may the invasion of railroads soon commence.

197. *Santa Cruz Sentinel,* September 24, 1870 (2:3)
RE-ADJOURNED MEETING.

As per announcement in last week's *Sentinel*, an adjourned meeting of the friends of the Orphans' Home and College was held in the Court-house on Saturday evening last. Rev. Mr. Ingraham and several other gentlemen spoke, discussing the location at length. A letter was read which had been received from the Location Committee, stating that that body would visit Santa Cruz among other places. R. C. Kirby, one of the gentlemen who visited Watsonville to solicit funds for the College, stated that the sum total received, not stopping to enumerate names, was $000,000 [*sic*].

The only objection mentioned that is supposed possible to exist, or that could be raised by the Location Committee, is want of railroad connection. Such objection is of short duration, as facts and figures can be produced that will prove that a railroad to Gilroy from Santa Cruz would pay if in existence to-day, and that if the College is located here steps will be immediately taken to build a railroad. Santa Cruz will certainly shortly have a railroad connection with the outside world, and the location of the proposed College in our midst, will hasten the consummation so devoutly wished. In speaking of railroads, E. L. Williams stated that the San Lorenzo Railroad Company would renew work on its road early in the coming spring, said road to be pushed to completion as fast as possible, and the terminus being at King's ranch, twenty miles from this place, the staging would be short to a connection with the Santa Clara railroad. The meeting adjourned to meet on Monday evening next at seven and a half o'clock, same place.

198. *Santa Cruz Sentinel,* **October 15, 1870 (2:1)**

[Report on selecting Santa Cruz as a site for the Odd Fellows' College and Home]

The barriers which separate Santa Cruz from neighboring towns towards the North and the interior have been represented as formidable. At present there is an admitted disadvantage in the fact that the place is approached from the metropolis only by sea, and by a mountain stage road from Santa Clara station on the line of the San Francisco and San Jose Railroad. Not forgetting that competing water and land lines insure permanently the benefits of cheap transportation, it may be said that the objection is a vanishing one. Competent engineers pronounce two or three routes for a railroad feasible without extreme cost. A charter has been obtained for one, the road bed partly graded and two or more other lines projected, for which charters have been sought. Without doubt the end of the present commercial depression will witness the active prosecution of at least two schemes, whose completion will shorten the time between San Francisco and Santa Cruz to three hours. One of the immediate effects of the completion of either of these lines, would be the multiplied value of real estate, and a greatly augmented population.

199. *Daily Alta California*, November 13, 1870 (1:7)

The *Times* of to-day states that work on the San Lorenzo Railroad will be resumed next spring.

200. *Los Angeles Daily Star*, November 19, 1870 (2:3)

Narrow Gauge Railroad.

We find the following in the San Francisco papers of the 15th:

The Narrow Gauge Railroad Company filed a certificate of incorporation in the County Clerk's office, yesterday. The objects of the corporation will be, to take contracts to construct, equip, and operate narrow-gauge railroads throughout the United States and countries adjacent thereto; and to receive pay therefor in cash, stocks, bonds, lands and properties, or securities of any kinds; as to this corporation may seem best: also, to own, hold, or sell the same, as may be deemed advisable by the Company. As such contractors, to build narrow-gauge railroads in such territories; and equip, operate, and by purchase, to own and operate the same, as the interests of the Company may justify. To generally transact any business in connection with the object sought to be obtained by the creation of this Company. The Trustees of the Company are L. L. Robinson, S. F. Butterworth, C. J. Brenham, Isaac Friedlander, Irwing M. Scott,

John Foster, F. MacCrellish, F. A. Hihn, and Phineas Banning. The capital stock shall be one million of dollars, divided into ten thousand shares of one hundred dollars each.

If these gentlemen are in earnest in their work, they will find a first-rate field for their operations in this part of the country. We directed attention to this subject lately; pointing out the advisability of constructing such roads as are contemplated by this company, through the Southern counties. We are glad to see that such a company has been formed; and hope they will turn their attention hitherward, in looking for their first field of labor.

201. *Santa Cruz Sentinel,* November 26, 1870 (3:1)

A convenience that has long been needed, and one that we hope will meet with a most generous support from the citizens of Felton and Santa Cruz, has just been established by H. W. McKoy, the moving spirit of the first terminus of the San Lorenzo Railroad. This enterprise is especially worthy of encouragement from the fact that Mr. McKoy has entered into an agreement with the postal department to carry the mail to Felton from this place, so soon as a post-office is established at the above-named point, which will be as soon as the papers can be properly filled out, for *nothing*. This work is necessary in order to secure a postoffice, and an express is put on to fill the contract. Whenever patronage justifies it a daily express will be run, and when the days are long the people of Felton can get the San Francisco papers the day they are published.

202. *San Juan Echo* via the *Santa Cruz Sentinel,* December 10, 1870 (2:4)

Route of the Southern Pacific Railroad.—The Southern Pacific Railroad Company are about to commence work on a section of twenty miles of railroad extending south from Gilroy. We have not learned that the final location of the sections of road beyond the points mentioned have yet been made. But the Sacramento *Record*, which is in a special sense, we believe, the organ of the Central Pacific Company, suggests the following route: The 3d, and the one likely that has been selected is that from Gilroy through a pass in the mountains to the Salinas Valley, Monterey county; up the Salinas to the boundary line of this county; thence to the Paso Robles Hot Springs; thence through a pass to the Santa Lucia Mountains to the Morro; thence through the Osos Valley; thence on down the coast to the Arroyo Grande; thence to the Huasna; thence up the Santa Maria river, through San Buenaventura Pass, to the coast; thence to the city of Los Angeles; thence down the coast to San Diego; thence through Warner's Pass to Fort Mohave. We have every reason to believe that this is the route, because the road then will pass through the most fertile and populous portion of Southern California.

203. *Santa Cruz Sentinel,* December 24, 1870 (2:1)

Our Railroad Prospects.

On Monday, the 2d day of January, 1871, the San Lorenzo Railroad Company will hold its annual meeting for the election of Directors, and the transaction of other business. This company has been organized over two years, under the general laws of the State, and has made considerable progress towards the completion of the San Lorenzo Railroad. The route has been surveyed to near King's farm—seventeen miles north-west of Santa Cruz, on the San Lorenzo River and the profile view, plans and specifications of the road completed. The working plan for the grade has been made, and a considerable portion of the grade is already built between Santa Cruz and Felton. The past eighteen months the work has been suspended, owing to a vexatious law-suit, which has lingeried in the Supreme Court for some time; but is now about to be determined in its finality, after months of litigation, in which the Railroad Company has gained its case in ever issue made. This last and final decision being favorable to the corporation, the Directors propose, at once, to go to work and complete the road as far as Felton the coming season.

Our object in being thus particular is to bring at this time, the subject of Railroad communications with San Francisco, into actual notice. It is well known that a Railroad Company has been organized in San Francisco, for the purpose of building a road to connect with the San Lorenzo *via* Half-moon Bay. The road will pass through high table-land, densely timbered, and capable of the highest cultivation. The supply of redwood, fir, pine, madrona, tan-bark (and other oak) laurel, &c., is almost inexhaustible. There are also vast quarries of limestone, granite and [garbled] on the route. Very recently a bed of blue-clay has been discovered, which will make fire-brick equal to the best imported article. In the vicinity of Capt. Staple's flint-sand (pure silica) capable of making white flint or Bohemian glass, abounds in mountain masses, and loads of quicksilver (cinnabar) have been discovered on the opposite mountain, while gold has been mined, in Deep Canyon, and Gold Gulch, in that vicinity.

The Odd Fellow's College and Home Committee will meet in San Francisco, on the 29th inst., and to that Committee would we direct investigation in reference to railroad communication with Santa Cruz, from San Francisco, Gilroy, Watsonville and other points. We do not lay our only claim on the San Lorenzo Road, or found our material hope on its enterprise, but claim that a road can and will be built along the coast, a distance of about seventy miles, to the town of Santa Cruz; in fact we are assured that a preliminary survey of this route has already been made, and that it has been selected as the route for the great National Southern Pacific Road, to connect with the thirty-fifth degree Parallel Road, passing through the Salinas Valley to San Luis Obispo, Santa Barbara, Los Angeles, San Diego, Fort Yuma and the towns along the Gila River. Taking the line of the coast from the estuary of the Purissimo to that of the San Lorenzo, there is not one good landing, in say, sixty miles. There are several embarcaderos; all other roadsteds are unsafe in rough weather, and the best of which are at New Years' Point, Pigeon Point, Davenport's and William's Landings. The agricultural land along the coast is a narrow belt of rich soil, bearing very nutritious grasses, and used for dairy purposes mostly; while the valley land produces those fine potatoes, vegetables and fruit so famous in the San Francisco markets. But the real wealth of this section lies, on an average, on from two to fifteen miles in-land, and consists of lumber, lime, bark, building stone and fire-clay. There are fifteen mountain streams already adverted to, entering the sea at about equal distances, from an easterly direction; while the San Lorenzo, with its northern curve, seems to take them all in its embrace. These streams coming south, are in rotation as follows: Purissimo, Pillareitos, San Gregorio, Pescadero, Butano, Deep Canyon, Garzas, Waddell Creek, Scott Creek, San Vicente, (Bias') Creek, William's, Laguna, Holy Creek, Baldwin Creek, Meader Creek, and the San Lorenzo, at Santa Cruz, the latter benign the largest and longest of them all. These creeks are all pure, limped streams of cold water, clear as crystal, and filled with brook trout. They head from ten to twenty-five miles in-land, near the divide of the Santa Cruz Range, and drain a section of country densely timbered with redwood, and other lumber trees. These virgin forests have hardly yet been explored, and only surveyed sufficiently to locate the range and meridians of the township lines, and sectionize and subdivide near the coast. But little of the land is claimed by Spanish grants, and that generally near the sea-coast, where the timber is not so valuable, and has suffered more wastage. It is to these great, undeveloped natural resources, that the attention of the Odd Fellows' Committee is directed, and to the enhanced value that will accrue to the institution and the country in the future, should our claim be favorably considered. Take for instance the town of Napa or San Jose, compared to Santa

Cruz. These towns have advanced in the past, owing to railroads to their utmost capacity, and have no future to predicate calculations on, while our town, and especially the country north-west of us, has everything for the future. The virgin soil has never been cultivated, and the timber forests have their primeval growth, standing in stately groves for centuries, undisturbed by the woodman's ax. San Francisco must have this timber, for lumber, manufacturing and firewood; the tanners must have the bark, and the piano makers and billiard-table manufacturers must have the laurel to finish the more elegant parts of their handiwork. Capital will supply this demand, and to do it this road must be built, and can be built at a comparatively small cost. The route is almost at a sea-level, and no tunnel (except ¼ of a mile at Waddell's Gulch) need by built. A narrow track road would [garbled] the timber-belt at the intersection of each one of these gulches, and be the feeder to keep the main road in supply, and thus every foot of land on the route (now only worth from one to twenty dollars per acre) would increase in value a thousand fold, just as it has increased in Santa Clara Valley, along the line of the Railroad. Our sea-coast land is just as good for cultivation, and more valuable for villa residences of the wealthy and fashionable, who delight in splendid views of land and sea scenery, that pleasure the eye and gratifies a cultivated and fastidious taste.

We also contend that this is *the* route that will eventually carry the freight from the Salinas Valley to the Metropolis. The Southern Pacific has now definitely determined to take its road through Panoche Grand Pass to the Tulare Plains; thence down the west side of the San

Joaquin River and the lakes to the Tejon Pass, to San Bernardino, and thence to Mohave. The Central Pacific has control of this road, and it cannot be expected that this Company will be allowed to monopolize the whole of the country, and impose a tax upon the people to keep its monopoly in force; and thus increase its power, therefore, this road will become a necessity, a counter-irritant, to thwart selfish schemes. For while an opposition road exists, the Company will not have absolute control. These are some of the reasons that will urge an early completion of the Railroad proposed.

204. *Daily Alta California*, December 27, 1870 (2:1)

A final decision in a suit, to which the San Lorenzo Railroad Company is a party, is expected soon and the Santa Cruz *Sentinel* says that if it should be favorable to the Company they will immediately commence work and finish the road from the county seat to Felton before the end of 1871. Part of the grading has already been done. The Company formed in this city to construct a railroad to Santa Cruz by way of Half Moon Bay, has done no work beyond the preliminary survey.

205. *Sacramento Daily Union*, January 6, 1871 (2:3)

San Lorenzo Railroad.—There was filed yesterday in the offices of the Secretary of State the following statement of the affairs of the San Lorenzo Railroad Company for the year ending December 31st, 1870:

Assets.

Reserved stock	$55,000.00
Unassessed stock	23,000.00
Assessment No. 1, due	2,050.00
Assessment No. 2, due	2,150.00
Assessment No. 3, due	2,250.00
Assessment No. 4, due	2,450.00
Expenses for 1867	-83,093.88
Expenses for 1869	-701,175.15
Cost of survey	1,962.02
Paid for grading	7,280.57
Right of way—deposit in Court	950.00
Salaries	115.00
Timber	603.95
Law expenses	821.25
	$102,901.82

Liabilities.

Capital stock	$100,000.00
Assessment No. 5, paid by stockholders	350.00
Assessment No. 6, paid by stockholders	350.00
Assessment No. 7, paid by stockholders	350.00
Assessment No. 8, paid by stockholders	350.00
Due Blockman & Cerf	700.00
Due C. Bern	800.00
Due E. Jones & Co.	101.82
	$102,901.82

206. *Santa Cruz Sentinel,* February 18, 1871 (2:1)

Railroad Interests.

That California needs railroads to develop the great agricultural and manufacturing resources of the State, none will deny. That these roads should be built by our own citizens, aided by the capital of the Eastern States, is also evident, but this is no argument that every county, city and town in the State, should impoverish themselves to aid monopolies, incorporated for the purpose of taxing individuals to build roads while the "companies," under a plea of legality, might reap all the benefits. A narrow track railroad from Menlo Park to San Francisco, is proposed to be built, and the necessary amount of $300,000 has already been subscribed--the distance being about thirty miles, keeping the line of the bay. This being the case, why not extend the railroad to Santa Cruz, via Felton, connecting with the San Lorenzo Company's road, at or near King's Farm? The gap would not be more than twenty-five miles, and as a narrow track road will admit of a short curve, the expense of crossing the mountains would not be so much as for a wide track road. Capitalists should examine into the feasibility of the route, and if practicable, adopt the plan, as it would cost very little more to grade the road through the hills 25 miles, than to drive piles along most of the bay route, thirty miles. The subject of narrow-gauge roads is getting to a point where we shall soon have actual working tests, according to appearances. The California and Arizona railroad Company intend adopting the narrow gauge, and the Nevada and Grass Valley Railroad Association have been talking and figuring on the matter. The Grass Valley *union* has given estimates, based on the nature of construction, where a 4 feet 8½ inch gauge would cost $24,000 to $30,000. It may be of interest to publish these estimates of the *Union*, for, although no definite figures can be given before the nature of the route is known, yet everybody desires to know "something about how much" it will cost. The estimate is per mile:

For 30lb rail, 53 tons @ 90	$4,770
Spikes and Fish-Plates, 6 tons, @ $120	720
Freight on above 59 tons @ $15	885
2,6000 ties, 6x6x5, 37 M feet @ $20	780
Grading and Laying Track (say)	2,500
Station and Platforms (say)	50
	$9,705

The grading may cost more or less per mile, according to the nature of the country over which the road will run.

The difficulty of making general estimates will be seen from the above, where, for instance, is included an item of freight on the iron, which amounts to about 9 per cent of the whole. In any given case there will be plenty of such items. The Stockton and Copperopolis Railroad, although only completed fifteen miles, is already working and paying a handsome income. When the road is completed, with branches to the Ione Valley, Murphy's and Sonora, a handsome profit on the investment will be realized. Why not try the railroad antidote experiment in Santa Cruz? It would certainly give life to our citizens. Trade would increase, and the assurance of a certain and speedy connection with San Francisco would increase our manufacturing interests, and lend a new impulse to local business. This is the age of railroads, telegraphs and steam. This is an age of progress, especially in the direction of science and what is understood by internal improvements. The human mind throughout the civilized world, is laboring constantly and earnestly in the field of science and improvement. New and useful adaptations of principles, complicated and important applications of philosophical, chemical and mechanical powers and principles, are daily conceived, and, after much labor, are brought forth in the shape of new inventions. Progress, in every direction, marks the age, and points the course to be pursued.

We propose to fall into line and to keep time, as well as we can, with the march of events in their onward movement towards that great and grand goal which civilization and progress must ultimately attain. All improvements by which the material interests of our city, county and State will be promoted, and our industrial resources be developed, and from which, general benefit will, in our opinion, result, will receive our earnest support and advocacy. We may differ with others in some things, as to the plans and policy by which our ends and aims are to be attained. But, in doing so, we shall be governed by what we conceive to be right and for the best, and shall accord to others the privilege of thinking and acting for themselves. We believe the construction of railroads and the establishment of manufactories throughout the State, and especially in Santa Cruz, are necessary to a proper and beneficial development of our industrial resources. Such results can not be attained by any other. Without such developments we must remain far behind the age, and be consigned to that position in the line of marching events which belongs to the laggard and the indolent. But we are proud to know that such is not the spirit which pervades our people. Already we have outstripped our sister counties in manufacturing interests, and all we want to further develop our great natural resources, is a railroad. We desire especially to see the road leading from Santa Cruz to San Francisco progress rapidly and prosperously. We are not among those who oppose everything done by the community to aid a railroad company, because a few individual stockholders or contractors may be benefitted. We believe such men as take hold of and push such enterprises *should* be benefitted. They deserve it. And, we also believe, that those who oppose everything of this kind are the *very last* who would undertake the prosecution of such valuable enterprises, unless they were sure of being personally benefitted and *paid largely*. We wish to see ALL work together harmoniously and vigorously to the end that all may be benefitted, and our city and county generally be raised to that position in the progress of the age to which our resources, locality and character, so richly entitle us. Our city is now at the most critical and important point in its existence. We are now at the turning point of our destiny. Shall we grow and become a large and influential manufacturing city? Or, shall we play the laggard in the race, and let others and more enterprising places snatch the prizes from our grasp? These are the questions to be answered by the citizens of Santa Cruz. The answer will forever fix our destiny, and determine whether or not we are to be the first and most powerful manufacturing city in the State,—the Lowell of the Pacific coast,—or whether we are to pay tribute to others. These are questions to be answered by our own citizens, and not by outsiders and those who have no further interests here than the amount of money to be realized. Let us then arouse ourselves fully and look to our own interests, and strive to make our city what it should be, even if we should have to give up some of our pet notions and individual opinions as to the best policy to pursue.

207. *The Pajaronian*, March 2, 1871 (2:4)
Railroad.

Many persons have spoken to us lately in regard to the probability of a railroad finding its way into the Pajaro Valley. The scheme—which is not such a great one—is not given up by any means, and we feel assured from various reasons that monied men are now looking with favor upon the construction of a road from Gilroy to Watsonville, and on to Santa Cruz. Let not our people despair. This fruitful and valuable section of country will not long be cut off from railroads, especially when a road is only 20 miles distant at the present time.

208. *Daily Alta California*, March 2, 1871 (1:6)

Santa Cruz, March 11th.—The certificate of the incorporation of the San Lorenzo Valley Railroad Company has been filed. Capital stock $300,000. It is the intention of the Company to set one hundred men to work on the road at once.

209. *The Pajaronian*, March 9, 1871 (2:2)
Southern Pacific Railroad.

The San Francisco *Bulletin* says that the passage of

the Texas Pacific Railroad bill renders it certain that the Southern Pacific, from Gilroy south, will be constructed at an early day. This road, for various reasons, has hung fire for a long time. But several routes have been thoroughly explored and preliminary surveys made. Between a point in the mountains east of Gilroy, and the head of the Salinas Valley, there are a number of passes in the inner coast range, all of which, we believe, have been examined with more or less minuteness. Through one of these the road will be carried into the San Joaquin Valley, thence through the counties of Tulare, Kern, San Bernardino, and Los Angeles to San Diego.

210. *Santa Cruz Sentinel,* March 11, 1871 (2:2)
RAILROAD MATTERS.

San Lorenzo Railroad.—We are able to give our readers this week a copy of the certificate of incorporation of the San Lorenzo Railroad Co. This is but the forerunner of more active measures, as it is the intention of the company to set 100 men to work at once on the road, and its early completion may be regarded as an established fact. The road this season will probably be extended from the Powder Co.'s Wharf the distance of sixteen miles, Felton being midway of the road, connecting with most of the saw-mills. A portion of the road to Felton has already been graded. The company hold a meeting to-day, and we shall be able to give full particulars next week. The earnestness with which the company has taken hold of the work is a good guarantee of its complete success, and the completion of the road will be hailed with satisfaction by all who have the future prosperity and wellbeing of our town and country at heart.

[For Articles of Incorporation, *see* Appendix Item H.]

211. *Santa Cruz Sentinel*, March 11, 1871 (2:4)

Mining.—Last winter two men, who were mining at Gold Gulch, the first station on the new railroad, took out $7.50 in one day. They were not able to test full richness of the claim, as the owner of a grain field would not allow them to run their ditch through it. Next year satisfactory arrangements will be made, and considerable mining carried on.

212. *Sacramento Daily Union*, March 17, 1871 (3:1)

San Lorenzo Valley Railroad Company.—Articles of association of the San Lorenzo Valley Railroad Company—organized to construct a railroad from Santa Cruz up the valley of the San Lorenzo river sixteen miles, to a point on Bowlder creek, near its junction with the San Lorenzo river—were filed yesterday in the office of the Secretary of State. Capital, $200,000, in shares of $100 each. The principal place of business will be in Santa Cruz. Directors—George Treat, F. A. Hihn, C. D. Anderson, R. C. Kirby, Lucien Heath, Henry Philip and Charles McKiernan.

213. *Santa Cruz Times* via *the San Mateo County Gazette*, March 18, 1871 (1:6-7)

The San Lorenzo Valley Railroad.

As will be seen by the articles of incorporation published on our local page, work is about to be commenced upon the San Lorenzo Valley Railroad. The gentlemen whose names appear as incorporates are a sufficient guarantee that the road will be pushed to completion at the earliest possible moment. This is an enterprise that will tend more toward our permanent prosperity than any movement that has heretofore taken place among us, and one which cannot be too highly valued by Santa Cruzans.

This road is to be built up the San Lorenzo for a distance of 16 miles, and eventually terminate at San Mateo, connecting at that point with the San Francisco and San Jose road. This will give us a direct rail connection with San Francisco in an almost air-line, and this connecting line once completed, the distance between that city and Santa Cruz can be traversed in about three hours. This will be a great saving over the present style of traveling, and business men will then be enabled to visit San Francisco, make a few purchases, and return the same day. To seaside visitors and pleasure seekers Santa Cruz will then offer greater attractions than any other point on the coast, and will become at once—as nature has situated her to become—the Nahant, Saratoga, New Port and Long Branch of the Pacific Slope. Families in all parts of the State will be glad to escape from the hot and unhealthy cities and towns of the interior, and will flock to Santa Cruz to regain health, enjoy our sea breezes, and the well-known hospitality of our citizens. The railroad once built business prosperity will return, our beach will be dotted with cottages, and our hotels will be crowded to excess.

The road will pass through the finest belt of timber land in the State, will develop thousands of acres of the best lands in the county, thereby increasing the flow of immigration to this point, and furnishing ready employment to the best class of population county can contain—the mechanic and laboring man. The production of lumber will be increased ten-fold, and the cost of transportation will be less than one-half the present price of hauling by teams. We will then be able to compete with Puget Sound, or any other lumber market on the coast.

But before all these advantages can be reaped by Santa Cruz, the road must be built, and to build the road the Company must have—*money!* The sweet strains of "chin music" will never buy a pound of iron, lay a tie, or grade a foot of the road. Men of enterprise, foresight, and business integrity have taken the initiative in this matter—men in whom our citizens have every confidence in the future prosperity of Santa Cruz by *investing their dollars* in the work about to be inaugurated. The shares are now $100 each—ten per cent. of the subscription to be paid down—and there is not a business man in the county but what can well afford to subscribe for one or more shares. The San Lorenzo Valley Railroad is a Santa Cruz institution, for the benefit of Santa Cruz Town and County, and the entire capital stock should be taken here. It is a home institution, and we believe that the people of this county will be unmindful of their true interests and not let this enterprise lag for want of financial support. The books of the Company will be opened in a few days for the purpose of issuing stock, and all will then have a chance to purchase and aid this enterprise. By so doing thousands of dollars will be expended in our midst the present Summer, hundreds of needy workmen will receive employment, and ere long the snort of the iron-horse will be heard on his swift passage up the San Lorenzo Valley, "sniffing the morning air," and making glad music on the ears of thousands.

214. *San Mateo County Gazette*, March 18, 1871 (2:2)

On the first page of this paper will be found an article which we copied from the *Santa Cruz Times*. While we are talking about building a narrow gauge railroad between Menlo Park and San Francisco, we thought it well enough to let our readers know what our Santa Cruz neighbors are doing in the way of railroading. They are now in earnest and mean business, and it may be set down as a sure thing that a narrow gauge railroad will be constructed in this direction a distance of 16 miles from Santa Cruz, within one year from this time. They talk of eventually extending the road so as to connect with the Southern Pacific Railroad at San Mateo; but Redwood City or Menlo Park are either of them better points for striking the Southern Pacific road. Whether the Menlo Park and San Francisco narrow gauge road is built or not, an effort should be made by our citizens to have the Santa Cruz road extended to Redwood City. There is no one enterprise which would help build up this town so much as the opening of a railroad between Santa Cruz and Redwood City. It would run through one of the finest and most valuable redwood forests in the world, and lumber could be landed in Redwood City at one-half the present price for hauling from the nearest mills. We presume that if a company should be organized in this county for the purpose of building the road from Redwood City to Santa Cruz county line, that the San Lorenzo Company would extend theirs so as to form the connection. The *Engineering and Mining Journal* says that the 3 feet 6 inches gauge road can be constructed on the prairies of the West, at a cost of from $8,000 to $10,000 per mile, with 36lb rails—which includes rolling stock, depots, and the usual equipments of a railroad. The Santa Cruz project is something worth considering by our citizens, and we have concluded to set the ball in motion with a view of inviting discussion upon the subject.

215. *Daily Alta California*, March 19, 1871 (1:7)

Commencement of work for the construction of the San Lorenzo Railroad is looked forward to as a relief to present Commercial depression.

216. *Santa Cruz Sentinel*, March 25, 1871 (2:3)
The Santa Cruz Breakwater.

The great desideratum of the numerous coasting vessels plying between San Francisco and San Diego, is a safe and commodious harbor, where storm-ridden steamers and sailing craft may find a refuge from the heavy storms, which at times sweet over the otherwise calm ocean. When we take into consideration that the passage of the bar at the entrance of the Golden Gate is not at all times practicable, without great danger to life and property, we see the absolute necessity for some harbor for vessels secure from the dangers of the deep. The Bay of Monterey is such a harbor. Should storms come from the south-east, then the Monterey side of the bay is secure, or should they come from the north, or any point not south-east, then the harbor of Santa Cruz is safe...

With a seawall one mile or less in length, Santa Cruz would have a safe harbor, accessible at all times, and secure from all storms, no difference from what quarter they may come. It is necessary—it is practicable! Nature has done much toward the construction of a breakwater at this place. From the point near the light-house a ledge of rocks extends into the bay for a distance of two miles, and a half mile from the bluff, at low water, this ledge is only four fathoms below the surface. By the completion of the San Lorenzo Railroad excellent facilities will be afforded for transporting granite from the inexhaustible quarries known to exist on the line of the proposed railroad, two or three miles up the San Lorenzo. This is an enterprise that should not only interest the people of this county, but of the entire State. Alexander destroyed Ancient Tyre by using it in the destruction of a levee to enable his troops to storm Insular Tyre. Ours is a more land able enterprise, and more benefits will accrue to commerce than by the destruction of a thousand Tyres. A side track from the San Lorenzo Railroad could be laid to the proposed breakwater, and the labor of construction is rendered easy. The project should be pressed upon our Representatives in Congress, and if necessary, our State Legislature should memorialize that body....

We do not look upon the breakwater as a strictly local issue or enterprise, but one in which the whole line of seacoast counties is interested. But even as a local enterprise, and for the sake of argument admit that it is, we required its construction to enable us, at all times, to ship our produce, and such manufactured articles as lime, leather, powder, paper, wood, lumber, etc. Let us be united on this question, and when the San Lorenzo Railroad is completed, the breakwater constructed, numerous mills and manufactories put in motion, utilizing the now unimproved water-powers of our streams, Santa Cruz will take her place among the leading manufacturing towns of the United States. Build the railroad and breakwater and the other improvements will quickly follow in their train.

In proof of the necessity of a breakwater at this port, through the courtesy of Dr. Kittredge, we are enabled to state that the arrivals and departures for 1870 were: steamers, 271; other vessels, 187; total, 418.

217. *Santa Cruz Sentinel*, March 25, 1871 (3:2)

San Lorenzo R. R. Company.—The annual meeting of the San Lorenzo Railroad Company was held Monday, March 20th, at their office, when the following named gentlemen were elected Directors for the ensuing year: H. Gushee, E. L. Williams, W. F. Peabody, Edmund Jones and S. A. Bartlett.

The directors then met and elected W. F. Peabody, President; Edmund Jones, Treas.; E. L. Williams, Secretary.

218. *San Francisco Bulletin* via the *Santa Cruz Sentinel*, March 25, 1871 (4:2)

A Local Railroad Problem.

For some years, some of the more enterprising citizens of Santa Cruz county have been agitating the question of a railroad connection with San Francisco. Opinions are somewhat divided. A few thought the most feasible way was to connect with the Southern Pacific Railroad by the way of Watsonville and Gilroy. Others preferred to obtain a more direct connection by way of the San Lorenzo Valley, thence over the "divide" into the Santa Clara Valley by way of Saratoga. This plan is much the most available one, and seems to be rapidly growing in favor with the citizens. Some work in the way of grading has already been done on the proposed road up the San Lorenzo Valley. We now learn that work will soon be resumed, and that an effort will be made to push the work along towards compilation as fast as means can be obtained. The valley is narrow, and for the greater part of the way is heavily timbered with redwood, fir and chestnut oak. Lime stone of the best quality abounds, and the waterpowers which would be made accessible are some of the best in the State. A road extend up this valley sixteen miles, would reach a point near where the crossing would be made over the ridge into the Santa Clara Valley. Sixteen miles more would make a connection with the Southern Pacific Railroad at San Jose; or extending it eight miles further tide water would be reached at Alviso. We premise that this road could be built on the narrow gauge plan, and stocked for $10,000 a mile, and that a road thus constructed would fully and profitably meet all the demands for freight and passenger transportation. The sixteen miles extending up the San Lorenzo Valley from the port of Santa Cruz, could be built and stocked for $160,000. The county subscribing for $100,000 of this stock and the citizens for $60,000 more, and the thing is done. A local railroad is constructed without subsidies, and is owned by the county and its citizens. It then twelve miles more of narrow gauge constructed from San Jose to a point at the foot of the mountains to the west of Saratoga, there would be a gap to be filled of something over four miles. The twelve miles on the Santa Cruz side could be built for $120,000. A good stage road could be made for the present, and stocked with coaches. At a future day, when the earnings of the road would justify it, this gap could be filled up with a railroad track, which would cost, of course, more than the easier grade of the valleys. Now it is quite within the ability of the two counties to construct this local road, and that without any dangerous strain. It is difficult to say which of these counties would profit most by it. All the passenger traffic between Santa Cruz, San Jose and San Francisco would be turned into this new thoroughfare. The route would be a quicker one by more than three hours, and far pleasanter than the one now followed by the stage coaches. For sixteen miles or more the railroad would furnish an outlet for the timber, wood, lime and bark at

Santa Cruz. On the other side of the ridge the same kind of freight would come down the mountain to San Jose, which is one of the best lumber markets in the State outside of San Francisco. The redwood lumber which supplies that market is now hauled from the western slope of the mountain by way of Lexington and the old stage road, a distance ranging from sixteen to twenty miles. And yet this lumber is sold at a handsome profit, after the cost of transportation to San Jose.

Now if the people of the two counties want such a railroad, they must make a liberal subscription for the purpose. The subsidy business—that is the making of direct gifts to half a dozen corporations of a railroad company—has come to an end. If half the money required to build this road can be raised by the two counties, bonds secured by a first mortgage would bring all the remaining funds needed. Talking will not construct this road, otherwise it would have been in operation before this time. But money and credit, backed with executive energy, will do the work.

219. *Marysville Daily Appeal*, March 26, 1871 (3:3)

At a meeting of the Board of Directors of the San Lorenzo Valley Railroad Company held at the Ocean House last night, the following officers were elected: Hon. F. A. Hihn, President; Edmond Jones, Secretary; Henry Philip, Treasurer and Engineer; work on the road will be commenced as soon as the survey is completed. The entire cost of the undertaking will be defrayed by local capital.

220. *Daily Alta California*, March 30, 1871 (1:8)

Santa Cruz, March 25th.—About the only excitement the Saratoga of the Pacific Coast is undergoing at present is relative to railroads, a company having recently been incorporated to push to completion the long-contemplated, neglected but invaluable San Lorenzo Railroad, whose course is up the river from which it takes its name a distance of about ten miles, terminating at the little village of Felton. About three years ago the initiative step was taken toward the building of the road, a franchise for twenty years having been obtained, work was commenced, and, after a few lawsuits by alleged enemies to the enterprise, the grading was finished and—that was all. For nearly two years it was in *statu quo*, as far as practical demonstration is concerned, and just as people were about to number it "among the things that were," lo! and behold, a new organization springs up and the most favorable indications of its imminent completion are manifested. When such men as the Hon. F. A. Hihn and G. B. V. De Lamater, Henry Philip, J. H. Besse and Geo. Treat (of San Francisco) are enrolled among its thirteen incorporates, we can but feel satisfied of a favorable result of the undertaking. With this railroad Santa Cruz will be one of the most thrifty, as it is now the most lovely, interior cities in the State. A large, and as yet comparatively undeveloped lumber and lime region, will be opened; the cost of transportation lessened, and the manufacturing interests of this locality brought forward in its true light.

The capitalist can see clearly where he is placing his capital, and look to the result with an assurance of success. Take it as a whole nothing can, or will be, as beneficial as the advent of railroads in this County, to the community at large, irrespective of wealth or station, and the company have the sympathy of all, and the aid of many, in furthering their commendable project.

221. *San Jose Independent* via *The Pajaronian*, March 30, 1871 (3:2)

Railroad Matters.

We have refrained from mentioning the new progress heretofore made in the preliminary arrangements for a railroad to connect San Jose with Santa Cruz. The project has now assumed so much of vitality that we congratulate our citizens on the prospect of an early commencement of the enterprise. Some forty of our most prominent citizens have already signed the preliminary papers. Among them we recognize a half dozen, anyone half of whom could build the San Jose half of the road from his own resources. The project is so feasible, that the only wonder is that it was not done long ago. In fact, the mountain range to be passed is so heavily timbered, that the expensive grading usually required in such cases, may nearly all be done away by substituting the trestle work of gigantic trees so abundant and so convenient for the purpose. This road may be narrow gauge, or of the ordinary width. It may go the Lexington or the Saratoga route. These and other important details will be discussed with Santa Cruz friends of the enterprise next week, when a committee of those interested here will visit our sister city to confer upon the subject. The terminus of the road on this side of the mountain is imperatively pointed out by the convenience of travel. It is equally adapted for persons wishing to use the road from the direction of Stockton and Gilroy, as from the direction of San Francisco, to say nothing of the freight and passage traffic which would inevitably increase to large proportions between this place and Santa Cruz. It used to be a rule in the Eastern States that when a stage line paid, it would pay to build a railroad, the freight and traffic always increasing in a rapid ratio with the increase of facility of transportation. We have no doubt the stock will at once be taken up here, because the line will pay very handsomely on the investment; and even if it only paid an ordinary return it would reimburse our citizens indirectly to the full value of the stock subscribed.

222. *Daily Alta California*, April 1, 1871 (4:1)

Santa Cruz, March 31st.—The surveying party of the San Lorenzo Railroad is progressing favorably and camped in the vicinity of Felton this evening.

223. *San Jose Independent* via the *Santa Cruz Sentinel*, April 1, 1871 (1:6)

ALVISO RAILROAD.–We are assured by one of the principal stock-holders in the Santa Clara Valley Railroad Co., that the late sale of the property of the California Steam Navigation Co. to the California Pacific Railroad Co., makes certain the speedy completion of the proposed railroad between this city and Alviso, and the opening up of a line of travel from here to San Francisco, by means of steamers connecting therewith and plying between the last named place and Alviso. Some time ago, we believe, the Santa Clara Valley Railroad Co. consolidated with the California Pacific; and as that company comprises a vast amount of capital with an enterprising spirit, we may expect that in a very short time the proposed line will really be in running order. In various directions throughout the State, the California Pacific is placing itself in opposition to the Central Pacific, and competing with it in securing railroad patronage; but on no line are its prospects better for such competition than on the proposed one of rail and steamer, via. Alviso, from San Jose and San Francisco.

224. *Santa Cruz Sentinel*, April 1, 1871 (2:4)
RAILROAD—FELTON!

The hope and much-needed necessity of this place has long been looked upon as a railroad with one of its termini at the Santa Cruz Beach. People have talked and talked and talked; have hoped and prophesied, and been prayerful. Business hunt in suspense, and many have said: "A railroad to Santa Cruz? Never!"

A few years ago the San Lorenzo Railroad Company was organized, surveys made and grading done, and on the strength of those indications the little town of Felton sprang into existence. Work stopped on the road—laborers were paid and discharged, shovels and picks housed. Little was said by property-holders. The prospects of railroading began to hang heavy. Feltonians learned from sore disappointment to look blue. Property, house lots and real estate generally, that had gone up in price like a rocket, hung heavy on the hands of new purchasers. Houses that had gone up in a night had an empty appearance in the day. Plans for magnificent hotels, public buildings and private residences, were the subjects of ghastly jokes. There was a change in the town—if not in appearance, in the hopes and prospects of its inhabitants, and some of them manifested a desire to sell. Even the staid and slow-going sawmill men who had calculated on getting their lumber freighted for one fifty, concluded that they had better do the work with cattle, and the woodman's ax and saw moved with a slowness that evidenced disappointment.

In the meantime legislative effort was made to pass an act that would authorize county aid in the construction of railroads. The plan was complete and magnificent,—a main trunk to Gilroy by the way of Watsonville, with branches up the Soquel and San Lorenzo Rivers. People, some people, got so fearful that we were on the eve or being railroad to death that they began to quarrel with their neighbor as to the width of the track and its exact location. Other liberal-minded gentlemen were in great dread that this one would get his hand into the railroad pie, and that his friend Mr. So-and-so would not get to be boss.

They were destined to quick disappointment. The

bill never got through the Legislature. Nobody hankered after stock. The outs were glad that they were out and the ins had all they wanted. Money was scarce and the prospects were discouraging. But the enterprising and public-spirited men who had conceived the San Lorenzo Railroad, had obtained its charter, surveyed its route, and expended somewhere near seventeen thousand dollars in grading, etc., bided their time in an unchanging faith in the wealth of Santa Cruz. Lawsuits and croakers obstructed but never discouraged. More stockholders and money were needed. The enterprise was canvassed by other parties in Santa Cruz and San Francisco. The Company made and received propositions. A new company was formed, including the old. Stock was rapidly taken, and at 12 o'clock on Tuesday last an engineer from San Francisco, assisted by surveyors T. Wright, M. V. Bennett, A. and P. McPherson, with any number of assistants, the latter numbering such men as were interested, commenced to re-survey in dead earnest, driving their first stake in Felton and working rapidly down towards the lower terminus.

The new Company means business—its stockholders have got the cash, and their interests, independent of the profits of the road, demand that the iron horse goes snorting to and beyond Felton. The President has the reputation of being a wide-awake, energetic and enterprising man, and a real estate holder to such an amount that he is justified in giving the road fifteen thousand dollars as a donation. But that is not all; the President is *President*, and as President he has too much at stake to let his name go down in defeat. The heaviest stockholder owns the Treat sawmill, and the immense Zayante Rancho that reaches Felton round about, and his subscription of twenty thousand as an investment on increase of property, is a monthly interest of two per cent., and principal at short call. Every person in this place is taking courage,—business men are taking courage, for every thing is seeming harmony and stock taken by interested money men. At Felton it looks cheerful. Tom Glynn and his amiable lady are busily engaged at the saw-mill boarding-house in preparing food for the surveying party, while Frank Turpin, the gentleman in charge of the mill, has all he can do to show the anxious and inquiring ones the lay of the land and the location of the road. Collins, Bennett & Co. have opened the San Lorenzo Turnpike, and carriages and wagons loaded with those desirous of investing in the embryo city, find no impediment. The Feltonians are alive to their interests and future harvest, and while they are pricking up their interests with brilliant business prospects, they have not forgotten to give their town with paint and white-wash a most clean and inviting appearance. The man of all business, store, hotel, express and postoffice has greatly improved his premises, while the store of Day & Hayes is well filled with the necessities of a varied community, while John Bassford "hangs out over the way." The heavy blows of Angus Frazer, the blacksmith, may be heard, proving that work by teamster and farmer is about to be commenced. Real estate is *rising* rapidly, and times bid fair to be lively.

225. *Daily Alta California*, April 5, 1871 (1:7)

Santa Cruz, April 4th.—...The survey of the San Lorenzo Railroad continues to be pushed energetically forward.

226. *Daily Alta California*, April 7, 1871 (1:3)

Santa Cruz, April 3rd.—Since my last communication surveyors have commenced the work of altering and improving on the proposed route of the San Lorenzo Railroad, and a week or ten days will complete their labors, after which, I am informed by one of the company, men and material will be placed in motion and the ball kept rolling until the consummation of the enterprise.

227. *Daily Alta California*, April 8, 1871 (1:7)

Santa Cruz, April 7th.—The surveyors of the San Lorenzo Railroad have found that by running a tunnel of 1,100 feet in length at Powder Mill Bend, on the San Lorenzo River, a saving in distance of one and a half miles can be effected.

The Committee appointed at the recent railroad meeting at San José to consult with the citizens of this place upon the ways and means of constructing a line of railroad from Santa Clara to this city, are in town and held an interview with prominent local capitalists to-day.

228. *Santa Cruz Sentinel*, April 8, 1871 (2:1)

Our fellow citizens F. A. Hihn and R. C. Kirby have gone to

San Francisco, and the supposition is that their visit is in connection with railroad matters.

229. *Santa Clara News*, April 1, via the *Santa Cruz Sentinel*, April 8, 1871 (2:4)

The Santa Clara and Santa Cruz Railroad.

After years of procrastination, events now seem to indicate the construction of a railroad from Santa Clara across the mountains to the sea port of Santa Cruz. A meeting of substantial citizens was held at San Jose a few days since, when the subject was fully and intelligently discussed, and the co-operation of the Santa Cruz people was invited. We can not say much for the enterprise of the people of that county, but we have an abiding faith that the whole of the capital stock necessary to secure the early completion of the road will be subscribed by our citizens. No enterprise can be suggested which promises better returns on the capital invested than this projected railroad. Without taking the passenger traffic into account, its freight list alone would place its success beyond a peradventure. Such a line of road would certainly command all the traffic of the region of country in the vicinity of Watsonville and Santa Cruz which, in the winter season is now deprived of a market for its grain, lime, wood and lumber, because the roads are impassible for teams. Hitherto Santa Cruz and Monterey counties have had no access to the great metropolitan market except by sea. And notwithstanding the almost insuperable difficulties which the people have encountered in hauling their various commodities to the landings, yet they have shipped enormous freights and given constant employment to the large fleets of coasting vessels trading between San Francisco and the several ports in Monterey and Santa Cruz counties. The trade, from a small beginning has now grown to immense proportions, and Goodall & Nelson, and owners of other steamboat lines have realized large fortunes by their enterprise. There is another view of this subject which directly affects the people of this valley, and that is that a railroad will speedily reduce the price of wood and other necessaries of life to about one-half the present prices. The mountains of Santa Cruz possess inexhaustible sources of wealth in timber, limestone and minerals, which only need development. We therefore earnestly hope that prompt measures will be taken to incorporate the Santa Clara and Santa Cruz railroad company, and that books of subscription will be immediately opened.

230. *Daily Alta California*, April 9, 1871 (1:6)

Santa Cruz, April 8th.—…The meeting of the San José railroad delegates and the promoters of the San Lorenzo railroad, held here to-day for the purpose of discussing the project of extending a line of railroad from some point of the Southern Pacific railroad to this city, resulted favorably to the scheme, although nothing definite was agreed upon.

231. *San Jose Independent*, April 9, via the *Santa Cruz Sentinel*, April 15, 1871 (1:8)

Railroad Across the Santa Cruz Range of Mountains.

S. A. Bishop, one of the Committee appointed from San Jose to visit Santa Cruz, for the purpose of conferring with citizens of that place in regard to the construction of a railroad between the two cities, returned along with other members of the Committee last evening. He informs us that the Committee were enthusiastically received in Santa Cruz and were given much more gratifying assurances of co-operation in the construction of the railroad than they expected to obtain. The capitalists are ready and willing to embark in the enterprise. Santa Cruz has appointed the following Committee, who will visit San Jose soon to let us know exactly what the people of that town are willing to do: F. A. Hihn, Henry Philip, Lucien Heath, E. L. Williams, Dr. Peabody. In the meantime the matter will receive thorough consideration in San Jose. From the present interest which is being displayed in the matter Mr. Bishop is confident that a permanent organization will soon be effected and that the road will be built within a very short time. We hope this may be so.

232. *Santa Cruz Sentinel*, April 15, 1871 (2:1)

San Jose Railroad.—The project to connect this place with San Jose by rail, is receiving earnest attention from the citizens of either end of the proposed route. The people of Santa Cruz want railroad connection with San Francisco, let it be by Gilroy, Soquel Creek, or Felton. They want the most practicable route. This information why must obtain by surveys. They have joined the San Jose people in an effort to survey the Soquel Creek route, R. C. Kirby circulating a subscription list to obtain the necessary money. The total expense is placed at $2,000; $750 Mr. Kirby readily obtained. The balance will undoubtedly be raised by the people of San Jose. yesterday morning R. C. Kirby and F. A. Hihn started for San Jose to bring the railroad business to a head. As the San Jose people have offered everything that is fair, and to give this end of the road the balance of power and the principal officers, we feel that they are in dead earnest, and should they succeed in their present laudable effort, San Jose will become one of the leading entrepots of the State.

233. *San Jose* Independent, April 11, via the *Santa Cruz Sentinel*, April 15, 1871 (2:4)

Santa Cruz Railroad.

D. S. Payne, Esq: Chairman of meeting of the citizens of San Jose, March 29th, for the purpose of appointing a Committee to visit Santa Cruz and confer with the citizens of that place relative to the construction of a railroad from San Jose to Santa Cruz, etc: *Sir*: Mr. T. Fallon and myself of the Committee appointed at said meeting have the honor to report that on Thursday, 6th of April, we visited Santa Cruz, and on the 7th had a talk with some of her most prominent and wealthy citizens, and principal men now engaged in a survey preparatory to the construction of a railroad up the San Lorenzo river. A deep feeling was manifested favorable to the project, and a meeting was held at the office of Dr. Peabody, and a resolution passed to have a Committee of five appointed, with power to meet a like Committee appointed by the citizens of San Jose, some time that may be agreed upon by said Committees for the purpose of a speedy organization of the citizens of the two places, and to take necessary steps for establishing the most practicable route for the construction of the proposed railroad. We would therefore suggest the importance of calling a meeting of the citizens of San Jose and vicinity to appoint a committee to meet the following named gentlemen, who constitute the Committee from Santa Cruz: F. A. Hihn, Henry Philip, L. Heath, E. L. Williams, Dr. Peabody. Hoping the people of both counties will enter zealously into the cause and unite their energies that they may result in successfully carrying out the projected enterprise, I am, sir, respectfully, &c. S. A. Bishop.

234. *Santa Cruz Sentinel*, April 15, 1871 (2:4)

April 12th.—An adjourned meeting of the Company was held at 2 P.M. at the office of D. S. Payne, Esq., to receive the report of the Committee appointed at a previous meeting to visit Santa Cruz and confer with the leading citizens regarding the practicability of the scheme. Payne in the chair and Tyler Beach, Secretary. S. A. Bishop made the report which has already been published in the *Independent*. Moved and carried that a Committee of five be appointed to meet the Committee from Santa Cruz to carry out the objects, for which they were appointed. S. A. Bishop, J. J.

Denny, Tyler Beach, Thomas Fallon and D. J. Porter were appointed as the committee, who are instructed to meet the Santa Cruz men, and if found practicable to join with them in forming a Company to build a railroad; also to raise money by subscription to pay for making the preliminary survey, etc.; adjourned.

235. *Santa Cruz Sentinel*, April 15, 1871 (3:1)

H. W. McKoy has opened a blacksmith shop in Felton, of which an advertisement will speak so soon as he can perfect his plans. On the completion of the San Lorenzo Railroad Felton will be one of the most thriving towns in the State.

236. *The Pajaronian*, April 20, 1871 (2:1)

Railroads.

All sorts of rumors are abroad in regard to the Southern Pacific railroad. The latest news is to the effect that the first section southward from Gilroy is being pushed ahead rapidly, and will be finished in a few months. A large depot is being erected at Hollister, and all is excitement in the latter town. But a short time will elapse, from present indications, before the Southern Pacific will be completed.

The talk of a railroad from Santa Cruz to San Jose, seems to become more and more serious from day to day. If we may judge from the character of the men at the head of the enterprise, there will be no halting, and the coming year will witness the completion of this road, thereby adding vastly to the wealth and importance of both counties.

The idea of a road from Gilroy to Watsonville has not died out. The company is still in existence, and the plan is as feasible as ever.

There is serious talk among business men of a road from Watsonville to Santa Cruz, in the event of the Santa Cruz and San Jose road being completed.

237. *The Railroad Gazette*, April 22, 1871 (45)

The San Lorenzo Valley Railroad Company was incorporated on the 11th ult. A road is to be built from Santa Cruz up the Lorenzo Valley and over to Santa Clara Valley. The connection of San Jose with Alviso and Deep Water has long been talked of, and it is said that the California Pacific intend taking hold of the project.

238. *Santa Cruz Sentinel*, April 22, 1871 (1:7)

New Incorporation of the Southern Pacific Railroad of California.

Sacramento, April 15th, '71.—There was filed to-day in the Secretary of State's Office an amended certificate of incorporation of the Southern Pacific Railroad Company, The directors of the new Corporation are Lloyd Tevis, Leland Stanford, Chas. Crocker, C. P. Huntington, Mark Hopkins, Charles Mayne and Peter Donahue. The capital stock is $70,000,000, divided into shares of $100 each, that sum being the actual contemplated cost of the railroad, including telegraph lines, rolling stock, motive power, shops, depots, etc. The object and purpose of the new corporation is to purchase, construct, own, maintain and operate a continuous line of railroad from the City of San Francisco, through the counties of San Mateo, Santa Clara, Monterey, Fresno, Kern, Tulare, San Bernardino and San Diego to some point on the Colorado River, distant 720 miles, as near as may be, from the point of beginning; also a branch road from Tehachape Pass, *via* Los Angeles, to the Texas Pacific Railroad, at or near the Colorado River, distant 324 miles; also a line from Gilroy in Santa Clara, and passing through Santa Cruz and Monterey counties to Salinas City, or some point near it, 45 miles; also such other branches as the directors may hereafter deem advantageous. The certificate is lengthy, and recites ample provisions agreed to the contracting parties for conservation of stockholders' rights in all corporations, consolidating and amalgamating therein necessary instruments duly enacted on the 11th instant., by Charles Crocker, President, and J. L. Welcutt, Secretary of the Southern Pacific Railroad. The other contracting parties, are the San Francisco and San Jose Railroad Company, and the Santa Clara and Pajaro Valley Railroad Company.

239. *San Jose* **Independent, April 15, via the** *Santa Cruz Sentinel*, **April 22, 1871** (1:7)

SANTA CRUZ RAILROAD.—At the last meeting of our leading citizens interested in the proposed construction of a railroad to Santa Cruz, a Committee of five was appointed, consisting of A. Poster, D. K. Porter, S. A.

Bishop, Thomas Fallon and Tylor Beach, to confer with a like number of Santa Cruzans on the practicability of the scheme. Yesterday the Santa Cruz delegation met at the Common Council room, City Hall. D. S. Payne took the chair and precisely stated the object that call them together, which was mainly to determine whether it would be advisable to incorporate a company. Considerable discussion ensued, some thinking an immediate survey should be made, and a preliminary organization perfected. A survey of three or four routes over the mountains would cost about $2,000. The company at Santa Cruz had already, before conferring with any of our citizens, a road in contemplation, to the San Lorenzo, sixteen miles beyond Santa Cruz; but they were willing to have a thorough survey and adopt any route that would prove the most advantageous to both cities. They were willing to stand half the expense incurred in surveying. Work should be commenced at once, in order that they join in with other contemplated railroads. Dr. W. F. Peabody and F. A. Hihn, of Santa Cruz, and S. A. Bishop and D. S. Payne, of San Jose, were appointed an Executive Committee, and are directed at an early moment to have preliminary lines run across the mountains to determine the most practicable route and take such steps as are necessary for a permanent organization.

240. *Santa Cruz Sentinel,* April 22, 1871 (1:7)

GRANITE.—We learn from one who knows whereof he speaks, that there are vast undeveloped granite ledges in the Santa Cruz mountains, near the proposed line of the railroad. At present the great expense that would be entailed by the cost of transportation, renders them almost valueless. The opening of the road, however, will develop the region about, and another avenue of trade will be opened to the State. This, with the gold mines that are said to exist there, will help to build up the enterprise and render it a paying investment.

241. *Santa Cruz Sentinel*, April 22, 1871 (2:2)

Railroad Survey.—On Thursday night the surveyors completed the survey of one of the proposed routes of the new railroad. It will run from Gann's house across the river to Kron's tannery; thence along the powder mill road to the house of William Corey. The engineer is somewhat in doubt whether to go around the bluff at this point, or whether to tunnel through it. If they decide upon the latter, the road will come out near Diesing's brewery; thence along by Scott's stable, down Rincon street near I. Hihn's barn to Chestnut street; thence down Chestnut street to the lagoon, one hundred feet to the left of Blackburn's old house; thence along the lagoon to the road passing under the bridge and along the brow of the hill past the residence of Mrs. Richards, to the powder mill wharf. Chief Engineer Stangroom has expressed the opinion that this the most feasible route yet surveyed, although the distance is eleven hundred feet greater. Another route has been surveyed around the bluff by Jones' house; thence to the powder mill wharf.

242. *Daily Alta California*, April 19, via the *Santa Cruz Sentinel*, April 22, 1871 (3:3)

Narrow Gauge Railroad.
A Coast Line from San Francisco to Los Angeles, and from Thence to the Colorado River.

The subject of narrow gauge railroads after a thorough ventilation, has received the endorsement of railroad builders, and capitalists are now prepared to invest in narrow gauge roads. Soon we may expect to see a meshwork of them over the whole country. A party of Eastern capitalists have decided to build, if it shall be found practicable, a narrow gauge railroad from San Francisco down the coast to Santa Cruz, San Luis Obispo, Santa Barbara, San Buenaventura and Los Angeles, and from there to the Colorado River. A surveying party of about twenty persons, under E. N. Robinson, Esq., Civil Engineer, started from this city a few days since to survey the route. They had arrived at Point Pedro yesterday, and will pus the work through as rapidly as possibly. Of the feasibility of building the road there seems to be no doubt. There will be but little grading required between here and Los Angeles, as the road will keep close to the beach most of the way down. Innumerable valleys will thus find an outlet, and without doubt the road will have all it can do to transport the fairy and farm products, grain, wool, hides, timber, etc., which will be offered. We trust the report of the Engineer will be such that it may be deemed advisable to commence the work of construction at once.

243. *San Mateo County Gazette*, April 22, 1871 (2:2)

Santa Cruz Railroad.

The San Jose people are moving in the matter of building a railroad from San Jose to Santa Cruz, and from present indications it seems quite probably that the road will be built within a short time—either by the way of Felton on the San Lorenzo creek; or by the way of Soquel.—The Santa Cruz people have already decided to build a road from Santa Cruz up the San Lorenzo to Felton, a distance of 16 miles, and the San Jose folks are talking about connecting with this road and thus bring the Santa Cruz lumber trade into San Jose. In reference to this project, the *Santa Cruz Times* of last week says among other things:

"It is highly probable that the activity exhibited by San Jose and her determined effort to build this road will arouse and stimulate the people of San Mateo, Redwood city, and Mayfield to a vigorous effort to build a road to the terminus of the San Lorenzo Valley Railroad, in order to secure the travel and freight in their direction, and thus whatever may be done in the matter will result in good to this section, and establishes the fact as inevitable that one if not both of these roads will be speedily opened, thus justifying the prediction that the future of Santa Cruz is filled with bright prospects of wealth and prosperity in the railroad era now dawning upon her."

If any one who was not pecuniarily interested in the prosperity and business of San Jose, contemplated the construction of a railroad from the line of the Southern Pacific road to connect with the Santa Cruz road at Felton, they

The Dream of Steam, 1854–1873

would never think of starting at San Jose, for the reason that it is entirely out of the direct route from Felton to San Francisco. As a matter of fact, Felton is but little (if any) further from San Francisco in a direct line than is San Jose from San Francisco, and parties who are familiar with the topography of the country say that the distance between Redwood City and Felton is no greater than it is between San Jose and Felton; If this is so, then it would seem that this is the proper point for making the connection with the S. P. R. R. by the Santa Cruz people, as they will save at least 18 or 20 miles in the distance between Santa Cruz and San Francisco, besides one hour in time. The San Jose movement is really a thrust at the S. P. R. R. for it is a part of the programme to run the road to Alviso and there connect with a line of fast steamers to San Francisco and thus turn the travel and freight of Santa Cruz county as well as that of a portion of Santa Clara, by the bay route. This being the programme, would it not be a good idea for the S. P. R. R. to step in and build a road from Redwood City to Felton, or Santa Cruz and thereby gobble up the Santa Cruz trade at one stroke. As an investment, there is no doubt but what it would pay a handsome sum to stockholders. San Mateo county could well afford to donate its $56,000 worth of stock in the S. F. & J. S. R. R. to an enterprise of this kind, for there would be four or five times that amount of money expended in the construction of the road in this county. The Santa Cruz and San Jose people are calculating upon assistance from the California Pacific Co. in the construction of their proposed road, and if the Southern Pacific wish to head off the California Pacific, their only show is to chip in for the Santa Cruz trade in the manner suggested. We hope to see a movement set on foot by our citizens for the immediate organization of a Co. with a view of putting through a railroad from Redwood City or Menlo park to Santa Cruz—or to form a connection with the Felton road. It will open up one of the most valuable and extensive timber sections in the whole State of California, and before the road has been in operation for twelve months, the value of the lumber brought out of the redwoods would amount to more than the cost of building the road. By all means let us have a railroad to Santa Cruz.

244. *The Pajaronian*, April 27, 1871 (2:2)
Railroad Matters.

The San Lorenzo railroad is progressing finely. We conversed with leading railroad men in Santa Cruz, a few days since, and all seemed to be hopeful and enthusiastic. The prospects of a road from San Jose to Santa Cruz were never better than now, but whether anything can be accomplished this season or not, beyond completing surveys, we are unable to say. Business men, however, have at length come to the conclusion that Santa Cruz county can be profitably connected with the markets of the State by rail, and that the enterprise will be a profitable one on the part of the projectors. Messrs. Hihn, Phillip, Heath, Peabody and Williams, are making strenuous efforts in the matter, and their labors are seconded by live men in Santa Clara county. The time is rapidly approaching when the iron horse will go bounding through our valley, like a thing of life, and improvements, and verdure and population, will take the place of solitude and desolation.

245. *The Pajaronian*, April 27, 1871 (2:3)
Southern Pacific Railroad.

Work commenced on this road on the 13th inst., at Gilroy. The road will pass through Hollister, near which place a large force is employed. Constant additions are being made to the 500 men and 150 horses now at work and a lively time has taken the place of idleness and quietude. The road will run in the direction of Watsonville, a distance of five miles, crossing the Pajaro river, it is thought about the fourth or fifth of May. Thus it will be seen we are brought within fourteen miles of road to connect the Pajaro valley with San Francisco by rail! The crops will be good this year, and the prospects for money making with all classes is good. Hence we feel that some effort will be put forth to build a road from Watsonville to the Southern Pacific—a move sadly needed as all will agree.

246. *Santa Cruz Sentinel*, April 29, 1871 (2:1)
The Railroad.—The surveyors, Mr. Stangroom and assistants, having completed the survey of the San Lorenzo Valley Railroad, the President of the Company is busy maturing the arrangements for an early commencement of the work. From the Paper Mill down to the beach, two routes were surveyed with deviations, one on each side of the river, and it has not been decided on which side the road will be built,

as the right of way must first be secured on both sides before the Board of Directors will act on the matter and finally locate the road. The San Jose people are making an effort to connect their road with the San Lorenzo road, but no decided action has as yet been taken by the latter company. Over $1,000 have been subscribed in San Jose, to make the proper survey and the services of a Mr. Arnold has been solicited to do the work. We are informed that it was the intention that Mr. Stangroom, and his efficient corps of engineers and assistants, would proceed to do the work, but we regret to say other engagements prevented the principal from accepting the proposition and we thus failed to secure his valuable services. According to the San Jose papers, the San Jose and Santa Cruz Railroad will be built in a very short period of time. May this be so in the wish of every one interested in the welfare of our mountain county.

247. *San Jose Mercury*, May 10, via the *Santa Cruz Sentinel*, May 13, 1871 (2:4)

Preliminary Survey.

Wm. J. Lewis, a first class railroad engineer and surveyor, has been secured to make the preliminary surveys for the San Jose and Santa Cruz Railroad. He was the superintending engineer of the Central Pacific Railroad, and is well known throughout the Coast as a master in his profession. A party of observation, merely, accompanied by Mr. Lewis, left this city yesterday for the Summit, where they will be joined by a like party from Santa Cruz. They will spend the remainder of the week in the hills, examining the various routes proposed and suggested, with a view to ascertain which are the most suitable and practicable for surveys. This done, there will be no delay in pushing the work promptly. The *Patriot* learns that the party will return to San Jose on Saturday or Sunday, when the regular surveying party will be organized at once. It will consist of Mr. Lewis, chief engineer, and his assistant, with the necessary chain men, flagmen, axemen, teamsters, teams, and the usual outfit of such business. The estimated cost of the survey (including three or four different routes) is from $1,5000 to $2,000; not to exceed the latter amount. The survey will begin on this side of the mountains, and Mr. Lewis is confident that he can complete the work in thirty days. Judge Payne, of the Executive Committee, is in receipt of letters from F. A. Hihn and others in Santa Cruz, Expressing the most favorable hopes for the enterprise.

248. *San Francisco Examiner*, May 15, 1871 (1:1)

Railroad Survey—Etc.

Santa Cruz, May 13.—The southern coast railroad surveying party, E. N. Robinson, chief engineer, arrived here this evening. The party have followed the line of the coast from San Francisco to this city. They report favorably as to the practicability of a narrow gauge railroad on that route.

249. *The Pajaronian*, May 18, 1871 (2:1)

Railroad Prospects.

From present indications, the prospects for a railroad

to this place are better than ever before. Ex-Governor Stanford, his brother and two other gentlemen were in town a few days since on business connected with railroad matters. From here they went to the Salinas, thence back to Gilroy. The road now being constructed to Hollister, from Gilroy, is completed to a point within 14 miles of Watsonville, and it is said that as soon as Hollister is reached, the whole force of workmen will be put on a road to this valley. Atherton has lately purchased land in this valley to the amount of $13,000, which fact is of itself highly suggestive. Other movements are being made, all tending to the same result—a railroad.

250. *San Jose Independent* via *The Pajaronian*, May 18, 1871 (3:1)

Santa Cruz Railroad.—The prospects of a railroad connecting San Jose with Santa Cruz, at the present time are flattering. The necessary subscription for the purpose of completing the survey, has been raised, and Mr. S. A. Bishop, one of the prime movers in the enterprise, and an energetic businessman withal, is now in San Francisco, negotiating with Mr. W. J. Lewis for taking the contract of the survey. Mr. Arnold failed to come to time, but should the company be fortunate enough to secure the services of Mr. Lewis, we may expect a careful survey, as that gentleman has made railroad surveys a specialty.

251. *Santa Cruz Sentinel*, May 20, 1871 (2:2)
Railroads.

That this is the age of railroads, we verily believe, and that Santa Cruz is not behind the age, may be inferred from the fact that there is not less than three different companies surveying roads in the county, connecting this town with all the world and the rest of mankind outside of our mountain and sea bound valley. First in importance is the Narrow Gauge Railroad of Robinson & Co., an English firm of immense wealth, seeking investments in railroads in California. This firm, it is said, have £80,000 subscribed to put into railroad improvements on the coast. The road will be a 3-feet-gauge, and will not, at any place, leave the water line over two miles, until they strike the Salinas, when they may keep that valley to San Miguel, crossing the divide to Santa Marguerita and other little valleys in that direction to the Santa Clara or Saticoy, and thence to Los Angeles or San Pedro, following the coast to San Diego, and eventually to Cape St. Lucas. Another branch will go to the Colorado, and thence down the Mexican coast to different points where interest or trade may direct. On Saturday last the engineers, going south, passed through Santa Cruz, making what is called a working survey. The line of road passes on the street north of the salt petre warehouse, at the powder mill wharf, and thence across the San Lorenzo river, south of Wood's Laguna, at the forks; thence to Soquel on a line with the Santa Clara and Santa Cruz railroad. The company will proceed as rapidly as possible, south, until they meet a similar company coming north, when each company will proceed on and revise each other's work, and report as soon as possible. It is said that the first section of the road, built, will be from Santa Cruz to Watsonville, and that the work will be commenced within one year. Some of the wealthiest men in the State and some of the heavy capitalists of San Francisco, are interested in the work and hold a large number of shares. It is said that Stanford and Crocker visited Watsonville last week, to prospect the chances for their road in that direction. The fact is, that unless the Southern Pacific railroad take the Salinas and coast route, the English company will tap their resources and take a fair share of their trade. As soon as the survey is made, we will give full particulars. On Wednesday last the San Jose and Santa Cruz Railroad Engineers, under the direction of Mr. W. J. Lewis, started from San Jose, to run the line *via* Soquel creek, to Santa Cruz, crossing the mountain near Burrell's farm. At the same time Mr. Thomas Wright, with another party, started from Soquel beach (tide water) to take the elevation from that point to the top of the divide. The route had previously been surveyed from Santa Cruz to Soquel. The road courses on the west side of the Soquel creek and passes near the road, through Barker's orchard, and in front of the Mason Grove Hotel. The elevation at that point is 219 feet, and 310 feet at the south corner of Cahoon's field (orchard) 60 feet north of the main road. The company were at work--eight men with teams and all necessary equipments for a thorough outfit--and it will be but a few days before we will be enabled to give all the particulars to our readers. The San Lorenzo and Santa Cruz Railroad Company, having completed their survey, are now busy securing the right of way, on both sides of the river, and will soon determine on which side it will be built. It is proposed to connect with the San Jose road, at or near the landing, but no definite action has yet been taken in the matter. As soon as the surveys are made and reports received from the engineers now running the lines over the divides at the head waters of the Soquel and Los Gatos creeks, a meeting will be held and then may be developed the route adopted and time of commencement.

252. *San Jose Independent*, May 18, via the *Santa Cruz Sentinel*, May 20, 1871 (2:4)

Santa Cruz Railroad.—The ball has at last started to rolling, and the work towards the construction of a railroad to Santa Cruz has commenced in earnest at last. The surveying party headed by Wm. J. Lewis Chief Engineer, John W. Johnson Assistant and eight others, started yesterday morning. The work will be hurried as fast as possible, and the most available route selected, without regard to favoritism. On this side of the mountains the party will be supplied by the San Jose delegation, on the other side by the Santa Cruzans, who are more solicitous for the railroad than even the people of San Jose. Mr. Lewis is a most competent engineer, and will manage the work carefully, and expeditiously. The road from San Francisco down the coast has commenced and there will be rank opposition, if any delay should arise on our side. So hurry up gentlemen and don't be laggards.

253. *San Francisco Bulletin* via the *Santa Cruz Sentinel,* May 20, 1871 (4:1)

Santa Cruz.
RAILROAD PROJECTS—THE REDWOOD FORESTS—
BEAUTIFUL SCENERY—NEED OF RAILROAD
COMMUNICATION WITH SAN FRANCISCO.
Santa Cruz, May 6th.

The commencement of work on the Southern Pacific railroad, and the agitation of various railroad schemes, have thoroughly awakened the town to the necessity of railroad communication with San Francisco. Everybody is in favor of a railroad connection with the Southern Pacific line, either at Gilroy, San Jose or San Mateo; but there seems to be no unity of opinion as to how it is to be made, who is to build it, or exactly where the money is to come from. It is proposed that the people of the two counties of Santa Clara and Santa Cruz should subscribe the money and build a road from San Jose; but the proposition, which was at first warmly received, does not seem likely to be carried out. The prevailing impression is that this would be the best plan, but somehow such projects never come to a head. After many meetings are held, articles are printed and speeches are made, and everybody is a unit for the scheme, it is discovered that Mr. A., a prominent citizen, is waiting to see what Mr. B. will subscribe. Mr. B. has his eye on Mr. A. for the same purpose, while Mr. C. watches both, and it finally ends in nothing being done. Local or private jealousy also often tend to produce this result.

Narrow Gauge Railroad and the San Lorenzo Valley.

I am assured, however, that a narrow gauge railroad, twenty miles in length, will be built northward on the San

Lorenzo Valley in which are some of the finest and largest red wood forests on the coast, and where there is the unfailing water power of the San Lorenzo river. The powder mills (with a capacity of 100 horse power) several tanneries and other manufactories are driven by this water power. Mr. Hihn, a twenty years resident of the county, assured me that there is plenty of room and water power for at least twenty other manufactories on the San Lorenzo river. The lumber mills of the San Lorenzo valley have a capacity of 100,000 feet per day, while those of the entire county have a capacity of 250,000 feet per day. The narrow gauge road through the San Lorenzo Valley would be a great aid to the local manufactories and be of vast service in developing the lumber interest, which is now in a very dull state, owing to low prices and small demand. In fact, from what I can gather here about prices, an advance on late city rates for redwood was really necessary, to allow lumber dealers and saw mills to live. The state of the market was tersely described to me by a store-keeper, who likewise owns some 30,000 acres of the surrounding land, which is mostly covered with red-wood timber.

Are the redwood forests being thinned out?

I had always heard and believed that the redwood forests of the Coast Range were being rapidly thinned out, but this statement Mr. John contradicts. He says that, in the vicinity of Santa Cruz the trees perpetuate themselves rapidly, unlike the pine, the redwood grows again from the stump. Mr. Hihn says there are plenty of trees here only fourteen years old which have diameter of fourteen inches and a circumference of forty-two inches.

Fifteen years ago the people of Santa Cruz county, he says, thought the tan bark or chestnut oak would soon give out, although its consumption in county tanneries was then but about 200 cords per year; now the local consumption and export is about 4,000 cords per year, yet the trees are as plenty as ever, the tan bark oaks like the redwood growing from the stump. Mr. Hihn thinks it would take sixty years at the present rate of consumption to cut down all the magnificent redwood forests of this county, and that the new growth will supply the waste. Redwood land is worth $2 to $10 per acre, but where rods are open and the location for shipment is good, it is worth $20 per acre. This last is an extreme price, and $10 per acre would be about the average. In many places in the San Lorenzo cañon, between Felton and Santa Cruz, the trees seemed to stud the ground as thickly as there was room to stand, I was glad to learn that these beautiful rain and fog condensers, which are the renowned guardian of our climate and agriculture, are in no danger of being thinned out.

How a railroad would develop manufacturing and lumbering interests.

When a railroad connects Santa Cruz and Watsonville with the Southern Pacific line, the water power manufactories of Santa Cruz and its lumbering interests must all receive a great impetus. In fact, I am quite sure that this country will then quickly become one of the richest and most prosperous counties of the State. Its forests are inexhaustible and their redwood of the best quality; its water power is extensive and unfailing, and as yet very little used; its ocean bathing is refreshing and strengthening; its scenery is always delightfully varies and beautiful, and occasionally rises into mountain grandeur. The sides of its mountains are generally draped in that undefinable purple haze, which would soften even the rugged features of granite, and which in this country makes Nature's beautiful face still more attractive and charming. Santa Cruz county is noted for good fishing and shooting. Trout still abound in its rivers, and deer, rabbit, quail and other game are plenty in its mountains, where bears are not yet strangers by any means. No county affords greater attraction to campers out.

Difficulty of access—beautiful scenery.

The great drawback is the necessity of stage riding from the Southern Pacific lines. This mode of travel the majority of men naturally dislike, while women detest it. I avoided staging to Pescadero last year by hiring a buggy in the city and driving through to and back from the pebbly beach and other attractions of that place, and this year I also avoided staging. I came through to Gilroy on the Southern Pacific cars, and hired a two-seated and two-horse buggy at the Gilroy livery stables of Dustin & Co., paying therefor but $5 per day. The city charge would be $10 to $15 per day, and the horses would be no faster, stronger or more gentle, and the general outfit any more comfortable and strong than that I secured at Gilroy. I drove to Santa Cruz *via*. San Juan, and will return *via*. Watsonville and the mountain stage road. The views from the top of the mountain on the latter are really grand, and few can be more varied and beautiful. The whole Pajaro Valley, from the mountains to the Pacific ocean, is spread beneath the feet, while in intervening lie tier

after tier of swelling hills, light and dark-green vales, and rugged and sombre tree-clad mountain dells. At least a week may be spent in drives around Santa Cruz. I could only spend one day there, which I occupied in a drive to the Big Tree Grove, returning to town by way of Felton and the San Lorenzo toll road. Some of the views down the depths of the San Lorenzo Cañon somewhat remind one of the grand sights from the Central Pacific Railroad line at Cape Horn.
Cheap traveling.

The cost of board and stabling for the horses is but $2 to $3 per day, and the hotel fare $2 to 2½ per day. A Party of four, with one or two children, can make such a week's trip for $30 to $35 each, while if they camp out and fish and shoot, they can make it for considerably less. A party with a buggy can start and stop when and where they please, and have a freedom, ease and enjoyment to which those who travel in stages are strangers.

A proposition by the Southern Pacific Railroad Company.

Santa Cruz can never rise to the importance to which it is entitled as a watering place and center of county manufactories until it secures railroad connection with San Francisco, at some point on the Southern Pacific line. I was told that the Southern Pacific Railroad Company has made a proposition to the people to build a road to Watsonville and Santa Cruz, which proposition is said to be reasonable, and should, and probably will be accepted. Such a road must soon be built, as it would add at least 30 per cent. to the traffic of the Southern Pacific line, while it would bring ten visitors where there is now one to Santa Cruz, and would quadruple the number of county manufactories and population within three years.

An attractive town.

There are few more attractive towns than Santa Cruz. It has everything that is needed to please the eye, engage the angler and sportsman, improve the health, and delight the swimmer. The Marine Insurance Companies of San Francisco recommend its selection by Congress as a harbor of refuge, there being no bar to cross. If this recommendation is acted upon, a large expenditure for a breakwater will be made. Santa Cruz only needs a railroad to place it in the foremost rank of society.

254. *San Jose Independent* via the *Santa Cruz Sentinel*, May 20, 1871 (4:2)

Santa Cruz Railroad.

The Committee appointed by the citizens of Santa Cruz and San Jose to have an examination made to ascertain the practicability of a railroad between the two cities, having secured the services of Wm. J. Lewis, who was formerly engineer of the three railroads terminating in this city, are prosecuting their duties with commendable diligence. Bishop and Beach of San Jose, with engineer Lewis, proceeded this week to make a reconnaissance of the lines on this side of the dividing ridge of the Santa Cruz Mountains, being met by agreement on the summit by Hihn, Kirby and Wright in Santa Cruz. They returned on Friday afternoon and report that there is no doubt about the practicability of the route for a narrow gauge railroad at a moderate expense, and with moderate grades by two or three different passes. Leaving

San Jose they crossed the almost level Valley of Santa Clara, to the foot of the hills at the village of Los Gatos, and thence passed up the west bank of Los Gatos creek along the toll road to the summit of the dividing ridge between Santa Clara Valley and the Pacific Ocean, which is at this point the divide between Los Gatos and Soquel creeks. The roll road first reaches this summit at Shulties' house, seven and three-fourths miles from the Ten Mile House, which is about one-quarter of a mile beyond the village of Los Gatos. The heights above the level of tide water at Shulties' Pass, at Taylor's Pass on the Toll road, about a mile beyond, where the toll road leaves the dividing ridge, and at Burrell's Pass, about three-fourths of a mile southerly of Taylor's, were also examined. These are the passes between the Los Gatos and Soquel creeks, and all of them are practicable; but which is preferable can only be determined by careful surveys. The gentlemen then proceeded westward along the crest of the Santa Cruz Mountains and examined several passes between the tributaries of Los Gatos creek and those of Soquel, Bear, Shearer's Gulch and Zayante creeks, and attempted to reach the head of Campbell's creek, which is opposite the head of the San Lorenzo creek, but found the ground along the crest of the ridge so difficult to pass over in any way that they concluded to make a separate examination of this pass by passing up Campbell's creek, from McCartysville to the summit. This they will do the coming week. Burrell's Pass is the lowest, Taylor's and Shulties' a little higher, and the passes west of Shulties' increasing in elevation as they proceed westward. The practicability of the route having been ascertained, two parties of engineers under Col. Lewis' direction, have been organized, one of which will start from San Jose and the other from Santa Cruz, uniting at the summit, and from the report of the two parties on the approach to the summit, the most advantageous route will be ascertained.

255. *The Pajaronian*, May 25, 1871 (2:1)
Narrow Gauge Railroad.

On Saturday a party of railroad surveyors, arrived in town, with their various wagons and other paraphernalia. This party are engaged in surveying a narrow gauge railroad from San Francisco to San Diego and beyond. We believe the enterprise is backed up by a wealthy English Company. It is their design to pass through all the Coast counties, touching at the various towns on the route, which will make the road one of great convenience and importance. The cost of such a road is hardly more than half of the ordinary railroads per mile, and in a style of road fast becoming very popular not only in Europe but in the United States. We cannot give any particular encouragement to our readers in regard to the construction of this road, but they Surveyors spoke in the highest terms of the feasibility of the route from the city to this place. It will be sometime before their report is ready, which, if favorable, will doubtless be accepted by the company, and work commenced. Indications are growing stronger and stronger for a railroad to this section—either the one mentioned above, or a branch from the Southern Pacific.

256. *San Jose Guide,* May 22, via the *Santa Cruz Sentinel,* May 27, 1871 (3:1)

END OF THE SURVEY.—We learn from M. Bishop that the survey of the route for the new railroad between San Jose and Santa Cruz, will be completed during the latter part of the week. Everything has progressed satisfactorily thus far. The altitude on this side is far below the grade expected, and will make the expense of construction considerably less than was anticipated.

257. *The Pajaronian,* June 1, 1871 (2:2)

Railroad.

We learn that prominent citizens of this valley are now endeavoring to raise a certain amount of money by subscription as a subsidy to the Southern Pacific Railroad, in order to induce the Company to run a branch road from Sargents' place near Gilroy, to this town. Whether the enterprise will succeed, we can form no definite idea, but from the character of the men at work, we have strong hopes that something will be accomplished. We have before expatiated on the benefits of a road, and have used our best arguments to induce subscriptions toward a road, feeling certain that each man's subscription would be returned to him four-fold. From present indications farmers in this section will do well, financially, this year, and this fact in itself is encouraging, as far as a road is concerned, for it is natural to suppose that farmers who have cash on hand will not so far forget their own interests as to refuse aid toward a road to this place, if called upon to do so. Perhaps by next week we may be enabled to say something definite in regard to the subject.

258. *Santa Cruz Sentinel*, June 3, 1871 (2:2)

Railroad Survey.—The Santa Cruz and San Jose Railroad Engineers are now below the Mason Grove Hotel, surveying a working grade to Soquel landing and Santa Cruz. They will be here next week.

259. *Santa Cruz Sentinel*, June 3, 1871 (3:2)

[Concerning the completion of the Saratoga Toll Road]

Soon there will be a post office established at or near the mouth of Bear and Boulder Creeks, and a village will spring up in that locality, making three post offices on the route, viz: Saratoga, Sylvey's and Felton. It will not be long before the San Lorenzo Railroad will be under contract, when an increased number of settlers may locate in the vicinity of king's farm and all along the timbered belt east and west of the valley.

260. *San Jose Independent*, May 28, via the *Santa Cruz Sentinel*, June 3, 1871 (3:2)

Santa Cruz Railroad.

The surveying party are over the summit and their wants are now attended to by the Santa Cruz delegation. There is much work yet to be done, and several weeks will probably elapse before the final report is handed in. The most available and practicable route seems to be that passing through Taylor's Pass. The altitude here is not so great as in other places, and the distance is said to be shorter. By this route the coast will be reached near Soquel. Another road, taking off a small portion of Scott's Valley, passing through Felton and crossing the San Lorenzo, is yet to be surveyed. Besides these two routes there is yet the Saratoga line to be surveyed, and considerable influence will probably be brought to bear by the interested ones in that region. The intentions of the company however are to select the best and most practicable route, without favoritism or ex parte motives. The projectors of the enterprise have got to work hard and sleep not to carry the scheme into successful execution. Some opposition will be met with, but with the energy, capital and brains that our railroad men possess, we do not fear the result.

261. *Santa Cruz Sentinel*, June 3, 1871 (3:2)

[Concerning the opening of the Saratoga Turnpike]

It will not be long before the San Lorenzo Railroad will be under contract, when an increased number of settlers may locate in the vicinity of King's farm and all along the timbered belt east and west of the valley.

262. *The Pajaronian*, June 8, 1871 (2:2)
Railroads.

During the last week this town and vicinity has been in a foment in regard to railroad matters. A few days since endeavors were made to raise some $50,000 to offer to the Southern Pacific Railroad Co., as an inducement to run a branch road to this town or to some point near by, and the subscriptions reached something over $8,000, when another paper came before the people, representing that if $50,000 was subscribed, the road would be run into this valley, but the depot was to be a mile and a half from the center of town, or a mile from the opposite, or Monterey side of the Pajaro river. As this latter was a new phase of the railroad question, the people of Watsonville, and surrounding country on the Santa Cruz side of the river, concluded to wait before subscribing more, until the matter could be more fully understood. Large subscriptions could be raised here in case the Company run the road on this side of the river, or even half a mile from the other side, but they did not feel so much like expending their money for a road that was to run and have the depot over 1½ miles from the center of the town of Watsonville. Hence the matter at this writing remains in abeyance.

In Santa Cruz, which place we visited on Tuesday last, the subject of railroads is the all-absorbing topic, and matters are at present in a flattering light, as regards the San Lorenzo road, as well as the proposed narrow gauge road from that part of the county to San Jose. We were informed by Dr. Peabody, one of the principal movers in railroad matters at that place, that the surveys for the latter road show conclusively its practicability. The former road, from all we could learn during the short time we remained, will soon be commenced, as a large portion of the stock is taken, and the company is composed of enterprising men. Since our item two or three weeks since about the arrival of the surveyors, employed by the English Company to survey narrow gauge road from San Francisco through all the east counties, we have heard nothing from them, but presume by this time they are somewhere in San Luis Obispo county.

263. *Santa Cruz Sentinel*, June 10, 1871 (2:2)

We are in Watsonville, the commercial center of Pajaro, livelier than we ever saw it before, and big with high hopes of railroad and hotel, every business house and residence filled, streets alive with teams and people, and real estate the burden of citizens talk. The residents of this town have long merited two things, a railroad and a first-class hotel. Governor Stanford was in Watsonville some time since, and admitted that he was in what was before to him an unknown country, in the "Garden of the State." Soon after his return to San Francisco a proposition was received from headquarters by the citizens of Watsonville, to have the cars in that place on the first day of September next, if the company was donated $50,000 and the survey of the railroad to near the town of Gilroy. The proposition was entertained, and Chas. Ford is successfully soliciting the required amount.

264. *Santa Cruz Sentinel*, June 10, 1871 (2:4)
Santa Cruz and San Jose Railroad.

The preliminary survey of this road having been completed, and the engineers preparing to report, we have interviewed Mr. T. W. Wright, who kindly furnished the following facts: The road will cross the mountain at Taylor's Pass, (which is near the crossing of the Soquel turnpike road) at an elevation of 1,541 feet, with a tunnel of 2,000 feet. The different passes have the following elevations: Schultie's (one mile west) is 1,592 feet; Burrell's (one mile east of Taylor's) is 1,539, as surveyed. By barometer, the Saratoga Pass is about 2,400 feet, and the pass on Bear creek about 1,800 feet. The preliminary line of the railroad, as surveyed, commences at San Jose and runs in a direct line to Los Gatos, keeping up the west side of Los Gatos creek and ascending the mountain to Taylor's Pass, crossing the divide at an elevation of 1,300 feet, with a tunnel 2,000 feet long through soft clay sandstone, sufficiently strong to stand without being timbered. The route then descends the southern slope of the mountain, at a grade of 132 feet to the mile, crossing the Burrell creek at the Soquel turnpike bridge, at an elevation of 1,210 feet; then following down Burrell's creek and the east side of the west branch of Soquel creek to the crossing of the road above Britton's house; from thence, at a grade of 105 feet to the mile (or 2 feet to the 100 feet) the road crosses the main or east branch of Soquel creek about 200 yards east of the Soquel Lumbering Co.'s sawmill; thence the road continues down the east side of the Soquel creek, at a grade of from 12 to 18 inches to the 100 feet, to a point near Rabel's tannery, from which point two lines of survey have been made to Soquel village, one line crossing near the tannery and running down on the west side, and the other on the east side at a very light grade. From Soquel to the powder-mill wharf at Santa Cruz, the line of survey made by Mr. Watson (of the Coast Line Narrow Gauge R. R.,) has been used.

The line is much better than supposed, and the road can be more easily constructed and at a much less expense than estimated. The shortest curve is 220 feet radius, and the most difficult point to pass is at the cabin of the Samuel boys, where there will either have to be a short tunnel or two bridges. The road has been so located as to make it available to transport all the timber and lumber from Soquel creek and its tributaries. The distance from Taylor's Pass to Soquel town, is 71,300 feet (at 5,280 feet to the mile) or about 13 miles, and from Santa Cruz to Soquel about 4 miles, making the entire distance from Santa Cruz to Taylor's Pass, about 17 miles, and about the same distance, with lighter grades, thence to San Jose—entire distance, about 35 miles. By increasing the tunnel 1,000 feet, the grade of the entire road will be decreased 2 feet on the mile. It is the intention of the company to build the road on a 3-foot, or narrow gauge track, which will enable them to work shorter curves and heavier grades, at a similar expense of construction. Col. Lewis, the chief engineer, having examined all the passes (From the Saratoga pass to Burrell's) finds the Taylor pass the best, and that the road can be constructed by that route at a much lighter cost than any other. The map, profile, estimate of cost and report of engineer, will be returned to the Company in a few days, when we will give a more extended report.

265. *Santa Clara Argus* via the *Santa Cruz Sentinel*, June 10, 1871 (3:3)

Progress of the Survey.—The engineering party of Mr. Lewis passed Taylor's Gap on Wednesday, and are now operating on the other side of the mountain.—The highest point on this route is 1441 feet. If this line is selected, a tunnel 1000 feet in length will be bored. The grade is found much easier than was anticipated.—Messrs. Wright and Bennett, civil engineers, conducted the survey on the Santa Cruz side, and met Mr. Lewis, chief engineer at the summit. The *Patriot* says; "The surveys on each side were made from the level of tide-water, and so remarkably accurate were they that on reaching the summit, and comparing notes of the two surveys, there was found only a difference of four inches and thirty hundredths of an inch in the elevation to be overcome."

266. *The Pajaronian*, June 15, 1871 (2:2)

Railroad.—We have nothing definite in regard to the road coming to this valley, but are informed by Mr. Thrift, that the road is approaching the town—that is, in order to get to San Juan, it is necessary to come three miles nearer Watsonville. This will bring us but eleven miles from the road, and we hardly think the Company will be so blind to their own interests as to go by without touching the Pajaro Valley—the garden spot of California. To sum up all the rumors, about the operations of the Company, we are under a strong conviction that the road is to be run to a point in or near the town of Watsonville.

267. *Daily Alta California* via the *Santa Cruz Sentinel*, June 17, 1871 (1:7)

A COAST LINE RAILROAD.

Letter from Gen. Roscrans—His Idea of the Proposed Enterprise—The Route, Grade, Cost., Etc.

Eds. Alta:—One of our direct needs is a railroad to open the southern coast counties to proper settlement and cultivation. They comprise a belt of land forty or fifty miles wide, and four or five hundred long, diversified with hill, vale, mountain and plain, having a mild, salubrious and most delightful climate. It is adapted to the culture and a great variety of valuable productions, such as wheat, barley, corn, fruits, vines, olives and nuts; to making butter, cheese, wine, dried fruits, silk, etc. But an industrious, intelligent, self-helping population, who can successfully develop these sources of wealth, will not settle in a country without railroads.

Alive to these things, on my return from Mexico in 1869, I endeavored to induce some of our leading San Franciscans to organize a company to secure the speedy construction of such a coast road, and, to save time and talk, prepared and had printed the enclosed statement.

It will be seen from this that I urged Gov. Leland Stanford and his associates to undertake the work; and when they declined for "fear of losing the Tulare lands," elicited from the Governor that, deeming the construction of such a road important for the enterprise of our State and city, he would not oppose, but would favor any organization of citizens which should undertake it.

No effective response to my paper ever came to me before leaving for the East. Our prominent men, whom I conversed with, feared the opposition of the Central, notwithstanding assurances, and thought there was too little prospect of a Southern Overland Railroad, connection with which was deemed essential to the Coast line.

I will not now detail how have been secured Congressional legislation, and a combination of business talent, capital, railway building and managing experience to construct that Southern Overland, unequaled in the world. What I now desire is, through our own press, to say to our fellow citizens that this certainty of the Texas Pacific being speedily built, and Gov. Stanford's assurance that he and his associates would not fight the Coast line, remove wo great obstacles to that much needed work, and that the time has come for the people of San Francisco and the coast counties to lend an effective hand to it.

"The gods help those who help themselves," and now is the time for combined and effective work to ensure that which more than any one thing will benefit San Francisco and the State.

An organization of some of your most respectable and useful citizens called "The California Southern Coast Railroad Company," was formed about a year ago to promote and assure the construction of a coastwise railroad, and has done effective and valuable service, and it is now at work, but needs to aggregate to it all the talent, influence and capital which ought to co-operate and ensure to San Francisco the control of a new avenue to a whole country that will soon fill up the thriving Eastern farmers.

Should prompt action be taken, I shall be glad to help, and think it safe to anticipate early and favorable result.

I hope our local press and the intelligent property-holders will take this matter promptly in hand, and let us show that we are equal to the situation.

W. S. ROSECRANS.

San Rafael, Cal., June 9th, 1871.

Description of the Line.

The following data relative to a route for a railroad from San Jose to Los Angeles is obtained from the report of Lieut. Parke, U. S.A. (vol. vii of *Pacific Railroad Explorations*), and is believed to be, in the main, reliable:

"Beginning at San Jose, the line runs along the Santa Clara Valley (via Gilroy) to the Pajaro River; thence along the Pajaro River (via Watsonville) to Monterey bay, thence around the foot-hills of the Gavilan mountains to the Salinas valley; thence up the valley and along the Salinas river (via Castroville, Salinas City and San Miguel Mission) to the Atascadero Creek; thence up the Atascadero to Santa Margarita valley; thence west of Santa Margarita to the San Luis Pass; thence along San Luis Creek and the Arroyo Grande to a point near the ocean; thence into the Guadalupe Largo; thence through the hills to the east of Point Sal to the Tres Alamos creek; thence down the Tres Alamos to the Jesus Maria Rancho; thence to the Santa Inez river; thence up the Salsipuedes creek to the Santa Cruz Pass; thence down a valley to the mouth of Gaviote creek; thence along the coast to the Mission of San Buenaventura; thence, leaving the coast, it crosses a plain and the Santa Clara river to Semi Pass; thence across the

The Dream of Steam, 1854–1873

San Fernando Plain and following the general direction of the Los Angeles river, to the city of Los Angeles, distant three hundred and ninety-six miles from San Jose."

The line, as above described, can be readily traced on Holt's Map of California.

General Character of the route.

"From San Jose to Santa Margarita valley, 177 miles, the work is very light; and the maximum grade required is but 18 feet to the mile to a point within 7 miles of the valley, where a grade of 70 feet to the mile is required. The work on the next 24½ miles, crossing the San Lis Pass, is very heavy. The elevation of the Santa Margarita valley is 978 feet; of the Pass, 1,556½ feet. Approaching the Pass a grade of 57 feet to the mile for 4 7-10 miles is required. The line then descends on a grade of 160 feet per mile for five miles to San Luis creek; ascends with the same grade for three miles and then descends to the mouth of the Arroyo Grande with two grades, one of 160 feet for 6 miles and one of 70 feet for 5½ miles. From the Arroyo Grande to the Jesus Maria Rancho, 32½ miles, the grades are easy and the cost of graduation moderate. From the Jesus Maria Rancho, the grade for 4 miles is 78½ feet per mile; thence to Santa Cruz Pass, the grades are light. From the Pass descending grade of 100 feet to the mile for 4½ miles is required. A large amount of earthwork and masonry will be required on this division, which is 35½ miles long. The next division (from Gaviote creek to San Buenaventura, 58½ miles) involves a large amount of heavy work. The line is located over an undulating terrace, at an average elevation of 110 feet above tide from Gaviote creek to

El Rincon, where the terrace disappears and the spurs of the Santa Inez mountains impinge upon the sea to within a short distance of the valley of San Buenaventura. From El Rincon to San Buenaventura the location is of a novel character, requiring, for 13 miles, a wall, or something of the nature of a riprap, to protect the road-bed from being undermined and swept away by the sea [this can be avoided—Gen. R.] The maximum grade on this division is 60 feet to the mile.

From San Buenaventura the grade ascends at 73 feet per mile for 5 miles; thence to Los Angeles there is no grade exceeding 32 feet to the mile. The only heavy work between San Buenaventura and Los Angeles—70 miles—is at Semi Pass, where there will be required a tunnel through soft sand-stone rock, 3,960 feet in length and 600 feet below the crest of the ridge. There are 4 grades of 100 feet to the mile, for 5, 3, 6 and 4½ miles, or an aggregate length of 18½ miles; six grades from 63 to 80 feet to the mile, for 28 7-10 miles, and on the remaining 348 8-10 miles, the grade at no point exceeds 40 feet to the mile. From San Jose to Atascadero—170 miles—the highest grade is 18 feet to the mile. The total estimated cost of the road is $19,468,750, which makes the average cost per mile, $49,163. [NOTE—It may be remarked that Lieutenant Parke estimated that part of the road between San Jose and Gilroy to cost $30,000 per mile. The actual cost of such work, including equipment, is less than $18,000 per mile.] No surveys have been made from Los Angeles to San Diego, but it is known that there is no formidable difficulties in the way. The distance is 120 miles. The superiority of the coast line over a line via the Tulare valley is manifest, especially if San Jose or Gilroy is made the starting point. The surveys of Lieutenant Williamson have made known the elevation and impracticability (except by using very high grades) of the passes at the head of the Tulare valley. These passes all lead into and through the deserts of the Great Basin, or involve recrossing the Sierras through New Pass at the head of the Santa Clara river. "Passes at the head of Tulare valley; Canada de las Uvas, elevation 4,256 feet—average grade, 302 feet per mile, for 5¼ miles; Tejon Pass, elevation, 5,285 feet—grades, 234 feet for 11¼ miles, 205 feet for 6¼ miles, 173 feet for 2 83-100 miles. Tunnel at summit, 1 15-100 miles in length."

From Los Angeles to San Diego, by personal inspection, I know three practicable routes, the relative merits of which can be determined by actual survey, viz:

1. From Los Angeles, southeasterly by the Chino Ranch and Laguna to Temecula, and thence via Pala or Santa Margarita canyon to vicinity of Buena Vista, and thence to San Diego.

2. From Los Angeles, via vicinity of Anaheim and the Santa Ana canyon, to Temecula, and thence as before.

3. From Los Angeles, via Anaheim to San Juan Capistrano, and thence to San Mateo, by Mission Vieja de la Paz, and then by the coast, avoiding the undulating table lands, to San Diego.

The total cost of this part of the route will not exceed $30,000 per mile, or $3,600,000. From Gilroy to Los Angeles the road will not, probably, average more, say in round numbers, for road and first equipment, than $12,000,000, or $15,000,000. Allow the San Bernardino branch, or connection with the Southern Overland, to cost $1,400,000, the total cost of the road and branch will be $17,000,000.

268. *San Luis Obispo Tribune*, June 17, via the *Santa Cruz Sentinel*, June 24, 1871 (2:3)

Southern Coast Railroad.

We had the pleasure on Thursday last, of making the acquaintance of Major Watson, the engineer of a new Company, which proposes to introduce English capital, already subscribed, for the purpose of constructing a narrow-gauge railroad from San Francisco, through the Southern Coast Counties, to connect with the Southern Transcontinental railroad, at some point between here and Los Angeles. We understand that the gauge is to be three feet; that it is to pass through Santa Cruz, Watsonville, Salinas City, the Salinas Valley, by way of San Benito, San Miguel, the Hot Springs; passing the mountain at or near the head of Moro Creek, and thence by way of the Osos and Laguna valleys to the Arroyo Grande. Major Watson assures us that all the capital needed is already secured; that the Transcontinental Railroad Company has agreed to pay to this Company $10,000 per mile for the laying down of an extra rail, enabling the wide-gauge cars of that company to pass over this company's rail and track. Also that the enterprise is already commenced and the track in course of construction; and that probabilities are that in four years it will be completed. This is good news for our county; and we congratulate our citizens upon the likelihood of the consumption of so desirable a work. The company seeks no subsidy, and can readily obtain the right of the way and necessary land for stations, etc., on the route proposed. We welcome the coming of the Iron Horse. His neigh will be music in the comparative solitudes of the Southern Coast Counties.

269. *Santa Cruz Sentinel*, June 24, 1871 (2:6)

Timber.—We have never seen a finer body of timber than is now standing on the San Lorenzo creek from the north of Boulder Creek to within two miles of the summit, along the Maclay road, the claim of the Chandlers are among the best. We are informed that the timber on Boulder Creek, which runs nearly parallel and west of the San Lorenzo, has a larger body of timber of better quality, growing more densely, on level land. If so, there is a wealth of natural resources in that vicinity that would pay to build the railroad from Santa Cruz to the mouth of Boulder Creek in a very short time.

270. *Santa Cruz Sentinel*, July 8, 1871 (2:1)

Railroad Items.

We are informed that on Saturday last a committee of observation, consisting of ten persons, among whom were some of the leading capitalists in the State, passed through Santa Cruz, viewing the route of the recently surveyed railroad, known as Robinson & Co.'s Narrow Gauge Railroad Company. It is the intention of the company to have 100 miles of the road completed within two years, which will carry the road into the Salinas Valley some where near the Elk Horn Slough. In the mean time the Southern Pacific, of Stanford & Co., are busy throwing out their feelers from Gilroy into the Pajaro Valley and soon the corps of observation will be one of occupation actually building the road, so as to tap the feeders and secure vested rights and favorable watering locations and shipping stations before het narrow gauge get their line under contract. The *Alta* of July 6th has the following:

On Monday, the Directors' car of the Central Pacific Railroad passed through here for Hollister, carrying President Stanford, Vice-President Huntington, General Superintendent Towne, Chief Engineer Gray, and others, making a trip over the line extension of the Southern Pacific. They return to-morrow.

From what we can learn the railroad interests of this county will soon take active advance. The San Jose and Santa Cruz railroad is quiet, at present; in a few days more the engineers report will appear, when a new impulse will be given to that route. We learn that capitalists are confident that the amount necessary to build the road can be secured by the time the road is finished, which will be less than two years, if no accident happens.

271. *San Louis Obispo Standard* via *The Pajaronian*, July 20, 1871 (4:1)

Route of Coast Line Railroad.

To a late letter of Gen. Rosecrans in the *Alta* is appended the following data relative to a route for a railroad from San Jose to Los Angeles obtained from the report of Lieut. Park. U. S. A. (vol VII of *Pacific Railroad Explorations*), and is believed to be, in the main, reliable. [*See* Article 267 above.]

It will be noticed that this route agrees in the main with that of the Narrow Gauge Railroad now being surveyed through this country. The only difference that we see, is that one begins at San Jose while the other begins at the city of San Francisco, and strikes the coast near the Cliff House, and then following the coast until it strikes the Pajaro river, at Watsonville. From this point southerly, both roads take the same general route.

272. *Sacramento Daily Union*, July 26, 1871 (3:1)

New Railroad Company.—Articles of incorporation of the San Jose and Santa Cruz Railroad Company—organized for the purpose of constructing and operating a railroad between those cities, a distance of about 38 miles—were filed yesterday in the office of the Secretary of State. Capital $500,000, in shares of $100 each. Directors—F. A. Hihn, A. Pfinster, S. A. Bishop, D. S. Payne and S. O. Houghton.

273. *The Pajaronian*, July 27, 1871 (2:3)

The Railroad.

Late news in regard to the railroad to Watsonville, is to the effect that several hundred men are at work, on a ten mile section, which will bring the road to a point within seven or eight miles of this place. From this point it is now uncertain as to which side of the river the road will pass. Of course we hope and expect that this side will be selected as the route, although an incalculable benefit will be the result of the advent of the road into any portion of the valley.

274. *Santa Cruz Sentinel,* July 29, 1871 (1:5-8)

Santa Cruz and San Jose Railroad.
Final Report of Chief Engineer.
San Jose, July 10, 1871.
To Messrs. Payne, Bishop, Hihn and Peabody, committee on the survey of the San Jose and Santa Cruz Railroad.—

Gentlemen:

As it is the intention of the citizens of San Jose and Santa Cruz to construct a narrow gauge railroad, connecting the two cities, and the surveys and estimates having been made with that understanding, it may well before entering upon the details of the operations of the surveying party, to briefly discuss the results of the recent improvements in the construction of locomotives and cars which may have already revolutionized the theory and practice of building and equipping railroads, and brought prominently into favor roads with a much narrower gauge than 4 feet 8½ inches, which has been most generally used both in the United States and Europe. These improvements are chiefly due to the ingenuity of Mr. Robert F. Fairlie of England.

To describe the peculiarities of construction of his engines would occupy too much space, and I must confine myself to a summary of the leading facts as far as they bear upon building and economically operating railroads.

The first locomotive designed by Fairlie on the new principal was intended to-run on rails laid upon common highways, or upon ordinary railways, and is described in Vol. I p. 401, Van Nostrand's Engineering Magazine, (May 1869).

It is called a locomotive car, being arranged so as to carry passengers. The calculated weight of the vehicle without passengers, but with fuel and water for a forty mile run, is under 14 tons, and with eighty passengers is 20 tons, of which more than one-half rests on the wheels of the steam bogie. The ratio of unpaying to paying load when the carriage is fully loaded is 2½ to 1, while as about 55 per cent of the total weight is available for adhesion, the carriage will be readily able to mount grades of 1 in 16 or 330 feet to the mile, the boiler being worked at a pressure of 140 pound to the square inch.

Although the total wheel base of the carriage is 57 feet, yet the actual wheel base, which has to be considered when estimating the capability of the vehicle for traversing curves is that of each bougie, or 6 feet only. With this base the carriage can be safely run around curves of two chains (132 feet) radius at moderate speeds, while running slowly a curve of 35 feet radius may be traversed. Thus by placing curves of 35 or 40 feet radius at the terminal stations, the carriage can be run around and the expense of turn tables avoided.

We have hitherto spoken of Mr. Fairlie's steam carriage as running by itself only, but it will be evident from what we have said that it possesses ample power, under ordinary circumstances, to draw another carriage behind it. (Van Nos p. 402).

We continue our extracts: "While on the subject we notice the Fairlie Engine Little Wonder which has been built for the Festiniog Railway Company, and which has obtained very considerable notoriety from its being the narrowest gauge passenger railway worked by locomotive, in existence. The line has been worked now about five years, and during that time there has not been the slightest accident of any kind. In fact it is considered a most extraordinary line, not only on account of its gauge, which is only two feet, but because of its success commercially. The traffic hauled the last year over this miniature line of twelve miles in length amounts to 130,000 tons of goods, and 145,000 passengers, which would be considered a very handsome traffic for a full sized railway of the same length, and the wonder is how it has been done. The credit is due to the able management of C. E. Spooner, managing director and engineer.

'The traffic has so increased that the ordinary engines are getting too small to pull the loads, and hence the adoption of a Farlie Engine, which at once enables the train loads to be doubled, without but in a small degree increasing the cost of each train.

"The Festiniog line is, for about eleven miles, one continuous ascent of about 1 in 80 (66 feet per mile) with very many curves some of which are as small as 100 feet radius.

"The Little Wonder, although weighing but nineteen and a half tons, fully equipped with fuel and water for the road, will haul after it 140 tons at a speed of fifteen miles an hour for the whole eleven miles, a feat, considering the gauge and weight, that could not be accomplished by other than the Fairlie Engine. The engine has eight wheels, in two separate groups of four each; each group being acted on by a pair of cylinders 8½ in diameter. The wheels in each group are 2 feet 4 inches in diameter, and are coupled together.

"The extreme wheel base is 18 feet, consequently the engine will run with remarkable smoothness. At the same time the wheel base of each bogie being but five feet the engine will pass round curves of 50 feet radius with the utmost safety, at 20 miles an hour.

"The principal in this respect is precisely similar to that of the steam carriage, passing curves 50 feet. The fact of either steam carriages or engines being constructed to run with perfect safety round curves of 50 feet, is unprecedented in the history of railways, and places the railway world under a considerable obligation to Mr. Fairlie, who has spared no pains to perfect a system which we wish every success."—V. N. Vol. I., No. 9. pp. 777–8. (Sept. 1869.)

An important paper read lately by Mr. Farlie before the British Association says: "It ought to be engraved on the mind of every engineer, that every inch added to the width of gauge beyond what is absolutely necessary for traffic, adds to the cost of construction, increases the proportion of dead weight, increases the cost of working, and in consequence reduces the useful effect of the railway."—V. N., Vol. IV, No. 30, (June, 1871.)

The 3½ feet gauge is the standard for Sweden and Norway. Two lines of this gauge are being built in Russia, and one constructed in Prussia of 31 inch gauge is a financial success. In Ohio, a 2½ feet railroad, 44 miles long, between Pequa and Celina, is about to be built. A system of small gauge railroads is projected from Toledo as feeders to the broad gauge railroad centering there, and it is now determined to build the line from Denver City to Santa Fe, more than 300 miles on the small gauge system.

I have embodied as much information on this matter as I could within the narrow limits of a report, and am fully aware that I have omitted much that is interesting and valuable; but I must content myself with adding one more extract. It is from Mr. Baird & Co., proprietors of the Belden Locomotive Works, Philadelphia.

"A uniform narrow gauge system desirable—For narrow gauge lines of any considerable length, and intended for both freight and passenger traffic, a gauge of 3 feet seems to have been generally agreed upon. If a system of narrow gauge roads is to be constructed in this country, (and such now seems to be the tendency), it is manifestly important that a uniformity of gauge should be established. The three feet gauge has the decided preference of railroad engineers and managers who have given this subject attention, and at this width has very important advantages in the designing of locomotives and other rolling stock, is believed that its adoption for the narrow gauge system would be advantageous. We may mention that the Denver & Rio Grande Railway now in process of construction, for 80 miles of its projected length, is to be of 3 feet gauge, and the Pennsylvania & Sodas Bay Railroad, another narrow gauge railroad 83 miles in length, has also adopted this gauge after careful investigation.

We subjoin, as pertinent to this subject the following figures, showing the comparative proportions of dead weight to paying load of full gauge and narrow gauge cars:

Full Gauge Eight-Wheeled Box Car,	Lbs.
Weight of car empty	20,000
Capacity	20,000
Weight of car loaded	40,000
Weight of Wheels and axles	5,400
Weight on all the wheels	34,600
Weight on each wheel	4,325
Percentage of dead weight to load	100

Narrow Gauge Four-wheeled Box Car,	Lbs.
Weight of car empty	4,500
Capacity	8,000
Weight of car loaded	12,500
Weight of Wheels and axles	1,200
Weight on all the wheels	11,300
Weight on each wheel	2,825
Percentage of dead weight to load	56¼

Full Gauge Eight-Wheeled Flat Car,	Lbs.
Weight of car empty	16,000
Capacity	24,000
Weight of car loaded	40,000
Weight of Wheels and axles	5,400
Weight on all the wheels	34,600
Weight on each wheel	4,322
Percentage of dead weight to load	66⅔

Narrow Gauge Four-wheeled Flat Car,	Lbs.
Weight of car empty	3,500
Capacity	9,000
Weight of car loaded	12,500
Weight of Wheels and axles	1,200
Weight on all the wheels	11,300
Weight on each wheel	2,825
Percentage of dead weight to load	38 8/9

Full Gauge Eight-Wheeled Coal Car,	Lbs.
Weight of car empty	6,690
Capacity	11,000
Weight of car loaded	17,500
Weight of Wheels and axles	2,300
Weight on all the wheels	15,300
Weight on each wheel	3,825
Percentage of dead weight to load	60

Narrow Gauge Four-wheeled Coal Cars,	Lbs.
Weight of car empty	4,000
Capacity	8,500
Weight of car loaded	12,500
Weight of Wheels and axles	1,200
Weight on all the wheels	11,300
Weight on each wheel	2,825
Percentage of dead weight to load	47

Design for narrow gauge freight cars by prominent manufacturers, show four-wheeled box, flat and drop-bottom, coal or ore cars. Their weights and capacity are dictated in the above figures.

For passenger service, eight wheeled cars with bodies 26

feet long and 6 feet wide are proposed as follows:

Second class cars with longitudinal slatted seats in centre, (passengers to sit back to back): capacity, 26 passengers.

First class passenger cars with seats and cushions like horse railway cars; capacity 30 passengers.

First class passenger cars with two rows of turning chairs with aisle between, etc.: capacity 18 passengers.

First class passenger cars with revolving back seats (double seat on one side of car and single seat on the other, the plan being reversed in the two ends of the cars; capacity 28 passengers.

All these cars to have wheels about 28 inches in diameter.

The cost of a mile of single track properly proportioned for a 4 feet 8½ inch gauge is $10,377, and for a 3 feet gauge $5,794.70, or in the ratio of 160 to 55.84; that is to say the superstructure of a 3 feet gauge costs a little more than one-half of that for a 4 feet 8½ inch gauge. In estimating the cost of graduating and bridging it is well to bear in mind the following facts:

1—Where the gauge corresponds nearly with the surface, the cost varies with the width of gauge.

2—Where deep cuts and fills are encountered, the formation of the side slopes being the same, but little is saved on the narrow gauge.

3—When the line is located on the slope of steep side hills, conforming nearly to grade, and where no embankment is allowable, the proportion is as the square of the width of base, or on narrow gauge, about one-half of work on broad gauge.

4—In the construction of bridges little is saved on general plan, but the weight being uniformly distributed, lighter structures may be adopted.

When these observations, which seemed to be necessary to explain the character of the work under consideration, I proceed to state what has been done and the results at which we have arrived.

As soon as possible I was notified of my appointment as engineer to make a survey to ascertain the practicability of constructing a railroad from San Jose to Santa Cruz. Bishop, Beach, and myself went from San Jose to the summit of the Santa Cruz Mountains, where we were met by Hihn, Kirby and Wright, of Santa Cruz, at Shulties, where the road from Lexington to Soquel first reaches the summit of the mountain. We followed along the Soquel road to Taylor's Pass (where the road leaves the summit) and went from there southeasterly about three-quarters of a mile to Burrill's house, where we found a pass of the same elevation as Taylor's Pass. Returning to Shulties we followed the summit northwesterly, examining the several passes, thence to the pass at the head of Campbell creek or Saratoga road.

Hihn, Wright and myself had each an aereoid barometer and the altitude of the several passes was approximately determined. Taylor's and Burrill's Passes are 1,540 feet above sea level; Shulties, 1,592; Bear creek, 1800; and Saratoga, 2,400. It was then agreed that I should start with a party for San Jose, and make a survey, taking the altitude to Taylor's Pass, while Wright should ascertain the altitude of prominent points between

Soquel village up and along Soquel creek, and thence to the summit of Taylor's Pass.

Commencing in San Jose at the intersection of San Carlos street with the Southern Pacific Railroad in Fourth street the survey followed San Carlos street to Delmas Avenue, when a direction was assumed to the mouth of the cañon near the village of Los Gatos, which is the point where we first strike the mountain country. This line was continued to Sta. 177 (3⅓ miles from the place of beginning,) crossing the Los Gatos creeks and lands of Splivalo, Sansevain, Naglee and Chapelle to George Treat's land. An angle to the right of 3½ degrees was then made, and the survey was continued through lands of Treat, Rucker, Johnson and Dougherty, passing between Dougherty's house and blacksmith shop and crossing Los Gatos creek at a short bend of the creek at Mr. Casey's house. Thence the straight line was continued to a point a little beyond the San Jose reservoir (which was 500 feet to the left of line, when it was found impractical to continue it further, it leaving the bluff bank of the Los Gatos creek. A line meandering along the foot of the bluff running through the village of Los Gatos and crossing to the Ten Mile House was then surveyed. Being satisfied from the survey and the observation of the land ahead that the railroad could not be located on the east side of the creek without seriously interfering with the flume of the Los Gatos Woolen mills, the survey was revised by running a line on the west side of the creek from the Ten Mile House back to the point P, nearly opposite the San Jose reservoir. This line crosses the Los Gatos on Mr. Robert's land. From San Jose to the crossing, the land is about as favorable as possible, and from the crossing to the Ten Mile House, the line is located on a gently sloping side hill, the graduation being less expensive than the construction of an ordinary wagon road. The grades are also very light, corresponding to the general rise of the valley.

From the Ten Mile House, the survey followed the toll road (which begins at this point,) through the cañon, which ends at Carnahan's creek, and through the village of Lexington to near the Forest House. With an expenditure of $4,457, the grade of the toll road through the cañon can be made to confirm to the grades and curves of the railroad, and, if suitable arrangements can be made with the turnpike company, I recommend the purchase and adoption of their road for that portion of the line. Indeed it may be adopted nearly to the Forest House, but if difficulties of any kind should arise, in passing through Lexington, the line may be located west of the village, giving a more moderate grade from Carnahan's creek to the summit.

From the Forest House the survey was made near the channel of Los Gatos creek to Coveli's burnt mill, and a line run thence transversely up the ridge to the north end of the tunnel at Taylor's Pass. The object of this survey was to obtain information as to the heights of the streams on both sides of the pass across the dividing ridge, so that a tunnel of greater or less length might be made as future results should justify.

The party under Mr. Wright had in the meantime

carried their levels to the Taylor Pass, while the party immediately under my charge, were making the survey between the Forest House and the summit. I joined Wright's party, and tunnels, both at Taylor's and Burrill's Passes were located. It was found that the tunnel at Burrill's Pass, while more favorable for ascent from the San Jose side, did not allow space for a descent along the west branch of Soquel Creek.

The slope of the Santa Cruz mountains from the summit to Los Gatos, is generally very gradual, and there is no difficulty in locating a railroad anywhere along it, with a very moderate expense of graduation.

To insure our descent towards Soquel, I established a tunnel at an elevation of 1,310 feet above ocean level and connected my survey with it. The tunnel and cut are 2,000 feet in length from grade to grade. The material is a soft sandstone rock, but I believe sufficiently firm to sustain itself without the necessity of timbering.

The parties were now consolidated, retaining Wright and two axmen. Wright having been for more than 20 years a surveyors in Santa Cruz County, is better acquainted with the topography of that section than any other man, and the axmen he brought to my aid were absolutely necessary, to enable me to make satisfactory progress between the summit and Soquel village.

The line on the slope of the side hill between the Forest House and the north end of the tunnel was not surveyed, it being evident that it was entirely practicable at a small expense. It does not differ far for a large portion of the distance from the toll road from the Forest House to

Shulties, and passes over ground of the same character. I carefully examined the work done on the toll road and have, with some additions, made a corresponding estimate for this portion of the work.

After the close of my survey southerly from the summit. I examined the ground west of Lexington and the Forest House and found a route with a lighter grade from the end of the cañon (Carnahan's creek), was practicable, but with a considerable increase of distance and at an increased cost.

The grade from a point sta. 733 (near the Forest House) to the north end of the tunnel, is 2.5 per 100 feet, or 132 feet per mile, is the maximum grade, on any portion of the survey.

Collating the results of Wright's survey it was thought necessary to adopt this grade descending southerly from the south end of the summit tunnel.

The descent on the west side of the dividing range is so abrupt, that it was necessary to follow a grade line running up the valley of the west branch of the Soquel creek to the bridge near Chase's saw mill, crossing the stream at that point, and then following down the left or east bank of the stream. This was followed to the village of Soquel. The side slopes are in many cases very steep, and, as will be seen by the estimates, much heavy work is encountered. The following are the most important point where we meet with extraordinary difficulties:

1—The curve at the bridge near Chase's saw mill has a radius of 239 feet, and considerable excavation must be made on both sides of the creek.

2—At station 241 we are obliged to cross a deep hollow, made by a former slide of the banks of the creek. We fortunately are able to cross this at right angles; but having on the south side a cut of 35.7 feet, extreme depth, and 430 feet extreme length from grade to grade.

3—At station 376 a high point projects up to the banks of the creek, behind which the bank recedes, requiring a tunnel of 160 feet in length and a cutting of 39 feet extreme depth on each side for an aggregate distance of 110 feet. This point is opposite Mr. Samuel's residence on the west side of the creek, and further examinations may prove that it is advisable to cross the creek at this point and recross it from where the wagon road from this place at the Lexington and Soquel road crosses the creek. The location of a portion of the road on the west side would undoubtedly accommodate a large district of country and add also to the profitableness of the road.

Proceeding from Samuel's road southerly, the grades are light and the land generally very favorable as far as station 525.40 near Rabel's tannery. Lane's creek and he east branch of Soquel are crossed without difficulty; the former by a trestle bridge 300 feet in length and elevation above the channel 55 feet, and at the latter by a trestle bridge 300 feet in length and elevation 56 feet above the channel of the creek. At Rabel's tannery a line was run across Soquel creek and connecting with a survey made by Mr. Wright on the western side of the Soquel valley, to the village of Soquel. The slopes are generally very small on this side, but, as the land is under cultivation, Mr. Hihn expressed his apprehension that there would be difficulty in obtaining the right of way on that side, while on the eastern side, the land would cost nothing. At his request the line was continued on the eastern side to the village of Soquel. A little beyond Rabel's tannery the creek sweeps to the left, and strikes an almost perpendicular bluff. The line can be carried around this bend protecting the base of the embankment by a rock embankment extending above high water mark, but I found that there was little difference in cost between this line and a straight line crossing and recrossing the creek, and making a much handsomer line, besides effecting a considerable saving of distance.

Hihn afterward made some examinations with a view to pass over the bluff. The height of grade at the crossing of the east branch of the Soquel creek is 250 feet, and this elevation is kept running level to the end of the cut, south of the crossing, to sta. 501. The top of the bluff opposite sta. 554, is 296 feet, so if we adopt a rising grade of 46 feet to the mile, we can pass over the bluff.

As the line is located on a side hill, there will probably be no difficulty in locating the road conformably to this grade, nor in running a line from this bluff to pass above the bluff about one mile ahead, at an elevation of 196 feet, where it will unite with the line shown on the map and profile.

As one of the most important sources of profit of the railroad will be the conveyance of lumber from the mountains to the village of Soquel to the Pacific Ocean at the Soquel landing, to Santa Cruz, to Watsonville and to the Pajaro and Salinas valleys, I think it advisable that there should be no ascending grade between Chase's mill and the village of Soquel, and I have marked the line and estimated accordingly, as I do not think the saving in cost

The Dream of Steam, 1854–1873

in passing over the bluff will compensate for the disadvantage of the rising grade.

The survey terminates at the village of Soquel, at station 706, and at an elevation of 65 feet above tide water. This is a convenient point for the divergence of a line running southerly to Watsonville and the Salinas valley. A line had already been run from the wharf at the Santa Cruz landing to this point by a party under the charge of Watson, and no question can arise as to the practicability of a railroad between these points. I expected to be furnished with the altitudes on this part of the route. Wright failed to receive them, but has given me information which enables me to make estimates that cannot be materially incorrect.

The length of the line from station 6, at the intersection of Fourth and San Carlos streets to station 706, at the village of Soquel, is 32.82 miles, and thence to the wharf at Santa Cruz, 5.3 miles, making the total distance from San Jose to the wharf at Santa Cruz landing, 38.12 miles. The map, profile, statement of grades and estimates in detail, are submitted as a portion of this report.

The maximum grade is 132 feet per mile and the minimum radius 230 feet, except for one point on the toll road through the cañon, between the Ten Mile House and Lexington, where a curve of 130 would save considerable expense. It has been shown that locomotives and cars will traverse curves of 50 feet radius, and I deem it unnecessary to incur an additional expenditure at this point.

The cost of the preparation of the road bed and for the superstructure of the line set forth in the above detailed estimate is $450,000.

From what I have already stated it must be evident that the cost of construction may be considerably reduced. From San Jose to the north end of the tunnel at the summit there can be little variation in expense. Should the company not have means to make the summit tunnel by adopting a higher grade the tunnel may be altogether avoided, and a cut of moderate depth at Taylor's summit substituted. There will also be a large saving between the summit and the village of Soquel, the particulars of which will be ascertained by subsequent surveys to be made before the line is finally located. The object of the present survey has been to ascertain the practicability of the route, and this I believe has been conclusively demonstrated, and that it can be made at an expense for preparation of road bed and superstructure, less than the mere cost of the superstructure on a 4 feet 8½ inch gauge.

The details I have given in regard to cost, will show that the construction of the road should be begun immediately. There are so many interests which I might specify which will aid the enterprise that I have no doubt respecting its early construction.

Referring back to the extract I have made from M. Band & Co.'s circular, it will be seen that the percentage of dead or non-paying weight on the narrow gauge is less than one-half of that on the ordinary or 4 feet 8½ inch gauge. Yet the Pennsylvania Railroad Company, carried their freight between Philadelphia and Pittsburgh, across the Alleghany Mountains in the year 1870, at an average charge of 1¼ cents a ton a mile, and made a small profit by the operation. I think I have proved that it is the policy of the citizens of the two counties to build the road themselves, and that placing the cost of transportation at reasonable rates they will receive a fair interest for their investment, besides the vast increase in the value of property at the termini and at every intermediate point.

Yours, very respectfully, Wm. J. Lewis,
Civil Engineer.

275. *Pacific Rural Press*, August 5, 1871 (76:4)
The Santa Cruz Railroad.

The final report of the Chief Engineer (Mr. W. J. Lewis) of the Santa Cruz & San José R. R. has been published. A line was run from San José (at the intersection of San Carlos street and the Southern Pacific in Front street), to near Los Gatos to the Los Gatos Creek, thence to Ten Mile House, along the toll road through the cañon, and through Lexington to near the Forest House. It then runs near the channel of Los Gatos creek and transversely up the ridge to a tunnel at Taylor's Pass, then down to Soquel and to the landing at Santa Cruz. The projected tunnel and cut are 2,000 feet in length, through soft sand rock. The total length of the line is 38.12 miles; the maximum grade, 132 feet; the minimum radius, 230 feet, except at one point where a curve of 130 feet would save considerable expense.

The cost of the road bed and superstructure is estimated at $450,000, or about $11,805 per mile. This may be reduced considerably. By adopting a higher grade, the tunnel at Taylor's Pass may be avoided. The object of the survey was to ascertain the practicability of the route for a narrow gauge road. This is demonstrated, and also the fact that the cost of road bed and superstructure of the narrow gauge will be less than that of the superstructure alone of the 4 ft. 8½ in. gauge.

276. *San Jose Guide* via the *Santa Cruz Sentinel*, August 5, 1871 (2:3)

Santa Cruz Railroad.—The articles of incorporation for the Santa Cruz Railroad have been sent to the Secretary of State's office, and as soon as they are filed, books will be opened for subscriptions to stock. The company will at once proceed to obtain the right of way and commence operations. A Committee will call on the landowners and represent to them the advantages of such a road, and by this means endeavor to obtain the right of way without resorting to law. There is no doubt that the right of way will all be donated, as no one will be more benefited by the building of the road than those who own the land along the proposed route.

277. *Santa Cruz Sentinel*, August 5, 1871 (2:4)

Letter from Watsonville.
Watsonville, Aug. 2d, 1871.

Mr. Editor:—During the past week the streets of Watsonville have been more than usually the scenes of busy life. Many strangers have visited us—capitalists, looking for chances of investment for money; pleasure-seekers, drifting along in the crowd, and a great number of men of small means, wishing to establish themselves in business in some growing town—merchants, mechanics, farmers, etc.,; and all drawn hither through the combined influence of the salubrity of our climate, the never-failing productiveness of our soil, and the building of the railroad.

Mr. Smith, one of the surveyors of the railroad, says it will be completed about the 15th of September. About twelve hundred men are at work on it. The prospective depot for this valley is not definitely known to us, but the general opinion is that its location will be about mile east of town, on the Monterey side of Pajaro river. Yet it may be built on this side.

278. *Stockton Daily Evening Herald*, August 8, 1871 (3:3)

Railroad Connection with Santa Cruz.—Articles of incorporation of the San Jose and Santa Cruz railroad have been sent to the office of the Secretary of State, and subscription books are to be opened at once. The completion of this road is of no little importance to Stockton and other inland points. It is some consolation to have direct railroad communication with a fresh sea-breeze and a good watering place without being obliged to go to San Francisco. Every point in the interior should congratulate itself on every indication of acquisition of a railroad to the sea-coast at some other point than San Francisco; and the more the better.

279. *The Pajaronian*, August 24, 1871 (2:1)
RAILROAD.

We are informed by Mr. Thrift, who receives his information from head quarters, that the cars will reach this place by the first of October. Thirty days and the Pajaro Valley will be in direct communication by rail, with the cities of the State, and National Good.

280. *Santa Cruz Sentinel,* September 2, 1871 (2:5)

We hear very little about the railroad now, and nothing about graveling the road to the depot, and building another bridge across the Pajaro river. The bridge will be built and the road graveled, however, some time this fall.

281. *The Pajaronian*, September 7, 1871 (3:2)

R. R. Ties.—On Friday last the first load of ties passed through town from the lumber regions north of this valley, *en route* for Monterey county, for the Southern Pacific R. R. Co. Messrs Ford & Sanborn of this place have entered into a contract for supplying 50,000, and Mr. Sanford 10,000. Thus can be seen even at this early day the benefit of the Railroad. This however, is but the commencement.

282. *The Pajaronian*, September 14, 1871 (2:2)
RAILROAD NEWS.

Workmen are engaged on the Southern Pacific about five miles from town. The whistle will soon be heard resounding among the hills that border the Pajaro. There is a rumor to the effect that the Company will continue the road on to the Salinas this year. Of course it is better for a town to be a terminus, but a road passing through this valley will be of vast benefits to all classes and will give an impetus to trade and agriculture which it would never received without a road. In the course of two or three weeks we shall take our place in the State as one of the important places, and receive a name worthy of this productive and beautiful section.

283. *The Pajaronian*, September 21, 1871 (3:2)
The Railroad—Freight.

The Railroad is still approaching, and we learn that it is the intention of the company to reach this place on or before the 10th of October.

In the meantime Mr. Bassett, Assistant Superintendent of the road, has been here and agreeable to this instructions, a storehouse of good width and a 160 feet in length, has been constructed, and Mr. Holbrook who has charge of the job, has commenced on another section of 150 feet long. The first section is already filled from sills to ridge pole with grain, and we doubt if the 150 feet additional will be sufficient to accommodate all the freight now being hauled there. But Mr. Bassett is equal to the emergency, and if necessary a storehouse long enough to reach to the foothills will be erected to accommodate our farmers. Large quantities of baled hay is being piled up in the railroad lot, ready for shipment to market. The farmers seem to enter into the spirit of railroad shipment with a will as the strings of teams to be seen any day will testify.

Freight Agent.—Mr. A. C. Bassett, Assistant Superintendent, has appointed Henry C. Pratt, son of Judge C. H. Pratt of this place, as Freight Agent at this point of the Southern Pacific Railroad. Mr. Pratt is a young man of good capabilities, ambitious, and we think will make an excellent agent. The position is a good and responsible one, and Henry doubtless feels flattered at being selected, considering that there were thirty or forty applicants. His numerous friends will wish him all manner of success in his new business. We think the appointment a good one and satisfactory to all.

284. *Daily Alta California*, September 23, 1871 (1:1)

The Watsonville Road.—The new branch of the Southern Pacific Railroad, building to Pajaro Valley, is now completed within seven miles of Watsonville. The contractor, Mr. Strowbridge, expects to have the road to that point in condition, inside of twenty days, to transport freight and passengers safely over it. A temporary road will be used at the point where the great tunnel is being pierced through the mountains at the head of Pajaro River. This tunnel will, we believe, be when finished, the second largest in the State. The people of the section are overjoyed at the rapidly approaching completion of the road, and land in its vicinity is now held and sold at double the rates ruling a few months ago.

285. *Ventura Signal* via the *Santa Cruz Sentinel*, September 23, 1871 (2:5)

Southern Coast Railroad.—The S.C.R.R. Surveyors, under Major Watson, broke camp here Tuesday morning, 7th inst., and are now on their way up the Santa Clara valley. E. N. Robinson, General Superintendent of the work, left Monday evening , and proceeds directly to the Colorado river, where he expects to meet the party from the East. All speak most encouragingly of the Coast route, and seem to think that there are no engineering obstacles that may not be easily overcome. Between this place and Santa Barbara, places that were thought to be serious difficulties in the way of building a railroad are pronounced to be in nowise difficult.

This survey is but a preliminary one, but it will satisfy those interested that the Coast route is not only a not impracticable, but in all respects a singularly favorable one.

286. *San Francisco Examiner*, September 29, 1871 (3:7)

Surveying Party—Etc.

Los Angeles, September 28—Watson's surveying party for the Southern Coast Railroad, are camped near the city. They leave next week to run the line to San Bernardino. Robinson's party left Soledad Pass on the 12th, for Camp Cady and Fort Mojave.

287. *Los Angeles Star* via the *Santa Cruz Sentinel*, October 7, 1871 (2:1)

Narrow-Gauge Coast Line Railway Survey.

The survey commences at the North Beach, San Francisco, and the length of the line from that point to a point on the Los Angeles river, above and near the mouth of the Arroyo Seco, is 448 75-100 miles. The heaviest grade on the line is 105 feet to the mile. Upon three-fourths of the entire line the grade will not exceed, on an average, more than twenty feet per mile. Eighteen miles from the initial point there will be required a tunnel of 5,500 feet. The line strikes the seashore at Nine Mile Point, and follows it to San Pedro, Spanish town, and Porter's Bluff, where it leaves the shore, and then up the North Fork of the Pescadero creek to Pescadero. Then to the shore, and along it to Santa Cruz; then a little from the shore to the mouth of the Soquel creek. Then, leaving the shore at the mouth of the Aptos creek, it follows up the Calabazas creek to Watsonville, one hundred miles from San Francisco. Then around the head of Elkhorn slough, leaving Castroville to the right, and passing on to the Salinas river to the crossing of the Santa margarita mountains. It is not yet determined whether the crossing of the mountains will be made at the San Luis or Moro Pass. In either case the line will strike San Luis, and pass on to the Arroyo Grande by the Cañada Yerbe, and passing the arroyo at the stage road crossing, and along the right bank of the Burros to the head of the Nepoma Val-

The Dream of Steam, 1854–1873

ley, and down that valley to the Santa Maria river, crossing which it follows it up on the right bank to Foxon's cañon. Then up this cañon to the summit at the head of the La Zaca, and down the La Zaca and the Alamos Pintados to the Ballard's station. Thence in a right line to the mouth of Agulia creek, from which point the line crosses the Santa Ynez river, and follows it up to the San Marcos pass, which is crossed near the line of the stage road by a tunnel two and a half miles in length; and then down the San Jose cañon, and along the foot-hills to Santa Barbara; and then along the line of the sea shore to San Buenaventura, from which point it follows up the Santa Clara river, on its left bank, to the San Fernando Pass to Los Angeles. A tunnel of half a mile will be required at this pass. The three tunnels along the line are all through the soft sand stone, so general along the coast of this state.

From the San Francisquito rancho to Fort Mohave on the Colorado river, Col. E. N. Robinson, Chief Engineer of the Company, has not determined yet over which of the several routes the road shall be located. All the routes will be surveyed and the most advantageous one selected.

The Chief Engineer of the Atlantic and Pacific Railway, Gen. Beckendorffer, with his party, from St. Louis, Mo., were encamped on the 16th ult., at a point fifty miles east of the Colorado river, and will strike the river at Fort Mohave, where his survey will connect with the survey now being made by Col. Robinson, from San Francisquito to Fort Mohave.

Major Watson will soon leave this city with his party, to survey the line from the Los Angeles river easterly, by the way of Cajon Pass, and connect it with the line surveyed by Col. Robinson. He will also survey the line through the San Gorgonio Pass, and connect it with Col. Robinson's line, east of the San Bernardino mountain.

288. *Santa Cruz Sentinel,* October 7, 1871 (2:3-4)
Railroad or No Railroad.

The oft recurring thought to persons interested in the growth, progress and prosperity of Santa Cruz is, shall we ever have communication with San Francisco by rail, and if so, how and when will it be consummated.

Some few years since, when a few of our most enterprising citizens set busily, and hopefully to work to construct a rail road up the San Lorenzo river, it was hoped that ere this time we should have been able to effect such communication by the most direct route. But that project so nobly begun, was thwarted, and there rests no longer a hope with our people that a road will very soon be constructed, as then designed.

Those were days of universal prosperity with all classes. The merchant, lumberman, and laborer, were alike profitably employed. How sadly does the present contrast with the few years that are passed. Then prosperity was of some fixed value, and houses sprang up in all parts of our thriving city. How is it now? Let those answer most interested.

Santa Cruz, with the most healthful climate in the world, surrounded with a scenery grand and sublime; the most centrally located town in the State, and altogether the most desirable place for a residence; having a forest of the most valuakind, covering an area of some two hundred square miles, and blessed with the privileges of the State, could to-day, with fostered enterprise, have been a city of ten thousand inhabitants. How is it that other sections less favored in every particular, with no other outlet than the mountain turnpike, can erect woolen mills and aid every laudable enterprise? It is because those most interested and most to be benefited are the first to assist in all that tends to the permanent up-building of the whole community. They don't stand idly waiting for the time to come when it shall be profitable for outside capital to build them up; they force conditions, and with the attending prosperity are ten fold remunerated for all the aid given to foster enterprise. Those who have risen from poverty to wealth in the community through its generous patronage, should be the first to reflect back a grateful assistance when opportunity offers, not sit hoarding their gold as if it was the most desirable thing of life and all of life.

It requires no extraordinary prescience to see why Santa Cruz has failed to become what she might have been, and the question now is, shall she remain in her lethargic mood until there shall be pasted on her approaching roads, "A town for sale." No, now is the propitious time of all times, when by the exercise of ordinary business sagacity, Santa Cruz, and the whole county may open new ways of prosperity, that shall be permanent and abiding as time. The only question is, how shall it be effected. With any reasonable degree of encouragement, the proprietors of the railroad in Pajaro Valley, will continue a branch to Santa Cruz. There are two ways only: the first, by subscribing to the stock; the second, by allowing country bonds, either of which can be done and have the cars running to Santa Cruz within six months. We propose to discuss for a moment the propriety of granting county aid, believing that in this instance it is wise and just to do so. Wherever the whole people are benefited by an enterprise, there certainly can be no good reason why all should not be willing to aid in fostering such enterprise. This county is long and narrow, the road will run immediately through the most valuable portions, and develop business in the most remote part of the mountains; without it, there will be no business, no development. We will assume that ten years more, will treble the population of the county, and more than quadruple the assessed value of the taxable property of the county. Let the bonds be issued payable for twenty years and the amount be $5,000 per mile, interest payable at even per cent. annually. This we believe will in no wise embarrass anybody or any- and if the aid is absolutely donated by the people, would return to them in that period with ten fold profit. Let us review the benefits to be derived: Every farmer and builder in the southern and eastern valleys, would be able to obtain all qualities of lumber for building and fencing, at from four to six dollars per thousand feet, less than at the present time, and which without completing the road, will constantly increase instead of diminish in price. This new market will afford a profitable margin for every foot of timber west of those valleys, and without doubt will assist very materially to induce outside capital to come and appropriate our vast water powers for manufacturing purposes of all kinds. Our lumbermen can now hope to compete with the up country dealers. Lumber is placed on the vessel there from three to five dollars cheaper than it can be placed on our beach, and these lower valleys are the only regions on the coast where other lumber than ours will not be taken. Again, what hindrance would there be to constructing large and commodious elevators in Santa Cruz, from which ships for foreign countries could be freighted as readily as in San Francisco, and with greater profits to the grain growers in the valleys below? If Santa Cruz does not make the move in this direction, soon, Monterey will, and which ever takes the initiative will hold the ascendency.

The farmer could with less expense send all his surplus produce to a coast market, and procure, because of increased facilities for transportation, much cheaper, the commodities used by him, that are not produced at home. There is not a farmer in Pajaro or Salinas whose annual savings on account of the road, would not amount to double the increased tax, and with many it would be an item of profit. On an average, a farmer uses in and about a farm 200 acres, 10,000 feet of lumber of all sorts annually, and this too after his first great expense of constructing buildings preparatory to farming.

Watsonville with constantly increasing population and extending business, and business facilities has not necessarily one vacant tenement; neither is there posted on every house or gate "this house for sale or rent." Contrast this with Santa Cruz, where there has been a constantly depressing tendency in business for over two years, until every branch of trade and industry complain of unexampled dullness. The prospect of a railroad has infused new life and vigor into the people of Watsonville, and the question now to be determined is, will Santa Cruz and other parts equally interested put forth an effort to effect railroad communications with San Francisco via. Watsonville. The route is not the most direct, to be sure, but is the most practicable and feasible at this time, and all considered, may we not rightly conclude, the most profitable. It will do much more for the general business of Santa Cruz, then a more direct road to the city, and will not materially lessen the travel that will be likely to visit this place. If any action is to be taken to give the aid of the county to the road, it must be done immediately. The Legislature to convene in December next, will repeal the five per cent. law very soon after organizing, and two months is sufficient to get this matter fairly before the people. The law under which to act, is in the substance as follows:

Sec. 1. The several counties, including the city and county of San Francisco, are hereby authorized to aid in the construction of railroads by the issue of county bonds bearing interest at the rate of seven per cent. per annum, and payable within twenty years from the date of there issue, and to provide by taxation for the payment of the interest and principal of said bonds; provided, that the whole amount of said bond herein authorized to be issued shall not exceed five per cent. of the value of the taxable property of such county, or city and county, according to its valuation on the assessment roll last preceding the time of the issue of said bonds.

Sec. 2. Before the granting of such aid, the Board of Supervisors of the county, or city and county, proposing to grant such railroad aid shall submit to the qualified electors of said county, or city and county at an election, of which election, at least thirty days notice shall be given, by publication once a week in a news paper published in said county, the question whether such railroad shall be granted, in which notice the day in which and the places where such election is to be held shall be stated; and the route for which aid is proposed to be granted shall be definitely described, and the amount of bonds to be issued shall be stated. All elections authorized under this act shall be conducted in the same manner as elections for State and county officers. No aid to railroads shall be granted unless a majority of the electors voting at such election shall cast their votes in favor of such aid.

A petition is already drafted and in circulation, asking the Board of Supervisors of this county to order an election pursuant to the above law. There is not the slightest doubt but that seven tenths of the value of this county will favor the project and vote all needful aid. Let the people carefully consider this subject and not decide rashly either way, but do that which seemeth best.

289. *The Pajaronian*, October 12, 1871 (2:1)
Railroad.

The *Call* of Sunday last remarks editorially that the Pajaronian has come to hand but "makes no mention of the railroad." We can assure our contemporary that we have not forgotten the fact that a railroad is rapidly approaching completion, and as near as we can learn will be completed and cars running about the first prox. We cannot obtain any definite knowledge, as the R. R. Co. prefer to keep their operations in the most profound secrecy. The location of the depot is not known to any outside of the railroad people. We suppose it will be placed about two miles from town, at a point almost inaccessible during the winter season. Why it is thus we know not. The ways of R. R. Cos. are past finding out. A petition has, we believe, been presented to ex-Gov. Stanford asking him to bring the depot near town. No answer has been vouchsafed to the petitioners as yet. We trust the Co. will locate the depot just where they please, without any regard to any one else.

290. *Castroville Argus* via the *Santa Cruz Sentinel*, October 14, 1871 (1:8)

Railroad.

The railroad surveyors have completed their work—the termination of the line from the Pajaro Depot hitherward being at a point distance about two hundred yards east of the present town limits of Castroville. This terminal point is adapted admirably for a depot, in which statement every impartial man will concur with us. We do not say this because of the proximity to our town of the spot indicated but on account of its special adaptability as regards altitude, centrality, and consequent convenience of access. But more potent than any language of our own, in proof of what we have stated, is the fact that railroad companies are little guided, if at all, by the location of towns in the choice of a route, which is selected with no practical reference to them, but with the single purpose being easily accessible by the patronage which such companies invite. We say, therefore, that the route and terminus are intrinsically good, else they would not have been chosen, and we expect to see soon tangible corroboration of what we are borne out in by the railroad company. The road will be completed in a few days to the Pajaro Depot, when work we are assured, will be commenced on the Castroville extension, a distance of eleven miles over a country almost level and requiring little grading or filling. The company is not unconscious of the fact that the road should be pushed speedily to this place and will act accordingly.

In connection with this laudable enterprise it is not inopportune to note the completion of the narrow gauge railroad survey from San Francisco to Los Angeles, which shows a proposed connecting distance of 448 miles, the heaviest grade being 105 feet to the mile for three-fourths of a mile. The report shows the feasibility of the scheme, and careful calculations made, leave no doubt of its being a success as a business enterprise.

291. *Santa Cruz Sentinel,* October 14, 1871 (2:1)
SANTA CLARA and SANTA CRUZ RAILROAD.

The surveys of this road being completed, and all the maps, plans and specifications of the road considered, the officers have determined to move in the matter of commencing the work. Mr. F. A. Hihn, the President of the road, visits San Francisco at this time with a route map of the road, for the purpose of making an exhibit and procuring aid, if possible, in prosecuting the work. On Thursday last we examined the map, and find many features more advantageous than at first supposed. Those who are skeptical should inquire into the matter, examine the route and figure on the natural resources of our mountain ranges, seacoast plateaus and tide-water levels, before risking an opinion against the enterprise.

According to the map examined, the Santa Cruz road forms a junction with the San Francisco and San Jose road, half way between the towns of Santa Clara and San Jose, which actually will be a central point when these two towns become one city, an event soon to be consummated. From this initial point the road is a straight line westerly five miles to the Los Gatos; crossing to the east side of the creek, the survey makes another straight line of five miles to the village of Los Gatos; thence, following along the east side of the Los Gatos creek to the crossing, two miles above Lexington, a distance of fourteen miles from the initial point; thence, curving along the creek at an easy grade, three miles to the tunnel, which is at an elevation of 1,100 feet above tide-water level. The tunnel will be 3,000 feet long, through sand-rock strong enough for self-support, without timbering or arching, although the rock is soft and porous, being cheaply and easily worked, and not dangerous to excavate. On the western slope the survey follows the west branch of the Soquel creek, crossing Chase's gulch, Dickens' creek and the east branch of the Soquel creek, following thence along the eastern bank of the main creek to opposite Hames &

Danbenbiss' flouring mill, where the line of survey recrosses the creek, and running thence, curving with the bench, on a direct line to Santa Cruz, making the entire distance from point to point 34 miles. The route is through a densely timbered section, affording ample water power for mills and machinery to cut all lumber and other timber on the route. Besides the natural resources, undeveloped, we might note a few of the improvements already made along the line of survey, or within a short distance of the route; We will not enumerate the valuable farms and vineyards in the Santa Clara Valley, but commence at Los Gatos, where a number of establishments afford profitable employment to many men. The most prominent is the woolen mills and a large flour mill. At Saratoga, but a few miles distant, are also considerable manufacturing interests, especially in the fine, large paper mills and tanneries. At Lexington, a very flourishing little town, or tributary to it, are two small saw-mills. Following up the creek is Doherty's large saw-mill, with a running capacity for cutting 200,000 feet of merchantable lumber per day. Chase's mill is next in order, cutting 5,000 feet of first class lumber per diem. Crossing the divide, the first mill on this side is the Dickens mill, cutting 16,000 feet per day; thence, continuing down, is the water-power mill of Mr. Charles W. Olive (we find his name on our subscription book, and therefore can give it in full), with a capacity of 3,000 feet per day; the Soquel River Lumbering Company mills cut 25,000 feet per day; Mr. Benjamin Cahoon's mill, 4,000; the Moore mill, 6,000; the Bates mill, 3,000; the Grover mill, 12,000, feet per day, and so on. [garbled] the shingle mills of Mr. Burns and others. The large tannery (formerly Rabel's) of Messrs. Funk and Wasserman, is also on the route, and not far from it the distilleries and vineyards of the Vine Hill section, belonging to Mr. G. M. Jarvis and others. At Soquel are the water-power mills (and no brand of flour in the California market is superior) of Hames & Daubenbiss, and Porter's steam flouring and planing mills, of a capacity equal to the largest in the county. Below Soquel Porter's tannery and a distillery are located. The tannery is one of the largest and best in the State, and famed for turning out superior leather of all kinds. In Santa Cruz (the Lowell of the State) we have three large tanneries (with one in Scott's Valley), two planing mills, one flouring mill (Santa Cruz City mills) where all the finer brands of best quality family flour are made, a glue factory, soap factory and other minor establishments. Near town are four large lime-making establishments, several saw-mills and shingle mills, besides the manufacture of staves, brooms, and almost everything that enters into household use or domestic economy. All this trade would be more than doubled or quadrupled in a few years after the road is completed. As an item worth mentioning, it is stated that the Bates gulch, east of Soquel, has forty millions of feet of first-class timber for cutting into lumber, which has never yet been touched by the woodman's ax. There are at least a dozen such districts on the line of this road, besides the timber on the main line adjacent to the road.

Of the Watsonville road, at this time we shall say but

little, leaving the people to discuss the question as seems best, owing to the fact that an effort will be made to build the road at once, and that by giving property holders a chance to aid the enterprise by a legal subscription. The Santa Cruz and Watsonville road will commence at the depot, about 1½ miles southeast of Watsonville; thence, crossing the Pajaro river near the center of the town, following along or near the line of the present stage road, next to the bay, to Aptos and Soquel. From Soquel, the road will run parallel with the San Jose track to Santa Cruz, a total distance of twenty miles.

292. *Santa Cruz Sentinel,* October 14, 1871 (2:3-4)
A Railroad Our Relief.

In launching so boldly, last week, the idea that something must be done immediately to rescue the impending decline into which business of all kinds and property of every description—except $20 pieces—is rushing, and has been tending for many months, we did it with some doubts as to how far, the general feelings of this people might be found to correspond with our own.

The very idea, to many, subsidizing a railroad, even though it was to carry them from perdition itself, would have to be cursed and rejected until the yawning depths opened before them as a stern reality or dread alternative. There are very many serious objections that can easily arise and grow from the abuse of this principle; but like everything fraught with great good when wisely divined, when perverted by the unscrupulous can become a wonderful engine of wrong and oppression. Our very existence, physically, rests in the careful observance of certain laws of life which tend, when unobstructed, to health, happiness and a more perfect manhood; still how many diseased, dwarfed, weak and abnormal conditions and temperaments do we find surrounding us on every hand; so little do we regard the first injunction of nature, "Preserve thyself," that we all are more or less the victims of some ailment engendered through violated laws.

Let this subject be viewed dispassionately; for it does not at this time afford the needed relief, then we know not whither to turn for aid.

We are surprised to find the general sentiment of the people so completely identical with our suggestions of last week, and so much in harmony with the idea that the only way out of our dilemma, is by urging, through some proper means, the speedy construction of a railroad from Watsonville to Santa Cruz. With one or two slight exceptions, the solid vote of Santa Cruz and Felton would be given in favor of any reasonable proposition that has for its object, the revivifying of industry and trade.

The idea that a few persons who have plenty—and to spare—should feel such a sudden deep concern for the poor taxpayer at this especial moment, is laughable in the extreme. It is the poor and medium classes who feel every depression of business and breath of adversity soonest and keenest; they work for their bread, and must find profitable employment to keep the wolf of starvation from their doors; they have no hoarded thousands to make them feel secure from want; their hands are their capital, and their personal welfare is as dear to them as is the wealth of Croesus to a Croesus. The poor tax-payers ask no such sympathy at this time; he wants labor for his hands at remunerative prices, that he may be enabled to meet his current expanses and retain to his family the little home his hard earnings have gathered together in more prosperous times. He realizes the fact that something must be done and is clamorous and willing to pay any reasonable tax imposed, if in return, he is to receive a corresponding benefit; he realizes, to be prosperous, is to be enterprising; fostering and favoring wise projects in every way that is reasonable and possible. We find these poor tax-payers are not averse to aiding a railroad, but mostly those who are able to and of themselves to build such roads; but who are very clear from giving aid in any way. On every hand, as it is and ever will be, there will crop out the verification of the old adage, that capital is aggressive, subversive and oppressive—tending to make the rich richer and the poor poorer. We can see very plainly why persons of wealth, in a community like ours, should throw hindrances in the way of every project that might enhance the value of property, when with a less value attached they might soon become possessed of every choice and valuable place. Such persons will always tell you that it is but a matter of time when every desirable resource of wealth and prosperity will come to them. This is very true, because such is the order of things; still cannot enterprise be forced and prosperity accelerated by a little timely aid? Who are to afford subsistence for the laborless and their families while these healthy financial times are snail like making their way in obedience to the order of things? We draw this picture as a true one, and which is sadly always about on the eve of any great movement that promises as much to others as it does to themselves. Santa Cruz, happily, has less of this class of persons than any place we have ever known; the instances are few, if any, with us where the wealthy are not open in their support of this movement. There are different ways suggesting by various persons; but all agree that if one method will not bring about the desired end, then the next best thing must be adopted. This is as it should be, and when this feeling prevails there is much to hope for. All agree that this is the moment when the effort to accomplish this will cost less and prove more effectual.

So far, we have only set forth the benefits to be desired, without particularly counting the costs. No good or safe financier would undertake or enter upon a project without considering the attending cost and inconveniences, as well as the benefits resulting therefrom; and none would consider him safe, if after so weighing his subject and finding chances equal, he should persist in hazarding an experiment fraught with no slight a chance for remuneration. If, after setting forth the result of experience, and the undeniable condition, that figures and reasonable statements indicate, it is not found that there is an ample and reasonable margin that in any contingency will render the experiment proper and safe, then we, with all other good citizens, will pronounce against the proposition to aid in building the road from Watsonville to Santa Cruz; but not until the subject has had a fair and impartial investigation, can we, in justice to the public which in a great measure we represent, obtrude our private opinions, which all know have been much against the general principle of subsidizing corporations. We must advocate that which seemeth for the best interests of this people and county, and if we err, it will not be because we desire to be wrong, but from a mistaken or immature judgment.

The following is the data from which we conclude this movement is opportune and wise: The assessed value of the real and personal property of this county for 1871 is $2,146,209.00. This is but one-third of the real valuation, which is $6,438,627.00. Then it is proposed to aid the road in some manner, either by giving or loaning County bonds, or subscribing to the stock in the sum of one hundred thousand dollars, which is five thousand dollars per mile for twenty miles—the distance from Santa Cruz to Watsonville. The bonds to become payable in twenty years and bear interest at the rate of seven per cent. per annum, interest payable annually; the interest amounting annually to seven thousand dollars, is just what, to a cent, the people will be taxed for twenty years on account of this road. Is there anything very alarming about that? The taxes for 1871 amounts to $64,361.69 and assuring them no more than 1872 the total tax would amount to $71,381.69, and this too with twenty miles of railroad completed valued at least worth six hundred thousand dollars, which of itself will pay three sevenths of the increased tax; then each man's tax would be just one sixteenth more on account of the road.

We must next consider the probable condition of the people and their capacity to meet the constant demand from year to year until the twentieth year, when the full burden of the aid must be paid. Is it too much to assume that our population will at that time be less than thirty thousand, and that the wealth of the country shall have increased more than four hundred per cent. making its prospective value reach the sum of $25,000,000. Will not the whole State increase in wealth and population in due proportion? and will not there be a great reduction naturally in both State and county taxes in proportion to the population and wealth of the State? Long before that day, the State and this county will have paid off every dollar of its outstanding indebtedness, and the tax instead of being $2.97 on the hundred dollars, will not exceed seventy-five cents on the hundred dollars to meet every expense of State and county government and pay off the then existing debt. To view this question properly we must not look at the future in the light of the present; everything with us is comparatively new, and we have not recovered from the first great expense of setting a new State and county government in successful operation., We of this county have considerable to show for our indebtedness in the way of expensive bridges, roads and county buildings, and the only way to reduce our taxes, is to increase the productive wealth and population of the county. No project, enterprise or undertaking will so thoroughly and completely accomplish this end as the completion of the proposed railroad.

There is not a mill property in the county, to-day worth one-half the first cost of construction, and the lumber is being sacrificed without any reasonable return to any one—more especially the manufacturer. When lumbermen from these parts are compelled to deliver lumber in San Francisco for seventeen dollars per thousand feet, they might better stop their saw-mills, for such is the sad waste of time and material. Neither does real estate find purchasers at the once desirable rates; there is a general stagnation of all business. It is hoped to modify and change this condition for the better, and establish business on a less transitory basis—giving some assurance to those desiring to come among us that there will not be a feast to day and a famine to-morrow.

How far our necessities correspond with our neighbors at Watsonville we are not fully informed; yet it does seem as though the benefits to be derived from a railroad connecting the remote parts of the county would be very considerable to them, and we trust this subject will receive due consideration at their hands. There is no truth in the statement that the company constructing the road into the Pajaro Valley contemplate continuing the road to Santa Cruz; they have simply viewed out the most available place from which to obtain what timber they require, and are not likely to come twenty miles when half that distance will do them. Those who peddle this idea are not doing so with good intent, or hope to benefit the present condition of things. If county aid is withheld, then the citizens must subscribe to the stock, or when will there come the desired relief? It being done, will afford profitable employment for laborers and mechanics; the roads will teem with a hundred well freighted wagons, and general thrift will usher in the hopeful future.

Our article would be too lengthy, did we treat this subject in all its bearings; we have said enough to set all parties to thinking seriously upon the subject and hope the effort being made to induce the Supervisors to order an election, will not prove abortive. We must believe that seven tenths of the voters of this county would be in favor of some kind of aid, and such a desire should weigh heavily with our Board when considering the subject.

293. *Santa Cruz Sentinel,* October 14, 1871 (4:1)

The Watsonville branch of the S. P. R. R. which starts at Junction, a few miles from Gilroy, it is expected will be completed to Pajaro, one mile from Watsonville, by the 15th inst. The distance between the two points is twenty-five miles. A depot is nearly completed, and the farmers are already storing their grain in the unfinished building, at this place, (Watsonville).

294. *The Pajaronian*, October 19, 1871 (3:2)

RAILROAD to SANTA CRUZ.
Subsidy of $100,000.

The last two numbers of the Santa Cruz *Sentinel* have each contained a long article favoring a railroad to that town from this place. The articles paint in very gloomy colors the present financial condition of Santa Cruz. The writer says the town is for sale—becoming bankrupt, and nothing will save it but a railroad from Watsonville. The writer's figuring, in order to make a flattering showing, is astonishing if not plausible. He says the assessed value of the real and personal property of this county is about $2,000,000, when it ought to be over $6,000,000. There's wisdom. Wants the county to give $100,000 to a railroad company. All very well to talk about, but what is to be done with the present county debt of sixty or seventy-five thousand dollars. But the writer of the articles referred to, sets the matter at rest forever, by asserting that the assessed value of the county, with a railroad 20 miles long to Santa Cruz, will in time be $25,000,000, and the population as countless as the sands of the sea, or something equally as ridiculous. We have heard of no responsible parties favoring the project, for the idea is utterly impracticable. If a Railroad company think a road will pay from this place to Santa Cruz, they will build it without a subsidy. And it will be the height of foolishness for the people of this part of the county to vote for a subsidy for a railroad to Santa Cruz, for we already have ample railroad facilities. Furthermore, every man in the county would be very foolish and near-sighted to vote in favor of a $100,000 mortgage, increasing taxes which are already enormous, in aid of a project that has not the first business-principle to back it up. Santa Cruz has ample port facilities, two splendid wharfs, three miles below, at Soquel, is another good landing, a few miles below Soquel, at Aptos, is still another landing, now what will there be left for a railroad to do, after all the vessels and schooners have taken their share. No lime, for the lime companies have wharf and vessels of their own; no powder, for the powder company also have a wharf and boats; no paper, for the concern is shut down the most of the time; no lumber, unless there should be a wet season in the lower country; no passengers, in addition to those who already travel, for a railroad never compels persons to journey unless they are willing. If we could see that the subsidy would be a good business investment, no one would be more earnest in its support than we. The School Fund of this county is barely sufficient to pay running expenses, and the Road Fund is bankrupt. The county is deeply in debt, and if we cannot keep our county roads in decent repair, we cannot see the sense in wading still further into difficulty by saddling ourselves with another debt of $100,000.

295. *Santa Cruz Sentinel,* October 21, 1871 (2:2)
FURTHER CONCERNING OUR RAILROAD.

Having had two weeks in which to canvass the proposition to aid in some way, through county assistance, the construction of a railroad from Watsonville to Santa Cruz, the people most interested and desirous of establishing such communication are expressing themselves quite favorably of the county subscribing $100,000 to the stock, which is thought the better way, as then the county will own that interest in the road and will receive back in dividends, saying nothing of the savings in transportation to the people, more than double the amount of principal and interest required in aid of this great project. What would Santa Clara and San Jose have been had not that county aided the railroad that has builded about them a city of happy homes, teeming with every shade of enterprise and business?

Read the following statement of facts published in the report of the Supt. Of the Los Angeles and San Pedro Railroad, and say whether you are prepared to let this favorable opportunity pass for securing this coveted prize—

"The Supt. Of the Los Angeles and San Pedro Railroad,

in a published statement of the business done by the road last year, says it transported 10,600 tons of merchandise and 5,800,000 feet of lumber to Los Angeles, and 1,410 tons wine and brady, 1,229 tons wool, 4,914 tons corn, 534 tons oranges and 1,933 tons miscellaneous produce from Los Angeles. The freight by rail on these things was $116,439.70, and by team, at the rate charged before the construction of the road, would have been $249.982.50, showing a saving of $133,482 for one year, or $2,007,642 for 15 years. The city and county together have promised to pay $562,500 to the Railroad Company, including the principal of the bonds and the interest for 15 years. By this calculation the county will make $1,445,142 by the transaction, and will have their stock in the road in addition."

The amount of lumber to be freighted into the valleys below will not average less than 10,000,000 feet per annum. The present price per teams is $6 per 1,000 feet, freight by rail will be about one-half, making a saving in the reduction in price of lumber to the farmer and builder of $30,000 annually, or $600,000 in 20 years. Then the advantages of shipping at Aptos, Soquel and Santa Cruz, will prove a saving, on the average, of one dollar per ton for all produce sent from the valleys, which saving, in the aggregate, will exceed annually the amount saved on lumber. If these are not considerations sufficient to induce our neighbors at the lower end of this county to favor county aid at this time, in the manner proposed, by subscribing to the capital stock in the sum of $100,000, then nothing can move them to a favorable consideration. All that is left for us is to submit the question to the people, and let those who oppose the project take the responsibility of defeating it if the election is carried against the measure. We have always thought that it would be mutually beneficial for Watsonville and Santa Cruz to be connected by a railroad communication, and believe so still.

It is thought advisable to insert the petition being circulated, and we accordingly give it place.

"To the Honorable the Board of Supervisors of the County of Santa Cruz, State of California.

"Gentlemen: The undersigned, your petitioners, respectfully represent and show to your Honorable Body, that the material interests of this county demand at your hands every consideration and reasonable effort tending, or that may tend to the upbuilding and development of the varied interests and resources of this county, and to this end ask your Honorable Body to favorably consider this our reasonable request and most earnest prayer, which is, that your Honorable Body call order and declare an election pursuant to An Act to empower the Board of Supervisors of the several counties of the State to aid in the construction of a railroad in their respective counties. Approved April 4th, 1870. And that such aid in the amount, not to exceed $5,000 per mile, be granted to any company that will, within the space of on year, construct and put in good working condition a railroad of proper gauge with T rail track, commencing at Santa Cruz, thence passing through, or near the town of Soquel, thence through the town of Watsonville, and connecting with some road being constructed, or to be constructed, into the Pajaro Valley, and which road shall establish railroad communication between the places named and the City of San Francisco. Said aid to be granted from the dividing line between the counties of Monterey and Santa Cruz, and extend for the distance of twenty miles.

"Believing that the people of this county will cheerfully approve by their suffrages any proper aid to such enterprises that your Honorable Board in its wisdom may determine and recommend.

"And to this end we will ever pray."

The petition, after being circulated a few days, has received the signatures of upwards of 500 of the taxpayers of the county; and what is most singular, out of all the number asked to sign only three refused. There will be 1,000 votes, at least, cast at this end of the county in favor of aiding the project, and there is not twenty-five persons in the county who will not be directly or indirectly benefitted by this line of railroad. It is a mistake that our farmers at this end of the county will oppose or vote against assistance, not one so far has refused to sign the petition, and all feel that the road will prove profitable as well as a great convenience.

The Supervisors meet on Monday next when the petition will be presented, and without doubt will result in giving us a chance to favor the most worthy project it has ever been this people's privilege to inaugurate.

296. *The Pajaronian*, October 26, 1871 (2:2)

Three Hundred Thousand Dollars to be Given Away!
TAXES TO BE INCREASED!

Our blinded Santa Cruz friends, are pushing their railroad scheme in a very energetic manner. A petition has been drawn up praying the Board of Supervisors to order an election under the provisions of the five per cent. law, and 500 men in Santa Cruz and vicinity have signed it. This Act embodied a principle fought against by the people of Santa Cruz at the last election, but with a lack of consistency seldom ever known before they are now, after only a few short weeks, as strenuously in favor of. We cannot say that we are surprised at this weather-cock changeability on the part of certain Republicans of Santa Cruz, but if Democrats should favor this unjust railroad scheme, our confidence will be destroyed in humanity as far as party men are concerned. We have never been a blatant Republican, but we can claim that we have ever been an honestly earnest and consistent as any one. We did not favor subsidizing Railroad Corporations (and especially the Central Pacific) before the election, neither shall we do so now.

Aside from the principle involved, the railroad scheme hatched up in Santa Cruz, is one of the most nonsensical moves in a business point of view we have ever heard of, and in all that we have seen written on the subject, there has not been one line to show that the road would pay, neither have we heard that the principal business men of Santa Cruz are in favor of it. In fact we know that many of the first business men of that end of the county smile at the absurdity of the idea. We heard a rumor to the effect that Mr. Hihn was active in pushing the matter forward, but we think it is not so. We have too high an opinion of his intelligence and business talents to believe that he would enter into such a foolish scheme.

It appears now that the enterprising and self-sacrificing

gentlemen of Santa Cruz wish to give away *only* $100,000; but we are assured from reliable persons that it is their real wish to issue bonds and tax the county in accordance with the five per cent law. This law says, "The whole amount of said bonds herein authorized to be issued shall not exceed five per cent of the value of the taxable property, of such county," etc. A writer in the *Sentinel*, favoring the subsidy, says the taxable property of the county is $6,000,000. Five percent of this sum is $300,000! Let us give the Central Pacific Railroad this latter sum, make over the county to them and then quietly move away to some place where taxes are not five or six dollars on every one hundred; where the road fund is not bankrupt, where the school fund is not always short, where all the people work together for the good of all, where one set of men because they happen to have a majority of votes, do not heap injustice on those districts having a minority of the voting population.

297. *The Pajaronian*, October 26, 1871 (2:3)

Railroad Subsidy.

"Ma, Johnny has got a whistle, I'm bigger nor Johnny, can't I have one!"

Such is the cry of Santa Cruz, now that we, in this primitive potato country, are soon to have railroad communication with all parts of the world, Santa Cruz excepted, hence a cry of distress goes up from the denizens of the city of the Holy Cross for the potato diggers to help them, as we have been derisively termed by the Santa Cruzans, especially during their reign of supposed prosperity, when they considered themselves independent of Watsonville and every other place. Santa Cruz with her powder and paper mills, lime and lumber interests, and above all her excellent hotels, splendid climate, a beach for sea bathing, Santa Cruz was to be the Queen of the Pacific, a second Newport or Saratoga. To question the future greatness of Santa Cruz was treason, every stage load of passengers was duly chronicled, their arrival of course, every object of interest in and around Santa Cruz was magnified into wonderful attractions; notwithstanding all this Santa Cruz has failed to attract many summer swarmers of late, the people are beginning to think that the meretricious show is not all that is necessary to build up a town, something more solid is required.

To retrieve their error and recuperate their fallen fortunes a Railroad is advocated from Watsonville to Santa Cruz. "Just the thing; we can build it easily by issuing bonds as a bonus and make the entire county pay for it." Very liberal of Santa Cruz, but excuse us we don't see it in that light.

A railroad to Santa Cruz may possibly be built in due course of time when it will pay; at present there is no company or corporation who will undertake to build the road unless a more liberal subsidy is given, than the one proposed, $100,000, and so soon after an anti-subsidy election, it is rather cool to say the least, to ask the people to vote for subsidy to a railroad, when they have just declared against subsidies. Another reason the entire people of the county do not desire to be taxed for the exclusive benefit of Santa Cruz.

There is in this end of the county quite a large amount of taxable property that would not be materially benefitted by the road to Santa Cruz, besides we do not need any such road either for export or import. As a general rule people do not buy anything they do not need, or can get along without; this may be applied to that proposed railroad with equal force.

We are informed that the good people of Santa Cruz are anxious to become better acquainted with us, to cement the bonds of friendship, etc. Strange that this should be thusly. Before the Southern Pacific concluded to run into this valley, we heard no complaints on the part of Santa Cruz. When the people of this valley, unaided and alone, were trying to build a railroad to connect at Gilroy, no offers of assistance came from the other end of the county, no suggestions thrown out that the county should take stock or issue bonds.

Now the case is altered, the sceptre is departing from Santa Cruz, times are hard, business is dull, houses and stores are to rent, stages come in empty; if bonds can be issued even if the road is never constructed, there will be a chance to make a corner on bonds, the scrip ring is hungry and must be fed at the expense of the public. We want none of the scrip or bonds, hence if the Supervisors are foolish enough to call an election for the purpose of fostering additional taxation on us, we shall vote against it and induce our neighbors to do so, and keep on voting against it, here, in					PAJARO.

298. *Santa Cruz Sentinel,* October 28, 1871 (2:2-3)
REASON FOR AIDING THE RAILROAD.

The more critically the question of the county's aiding the railroad between Watsonville and Santa Cruz is examined, the more apparent becomes the reason, justice and necessity of so doing. And to no part of the people is it of greater importance than the citizens of Watsonville and surroundings. The proposed road will pass immediately through the town of Watsonville, and afford the coveted advantage of a depot, for which its citizens proposed to give the Central Pacific Company $50,000, and which bid was declined, leaving our friends to travel over one mile to make connection with the cars; this may be very desirable for Watsonville, but generally such disadvantages and inconveniences are not highly prized. The road will touch every prominent place and point in the county; Santa Cruz, Soquel, Aptos, Corralitos and Watsonville, and at each place establish stations or depots, affording the usual railroad facilities. One thing is very certain; if this project should fall for want of support from the people of Watsonville, there is but one other course left for Santa Cruz and Soquel, which is, to try and construct the road now surveyed, and which will connect with the road at San Jose.

The stimulus which a defeat would afford would cause sufficient stock to be taken in Santa Cruz to insure constructing the road; still, aside from the saving of two or three hours travel, between Santa Cruz and the city, we believe the people generally prefer the road via Watsonville. It is a foregone conclusion that we must have better, cheaper and speedier connection with other parts, and if the people are going to pay personally for a route, they will accept the most direct, especially when all that is asked of them is $50,000. The road to Watsonville will never be undertaken and completed without county aid. There is not capitalists enough in this county who will hazard an investment to justify an attempt to raise $500,000 to build the road, and any other company would be extremely foolish to put money in the pockets of those who refuse to help themselves. The Central Pacific have done nobly in running their road into the main valley, and now, if we are so exacting as to demand further assistance from them, we must not be frightened at their refusal. We feel confident that the people, when understanding this subject, will come to its relief in sufficient numbers to save the project.

Now in order to show the importance, practicability and necessity of our sustaining the proposition to aid the road by issuing county bonds, payable in twenty years, in the sum of $100,000, bearing interest at seven per cent per annum, it will be necessary to make use of some facts and figures used in former articles on this subject. We have taken the pains to interview our late county Assessor, Mr. Taylor, on the subject of assessments, and he informs us that the assessments of the real and personal property of the county is upon the basis of a one-third valuation. The assessed value being, $2,146,200, confirms our statement, at which the learned editor of the *Pajaronian* becomes more frightened than hurt, that the actual value of the property real and personal of the county, exceeds, $6,000,000. Mr. Taylor also says that there is over $600,000 mortgages in this county unassessable. In all probability this unjust exception and pandering to wealth will be suspended by a law compelling all kinds of property to be assessed at its true value. Then our ability to meet the exigencies of taxation in the event the road is constructed would stand thus:

Real and Personal property, (true value)	$6,438,627
Mortgages (unassessed now)	600,000
<u>Twenty miles of Railroad</u>	<u>500,000</u>
Total	$7,538,627

The State and county taxes for 1871, amount to $64,381.69; add to this $7,000 required to meet the interest on the bonds, and the grand total of taxes for 1872, assuming them to be no greater then than now, will amount to $71,361.69.

If all property is assessed at its actual value in 1872, the tax to meet every demand will amount to just ninety-five cents on the hundred dollars. It will be seen from this showing that the $600,000 of unassessed mortgages, and the $500,000 the value of the road, constitute $1,100,000 new property to be assessed, and which, at the aforesaid rate, will return, in taxes, $10,450, more than enough by $3,450, to meet the interest on the bonds given in aid of the road. This establishes the fact that, with the road, and just laws respecting assessments, the people who pay the taxes this year, will have less to pay next, by $3,450.

The road will pay an annual tax of $4,750 towards liquidating the $7,000 interest on bonds. In twenty years at this rate the road will pay back to the county in taxes $95,000. Those taking sides against the road do note deal fairly; they only show what are seeming inconveniences, and never point out the advantages.

We now proposed to show that without the road, the farmer will ultimately bear a greater burden; that the bulk of the taxes will be shifted from the towns to lands that are growing in value every day. In 1868 Santa Cruz paid one-fourth of all the taxes of Santa Cruz County; in 1871 she will not pay one-seventh, and if her real estate continues in its present decline, she will not pay one-twelfth the tax in 1872. We reason thus: If the farmer would lessen his taxes, he must foster such enterprises as will enhance other property than farming lands. With a rail road Santa Cruz will, in three years, double in population and wealth and then would pay one-third the tax of the county; so also would the town property of every place touched by the road increase, and the tax on farming lands would constantly be lessened, as city wealth accumulates much faster than rural wealth.

Having shown our ability to meet every contingency that can possibly arise from aiding the road, we will pause to consider the profit and benefits resulting to the whole people from the road.

Santa Cruz, Soquel and Aptos will be enabled to place their millions of feet of lumber in competition with Ford & Sanborn, thus reducing the price of lumber four dollars per thousand. With this reduction there would be a good market for ten million feet annually, with an absolute saving to consumer of $40,000. You will find these home monopolists crying out against exorbitant taxation, never telling you that this $40,000 might be saved if reasonable competition was allowed; in ten years this saving alone, would nearly build a road as proposed. About one-half to meet the interest on the bonds, will be paid by the road. In no possible contingency, can the tax-payers at the lower end of the county have their taxes increased more than fifteen hundred dollars on account of the road, and why a people should be so blinded and unreasonable, as to oppose a thing for their immediate relief and benefit, is strange indeed. Do not the farmers know that if they should ship every pound of grain by rail to San Francisco, they would be benefited by the reduced transportation this line of road would cause, because of the convenience afforded to ship by water from Aptos, Soquel or Santa Cruz. Mr. Titus Hale says, and he is good authority, that the reduction in freight would not be less than one dollar per ton on every ton of produce grown in the Pajaro Valley. Then in this item of reduced freight there will be a saving to the producers of some fifty or sixty thousand dollars annually. Economists tell us the best way to make money is to save it, and if the saving of some hundred thousand dollars per annum to the farmers of this county is not worth considering, what in the name of reason is? At the present rate of freight by water, vast fortunes could be made by rail; the way to prevent these conveniences and great necessities from becoming engines of wrong and oppression, is to create antagonism and competition. Set them to bidding for patronage, and the patron will receive a fair equivalent for his money.

The Dream of Steam, 1854–1873

There is also received over the wharf at Santa Cruz, 650 tons freight per month, and quite as much, exclusive of Davis & Cowell's lime, sent off. A railroad would reduce the freights one dollar per ton, saving to Santa Cruz in the item of freight some $15,000 per annum. Add to this the profits of a revived lumber trade, and traffic, with an increasing population, and no sane man in these parts could, in justice to the community in which he lives, cast his vote to send us backwards. If there is any person in the county who is possessed of large landed interests that are held for posterity, these will be somewhat annoyed, and may be compelled under the new regimen to allow such property to contribute to the productive wealth of the county. Such persons will of course be found working against the interest of any place or people that strive for progress. Santa Cruz is considered by our farmers the best market in the State for all they have to sell. Everything could be sold at higher prices than in San Francisco, with the still further saving of transportation, storage and commissions. With business for all our teams, labor for all classes, and business for the merchant, will not our farmers find an ever profitable and increasing market for their produce? A railroad will do this for them, and by increasing the wealth and population, the county will largely lessen their taxes. Let every man who speaks against the project, reflect on what he is doing to whole communities, whose only hope for business depends upon its consummation. If Santa Cruz does not do something to afford profitable employment for her laborers and mechanics, there must two hundred with their families move away the coming season, if they would find work for which to live without going in debt.

Nobody can be very badly affected by the additional tax of $7,000, and in twenty years, when the bonds become due, how many now here will be present to help pay the debt; and if they should, we venture the prediction that they will not be those who oppose every public enterprise, or who opposed this.

299. *The Pajaronian*, November 2, 1871 (2:1)

One of the arguments in the *Sentinel*'s Railroad article, of last week is to the effect that if the Railroad was constructed from this place to Santa Cruz, the lumbermen of Aptos, Soquel and Santa Cruz would be enabled to compete with Messrs. Ford & Sanborn of Watsonville, in the lumber trade! We never thought of that view of the railroad question before. A mighty argument, to be sure.

300. *The Pajaronian*, November 2, 1871 (2:1)

The Sacramento *Union* of the 30th ult, contains the following sensible remarks, evidently based on our railroad editorial of last week:

The Santa Cruz Railway Scheme.

Santa Cruz desires railway connection with the San Jose and Gilroy lines. The road out would be short and somewhat difficult. It would probably cost half a million dollars, possibly more. The county has $6,000,000 worth of taxable property at a fair valuation. It is figured by some of the citizens of that town that the county levy a tax of five per cent. under the law of April, 1870, which would yield $300,000, and offer that sum in subsidy to the Central Pacific to build the coveted road. If our advice could avail we would give it against such a course. If the county can afford to *give* away $300,000, it can far better afford to add $200,000 to the amount and own and control the road itself. It would thus insure the lowest rates of fare and freight, add several millions to its taxable property and keep clear of a company which only receives such gifts to oppress the giver. The same law that authorizes a county to build, own and control a mud road or a macadamized one, authorizes it to build, own and manage a railway. If rates of transportation are cheap, every interest will benefit by the construction of the road; if dear none will benefit. If the Central Pacific owns the road, there is nothing in the future surer than they will charge the highest rates; but if the county had it in its own hands, the people would unanimously demand the lowest practicable rates and the town and county of Santa Cruz would soon feel the beneficial effects of such a management.

301. *The Pajaronian*, November 2, 1871 (2:2)
Railroad Subsidy.

From all we can learn many of the citizens of our "Sister City," Santa Cruz, have laid aside their usual good judgment and forethought, and are permitting themselves to be led by a few interested parties in a direction contrary to their best interests. We refer of course to the $300,000 railroad subsidy now being strenuously pushed forward by land owners and scrip speculator.

We learn that a majority of the Board of Supervisors are in favor of ordering an election, their meeting tomorrow being exclusively for that purpose. During the agitation of the subsidy question the citizens of this portion of the county, who pay one-half of the taxes, have not been consulted, and it has only been by strict inquiry that we could ascertain what was going on. We cannot look upon the proceeding in any other light than that of a purely selfish operation, and an outrage on the people of one-half of the county. We are sorry to think so, for our memories of Santa Cruz are ever pleasant and we dislike to think that men in whom we placed confidence should not display a spirit so utterly at variance with charity and good fellowship. We are inclined to think that the whole thing from its first inception was instigated by jealousy— a fear that Watsonville, which has always been second to Santa Cruz, would in a few years stand first in the county. That the Court House, and fine hotel, and skating rink, and Farmer's clubs, and churches would be removed to the Pajaro, and that town be left in denuded state, with nothing left but the jail.

To show our friends how subsidies sometimes operate we will cite one well known instance. Calaveras county, some years ago, began to fall into debt (the same as Santa Cruz county has done) business became dull, settlers came slowly, and old residents one after another sold their homesteads and sought other localities. A multitude of stores and dwelling houses were lying idle, and all classes of business grew dull and men struggled along hoping against hope. At length a few land owners and speculators conceived the idea of building an immense wagon road over the mountains and induced the already groaning county of Calaveras to issue bonds to the extent of $250,000 to help construct the road which speculators were so anxious to see made. The road was built. A few rich men became richer, but the county was bankrupt. Poor men stood up manful under the enormous taxation the road had entailed, and at length, dispirited and cursing, almost gave their property away and left. Persons searching for locations avoided Calaveras as they would a cholera district and settled in Amador county adjoining. The consequence is, that while Amador is progressing, Calaveras, with equal advantages and the same climate, is still tax-ridden and bankrupt, with no signs of prosperity to encourage its scattered and depleted population.

Let the people of Santa Cruz county think carefully for themselves on this subsidy move, and go for no measure that will entail greater taxation upon then, without first securing more convincing proof of a corresponding gain in their financial prospects. But build the road, give away immense sums of money to a corporation, and our beautiful county will become what Calaveras now is—an object of charity.

302. *The Pajaronian*, November 2, 1871 (3:1)

The railroad to this place is progressing satisfactorily. A large quantity of grain has already been taken from the edge of the valley, some six miles from town, and it is expected that by Saturday the construction train will reach near the site of the depot. It will probably be some weeks before passenger trains will run, but freight trains will probably commence running next week. Work is progressing rapidly at the depot grounds, and but a short time will elapse, before the road will be entirely finished.

303. *San Francisco Bulletin,* October 30, via the *Santa Cruz Sentinel,* November 4, 1871 (1:7-8)

THE PAJARO VALLEY RAILROAD.

The stage coach is doomed, its days, at least in the Pajaro Valley, are numbered. Already the locomotive thunders down its sunny slopes, and the shrill engine whistle awakes the echoes in its sequestered glens. In company with Col. Geo. E. Gray, Engineer-in-Chief of the Southern Pacific Railroad, the writer of this found himself on board a supply train at Gilroy, bound for Watsonvilleward. For some two miles we follow the line of the Southern Pacific toward Hollister; then turn sharply to the right over a rich and comparatively level country. We cross the Pescadero and one or two minor streams, and after a short exhilarating ride we reach the Pajaro River, along the right bank of which we run for several miles. The Pajaro, a foaming, roaring, rampagnant stream, lawlessly running away from its bed and breaking things generally in winter, is very docile now. A child may play with it; a donkey made wade through it without so much as wetting the tip of his tail. Now its sluggish water stands in pools; now its course is marked by long reaches of bottom, as dry and dusty as the highway itself. As we descend, the valley alternatively widens and contracts; now stretching out into fertile plains,

The Dream of Steam, 1854–1873

now shrinking into a mere cañon, the track winding between precipitous rocks, skirting the base of mountain peaks, hanging, as it were, on the verge of gorges that make the head swim to look down into. There are at several points considerable engineering difficulties, which have been skillfully overcome; several cuts and fillings which in the earlier days of railroad building would have been considered formidable.

ACROSS THE RIVER.

About 12 miles from Gilroy, the road crosses to the left side of the river by a bridge from 300 to 400 feet long, at an elevation of 65 feet above the level of the stream. It is a wooden structure, strongly built, over which a train passes with-hardly a perceptible tremor. Beyond for some little distance, the cañon is very narrow, the hills abrupt, the scenery wild but beautiful, the track running close to the river bed but high above it. Beyond, the valley widens, the river turning to the right and making a detour. The railroad leaves it, cutting this section of the valley at right angles, heading straight for Watsonville, in defiance of the fact that a large hill lies straight across its path. The cutting through this hill constitutes the heaviest work on the line. When it is completed to the normal grade, it will be 80 feet deep—the heaviest single cut on any railroad in California. At present, however, a temporary track will be laid over the cut at a point considerably above grade. This is rendered necessary by the accumulation of freight waiting transportation at Watsonville.

AT THE FRONT.

The track was laid Thursday morning, to within five

miles and a half of Watsonville. The scene at the front as we arrived there was lively. The fields were dotted with tents; a construction train with all the appurtenances of boarding-house quarters, supplies of various kinds, materials for track-laying, etc., etc., stood on the track ready to "move out" close in the wake of the work. A few yards ahead a small army of track-layers were hammering and pounding and cutting away with might and main. Further on the road bed was being levelled, and ties being put in position. Still further on the graders, hundreds in number, were digging away at the great cut. Here Strowbridge, famous in the annals of railroad building "across the continent," was found overlooking everything, directing everything, making himself manifest through competent foremen, through every part of this busy hive. John Chinaman, complacent, moon-eyed, broad-hatted and dirt-begrimed, was there in force, shoveling, digging, picking, drilling, dumping dirt out of carts, urging, with barbarous phrase, fagged out horses, doing his work methodically, mechanically—himself a part of the great machine. It is expected the cut to the temporary grade will be finished by Tuesday next.

BEYOND.

From the great cut to Watsonville, a distance of five miles, the road makes nearly a straight line. The graders were far ahead—one party nearly two miles from the cut—while the line of the road marked by the plough furrows was visible some distance beyond. The work the remainder of the way is of the easiest. No more cuts, no more filling, no more gorges to cross, or ravines to span—but a bed as "level as a barn floor."

WATSONVILLE.

Watsonville was agitated to its centre by the question of the location of the railroad depot. Speculators were in the throes of suspense, real estate sharps were at their wits end. In the meantime, the railroad officials are cruelly reticent, and insist on keeping their own counsels. But shred guessers even now might forecast the location without serious fears of being set down for false prophets. The graders will be there next week, when all doubt will be at an end. Watsonville is thrifty. It is moved by a new impulse of activity by the advance of the iron road. Business is good; money seems to be reasonably plenty, and everybody is looking for great things ahead. A large number of elegant residences are going up, and a hotel, one of the largest in the State outside of San Francisco, is in process of erection. It is built and owned by Messrs. Alexander & Billings, who propose to make it in every respect a first class house. It is three stories high, with Mansard roof, and will have all the modern improvements of gas, water, bath-rooms, etc. They hope to have it ready for the accommodation of guests in about three weeks. The climate of Watsonville is considered among the best in the State, and with a good hotel can hardly fail to become a popular place of resort.

THE PAJARO VALLEY.

The Pajaro Valley is famed for its beauty, and its fame does not belie it. It is no exaggeration to call it one of the garden spots of the world. The scenery has a sort of quiet beauty all its own. It reminds one now of Savoy, now of North Wales, now of the Mohawk Valley. It has a matured, settled look, as if the people who lived in it were satisfied with their choice of a home and meant to stay. One no longer sees the miserable, unthrifty California ranch hovels, but tidy, tastefully designed farm houses, with pretty lawns and garden plats and flower beds in front. It takes one back to Central New York. The eye is not lost in a wilderness of floral sweets. And the soil is so wonderfully fertile. Life oozes from every pore. "We never missed a crop" is the universal boast of the people. Such a wealth of fruit and flower—of cereal and vegetable! It is Nature squandering her treasures. Everything that grows seems to grow with all its might. The pumpkins are colossal, the corn-stalks Brobdingnagian. Think of fifty and sixty bushels of wheat to the acre in this year of grievous drought!

PRICE OF LAND—STORAGE OF GRAIN.

The railroad company have built two immense warehouses for the storage of grain, about a mile to the west of Watsonville. They already contain some 26,000 sacks, and when the last lot is in will have about 30,000 sacks. This will be put on to the cars as soon as the track is laid to Watsonville, and taken to market. The price of land has greatly advanced in the Pajaro Valley within the past year. Prices for the best lands have ranged from $40 to $200, the latter price having been recently paid for a very choice piece near the town.

THE FARMERS AND THE RAILROAD.

There will always be croakers. A few desperate old fogies look askance at the railroad as a harbinger of evil, and a few people living on hired land complain that under the new stimulus rents have advanced to a burdensome figure. But the great mass of farmers look to the advent of the locomotive as the dawn of a new and better era. A very intelligent tiller of the soil, with whom we conversed, said: "You see, the railroad will do great things for us—at least, if the Company pursue a liberal policy. It will bring us directly to market. It will break up the tyranny of middlemen. Heretofore we have been compelled to take our grain down to the embarcadero—a distance of several miles. Here we were compelled to wait oftentimes a week or two for transportation, to pay heavy warehouse charges. Then heavy freight charges by steamer or sailing vessel, a passage of several days to San Francisco; consignment to a commission merchant; wharf charges at San Francisco; cost of storage, etc., until the profits were eaten up in charges, and we found it cost about as much to raise and get our grain to market as we got for it. As a consequence, the farmer was always in debt, always borrowing money, and always poor in the best grain raising country in the world. All that will be changed now. He will put his grain bags on board the cars in the morning, and by night it is in 'Frisco. He will sell at the market price as soon as he arrives, and the next day will come home with his money in his pocket.

304. *Santa Cruz Sentinel,* November 4, 1871 (2:1)

Our Railroad.—The Railroad subsidy question is the topic all over town. The opponents to the subsidy, although few in number, are active. Unfortunately for them they can bring forth no arguments to sustain their opposition. They claim that the Railroad Companies will take our Bonds without building the Railroad. To refute such an argument we copy the law:

"Section 1. No bonds shall be issued by the Supervisors of any county, in aid of the construction of a railroad, until at least five miles of such railroad shall have been constructed, and then only in such an amount as the distance of railroad constructed shall bear to the whole amount of aid to be granted."

305. *Santa Cruz Sentinel,* November 4, 1871 (2:2)

Why Watsonville Opposes the Railroad.

The question as to whether this county shall donate to some company $100,000 of its bonds payable in twenty years with interest at seven per cent. per annum, has now reached that climax of interest where it behooves us to speak plain, and unveil the latent designs and desires of our rival neighbor Watsonville. We have hitherto looked upon the removal of the County Seat from Santa Cruz to Watsonville as mythical, and also looked with favor upon the question of extending our county boundaries so as to include some fifty thousand acres of the adjacent territory of Monterey county; but since the advent of a railroad into the Pajaro Valley, the shaping of things so as to ultimately accomplish the removal of the County Seat is considered very possible, and as appearances now indicate, looks very probable. There is little doubt but that sooner or later all that vast region of fine agricultural land included in the valley east and south of Watsonville, embracing an area of 50,000 acres, thickly settled and well farmed, will be annexed to Santa Cruz county.

The territory, we believe, should belong to this county; but we do not desire it at a sacrifice of all that tends to sustain a just equilibrium between the different sections of the county. If Watsonville desires this annexation of territory merely for the advantage it affords her for removing the County Seat from Santa Cruz to Watsonville, then for this reason, we shall be obliged to propose the measure. Santa Cruz is beginning to understand Watsonville, and now more than ever. Our desire for railroad communication with that place, calls forth such a unanimous opposition, that none can be so blind as not to see the real cause behind their subterfuge. Everybody must know that Watsonville will be as much benefited as it could wish, and without it, become the prey of a few grain and lumber speculators.

The real cause of her opposition is, she knows that with the railroad, Santa Cruz will always be the most populous part of the county, and thus defeat the wish to take from her the County Seat. The antagonism now so apparent, must unite our people, and keep them as one man in support of enterprises tending to develop and build up all parts of the county, giving to no section that dangerous advantage of superior numbers, that might in utter disregard of all principle, be constrained to commit acts of great injustice to other sections, without any corresponding benefit. If we were not confident that the benefits resulting from the proposed aid to build the railroad from Watsonville to Santa Cruz, were equal, or as nearly so as human agencies can render them, we would not urge so strenuously the necessity of building the same, notwithstanding we believe no road will ever be built without aid from some sources.

We would not incite ill feeling towards our neighbor Watsonville, but must bring to the notice of Santa Cruz the fact that envy, jealousy and antagonistic feelings prevail to a great degree among the people at the lower end of the county, and if we do not protect ourselves by the use of every honorable means, there will be occasion for much ill feeling on the part of Santa Cruz. There is no denying the fact that Watsonville has her heart set on obtaining the County Seat; and see how easily it will be accomplished after the acquisition of a portion of Monterey county. That 50,000 acres has now a voting population of 400 and is capable of sustaining a population of 5,000. The railroad is surveying off a town which must soon number hundreds of voters; then with the increasing population the road will naturally bring to Watsonville and surrounding country, this end of the county will very soon lose the power of retaining the County Seat. Do you not known that the people of the section proposed to be annexed to this county have already taken steps to have the next Legislature annex them? and do you not know that the Honorable Gentleman representing this county in the next Legislature, both Senate and Assembly, are both from Watsonville, and are largely interested in real estate—especially Representative Bockius, who has about one hundred acres, called Bockius' addition to the town of Watsonville, which, in the event, a change of County Seat could be effected, would increase his financial prospects some $60,000 and our friend, Senator Beck, not quite so much?

Are these not considerations which naturally move men when backed by a goodly number of their constituency?

The power to effect the annexation of that desirable

portion of Monterey, and to secure a law putting to vote, the County Seat question, rests in the hands of these two gentlemen. Our ability to retain the County Seat under this contingency, must rest upon our power to out-vote the three precincts below.

The vote of the county will stand then about as follows, taking the poll lists of the Judicial Election as a criterion of our relative strength.

Watsonville Precinct, 558; Corralitos Precinct, 152; Annexed District, 400; Total, 1,110.

Santa Cruz Precinct, 811; Soquel Precinct, 326; San Lorenzo Precinct, 210; New Years Precinct, 75; Scott's Valley Precinct, 110. Total, 1,570.

Thus it will be seen that an influx of five hundred votes to Watsonville, the new railroad town and the annexed territory will suffice to carry the election against Santa Cruz. With the advantage Watsonville now has over us, there will, within about one year, be more than enough to turn the scale, and such is undeniable the design of our neighbors, their denial to the contrary notwithstanding. Every move unmistakably points to that end, and it behooves our citizens to stand on the defensive and defeat this infamous design. Those among us, who are playing in to the hands of Watsonville, are also largely interested in property and business there, which accounts for the milk in the cocoanut.

It is the universal feeling among Santa Cruzans, that the defeat of this aid to the railroad, will ensure the removal of the County Seat, and the vote at this end of the county must be as near unanimous as possible, for no scruples will be spared to defeat us below. We hear there is a purse of $5,000 raised to be expended in defeating the project. We need no such corrupting means if every man will act wisely and justly in the premises.

We begin to see why Watsonville accorded Mr. Beck such a warm support, and cannot blame brother Cummings for going back on Dr. Flint and the Republican party.

306. *Santa Cruz Sentinel,* November 4, 1871 (2:5)
PAJARONIAN AND THE RAILROAD

The *Pajaronian*'s article entitled "Three hundred thousand dollars to be given away," neither treats the question of aiding the railroad, with fairness or intelligence. The writer proves conclusively that he knows nothing of the law under which the Supervisors are to act, nothing of the wants and necessities of the people at this end of the county, and apparently does not care to better inform himself. He takes the narrowest and most selfish view of public enterprises; seems to think that because Watsonville has a railroad within two miles of town, the rest of his patrons have no desire or use for better and speedier facilities for business and travel.

If the editor has not learned that the principal business men of Santa Cruz favor this project, we will tell him that every firm and business man in town—except two—have signed the petition and are more intent to-day than ever on having the road as proposed in their petition. Santa Cruz would give a solid vote in favor of the railroad and so would Soquel, if an opportunity is offered, and we confidently believe and expect that one third of the voters of Watsonville Precinct will not be foolish enough to oppose a measure that will do more for them than the road now about to connect them with the rest of the world. One would suppose that the editor was merely running his paper in the interest of a few private speculators, whose occupation of fleecing the farmers of Pajaro and surroundings to the tune of $80,000 annually, through excessive prices for lumber and high freights was in some danger of being brought to a termination if reasonable competition was permitted. Did not that paper know that Santa Cruz and Soquel will be glad to furnish merchantable lumber at Watsonville at $4.00 per M and dressed lumber at $10.00 per M less than the present prices prevailing there? No man, capable of estimating the business of the proposed railroad, has ever dated to dispute the fact that the road would be a paying institution; and those two citizens here who oppose the road, do not do so on the ground that it would not pay, but that the road will come to them within a short time without aid or expense to the people of the county. If we had not the positive proof that the road will not be constructed without aid as proposed, we would never lend our paper or influence to procure the demanded aid; but those who oppose the project here are able to wait one, ten or twenty years for its coming, while others will have to go elsewhere to find bread and employment. In due time we will give the public the facts and figures in a manner so fair and undisputable, that no honest or unbiased man in the county can fail to vote the required aid.

If the editor had ever read the laws of the last Legislature respecting aid to railroads, he would have found that in no cause, can a county grant more than $5,000 per mile to any railroad, and it cannot grant that amount, if said aid should exceed in the aggregate five per cent. of the real and personal property of the county, according to its last assessment roll. According to the assessment roll of 1871, this county has real and personal property valued at $2,146,209, five per cent. of which would be $107,301.46. The petition asks for only twenty miles of road and cannot in any event, obtain aid to exceed the above amount.

The *Pajaronian* has no rights to treat its patrons at this end of the county with such intentional unfairness. They feel this a great necessity, and see wherein their neighbors at Watsonville will be equally benefited. This is no attempt to force on the people of Watsonville an unwelcome or undesirable project, neither an attempt to make them pay for what they do not receive a corresponding benefit. We know that if the majority of the people of this county are not benefited by this road, they will vote it down, and many who are largely benefited may vote adversely; so if it should be put to a vote and carried, over all opposition, what right has Watsonville to act so badly? If there is any humanity in one-half of a people prospering off of the misfortune of the other half, we fail to see it; and it becomes a public journalist to set public enterprise properly before its readers and the world, letting them judge whether they, from the light before them, can better afford to oppose then aid them.

If we fail to act as we herein indicate, we do not know it, editors and papers are not altogether infallible, and the more we read the *Pajaronian*, the more settled become our convictions.

307. *Santa Cruz Sentinel,* November 4, 1871 (4:2-3)

Election Proclamation.

County Seat of the County of Santa Cruz, and office of the Board of Supervisors thereof.
Santa Cruz, Nov. 3d, A. D. 1871.

In accordance with the call entered herein on Oct. 28th 1871, for a special meeting of the Board of Supervisors, the Board of Supervisors of said County met pursuant to said call. Present, Supervisors Jacob Parsons, P. F. Dean, George Anthony and the Clerk.

The Board now considering the petitions for and remonstrances against rail road aid and

Whereas, In the opinion of this Board, it is of great importance and advantage to the County of Santa Cruz and the citizens thereof to have railroad communication and connection from the town of Santa Cruz to and with the Southern Pacific Railroad, at or near the town of Watsonville, in said county, and

Whereas, This Board believes it to be for the best interest of the said county to donate the sum of One Hundred Thousand Dollars ($100,000) to any Railroad company now or hereafter to be organized, that will soonest construct and stock a railroad, connecting said town of Santa Cruz with the Southern Pacific Railroad, as aforesaid, of the same gauge therewith, to-wit: four feet eight and one-half inches gauge, as near as practicable on the following general route, to-wit:

Commencing at the southern boundary of the County of Santa Cruz, at or near the town of Watsonville, on the Pajaro River; thence running in a north-westerly direction to, and crossing the Aptos Creek, near the residence of Rafael Castro; thence to and crossing the Soquel river at or near the town of Soquel; thence to the town of Santa Cruz; *whereas*, it appears to us from the last assessment roll of said county.

Now in evidence before this Board that the value of the taxable property in said county, as appears therein, amounts to the sum of $2,147,309, and that five per cent. thereof exceeds the said sum of one hundred thousand dollars, together with all sums granted to any railroad company whatever.

And *Whereas*, we, the Board of Supervisors of said county propose, on behalf of this county, to enter into a contract with any Railroad Company now organized, or which may hereafter be organized to build said railroad on said line, and connecting the points and aforesaid, at or near the town of Watsonville, being a distance of about twenty miles, of the gauge as aforesaid, and in consideration thereof, to donate to any such railroad Co., the sum of $100,000 to-wit: One hundred Bonds of said county, of the sum of $1,000 each; said bonds to be payable to the holders thereof twenty years from the date thereof with interest thereon at the rate of seven per cent. per annum, both principal and interest payable in gold coin of the United States; said interest to be paid semi-annually on coupons to be attached to said bonds; the said bonds to be issued under the seal of said county and signed by the clerk thereof and also by the President of the Board of Supervisors, and to be delivered to any Railroad Company that shall construct said Railroad, *pro rata*, upon the completion of each and every give miles of said road, commencing at the southern line of the county ,at or near the town of Watsonville, and continuing into the town of Santa Cruz, and connecting therewith, and the completion of said road shall be construed to include the running an engine and cars over the same.

And now, whereas this Board hereby decide to submit to the qualified voters of said county, the said question of the donation of said one hundred thousand dollars as aforesaid, in the manner aforesaid, under and by virtue of the provisions of an Act of the Legislature of the State of California, entitled an "Act to empower the Board of Supervisors of the several Counties of the State to aid in the construction of a Railroad in the respective Counties," approved April 4th, 1870, and the Acts supplemental thereto, and amendatory thereof.

Now, therefore, it is ordered that the question whether the aid aforesaid as proposed and in the manner aforesaid shall be granted, be submitted to the qualified voters of said county at an Election to be held on Monday, the 11th day of December A. D. 1871 at the following places, in the different Precincts of Santa Cruz county, to-wit:

At Santa Cruz Precinct, at McPherson's building

At New Year's Point Precinct, at David Post's Half Way House.

At San Lorenzo Precinct, at the School House.

At Soquel Precinct, at John Hame's building.

At Coralitos Precinct, at the School-House.

At Pajaro Precinct, at Hy Jackson's Store.

And it is further ordered that at said election, the ballots to be cast thereat, shell be in the following form, to-wit:

Railroad Aid, Yes.

Railroad Aid, No.

And that if there shall be a majority of the ballots cast at said Election containing the said word "Railroad Aid Yes," then it shall be the duty of said Board to prepare, issue, donate and deliver the said bonds aforesaid.

It is further ordered that said election shall, so far as practicable, be held in the same manner as elections for State and County officers, and the returns canvassed and ascertained in accordance therewith.

It is further ordered that notice of said election and the foregoing orders be published in the *Pajaronian* and Santa Cruz Sentinel, two newspapers published in this county, at least once a week for the period of thirty days prior to said election.

The Clerk is hereby ordered to notify the Clerks of the Board of Registration of the different Precincts of said county of said election. Attest ALBERT BROWN.

Clerk, JACOB PARSON.

Chairman, GEO. ANTHONY.

308. *The Pajaronian*, November 9, 1871 (2:1)

From Argument to Abuse.

The railroad "sharp" who has been for some weeks past writing for the *Sentinel*, has utterly failed to keep up his side of the Subsidy argument—the *Pajaronian* routing him completed from all of his strong holds, so he has now dropped argument, and resorts to abuse, to get out of untenable positions. He finds that arguing in favor of county subsidy at a time when our county is deeply in debt and groaning under heavy taxation is a thankless and up hill occupation. The abusive manner in which he rails at Watsonville and her people, reminds us of a two year old child endeavoring to cut down a white oak tree with a dull jack knife. He says we are antagonistic to Santa Cruz that we wish to rob them of the Court House; that we are plotting like fiends to advance our own interests at the expense of Santa Cruz, and almost hints that the virtuous citizens of that city of the Holy Cross would be in personal danger should they visit this section! He says it is no use for the people of this end of the county to deny that they are "picking on" Santa Cruz, and calls on the citizens of that burg to stand bravely on the defensive. Whether there is any truth in the report that a delegation of pale and trembling Santa Cruz citizens went to Sacramento last week to see Governor Haight and secure the services of the Amador veterans, we do not know; but from the excitable article in the *Sentinel* we judge it to be so. The writer of the article quoted from admits that Watsonville has Santa Cruz in chancery, but we wish to assure all those at the other end of the county who are like the writer of the article, trembling with vague fears and grim visaged apprehensions, that we of Watsonville, unlike many at Santa Cruz never kick a fallen foe. The article in question created here a mild feeling of contempt mingled with amusement, and many expressed strong pity for the writer, and a friendly wish that Science would supply him with a new set of brains. Don't do so any more, Broughton, for we still have a high regard for you and would weep vociferously to learn that you had been taken to Stockton. Don't gush any more, dear friend; think twice and then don't say anything. Pay a more tender regard to Truth, and grammar, and logic, and orthography, and manliness and liberal thinking and all that sort of think you know."

309. *The Pajaronian*, November 9, 1871 (2:2)

After Us.

The gushing, verdant and muddy writer on railroad matters, who has been airing his limited knowledge in the *Sentinel* for several weeks past, made a wicked pass for our scalp last week. He fell into the mud of his own slang, however, and we are yet safe. Other parties are brought into the article in a very ungentlemanly manner. Lumber and Law are frequently mentioned by the writer. Of his legal attainments the less said the better. As a lumberman, we have to say that a wooden headed man would naturally have more genius for chopping or sawing wood and discussing like subjects than a man possessed of a more sensitive head piece. We don't blame Kooser for publishing the trash, for we know the temptations that sometimes beset an editor, to "fill up" with almost anything that comes along. If the writer imagines that he is the mouthpiece of Santa Cruz, he is terrible mistaken, for we conversed with numerous better men than he, who deprecate the twaddle in the *Sentinel*. Still we rather like the writer, in some respects, and this liking we have for him prompts us now to notice him. We can imagine with what pride he will show this week's *Pajaronian* to all his acquaintances and say, "Cummings noticed us this week, the first time any one ever deigned to pay attention to any thing we ever said. Cummings is a good fellow after all."

310. *The Pajaronian*, November 9, 1871 (3:1)

Surveying has been stopped on the Watsonville and Santa Cruz railroad until after the election on the 11th prox.

The construction train will reach the depot to-morrow or next day we are informed.

Commenced.—Surveyors commenced Tuesday last to survey the route for a railroad from this place to Santa Cruz. The present route runs along the northern side of the town limits.

Supervisor Dean.—We learned while in Santa Cruz last week, that Supervisor Dean worked hard and skillfully against the passage of the order calling an election in this county in regard to giving aid to a railroad. But the order passed and the election will be held in accordance with the Election Proclamation.

311. *Santa Cruz Sentinel*, November 11, 1871 (2:1)

POWDER COMPANY AND THE RAILROAD.

What better or more convincing proof can the tax-payers of this county have presented them, to show that fostering enterprises and building up general business, reduces taxation by augmenting the taxable property, and increasing the people to be taxed, than the fact that such large and valuable establishments as the California Powder Company favor, very decidedly, the project of aiding a railroad by donated County Bonds, in the sum of $100,000.

This Company, for the past few years, has paid more than *one thirtieth* of the entire State and County taxes of Santa Cruz county, and now, as a business transaction, without expecting to ship one pound of powder by rail, they say they are confident that the road will very soon double the value of taxable property of the county, and more than double the population of Santa Cruz and the county; thus lightening the burden of taxation in two ways—first by increasing the taxable property, and second by increasing the number of person to pay it. They say further, that the competition between the railroad and vessel transportation, will lessen considerably the price of freight now prevailing, and which must continue to prevail, unless competition is created; and that a railroad is the only hope of effecting this result.

We are informed that every company manufacturing leather in this county, take about the same view of the subject, and favor the aid for like reasons. They have a direct interest in a railroad, for it will enable them to ship leather at all times of the year.

Bennet & Co., lime burners, will ship large quantities of lime by rail, to the customers of the line of the road; San Jose, Haywards, San Leandro, and Oakland, and not being interested in vessels, will secure a cheaper transportation by water.

The same course of reasoning bids us to conclude, that with freights reduced, there will be a profitable and extensive business carried on from our wharves in the wood, lime, a branch of business which in time must prove very advantageous to Santa Cruz, Soquel, and other points. With freights reduced one dollar per ton, there is hardly a business that will not be prospered, and become lucrative. If the wealth and business of the county demand this road, and are so willing to pay taxes to meet every demand required to effect it, what can the poor man and small tax-payer say who will be enabled to find constant employment or sale for all his produce; certainly not that he will oppose aid enterprise so much demanded by all our people.

312. *Santa Cruz Sentinel,* November 11, 1871 (2:2-3)
Railroad Aid Submitted to Vote.

The Board of Supervisors, having held their special meeting called for Nov. 3d. for the purpose of fully and finally considering whether, all things considered, it would be proper, just and wise to order an election, putting to vote the proposition [...] to donate $100,000 in County Bonds, payable in twenty years, bearing interest at seven per cent. per annum, and payable semi-annually, to the railroad company that would contract to soonest complete a railroad of the gauge of the Southern Pacific road, from the town of Watsonville to the town of Santa Cruz, a distance of twenty miles, concluded the session by making the order found in this issue, calling the election for December 11th, 1871, which submits the proposition to the qualified voters of this county.

Supervisor Dean, the member from Pajaro dissenting,

presented his objections to ordering the election, in a manner becoming the dignity of a Supervisor, and in strict accordance with the wishes of his constituents.

Supervisors Parsons and Anthony could not, in justice to those they represented, have acted otherwise; for a great majority of the people at this end of the county very decidedly ask the opportunity of voting on this subject. The election involves no great expense, and the people will have to be contented with the result.

The question is fairly and legally before the people, and it is hoped that they will give it that consideration the importance of the occasion demands; let those who entertain prejudice against the general principle of subsidies, reflect upon this especially instance of the application of what they may in other forms justly proclaim pernicious, and see if there is not sufficient merit in this divergence to warrant a cordial support.

We can in no better way give our views of the benefits resulting to a county from the assistance the people may feel themselves justified in according public enterprises, than by quoting from the *Alta* of Sept. 13th, the following facts concerning railroads in Illinois.

"A remarkable instance of the great benefits that railroad land-grants are to the people, the State and Government, is illustrated in the Illinois Central Railroad. In 1850 that State had 851,470 inhabitants, and the State was very sparsely settled. The population was only 250,000 more than that of California now. The Federal Government held then 19,000,000 acres of land in the State, which had been thirty years under proclamation without finding settlers, because that land, like that of that now in California, was inaccessible to market. It was felt that the land never would be settled unless a railroad was built through it. But who would build a railroad through an unsettled country? If the land could be settled the 19,000,000 acres would become taxable by the State and give its resources which would lighten the general burden. The people wanted to settle the lands, the United States wanted to sell them, and the State wanted to tax them—a state of affairs which now exists on a broader scale in California. Congress then determined to give the State 2,595,000 acres of that unsaleable land to have a railroad built. The State incorporated the Illinois Central Railroad and turned the lands ever to it in 1850. The road was built; the Federal lands were immediately taken up by settlers, giving the United States $25,000,000, purchase money. The State's population increased to 1,711,951, or more than doubled in 1860, and to 2,529,410 in 1870. The State revenues from the lands became very large. The State revenues from the lands became very large. The railroad drew vast freights from the land, the business of Chicago increased $10,00,000 per annum by produce brought down and goods sent up, and the railroad has sold off its grant, 2,179,000 acres for $24,900,883, and has 415,610 acres left worth $12.50 per acre, or $5,225,905, more than meeting the whole first cost of the construction of the road. All these immense benefits have resulted in twenty years from the judicious use of a portion of the public lands to give value to the remainder. That is the state of affairs now awaiting California. The vast tracts of fertile public land are awaiting the intervention of railroads to promote the general interest of the State, the city of San Francisco, the people, the Federal Government and those interests which depend more immediately upon railroads, and the elements are at work to produce that combination.

The question often presents itself, why has not Santa Cruz, of late years, made the same progress it did in former times? There are several causes, but the chief cause is, we have not kept pace with other parts of the State less favored and endowed with natural facilities. So long as other places on this coast were only accessible by the same facilities we now possess, Santa Cruz pushed forward and was prosperous; but when every inland town or point of considerable note or importance effected communication with San Francisco by rail, except Santa Cruz, she no longer attracted the attention necessary to keep her in the line of prosperity established and enjoyed under a different order of things. We are approaching that period in the history of our State, when to be without a railroad is to be sadly deficient of the elements of prosperity, and we can not hope for better times or more prosperous business until we possess the power of making those now resident among us feel secure in the means of making a living. A railroad will open up, bring to notice, and develop the resources of this county, beyond our most sanguine anticipations. The mere talk about the road has infused new life into the people, who begin to feel that with the success of the present project rests every prospect of the future for them and Santa Cruz.

We admit that the taxes of this county are high, and no prospect of their being any less, even though we have no railroad. The farmer complains of increasing taxes, and fails to see the cause, which rests with the depreciation of town property, it becoming of less value every year, the farmer must make up deficiency, now if the farmer wishes to lessen his burden, there is but one way to do it, and that is, to do that which will enhance the value of other than farming lands. There can be no doubt but that a railroad would effect this speedily and completely. The most valuable property, intrinsically, in this county, the timber lands, is assessed at almost nothing. We have taken much pains to learn, as near as possible, the number of acres of timber land in the county, and find it to amount to about 200,000 acres, which at present is not paying an average of forty cents per acre, taxes. This body of land will yield about 10,000 feet of saw timber per acre, exclusive of wood, tanbark, &c., which amounts in board measure to 2,000,000,000 feet, which should pay the owner, when manufactured, fifty cents per stumpage, amounting in the aggregate to one million dollars. If this body of timber was manufactured and shipped at the rate of 50,000,000 feet annually, it would take 40 years to exhaust this resource of lumber. It is not contented that all this vast region of timber will find outlets along the proposed line of railroad, but that this amount will be made more available and valuable in consequence of the road, and consequently pay a just proportion of the taxes. There is no reason why every acre of timber land, in five years, should not be assessed at $29 per acre, thus increasing the taxable property $4,000,000. If a railroad is not constructed, it will be many years before the timber lands pay any considerable portion of the taxes.

Yet all the time they are spoken of as being of immense value. It is apparent to every one who will carefully and candidly study this subject, that with a railroad to aid in making immediately available the natural resource of the county, the value of every species of property will be enhanced, and in just that proportion will taxation be reduced. If there is now $7,000,000 of property in this county, to pay the present amount of taxes, and in five years could be made to amount to $14,000,000, it is not plain to see that the rate per cent. would not exceed half the present rate. Many have an idea that their taxes increase in proportion to their wealth. That is not so; if all property advances simultaneously, it is just the reverse, and that community acts wisely who sets themselves at work fostering enterprises which tend to augment rapidly the value of all property. San Jose affords an instance of this kind; there is property in that town that was offered for sale at $10,000 before the railroad was completed to that place, and which, since its completion, has advanced, until the same property exceeds $100,000 actual value to-day. Every other town in the State to which roads have been constructed are in the same thriving condition of San Jose and Vallejo, and those places where people are waiting for roads to come to them, are lacking in every thing that makes a community prosperous and contented.

We are pleased to learn that the people below are thinking more favorable of this matter, and that there is a great prospect of receiving a fair proportion of their votes in aid of the project. If the aid is voted, the road will be constructed to Santa Cruz within one year, affording the farmers every facility for shipping their produce by water or rail at a much reduced price over the present rates. Steps are being taken, we hear, to organize a company in this county, to take the aid, if voted, and build the road; this view seems most in favor with the people of Watsonville. Santa Cruz is not particular who gives her the road, but desires its completion in the shortest possible period. If Watsonville and Santa Cruz can work in harmony for their mutual interest in this matter, there can be no doubt of the success of the election, and the speedy benefits resulting to both places.

313. *Santa Cruz Sentinel,* November 11, 1871 (2:3)

Lawyer Craig and the Rail Road.

During the late term of the County Court, we listened to some of the most sensible talk concerning the railroad from Watsonville to Santa Cruz, by lawyer Craig of the former place, it has been our privilege to notice. Mr. Craig takes the position that the farmers of Pajaro, will be materially benefitted by the road as it will afford them outlets for produce, and cheaper facilities for shipping than they now enjoy or can hope to have unless the road is constructed. He says Santa Cruz being a manufacturing place and country entirely, has afforded with her present sparse population, the best market in the State, for the farming product of the Pajaro valley; quite one third of which found its way to Santa Cruz, and was disposed of free of storage commission wastage, ratage &c. He contents that with a railroad Santa Cruz will soon reach a population of 10,000, and the increasing settlement of timber lands and appropriating the manufacturing facilities adjacent, will require a population of half as many more, and that this will constitute a market for one-half if not more, of the entire product of the valley. In return, the farmers must have lumber for building and fencing, which in a very short time must come from Santa Cruz, as the timber now furnishing the valley is fast becoming absorbed, and soon will be inadequate to meet the growing demand of the people; then, if there is no road as proposed, the price of lumber, which must be considered a very important matter, will increase instead of decrease, as with a railroad it certainly must.

Again Mr. Craig argues; if this road is not constructed from Watsonville to Santa Cruz, the Santa Cruz people would be very foolish if they did not effect communication with San Francisco by some other route, and this route being through the Santa Clara Valley, will entirely cut off the Pajaro Valley from every benefit to be derived from Santa Cruz as a market for it will be a very easy matter, and quite acceptable too, for the farmers of that valley to furnish Santa Cruz all the produce required and take lumber in return. Santa Cruz will be the gainer, for then Pajaro must compete with Santa Clara, and what can be realized after doing the reining by teams, or what can be the value of lumber hauled 20 miles by wagon.

We were so forcibly struck with the cogency of Mr. Craig's remarks that we give them to our readers as the best cause of reasoning to convince the people of this country, and especially the farmers of Pajaro valley, that it is for the interest of all sections to favor the aiding of the proposed railroad, and force its completion in the shortest possible period.

The issuing of County bonds payable in 20 years, only involves an expense to the County of $7,000, annually, until the bonds mature, and this increased tax will be about one-half met by the railroad property itself, and if the entire amount was paid by the taxpayers independent of the road, the amount is but insignificant when compared with the resulting benefits.

314. *Santa Cruz Sentinel,* November 11, 1871 (2:5)

Bro. Cummings, of the *Pajaronian*, gets personal in his enthusiasm against Railroads. Confine yourself to facts, argument and statistics Bro. C. and you will do well. The cow that jumped over the moon went through the "milky way," and probably the firm which controls the *Pajaronian* have been sucking some of that lacteal fluid through a "Clear Quill." Where, oh where, Brother C. are those fine articles in favor of Railroads, which you promised when here, stating that you saw things in a different light since an explanation was made? why don't you correct that error, when you state that the subsidy was to be $300,000, or when $100,000 was the utmost amount? For what reason do you fail to call the voter's attention to the Election Proclamation, published in your litigant columns, explaining the true nature and facts of the proposition? Were it to find room for flippant articles against the *Sentinel*, a paper that *not* only reflects the opinions of this community and the Republican party, through the absolute control of the person whose name may be found at the head of the editorial column.

315. *Santa Cruz Sentinel*, November 11, 1871 (3:2)
Santa Cruz Will Not Build Itself.

Santa Cruz will not make its people, but the people must make the place. To be sure nature has done a great deal for it—these balmy skies—these healthful airs—these cool ocean breezes—this diversified scenery. All these things make it a place of unrivalled attractions for summer resort—Nature has done much.

But the people must make a way to get to it. People in the heated interior, in the cities, and all over the plains, multitudes of them will want to come, but a way must be made for them to get here.

Once a stage coach would do, but it won't do any longer. That day is gone by. A place that don't provide its railroad now, will not be frequented. Excursionists, tourists and visitors will go where cars will take them, and they won't go anywhere else.

If the people of Santa Cruz want to make the town the watering place of the Coast, they must make it accessible by cars. That proposition is too plain to need argument.

And, what is more, there is no time to be lost. Other places are connecting themselves with the great cities by rail. Those places will grow, and they will draw away the people from those that have no roads. They will take away the business; they will leave them to decline in value. This is just as certain as that water will run down hill.

To sit still and wait for some miracle to prevent it, is simply to lose opportunity and give rivals a chance to distance all competition. And they will make themselves busy enough in doing it.

Nature has made Santa Cruz a delightful place to live in, but the people must establish something to live on. The land will employ some in farming, but they must have consumers for what they raise. Trade will employ some, but they want more customers.

Manufactories would solve the difficulty; they would make work that would pay. People could live here, and earn something to live on. Young people could stay at home and find something to do.

But manufactories won't grow up of themselves. Ingenuity must plan them; Enterprise must build them.

Why not have cotton mills, leather manufactories, woolen factories, iron foundries, perhaps silk manufactories, sugar refineries, carriage shops, furniture manufactories, machine shops, and the like in Santa Cruz. These things have made many of the most prosperous cities in the world.

Nature has done a great deal for Santa Cruz, it would seem as if the people might do the rest, and make it a busy, prosperous city.

Those streams of pure, cool, sparkling water, that come pouring down the mountain sides, Nature seems to have put them there on purpose, to be brought down and conducted through all these dwelling and public buildings and streets, and ornamented grounds. What health, what beauty, what elegance, what luxury, what convenience would water so distributed bring? And what safety, as well? For its reservoirs could be on these high terraces, giving it such a pressure blow, that it could be used in case of fire to and forced over the tops of the buildings without any engines.

There came near being a fire in the Ocean House a while ago. If there had been, and that building had burned, the loss would have probably been enough to have paid the entire cost of beginning a permanent water works, that would have been a perpetual security to the whole town.

Then cheap water could be used freely by the poor as well as the rich, and yet yield an income sufficient to pay the cost of the water, and interest on the cost of construction.

There never was a town that had greater advantages for furnishing all its inhabitants with pure soft water, under pressure, so as to be used freely, at small cost, for every purpose.

Santa Cruz has these rare advantages without being offset, as is often the case, with disadvantages.

But it is in the hands of its people. They must build it up or it will not enrich them.

Connect it with other places by rail, and then see what will be the price of property. Start manufactories, and see if you can find "to let" on the houses.

Distribute cheap, pure water through the place, and then see if the market value is not well nigh sixty per cent. advanced.

It is a place of favorite resort now, then it will be thronged. There is not a place on the coast that can enrich itself at so small a cost. There is not a place that will be so desirable for residence when it is done.

316. *Santa Cruz Sentinel,* November 11, 1871 (3:3)
Citizens Railroad Meeting.

On Saturday evening, Nov. 4th, the citizens of Santa Cruz assembled in Anthony's Hall for the purpose of systematizing their efforts to secure a favorable consideration by the people of the subject of voting the aid set forth and required by the Proclamation and order of election issued Nov. 3d, by the Board of Supervisors, and which order sets the 11th day of December next, as the time when the qualified electors of this county are permitted to express their views through their ballots upon this all important matter donating $100,000, in County Bonds, payable in twenty years, to the company that will the soonest construct and complete a railroad from Watsonville to Santa Cruz.

The meeting selected the following committee to draft an address to the people of the county, setting forth the advantages and necessity of the road, and which will in due time, be placed in the hands of every voter. Rev. Mr. Tuthill, Bernard Peyton, Supervisor elector for this township, E. L. Williams, B. F. Porter, Titus Hale and T. W. Wright. No better selection could have been made, for all these gentlemen are intelligent and well posted in the resources of the whole county, and know the great advantages of railroads in general. We expect a most convincing address upon the subject.

The meeting also took steps to select a committee of thirteen from all parts of the county, and whose duty it will be to take general supervision of all matters pertaining to the success of the election. Our folks are getting terribly in earnest over this railroad question, and don't propose to relax their energy until sun down December 11th, 1871, when we bespeak a most triumphant victory to the friends of enterprise, progress, and humanity.

317. *San Francisco Bulletin*, **November 8, via the *Santa Cruz Sentinel,* November 11, 1871 (3:3)**

Railroad from Santa Cruz to Watsonville.

The Southern Pacific Railroad, or a branch of the same, having been extended from Gilroy to Watsonville in the heart of the Pajaro Valley, the people at the other end of the county are considering by what means they can connect the town of Santa Cruz with the railroad. The distance between the two towns is about twenty miles. An election has been called in that county to vote upon the proposition to aid the construction of this twenty miles of railroad by an issue of $100,000 in bonds. The cost of constructing these twenty miles will be not less than $500,000, or $25,000 a mile. If aid to the extent of one-fifth were furnished by the county the building of the road would be insured.

Santa Cruz has suffered of late years from its isolated position. While it is near, as to the number of miles to be traversed it is very remote. By railroad to Santa Clara, and stage road thence over the mountains, the distance is a round 80 miles—33 miles of which is by stage. It is a fatiguing day's work to make this journey from San Francisco to Santa Cruz. In good weather steamers ply with considerably regularity between the two points; and a number of sailing vessels are engaged in the freighting business. But during the heavy weather or winter there may be ten days or more when no vessel can touch at that point; and we have known mail facilities cut off for an equal length of time, the road over the mountains having been carried away by the floods.

The distance from this city to Santa Cruz by way of the proposed railroad would be about 120 miles, it being an even hundred miles hence to Watsonville. The distance by railroad would be about 40 miles more than by the stage route across the mountains. The fare by this route averages $5, and passengers are not set down in Santa Cruz much before 5 o'clock in the evening. With the railroad by way of Watsonville, the time would be materially shortened. The down train now arrives at Gilroy a little before 12 o'clock P.M. It will require say one hour to make the distance from that point to Watsonville, and another hour thence to Santa Cruz. By this means passengers would be set down in the latter place as early as 2 o'clock P.M. The fare would probably be somewhat less than is now charged by railroad and stage. The other substantial advantages would be an outlet for freight into the Pajaro and Salinas valleys, and still further south. Sailing vessels and small steamers furnish very good facilities for bringing freights from Santa Cruz to this city. And it is doubtful if the railroad could transport freight between the two points at cheaper rates. But the consumption of lime lumber and other heavy articles is large in a southerly direction, at points which cannot be reached by water. Coming up from the southern counties, the nearest point where redwood lumber and lime can be procured is at Santa Cruz. The demand for these and other bulk articles which swell freight-bills, is constantly increasing with counties further south. All this freight would go by railroad if connection in this way was complete. These are the leading considerations which move the people of Santa Cruz county to secure a railroad connection, not only with this city, but with the rich vallies in a southerly direction.

318. *The Pajaronian*, November 16, 1871 (1:5)

THE RAILROAD.

All hail to the Railroad! We view with delight
The steady advance of the track,
And the huge Locomotive exulting in might,
Pressing close to the spike-driver's back.

Joy, joy! for the Railroad will soon be completed
And stage be needed no more.
To go round by San Juan with three crammed in a seat,
Which by all is accounted a "bore."

Then welcome the Railroad. Farewell to the stage;
Though gratitude clings to the smiles
Of the good-natured drivers, which served to assuage
The toils of the wearisome miles.

A. K. Crawford.

319. *The Pajaronian*, November 16, 1871 (2:1)
Watsonville and Santa Cruz Railroad.

Our Santa Cruz friends are very much in earnest in regard to voting a subsidy of $100,000 for the above scheme. They argue well and earnestly in its favor, and seem to think that a railroad is all that is required to dispel the dark financial cloud that now temporarily over-shadows that beautiful section. We have lately had several "talks" with Mr. Hihn and others on the subject, and while we admire their logic and arguments in favor of the move, yet we cannot entirely dispel the fears of the consequences that may beset us, should the debt be thrown upon us. We fear that the citizens of Santa Cruz, in their enthusiasm for the cause, are picturing the present condition of their town in colors far too dark. That place has prospered wonderfully during the past few years, and now because there is a lull in its prosperity, discouragement predominates where cheerfulness should preside. No town in our knowledge has continuously prospered for a succession of years. Santa Cruz is no exception, but the present dark days will most assuredly give place to sunshine as soon as the surrounding country is more thickly settled, and the *demand* for lumber, lime, leather, etc., is greater. The rates of transportation are very low from Santa Cruz to all parts of the coast, and we cannot see how the railroad will materially increase the present demands for their productions or make the rates of freight any the less. It is argued in Santa Cruz that the road will increase the value of property in that section to such an extent that this end of the county will pay far less taxes. This argument is a very lame one when examined carefully, for property in Santa Cruz has been held for years past at a fictitious valuation the result of a sudden excitement, and if the railroad gave another sudden impetus to the price of property for a year or so, it is bound to fall to its real value again and the result in the end will be far worse than at present. They say that a railroad from this place to Santa Cruz will give a greater market for our products. The freight shipped to Santa Cruz in a year would not amount to a hundredth part of what is used here, so no material advantage can be derived on that score. Many other arguments—seemingly fair propositions, are made use of by them which we have not space to repeat. Besides we expected to receive a communication this week setting forth their views, as we urged several parties to favor us with their opinions, which would be willingly published.

To sum up we are asked to vote a subsidy for a road the route of which has not even been established. We are asked to place our county under an enormous debt for the benefits of a company not yet found to take the subsidy. We are threatened that if we do not. Vote for it here and the measure carries, Watsonville will be entirely ignored by those who construct the road. This threat, we will have the fairness to say, is only uttered by a few ranters whose tongues are as ladened with bitterness as their minds are with envy. Furthermore the people of this section are urged to go for that which they fought against only a few weeks ago! Consistency, thou hast departed from that gem of the Pacific—the city of the Holy Cross. We are asked to give a large amount for a railroad through this county when the Southern Pacific, without a subsidy, contemplate building a road to Aptos; and survey has already been made for a narrow gauge from San Francisco, though Santa Cruz county to Los Angeles. Above all we are asked to enter into a business venture, involving the expenditure of $240,000 in twenty years, that no one has yet said would pay a company for the investment. We have nothing against the Southern Pacific Railroad; we believe in the national subsidies that have already been given; we have watched counties that have given subsidies and have noted their struggles. We have thought seriously on the subsidy now under contemplation, have conversed with prominent men of all parts of the county, and after all we feel that we are personally interested in the investment and we can not see that the movement is a safe one. We can feel no different now in regard to the subsidy than we did a few weeks ago when we advocated the election of anti-subsidy men for office. And right here we wish it distinctly understood—to correct false impressions at Santa Cruz—that all good citizens of this place, so far as we can learn, as well as the editor of this journal, look to the welfare of the whole county in arguing this subsidy scheme, and are not blinded with prejudice or selfishness as has been represented by a few persons in Santa Cruz. We think for ourself on all matters, and shall give utterance to those thoughts when we deem proper, and all we can ask of the people of this county is to do the same, whether subsidy, or any other matter of importance is before them, and then act as they please.

320. *The Pajaronian*, November 16, 1871 (2:3)

Give Us a Bridge.

Now that the Railroad has arrived in our valley, and Watsonville is rapidly becoming more important as a mercantile center, it is necessary that a bridge, over which two teams may go at once, should be constructed. It may be that the present bridge can be widened six or eight feet. If practicable, we think the Board of Supervisors of both counties should take the matter in charge, and make necessary repairs and enlargements. We need one good bridge at least at this end of the county, and we hope the Supervisors will see that we do have.

321. *Santa Cruz Sentinel*, November 18, 1871 (2:2)

PROGRESS OF THE RAILROAD ISSUE.

Nothing gives more hope for the future of Santa Cruz, or more encouragement to those laboring to give this county a line of railroad, connecting the principal towns with San Francisco, than the favor with which the people received and welcome the proposition to vote $100,000 in county bonds, as a donation to the company that will soonest consummate the work of constructing the proposed railroad from Watsonville to Santa Cruz, a distance of twenty miles.

Many of our most worthy citizens at first looked with distrust upon the proposition to aid even this railroad, so long needed and much demanded, and declared that consistency with their pre-conceived notions upon this subsidy, forbid their entertaining the proposition, or according it that consideration they believed it merited; consequently, for a few weeks, such persons assumed the position of opponents of the measure, giving to not a few the idea that no considerable portion of the people would support or favor the measure. The three or four weeks which have intervened since we first mooted this question, have found such persons one by one wheeling into line, until those whose conversion seems hopeless in this end of the county can be counted on one's fingers. There are few who cannot see wherein this road will prove a great advantage and blessing to every part of the county, and to all persons. The farmer is much interested in building up towns and occupations, requiring consumers for his produce. If all were farmers who would consume the surplus? And what better way can the farmer advance his own interests than by creating a home market where he can do his own selling; saving freights, storage, wharfage and commissions? There should, in ten years, be a population in this county capable of consuming four-fifths of the produce grown in the county. But such will not be the case, unless we adopt the progressive ideas and measures which have transformed the western wilderness into marts of commerce and great centres of productive enterprises. Those parts of the United States most favoring the construction of railroads, have grown in population and wealth beyond the hopes of the most sanguine. The great State of Illinois is dotted all over with thriving towns and beautiful cities, comprising a population of nearly three millions, where before the advent of railroads there were no settlements, and must have remained for all time one vast range for stock, yielding no tax, and adding no wealth to the State.

Broad prairies, without wood or water, have become densely populated wherever a railroad offered facilities for marketing the products of their broad acres. For such energizing instances, the people can afford to pay, and none better than those who cannot hope for market, employment or business without them. Santa Cruz has reached this point exactly; she has done well, done much in the past, but must keep pace with the other places on this coast, rivaling her in scenery, climate and industrial advantages, or her population occupied in other pursuits than farming, will go where labor is more abundant and remunerative. We believe a railroad is her only relief, and will bring with it a health state of things, an influx of people who will see our great natural advantages and turn them to profitable account. If our citizens of wealth were infused with a just spirit of enterprise, Santa Cruz would ere this have had fine and spacious woolen mills, giving employment to five or six hundred operatives; we have every convenience and advantage for these and kindred enterprises, which must become fruitful when the town becomes more widely known and less difficult to access. The great papers of the State always speak in the highest praise of this county, but never fail to tell the traveler that there is a tedious and fatiguing drive of thirty-five miles over dusty roads and dangerous mountains before reaching it.

This we would obviate by a railroad, and although not the most direct route, still, all considered, is the best for the future of Santa Cruz, and the county; persons cannot but be favorable impressed with the beautiful and productive Pajaro Valley, the thrifty and well-ordered town of Watsonville, when making the pleasant circuit by rail to Santa

Cruz, which will in all probability be the terminus of the road, and where the principal train from the city will make its head-quarters. This will be a matter of great moment to Santa Cruz than many suppose. There are always a great many excursionists and pleasure seekers who will prefer Santa Cruz as a place of resort for pleasure and relief to any place on the whole line of the road.

A road up the coast, or over the mountain, to intersect the San Jose road, would leave Santa Cruz a common way station, and afford simply the ordinary conveniences of grand trunks, while as a terminus the road will give greater prominent and importance to the place than a half dozen roads with way stations, and induce men of means to seek this town and county as a place for profitable investment.

It will be but a short time when the high rates of interest prevailing on this coast will fall to the standard of the east, and then it will pay capital better to be employed in manufacturing enterprises, than producing simple interest. When that period arrives, be it nigh or remote, the wealth and population of the State will increase with unexampled rapidity. Railroads are great equalizers, and what California requires is a standard of prices comparing with the east, then manufacturing enterprises established at every eligible point on this coast, will pay. There is no reason why this condition of things should not be speedily brought about, if the people of the different parts of the State will grant such timely aid to enterprises as will insure their permanency and prosperity. It is now left with our people to say how far they will go to aid or thwart the worthiest project or enterprise it has been their privilege to secure.

Governor Stanford, of the Central Pacific Company, assures this county that if the vote to donate the aid requires is favorable, that company, if preferred, will complete the road as per order of election, in time for use next year. This is precisely what we want, and our people, as a mass, are not particular who builds the road, or who receives the aid, if votes; what they require is, its completion in the shortest possible period. And who can do it so speedily or cheaply as a company with every convenience and facility for constructing railroads? There is now no doubt but the Central Pacific will be awarded the contract, and it is proper the people know this before voting, that they may not claim to have been deceived. Every idea of forming a company in this county for that purpose must be given over, and all who are favorable must feel this the wisest and most prudent course to pursue.

We believe every person working and wishing for the success of the road, is doing so in the most unselfish manner, and for the general good of this county, irrespective of any personal considerations.

322. *Santa Cruz Sentinel,* November 18, 1871 (2:3)
UNEQUAL TAXATION.

The first great object and duty of a community should be to so order and adjust taxation as to make that burden bear as equally and evenly upon all classes as it is possible for human experience to establish and arrange.

No system establishing a perfect equality is possible,

where values are established through man's imperfect judgment, and no system is more imperfect than that now in practice in California.

We not unfrequently hear complains that property is assessed for all it would sell for at forced sale, while other property is not assessed at one-tenth of its actual cash value. This disparity of assessment arises from the imperfect judgment of those whose duty it is to establish valuations, and is the fault of the law which clothes a person with such a dangerous power.

All admit that the present system can be much improved, and the incoming administration would do well to pay especial attention to this all important subject.

We have heard many express a wish that all property, real and personal, could be assessed at its actual value, believing that such a system would give less cause for complaint, and less room for imperfect valuations. It is much easier to establish general rules than work satisfactorily by those of a special character. The duty of the Assessor would be much easier, and less open to censure.

There seems to be very little equality between the valuation of town property and farming lands.

A house and lot costing but a few hundred dollars, is found valued or assessed as high as ranches of hundreds of acres, from which the owner receives an income annually, amounting to about as much as the city property is worth. An inspection of the Assessment Roll of this county, will astonish any person taking the trouble to satisfy himself of this fact. We do not know that this seeming inequality can be remedies, and do not pretend to say that every other State is afflicted with like grievances. We bring this fact to notice, more particularly to show our farmers that their real interests lie in building up towns and thriving communities, where wealth concentrates, and property becomes of greater value, and proportionately relieves them from the burden of taxation which, which, without this aid, would make taxes almost unbearable. If the farmer thinks this a drawn and farfetched fact, let him take from the assessment roll the value of the property included within the incorporate limits of Santa Cruz and Watsonville, and add to outside property the tax these two towns pay, and each farmers tax would be almost doubled. It must be remembered that the farmer is not taxes for any public improvement made within the limits of these places, and that the towns are assessed as much for State and county purposes as the farmer, and that without these places, the taxes would not be very much less.

Need we say more to prove to the farmers of this county conclusively that the construction of a railroad, even with the county's aid, in the sum of $100,000, will, at no distant day, lighten their taxes, by transferring them to the towns and manufacturing enterprises, sure to follow in the wake of this first great necessity of the people.

323. *Santa Cruz Sentinel,* November 18, 1871 (3:2)
Watsonville and the Railroad.

The railroad question is being discussed with much more coolness and consideration, by our Watsonville neighbors than when, first presented them. The sober second thought brings to its support many of the most prominent men in the Valley, who are now ready and willing to admit that the road is a great necessity and will do more to develop and settle Pajaro Valley than all former influences and enterprises combined. Watsonville can not afford to lose this opportunity of uniting herself with Santa Cruz, and thus secure a railroad into the town. This is what all our people desire, and will labor for; it would be an act of folly and injustice to build this road avoiding Watsonville. There is room for one town only in that end of the valley, and want that place to be Watsonville. A little timely co-operation will settle all the preliminaries necessary to place the road precisely where the greatest good to the greatest number of people will result, and we believe that mutual effort in this direction will be regarded by those moulding opinions in Pajaro as the best and wisest course to pursue. The aid required is too significant to deceive or secure any man into opposition, and the election too sure to encourage any very vigorous effort to defeat it. Watsonville is the only point in the county where there will appear any opposition whatever, and very many of her farmers are heartily supporting the measure. Many more would support it if they had not been made to believe that the road will be constructed without the aid. Do the people in Pajaro Valley think or believe that the people at this end of the county are less mindful of their own interest and desire to pay for what they could get free? Our folks have taken every precaution and made thorough investigation of this matter, and have every proof to convince us that we cannot hope for railroad facilities without this aid or by constructing ourselves the road over the mountain. If the latter was done, what benefit would one-half the county receive from the road? Is it not better that a road pass through the most valuable portion of the county, than across one corner and damage the balance?

324. *The Pajaronian*, November 23, 1871 (2:1)

Narrow Gauge Railroad.

TO BE BUILT FROM SAN FRANCISCO TO THE COLORADO RIVER

A Subsidy Unnecessary.

It is now established beyond a doubt that the narrow gauge road from San Francisco to the Colorado River, *via* Santa Cruz and Watsonville, is to be constructed, and from all information we have been able to obtain on the subject, the work will be commenced about March next. Of course the Santa Cruz Subsidy movement is already a thing of the past and will fall to the ground. Prominent subsidy men of Santa Cruz have come to the conclusion that the movement was premature and think it best to say no more about it. A wise conclusion under the present aspect of affairs. Knowing that the narrow gauge was to be constructed as soon as Major Watson, the Company's Engineer, had completed the survey, we have felt the subsidy movement to be a very foolish one, and a scheme calculated to entail great wrong on the people.

325. *The Pajaronian*, November 23, 1871 (3:2)
JAKE PIPPS.
FAVORS THE SANTA CRUZ SUBSIDY.
Talks to the Citizens of Picketville.
Picketville, Nov. 19, 1871.

Mister Eddyter:—Yesterdy, wich wuz Saterday, I arrove hum arter going ter Santa Scruze ter pay my taxes, and while thar was konvarted tew think ez them fellers up thar say they think on the Ralerode Subsidey. Larst nite arter gitten my hoss staked out, I shuffled round amung the fellers here and called a ralerode meetin ter take place in the skewl house which wuz manufactered last year nere that old holler redwood stump whar the grizzly bar cum durned nere chawin the inter sassenger meat last year, and the skewl marm is az pooty a gal az I ever sot eyes onto. Bout seving or a quarter parst nigh onto fifty hed come, an' the meetin wuz called ter order, me ez Presidunt and Bill Lufkin ez Secertary. Arter considerabul gassin amung the boyz I riz and got up and sez I,

Gentlemun uv the ralerode meetin. I am a subsidy man frum the ground up. I hev jest cum frum Santa Scruze and—

Whar's Santy Scruze? sez one feller with his cow hides histed onto the stove.

Shet up yure jaw, and let mister Pipps perceed, yelled Jim Tiblins.

Order, sez I, the feller as wat axed the question hant bin in this here county moren few year and uy corse kant expected ter know. As I sed afore, I kontinnered, I hev jest cum frum Santa Scruze and I heered sum pints thar on the one hunderd thousan dollar subsidy thet wourd jest make old Logic git up and howl like a hyeeny. Whar would this here kentry be without no ralerodes up tew Santa Scruze? What would conducktors dew fer a livin ef thar wuz no ralerodes ter Santa Scruze? I ask yew agin, my feller siterzens, how could tha? Look, my frends tew the kondishen uv Picketville at this here period. Look at this here place which hez a klimate that would kill a grizzly bar in tew month; look at the senery; just look out uv that are back winder and then grit yewer teeth with the disgustedness at the gloomy scene; look at wat we air dewin here—tew or three cords uv wood thar, a load uv pickets here, and a patch of pea beans in tother place. How is it about populashen in Picketville? Thar air bout sixty nine pussons hear, the whisky iz the wust I ever seen, an thar air more babys an fewer marryages than enny place I ever struck.

Hoo yew lookin at, hollered a feller in the krowd. I lows no persenalitys round this here—

Jest then I gin a wink at old Murphy's boy Pat, an he went fer the feller wat hollered, sayin, Cum on me feine fellers, the sappleen iz formust the blessed sub*say*dies, an quickern Jim Tiblin's old mule culd wink her blind eye the feller was cuten the house, with a pison face onto him. Arter things was stiddy agin I continnered:

How, my talunted frends, would it be in Picketville ef we hed a ralerode runnin threw hear; how would it I obsarve agin. Why, yew would cumbine in Picketville the scneery uv Italy, and Rooshy, and Washoe, the attrackshens uv Nantucket and Canaday East, and Long Branch, the industrys uv Mane, and Loell, and Lexintun, and

Lawrunce and Lions, and—and—Soquel, and—San Andreas and awl the rest uv em, the productiveness uv the Western plains, the frutes uv France and the grand Rocky Mountings, and Pikes Peek, one hundred thousan peeple, free whisky, an nothin tew dew but git married and dig holes tew put yewer munny into.

Horray, Horray, Horray, yelled awl the fellers.

Mister Pipps, sed a man which wuz a standin in the door, an a cold chill run down my back fer I knew be wuz a clare heded chap frum Whatsonville, which I hadnt saw before, an wich wuz awl the time axin conundrums bout rale rodes.

Mister Pipps, sez he agin, don't yew think a ralerode subsidy iz a dern foolish thing when a kumpany wih build a rode without nu munny bein given 'em?

I gin anuther wink few old Murphy's boy Pat, an he went for the Whatsonville feller, sayin,

Cum on me feine fellers, the sappleen iz ferninst the blessed sub*say*dies.

Pat iz sum better, but it will be a munth yet afore he kin leve hiz bed.

By order uv the Kommittee, JAKE PIPPS, Cheerman.

326. *Santa Cruz Sentinel,* November 25, 1871 (1:6)

LETTER FROM SAN FRANCISCO.

...Laying aside politics for railroad matters, of which it appears is the all-absorbing question in your county, I understand from those in the secrets of the Coast Narrow Gauge, that if you county vote the subsidy for building a road between Santa Cruz and Watsonville, the Directory of that road will bid for the subsidy, and build their road through Watsonville, otherwise they will leave that down to the left, crossing the Pajaro river near its mouth, going direct to Castroville, which, if the road is built through Watsonville, will be left to the left, the road running direct to Salinas City to Watsonville. The company are in earnest, they have demonstrated the certain feasibility of the road, and will, proceed as soon as the necessary arrangements can be made, commence the construction of this road. If they obtain your subsidy, they will commence the construction of that section of the road at once, and probably build both ways from your town, otherwise they will begin at San Francisco, building south. OBSERVER.

327. *San Francisco Chronicle* via the *Santa Cruz Sentinel*, November 25, 1871 (1:7)

The Narrow Gauge Railroad from San Francisco to the Colorado River.

Major Wm. S. Watson has just returned from his arduous labors in locating a route for a narrow gauge railroad, from the northern part of San Francisco to the Colorado River, a distance of 700 miles. The Narrow Gauge Railroad Company was incorporated under the laws of this State about a year ago. The principal men engaged in it are Mr. Hayes, President of the Bank of St. Louis; Mr. Stout, President of the Shoe and Leather Company's Bank, of New

York; Mr. Crocker, President of a Bank in Boston; Mr. Coffin, the President of a Bank in Boston and deeply interested in railroads in all the Eastern States, and other prominent Eastern Capitalists.

J. P. Robinson and L. L. Robinson are among the Directors, and E. N. Robinson is Chief Engineer, with his office in the city of San Francisco.

THE ROAD.

The proposition is to build a road from the northern part of the city of San Francisco along the coast line to a point twelve miles south of Santa Cruz—running thro' Pescadero, Spanishtown and Soquel to Aptos; from there they leave the coast and run to Watsonville in Pajaro valley; thence to Castroville and Salinas city in Monterey county; thence up Salinas river to Pasa Robles, in San Louis Obispo county; thence crossing the San Marguerita range to the town of San Luis Obispo, the county seat; thence to the Aroyo Grande, the Las Berros and the Napoma Valley; Crossing the Santa Maria river at its outlet; thence following that stream to the mouth of Foxens Cañon; thence along the canon to Zaca river; along that stream to the Alamos Pintados and Santa Inez river, crossing at the Los Angeles stage road; thence along the south side of the Santa Inez to the Mission San Marcos; thence across the Santa Inez range of hills by Hampton and San Jose cañons to Santa Barbara city in Santa Barbara county; thence along the coast to San Buenaventura; thence along the Santa Clara river and valley to its headwaters.

MOUNTAIN PASSES.

From this point there are two lines run. No. 1 runs by

the Soledad Pass. Lanes and Point of Rocks, along the Mohave river to Soda Springs; thence bearing south of the old military road through a level country to a point on the Colorado river known as the Needles, where a bridge can be thrown across high above the tallest masts or the smokestack of any steamboat that may be running on that stream.

THE SECOND PASS.

No. 2 is another line running from the Santa Clara river, crossing the San Fernando mountains at the San Fernando Pass and Mission; thence to Los Angeles; form there they run eastward to San Gregorio Pass in the San Gregorio mountains; thence from the summit of Morongo to the "29 Palms," and from thence to the Needles, as before, which is about 45 miles below Fort Mohave. No. 2 is 750 miles long, while No. 1 is 700 miles long, and the latter will in all probability be established as the line for the road.

THE DISTANCES.

Are: From San Francisco to Watsonville, 100 miles; to St. Marcos Mission, 200 miles; to San Luis Obispo, 300 miles; to Los Angeles, 446 miles; to San Bernardino, 500 miles; to mouth of Morongo, 554 miles; to "29 Palms," 595 miles; to the Needles, 751 miles. This is the middle route, and might be adopted, but it is not likely to be the case. The greater portion of the road needs very little grading; the highest grade will be about 105 feet to the mile for nearly four miles in different places; 75 per cent. of the whole distance will be less than 30-feet grade to the mile. The cost will be about $37,000 per mile, or an aggregate cost of $25,900,000 to complete the road and put everything in running order. At the Santa Inez mountain there will be

A TUNNEL OF TWO MILES,

Through the Santa Marguerita mountains three-quarters of a mile, and San Pedro Point one mile, all of which can be done by the time the balance of the road is made. There is plenty of money among the stockholder, and they seem determined to build it an early day. We cannot begin to calculate the advantage of this road to San Francisco, as the great center of Pacific Ocean commerce. The road east of the Colorado will soon be an established fact, and then we shall have a through line oi trade and travel direct to the Southern States.

328. *Santa Cruz Sentinel,* November 25, 1871 (2:2)

HOW A RAILROAD WILL AFFECT TAXES.

The peculiarities of human nature are such, that in order to advance public measures through the agency and aid of individual effort, it is necessary to demonstrate that individual considerations are involved, as well as those of the general public.

Mankind are not so self-sacrificing as to give over the hope of immediate gain, simply to secure to posterity some ideal blessing, and seldom lay plans for the future greatness of a people, unless they find a way to weave themselves securely into the superstructure as trustees, or well-paid guardians; the much talk and concern about those to come after us, is generally caused by some hope or wish to advance the immediate present, and avoid, if possible, the result of an approaching and unwelcome contingency.

We are so constituted, that wile we wish well for the future, we absolutely need much for the present, whose wants must be supplied, and well being secured, before posterity can claim any considerable attention for its betterment; and while we would not ignore the future results of projects, we cannot let their consideration stultify our judgment, and thwart our efforts to aggrandize the present; for with the present we have to deal, and can only make the future secure by advancing the interests of to-day.

The expediency or inexpediency of aiding public enterprises by means that must be met through taxation, is worthy of a consideration that requires considerable time to determine wisely; and too much care cannot be exercised to render lucid every argument urging affirmative action.

For five weeks we have labored to convince this people that the depressed times and burdensome taxation could find immediate relief, by taking such action as would ensure the speedy construction of a rail road from Watsonville to Santa Cruz, and which road would effect communication between all parts of this county, and the great commercial centres of the State. Our first efforts were crowned with success when the Board of Supervisors made the order of election, submitting the question of aiding this road by a donation of $100,000 in county bonds to a vote; and it is now left to be seen whether the people will approve the wisdom of the Board, by voting the aid as recommended, on the 11th day of December next.

The question has become reduced to an earnest desire to know how the railroad will effect taxation. Figures are no longer necessary to settle this question in the mind of an unbiased, thinking man, since the publication of the Rev. Mr. Tuthill's address to the voters of the county, on this subject. It is the most exhaustive, and proves beyond the possibility of a doubt, that our taxes will be considerably less with a road than without it. After arguing the whole question with a clearness evincing an acquaintance with even the least of our wants, a statement of our condition with and without the road is submitted in the following form:

Exhibit A.

Showing the increase of tax for want of a railroad.

Amount annually required to defray expenses .. $75,000

Present value of taxable property 2,500,000

Deduct next year for depreciation in saw mill property 75,000

Depreciation on timber land 75,000

Depreciation on town property 200,000

.... $350,000

Total value of taxable property in 1872 .... $2,150,000

Rate of tax required, $3.50 per hundred.

Thus a laborer who pays now an annual tax of $10 will have to pay $11.40, or the well to do farmer, who pays $100 will have to pay $111.40 per year.

It is very correctly assumed that the next assessment roll will show a very great reduction in the value of saw mill property and timber lands. There is not a saw mill in this end of the county out of more than twenty that cannot be purchased if this road is not secured, for about the amount assessed this year, which is two-thirds less than its reputed value one year since. In fact, such property is not salable at any price, for it will not pay to run them unless relief comes speedily. In the item of town property, we will cite one instance, to show how values have been reduced for want of better business prospects. A gentleman purchased a lost at a cost of $800, built a house at a cost of $3,500, and at private sale was able to get but $3,000 for both house and lot, and this was a fair price according to the times; an absolute loss of $1,300 in one year. This will be about the reduction to be made on all our town property, unless the people can be made to believe there is a prospect of reviving business. This reduction in town property will exceed the amount stated in Exhibit A, and other property, such as farming land, which is steadily increasing in value, must make up the deficiency. These are facts and conditions that actually exist, and no amount of coloring can make the fact less apparent.

Some fifteen or twenty of our best and oldest citizens, blacksmiths, wheelwrights, carpenters, lawyers and doctors, are now in search for a place in the lower counties, where they can procure land and establish permanent homes, not one of whom would ever thought of leaving Santa Cruz. Again, we publish the bright side of the picture, as set forth by Mr. Tuthill's circular.

EXHIBIT B.

Showing increase of taxation to provide for the payment of interest on $100,000 of railroad subsidy bonds without estimating benefits.

Total present value of taxable property in county............
.... $2,500,000

Rate of tax $3 per hundred

Total tax	$75,000
Interest on R. R. bonds	7,000
Less amount of tax on twenty miles of track, rolling stock etc	4,500
Balance to be provided for by taxation	2,500

A tax of 12 ½ cents on 100.

Thus a laborer who pays now an annual tax of $10 will have to pay $10.40 or the well to do farmer who pays now a yearly tax of $100 will have to pay $104 per year when the railroad shall be completed.

If the aid be voted, not one person would be willing to sell his property at twenty-five per cent. advance, within the town limits; and the dissatisfaction, discontent and depressed feeling now so general, would vanish; the future would appear more hopeful and full of promise. If the aid is secured, the Central Pacific Company will commence immediately, weather permitting, on this line of road, and with their appliances at hand, can and will complete the same to Santa Cruz by July 1st, 1872. Talk about taxes; this town alone could well afford to raise by subscription $7,000 annually to meet the interest on the bonds. So all could Watsonville; either place will be benefited in two years by increased business, beyond the entire cost of this road to the county in twenty years. In five years after the completion of the road, the principal towns, Santa Cruz and Watsonville, will pay more than five-sevenths of the entire tax collected in the county. The great advantage the road will be to outside lands, is to cause their settlement and cultivation, and to equalize their value, thus in two ways, relieving the farmers taxes. First, by creating business centres, such as towns and cities, and second, by equalizing the value and securing the settlement of non-resident lands.

With a revived business, it will be much easier for the people to meet an enlarged tax, than with no business to meet any demands, however small.

329. *Santa Cruz Sentinel,* November 25, 1871 (2:4)
NARROW GAUGE RAILROAD.

We publish on the first page of to-days issue, the long and interesting account, given in detail in the San Francisco papers, of the beginning, course and terminus of the projected narrow gauge railroad, which, according to the survey, will pass through the entire length of Santa Cruz county, a distance of forty-five miles, touching at every prominent point about the Bay of Monterey, thence south-east, touching all the coast towns, and extending forty-five miles below Fort Mohave, Arizona, a distance of 700 miles, at an estimated cost of twenty-six million dollars.

A road of this character may be constructed some day, but will depend very materially upon the progress made in the development of the agricultural resources of the Southern country, which, to-day, find cheap and ample means of transportation by water. Colonel Hollister, of Santa Barbara, states that freight from that county to San Francisco per ton, does not exceed $3, and which is much cheaper than any railroad can afford to carry it. While we hope that this company may find it expedient to hasten on the work of this road, we must express our doubts about its being undertaken or completed for many years to come. $26,000,000 will not be expended without some better showing for profitable investment.

Santa Cruz, in our opinion, would wait many years for railroad facilities, if her only prospect hinged upon the narrow gauge project. We have a fine opportunity to secure a road at moderate cost to the people, and no speculative notions should lessen our zeal in carrying out the undertaking so wisely recommended by the Board of Supervisors. A road is the immediate demand of the whole county, and all efforts to defeat the present prospect by urging assistance to the narrow gauge, will prove abortive.

Let us finish up what we have so worthily undertaken, lest in attempting to obtain too much, we fail of securing anything. By united effort, Santa Cruz can have a railroad in full operation by July 1st, 1872, leaving Santa Cruz the terminus of the road.

330. *Santa Cruz Sentinel,* November 25, 1871 (2:5)

Address to Voters.—The committee appointed at the public meeting two weeks since, to draft an address to the voters of this county on the railroad question, has concluded its duties, and we have before us a most exhaustive argument in favor of voting aid to the railroad as recommended and proposed in the order of election.

The address will be placed in the hands of every voter in the county, and cannot fail of producing the desired effect, that of carrying the election by a handsome majority.

What a glorious day for this county, when we can feel that the people are a unit on some great measure, and have acted with that unanimity necessary to accomplish this result. The committee of thirteen are vigorously at work, and feel sure of carrying the election by a large majority.

331. *Santa Cruz Sentinel,* December 2, 1871 (2:2-3)
BENEFIT OF RAILROADS.

The rapid settlement and development of the Pacific States is bringing the country fast to the level and standard of the East and West, and is forcing like conditions and considerations upon our people.

In the East and West experience has demonstrated that progress and prosperity follow speedily, permanently and satisfactorily wherever the wisdom of the people has led them to foster public enterprises, such as churches, colleges, railroads, manufactories, etc. It was found, as a consequence, that lands of little worth and paying no tax, soon became occupied, cultivated, and added to the wealth of the country by their productions, as well as enhanced value. Railroads annihilate the distances between producer and consumer, and by cheap and enlarged facilities for transportation, render farming as profitable as manufacturing; so that corn, wheat, and all farm produce, which before had no market and no value, were of immediately and profitable exchanged for cash. This rapid and wonderful revolution in the condition of the West, has made its people the most progressive, philanthropic and liberal of any on this Continent.

It is undeniable that railroads have done more than all else combined, to facilitate the spread of this spirit and enterprise and progress; by the people of remote parts are made near—their intercourse and reciprocity of thought and feeling create a laudable pride and just spirit of emulation until the American has been and is entitled to be termed Cosmopolitan.

California will not remain long in the unenviable condition of the territories, isolated and almost unapproachable. The few roads constructed and being constructed within her borders, have wrought a marvelous change in the opinions of the people, and all sections are alive to the great need of them, and the benefits flowing from their timely advent, and ask the privilege of aiding and hastening their construction. There is no place on this coast where roads are in operation; that is not prospering beyond all precedent, and with a promise of permanency; while those parts without them are languishing, business unprofitable, the people discontented and unprosperous, taxes burdensome, valuations declining, and population decreasing. Is not this the exact condition of this end of Santa Cruz county? And how does it contrast with our neighbor Watsonville, with railroad facilities, only twenty miles below us? This whole railroad problem is solved within this little country, and he who is too blind to perceive it, deserves no commiseration.

If any person thinks that railroads exercise no wholesome or beneficial influence over the business and general prosperity of places favored with them, let such pass a few days in and about Watsonville, and then speak honestly. That place, with no rival over the river, would in three years more than double in wealth and population. Already extensive Homestead Associations on both sides of the river are being formed with a view to this end; and while we do not envy our neighbors their prospective greatness, we wish they could see the great good apparent to us in the construction of the Santa Cruz and Watsonville continuation of their railroad. Santa Cruz would then enter upon a line of progress which should be as pleasing to Watsonville as profitable to us.

The Los Angeles *Express* states some important facts showing the benefits to Los Angeles County of the Los Angeles and San Pedro Railroad, which is twenty-one miles in length, and has been operating less than two years. The taxable property of that county in 1868, the year the project was undertaken, amounted to $3,764,045, and in 1870 had increased to $6,918,074, a difference in favor of the county of $3,154,029, or nearly double the assessed value of 1870. This increase in taxable property is mainly attributed to the good results flowing from twenty-one miles of a railroad. The *Express* says:

"When the survey was made of the route on which the road was built, there were only three mud houses in sight of its present location, and these were occupied by native Californians. Not one acre of soil was under cultivation; not an American lived near it;; and land which at that time sold for five dollars per acre, has since changed owners at twenty-five and fifty-dollars, and in some cases as high as one hundred dollars per acre. Many large stores and dwellings that were not thought of two years ago, have been erected in the city, and now pay a handsome interest on their cost. A large brick grist mill, and a first class steam planing mill have been constructed, and are doing well.

Lumber has decreased in price $7.50 per thousand feet, and the rate of freight on each ton of grain is now five dollars less than it was two years since, and consequently it is worth that much more to the producer."

This wonderful progress and prosperity of Los Angeles county, was all accomplished in two of the driest years known to the inhabitants of the county, therefore, cannot in justice or reason be believed to have resulted from any other cause than the railroad.

Does this not argue well for railroads? And where would the people of this county look for a fairer parallel to more conclusive evidence to induce them to aid in constructing our road, of about the same distance, and with ten-fold greater prospects of benefiting the whole county, than to that road, running almost entirely through an uninhabited region, while ours traverses the most valuable and populous portions of the county. The further fact that the Los Angeles and San Pedro Road was aided by city and county bonds, amounting in the aggregate, in fifteen years, to $562,500, more than double the entire cost of our project to this people in twenty years, is a still further evidence of the wisdom and enterprise of those urging county aid in the sum of $100,000 to the Santa Cruz and Watsonville road. We quote further the *Express*:

"The Superintendent of the Los Angeles and San Pedro Road, in a published statement of the business done by the road that year, says that it transported 10,600 tons of merchandise, and 5,800,000 feet of lumber to Los Angeles, and 1,410 tons of wine and brandy, 1,229 tons wool, 1,314 tons corn, 564 tons oranges, and 1,933 tons miscellaneous produce from Los Angeles. The freight by rail on these things was $116,430.70 and by team at the rate charged before the construction of the road, would have been $249,982.50, showing a saving of $133,551 for one year, or $2,003,265 for 15 years. The city and county together promised $562,500 to the Railroad Company, including the principal of the bonds and the interest for 15 years. By this calculation the county will make $1,440,765 by the transaction."

What that people saved in reduced transportation, and reduced prices of articles used in and about their homes and business, must certainly be set down to the credit of the cause effecting such wholesome results.

Thus we find the people of Los Angeles county acknowledging that their twenty-one miles of railroad will, in fifteen years pay the debt, and net them $1,445,142, or nearly three times the cost to them of the road, in reduced prices and transportation alone; and this calculation is based upon the first two years' work of the road, which certainly brings the conclusion within the bounds of things so probable as to be considered a just conclusion.

Accepting these results as a fair criterion to guide us in calculating the benefits resulting from a like project in this county, we have only to show a like condition to make our position tenable.

Santa Cruz county is very materially in advance of Los Angeles county to-day, in the development of her agricultural and manufacturing resources, and consequently demands enlarged conveniences for transportation and travel. We also require an outlet and a market for the vast millions of feet of lumber covering our mountains, which market, in future, with this road, will be the southern valleys, into which no other lumber can be taken so cheaply. In return, those employed in our forests and manufacturing establishments, will require the articles of living produced by the farmer.

Our statement then, is this: The assessed value of the real and personal property of this county, as per Assessment Roll of 1871 on the basis of a one-third valuation, is $2,146,000, or in actual value $6,438,000, allowing the rates of increase in valuation to equal that of Los Angeles, and in six years the actual value of the property of this county will exceed $19,000,000, one half per cent. of which will afford a tax of $95,000 per annum; then considering the State and county demands, including the interest on bonds, no greater than the tax of 1872, which will be, with the road, $71,361, leaving a balance of $22,639, which if used as a fund to liquidate the county's outstanding bonds, will, in seven years, being 1885, more than pay every dollar of the county indebtedness. It must be borne in mind that during this time the rates of increased valuation is advancing, and taxation as a result becoming less.

This is no chimerical sketch of possible results, but precisely what has transpired in a county not half so eligible to progress as Santa Cruz county.

Twenty-one miles of a railroad, entirely disconnected with any other road, has accomplished all this for Los Angeles county, and may we not predict even greater progress from being connected with the whole net-work of railroads of this State; yes, of the United States.

332. *Santa Cruz Sentinel,* November 25, 1871 (3:1)
FURTHER CONCERNING THE NARROW GAUGE ROAD.

The canvass on the railroad question is becoming quite lively. The vast advantages to be gained by the whole county from the construction of a railroad from Santa Cruz to Watsonville are becoming so apparent, that many who at first honestly opposed the proposition for a subsidy, are now its warmest advocates. We are assured that this is particularly the case in Watsonville, and in the Pajaro Valley. A few can yet be found in nearly every neighborhood who oppose subsidy. They generally belong to that class who oppose every public improvement, and who opposed the building of roads, school houses, churches, &c., and whose names never appear on subscription lists for charity, or for any measure tending to the public good, who can see nothing good in anything but themselves. That class you can never convince that, with a railroad, the wealth of our county, consisting of land, mill power, muscle and money, can and will be made available, while without a railroad we are paralyzed. But if we would accept as true the assertions of this class, they are now most strongly in favor of a railroad, not alone from Santa Cruz to Watsonville, but also from Santa Cruz, by the coast, to San Francisco. That is the route they favor now, that is the road which will be constructed without a subsidy, that is the road to grant aid if needed.

Who believes such trash? What assurance have they for such assertions? Why impose them upon public notice at this particular time? Does not their every act betray their lurking desires?

As journalists we have copied from the San Francisco *Chronicle* of Nov. 19, the report of the Survey of the Narrow Gauge Railroad from San Francisco to the Colorado river; we consider, and have evidence that it is highly colored, and that the truth is very much mixed with fiction; in fact we believe that its publication at this time is for the purpose of distracting the friends of a subsidy for the road from Watsonville to Santa Cruz. The report says: "The greater portion of the road needs very little grading, there is plenty of money among the stock holders, and they seem to be determined to build it at an early day." This is sheer nonsense. There is no route on the continent which offers more engineering difficulties than the greater portion of this route, and as to the stock holders, they may have plenty of money, but instead of being determined to build the road at an early day, they say "the outlay necessary is very large, that the country is mountainous; large cañons and ravines will have to be bridges, large excavations made and long tunnels run, and that without local aid no company of ordinary prudence would undertake it."

'We copy the above from a letter of Francis B. Hayes, President of the Atlantic and Pacific R. R. Co., to Wm. Alvord and others, dated July 15th, 1871, and published in the *Alta* of 22d of July last.

It must be borne in mind that this letter was written by Mr. Hayes on his return to San Francisco, after a personal inspection of this route, long after the alleged incorporation of the Narrow Gauge Railroad Company. Mr. Hayes has returned to St. Louis, the whole project is abandoned, and the Company does not, in fact, exist, except on paper.

333. *Santa Cruz Sentinel,* November 25, 1871 (3:3)

Railroad Progress in California.

ROADS THAT ARE BUILDING AND ROADS THAT HAVE BEEN BUILT—SOME SIGNIFICANT FACTS—NUMBER OF ROUTES IN OPERATION.

We have from time to time says the San Francisco *Bulletin*, of November 22d, published facts relative to the State railroad progress. Annexed will be found a full abstract of the progress of each road, the number of miles built and the total length of railroads now in operation in California. Laborers are in increased demand for railroad construction. In fact more men, are being employed at present in building State railroads than at any period since the great Pacific Railroad race between the Central and Union Pacific roads...

Watsonville Branch.—the Watsonville branch of the Southern Pacific road is about completed, and there is every probability that the people of Santa Cruz county will induce the company, by a subsidy of $100,000, to extend the road through their county and to the town of Santa Cruz, a distance of 20 miles....

It will be seen that the Narrow Gauge road is not even mentioned as among the probable roads, in the above article on railroads taken from the *Bulletin* of 22d inst., and bears out the general opinion that there is no prospect and less hope of its becoming a thing of any importance for years to come. Our people must not look upon this mythical project as a fixed fact, because of its favorable mention by a sensational paper nor because some of the opponents of our present efforts to secure immediate railroad facilities, advocate the narrow gauge road, as the best means of dividing the friends of some railroad, and who imagine such division will defeat aid to any. If such persons are sincere, why not come up and work manfully for the road you know, will and can be constructed, if aid be voted, in time to relieve the people of the whole county the coming year. If the completion of this road is to be deferred for two, three or five years, and the voters become aware of the fact, not one in ten will accord it their support. One year is all the time the Central Pacific Co., requires to give us this road, and the people will consent to be taxed only in the event of its speedy construction.

334. *The Pajaronian*, November 30, 1871 (2:1)

Railroad Subsidy.

We propose to state succinctly some of the reasons why we oppose the proposed donation of one hundred thousand dollars to the Central Pacific or another company, as an inducement for them to build a railroad from Watsonville to Santa Cruz.

First—Because we believe that all subsidies of the nature and kind proposed are fundamentally wrong in principle. If each or any citizen of the county desires to make a donation of his won individual property to said company, no one has a right to complain. But when any person or combination of persons by any means compels us against our will and consent to make such donation through the medium of taxation or otherwise, the act it seems to us, differs but little from that of the highwayman, the only difference is that one is *legalized* robbery, or rather is invested with the sanctity of the *form* of law. We say the *form* of law knowing that our Supreme Court has decided that the act in question or a similar one, is not void as being in conflict with the letter of the State Constitution, and we bow with deference to the decisions of our Court of last resort, while we also know that the Supreme Courts of Michigan and others states, with similar Constitutions have declared—as we think with better argument and reasons—that similar acts are unconstitutional and void. We are finding no fault with our Court, however, the question with us now is, not whether said act violates any express provision of our Constitution, but is it a just, wise politic and expedient act and should it be enforced generally or in this particular instance? Why should this attempted application of it be deemed an exceptional case, if it be conceded that the principle is wrong and impolitic? What arguments or reasons can be urged in favor of its application here, that cannot with equal force and consistency be urged for its general enforcement? That said law is impolitic and the principle of it wrong, the people of this State has most solemnly and emphatically and with a singular unanimity declared. If there was any local issue preeminently before the people of this State during the late canvass, it was this subsidy question. Each political party vied with the other to show to the people that it was more heartily and consistently opposed to the principle than the other. The expression of the people of the whole State, of all parties and sections, against it, was most emphatic and overwhelming.

Second—Because we believe that the county is already

sufficiently involved in debt, and that the burden of taxation is as great as the people can and ought to bear.

If the argument of the advocates of the measure, *vis*: that the payment semi-annually of the interest on said sums, and eventually of the principal, by the county, will reduce taxation, is good, we would respectfully suggest whether the payment of four or five times that amount would not wipe out taxation altogether.

Third—Because said sum, though large for our small and indebted county, is but a drop in the bucket to the Company would build said road, and while as a matter of course, any company would gladly accept of such a donation, it would be no inducement for them to build the road; they would build it just as quick without as with that, to them, trifling sum.

Fourth—Because we believe that the Southern Pacific Company will be compelled to build said road at once, without subsidies, as the timber which it will give them access to, is of vital importance to them. That one hundred thousand dollars will thus be saved to the county, and withheld from a rich monopoly that has already received more subsidies than it should have done.

Fifth—Because we believe, that if the Southern Pacific Company does not build said road the Narrow Gauge Company will, and they ask no subsidy.

Sixth—Because we believe generally that when the wants of a county demands a railroad, and capitalists can be made to see that it will pay, private enterprise will build it.

Seventh—Because we believe that if private enterprise cannot or will not alone build a needed road, and that

County aid should in any manner be extended that such aid should be given in the way of taking stock in the Company by the County to the proposed amount so that the County might own and control the road to the extent of its subscriptions for if the County aids in building a road it should see to it, that the fares upon it and the management of it are such that it will benefit and not oppress the people.

335. *The Pajaronian*, November 30, 1871 (2:2)

Editorial Correspondence.
Santa Cruz, Nov. 29th, 1871.

Since our arrival in this place last Sunday morning, we have been sick in bed—so sick in fact that Dr. Peabody deemed it necessary to call four or five times a day up to yesterday. We are not yet able to sit up but write this bolstered up by friendly pillows. While we were in our most critical and painful state, and mental and bodily quiet had been ordered, a man by the name of McDermott of this town, rushed to the door of our house through a pelting rain, gave a loud knock and delivered a ponderous package to our half worn out nurse, addressed to us. Opening it we found a long card from D. Tuthill, whose name was attached to the subsidy circular which we referred to last week, and whom we in the same article criticised severely and accused of lying about Watsonville. Tuthill's card was a forcible demand for an apology for our attack on him. Said demand being accompanied by another card signed by 26 of the first subsidy men of this place, who also demanded that we take back what we had said in regard to Tuthill and the subsidy circular, as *they* were entirely responsible for said circular! In the fact of so much proof of Mr. Tuthill's innocence we can do nothing less than to take the lie in regard to Watsonville contained in said circular, from Mr. Tuthill's shoulders. So we apologize to Mr. Tuthill for calling him a liar, and he is now at liberty to call us the same name if he so desires. But the lie is still out, and whether the 26 subsidy men we have referred to are collectively or individually responsible for it we do not know.

Mr. Tuthill says we did him a wrong when we said that he was only a transient resident of the county with no financial interest here except his monthly salary, for he has resided here over two years and is one of the owners of the Santa Cruz Gas Works. We were simply misinformed and stated what we believed to be so, with no intention of doing him injury.

He says he did not write the scurrilous article against Watsonville and her citizens which appeared in the *Sentinel* a few weeks since. We never said he did write it. To sum up all, we were hasty in speaking of Tuthill so severely, but our information was as exact as could be obtained from the short time we had and as his name was signed to the circular we supposed him to be the author, a very natural mistake, we think. But as we have said before, the 26 noble committee men claim the whole trash and Mr. Tuthill's name, we are glad to know stands free from odium, and we regret that we should have lost our usually even temper and caused Mr. Tuthill any uneasiness.

The whole active Subsidy portion of this community

are now roused to a violent pitch of anger against the editor of the *Pajaronian*, for, they say, if the subsidy measure is defeated, "it can all be laid to Cummings." But we claim that we have a perfect right to our opinions on subsidies, or politics; we shall not join with the old line party stampeders and bolt from principle entirely, and if we get into trouble with a man we really cannot see why the whole community should set up a doleful howl of horror. They would not do it did they not know that their pet subsidy scheme was virtually lost. During all the discussion of this miserable, thieving subsidy question, we have never lost patience until last week, and we have never yet referred to Santa Cruz or to her citizens except in terms of respect and praise—fought for our friends in this place the same as for friends in Watsonville, referred to the erection of elegant structures here with the same pride as though in our own town, but during the late subsidy wrangle the manner in which Watsonville has been spoken of has simply been cowardly. Our financial interests, and friends, are in Watsonville. It was there we went three or four years ago with nothing, and with the aid of a kindly and noble class of people to stimulate our industry we have at length got above the more rugged ways of poverty, and while we reside there we shall resent any insult offered to the people or place.

We would say more, but as it is uncertain when we can get out of this very excited place and we may be [moved] two or three times before we do succeed in eluding the watchful eyes of the Subsyites, it is best for us to wind up our note before our physician arrives, or a blunderbuss is poked in through the window and shot off at us.

We will say, however, that our views as expressed last week in regard to the "Address to Voters," remain unchanged—said address being a jumbled mass of uncomprehensiblities figures run mad, and imagination stretched to bursting. That "Address" alone a burlesque in itself, will deter every man who reads it, from voting in favor of the Subsidy, if nothing else will.

As it is so late in the week we will not have the *Pajaronian* kept back by trying to publish the papers with which we have been served—Mr. Tuthill's card and the card signed by the faithful 26. But propose to publish them next week.

We wish to say to our friends there, that though sick, and encompassed with danger, we have a first-class physician, and ammunition enough to last a day or two.

CUMMINGS.

336. *The Pajaronian*, November 30, 1871 (3:1)

Hurrah for the Railroad.

At length the long expected, much talked of Pajaro Branch of the Southern Pacific Railroad has reached its terminus. For nearly three months we have been informed almost every week, by parties who received their information from various sources, that this desirable event would take place in "ten days." Consistent with this expectation men have made business arrangements, and have disappointed, and some have been accommodated by the "construction train," and so relieved in their disappointments.

Not being possessed of foreknowledge the *Pajaronian*

has neither been able to contradict or confirm these predictions. The Celestial operators have kept up such a tremendous dust in that wonderful cut at the upper end of the valley, that not even the Superintendent of the grading could see how many rocks were underground.

It is not the duty of the prophets of this dispensation to predict future events, this vocation, we are told, is to preach, or teach, to worship and give thanks. Now, if on this Thanksgiving day, we may venture forth as "Saul among the prophets" we would suggest as a subject of gratitude and thanksgiving, the completion of this enterprise.

On Monday the first train arrived, and every day since we have received our mail by the same conveyance, about three hours earlier than we could have had it by the stage.

The trains for the present will run as follows: Leaving San Francisco at 8:10 A.M., arriving at Pajaro at 1:30 P.M., returning leave Pajaro at 12:00 M., arriving at San Francisco at 5:30 P.M. This time table will be published next week.

If our necessities demand it there will doubtless be more trains run for our accommodation; but for the present we may be very glad of what we now have. The Depot is going up with California speed, and will be a good respectable building for the purpose.

337. *Santa Cruz Sentinel,* December 2, 1871 (2:4-5)
NARROW GAUGE AND ITS CONVERSE.

The advantage claimed for the narrow gauge road, cannot be considered as even approximating that degree of certainty warranting its adopting in preference to any other. The only considerations favoring their construction, are their cheapness, and their facility with which they make sharp curves and unusual grades. It is not contended that they meet the demands of extensive trade or travel, likely to bring them into favor, or general use, where other and broader gauges are possible. Those sections of the country favorable to cheap roads, the valleys and plains, are precisely where the requirements of trade and travel demand greater speed and capacity for freighting; and no road has ever met these demands so satisfactorily as the broad gauge.

A glance at the average freights per ton per mile of the Central Pacific Company within this State, will convince any person, that this road is proving a great blessing, as well as a convenience for the people, notwithstanding the attempt by some papers to convince then that his company is arrogant and oppressive, and exercising a great disregard of its patrons' interest; it has reduced its freights below the standard of Eastern roads of the same gauge, and which is by all odds, the cheapest means of transportation through the country, until at this date, its average freight per mile per ton is less than two and one-half cents—and this, too, in the face of a law which allowed them to charge fifteen cents per ton per mile. Eastern roads, with much more business and greater facilities for constructing and repairing cheaply, charge an average of four cents per ton per mile. Is it not time, then, that this howl against these benefactors of the people be discountenanced until it is shown wherein the people are wronged and their rights disregarded?

During the last political campaigns, much was said to prejudice the people against railroad corporations in this State by both parties, when the principle against which they were wailing, State and national subsidies, did not in justice, embrace the principle of aid to local railroads. There is much reason in one part of the State not being willing to be taxed to aid a road in another part; but when the people benefited, foot all the bills, so far as taxes are concerned, the question then, becomes one to be governed by ordinary business ideas.

If it is required, the people should make an effort to obtain it, and not hesitate to render even individual assistance, much less that greater aid, with less embarrassment because of an equalized burden, a general tax.

A little reflection has done much to restore this people to a normal condition of mind; they are now fairly considering what is required, and have come to the conclusion that among the many things needful, a railroad stands the first.

As a matter of much interest to our farmers, we take from an up country paper, the following list of grain rates charged by the Central Pacific Company in this State, also comparisons with Eastern freights from Watsonville to San Francisco, will not, when the road is in complete working order, exceed two dollars and fifty cents per ton, and from Santa Cruz, not more than two dollars and seventy-five cents.

GRAIN RATES TO SAN FRANCISCO.

From	Distance	Rate per ton.	Tonnage per mile
Mokelumne	193	$2.502	43-100
Elk Grove	123	2.752	24-100
Marysville	190	4.402	23-100
Chico	234	5.602	39-100
Tehama	251	6.002	29-100

Thus it appears that the rates charged by the Company in no case instanced equal 2½ cents per ton per mile, and fall as low as 2¼ cents.

As a matter of fact they do not exceed 2½ cents, and this without any legislation whatever; but simply as a result of common sense acting upon a business proposition.

Now for a comparison of these rates with those on some of the Eastern railroads. Iron and coal are the cheapest kinds of freight.

We find on reference to the statistical reports of Eastern lines, that for distances varying between forty and sixty miles the following rates per ton are charged by the roads mentioned:

For coal, the Housatonic charges $3.40; the Providence and Worcester, $2.80; the Fitchburg, $3.20; the Boston and Maine, $2.50; the Old Colony and Newport, $3; the Boston, Hartford and Erie, $3.40; the Norwich and Worcester, $3; the Vermont and Massachusetts, $4; the Connecticut River, $3; the New Haven and Northampton, $2.80. All these ,remember, are charges, for distances between forty and sixty miles. *The Central Pacific Company carries grain 103 miles for $2.50 per ton*. The Eastern charges on coal are nearly as high as those quoted on iron. Thus the Providence and Worcester road charges, $2.80; the Fitchburg, $3.20; the Boston and Maine, $2.50; the Old Colony and Newport, $3; the Boston, Hartford and Erie, $3.40; the Norwich and Worcester, $3, etc.

The same paper, speaking of the wonderful advantages of this road to Placer County, says:

'If the popular vote of Placer county, or the whole State were taken to-day, it would be unanimous in favor of the railroad. The people of Placer county need not be told that private property has been increased in value ten fold since the completion of the Pacific Railroad through that county. They knew it already. They know likewise, that thousands of what were supposed worthless lands have been made remunerative beyond expectations.

'The permanent settlement of the people; the extensive purchase and profitable culture of the soil, and the consequent benefit to other pursuits have jointly flown from an enterprise against which the puny quill of the *Herald* flings his hebdomadal maranathas.

'The annual tax paid to Placer county by the Central Pacific Railroad Company is sufficient to pay the salaries of the County Clerk, Recorder, Sheriff, Treasurer, District Attorney, County Judge and Assessor, leaving a balance of several hundred dollars.

If the salaries of those officers are *small* as those of like officers in this county, the road pays a taco f over $15,000 annually, and which doubtless comes quite acceptable in liquidation of taxes.

It is this same company which has done so much to develop the counties through which it passes, that offers to give this county twenty miles of the same kind of road for the inconsiderable sum of $100,00 in County Bonds, payable in twenty years, and which road will cost the company at least $600,000. More than one-half of this amount will be expended in the county during the progress of construction, and the road will pay back to the county in taxes, in twenty years, about as much as the original aid. The county, then, is simply required to meet the interest on the bonds, $7,000 annually, which certainly is no proportionate return for the advantage of the road.

On being interviewed respecting the probably result of the two gauges being contiguous, the projectors of the Coast Narrow Gauge Road, say that money is uselessly expended in their road if it be thrown in competition with the broad gauge. The speed being more than double that of the narrow gauge, no one would think of preferring such slow means of travel or transportation to the quicker and cheaper rates of the broad gauge.

The broad gauge is capacitated, through size, power of engine, cars, track and calibre of rail, to move at great speed, long and heavily freighted trains of cars, against which, it is not claimed by the friends of the Coast Road, a narrow gauge could compete; its speed at greatest—not exceeding twelve miles per hour.

Some of the opponents of our proposed road, have very suddenly been converted to the practicability of narrow gauge, and would make us believe that their advantages to communities were superior to the broad gauge, and as we prefer to show good reasons for our advocacy of the larger roads, we can do so in no better way, than by publishing the remarks of Mr. Seymour, a very eminent engineer, to Marshall O. Roberts, the controlling spirit of the "Texas Pacific Railway," showing the superiority of the broad gauge over the narrow gauge roads. He says:

A train, like a wagon, may be hauled much easier with wheels of large than small diameter. This width of gauge allows of considerable larger wheels under its ordinary rolling stock, than are admissible upon the narrow gauge; but with this proposed redacted height of cars upon the wider gauge, the wheels may be made to much larger than a very material saving will be effected in power.

Having a greater base of track in proportion to the height and width of your cars, the irregularities in the track would be less apparent; and you could certainly make as fast time with greater safety, or faster time with equal safety than you could upon the narrow gauge.

This is the testimony of every experienced engineer when asked to express an opinion touching the relative value of the two roads.

If the narrow gauge is good, the broad gauge is better; and to secure it is our privilege if we act wisely in voting

RAILROAD AID, YES

On the 11th day of December—one week from Monday next.

338. *Santa Cruz Sentinel,* December 2, 1871 (2:5)
RAIL ROAD.

The Executive Committee meet every evening, at the Club Room, over the store of I. Blum & Co. The friends of the Rail Road are requested to drop in.

Wm. P. McDermott, Secretary.

339. *Santa Cruz Sentinel,* December 2, 1871 (3:1)

Mr. Martin,

Our old foundryman, has just completed and furnished his new machine-shop with a view to secure the contract for railroad work. Santa Cruz being the terminus of the road, must provide such an establishment, or the company will be compelled to do their own work.

Parties from Different

Parties of the State have engaged every vacant store in Santa Cruz, so we are informed, and will open in business soon as it is determined that we shall have a railroad. We see the reasons why all the shingles "to rent," have been turned round.

Second Address,

Our railroad committee have issued a second address to the voters, which very ably and correctly concludes that our only relief is in the speedy construction of the railroad.

—The construction of a new hotel is in contemplation; we suggest the propriety of calling it the "Railroad House."

—A gentleman in Massachusetts lately recovered $15,000 from a railroad company for injuries sustained by his wife. He has ever since considered railroads a great blessing. We wish he was here to vote railroad aid—Yes—on the 11th inst.

Would it not be Advisable,

To hold a public meeting to determine at what point the Depot had best be located? It will very materially assist the vote.

The New Pavement,

Being put down by Mr. Hihn, has been dubbed the "railroad pavement."

340. *Santa Cruz Sentinel,* December 2, 1871 (3:2)

Undignified and Unprofessional.

The clever editor of the *Pajaronian* gets ugly, wrathy, personal and abusive over the very excellent address to the voters of this county on the railroad question by the Rev. Mr. Tuthill, and says some very unwise, indiscreet things, all of which we believe he is heartily ashamed of ere this. If such is the argument used by the opponents of the road, it certainly indicates a very bad cause, for such language never convinces anyone of anything but the absolute unworthiness of the measure advocated. Mr. D. Tuthill is one of the most worthy, exemplary and excellent gentlemen we have ever met, and withal, a man of refined tastes and extensive culture; for integrity, probity and business solidity, Mr. Tuthill has no superior in this community or any other, and the good people in this community will endorse what we say. Mr. Tuthill issued that address to the voters at the earnest solicitation of the solid men of Santa Cruz and Soquel, and if the arguments were too sound and conclusive to suit the opponents of the road, it would have looked much better to have said nothing. One of the most important enterprises in the county, the gas works, is largely owned and entirely superintended by Mr. Tuthill; he therefore has some slight interest in the prosperity of this people, and responded ably to their wishes when asked to "state the question."

Mr. Tuthill has never written a line, on railroad matters, for the *Santa Cruz Sentinel,* and it is undignified and unprofessional to attack any one but the proprietors or editor of the paper for articles which appear as editorials. If it also wrong to blame the Committee or their Executive for what appears in this paper. We are not advised by nor do we consult the Railroad Committee before writing on the subject.

341. *Santa Cruz Sentinel,* December 2, 1871 (3:3)
Subsidy Bugaboo.

It will be seen by the following, that the people of the southern counties are not so badly afflicted with the anti-subsidy mania as to thwart every enterprise tending to their prosperity. The people of San Diego and San Bernardino, like the people of Santa Cruz county, see no impropriety in induing rail road men to come among them, even though it requires a small tax to effect desired results:

The San Diego Union published the 18th ult, says that a petition is being circulated by the San Diego and San Bernardino people for the purpose of obtaining signatures, which requests the Board of Supervisors to order an election for the purposes of deciding whether a subsidy of $100,000 shall be granted to The San Diego and San Bernardino Railroad Company.

Now that the sober second thought is obtaining among the people, and they begin to see that much good can result from property aiding the construction of railroads, it would be well to ask the Legislature to not entirely repeal the fiver percent law, but so modify and restrict the power it places in the Board of Supervisors, as to make it less objectionable to the public. It would be unjust to leave every county or community powerless to aid themselves, did they desire, by forcing them to wait for special Legislative sanction. What may seem improper to day, may, one year hence become an absolute necessity; and the people should be their own judges, so long as they are willing to foot the bills. The law can so be amended that their will be no danger of Colonizing to defeat the will of the rightful citizen. Don't let the progress and industry of the state be paralyzed to satisfy the caprices of demagog politicians who are, often all, nothing but cormorants, a sort of political fungus, kept alive by imposing themselves upon the people. By your own judges of what is necessary to advance your material interests, and ask for laws that will permit you to act in time to avoid impending danger.

342. *Santa Cruz Sentinel,* December 2, 1871 (3:3)

Outside on Our Railroad.

Mr. A. A. Hecox, Lighthouse keeper at this port, allows us to wake an extract from a letter from Mr. L. H. Dimmick of Illinois under date of Nov. 3d, 1871, as will be seen. The great hinderance and draw back to Santa Cruz, is the lack of railroad facilities, and men over the mountains are watching and waiting for the line to come, when these healthful and beautiful localities will be made easy to access. The gentleman asks: "What are the prospects for a railroad to connect Santa Cruz with the outside world?'

I see by the Weekly *Bulletin*, which I take, that the road to Watsonville from Gilroy is being built.

"I feel some interest in Santa Cruz, not knowing but I may decide to make my home there, but I do not like to get away from railroad facilities."

This is the enquiry and this the feeling of every person wishing to locate in this State; other places are alive to this great source of settlement, and are building roads in every direction. We will soon have one to Santa Cruz.

343. *The Pajaronian*, December 7, 1871 (2:1)

We learn from good authority that money is being used to carry the Subsidy measures next Monday. A man in this section was approached by a subsidy emissary on a money basis, but the emissary could not make an impression. Who supplies this cash? We shall try and ascertain who the rascals are who thus endeavor to place the county under a needless debt by the use of money, and shall deem it our duty, as a fearless journalist, to expose all such low and underhanded operations.

Vote on Monday next and save the county from debt and difficulty.

344. *The Pajaronian*, December 7, 1871 (2:2)

The Subsidy and the *Pajaronian*

A few weeks ago a scheme was hatched in Santa Cruz by some party or parties unknown to the writer, to run this county into debt to the amount of $100,000—in other words to issue bonds to the amount of $100,000, interest at 7 per cent. to be paid annually, and the principal in twenty years, as a gift to any company that would construct a railroad from Watsonville to Santa Cruz. The *Pajaronian* opposed the movement from the first. Not that we were opposed to railroads in general or to the proposed road to Santa Cruz in particular, but because, we are and have been for a long time past opposed to the principle of subsidies; we believe that the people should, as a duty, watch with a jealous eye the great monopolies now exerting such a vast influence in the United States, and endeavor all that is in their power to keep themselves free and untrammeled of all grand railway combinations. The history of various counties in the West, as well as counties in this State, which we have heretofore cited, will show the danger of subsidies and the evils they often bring. We opposed the Santa Cruz movement, because it was premature—for the reason that a *road will be constructed without a subsidy*. And here we wish to say on this point. A gentleman well known in railroad and other business circles of this State was in our office on Tuesday last. He is familiar with all the railroad operations of the coast, has large landed possessions in this county and is in favor of subsidies. In speaking of the Santa Cruz subsidy scheme, he said that from his knowledge of the railroad operations in this section, and from what prominent railroad men had said to him, it is the intention of the Southern Pacific Company to build a road to the Aptos, subsidy or no subsidy—"it will be a mere matter of time—a few months more or less." Again, this selfish Santa Cruz subsidy scheme seemed to be the result of a sudden excitement, and names of committees and reports of meetings have been kept in the dark, the document to be voted on is loosely drawn, and the whole thing seems to be without a head, an irresponsible scheme that will not bear close inspection—a scheme of danger that voters should never think of encouraging. We have various other reasons for opposing the subsidy, good and cogent ones—which have already appeared in our journal. During all of the opposition, we have been conscientious, and earnest, and have talked seriously when sober language was required, with no idea but that of benefiting the whole county.

345. *The Pajaronian*, December 7, 1871 (2:2)
Keep Cool Gentlemen.

During the past two weeks the *Pajaronian* and its editor have received a good level of abuse at the hands of persons in Santa Cruz. The vilest language has been used in regard to us as well as threats, and prophecies of our rapid ruin. This excitement was created by our criticism of a certain subsidy circular, in which a citizen of Santa Cruz was mentioned. We never yet said one word adverse to Santa Cruz or its citizens, and many of those who now entertain such harsh feelings towards us are persons whom we have often mentions in our paper in the most flattering terms. We have done no evil. We have said nothing against Santa Cruz or its inhabitants. We have simply and honestly opposed the subsidy believing that it was wrong and would work injury to the county of Santa Cruz. But a few excitable parties in Santa Cruz have allowed their prejudices to gain the mastery, and their whole souls are green with jealous bitterness, and we happened to be there and they knowing that we were sick, they concluded they would have a good and *safe* opportunity to vent their spleen. The vilest and meanest language was used to our face by a coward of that place, at a time too when we were incapable, from a severe illness, of resenting insults of the kind, and for no other earthly reason than that we opposed the subsidy. Now this bitter feeling does not speak well for the subsidy cause, or those who thus allow their angry passions to become excited. Keep cool gentlemen, and when we attack you or your town it will be time enough for you to squirm. In view of the fact that we apologized to Mr. Tuthill, last week, and he is now out of the fight entirely, and that we have been wrongfully abused and injured by certain of the subsidy citizens of Santa Cruz, we shall decline to publish any and all cards relating to the subsidy, unless they be apologies to us.

346. *The Pajaronian*, December 7, 1871 (2:2)

Read It.

We would be pleased if each man in the county could read the Subsidy Circular issued a couple of weeks ago. We are grieved to know that it originated in our lovely county. If it had been issued as a laughable burlesque, it would have been a success. But it was printed and circulated, as a sober business document, backed up by a committee! We hope that none of our old friends were connected with that committee, for we should feel sorry for them. We hope all the thinking men of the county will pay it half an hours' attention. It has and will do more to defeat the subsidy scheme than all the eloquence we have used.

347. *The Pajaronian*, December 7, 1871 (2:2)
Can Be Defeated.

The odious subsidy scheme, can be defeated. We are satisfied of this. All that is necessary is for the voter to come out on Monday next, to refuse to run our county needlessly into debt, and vote accordingly.

348. *The Pajaronian*, December 7, 1871 (2:3)
Ignored.

While Santa Cruz Subsyites are damning us for opposing their pet scheme we wish to inform them this. Three or four times during the subsidy wrangle, we asked Mr. Hihn, to send the names of the railroad committee to our paper, also proceedings of their railroad meetings and we should be glad to publish them. We also said to him on one occasion, that we should be pleased to receive communications from him or any other responsible man, in favor of the subsidies, all of which we would publish for the public benefit. We were anxious and willing to give all sides. But from that day to this the subsidy committee (if there is such a committee) entirely ignored our paper and this end of the county. We made requests as above of Tom Wright. But no names of committees, no communications, no word of any kind has been received at this office. And furthermore, when that brilliant and immortal subsidy circular was scattered over the county, the editor of this paper as well as numerous other anti-subsidy citizens of this place, were not favored with a copy. We procured one of a friend in Santa Cruz. We think those who directed the circulars became ashamed at the whole thing and sent as few as possible. We admire their delicacy. There is a passage in the Bible about those who work in the dark, which we think will apply to the mysterious cabal yclept "Railroad subsidy committee."

349. *The Pajaronian*, December 7, 1871 (2:3)

The Road Fund.

At this time only a few weeks after the collection of Taxes, there is but $500 in the road fund of this county! The roads are in a terrible condition from one end of the county to the other, and are getting worse all the time. We have told the people from time to time that this fund was short, and now there is comparatively nothing in the treasury with which to repair roads, bridges, etc. In the face of the above fact, and in the face, too, of the fact that the county is in debt close to $75,000, a few selfish men are endeavoring all in their power to plunge us into a further. Debt of one Hundred Thousand Dollars! Let each man in this county who is a voter, think seriously before he helps entail the debt upon us.

350. *The Pajaronian*, December 7, 1871 (3:2)

The Railroad.—We print this week the Railroad Time Table. As the cars run at present the traveling public can find no fault, and the time made is very good considering the nowness of the road. Mr. Bassett, the Assistant Superintendent, makes frequent visits here, and as might be expected from his character as a prompt and energetic business man, the depot and other buildings are being pushed rapidly forward.

351. *Santa Cruz Sentinel,* December 9, 1871 (2:1)
THE CRISIS.

The time is nigh at hand when the voters of this County must determine by their ballots, the fate of Santa Cruz, and in a great degree, the fate of the whole County.

Since the seventh of October, the date of our first mention of the Watsonville and Santa Cruz Railroad, we have endeavored, and believe we have, presented every phase, shad and bearing this question has to the material interests of the whole County. While we have perhaps more especially dilated upon the necessity of a Railroad to relieve the immediate wants of Santa Cruz and surroundings, we have not failed to take the broader view and present the case as it affects the remotest parts of the County, and in so doing, we have never been confronted with one valid or well-timed argument in refutation of what has, through the columns of the *Sentinel*, reached the public.

The majority of the voters of this County, without doubt, desire to aid in the construction of this road, knowing that without it, every profitable industry or enterprise in this part of the County will become hopelessly paralyzed, and property so valueless as to pay no just proportion of the taxes.

With great unanimity the people of Soquel, Santa Cruz, San Lorenzo, Scott's Valley and New Years are favoring the project to aid the road, believing that it is the only means that will induce its construction for years to come. It is the present that affects the more moderate in circumstances, and these are hopefully holding on to their little homes, thinking and wishing for some revival in business to come about, when they may continue to earn a living in a place and County they prefer above all others. For two years this class has waited, until their immediate demands are pressing, and this road being the only relief offered, they are found to a man, urging a favorable vote on the question of aid, to be decided on Monday next.

The more able have also become convinced that the longer delay of an effort to make Santa Cruz County what it is destined to become, will place it so far in the rear of the balance of the State, as to require a superhuman effort to wrest it from the impending decline. Thus, all are found, with us, favoring the proposed aid, which after careful investigation forces us to conclude that the road will absolutely be the means of reducing future taxation, when compared with the enhanced valuation of property occasioned by the road.

Let no voter who has the welfare of this community or the County at heart, cast his vote to retard what little of progress will flow from this enterprise. No reasonable expense can be urged for keeping our prosperity a thing of the distant future.

If this vote be favorable, fifty new dwellings will be constructed in Santa Cruz the coming season, which, together with the bridges and depots required by the road, will afford work for every available laborer and mechanic in the County.

More than $250,000 in cash will be expended among our people in the short space of one year, if the road is induced to come through the County, and if not, more than two hundred of our best people will leave for more propitious parts. Santa Cruz cannot stand still; she has done so for two years; she must either make progress or enter more speedily on the way of retrogression. We must receive as by induction this spirit of progress so general throughout the State, or pass dreamily over to the future some of the best privileges with which a people were ever blessed. A glance at the progress made and being made in the line of railroads, will demonstrate how essential it is that we do not let pass this most favorable opportunity for securing the continuation of the finest and most substantial road in the State.

California has, at this time, nine hundred and two and a half miles of railroad in active operation, as follows:

Main Central Pacific Road (to State line), 293; California and Oregon branch of same (Roseville Junction to Red Bluff), 115; San Joaquin Valley branch of same (Lathrop to Bear creek), 58; Southern Pacific Railroad (to Hollister), 100; California Pacific (Vallejo to Marysville), 95; Napa Valley, branch of same (to Calistoga), 33; North Pacific (Donahue to Healdsburg), 42; California Northern (Marysville to Oroville), 26; San Pedro and Los Angeles (to Milton), 48; San Rafael and San Quentin, 3½ miles. It is safe to say that in another year two or three hundred miles more of roads will be added to the list.

This does not include the road into the Pajaro Valley, and which will soon be followed with a continuation to Castroville and Salinas City, and to Santa Cruz if aid be voted.

We have shown heretofore precisely how this road will affect the lumber interests, manufacturing interests and farming. It is therefore not necessary to recapitulate at this time, for those who are undetermined after the opportunity afforded to become posted, will only be convinced when the cobwebs of doubt are cleared away by the hum and activity of revived business, following in the wake of this first great want of the people.

The *Real Estate Circular*, viewing donations to roads in a very rational light remarks as follows:

"Diligent raking, of the country from Maine to California with a fine-tooth comb would have utterly failed to find any man or body of men, outside of a lunatic asylum, who would, before the railroads were built, have given five cents an acre for the land that has since been made valuable by the presence of the locomotive. This old railroad land gag has served for a text so often that it has grown gray with absurdity. It should, therefore, be put on the retired list of superannuated humbugs and never asked to blush at its own folly in type again."

Don't let the cry of consistency over this exploded subsidy humbug deter you form marshalling a just courage and giving your vote and influence to aid this very essential and worthy project. Every man mindful of the responsibility resting on him at this juncture, must prove untiring in his efforts to determine the contest in the interest of business, progress and prosperity.

352. *Santa Cruz Sentinel,* December 9, 1871 (3:2)
Railroad.

The vote, to grant $100,000 in County bonds to aid in the construction of the Railroad from Watsonville to Santa Cruz, comes off on Monday next. Let no good citizen fail to be on hand to vote on that important occasion, in the affirmative. The decision *will* be *favorable* if the friends of the road come out and vote. This, to *you all*, is a matter of greater interest than any election held this year, and should tax your energies quite as much.

353. *Santa Cruz Sentinel,* December 9, 1871 (3:3)
Hay.

This article is steadily advancing, and will be $20 per ton before Spring. Since the railroad reached Watsonville hay has advanced from ten to twenty dollars per ton.

354. *The Pajaronian*, December 14, 1871 (2:1)

The Subsidy Carried.

The election last Monday resulted in the triumph of the Subsyites, by a majority of seven hundreds. In this precinct the vote stood, 848 against aid, and 25 for aid to the Road. No excitement worth mentioning, as far as we can learn, transpired at any of the polling places. As the Subsidy is carried, we can only wish, should the road now be commenced that the benefits resulting to Santa Cruz and the county generally will fully come up to the expectations and calculations of our Santa Cruz friends. We will moralize no more on the principle of the thing, nor discuss causes or effects—but simply express a hope that the people of such precinct in the county will set as one man to aiding our Board of Supervisors to ward off all troubles that may arise, pay their taxes cheerfully—work together, in fact, for the good of the whole county.

355. *The Pajaronian*, December 14, 1871 (2:1)

The *Sentinel* says we acted very "unwrong" toward 26 gentlemen in Santa Cruz who endorsed the act of Mr. Tuthill." The 26 gentlemen informed us through a frightful letter done up in a huge envelope that Mr. Tuthill had done *nothing*, but that they were the parties responsible. Now there is not a man of the 26 to whom we referred, who if he was in difficulty we would refuse to aid if in our power. Furthermore we believe there are a number who signed that letter to us who would not have done so if they had read it a second time. But notwithstanding all that has passed, we freely and unqualifiedly forgive them. We hope the *Sentinel* will not ask more at our hands.

356. *The Pajaronian*, December 14, 1871 (2:1)

Bro. Morehouse, of the Salinas *Standard*, reads us a little lesson on the subsidy, and intimates that we of this town feel puffed up over our railroad facilities, and look down on the beautiful town of Santa Cruz. You are wrong Bro. M. The people of this place are not so narrow as to take a selfish view of the matter, and the *Pajaronian*'s opposition was based on principle, actuated only by honest and conscientious motives.

357. *The Pajaronian*, December 14, 1871 (2:2)

The Five Per Cent. Law.

The *Sentinel* is somewhat dubious about the late subsidy burlesque resulting in a railroad after all. It fears that the five per cent. law will be repealed before a company is found that will take the contract for constructing the road. The above journal also thinks it "would be an act of injustice to repeal the law without exempting Santa Cruz county!" At the general election held but a few weeks since the whole county—Democrats as well as Republicans—expressed anti-subsidy sentiments and in working and voting for county and State officers we as well as others worked and voted for them because, among other reasons, we thought them to be against subsidies. We cannot believe they have changed so suddenly. Men like Hihn and others, who belong to no party and have extensive landed interests, are expected to flop and flip-flap from side to side, according to the weight of dollars and cents dangling from one beam of the balance or the other. But we feel safe in asserting positively that Senator Beck and Assemblyman Bockius, still hold to the principles they professed during the above election, and we believe they will vote for the repeal of the five per cent. law, as recommended by both Governors, and many of the first minds of the Legislature. The *Sentinel* says—and truthfully too—that two-thirds of the vote of this county was in favor of subsidy. But the people were deceived. They were led to believe that the Southern Pacific Railroad Company would commence constructing the road as soon as the subsidy was carried. As we told the people at the time, no company can now be found to take the job. In reviewing the subsidy election, we feel honest in the assertion that a fair expression of the people was *not* obtained, and that this county should no more be exempted in the repeal of the five per cent. law, than any other portion of the State. Let our Legislature feel no hesitancy in regard to voting against the law, for the people of this county desire no longer to be living over a subsidy mine that may explode at any time and ruin them and the county. The whole thing will be in the hands of a few, and the people will dance to the tune they play on the subsidy trombone. Repeal the law, and the people of this county and the State generally will breathe more freely.

358. *Santa Cruz Sentinel,* December 16, 1871 (2:1)

Sequence.

The election which came off on Monday last testing the question of aid or no aid to the proposed railroad, called out, in proportion to the numbers enrolled, a larger vote than the last general election, and resulted as any careful observer must have believed, in the completest victory ever gained in favor of any issue presented to this people. Think of it: out of 716 votes cast in Santa Cruz Precinct, only 22 votes against aid; out of 134 votes at San Lorenzo only 7 voted no; and of the 58 votes in Scotts Valley there were but 4 against aid. Who shall say hereafter that the people are not competent to express their wishes through their ballots? If no further hindrances are interposed we shall have railroad communication with San Francisco by July next. An attempt will now be made to repeal the five percent law before closing the contract with the company that shall build the road, as without such a consummation it is thought the success would be a defeat after all.

Now that the vote is taken and that a two third vote of the county favor the subsidy, would it not be an act of unparalleled injustice to repeal the law without exempting Santa Cruz County? The representations from this County, Senator Beck and Assemblyman Bockius, certainly should not hesitate to represent the expressed wish of their constituents in this matter, no matter what their private opinions may be concerning the principle. This was no party affair: the whole county irrespective of party, voted upon this question as one involving the very existence of future business prospects and will hold in pleasing remembrance those who see that no injustice is wrought at this propitious boar. The majority of the county in favor of the road is 602, the total vote cast being 1613.

359. *Santa Cruz Sentinel,* December 16, 1871 (2:2)

Coaches.

The trip from San Francisco to Santa Cruz, is shortened about three hours, in consequence of the railroad into Pajaro Valley. When it reaches Santa Cruz, four hours time will be saved. What a convenience!'

360. *Santa Cruz Sentinel,* December 16, 1871 (3:2)

ELECTION RETURNS

The following is the official canvass of the votes cast at the special election in aid of the Railroad, held in Santa Cruz County, December 11th, 1871:

PRECINCTS.

	Santa Cruz.	Watsonville.	Soquel.	San Lorenzo.	Corralitos.	Scott's Valley.	New Years.
Aid Yes..........	694	25	171	134	8	58	19
Aid No...........	22	343	51	7	64	4	16
Total................	716	368	222	141	72	62	35
Maj'es Yes.....	672		127	127	...	54	3
Majorities No	......	318	......	......	56	...	...

Total Majority Yes............................ 602

361. *Santa Cruz Sentinel,* December 16, 1871 (3:2)
Responsible Parties.

Query—does not brother Cummings, of the *Pajaronian*, yet realize that *some responsible parties* favor aid to the railroad from his town to the *City of Santa Cruz*—or does the 22 *influential persons* voting against aid in Santa Cruz constitute his ideal of responsibility? No person is so blind as he who has eyes and refuses to see. Does not a majority of over 600 in this county in favor of aid rather settle the mixed question with our contemporary? Make an honest confession, and ask pardon for the sins of the past month, Brother C—, and when the road is completed, we will bring down our Executive Committee, and present them to you *scriatim*.

362. *The Pajaronian,* December 21, 1871 (2:2)
Railroad Affairs.

That pernicious Act known as the Five per cent. Law should be repealed. Both Governor Haight and Governor Booth strongly recommend its repeal, and we doubt not, ere many weeks, it will be erased from our Statute books. Rumors now reach us of trouble ahead in regard to finding a company who will take the Subsidy and build the road from this place to Santa Cruz—that the Central Pacific will not touch it until the right of way has been obtained free between the two places, and a thorough survey and careful estimate as to the cost of the road has been made. We patiently await the result of the Santa Cruz railroad *fiasco*.

363. *Santa Cruz Sentinel,* December 23, 1871 (3:1)

Railroad.

The engineers would have had the route surveyed this week, had not the storm prevented. We are assured that work will soon commence, the weather proving favorable. Our prediction that the railroad will be completed by July 1st, will not fall far short of the proper time, as the company intend hastening the work to Santa Cruz.

364. *Santa Cruz Sentinel,* December 23, 1871 (3:2)

Land for Sale.

Those who are desirous of securing farming, grazing or timber lands can do so at this time, in this county, on better terms than ever before. This county never fails of a crop, and the railroad being constructed to Santa Cruz will make it one of the most thriving counties in the State. Some of the most beautiful and eligible farms in this county are now for sale through the Santa Cruz Land Agency, also very desirable city and suburban sites, all of which are advertised in this issue.

365. *Santa Cruz Sentinel,* December 30, 1871 (2:2)

The people of the county have determined to inaugurate a more progressive period, and have, with this view, voted $100,000 to aid in the construction of twenty miles of a railroad, from Santa Cruz to Watsonville, which will put this county—Santa Cruz in particular—in direct communication with the great business centers of this coast. This we look upon as the most desirable and necessary enterprise this people could undertake. Santa Cruz will be greatly benefited, and business, the approaching season will assume its old familiar hum, when every willing hand found work at remunerative rates, and every merchant and manufacturer was content with the prosperity attending his business.

366. *Gilroy Advocate* via the Santa *Cruz Sentinel,* December 30, 1871 (2:3)

The entire county south of Gilroy has been a perfect sea during the greater part of this week. The railroad company has suffered severely. We sincerely regret to see so much labor and capital swept away.

The new road from here to Watsonville is almost all washed away; from the Pajaro bridge there is scarcely any road left. The company, with characteristic energy, put an army of workers on the road repairing damages.

367. *Santa Cruz Sentinel,* December 30, 1871 (3:1)

The Railroad.

Owing to the heavy storm and flood, the Central Pacific Company have been unable to set their engineers to work surveying the route, but as soon as the company can repair the immense damage their various roads have sustained by the flood the work will commence, and be prosecuted with vigor. Mr. Stanford says he intends we shall have communication with the city at an early day, and has also concluded to run the line as near the town of Watsonville as their people desire. This is what all are pleased to learn.

368. *Santa Cruz Sentinel,* January 6, 1872 (3:3)

Rail Road Hotel.

The Railroad is coming and soon the whistle of the locomotive will waken up hungry customers, early, to go to Chris Patten's Rail Road Hotel and get an early breakfast before leaving for San Francisco. See the new advertisement of the Railroad Hotel in to-day's paper.

369. *Santa Cruz Sentinel,* January 20, 1872 (2:8)

RAILROAD HOTEL.—Chris. Patten...Prop'r

Having leased the splendid two-story building of Dan. Wente, on the corner of Front and Cooper streets, I have replenished and fitted it up as a first-class hotel, to accommodate the public with either single meals or boarding and lodging. Everything to be found in the market, in season, will be daily supplies, and cooked to order in the best style at the following low rates:

Board and Lodging, per week $5.00
Board, without Lodging $4.00
Single meals .... 25 cts.
Beds furnished at 25 cents each.

370. *Santa Cruz Sentinel,* January 20, 1872 (3:2)

RAILROAD MASS MEETING!

At Court House,
Saturday Evening Jan. 20, at 7 o'clock

The Public are invited.

371. *Sacramento Union*, January 19, via the *Santa Cruz Sentinel*, January 27, 1872 (1:5)

Incorporated.

In the Secretary of State's office, there was filed January 18th, 1872, the certificate of incorporation of the Santa Cruz and Watsonville Railroad Company—organized for the purpose of constructing a railroad from a point on the line of the Southern Pacific Railroad, in the county of Monterey, at or near the Pajaro depot; thence passing in a westerly direction near or through the town of Watsonville, to or near the residence of Rafael Castro, on the Aptos; thence westerly, passing through or near the town of Soquel, to and within the corporate limits of the town of Santa Cruz. The length of the road will be twenty miles. Capital stock, $500,000, in shares of $100 each. The principal place of business will be in the town of Santa Cruz. Directors—Elihu Anthony, W. F. Peabody, Titus Hale, F. A. Hihn and Samuel Bartlett.

372. *Santa Cruz Sentinel*, January 27, 1872 (1:6-7)

RAILROAD CONTRACT.

[Agreement of Santa Cruz and Watsonville Rail Road Company with Santa Cruz County. Filed January 18th, A. D. 1872, and recorded in full by the Clerk.]

This agreement, made and entered into this the eighteenth day of January, A. D. 1872, by and between the "Santa Cruz and Watsonville Railroad Company," a Corporation duly organized and existing under and by virtue of the laws of the State of California, and known by its corporate title as the "Santa Cruz and Watsonville Railroad Company," and having its principal place of business located at the town of Santa Cruz, State of California, party of the first part and the County of Santa Cruz, State of California, and the Board of Supervisors of said County, acting in and on behalf of said County of Santa Cruz (which said Board is composed a follows, to wit: Jacob Parsons, Chairman thereof, and George Anthony and P. F. Dean,) party of the second part, *Witnesseth,*

1st. That said party of the first part, being heretofore duly authorized by its lawful authorities, hereby agrees to and with said party of the second part for and in consideration of the sum of One Hundred Thousand Dollars, and other considerations hereinafter set forth, to build, construct, run and maintain a continuous line of Railroad, connecting the Town of Santa Cruz, in said County, to and with the line of the Southern Pacific Railroad, said road to be built, constructed and maintained as near as is practicable upon the following general route, *to wit*;

Commencing on the line of the Southern Pacific Railroad at or near the Pajaro Depot thereon, in the County of Monterey, thence northwesterly, and intersecting the southern boundary line of the County of Santa Cruz at or near the Town of Watsonville, thence running in a northwesterly direction to and crossing the Aptos Creek, near the present residence of one Rafael Castro, thence to and crossing the Soquel River at or near the Town of Soquel, thence to and within the corporate limits of the Town of Santa Cruz.

2d. That said Railroad Company will so build and construct and finally complete a Railroad over and upon said route within the period of two years from the date of these presents, and pass and run an engine and cars thereon and over said Railroad within the said period of time; and, furthermore, will commence the construction of said road within six months from the date of these presents, said Railroad to be built and constructed of a like gauge with the Southern Pacific Railroad, that is to say, having a gauge of four feet eight and one half inches, with all necessary signals, switches, side tracks, etc., for the general and proper conduct and running of the same, said line to be constructed without any dictation or demand from said Board of Supervisors, about the mode and manner of constructing the same.

3d. That the said party of the first part or its assigns will commence the building and construction of said Railroad line at the southern end thereof, and continue the same from thence to and within the corporate limits of the said Town of Santa Cruz until the whole line is completed, and the completion of the same shall include the running an engine and cars over the same.

Now, therefore, in consideration of the agreements and covenants aforesaid, to be done and performed by said party of the first part, the said Board of Supervisors for said Board and for and behalf of said County of Santa Cruz, hereby agrees and covenants, to do and perform upon the part of said Board, and on the part of said County as follows—*to wit*:

4th. That upon, and at the time of the construction and completion of the first five miles of said road, which shall lie within the limits of the County of Santa Cruz—commencing at the point where said railroad line shall intersect the Southern boundary of said County, at, or near the Town of Watsonville, (which said point of intersection shall be the initial point from whence said line shall be measured) by said Railroad Company, or its assigns, in a fit and proper condition for the passage of an engine and cars over the same; then the said Board and the said County, agree to issue and donate to said Railroad Company, or to its assigns, twenty-five bonds of said County, of the amount, or denomination each, of the sum of One Thousand Dollars, being for said five miles so built, the sum of Twenty-Five Thousand Dollars payable to the holders thereof; and said party of the second part, for itself and for and on behalf of said County, further agrees that for each and every additional five miles of said road that said party of the first part, shall build or cause to be built as herein-before stipulated upon said general route, there shall be issued therefor, the number of twenty-five bonds of said County of the sum or denomination, each of One Thousand Dollars—payable to the holders thereof ; said bonds to be issued as hereinafter set forth, provided, however, that the said party of the second part, does not agree to issue, or donate the bonds of said County in any amount, exceeding the sum of One Hundred Thousand Dollars, as the total amount to be donated as aid to said Railroad Company, or its assigns.

5th. And the said party of the second part further agrees, and covenants to and with the said party of the first part, that if when the last or fourth section of said road shall have been built and constructed, on said general route, connecting the points aforesaid, the same be of less distance than five miles, then, in that event, the Bonds of said County are to be issued to said Railroad Company, or to its assigns, to the number of twenty-five Bonds of the sum, or denomination, each of one thousand dollars, for said last section, the full intention and agreement herein being that the aid or donation herein given and granted to said Railroad Company shall in any event amount to but not exceed the aggregate sum of one hundred thousand dollars, for the entire construction and completion of a railroad upon the said general route, connecting the point aforesaid.

6th. And it is further agreed herein that the said Bonds shall be of the respective denomination of one thousand dollars each, and shall be payable to the holders thereof, twenty years from the date thereof, and all to bear interest at the rate of seven per cent. per annum, both principal and interest, payable in gold coin of the United States, said interest to be paid thereon semi-annually, on Coupons to be attached to said Bonds, and said bonds to be issued under the seal of said county, and signed by the Clerk thereof, and also by the President of the Board of Supervisor and to be delivered to said Railroad Company, or to it assigns, without any expense to said Railroad Company or to its assigns.

7th. It is further agreed herein, that in case the said Railroad Company or its assigns should, for any cause fail or neglect to carry out or perform the agreements and covenants hereinbefore set forth to be done and performed by said Railroad Company, then, in that event, it is hereby agreed and stipulated that the amount of damages which said

County or said Board shall be entitled to recover therefor, of and from said Railroad Company, shall not exceed the sum of one hundred dollars.

In witness whereof the said party of the first part has hereunto caused their Corporate Seal to be affixed, and these presents to be subscribed by its President, and Secretary. And the said party of the second part—by Jacob Parsons, Chairman of the Board of Supervisors of said County—being hereto duly authorized in all things to sign, execute, seal and deliver, these presents for said County, and for, and on behalf of said Board of Supervisors, by a resolution of said Board of Supervisors, spread upon the minutes of said Board, this day, for, in the name of, and on behalf of said County of Santa Cruz, and for, and on behalf of said Board, for the purposes aforesaid, has set his hand and seal, and has caused the seal of the said county to be affixed hereto.

F. A. HIHN, President of the Santa Cruz and Watsonville Railroad Company.

D. TUTHILL, Secretary of the Santa Cruz and Watsonville Railroad Company.

JACOB PARSONS, Chairman of the Board of Supervisors of Santa Cruz County.

373. *San Mateo Gazette*, January 27, 1872 (1:5)

Mr. [Wm. H. Chandler] values his claim of 160 acres at $2,000, and to any one wishing to take advantage of the Santa Cruz Railroad that will be built the present season, it is a cheap bargain. We are going down hill, and no time is lost in passing over one claim to another. At the forks of the San Lorenzo and Bear Creeks, the proposed terminus of the San Lorenzo Railroad, is a clearing being made for the location of a town.... The topics of conversation are railroad and storm, storm and railroad.

374. *The Pajaronian*, February 1, 1872 (2:1)

A railroad meeting was held in Santa Cruz on the 20th ult., and among a lot of verbose and highfalutin Resolutions and Whereases, the following was introduced in regard to the railroad company lately formed in that place:

Whereas, The said company is composed of substantial citizens resident of this County, and in our opinion, will of said aid to be granted, build and construct said road—as proposed to said Board.

We venture the assertion and predict that if the Road is commenced, the company formed in Santa Cruz will not construct it. We also feel safe in asserting that it is not nor was it ever the intention of the said Santa Cruz Company to build the road, but to sign the contract, then transfer the said contract to the Southern Pacific, if the latter company will take it.

375. *Castroville Argus* via *The Pajaronian*, February 1, 1872 (2:2)

Railroad to Santa Cruz.—We report elsewhere the incorporation of a company who propose connecting Santa Cruz with the Pajaro extension of the Southern Pacific railroad. During a recent visit to Watsonville we were informed that a contract has already been entered into by two of the Santa Cruz county supervisors, but that Mr. Dean, the Watsonville Supervisor, not having received the notice required to be given by law to attend the special meeting at which the contract was made, the validity of the same will be called into question.

376. *Santa Cruz Sentinel,* February 3, 1872 (3:1)

Improving.

It is remarkable the progress Watsonville is making since the completion of the railroad into the Pajaro valley. A few years and her citizens will be numbered by thousands. When our branch road is completed, Watsonville will become the most thriving inland town on this coast.

377. *Santa Cruz Sentinel,* February 3, 1872 (3:3)

The prospects of a Railroad at an early day, has made a demand for town and suburban real estate, not heretofore known in this town.

378. *Santa Cruz Sentinel,* February 10, 1872 (3:3)

Santa Cruz Extending.

The railroad which is sure to reach us during the coming Summer, will develop a deep interest in this locality, and throughout the State, much to the advantage of Santa Cruz county; and the sooner our people prepare to turn this to their advantage, the sooner will the town enter upon the highway to prosperity.

379. *Santa Cruz Sentinel*, March 2, 1872 (3:1)
Railroad Affairs.

As soon as the Legislature adjourns, and our railroad interests placed beyond danger of being interfered with the coming two years, the railroad folks intend entering upon the surveying and constructing of the Santa Cruz and Watsonville railroad. It is not certain now that the road will pass Watsonville at a point nearer than one and one-half miles to the north. Every effort on the part of our citizens will be made to have the road pass at a point most in harmony with the people of Watsonville; these railroad Kings go pretty much where they like.

380. *The Pajaronian*, March 7, 1872 (3:4)

The Southern Pacific Railroad Co's Depot and other buildings are excellent edifices. The Depot is ample, substantial and well arranged. Other improvements will take place on their property as soon as settled weather comes.

381. *Santa Cruz Sentinel*, March 9, 1872 (3:3)
Sawmills and Lumber.

The railroad will soon be commenced, and then a large demand will spring up for ties, stringers, bridging and trussel-lumber and timber. We would not be astonished to see fifty or sixty miles of railroad track laid in this county within the next three years.

382. *Santa Cruz Sentinel*, March 16, 1872 (2:1)

Letter from San Francisco.

San Francisco, March 12, 1872.

Ed. Sentinel:—Our pioneers concur in the opinion that we have just passed through the most severe winter that they ever experienced on the Pacific Coast. Such protracted cold weather and high winds as we suffered during the last two months is particularly a rare event in California. The winter of 1872 has demonstrated one very important fact, and that is, that the Central Pacific Railroad is utterly unreliable during a tempestuous season. It can neither be depended upon as a mail route, nor as a means for the transportation of munitions of war. In any sudden emergency like that of war, the country demands that the means of transportation from the Atlantic to the Pacific shall be absolutely certain at all seasons of the year. The sudden descent of an enemy on this coast might render it necessary to move large bodies of troops of war material with great celerity, and since it has appeared that this great trans-continental railway is liable at any moment to be blockaded during the stormy season of winter, it is reckoned, especially by military men, as a failure. The consideration for which large tracts of the public lands were donated by the Government to a railway ring, has therefore failed forever, and the question now is, whether the domain thus squandered can be recovered and restored to the people.

The collapse of the northern route will, however, be productive of some good result, and that is the speedy completion of the Southern Pacific Railroad along the 45th degree of north latitude, from San Diego to St. Louis, Mo.

[The truth is, as reliable information says, the Texas Pacific railroad, and St. Louis and San Diego route, will be united and constructed at once. From San Diego to San Francisco the route will take the line surveyed by the Robinson company. Maj. W. S. Watson has charge of the first section. He is a first-class Civil Engineer, and the Atlantic and Pacific railroad will place his party in the field in a few days—his section extending to San Buenaventura, through Spanish town, Pescadero, and Santa Cruz, along the coast, touching at Soquel, Aptos, Watsonville, and Salinas City. The Construction Department will start out as soon as the alignment grade is surveyed and stakes set. The graders and track-layers, with competent engineers, will follow in due time. The depot will probably be at the south-western suburb of your town, near the coast. San Francisco will probably subscribe six millions of dollars as a subsidy to this road, but will not give one million at this time to bridge the bay. Further bonds of several millions will be issued to aid the Atlantic and Pacific Company to construct their locomotives and cars in this city, under the plea of aiding home manufacturers, as will be seen by our Board of Supervisors.]

Railroad lobby at Washington has made and will continue to make powerful efforts to prevent any concession of

Government aid to the Southern Pacific railroad, but judging from the present tone and feeling of capitalists, I think it certain that the southern route will be pushed to an early completion, even if Congress denies it any of that assistance, which was so generously but injudiciously extended to the northern companies. Meantime, Leland Stanford, the President of the Central Pacific, has aroused a powerful opposition in this city by his attempt to obtain a cession, by Congress, to the Central Pacific Company of Goat Island—a property valued at millions, and located in the very centre of the harbor of San Francisco. It seems that animals on the land are subject to the same vicissitudes as animals in the water; in both cases the big fish eat the little ones. It is the old story of the sardine and the whale.

The adoption of the new civil and penal codes, which have been prepared by the Commissioners and submitted to the Legislature, promises to create a revolution in the practice, pleadings and proceedings of our courts of law. Lawyers and Judges will require a vast amount of study and preparation to fit them for the new order of things. I conceive that the most important effect of the new system will be to weed the legal profession of thousands of men, who were never fitted for it by nature or education. Men of the highest qualities can alone hope to win honor in the profession of the law, as it will be hereafter practiced and conducted.

Many of our leading citizens intend to visit Santa Cruz with their families, this Summer, and they have learned with satisfaction of the proposal to construct a first-class hotel in the vicinity of your beautiful city, children and families require an abundance of air and green fields; when you add to these a view of old ocean with opportunity to bathe in its limpid waters, then you complete the enchanting picture. Neither Newport nor Long Branch can offer more than these.

Among your visits will be Mr. P. M. Bowen, of the great firm of Bowen Bros., wholesale and retail grocers, on Pine Street, in this city. Mr. B., the head of the house, is one of your warm personal friends, and you will be rejoiced to hear that he has quite recovered from the effects of the injury he suffered several months since by the breaking of the [pale] of his carriage. The house of Bowen Bros., 432 Pine Street, stands to-day where it has stood for years, at the very head of the wholesale and retail grocers' trade in California. Capt. M. R. Roberts is another of our prominent citizens who has informed us of his intention to find a home in Santa Cruz for his family during the summer. Many will take their tents and camp on some of the pretty streams which find their way from the mountain ranges and debouch into the sea at various points on the coast line between Santa Cruz and Pescadero. C.

383. *Santa Cruz Sentinel*, March 16, 1872 (3:1)
Real Estate Sales.

This fall, when the railroad cars are running past our doors, real estate in the new town of Santa Cruz will be as high as it is at present in and around the flourishing city of Watsonville.

384. *San Francisco Examiner*, February 16, via the *Santa Cruz Sentinel*, March 23, 1872 (1:8)

Atlantic and Pacific Railroad.

Croakers have freely circulated a report that the Atlantic and Pacific Railroad is a myth, having neither reality nor vitality—merely gotten up to be bought off by the Central and Southern Pacific Railroad Companies. There is not, in our opinion, the slightest foundation for any such belief. Major W. S. Watson, Civil Engineer, informs us that he has been officially directed to form his corps of engineers and assistance to be ready and commence work on the 15th of March, 1872. The road is divided into three, nearly equal divisions, the first is between this city and San Buenaventura, a distance of 260 miles; the second division is between San Buenaventura and Soledad; the third from Soledad to the Colorado river—the whole distance being 746 miles. Major Watson has charge of the first section, the others, it is expected, will be under the control and management of engineers from St. Louis.

We are assured the company is under such management as to secure its construction without looking to San Francisco for any assistance; but they can and would built it in less time if such assistance were granted, and, which they inclined to think will be done. This road is to be made on the 35th parallel. It will be the great Southern road. Its trips will never be disturbed by snow blockades. It is much shorter than the central, and will open one of the most desirable mining countries known to the world—a country that abounds in mines of gold, silver, copper, lead and iron. It will run through a large amount of country, where the land is worth nothing, but, as it has been proven by practical experience, that plenty of water can be obtained by artesian wells, we may reasonably calculate that much of such land will be redeemed by irrigation, which would make it a paradise, equal to Los Angeles or Anaheim, where oranges, limes, lemons, figs and other tropical fruit is now grown in abundance.

Our citizens, owning large amounts of real estate, will see at once the importance of such a road, particularly when we consider the fact that the main trunk from San Francisco to St. Louis will be tapped by the Texas road, and thereby bring us much of the trade of Texas, Louisiana, Mississippi, Alabama, and of several of the Territories. If the Southern Pacific "has vitality" enough to build its road so much the better. It would greatly increase our trade and hasten the glorious destiny of this great center of commerce. The time is not ten years off when the Northern Pacific, Central Pacific, Southern Pacific, and the Atlantic and Pacific will all empty their freight in the lap of San Francisco, and our merchants, manufacturers and capitalists ought to urge forward an enterprise that will confer immense advantages on San Francisco.

385. *Santa Cruz Sentinel*, March 23, 1872 (4:1)

The Texas Pacific Railroad.

The accession of Col. Thomas Scott, of the Pennsylvania Central Railway, to the Presidency of the Texas Pacific, is accepted in the East, as well as here, as evidence that real business is meant, and that in the hands of an intelligent management, the road will be pushed to completion with gratifying celerity. Illustrative of Eastern opinion, we present the following extracts from a late article in the New York *Bulletin*: "The acceptance by Col. Scott of the Presidency of the Southern Pacific, or more properly, the Texas Pacific Railroad, secures the prosecution of the work with all possible energy and dispatch. For some time past, little or nothing has been done on this line. The Texas Pacific Company succeeded to a Fremont legacy of blunders, which it was necessary to rectify. A large amount of bonds had been placed in the Paris money market, and there were also some outstanding obligations in this country that required amicable settlement. The operations were also seriously embarrassed by the ill health of Mr. Roberts. The interest of that gentleman in various Southern railroad lines was about $1,500,00, and it is understood Col. Scott has taken on himself the payment of that sum. Whether Col. Scott takes the control of the Texas Pacific Railroad on his own responsibility, or on behalf of the Pennsylvania Railroad, or the new Southern Railroad Security Company, does not yet appear. The probability is that he represents all these combined interests, and that the new trans-continental route will be constructed and run in connection with the great Pennsylvania Railway, rather than under its direct control. It is rumored, and with strong appearances of probability, that Col. Scott will not retire from any active management in the other concerns in which he is interested, and devote his whale time and energy to the construction of the new line. The

Texas Pacific (Transcontinental) Railroad commencing at Marshall, near the Texan line, is to run via El paso, Mexico, to the town of San Diego, California, about 400 miles south of San Francisco."

'The Texas Pacific Railroad is entitled to a Congressional land grant of 13,440,000 acres, and is also entitled to other grants which it is expected will suffice for the construction of the road."

386. *Santa Cruz Sentinel*, April 6, 1872 (3:1)
Santa Cruz and Watsonville Railroad.

Mr. F. A. Hihn has just returned from San Francisco, and informs us that Mr. Stanford has given his verbal promises that he will be in Santa Cruz very soon, and proceed to make a preliminary survey, to be followed by the construction of the road. We hope this may be true, as nothing but a railroad will enable our people to go prosperously ahead.

387. *The Pajaronian*, April 11, 1872 (3:1)
Santa Cruz and Watsonville Railroad.—Mr. F. A. Hihn has just returned from San Francisco, and informs us that Mr. Stanford has given his verbal promise that he will be in Santa Cruz very soon, and proceed to make a preliminary survey, to be followed by the construction of the road. We hope this may be true, as nothing but a railroad will enable our people to go prosperously ahead.—*Sentinel*.

And the above is all the encouragement that Hihn

can offer in regard to the above railroad, after all the expense and hard feeling and underhanded operations that have taken place in voting the $100,000 subsidy! Hihn and others gave out to the people before the election that permanent arrangements had been made with Stanford to build the road immediately. That the only thing required from the people was to vote the subsidy! Now after months have passed away, he offers the above flimsy dose and expects it to be swallowed by the people. If a railroad is all that is required to make Santa Cruz prosperous, we earnestly hope that they may get it. But we do object to speculators bolstering up chimerical schemes for their own benefit—we object to anything to deceive the people, whether in politics or any other times.

388. *Santa Cruz Sentinel*, April 13, 1872 (2:1)

New Laws.

From a supplement of the Sacramento *Record*, we extract the following laws which have a local interest in this county:

Chapter 335—An act to repeal an act entitled an act to impower the Board of Supervisors of the several counties of the State to aid in the construction of railroads in the respective counties. The counties of San Francisco, Santa Cruz, San Diego, Santa Barbara, San Luis Obispo, San Bernardino, Marin and Los Angeles, in all of which said act shall remain in force.

389. *Santa Cruz Sentinel*, April 13, 1872 (2:3)
Atlantic and Pacific Railroad.

On Tuesday last our town was visited by Mr. J. Blickensderfer, Jr., Chief Engineer of the Atlantic and Pacific Railroad from St. Louis, accompanied by E. N. Robinson, Chief Engineer on the Pacific slope and Coast Line. These distinguished visitors were making their final observation before ordering a working survey. We are also assured that 150 miles of working survey has already been made from Los Angeles, via. Gaviota Pass, northward. We are assured that the company contemplate building the road in time to secure the $100,000 voted by this county, and that the route will be along the coast, via. Half Moon Bay, Pescadero, Santa Cruz, Aptos, Watsonville, Salinas City and the Salinas Valley to the Warm Springs. The San Francisco *Bulletin* of April 10th has the following, which will enlighten our readers on the subject:

"Saturday afternoon, twenty gentlemen, well known citizens of San Francisco, met in the Chamber of Commerce for the purpose of conference upon the railroad interests of the city. An organization was effected, and seven men, S. P. Dewey, Alex. Austin, H. A. Cobb, E. F. Northam, James Otis, Alfred Wheeler and R. B. Swain, were appointed a committee to choose another committee of one hundred citizens to take steps for the general protection of San Francisco's railroad interests. Yesterday afternoon the committee of seven was in session with closed doors, but, aside from a general discussion of the situation, it did not transact any business save the canvassing of the names submitted for the committee of one hundred. The public will watch the proceedings of the committee of seven with a lively interest, making such suggestions from time to time as may be worthy of consideration. In the selection of the committee, care should be taken to secure honest, intelligent un prejudiced citizens, who will serve the interests of the city without fear or favor; men in whom the public can place implicit confidence, and whose propositions will be met in the proper spirit. Within the next thirty days, the Directors of the Atlantic and Pacific railroad and the Mayor of St. Louis, will visit this city to ascertain what our citizens are willing to do to aid the projected railroad. It is of the greatest importance that the committee representing San Francisco meet these gentlemen from the East, discuss the railroad question, and make a showing of facts that the community at large will endorse as strictly correct. This committee of seven, then, has a difficult task to perform in selecting the citizens' committee, and should act with the utmost prudence and caution."

390. *Santa Cruz Sentinel*, April 20, 1872 (2:2)

Change of Route.

The telegraph informs us that Senator Cole has introduced a bill to allow the Southern pacific Railroad Company of California to change the route of the road.

It has long been understood that Stanford would apply to Congress for permission to change the route of the

Southern branch of his road from the present location. A few weeks ago San Francisco papers referred to this matter, and the *Bulletin* asserted that it was almost certain that the company desired to "deflect their route westward from Gilroy, via. the Watsonville branch into the Pajaro and Salinas Valleys, thence through Monterey county, to a point in the Coast Range nearly due west of Tulare Lake, where there is a path leading into the Tulare Valley. This route has the advantages which belong to a very productive valley, fast filling up with people, and already containing numerous thriving settlements and several growing towns. It is also on the direct line to Los Angeles, and offers close connection with the railroad projected from that city and San Diego up the coast.

The Fresno county *Expositor*, however, in an article which appears to have been based upon some authoritative information, stated as long ago as the first of February last that the Southern Pacific route was about to be practically abandoned, and that the San Joaquin Valley branch would really be the Southern Pacific line. And, more recently, the San Jose *Patriot*, in a well considered article on the subject, uses the following language:

The fact is clear to observing minds that the persons having the control of the construction of the Southern Pacific Railroad have determined to carry that road east of the Coast Range counties, and through the great San Joaquin Valley, from Stockton southward. The Directors of the road amused and deceived our people, by making a show of locating the road through this Valley, and the Valley of the Salinas, crossing the mountains into San Joaquin Valley near

Tulare lake. On this proposed route, the road was carried on and constructed as far as Hollister. There it stopped, and will remain stopped on that line for an indefinite time. While nothing is being done towards extending the road south of Hollister, the Directors are pushing the construction of the road in the San Joaquin Valley southward with extraordinary energy.

We believe with the *Expositor* and *Patriot*, that it is the intention of the Company to abandon indefinitely the construction of the road from Hollister, and make the San Joaquin Valley branch the real Southern Pacific road. Every movement indicates this purpose. The road from Lathrop southerly, through the San Joaquin Valley, is being pushed forward to Visalia with great rapidity, and is expected to reach the latter point during the coming Summer. The San Joaquin and Tulare valleys offer independent local inducements for a railway, sufficient at the present time to warrant the completion of the one under way. From Visalia the road will probably be carried on to Los Angeles, with what speed will depend upon the alacrity with which the people respond to the appeal for subsidy. The connection of Stanford's road with the Texas Pacific will, we believe, be made at Los Angeles, if it is made at all; although there is a possibility that the Central people may think it worth their while to build 125 miles further to San Diego; but as we have before said, we think it is hardly probable.

We think it improbable that Sanford will come hither to connect with the Texas Pacific, because, while San Diego will be the western terminus of the latter road, and the point at which its freight business from China and Japan will be received, it will certainly be extended along the coast route to San Francisco. Stanford has little, therefore, to gain by any connection with the Texas Pacific. Certainly, the talk of a connection at Fort Yuma, sometimes indulged in, is the purest nonsense. Unless, indeed, Stanford & Scott are going into partnership, which is a preposterous idea.

391. *Santa Cruz Sentinel*, April 27, 1872 (2:1)
Atlantic and Pacific Railroad.

The San Francisco *Alta*, of April 23d, in answer to an inquiry from the *Examiner*, verifies all we have said the past six months on the subject of the Coast Line of Railroad. We believe the road will be built, unless Stanford & Co., should sell the San Jose, Gilroy, Hollister and Watsonville roads to the company. In that event, the coast line as far as the Salinas Valley, would at present not be built, and the road would be continued south from Watsonville as rapidly as money and men could be procured. It is reported that surveyors are at work this side of Watsonville, for the Stanford company, making an alignment survey; if so, the chances are that we will have two railroads, with branches, up Soquel and San Lorenzo creeks. We welcome them all; the more the merrier. The *Alta* says, in speaking of these two main roads:

'We can state by authority that the Thirty-fifth Parallel or Atlantic and Pacific Railroad Company have surveyed and filed their route or line in the office of the Secretary of the Interior at Washington, from San Francisco to Springfield, Missouri. Their route in California, as filed, is from San Francisco to Santa Cruz and Watsonville;

thence up the Salinas Valley to San Miguel Mission; thence to Santa Margarita and San Luis Obispo; thence to Nipoma and Purissima Mission; thence to Los Pueblos and Santa Barbara; thence via San Buenaventura to the Santa Clara river; thence up the valley of the Santa Clara via the Soledad Pass to the Desert; and thence direct to the Needles, on the Colorado River, below Fort Mohave. Distance about 650 miles.

From the foregoing description of the route of the Atlantic and Pacific Railroad it will be seen that the line passes within about thirty-five miles of Los Angeles, to which point a survey has been made for a branch road.

The original survey and location of the Central Pacific or Southern Pacific Railroad of Messrs. Stanford, Huntington and Hopkins, as filed by them at Washington, and along which the lands were withdrawn, is from San Francisco to San Jose and Gilroy; thence, *via* San Benito Valley, across the Mount Diablo range of mountains, to Tulare Valley; thence, *via* Tehachapi Pass, to Colorado Desert and to the crossing of the Colorado river, at any point where the Atlantic and Pacific Railroad may cross that river; with a branch from the desert down through Soledad Pass, *via* Santa Clara river, to San Fernando, and across to Los Angeles; thence, *via* San Bernardino, to Fort Yuma, to intersect with the Texas Pacific Railroad wherever that road crosses the Colorado river, at or near the 32d parallel.

Since the location of the Southern Pacific road was filed, the Company have constructed a branch from Gilroy to Watsonville, and now wish to abandon their original location via San Benito Valley to Tulare Valley, and have had a bill introduced into Congress, giving them the right to change their location, abandon the San Benito route, avail of the Watsonville branch, and extend the road over the same route occupied by the Atlantic and Pacific road up Salinas Valley to San Miguel Mission; thence up the Extrello Branch of Salinas, across the Mount Diablo Range, via Pollonio or Chalamo Pass, into Tulare Valley.

392. *Santa Cruz Sentinel,* April 27, 1872 (3:3)

A Washington date states that the Pacific Railroad Committee has reported favorably on Blain's bill extending for three years the time for the completion of the Atlantic and Pacific Railroad.

393. *Santa Cruz Sentinel,* May 11, 1872 (3:2)

Our New Town Visit.

Last Thursday afternoon we jumped into the buggy of a friend, and after a few minutes' ride had the pleasure of interviewing a few of our subscribers in the new town of Santa Cruz [on the West Side between Garfield Park and Neary Lagoon]. Approaching the tract, we were struck with the bustling air of improvement observable on every hand; houses erecting here, fencing there, well-digging yonder, neighbors chatting and laughing over the bright prospects of the new town, with the numerous ladies and gentlemen engaged in selecting, measuring and buying lots of the indefatigable agent, who, map in hand, was on the ground ready and willing to accommodate them all. Truly, to us, the sight was quite refreshing.

The most remarkable thing connected with all we saw, was the apparently happy condition of those who are now located in the new town. This feeling we attribute to the confidence inspired by the knowledge that in buying lots in the new town they made a first-class investment. The land, they know was sold to them for a mere fraction of its value, to start the enterprise; and is as sure to increase shortly to a fabulous value as that the sun will shine to-morrow. The Atlantic and Pacific Railroad, to be built at once with the united capital of St. Louis and San Francisco, will have its depot, for Santa Cruz, on the site of the new town; in fact, one of our prominent citizens is now in the city, conferring with the Committee of One Hundred in regard to the offer of land, right of way, etc., in the new precinct; so that the gift of prophecy is not required to foretell what we assert.

394. *Santa Cruz Sentinel*, May 11, 1872 (3:4)
Railroad Land.

The enlightened and enterprising proprietor of the tract over which the new town of Santa Cruz is so rapidly extending, has, with his usual promptitude and liberality, set aside, and now offers to deed to the railroad company that shall be the first to lay its track to this point, four acres of land, for terminal uses of said road, on the site of the new town of Santa Cruz. This pioneer movement on the part of the sagacious proprietor of the new Town Tract, is one in the right direction, and if followed up, as we hear it is sure to be, by other land owners in the same neighborhood, will do more to hasten the construction of a railroad to our town, than all the frothy talk in the world could accomplish.

395. *Santa Cruz Sentinel*, May 18, 1872 (1:5)
THE COAST RAILROAD.
Half Moon Bay, May 10th, 1872.

Editors Alta*:*—In confirmation of the views expressed by your correspondent, "K," and myself, regarding the vast advantages to at once result from the formation of a coast railroad, I beg to furnish your readers with a few statistics, which I have taken some pains to collect, relating to the products and export trade of this district—a comparatively small section of the Pacific seaboard. The present population of Half Moon Bay, or the fifth township of San Mateo county, according to the last census, amounts to 1,300 inhabitants. From the San Pedro Rancho, on the northern, to the San Gregorio Creek, on the southern boundary, in an area of 24 miles long by six wide, about 20,000 acres of land are annually planted with grain and potatoes; over one-fifth of this crop consisting of the latter esculent, the average yield, in weight, to the acre is heavy, say two tons. This would give us 40,000 tons of transportation to the San Francisco market, and the cost of carriage being fully $4 per ton, $160,000 is the sum yearly expended in conveying our products hence.

Lying some four miles back, between the township's eastern boundary and the summit of the Coast Range, is a further area of 5,000 acres of uncultivated land, which a railroad would tap. Producing two tons to the acre, at an increase cost of transportation, of six dollars per ton, this portion of country pays the sum of sixty thousand dollars per annum for land and water carriage. This high rate acts as a positive drag on agricultural industry in such localities, amounting to almost a prohibition. Were railroad facilities afforded, the production would soon be more than doubled. Even as it is, large tracts of new land are being yearly broken up in the extensive cañons, and on loamy, rolling hills, where the soil is as deep and fertile as the rich diluvium of the adjacent valleys.

Our farmers are proverbially poor, and the seeming anomaly is easily accounted for. Possessing unrivaled soil, and the most abundant of harvests, the fruit of their labor is eaten up, the profits completely absorbed by the exorbitant cost of transportation.

The rehandling of produce at the warehouses, at the railway depots of San Mateo and San Francisco, is attended with considerable damage and expense, enhancing thereby the prime cost of the producer. This would be entirely obviated by the Atlantic and Pacific Railroad Company, who intend to have freight trucks shunted off the line at convenient intervals, to receive the farmer's products at his very door, and if this Company, with all its fit appliances, cannot contend to as great advantage with four and six dollar freight, as did the San Francisco and San Jose Railroad Company with a ship freight up the bay, of one dollar, then the sooner the scheme is abandoned, and forever, the better.

But another extensive revenue will be derived from the dairy and farmyard, the yields from which are now being conveyed to the city by a light-goods express company and by private teams, at a cost of from one cent, to a cent and a half per pound. Ten tons of this description of loading are weekly taken over the mountains, or over 500 tons in the 12 months, costing $12,500.

About 5,000 head of cattle, hogs, etc., are yearly driven from thirteen to thirty-five miles, to the San Mateo depot of the Southern Pacific Company, or direct to San Francisco, at great inconvenience, trouble and expense to the owners. The Southern Pacific Company charge $15 per truck for the conveyance of stock to San Francisco.

Kitchen garden productions; owing to the dearness of transport, are excluded entirely from all outside markets. It would be impossible to estimate what the revenue on the carrying of vegetables would amount to, but that it would be immense and continuous is certain, seeing that fresh supplies in superabundance can be raised the whole year round. Neither can be approximated the receipts on redwood lumber, as the commodity has never been exported extensively, although the forests contain an almost inexhaustible supply.

In summer the passenger traffic is large. Two coaches, and frequently extras, leave Half Moon Bay daily for San Mateo. During winter, owing to bad roads, there is less doing, but, as passenger travel by railway can never be brought into comparison with that of the slow, old-fogy stage coach, I will not presume to anticipate results which must be obvious to all.

The figures I have here employed have reference to but a very small extent of country, a mere "flea-bite; of the Pacific coast, but similar results will be found to obtain in a somewhat similar degree as far as products are concerned, and in a much greater measure, as regards cost of transportation, as we advance southward, from San Gregorio to Pescadero, and from Pescadero to Santa Cruz, where, as everyone knows, there is a rapidly rising, well established manufacturing town of considerable magnitude, commercial importance, governed by energetic, live, go-ahead business men who, with the inhabitants of the coast generally, will come forward to render all the assistance in their power to the Atlantic and Pacific Railroad Company. Yours, etc., BORAK.

396. *Santa Cruz Sentinel*, May 18, 1872 (2:1)

Our Railroad Prospects.

The Atlantic and Pacific Railroad Company have filed their location of route, from the city of San Francisco, southerly, to San Miguel Mission, in the Upper Salinas Valley. The route selected follows along the coast from San Francisco to Aptos, a distance of about 85 miles; thence leaving the immediate coast line and passing through, or near, the town of Watsonville and through Castroville and Salinas City, in Monterey County.

This line of road, if constructed, will pass through our County from its western to its eastern boundary, and will be of much more advantage to us than a branch road, connecting our town with the Gilroy and Watsonville road, as it will develop all the resources of our county, which the other will only do in part.

It has been urged by some that the route located is too

rough; that the country adjoining has no resources; and that the additional cost of construction would greatly overbalance the advantages which would otherwise be given to this location. With the cost of constructions we have nothing to do, that is a question for the Company and its engineers. Competent men have said that no great obstacles will have to be overcome. The matter for us to consider is: What can we do, and what resources can we show? Companies generally build roads where it is most to their advantage to do so, and though we may not be able to do much we can certainly do something. We have a subsidy of $100,000 waiting to be given to the first company that reaches us with a railroad; the right of away can be given; parties owning lands over which the road may pass will be none the poorer for giving the right of way, on the contrary they will find the value of their property much enhanced thereby. And though our county is small we have many resources. We have about 400 square miles of territory that will be directly benefited by such a road, one-half of this is farming and grazing land, the remainder is heavily wooded with all kinds of valuable timber; lumber is now one of our leading articles of export; our limestone is of the finest quality and practically inexhaustible, with a lasting supply of fuel for its manufacture. We also manufacture powder, leather, lime, paper, safety-fuse, glue and soap. All these manufactures would be much increased, and other established, as our mountain streams furnish abundant water power for manufacturing purposes.

From San Francisco to Santa Cruz there are no shipping places that are safe throughout the year, even our town is not entirely safe during the winter months, this inconvenience would be remedied by inland transportation. In fact from Santa Cruz up the coast shipping can only be done at much risk to the vessels employed. In addition to these advantages, this line would be the only road leading out of San Francisco and following directly along the coast. Our County has a fine climate and fine scenery and everything that could invite travel, protected as we are from the cold winds which make San Francisco so disagreeable, and not oppressively warm. Our town is already a place of much resort during the summer months, and how much more so will it be, place us on a great National thoroughfare with one-half the commerce of the Pacific passing before our doors and within three hours travel of the city of San Francisco.

397. *San Francisco Bulletin* via the *Santa Cruz Sentinel*, May 18, 1872 (2:1)

A Coast Road Survey.—The survey of the Atlantic and Pacific Railroad Company, follows the line of the coast from San Francisco to Pajaro Valley. The distance by this line is 100 miles, or exactly the same distance as by the way of San Jose and Gilroy. The belt of country along the coast, although rough is very productive. The lumber resources are very large, but at present the cost of shipping the lumber is so great at many points, that there is little or no profit in the manufacture. At some points the cost of getting it on board of a vessel by means of a hawser, is not less than four dollars a thousand feet. Add to this the cost of hauling, and the cost of manufacture, and with the present facilities, very little can be made at present. From the Cliff House to Santa Cruz, there are no safe landing places. The best is probably that under Point New Years. At Santa Cruz there are wharves, and the facilities for shipping lumber from that district are very good. The crops are generally very heavy along the coast line, and the amount of local freight is very great. Schooners stop in here and there, and take advantage of favorable weather to take in freight, but are frequently obliged to slip their moorings and go to sea with only part of a load.

If the coast line is rugged, as compared with the Santa Clara Valley, there is the balancing advantage of inexhaustible resources along the whole route. Nearly every mile of the way will contribute freight. The physical obstacles are not insurmountable, although the cost of constructing a road would of course be enhanced by the ruggedness of the country. Santa Cruz county has already voted a subsidy of $100,000 for the purpose of connecting the county seat with a railroad. This large subsidy is just now in abeyance, awaiting further developments; but it could probably be made available for the Atlantic & Pacific Railroad, which is located through the entire length of that county. And although it would only be but a drop in the bucket, yet every hundred thousand dollar drop is a substantial gain. In the first hundred miles, following the coast line, the Atlantic and Pacific road, as now marked out, would have no other competition than that furnished by water craft. Nearly every foot of arable land is already turned in some way to account, and the forest are full of lumbermen who have been looking for years for just such facilities as this road would give them.

398. *The Pajaronian*, May 23, 1872 (2:4)

The following is taken from a correspondence in the Sacramento *Record*:

"The town of Watsonville is the present southern terminus of the Southern Pacific Railroad, and the flourishing seat of trade of the fruitful Pajaro valley. Being a railroad terminus it is reaping much profit thereby, and will continue to thrive even after the road is extended, as it is the center of a rich region, the resources of which are not yet half developed. But settlers are filling up the back country of late, and every year will add to the wealth produced there and contributing to the general prosperity of the State. Lands between Watsonville and Gilroy are generally very beautiful and suitable for the cultivation of almost everything grown in this State, as well as to stock raising. In some of the valleys, the dairy business will now be carrier on with prophet, as the people, unlike the times formerly, are near to a market for their wares."

399. *Santa Cruz Sentinel*, May 25, 1872 (2:3)

Santa Cruz Scenery.

Mr. Charles Nordhoff, writing illustrated papers for *Harper's Magazine*, in the June number, thus refers to Santa Cruz and the scenery around the bay, and along the coast, to Pescadero, over the track, as located, for the Atlantic and Pacific Railroad.

400. *Harper's New Monthly Magazine*, June 1872 (76)

From Santa Clara, or San José if you return thither, the train will take you, by way of Gilroy, to Watsonville, where you may see wheat growing luxuriantly almost to the sea-shore; and by stage through a charming country to Santa Cruz, one of the pleasantest watering places of California, on the bay of Monterey, the old capital of California. You can not do better than to ride up the coast, through lovely scenery and pleasant villages, to the famous beach of Pescadero, and back to San Mateo, where you take the railroad to San Francisco. This is one of the most delightful of the excursions to be made around San Francisco, and it will give you an excellent example of the agricultural wealth of California, as well as of the picturesque beauty of its scenery. In May and June the whole country is covered with lovely flowers. The brilliant yellow and orange of the eschscholtzia, or California poppy, and the tender blue and white of the lupine, line the road and cover the fields in broad masses, which give a perpetual delight to the eye.

401. *Santa Cruz Sentinel*, May 25, 1872 (3:3)

Railroad Prospects.

There is no special change in Railroad matters. We still adhere to the opinion that a road will be built, from San Francisco, down the coast; capitalists will see that interest directs and duty impels them to take the route through Santa Cruz county; it is the nearest, best and most desirable for a constant and reliable way-trade, in passengers and freight. The St. Louis committee (sent by the committee of 100,) have telegraphed that everything is substantially correct, as represented. A company has been formed, in San Francisco, with $25,000,000 of capital and been organized. That the road will be built we have no doubt.

402. *San Francisco Bulletin*, May 23, via the *Santa Cruz Sentinel*, June 1, 1872 (4:1)

San Francisco and Atlantic Railroad.

At a meeting of the Executive Committee of One Hundred, held yesterday afternoon, the Committee of New Railroads presented a plan of organization of a railroad from San Francisco to the Colorado, to be named the San Francisco and Atlantic Railroad Company, under the laws of the State of California, and the details were discussed and determined upon. This plan embraces a corporation having a capital stock of $25,000,000, with a Board of thirteen Directors. The capital stock to be apportioned for subscription among the counties which have the right to aid in its construction, under the Act of April 4, 1870, in proportion to the amount of assessment rolls of the respective counties. Every taxpayer in such counties to have the right to subscribe for an amount of stock bearing the same proportion to the whole number of shares set apart for the county as taxes paid by him for the fiscal years 1872–1873 bear to the whole county tax for that year. All contracts for construction for materials, Grading, &c., &c., to be let to the best and lowest bidder, the road to be free for the use of trains of other companies on payment of tolls fixed by the Board of Directors. All aid or subsidies granted to the Company under the Act of April 4, 1870, shall be credited to the body contributing the same, no dividends exceeding ten per cent. per annum on capital stock, to be paid until such credit be extinguished.

The proposed plan was adopted, and the subject referred to the Committee on Railroads to select the Board of thirteen Directors and organize the incorporation....

403. *The Pajaronian*, June 6, 1872 (2:2)

The Southern Pacific.

The San Francisco *Call* says the contract has just been let for the construction of an additional fifty miles of the Southern Pacific Railroad southward from its present terminus, near Watsonville. Work will be commenced at once, and pushed forward vigorously through the Salinas Valley. This will be good news for the people of that region, who have long been wanting an outlet for their farm products. We believe the iron is already on hand, and the track will be laid without unnecessary delay.

404. *The Pajaronian*, June 27, 1872 (2:2)

The Subsidy Again.

All our readers will distinctly remember the great subsidy excitement in this county a few months ago. It will also be remembered that this journal opposed the movement not on account of opposition to railroads, but for the reason that no company was ready or had ever signified their willingness to take the subsidy and build the road, and the expense and trouble to the county was unnecessary and wrong; that the men who pushed the measure through were entirely ignorant of railroading and simply desired to make capital on the outside for their own financial gain. During the controversy a great deal of bitterness was engendered, and the editor of this paper received a great deal of abuse from Hihn and others, and suffered great loss financially, by losing Hihn and Heath from his subscription list. We have partly recovered, however, from the loss thus sustained and can doubtless entirely recuperate in time. We are only thankful that Hihn with his unbounded influence, did not come to Watsonville and prohibit us from ever issuing another paper unless we consented to advocate his interests right or wrong.

The subsidy passed, by a large majority, through grossest misrepresentation, and a reckless stirring up of bitter and rival feelings between the two principal towns of the county, by certain parties in Santa Cruz. The subsidy passed as we have said, and great was the rejoicing among the few who carried it, and all that was next necessary was for the Southern Pacific to go right to work, build the road straight into Santa Cruz and take the cash, But, strange to relate, Stanford did not seem to think the scheme a practical one—would not commence, and a flutter again took place in Santa Cruz. Hihn called a council of war and by asserting in eloquent terms that "the thing is just dis way here," succeeded in forming a local company which proposed to build the road and grab the spoils. This movement was inaugurated, of course, to gain time. They have not commenced work and on the 18th of next month, the contract runs out by limitation, and the great subsidy humbug falls still born at the feet of Hihn and others—unless something can be done. Again there was a flutter in Santa Cruz, and the principal movers turned somersaults and stood on their heads in agony, for fear that the whole thing would be a failure. Another council of war was held by the faithful, Hihn again eloquently asserts that "the thing is just dis way here," and the result was as follows:

Hihn went before the Board of Supervisors and endeavored to renew the subsidy contract for the period of eight months in anticipation of the Atlantic and Pacific Railroad Company, commencing to build the road along the coast.

The Board rightly and promptly voted down the proposition to extend the time, and unless the road is commenced within the time specified above, the subsidy swindle falls to the ground, and will ever lie there, as a sign of the uncertainty of human events and a lasting reproach to the boyish and foolish schemes of men who would, if they could, be Stanfords, but who, when they try, make ignoble failures.

By extending the time so that the Atlantic and Pacific company could take the contract from the hands of the local company, the road would be built by the former if it is determined t go the extreme coast route and the subsidy would go into their hands of course. But they propose when passing through those counties where subsidies have been voted, to give in return for the subsidy an equivalent in the *Stock* of the road to the county. So it will readily be seen that, as the Hihn crowd have the subsidy contract in their own hands, they could transfer to the Atlantic and Pacific and receive $100,000 worth of stock in return, while the county might whistle while paying the interest and principal. A shrewd trick on the part of one or more men to make $100,000l but we do not think it will work this time.

Should the subsidy swindle fall to the ground, this is what we shall say over its demise:

'Vale! Vale! Subsidy. Hihn and others, we cannot gloat over you, for we pity you, and tears fall unbidden upon the page as we write, with thoughts of your struggles, and failures and bitterness of spirit. Come home to your father's house. Apologize to the editor of the *Pajaronian*, and he will renew your subscriptions; and if you should ever do a good and noble act for the benefit of the *whole people, if* you ever do, we say, in the long and brilliant future before you, we will take pride and pleasure in making a note of it. Good-bye dear friends, and God bless you.

405. *Castroville Argus*, June 15, via *The Santa Cruz Sentinel*, June 29, 1872 (1:6)

The Coming Railroad.

Let our people rejoice! The great blow that is to build up our town—the blow for whose sound we have all been so anxiously awaiting—has been struck at last. It fell a few days ago upon the yielding ground of the railroad route between here and Watsonville, and already, scattered between the toll road crossing of Elk Horn Slough and the depot at Pajaro, hundreds of strong armed men are building the highway that is to connect Castroville with the outside world—that is to make her the first town in the county.

The liberality of our esteemed fellow-citizen, Juan B. Castro, Esq., has assured us that, not like Watsonville, will be left at a distance, but that the depot and other buildings of the Company will become an integral portion of the town, and that, whatever benefit accrues from such advantage will be surely gained by us.

During a trip to Watsonville, Wednesday, we passed the scene of labor—and a busy scene it was—here, men at work plying the shovel and pick; there, others pitching tents, digging wells, building boarding houses, while all along the road were scattered blacksmith shops, horses carts, plows and other implements of labor, in vast quantities. Of course, we picked up a few items—to the effect that it was the intention to complete the road to this place in fifty days; that white laborers were in great demand; that the *Call*'s statement of the letting of a contract for building *fifty* miles of the road from Pajaro depot was premature; that Elk Horn slough was to be crossed by a pile bridge five hundred feet long, and that the engineer in charge of the work was a pleasant, social gentleman, rides a fine trotting horse, in power, speed and action almost equal to a locomotive.

406. *The Santa Cruz Sentinel*, June 29, 1872 (2:1)

Our Railroad.

From the report of the investigating Committee sent by the Committee of One Hundred, to St. Louis and Boston, to inquire into the affairs of the Atlantic and Pacific Railroad Company, we are inclined to think that the prospects are good for a speedy completion of the road. From the lengthy report we learn that the Company is sound and reliable, and have ample means to finish the road to the California line. Already 370.25 miles of the road is completed, from St. Louis to Vinita in the Indian Territory, and in running order. The distance through the Indian Territory, along the Canadian river bottoms is 305.25 miles. In Northwest Texas, between 10 and 103 degrees of longitude, the distance is 199.46 miles. In New Mexico 445.67 miles. In Arizona 397.38 miles. And in California 656 miles, from the Needles at the crossing of the Colorado river to San Francisco. The California section of the road, according to the survey of *reconnaissance*, which may be much improved by running other and working surveys, is reported as follows:

Length of line from Colorado River to San Francisco, 656 miles.

ALTITUDE OF IMPORTANT PLACES

Watsonville 28
Ridge between Watsonville and Santa Cruz 400
Santa Cruz 29
Tunnel near Pescadero creek 252
Total length of line from St. Louis to the Colorado river
.... 1,732.01
Less already constructed 370.25
Length to be constructed 1,361.76
Do. in California 656
Total to be constructed 2,017.76
Add to the line already built 370.25
Whole distance from St. Louis to San Francisco ....
.... 2,388.91

Estimated cost of building 2,017.76 miles of new road $80,000,000.

407. *The Santa Cruz Sentinel*, June 29, 1872 (3:2)

T. W. More, an old settler, visited Santa Cruz the past week. Tom is quite sanguine the railroad will be built along the coast from Watsonville to San Francisco. We hope so, and infer that no interest can influence a change of the route, filed and accepted, mapped out in the U. S. Land Office at Washington, by which the Company are allowed 1,700,000 of lieu lands, worth $4 per acre, provided they keep the coast side of the Santa Cruz range. The principal Depots will be in Spanish Town, Pescadero, Stelle, Waddell, Davenport, Laguna, Santa Cruz, Soquel, Aptos, Calabases, Whisky Hill, [Hillsburg], Watsonville, &c. The Company expect liberal encouragement, from towns, and will extend every facility to the people in return that courtesy and interest will permit.

408. *The Santa Cruz Sentinel*, July 6, 1872 (3:4)

Railroad Meeting.

It is about item that we hold a railroad meeting to cooperate with the San Francisco Committee of 100. A little action now may secure us the road. We are prepared to show a subscription of $250,000 for this county if the road comes down the coast, with free right of way and donated lands for stations and depots.

409. *The Santa Cruz Sentinel*, July 13, 1872 (1:8-9)

Coast Railroad.

As the citizens and the Southern Coast Counties of California cannot be indifferent to any intelligence which promises the construction of a railroad through this section of the State, we publish the following extracts from the *Bulletin* and *Alta*. Both journals claim to speak by authority, and it is quite certain that the letter of the Commissioners of the General Land Office published in the *Bulletin* article that the route is definitely located as far as San Miguel; and the *Alta* declares that it speaks "by authority" when it gives the continuation of the route south "to the Needles on the Colorado River, below Fort Mohave." We quote the *Bulletin* of May 3d.

A New Railroad Land Reservation.

The Atlantic and Pacific Railroad Company have just completed their surveys of the Pacific end of the route. The road is definitely located from San Francisco to San Miguel Mission on the border of San Luis Obispo county. For the greater part of this distance it is substantially a coast road. The contour of the coast is closely followed until the line passes around Monterey Bay. Thence southward the line bears away from the coast fifteen miles or more until San Miguel Mission is intersected. It appears that a plat of this location was filed in the General Land Office at Washington on the 12th day of March last, and a duplicate showing the line of the road, together with a map definition the twenty-mile reservation of public land and ten miles additional for lieu land, was filed in the Land Office in this city to-day, together with the following letter:

DEPARTMENT OF THE INTERIOR,
General Land Office, Washington, D. C., April 22, 1872.

Register and Receiver, San Francisco, Cal.—Gentleman:—I transmit herewith a diagram showing the definite location of the Atlantic and Pacific Railroad, under Act of July 27, 1866, Stat. Vol. 14, p292, from San Francisco to San Miguel Mission, Cal., showing also the twenty and thirty mile limits of the land grant under said Act; and you are hereby directed to withhold from pre-emption or homestead entry, private sale or location, all the odd numbered sections falling within those limits, both surveyed and unsurveyed, not reserved, sold, granted, or otherwise appropriated, and free from pre-emption, or other claims or rights, at the time the line of said road was designated by filing a plat thereof in this office, which was March 12, 1872.

The even numbered sections within the twenty mile limits, you will increase to $2.50 an acre, and dispose of them at that ratability; and only under the pre-emption and homestead laws. The even sections outside of the twenty mile limit are not affected by this withdrawal.

Claims initiated by settlers under the pre-emption laws prior to the right of the road attaching, March 12, 1872, are not affected by this order.

Yours respectfully,

WILLIS DRUMMOND,
Commissioner.

Few persons, we apprehend, were aware that the Atlantic and Pacific Railroad Company had any land within the limits of this State. But turning to the Act of July, 1865 [*sic*], by which the Company was incorporated, we find the following requirements as to location:

Beginning at or near the town of Springfield, in the State of Missouri, thence to the western boundary line of said State, and thence to the most eligible route as shall be determined by said company to a point on the Canadian river, thence to the town of Albuquerque, on the Rio Del Norte, and thence by way of the Agua Fria, or other suitable pass, to the head waters of the Colorado Chiquito, and thence along the thirty-fifth parallel of latitude, as near as may be found most suitable for a railway route to the Colorado river, at such point as may be selected by said company for crossing; thence by the MOST PRACTICABLE AND ELIGIBLE ROUTE TO THE PACIFIC.

By the charter the Company is authorized to build a road from Springfield, Mo., to San Francisco, the latter being the most eligible point on the Pacific.

The second section of the same Act grants the right of way, with the usual privileges. In the third section of the same Act there is granted to the Company *twenty* alternate sections per mile on each side of such line as may be adopted through the Territories of the United States, and *ten* alternate sections per mile on each side of the located line where it passes through any State. When the public lands have been exhausted in the States, the right is extended to take the ten sections within ten miles beyond the first limit.

We find a chartered line of railroad under this Act from Missouri to an indefinite point on the Pacific, with the privilege of reaching that point by the most eligible route. The route and the point have been determined by the Company, and in conformity therewith the plats have been filed and reservation made. It is clear also under the Act cited, the land grant runs with the entire line of the road from Missouri to San Francisco.

There is very little available Government land between

San Francisco and Monterey Bay. The lands once sought to be made available for the San Jose Railroad Company as a part of the Southern Pacific, were not allowed by the Department. But south of San Jose the lands marked as reserved on the plat filed by the Southern Pacific Railroad Company, with the additional ten miles limit, extended for some distance nearly to the ocean, overlapping as it would seem the lands now designated in the plat filed by the Atlantic and Pacific Railroad Company. But further south, the lines of the two roads as designated by the plats filed, diverge so far that one does not appear to interfere with the other.

In San Luis Obispo, Santa Barbara, and other counties there are some bodies of public lands still held by the Government, and which could probably be made available for the construction of the Atlantic and Pacific road. The country within which selections may be made is thirty miles wide, and probable within those limits considerable grazing lands will be found. The resuscitation of the grant so far as it relates to California, is a fact of much significance.

The San Francisco *Alta California* says:

"We can state by authority that the Thirty-fifth Parallel or Atlantic and Pacific Railroad Company have surveyed and filed their route or line in the office of the Secretary of the Interior at Washington, from San Francisco to Springfield, Mo. Their route in California, as filed, is from San Francisco to Santa Cruz and Watsonville; thence up the Salinas valley to San Miguel Mission; thence to Santa Margarita and San Luis Obispo; thence to Nipoma and Purissima Mission; thence to Dos Pueblos and Santa Barbara; thence via San Buenaventura to the Santa Clara river; thence up the valley of the Santa Clara via the Soledad Pass to the Desert; and thence to the Needles, on the Colorado river, below Fort Mohave. Distance about 650 miles."

410. *The Santa Cruz Sentinel*, July 20, 1872 (2:2)

Railroad Views.

We almost despair of having the Atlantic and Pacific Railroad built, by aid from San Francisco, down the coast through our beautiful county. A majority of the Committee of 100 is evidently controlled by Stanford and the Stockholders in his road, and as a matter of safety they have to adhere to the interests of the Central Pacific; hence all their railroad talk, is mere moonshine. So far as San Francisco *large* capitalists are concerned, they are willing to subscribe freely, provided they can control the road, and lay it at the feet of their royal master wherever he makes it to their interest to do so. They want to purchase the San Jose, Gilroy, Hollister and Pajaro roads, because they own large amounts in stock; and can pay that stock (which would be comparatively worthless, if an opposition road was built down the coast,) in, to liquidate their subscriptions. The same old beast, with seven heads and ten horns, is visible in this squabble over subscriptions, routes, &c., backed by personal debates that would disgrace a fish-market hags, or dissolve a county debating society. Each honorable member wants a tape-worm line of road to pass his own barnyard or fish pond, so that his estates will be enhanced in value, thousands for his hundreds subscribed and unless he can accomplish this, he will oppose all railroads, and throw cold water on the Atlantic and Pacific enterprise, as surveyed on the coast line.

The people of St. Louis, Boston and Tom Scott, will eventually build the road; but, as its construction is from the Eastern end, it will be several years before we can expect it finished through to San Francisco, on the line of survey filed in Washington. The San Francisco *Bulletin*, a friend of the Santa Cruz or coast route, thus places the question:

There are two plans of building railroads—one safe and practicable; the other wasteful and tending directly to corruption. The latter plan was brought prominently before the public in the construction of the Central Pacific Railroad. It was a subsidy road from beginning to end. It reversed all the experiences of railroad building for the last quarter of a century. Before that time the building of a railroad required the united action of a large number of stockholders. They came together, put down their subscriptions in good faith, and paid the money over according to agreement. If their subscriptions were not sufficient back bone. Mortgage bonds were good for whatever was lacking. A large body of intelligent capitalists and business men had a direct interest in the road. They had put in their money, and they were guarantors to the public, of good faith on the part of the railroad company. Fifteen years ago, no sane man thought it desirable or possible that a subsidy or free gift should be bestowed upon any railroad corporation. But the Central Pacific, having been successful with its subsidy scheme during war times, we have now this vicious system fastened on to us even to the point of strangulation.

The proposition to build the western end of the Atlantic and Pacific Railroad, did not involve any direct subsidy on the part of this city, nor on the part of the counties along the proposed line. The plan has been to build it by private and public subscriptions. If a county subscribed $200,000 it was to have the equivalent of that in stock. If San Francisco as a municipality subscribed $5,000,000 or more, the stock was to be allotted to the city as its just equivalent. That was deemed a safe and just way of dealing with the public. No subsidies, no free gifts were asked. It was a return to the old plan of railway construction. But, just there came in the Central Pacific Railroad influence. If a railroad was thus built without subsidies, it would be a standing reproach and menace to a corporation built up on subsidies. The city would own $5,000,000 or more of stock and would have a vital interest in railway management. Citizens would own as much, obtained by paying out dollar for dollar, and they would have a right to look into the management. It would never do it give up the subsidy and free gift business in that way. If once the city should vote a subscription that would put an end to subsidies. The two plans of building railroads are now before the public. The Central Pacific comes in, procures the organization of a railroad company to the Colorada river, invites subscriptions with the private understanding that they are never to be paid, and in fact that they will not be necessary if a ten million subsidy can be procured from the city. With that subsidy the road can be sold, consolidated or otherwise disposed of so that the paper stockholders who have never paid a dollar will have a chance to make something handsome in the operation. It is the Central Pacific subsidy policy right over again. It does not mean an independent road connecting San Francisco with St. Louis, which is the most important public project ever suggested in connection with this city. But it means an isolated, subsidy road or the absorption of the Southern Pacific for the present, and the re-absorbing of the same road by the Central Pacific at a future day when a majority of nominal stock is consolidated and the tide sets just right.

The original proposition put before the people, and which we believe accords with their intelligent convictions, is to construct the western end of the Atlantic and Pacific between the two cities as soon as possible. The other plan does not involve any such results in a direct and straightforward way. It is a dilatory, temporizing expedient, with a road into the desert at a future day if a subsidy will build it, and until that time a paper railroad.

411. *The Pajaronian*, August 1, 1872 (2:2)

Narrow Gauge.—We hear a rumor to the effect that a narrow gauge railroad is seriously contemplated from this place to Santa Cruz. We have no opposing words to utter—but if it will pay to build a narrow gauge, why will it not pay to build a broad gauge, thereby saving an important item in regard to handling freight? We do not know, as yet, who project the movement, and can only learn that it is proposed to vote a subsidy of 5 per cent. on the taxable property of the county in and of the road. Mr. Hihn, as one of the principal moneyed men of the county, probably has something to do in the matter. If the plan, after being made public, is a feasible one, and is calculated to benefit all the people of the county, we shall take great pleasure in advocating the construction of the road. Otherwise, we shall fight it, as we did the last subsidy swindle. Let us know your points, gentlemen.

412. *The Pajaronian*, August 1, 1872 (5:2)

Southern Pacific.—The Southern Pacific Railroad is being pushed rapidly to the Salinas, and it is expected that by the first of October the road will reach the town.... After all the talk about subsidies and immense land grants, California would be far, far, behind the times without her splendid railroad facilities. The Pajaro Valley already sensibly feels the impetus of railroad communication, and, as years pass on, benefits will rapidly multiply by such advantages.

413. *The Santa Cruz Sentinel*, August 3, 1872 (1:7-8)

The railroad depot is in Monterey county, one mile south of Pajaro river, and it is of little convenience and no direct benefit to the town [of Watsonville]; in fact it has in a degree injured the place, by unsettling fixed rates and values of Real Estate. In the valley at large, there is no doubt that the railroad has been a great advantage, and brought many new men with money into the place, and increased the population by immigration, and the amount of cultivated land. This fact has had a tendency to increase trade in the town, and the consequence is more teams, wagons, stages, hacks and buggies may be seen dashing to and fro in all directions. But then, there is a general distrust; outsiders will not purchase Real Estate freely in the town, they are afraid of the railroad building up a rival city. Lots, at the Depot, remain unsold, as people are distrustful of the Railroad Company moving the Depot elsewhere, and they point at the temporary structures and hencoops of station houses, (where lumber is so near, cheap and abundant,) already erected. In truth, they know a railroad will eventually go to Santa Cruz, and then the great city of the Pajaro Valley will be at the junction of the two or three roads—"mugby" junction, it may be, but still it will capture the trade and be the main city of the valley. The fact that the bay landing is five miles distant from the Depot, though a rich valley, is evidence that there is a future in a distance as well as time for the railroad Depot. At present the railroad is progressing southward, along the Elkhorn Slough to Castroville. From the stage road we saw the newly graded line, and tents of the (Chinese) workmen along the laguna. The track crosses the slough far below, and the great long piles (all peeled) passing through Watsonville on huge wagons, were for the bridging and trestle work. It is said some of these piles had to be driven down 139 feet in the deep water and soft mud before a firm bottom could be reached. The railroad will be finished by October to Castroville, and in fact within a year to Salinas city and New Republic, but will, probably, not go within a mile of the latter two places, preferring in each instance to build their own city and derive all the speculative value from the sale of lots; as for instance Watsonville, Visalia, Red Bluffs, Stockton, Woodbridge and other places. It is said that the road is under contract to be completed to Alisal, near the Gabilan (Jesse D. Carr's ranch) within one year; if so, the whole valley will be at the mercy of the road, so far as town property is concerned, just as Pajaro Valley now is. But then the road will be a benefit, in the end, to the country, by bringing population, and adding to the taxable property and material wealth of the valley.

414. *The Santa Cruz Sentinel*, August 3, 1872 (2:1)
Atlantic and Pacific Railroad.

In San Francisco, up to Thursday last, 972 persons had subscribed $664,950. The object of the incorporation is to get as many small amounts subscribed as possible, in order to control the subsidy vote. The road will no doubt be built through this county, down the coast. We are convinced that a subsidy of $200,000 will be subscribed by this county, with twice the amount of private subscriptions, should the road go through Pescadero, Santa Cruz, Soquel, Aptos and Watsonville, thence via. the Coast to Moss's Landing, skirting east of the Salinas river to the Mission of Soledad. This is the course of the Genuine Atlantic and Pacific Railroad. All others are not in the interest of the people, or the settlers and towns on the route.

415. *The Santa Cruz Sentinel*, August 10, 1872 (2:1-2)
The Coast Route Considered.

In the *Alta* of August 2d, we find an elaborate interview with John T. Doyle, one of the "100" who are now seeking ways and means "how not to do it," in assisting the Atlantic and Pacific Railroad. According to the interview, Mr. Doyle is opposed to the Coast Route, west of the Santa Cruz range of Mountains, and seems to think there is but one way to grade, and that is down the Santa Clara Valley. The location of the route is the whole pith of the trouble in reconciling railroad matters in the city. Heavy capitalists like D. O. Mills, Hayward, Latham, Howard, Donahue and others, want the road to pass their own residences or milk ranches, and they don't care whose interests suffer or how much gerrymandering surveyors make, provided the tapeworm line enhances their rural possessions five hundred fold in value. They also own, largely, stocks of the San Jose, Gilroy, Hollister and Pajaro roads, called by courtesy, (or a fiction of floated location), "the Southern Pacific." The main object is to prevent opposition to their interests in the road, and thus save their stock from depreciation. It has been asserted that the Southern Pacific—so called—is worth but bout $40,000 per mile, rolling stock, turn-outs, depots, and right of way included; and that there is a debt of twice as much against the road. If this be true, or only a part truth, it easily accounts for the anxiety of the world be millionaires for their property. In this very natural emotion, they are backed by homestead association in the city. Hundreds of real and fictitious companies own homestead tracts all along the Santa Clara route to Redwood city and even to Mayfield. The Shares of these genuine and bogus companies are disseminated in every direction, among all classes in the city and on the proposed route; this is another reason why our interests and the interests of the Atlantic and Pacific road, are cast aside, through interested motives, by speculators in San Francisco. They care nothing for the franchise or charter of the road, and would sacrifice the great National subsidy of six or seven million dollars worth of land—or lieu land—(which the road is entitled to if it adheres to the route of the survey filed and accepted in Washington,) merely to make a few paltry dimes for their own interest. Mr. Doyle is aware of this fact, and panders to the appetite and wishes of the homestead interests, regardless of the interests of the coast route and St. Louis people in their great Railroad enterprise.

We admit, for sake of argument, that the coast road would cost 25 per cent. more to grade the track, than the valley route. But would not the cost of timber for ties, stringers, trestle work, &c., and the price of land for right of way, depots and side track, cost more in Santa Clara Valley, than the additional grading expense on this side the mountains? Railroad Engineers and road-builders know very well that trestle-work and bridging is less expensive, in a rough country, than grading; and that a road once graded, where hillside and rocks are abundant, giving ample drainage, is far better and more permanent, than a road on level adobe or alluvial ground, liable to overflow or settle down by the winter floods. Once build the road along the coast, and the incidental expenses for the repairs, would not be half as much as through the low, boggy lands in the Santa Clara, Gilroy and Pajaro Valleys. The streams on the coast route, are all mountain torrents, of pure, cold water with high banks, and deep gorges to cross. The grading of the banks would fill up the ravines and make a durable, permanent road, not liable to destruction, as were the Yolo road and the Gilroy and Pajaro roads last year. As to way trade, we contend there is five hundred per cent. more in wood, posts, pickets, shakes, staves, lumber, shingles, bark, hoop-poles, lime, leather, powder, safety-fuse, soap, glue, butter, cheese, coal, granite, lime rock, iron ore, silver ore, and a hundred other articles of manufacture and natural resources on the coast, than on the Santa Clara route; and before the road would be finished, such a large passenger trade would spring up, as would astonish every one, and more than double the present divided passenger trade of Santa Clara valley—we say *divided*, for there are now three traveled routes from Santa Clara and San Jose to San Francisco, and when the Alviso and San Jose railroad is built, there will be three effective railway communications, twice a day and oftener. We ask, in all sincerity, would a *fourth* railroad track pay, over the same field of trade? We think not, and Mr. Doyle will no doubt agree with us if he is honest in his convictions and argument.

Another railroad, along the Santa Clara Valley, would not materially enhance farming land south of Mayfield, as the route would necessarily have to be very near the roads already built, and therefore would be of little convenience as an outlet to a market, or for travel. On the contrary, in many places the roads would have to run parallel within from two hundred feet to a mile of the Southern Pacific road, thus cutting up the land so as not to afford a calf-pasture between the two routes. This narrow strip of land would not be worth the tending for agriculture, and the railroad would have no use for it as depots or side track conveniences, consequently the land would be depreciated in value. Who is to stand the expense? The railroad company would settle that question, only at the termination of expensive and vexatious law suits.

We consider the assertion of Mr. Doyle, that the coast route through Pescadero to Santa Cruz, is too difficult and expensive, in view of all the facts—mere moonshine. The surveyors of the Atlantic and Pacific railroad agree with us, and every one of their resorts recommend the coast route; accordingly that route was accepted, adopted and filed by the company in Washington, and the Secretary of the Interior therefore issued his certificate of charter, which must remain intact, as the Act of Congress granting the lands, is inviolate, or the whole company will be illegal and a fraud on the people and the Nation, so far as the location of route is concerned. Let the [???] travel over the coast road and examine the shady nooks, rich table lands and splendid alluvial valleys all along the coast, from Half-moon Bay. There is Purissima creek, San Gregoria, Pescadero, Butano, Waddell, Scott, Big, Blass, Laguna, Majors', Meader, San Lorenzo, Soquel, Aptos, Corralitos, and their tributaries, and numerous smaller creeks, all full of speckled trout, with ample water-power to drive machinery, on or adjacent to the route; it will be plain to the thinking and candid mind (if not Mr. Doyle) that there is really more wealth on the coast route than any other north or south of the Bay, from San Francisco to the Salinas Plains. There is almost a continuous succession of dairies and grain fields on the route, for ninety miles, and the entire distance is through a country underdeveloped, of richest natural resources indispensable in the San Francisco market, especially in building material and subsistence supplies. The hunter and angler, can here find rare sport on the coast, or trout fishing; and in the higher hills, where deer, bear and small game—especially quail, doves, hare, rabbit and mountain squirrel—are abundant. Those who seek diversion in gathering algae, sea-shells, or dazzling pebbles—brilliant as Arizona diamonds, and more valuable—can stop at any of the depots on the route. Another beauty and pleasure is the abundance of wild berries and hazelnuts at certain seasons, also pine-cones and myriads of rare and choice wild flowers and ferns, growing to perfection, in nature's own garden, and in the dark, deep cañons, amidst precipitous rocks, overhanging cliffs, and alpine heights, and in places within a short distance of the road. All these rich and rare curiosities may appear trifling advantages, too tedious to mention, but a city population takes them into account, and it is these minor inducements which tempt an over worked and business-exhausted people to go forth into the country to ruralize. Thousands of picnic parties would annually make excursions along the coast, clear down to Sant Cruz, had they railroad facilities to enable them to go and return the same day—allowing six or eight hours for enjoyment.

We close without giving a tithe of the many advantages of the coast route; but would admonish the committee of 100—especially John T. Doyle, Esq.—to examine, and more particularly inspect the subject.

416. *The Santa Cruz Sentinel,* August 10, 1872 (3:4)

Good Investment.

The Atlantic and Pacific Railroad Co., are receiving subscriptions daily in San Francisco. About one million dollars have already been subscribed, mostly in $100 subscriptions, by some 700 persons. There is forty millions of dollars belonging to the laboring and producing classes, in San Francisco, now returning an interest of from eight to ten per cent. per annum. This money should, in part, be put into the railroad. The interest would not at present be so large, but in a few years the stock of the company would make up the difference by enhanced value. Build the road, and every foot of land in San Francisco (outside lands) would treble in value every year for five years to come.

416. *The Santa Cruz Sentinel,* August 17, 1872 (1:8)

A Plea for the Coast Route.

Half-Moon Bay, August 5th.

Editors *Alta*:—I have just perused the interview between your reporter and Mr. John T. Doyle, reported in your paper of the 2d inst., in which Mr. Doyle defines his objections to the Coast route of railroad. I here state with all candor that his views are not becoming his reputation for good judgment. Do the people of San Francisco propose to drive an opposition to Stanford & Co., without the view of benefitting themselves? If they do, then Mr. Doyle's argument is good, but if they propose to have a paying line from San Francisco to St. Louis, with an eye of general benefit to both St. Louis and San Francisco, and to the company that builds the road, his suggestions have no virtue. He says that the first twenty miles built from San Francisco would be an opposition to Sanford & Co., that the Coast Road will bring no business, but what they now have. I say that the coast freight would double its present traffic, and at very high tariff, and a company would get the right of way free.

I ask Mr. D. can the proposed company or any other company get the right of way from San Francisco down as far as Gilroy through the Santa Clara Valley free? I answer no, and on the contrary it would cost more to obtain the right of way and build the road through the Santa Clara Valley than it would cost on the Coast route. I ask Mr. D. what he expects the road would pay, running parallel and in a quarter or half a mile of the Southern Pacific Road? It would not pay the taxes on the property. But I say and can convince any reasonable set of men that the Coast Road would be a good paying route. The country is very rich in soil, dairies and timber, and with no harbor to ship, only about six months in the year, from May to October or November, and at a schooner or steamer freight at an outrage of $4 per ton from Half-Moon Bay to Monterey, and where there is an abundance of freight, why won't it pay? Mr. D. is ignorant of what he states, or he evades the truth in saying that the Pajaro freight is taken to Oakland for Goat Island. That freight comes on the Southern Pacific, and is landed at the depot in San Francisco; but if Mr. D. is correct, would not the Coast Road necessarily have to run through Pajaro Valley, and tap Messrs. Stanford & Co.?

Taking Mr. D.'s views altogether they are without

truth or argument but, through private or other interest to me unknown, he is bound to the Santa Clara Valley route *perfast ni fas*. D.

417. *Missouri Republican*, July 25, via *The Santa Cruz Sentinel*, August 17, 1872 (1:9)

Atlantic and Pacific Railroad.

The popular movement in San Francisco and California to aid the construction of the Atlantic and Pacific railroad has very naturally excited the opposition of the Central Pacific Company. This was to be expected, but it is satisfactory to know that the movement is progressing steadily notwithstanding the misrepresentations and sinister schemes of unfriendly parties. Advices received in this city yesterday stated that the enterprise was progressing most successfully and that private subscriptions were being made rapidly by merchants and others. Quite a number of firms had put down their names for sums ranging from five to ten thousand dollars, and the list was swelling each day. One effort by the opposition originated, on paper, a new company to construct an independent road to connect somewhere, with the Atlantic and Pacific or Texas Pacific. This scheme attracted attention for a few days, but gradually businessmen began to understand its character, and to distrust its pretensions. It has very properly fallen into the background. We trust all similar attempted diversions of the enemy will meet a similar fate.

In the Atlantic and Pacific railroad the only substantial prospect is opened to the people of California, and of St.

Louis and the West, of establishing a suitable and permanent railroad highway across the continent. Of course no grand project of this character was ever worked into a livering fact without misrepresentations and opposition, but in this case, we believe, the earnest men of two great sections of the nation cannot be successfully hood-winked and deceived. The charter of the Atlantic and Pacific is the only charter in existence under which a trans-continental railway commensurate with the country's wants can be built. The route of the Atlantic and Pacific railroad along the 35th parallel, is the only proper route for such a road to occupy, and this is established by all the practical knowledge of fifty years' exploration of the continent has afforded. No other route, either farther north or south, offers the same advantages, not only of climate, but as a means of national settlement and commanding the trade of the interior.

These two simple and naked facts should be enough to dispose of all hollow and selfish opposition. Their logic is irresistible, and the only question for all who are in earnest in this matter to discuss, is the means of carrying out this great work. Here, we confess, are grave problems to consider without wasting strength on immaterial and frivolous suggestions. But the difficulties presented are not insurmountable when the great agencies and energies of the people are brought to bear against them. Let the people of California combine their powers to assist the present movement, and with the moral and practical co-operation of St. Louis and the Mississippi valley, success must be accomplished. It takes some time and indeed education of opinion to consolidate the energies of communities towards a particular object, but, in reference to this matter, a spirit of earnestness and determination is abroad that must eventually achieve that result.

418. *The Santa Cruz Sentinel*, August 17, 1872 (2:1-2)

Our Railroad System.

The following is an extract from E. N. Robinson's answer to Mr. Goddard's letter published in the *Bulletin*, Jul 23d. We copy from the *News Letter* of August 10th. It will be seen that Mr. Goddard was mistaken in many important points and consequently his views are not substantiated by facts:—

I have, what Mr. Goddard may consider an insane idea, that a railroad projected between any two points, should seek that route between the points (Pajaro Valley and San Francisco) that will most benefit the immediate country, even at a reasonably increased cost and length of line—the same to be determined by the relative value of the various routes, for local trade combined with a thorough traffic, etc.; in other words, any new road from here to the Colorado River should be built upon that route (not covered by an existing line, completed or projected), that will offer the greatest accommodation to the largest number of people; a route that will assist to build up our coast counties that already "bloom as the rose," and only need a line of rail to make the bloom profitable, and break down the last stronghold, where the great monopoly of the present battle against this city and her most important interests. The benefits that must accrue to this State, from a close and rapid connection

The Dream of Steam, 1854–1873 581

by rail with the magnificent counties that lay between this and the Bay of San Diego, along and in close proximity to the coast, can hardly be estimated—a large extent of which the Southern Pacific, or the suggested route by Mr. Goddard, will not benefit in the least.

Mr. Goddard is wrong when he says the Atlantic and Pacific survey commences at Mission Bay and follows the City Front to Fort Point. He is wrong when he says the survey follows the sinuosities of the coast to the Salinas Valley; wrong when he says it has grades of 112 feet per mile. He is 2,564 feet wrong if he says we rise to 5,189 feet at any one place on our entire line to the Colorado. He is wrong in making statements that are not true. He is wrong, as an engineer, in starting out on his wild career before overhauling the maps and profiles open to the examination of all at the office of the Atlantic and Pacific Railroad Company.

The surveyed route of the Atlantic and Pacific Railroad (subject to alterations and modifications, as the interests of this city may require), commences at the foot of Broadway, and following around the north shore line reaches North Beach, where it is proposed to locate the machine shops, car shops, round houses, cattle sheds, side tracks, etc., with a ferry landing for a connection with the Northern Pacific Coast Railroad to Sausalito. From North Beach the line crosses the range of hills back of the Presidio and reaches the coast at Nine Mile Point via Lake Honda and south end of Lake Merced. The heaviest grade for a short distance on this part of the line is 104 feet on leaving the Presidio. It can be reduced to about 90 on final location. From Nine Mile Point the line follows the coast to a point on the south bank of Pajaro River, 100 miles from San Francisco, the highest elevation reached being 460 feet, near Lake Honda, 250 feet near Pescadero, and 385 feet between Watsonville and Santa Cruz. Two of these elevations can be avoided by a change of line that would ignore the valley and town of Pescadero, the valley of the Pajaro, and the city of Watsonville. With the exception of the points and elevations named, the intermediate country between here and Watsonville lays upon a very uniform plain, the formation of the coast being not unlike two plateaus, one having an elevation approximately 40 feet, and the other 80 feet; and upon these we located our route— having run but a single preliminary line. We are convinced that, upon location, we can improve both grades and alignment. However, for the purposes that the survey was intended it answered well, and the company for whom the survey was made were satisfied.

On this, the *First Division*, the grades are light and uniform. The country along the coast will justify the building of a very expensive road and with a line of rail to San Francisco, will in a few years, be the most thrifty part of California.

The Second Division lays in the Salinas Valley, the same as Mr. Goodard's proposed route from Watsonville to San Miguel Mission, and as *he finds no fault with the same*, we will admit it is right, and pass to the *Third Division*, which offers about fifteen miles of *the only heavy work for the entire line from Watsonville to the Colorado River*, and that is on the range dividing San Luis Obispo Creek and Santa Margarita. This range will be pierced with a tunnel 4,000 feet long; the line will reach an elevation of 1,324 feet on this ridge. The preliminary survey established a line with 105-feet grades for about seven miles, 2.3 going up, and 4.96 down, going south. A careful final location will reduce these grades to about 100 feet.

From San Luis Obispo to the 400-mile stake in Santa Clara River Valley, east of San Buenaventura, there are no grades, by the amended line, that will exceed 53 to the mile.

From San Buenaventura, elevation 24 feet, the line follows up the valley of the Santa Clara River for 50 miles to the Owens River road, at which point an elevation of 1,120 feet is attained. From this point the summit of Soledad (elevation, 3,315 feet) is reached in 27.5 miles; this amount of 2,195 feet can be overcome with a maximum grade of 96 feet to the mile for a short distance. From the summit the line is an easy one for the entire distance to the Colorado River.

The highest point reached between the Mohave and the Colorado River, is 3,623 feet on Pluts Pass. Mr. Goddard's blunders originated from his ignorance of the fact that our final survey was not completed until June 20th, last, and the full notes have but lately been received at this office. The figures and data from which Mr. Goddard obtained the valuable information that he has (uninvited) spread before the public, were undoubtedly obtained from the report of the California Commissioners on the Atlantic and Pacific Railroad, who predicated the same (as far as the survey was concerned) upon the maps of the preliminary surveys sent to St. Louis from time to time, that they might be acquainted with progress of work, etc. Among those maps was showing a traverse line *via* Cedar Pass, an experimental line only, over which it never was proposed to build the road, although that line was practicable. If Mr. Goddard has read said report carefully, he must certainly have observed the following appendix to that report, relating to elevations, and which reads:

ALTITUDE OF IMPORTANT PLACES.

Western Colorado River bank	664
Summit Cedar Pass	5,187
Crossing Mojave river	2,400
Summit Soledad Pass	3,315
Junction of Soledad Pass and Coast Range lines on Santa Clara river	1,120
San Buenaventura	20
Santa Barbara	825
Summit San Marco Pass (tunnel)	868
Santa Inez river	532
Summit Foxen Cañon (tunnel)	1,444
Santa Maria river	200
San Luis Obispo	134
Summit Moro Pass	1,375
Nacimiento creek	600
Watsonville	28
Ridge between Watsonville and Santa Cruz	385
Santa Cruz	20
Tunnel near Pescadero creek	250
San Francisco	Pacific Ocean

The maximum grade on line in California is 112 feet per mile, for a length of 5.39 miles descent from Moro Pass Summit towards San Luis Obispo.

	MILES.
Total length of line from St. Louis to the Colorado river	1,732.01
Less already constructed	370.25
Length to be constructed	1,361.76
Do. in California	656
Total to be constructed	2,017.76
Whole distance from St. Louis to San Francisco	2,388.91

Estimated cost of building 2,017,76 miles of new road $80,000,000.

In conclusion, I can only say that the route will stand before the people upon its own merits, and I have grave doubts if the judgment of the gentleman named will stand the same test.

E. N. ROBINSON,
Engineer in charge of California Division of the Atlantic and Pacific Railroad.

419. *The Santa Cruz Sentinel,* August 17, 1872 (3:1)

Narrow Track Road.

Considerable discussion is going on about building a narrow track railroad from Watsonville or Pajaro depot to Santa Cruz. We are informed that farmers in the Pajaro Valley desire such a road, to ship grain at a low rate of freight to Santa Cruz, and thus reach a foreign market. We consider this narrow track enterprise, a snare and delusion, to injure the Atlantic and Pacific road. We have a good prospect that the main road will be built along the coast, especially if we save our money to help it. Once let a subsidy go into a side road, and the old San Jose road—built by Newhall, Polhemus & Co.—would soon gobble up our road. Investigation appears to show that the title in the San Jose road has never passed to the Stanford cormorants; the conditions of the transfer having never been complied with. If this be a fact, we would even have a harder taskmaster than Stanford & Co., were we to get into the legal meshes of the Southern Pacific. At any rate it shows why the Bank of California and its retainers are to establish an independent railroad company from San Francisco to the Colorado. The San Jose railroad company would own and control the road, and get a six or ten million subsidy for doing so. It would only be transferring the saddle from an old, broken down jade to a new courser, and the same race, for enslaving the people, would go on as usual, with renewed energy and enhanced capital.

420. *San Francisco Chronicle*, August 17, 1872 (3:4)

The Atlantic and Pacific.

Meeting of the Stockholders Yesterday.
A Plan of Operations Agreed Upon.

The subscribers to the capital stock of the California, Atlantic and Pacific Railroad held a meeting yesterday at the rooms of the Chamber of Commerce. R. G. Sneath presided. He said that the object of the meeting was to hear the reports of Committees which had been appointed by the stockholders and the Committee of One Hundred respectively, to organize the company and make the necessary arrangements for its incorporation. Mr. Sneath read the

ARTICLES OF INCORPORATION

Of the California, Atlantic and Pacific Railroad Company, which provide that it shall be constructed from a point on the west side of the Bay of San Francisco, through the counties of San Mateo, Santa Clara, Santa Cruz, Monterey, San Luis Obispo, Santa Barbara, Los Angeles and San Bernardino, to a point on the Colorado river, near the thirty-fifth parallel of latitude.

The Trustees are thirteen, ten of whom are as follows: A. Hayward, J. Seligman, — Steinhart, L. B. Jones, M. J. O'Connor, Richard Tobin, L. B. Benchley, Albert Dibblee, Judge Hager, and R. G. Sneath, of the city of San Francisco, and Mr. Coffin of St. Louis. Two more St. Louis men are to compose the Board. The capital stock is to be $30,000,000, divided into 300,000 shares of $100 each.

Mr. Sneath then read

THE PLAN OF ORGANIZATION.

He first said that the documents set forth only the general plan. The details could not be mentioned yet; but the whole of the plan would be submitted to the approval of the subscribers before application would be made to the Board of Supervisors for a subsidy. It was the design of all the promoters that everything connected with the management of inauguration of the scheme should be open to the public, to the minutest detail. He then read the plan as follows:

We, the undersigned, do hereby subscribe for and agree to take the number of shares set opposite to our names respectively, in the capital stock of the California, Atlantic and Pacific Railroad Company, and to pay for the same in such installments as may be called for by the Board of Directors of the company.

And we agree and consent to the following terms of subscriptions as constituting a contract of organization, which shall be binding upon, and control now and forever the company, and all subscribers and stockholders thereof and their assigns, and shall run with the stock to all owners and holders thereof:

TERMS OF SUBSCRIPTION:

First—There shall be reserved until after the general election of the year 1872, shares of stock corresponding in normal value to the aggregate aids or subsidies authorized by the Acts of the Legislature of the State of California, empowering the several counties to aid in the construction of railroads. Any aid or subsidy granted to the company under said Acts shall be credited on the books of the company as received to such aid or subsidy, with the name of the county, or city and county, by which the same was granted; and the company shall, in consideration thereof, issue stock of corresponding amount as full paid and unassessable stock to fifty Trustees, jointly, in trust to hold the same, and to receive and dispose of the dividends thereof for the benefits of the body politic granting such aid or subsidy, whenever such body may become authorized to accept, and shall accept, the beneficial interest of said stock. The said Trustees shall vote upon and represent the stock to issue to them, and shall have power to fill vacancies in their own number.

Second—All contracts for work or material shall be open to free competition.

Third—No Director or officer of the company shall be interested in any contract let by the company.

Fourth—Consent is given that the Directors of this company, by a two-thirds vote of their whole number, may amalgamate and consolidate this company with the Atlantic and Pacific Railroad Company, or the capital stock, debts, property, assets and franchise of the one company with those of the other company; or may, by a like vote, make subscription to the capital stock of the Atlantic and Pacific Railroad Company, and make payment therefor by a transfer of the capital stock, property, assets and franchise of this company; or may, by the like vote, make the other transfer or disposition thereof to effectually accomplish a union with the Atlantic and Pacific Railroad Company for the construction of a through line of road from San Francisco to St. Louis. But such amalgamation, consolidation, subscription, transfer or disposition shall only be upon the following conditions:

HOW THE MONEYS ARE TO BE EXPENDED.

First—For each one hundred shares of the preferred stock of the Atlantic and Pacific Company subscribed for there shall be issued to this company one hundred shares of said preferred stock, and thirty-three and one-third shares of the common stock of the Atlantic and Pacific Railroad Company.

Second—All moneys so expended shall be under the control of California Directors and within the State of California.

Fifth—All certificates of stock shall bear a general reference to these terms of subscription and the whole of article fourth.

Mr. McRuer said it ought to be understood that the

large subscriptions had been made not for the purpose of controlling the organization, but merely to supply the necessity of perfecting it.

On motion the report of the Committee was adopted, and the papers approved.

MR. FAY'S RESOLUTION.

Mr. Caleb T. Fay offered the following resolution, which on motion of Mr. Hatch, were unanimously adopted:

Resolved. That seventeen hundred subscribers to the California, Atlantic and Pacific Railroad in the short space of twenty days is evidence that the people desire to own and operate a great through competing railroad line to the East, through the Atlantic and Pacific Railroad, and in their own interest.

Resolved. That the policy of the Atlantic and Pacific Railroad Company shall be to foster and protect and employ *home labor* in all its branches—the farmer, the mechanic, the laborer, the merchant.

Resolved. That the alacrity with which the masses respond to the call for subscriptions to this road is a source of congratulation, and the distribution of the stock is a solid guarantee of good faith toward the people.

The meeting then adjourned.

421. *San Francisco Bulletin*, August 14, via *The Santa Cruz Sentinel*, August 24, 1872 (1:9)

The Difference.

The fact that about fifteen hundred of our citizens have

subscribed about $800,000 towards the stock of the California Atlantic and Pacific Railroad Company, in advance of its formal organization, indicates the popularity of the movement for a direct competing railroad across the continent. In contrast to this fact, we see the Colorado River Company, with only a score or so of subscribers; confessing that it cannot do anything without a subsidy of ten millions, and aiming at no more than to build without a subsidy from the city, if this Company does not take it off their hands. The projectors of this Colorado river scheme have subscribed nominally four or five millions, but their subscriptions do not represent as much investment of private money as the lesser subscriptions to the California Atlantic and Pacific. The latter are made on a strict cash basis, and do not contemplate a transfer of Central and Southern Pacific bonds. Whatever the city votes in aid of this road she will not offer as a gift, but put into the stock as an investment, under her own control, securing thereby a genuine competing railroad, on a direct route to St. Louis and the Atlantic.

422. *The Santa Cruz Sentinel*, August 24, 1872 (2:3)

Coast Railroad Meeting.

Spanishtown, (Half Moon Bay), August 20th.—A Coast Railroad meeting was held here last night. The citizens of Half Moon Bay and Pescadero met at Pacific Hall, Half Moon Bay, and appointed an Executive Committee to correspond with Santa Cruz and San Francisco, and to open books for subscription. The people are determined to have a Coast Road.

This is the proper course to take. Now let Santa Cruz follow suit. We should hold a public meeting and show the people of San Francisco that we are alive to interests of the Atlantic and Pacific road, and will vote $250,000 worth of stock, and subscribe as much, provided the road is built according to the route surveyed by the company, and the plat filed in Washington and accepted by the Government. We believe enough money could be raised along the coast and from this county and San Mateo, to grade the route (outside of the two tunnels and bridging) the entire distance. The right of way and land for depots, stations, side tracks, turntables, turn-outs, watering tanks, &c., would be donated free of cost in [tn s] county, and mostly in San Mateo. Residents along the coast, adjacent to the line would do the work, and furnish ties, lumber, &c., at a low rate payable in stock, and everyone would put their shoulder to the wheel to aid the enterprise. No one doubts this, and let the company send or come and they will find it so. We have already $100,000 voted, which could be made immediately available, and $150,000 more would be added this fall election, and the work would be accomplished. The taxes on forty-five or sixty-five miles of railroad in this county, would almost pay the enhanced taxation, not taking into account the new property accumulated, and additional number of tax-payers to be added, besides the increased value in land and products all along the line, and west of the Santa Cruz range of mountains. Let us start a call for a public meeting and appoint a committee to aid the citizens of Half Moon Bay and Pescadero in their efforts. We want no other road but the coast railroad now, and let us all work for it, talk for it, and act for it. It is time enough to talk about branch lines up Soquel, San Lorenzo and other creeks, or a narrow track road to Watsonville, after we fail (if fail we must) in our present effort. We care northing for the committee of a "100" or the squabbles of the city in this matter; sour interests are at stake and we must be alive or the golden opportunities will vanish before united action can be taken and a fair showing made. A vast coal field has just been discovered on the line, or near it, of the road, this side of the mountain; let that fact be made available; another inducement is a large body of iron ore, between Pescadero and Santa Cruz, sufficient to furnish iron to build the road. A Mr. Brooks is our informant, and he says there is abundance of iron both in grains and large masses to open manufacturing establishments. This is probably the belt of ore referred to some time ago, by a member of the Natural Sciences, San Francisco. That we have abundance of both coal and iron we have no doubt, and Mr. Lockhardt, an eminent mineralogist who has just inspected the prospects, will in a short time report even more favorably than we could expect. There are five different stratas of coal underlaying the sand and slate ledges, from the headwaters of the San Lorenzo creek, to way south of Peach Tree Valley in Monterey county, so says prospectors who have explored the minerals and tested their merits.

423. *The Santa Cruz Sentinel*, August 24, 1872 (2:4)

The Peoples' Railroad.—What the people think of the contract proposed to be neutered into between San Francisco and Stanford & Co., is shown by the gain in subscriptions to the California, Atlantic and Pacific road. Since the proposition was announced, there has been one hundred and fifty-two new names added to the list, aggregating $112,600. The total subscriptions now amount to $995,300. It really begins to look encouraging.

424. *San Francisco Examiner*, August 27, 1872 (3:3)

BOARD OF SUPERVISORS.

The San Francisco and Colorado River Railroad Asking for a Subsidy.

The regular weekly meeting of the Board of Supervisors was held last evening, Mayor Alvord presiding. Petition and protests were received and various referred...

Colorado River Railroad Company.

The following petition was read and placed on file:

To His Honor the Mayor, and to the Honorable Board of Supervisors of the city and county of San Francisco:—Your petitioners, the San Francisco and Colorado River Railway Company, respectfully represent that they are duly incorporated under the laws of the State of California, for the purpose of constructing and maintaining a first-class railroad, commencing at the harbor of the city and county of San Francisco, in the Bay of San Francisco, on or in Mission Bay, connected therewith running thence on or near the water of said county of San Francisco to the intersection of the line between said last named county and the county of San Mateo; thence through said county and along or near the bay first named, passing through or near the town of San Mateo, until the line between the county last named and that of Santa Clara is intersected; thence, in its general course southeasterly, to the city of San José; thence southerly, or nearly south, to the town of Gilroy in said county; thence nearly south to the line dividing the last named county and the county of Monterey; thence its general course southerly to the town of San Juan; thence, by general course southwesterly, to the Salinas river, passing at or near Salinas city....

Wherefore, your petitioners pray that aid may be granted by said city and county in the construction of said railroad, by the issue of bonds to the amount of ten million dollars, payable in gold coin of the United States twenty years after the date of issue and bearing interest at the rate of six per cent. per annum, payable semi-annually, in like gold coin; and that your honorable body submit the question of granting such aid to the qualified electors of said city and county at the next general election in accordance with the statutes in such cases made and provided. Signed: J. Mora Moss, Peter Donahue, John Parrot, H. M. Newhall, W. C. Ralston, W. T. Coleman, Geo. H. Howard, R. B. Woodward, John O. Earl, Josiah Belden, Michael Reese, Albert Gansl, H. D. Bacon....

A petition was read from the California Atlantic and Pacific Railroad Company asking for a $10,000,000 subsidy.

425. *Sacramento Bee*, August 27, 1872 (3:7)

There is now little doubt that the order introduced in the Board of Supervisors last evening, and referred to the City and County Attorney, providing for submitting the question of a ten million dollar subsidy to a vote of the people at the November general election will be adopted at the next meeting of the Board. The action of the Board, in placing on file, without reference, the petition of the Atlantic and Pacific Railroad for a subscription of ten millions to its capital stock, apparently indicates that the proposition is not in favor with a majority of the Board.

426. *The Pajaronian*, August 29, 1872 (2:1)

Rumors from time to time reach us regarding a narrow gauge railroad from this place to Aptos, and perhaps to Santa Cruz. The question is yet in its incipiency, and not much can be said in regard to the matter. We should be in favor of the road if the people are not to be unduly oppressed in its building—in other words, if the scheme will pay, push it through. We shall have more to say hereafter on the same subject.

427. *The Santa Cruz Sentinel*, August 31, 1872 (2:1-2)
RAILROAD MEETING.

On Wednesday evening last a large, respectable and enthusiastic meeting was held in the Court House, to "aid in assisting the location of the coast line of Railroad." This meeting, according to our notion, was called, auxiliary to the meeting held at Halfmoon Bay, of citizens along the coast, from Pescadero, in San Mateo county, to make a showing to the Atlantic and Pacific Railroad Company, of our willingness to aid the enterprise. That the Halfmoon Bay meeting was a success, will be seen by proceedings printed on our first page, and had the meeting in the Court House adhered to the same line of policy, our meeting would have been fruitful of glorious results. It may be that the General Committee appointed, will redeem this want of action, and still crown the meeting with success. The Committee is very good, in part, but it contains names who are non-progressive, and would just as soon as not that Santa Cruz should plod ahead in her own slow way, as long as money is worth 1½ per cent. per month, and goods can be sold at 50 per cent. profit. We have every confidence in Mr. D. Tuthill, the Chairman of the General Committee, that he will do what is right, guided by the lamp of wisdom and experience, and shall expect a hearty co-operation with San Mateo County residents, on the coast, who held the Halfmoon Bay meeting. To do this it is desirable to have an Executive Committee to visit settlers and land-owners on the proposed route, and acquire the right of way and secure sufficient land for depots, watering places, turn-outs, side-tracks, &c.; also ascertain the amount all tax-payers would be willing to subscribe, (in stock) and the county give (in stock) as a subsidy to secure the road. We contend that the county could afford to take $250,000 in stock, and individual tax-payers would find it to their advancement to subscribe 5 per cent. of their assessment returned this year. Our property assessment is $7,225,978.00 or over, and this plan would probably give a subscription of five hundred thousand dollars, which with the subsidy and a free right of way, and donated lands for depots, terminus &c., would undoubtedly secure us the road. The importance of the road is, at all events, sufficient to prompt a trial and an effort to accomplish the object. We firmly believe that the road will be built down the coast, if we aid to the extent foreshadowed. Is the road with the required amount, is a question for tax-payers to determine.

The meeting held on Wednesday evening was well attended by our best men, and we are sorry to say there was a spirit of opposition disseminated to divide and destroy its usefulness. That any man in his *sober* senses (one of the speakers is exempt from the *italic* allusion) should have done anything, or said a word in the meeting against the coast road (to aid which the meeting was called) we are astonished. Men rose from their seats and advocated other routes narrow-track roads, 3-foot gauge roads, &c., which distracted and confounded the friends of the Atlantic and Pacific road, as surveyed along the coast. Men came there cocked (or half-cocked) with cut and dried speeches, and committees primed to pervert the real intent of the meeting, in order to gain strength, for some pet measure, or private scheme to build some other road. Some said it was "too late," the route had already been located on the other side of the divide, and the petition to the San Francisco Board of Supervisors by the company had been sent in defining the route. We admitted such a petition had been sent in, but has that subsidy or any other been voted? There are four subsidies now being discussed by the "One Hundred" in San Francisco—one for the northern route, one to build a bridge for the Central Pacific, one for the San Francisco and Colorado, and one for the California

Branch of the Atlantic and Pacific—and it is very questionable, whether either road, at the coming election, will be voted a subsidy, because Stanford controls the elements of the Committee, or city, and will have his grist ground first, or the mill shan't run. Now, Elihu Anthony, R. C. Kirby, F. A. Hihn, S. W. Fields, and others, who gave their views at the meeting, should know that the only company that will get a subsidy is the California branch of the Atlantic and Pacific road, and that, if we act liberally, in good faith, the road will come down the coast, or the offer will be plainly rejected for good reasons. The subscriptions, in San Francisco, already amount to a million and a half, subscribed by over two thousand tax-payers; before the lists are all taken in and subscriptions closed, it is expected there will be 3,500 names on the list, subscribing over three millions of dollars. Then they will commence business in earnest by electing a President, Vice President, Secretary, Treasurer, and Board of Directors. The next step taken will be to locate the road, and every subscriber will have a vote, Santa Cruzans as well as San Franciscans and residents of San Mateo county. Suppose each man has a vote for every hundred dollars he subscribes, for officers and location—who will be elected, and what route adopted? Let those who asserted "It is too late," "We c-a-n-'-t do it," answer the question.

It is a straw in our favor that the terminus of the Atlantic and Pacific will be located at North Beach, San Francisco, and not at Mission Bay, or China Basin, as first contemplated. This is done to the more readily connect with the Northern Pacific terminus at Sausalito, and facilitate the entrance into the city, by tunneling Russian Hill, or getting part of the Presidio reservation for depot sites. There is no telling what railroad men intend doing, and it is idle to talk and foolish to say: *"We can't do a thing"*— *"It is too late"*—when no trial has been made or offer extended. Never despair, say we, and to pull your longest and strongest on the last dip you make, before sinking is a good rule to act on in this matter. We want a railroad, and must have it; the best road for our interest, at present, is the coast road; let us all work unitedly together to secure it, and we firmly believe it will be built, right in front of our doors. Never give up until the last button is gone, then we will congratulate each other on the fight, if not on success, and turn our attention to other schemes and roads, which formed the apple of discord at the recent meeting. If it is a narrow-track road, so be it; if it is a three-foot gauge or Watsonville branch, we are content; or if the Soquel route to Santa Clara is adopted, as being feasible, so much the better, it puts us in more *direct* communication with San Francisco. But if failing in all these, we have no other recourse, let us build a road of our own and connect with San Diego. Tom Scott may put on a line of steamers from Japan, China and Australia, and make San Diego in a few years, the metropolis of the Pacific Coast, then our interest will be in that direction, and it will be to them we must look to for aid and protection. That will, in such contingency, be the market for our powder, safety-fuse, paper, lime, leather, glue, soap, and many other manufacturers.

There are men here who "pooh-pooh" at the idea—men who are interested in keeping the price of wood and lumber down, because they are dealing in it, and shipping to the lower country; they too, will see in time that burlesquing a railroad meeting was not as profitable as they had expected. We want a market for our manufactures and products, that is constant, reliable and tangible, and the only road, we infer, that will give it to us with quick dispatch and full returns, is the Atlantic and Pacific Railroad along the coast.

428. *The Santa Cruz Sentinel,* August 31, 1872 (2:2)
Railroad Meeting.

A meeting of citizens of Santa Cruz, was held at the Court House, on Wednesday evening, August 28th, to adopt such measures as might be deemed necessary to induce the Atlantic and Pacific Railroad Company to construct their road down the Coast.

On motion, J. S. Green was elected Chairman and Roger Conant, Sec'y. The Chairman of the meeting stated that the object of the meeting was to devise some plan to obtain a railroad through this section of the country along the coast and to correspond with other parties along the route on the subject.

Mr. Adams said several letters had been received, on the subject, by Mr. Besse—should like to hear them read.

Mr. J. Green—The letters are in the hands of Mr. Besse who has produced them in the meeting.

Col. Heath—I move that an Executive Committee of five be appointed, consisting of A. Pray, Sr., Wm.

Cooper, D. Tuthill, E. Briody, R. C. Kirby and J. N. Besse, to take charge of this matter.

Mr. Kirby, Mr. Hihn and Mr. Anthony, advocated the construction of the road from Santa Cruz to Watsonville, and in favor of petitioning the Board of Supervisors to increase the subsidy from $100,000 to $250,000, and also the taking of stock by the people, and also to change the road from a Broad to a Narrow Gauge.

Mr. Kooser and Col. Heath spoke in opposition to this plan, and in favor of getting the co-operation of the Atlantic and Pacific Co., to build a road down the coast. The resolutions of Half Moon Bay were read, after which a general committee of seven, consisting of D. Tuthill, G. B. V. DeLamater, J. N. Besse, A. Pray Sr., L. Heath, John Werner, Edward Briody, with power to add to the committee, so as to have the different sections through which the road would pass, represented, was approved. On motion, the chairman, J. S. Green, was added to the committee. The committee were instructed to correspond with committees in other sections, as to right of way, and to appoint such special committees as might be deemed necessary to secure subscriptions &c.

On motion the meeting adjourned.

R. CONANT, Secretary

429. *The Santa Cruz Sentinel*, August 31, 1872 (3:1)

Nil Desperandum.

One of the speakers at the Railroad meeting said, "we can't do it"—"we are too late with this Railroad meeting to effect anything." We say it is not too late, and we can yet accomplish something. Let a committee be appointed on right of way—such men as A. Craig of Watsonville, Claus Spreckels of Aptos, Ben Porter of Soquel, G. W. Davis (the architect), Mr. Baldwin (of Wiley & Baldwin), Geo. P. Laird of Davenport's Landing, W. W. Waddell, Omar Steele and others in this county—and after they have viewed the route, secured the right of way and a promise of subscriptions, they can confer with the Half Moon Bay committee, who would join in a report to the San Francisco committee of the California, Atlantic & Pacific road. Let us see what befell a "can't do it." In 1864 a party of four men started from Mono Lake across the desert to Carson Valley; they lost their way, foolish counsel bewildered them, and they were perishing for want of water. One of the party proposed to dig for water, they had picks and shovels with them; the "can't do it" man laid down and said to the "it is too late" man, I can go no further. Well, says Dubious Doubtington, the third, we will proceed any how with Mr. Try-it-to-the-last, and see what can be done. They started, and returned to seek "can't do it," who they found, with mining tools—pick and shovel—dead where they left him. They immediately proceeded to dig a grave and bury him where found, when, to their surprise, after digging two feet deep, the water rushed into the hole so fast that they had to seek higher ground and dig a new grave. Now this is a fact, and only shows that it is never too late to try. It was the cry of "can't do it"—"it is too late" that caused the death Had the party dug for water or made a good, manly trial, the man would have been saved. This little story is no fiction, but the actual truth. Our local "can't do it" and "it is too late" speakers should apply the moral.

430. *San Mateo Gazette* via *The Santa Cruz Sentinel*, August 31, 1872 (4:1-2)

Our Coast Railroad.

Pursuant to a very short notice a public meeting of the inhabitants of this township was held on Monday evening in the Public Hall. Messrs. Brad. Weeks, Alex. Moore, B. Hayward and B. V. Weeks attended as a delegation from the citizens of Pescadero, who had been invited to be present. The meeting was called to order by C. E. Kelly, and presided over by S. Walker, J. P. W. H. Campbell, having been appointed Secretary, read the notice concerning the meeting, which was signed by S. Walker, J. P., Alex. Gordon, C. E. Kelly, A. Guerrero, John Johnston and John Higgins, the business mentioned therein being "To consider the best means of obtaining railway accommodation, and to take such steps as may be deemed most advisable towards promoting that object." A letter from E. N. Robinson, C. E., engineer of the Atlantic & Pacific R. R. Co., endorsing the Coast route, and making some important suggestions, was also read.

The Secretary proceeded to point out the importance of immediate action being taken, if they wish to secure any railroad, but especially if they were desirous to have the main track, competing eastern line, brought along by the Coast, which was in fact the only real, legitimate, available, competitive route, geographically or beneficially speaking. Why, if the Atlantic & Pacific Co.'s surveyed narrow gauge way, be not an opposition to Stanford & Co., "a benefit rather," Mr. Doyle would have it, why is it that the friends, backers and sympathizers of the Central Pacific Railroad Company totally ignore and try to blot out "the absurd Pigeon Point route?" Because they know that after it is built the existing company's occupation is like Othello's in the passenger traffic at all events, for at least six months of the year. They would like, wouldn't they, to have the San Jose road taken off their hands, and with San Francisco's subsidy and the people's subscription, pay off the old proprietary?

The San Francisco people he hoped were not so green, however, as to be snared thus; the present compromise going on in the city was a farce. The citizens there would not tolerate it. Let them be up and doing and get the people of San Francisco to take an interest in their road by taking an interest in it themselves. The Coast folks had been slumbering in blissful ignorance and security, having relied on the management of the People's independent line adopting, as a matter of course, the surveyed track of the A. & P. Co. But they had "reckoned without their host," as daily events in San Francisco clearly indicate. If they wanted a railroad they must put their hands in their pockets—in the nineteenth century this was the only way of going about business to be successful—and assist the Atlantic and Pacific Co., or any other Company that is willing to open up communication, past their doors, and between San Francisco and the Colorado River. Some of their leading men were coming forward with handsome subscriptions. Mr. Gorlon who, he regretted, was unavoidably absent, had promised $10,000.

Judge Templeton, who was here yesterday favored the movement. Dr. McLean, a San Francisco gentleman, will give $1,000 at least, and Messrs. L. Cockburn, Orrin Brown, Major Downing, F. C. Gilbert, and many others not here to-night, had offered their aid in the enterprise. In fact, he knew not a single land-owner who would refuse to contribute. He was not a property-holder, himself and would probably be leaving the district in a few weeks, but he felt an interest in the prosperity of a neighborhood in which he had resided for four years. During that four years they had been languishing, standing, still comparatively, and if they lived there four hundred years, things would just be in the same state, without the great prosperous civilizing advantages of railway communication.

Mr. C. E. Kelly entered into figures to prove that a Coast road would be a paying one from the very commencement, after its completion to the farming district; the cost of carriage from hence being at present from $4 to $5 per ton, while the Bay freight against which the San Jose cars had to contend was only $1 per ton. The traffic between San Francisco and Santa Cruz, he believed to be greater than that between the metropolis and San Jose when the railway between those latter places was about to be built.

He failed to see how Mr. Doyle could make a competing line, down by San Mateo, pay after the first twenty miles were constructed. They were weak over here compared to the Ralstons, the Haywards, and the Parrots of the other side of the mountain, but they had still some pluck and energy, and commercial enterprise amongst them, and united, he thought they would sum up one or two Ralstons or Haywards at all events. Let them then stand forward and subscribe to their utmost capacity, and Eastern or English capitalists will soon come to their aid, and put their road through.

Mr. B. Hayward said the people of Pescadero are in favor of the project, and will subscribe to the full extent of their means. Even small property-holders will take $1,000 in stock. He himself was not an extensive landowner, yet he would put his name down for $4,000, perhaps more. The calculation is that at least thirty Pescaderians will average $5,000 apiece. Santa Cruz was in favor of the Northern Coast route and would soon abandon the Pajaro scheme, which was something like making a right-angle to get to San Francisco. Mr. H concluded by throwing out some valuable hints as to united action with Santa Cruz and his town.

Mr. Guerrero considered it would be desirable to consult with the property-owners of the San Pedro ranch, also with those citizens of San Francisco, who from interest or knowledge of its advantages, were favorable to a Coast line. He was sure Mr. Tobin, Mr. Mahoney and others would exert themselves on behalf of the shore railroad.

The following resolutions were then put the meeting and carried *nem com*.

1—That this meeting, believing in the necessary which exists for immediate railroad accommodation along the Coast, pledge itself, on behalf of the inhabitants of this section, to use every means in its power to carry out this object.

2—That for this purpose subscription lists be now opened to the capital stock of the Atlantic and Pacific R. R. Co., or to that of any railroad company local or foreign that will construct a coast railway forthwith, along or as near thereto as possible, the route surveyed by E. N. Robinson, viz: From San Francisco, southward by way of the San Pedro Creek, Half Moon Bay, Pescadero and Santa Cruz, such railway to connect with the 35th or 32nd parallel road.

3—That a committee, consisting of J. Walker, J. P., A. Gordon, C. E. Kelley, A. Guerrero, John Johnston, John Higgins, J. Downing, W. Griffith, R. H. Hatch, A. Dobbel, W. Raynor and W. H. Campbell, with power to add to their number—be formed for the purpose of canvassing the district for subscriptions, and for conducting such executive business as may be necessary for the promotion and furtherance of the contemplated railroad organization.

4—That the citizens of San Francisco, Pescadero and Santa Cruz, be invited to co-operate in this movement to establish a coast road, and develop the resources of the hitherto neglected seaboard of California.

5—That this meeting be adjourned till Friday next at 3 p.m.

The committee have commenced canvassing this morning. Next week I hope to be able to report good progress.   BORAK.

Half Moon Bay, August 20th, 1872.

431. *The Santa Cruz Sentinel*, September 7, 1872 (1:8)
Railroad Meeting at Pescadero

At a Railroad Meeting held in Pescadero, August 23d, to take action in regard to a coast railroad running from San Francisco to Santa Cruz, I. C. Steele was elected President, and I. R. Goodspeed, Secretary.

Resolved, That this meeting, believing in the necessity which exists for immediate railroad accommodation along the coast, pledges itself on behalf of the people along the coast, to use every effort in its power to carry out this object.

Resolved, That we are in favor of an independent railroad from the City of San Francisco, running south on the coast to connect with either the 32d or 35th parallel, and if any railroad company will give the proper guarantee and assurance that it will build such a railroad, we will give to the extant of our ability for this purpose.

But it appears that none of the railroad companies will build their road on the coast, then we are in favor of an independent, narrow gauge railroad, to be *commenced* within *one* year.

A committee of ten was appointed to solicit subscriptions to the coast railroad, consisting of Braddock Weeks, I. C. Steele, Alex. Moore, John McCormick, John Anderson, B. Hayward, S. J. Finney, George Harrington, S. H. Prebble, B. M. Scofield.

The Secretary was instructed to correspond with Santa Cruz and Half Moon Bay to see what action they will take in calling a general Railroad Convention, to be held at Pescadero as soon as possible, to unite on some definite plan to pursued in regard to a coast railroad from San Francisco to Santa Cruz, or to connect with the 32d or 35th parallel road.

Adjourned to August 30th.

R. GOODSPEED, Secretary.

432. *The Santa Cruz Sentinel*, September 7, 1872 (2:1)

Narrow Gauge Railroad.

To the Committee on Railroads:—The Atlantic and Pacific R. R. Co,. having changed their route, and the owners of the Southern Pacific Railroad Co. not complying with their promise to build a wide gauge Railroad, from Santa Cruz to Watsonville, we are forced to conclude that if we want a Railroad *we must build it ourselves.* A wide gauge railroad from Santa Cruz connecting with the Southern Pacific Railroad, near Watsonville cannot be built for less than $25,000 per mile, or, say $500,000. In addition to the subsidy granted for this purpose, amounting to $100,000, the further sum of $400,000 would have to be raised by private subscription and loans. This is impossible.

We must therefore build a cheaper road; a narrow gauge (3 foot wide) Railroad can be built from the Pajaro depot to Santa Cruz, for $12,500 per mile, with equipment, or, say $250,000, and can be continued further along the coast to the northern line of our county, without equipment, at a cost of 12,500 per mile, or, say $250,000 more, The utmost amount of private subscription for any railroad now obtainable in this county, and from non-residents interested, is $100,000. The balance must be raised by county aid and by loans. In order to get county aid, we must make it to the interest of every taxpayer to grant such aid. It is therefore proposed that a company be organized to build a narrow gauge Railroad, commencing on the line of the Southern Pacific Railroad, near the Pajaro river, and running thence along or near the survey of the Atlantic and Pacific Railroad, along or near the coast to the Northern Boundary line of our county, a distance of about 40 miles. That county aid be solicited to the amount of $6,000 per mile, such aid to be in lieu of the subsidy already granted. That subscriptions to the stock of said company be solicited from every person interested in this county. That the right of way and necessary depot grounds be secured, and that the citizens of all the coast counties from San Francisco to San Diego, be invited to organize like companies in their respective counties, in order to secure the construction of a 3 foot gauge Railroad, from San Francisco along or near the coast, to the southern line of the State.

Santa Cruz county should certainly take the initiative in such a movement, because if even partially successful, or in other words, if we should only secure the construction of such a railroad from Watsonville to Santa Cruz, it would be of an immense benefit to the county at large, by the development and opening of the varied resources of more than three-fourths of our county, and by the large increase of taxable value. But it is reasonable to expect that if a narrow gauge Railroad constructed from Watsonville to Santa Cruz should prove a financial success, of which there is hardly any doubt, the means would not long be wanted to extend the road both North and South, and thereby the permanent prosperity of our county would be secured. F. A. HIHN,

Santa Cruz, September 4th, 1872.

433. *The Santa Cruz Sentinel*, September 7, 1872 (2:1)

Committee Railroad Meeting.

Santa Cruz, Friday Evening, August 30th, 1872.

The Executive Railroad Committee appointed at a meeting of citizens of Santa Cruz, held at the Court House, Wednesday evening, August 28th, met at DeLamater's Hall at 8 o'clock. Present—J. N. Besse, D. Tuthill, A Pray, G. B. V. DeLamater, John Werner, L. Heath. Absent—J. S. Green.

D. Tuthill, who was appointed Chairman of the committee, by the original meeting of Wednesday last, called the committee to order, and on motion of G. B. V. DeLamater was elected Secretary.

On motion of J. N. Besse—The Secretary was instructed to correspond with parties at Halfmoon Bay and Pescadero, and to state to them that it is the opinion of a majority of this committee, that Santa Cruz county—in case the coast Railroad was built—,would give a subsidy of two hundred and fifty thousand ($250,000) dollars and right of way; and perhaps double that amount. And also request of them to report to this committee, the amount their county would give in subsidy and subscriptions for a Railway from San Francisco to Watsonville, by the route proposed; and if right of way would be given.

On motion, D. Tuthill was appointed a committee of one to report at the next meeting of this committee, what has been done by the Santa Cruz and Watsonville Railroad Company? What that company propose doing? Whether any surveys have been made, and whether any measures have been taken to secure the right of way from here to Watsonville?

434. *San Francisco Post*, September 2, via *The Santa Cruz Sentinel*, September 7, 1872 (2:1)

A Subsidy for Coast Road.—Two more applications for subsidy were made to the Board of Supervisors last evening—one from the North Pacific road, which will run out of Sausalito through the coast counties; and the other the Santa Cruz road. The latter road is one that, in some way or other, our citizens ought to build, as it will open up all the rich coast valleys [too faint to read] do better than to give it something.

435. *San Mateo Gazette* via *The Santa Cruz Sentinel*, September 7, 1872 (4:1-2)

Our Coast Railroad.

The adjourned public railway meeting took place at the Pacific Hall, on Friday afternoon. Samuel Walker, Esq., occupied the chair. After the reading and confirmation of the minutes of the meeting held on the 19th instant, the Secretary (W. H. Campbell) reported that he had communicated with Hon. F. A. Hihn and J. N. Besse, of Santa Cruz, and with gentlemen in Pescadero and San Francisco favorably to the movement, which they all had so much at heart. He had also sent communications to the San Mateo *Gazette*, and to the principal San Francisco journals. At a meeting of the executive committee, held on Tuesday, a written heading to the subscription list was submitted and approved. Books had been got ready and were being distributed amongst the collectors. Since last they met Governor Purdy, on behalf of the San Francisco, San Mateo and Watsonville Railroad Co., had paid the town a visit for the purpose of securing a right of way for his company, that being the one which originally had the coast survey made by E. N. Robinson. This company had already a subscribed capital of $1,000,000. Its proprietary were well known men of wealth. They expected a small subsidy, say of $1,300,000, from San Francisco, and Santa Cruz would also help them. Less than $3,000,000 would build the road, which would be a narrow gauge one; ties being put in, whereby a broad gauge track could be added by the laying of a single rail. Now they were bound to assist this company all in their power, provided they did the fair thing by them. He believed in their *bona fides*, and that they meant business, but in case they were slack in coming up to the mark, why they had the great Tom Scott now in San Francisco to appeal to. It would do well to direct the attention of "the railroad king" to the advantages of the coast route. He questioned if Col. Scott had ever been informed of these advantages. Possibly he entertained the notion, held by so many Californians, that the Pacific seaboard, between San Francisco and Santa Cruz, consisted of rocks, mountains, chaparral and grizzlies.

The Dream of Steam, 1854–1873   615

Mr. A. Guerrero, as the representative of the largest landowners in the district, was perfectly willing to grant a right of way to the San Francisco, San Mateo and Watsonville Railroad Co., or to any other company which might apply; but only on satisfactory assurance that the work would be commenced within twelve months, and carried steadily on until completed. Further, that no transfer be made of such title to any other company. Thus the proprietary now procuring the right of way could not possess the same for more trading or speculative purposes. He was perfectly satisfied in the ability of the gentlemen, whose names Governor Purdy had mentioned, to carry out any enterprise which they took in hand. With such names as R. Robin, J. B. Felton, D. Mahoney and Michael Reese, interested in and associated with the project, it could not fall through. The Guerrero and Denniston ranches had already subscribed $15,000 to the stock of the first company that broke ground; and perhaps when things were in a little more forward state, they would double the amount.

Mr. D. McPherson (Redwood City) remarked that from the present isolated position of this portion of the coast, but very imperfect knowledge of its natural wealth, advantages and resources, existed outside the few whom business, pleasure or accident brought over the mountains. The people of Redwood City knew what they wanted and sympathized with them in their efforts to get a railroad; but the residents here must show what they mean, by making active exertions, particularly in the way of taking stock, when called upon so to do. He meant himself to be a stockholder in their line. They had among them men of substance. Capital is well represented here. Your rich soil is capital. Contribute then in proportion to your capital and ample funds might be raised within the people of the coast to construct a road. Santa Cruz, surrounded as she is by great factories, had already granted a subsidy of $100,000, which would be increased by subscription to $200,000. This sum would be available for the coast road, as the $100,000 is in the hands of a local Co., who incorporated only to hold the money that it might not lapse to the county. Hon. F. A. Hihn was President of this company, and every body knew who is familiar with railroad efforts in Santa Cruz he was a worker in earnest. Probably he (Hihn) would take $50,000 stock himself. The people of Santa Cruz would subscribe liberally, being much exercised over the question. The larger the number of subscribers' names obtained and the bigger the gross total amount contributed, the greater the chances of success, for these are but substantial endorsement of public opinion on the subject, besides being an encouragement to capitalists to come to their assistance. They must agitate the great railroad question. Such subjects have to be talked over a good deal. It took ten years talk ere the Central Pacific was started; and after all their talk, it was left to the energy, perseverance and courage of some Sacramento folks to put it through. Their watchword should be, "agitation, subscription, representation." Money was cheaper now, and more easily obtainable than formerly. The road must go through. Railways are a power in the land co-equal with the Government or legislature, oftentimes more powerful. Besides, they are a paying investment.

The San Jose road cost $1,500,000 and was sold for double that price. No railroad would pay better than a coast one, if properly built and managed. Whether as a power in their midst, a greater civilizer and developer, or as a good, payable investment, he equally supported and recommended his project.

After a few remarks from Messrs. R. H. Hatch and Fay, who both subscribed to the railway fund, the meeting adjourned *sine die*, to be called together again by the President after Pescadero and Santa Cruz are heard from, and when the subscription books have been brought in by the collectors. BORAK.

436. *San Francisco Bulletin*, September 4, via *The Santa Cruz Sentinel*, September 14, 1872 (1:8-9)

Competition on Short Lines.

On more than one occasion we have expressed the idea that San Francisco, out of the gross amount she may decide to expend for securing railway competition, should apportion one or two millions in aid of local lines, running up and down the coast. To this end we thought that a subscription of about seven and a half millions would be enough for the California Atlantic and Pacific, leaving a margin for help to minor enterprises within the limit of the sum proposed to be subscribed to one company alone. As, however, the California Atlantic and Pacific Company now propose to extend its track around the city front, from the South part of the city to North Beach, a larger amount than seven and a half millions will not be unreasonable. We would still, however, like to see the city subscribe in aid of the railroads that would accommodate the upper and lower coast counties, and that would extend the competition with Stanford & Co., opening new regions to our trade and benefitting communities that need and desire our help. Relying upon the existence of such a feeling among our people generally, two organizations—the North Pacific Coast Railroad Company and the San Francisco, Santa Cruz and Watsonville Railroad Company—present petitions for subsidies to the amount of one and one and a quarter millions respectively. It would be sound policy to help these companies, if such help can be given on conditions similar to those agreed to by the California Atlantic and Pacific—if in each case we can have an organization commanding public confidence, and providing for the city to be represented by Trustees carefully chosen. It is possible that the organization already effected, after so much laborious selection among men, might be used to secure the city should it be thought best to subscribe to the stock of the coast roads. Unquestionably much benefit would result to San Francisco from narrow gauge roads, costing not over $15,000 per mile, penetrating the lumber and dairy regions of the upper and lower coasts, and bringing their product cheaply to the market. But what is spent to help such roads should not be spent recklessly. It should be in the shape of subscriptions, giving the city a right to a voice in the management, and held by a good body of Trustees. Money so expended would be returned. Such roads would earn dividends sufficient to pay the interest on the bonds, while the stock would ultimately be sold, if thought desirable, to pay the principal. San Francisco can as well afford to put money in railroads, after this prudent, business-like manner, as Baltimore, which is now reaping an income from her wise investment.

437. *The Santa Cruz Sentinel,* September 14, 1872 (2:1-2)

Letter from E. N. Robinson.
San Francisco, Sept. 9th, 1972.
Mr. R. Thompson, Santa Cruz,

Dear Sir:—Your favor of the 5th inst., came duly to hand. I regret exceedingly that I was not enabled to be present at the railroad meeting held in Santa Cruz on the 28th ult. You are aware I presume that I have always advocated the Coast route from this city south, and have no reason to change my mind in that respect since I first completed my survey to Watsonville, and thence south as far as the Colorado River, where I connected my surveys with those of the Atlantic and Pacific, or 35th Parallel Railroad, at or near Fort Mohave, in June last.

I believe the Coast line between here and Watsonville offers a field for a remunerative railroad enterprise *not equaled in any other part of California*. This is my present idea, and I gather my conclusions from a thorough and accurate survey of the country, a detailed estimate of its resources, and a carefully prepared estimate of the cost of placing a standard gauge railroad between North Beach, in this city, and Watsonville, in your county.

The fact that a strong Mission Bay and Menlo Park suburban property influence, with a strong Central Pacific seasoning of *bridge* at Ravenswood sprinkled *over both* with a liberal hand, has made the *railroad* salad so hot here of late that you can understand why the California Atlantic and Pacific Railroad Co. have decided to follow the present construction line to Watsonville, (113 miles) via the Bay, in preference to the Coast line, which is only 99 miles.

As a railroad proposition the second Bay line is a foolish one, although for *politic reasons* it may be a good one. It seems plain to me that a dozen lines of railway between this city and Watsonville, via Menlo Park, Santa Clara, San Jose and Gilroy, will not improve the country, increase the population, or really benefit the inhabitants along the said route one farthing. No one can honestly find fault with the passenger and freight tariff between here and Watsonville over the present line of rail; the equipment and management is good, and there seems no reason in my mind to adopt "the dog in the manger" policy towards this short local line. Mr. Jones, and his neighbors at Menlo Park, see in this second line of rail a chance to ride home for fifty cents instead of a dollar, and with them it is self and a dollars and cents proposition (which I must acknowledge seems the ruling principle of the present generation), the railroad men who have controlled and are controlling the railroads, legislature and policy of this city—be they for one route or the other out of this city—should look at it in the latter light and consider for every dollar investing how many are we going to get in return? and while benefitting ourselves how can we benefit others?

You are aware that for many miles south of this city, along the Bay line, land is held at fancy prices for fancy purposes, at such prices indeed that it is no asylum or land of promise for the ordinary farmer or seeker after land with intent to plow, to sow and to reap. The land is placed on a high shelf, far above the reach of such men as follow in the path of railways, and who by hard work, energy and industry, build up towns, increase population and generally improve and benefit a country in which they settle. I say there is no such field along the Bay line and never can be under the present rule; and any second line of railway from here to Watsonville, through the Santa Clara Valley, will be as useless and unremunerative as a stage line. Along the Coast it would be different, for between this city and Watsonville, west of the Coast range, there is a section of country, approximately 300,000 acres, of productive soil suited for grain and never subject to San Joaquin or any other kind of drought; a land that produces as often as the seasons roll around. You hear no complaints coming from the Coast of a lack of moisture to satisfy the requirements of the field. The only cry is for a sure, rapid, convenient and reasonably cheap transportation to a market. From November to May many of the people along the Coast between San Francisco and Watsonville are debarred from any connection with San Francisco, excepting at the expense of a heavy cost over the mountains.

With a railway down and along the Coast, population would flock in and settle on the broad and prolific tablelands that lay between the mountains and the sea. Hundreds, yes thousands of people would fill those beautiful valleys that reach for miles back from the Coast into the range of mountains skirting them. Industries of all kinds would spring up and prosper on the many water-courses on the western water shed of the Coast range. Timber, lime, granite and building material of all kinds, that exist in inexhaustible quantities along the coast, would enrich the corporation owning and controlling the avenue through or over which such material could be expeditiously transported to a market. Our merchants would then seek the sea shore for their summer residents, and our poorer classes could breathe the sea air from cottages on land of their own, at a cost that would not purchase them turning room on the Bay side, at present prices of land. Land in Santa Clara Valley is held at from $200 to $700 per acre; better land can be had on the coast at $10 to $30 per acre. The Coast land will produce yearly, the Santa Clara Valley land semi-occasionally.

The Bay and its Sloughs from San Francisco to Alviso, offers a present and everlasting opposition, by water, to the present Railway. On the coast, embarkation is so uncertain, that opposition by water amounts to nothing, even if it did, I contend that, allowing all the present freight that accumulates along the coast to seek water transportation, a line of rail will create enough extra to keep itself busy at remunerative prices.

It is claimed that the line from here to Watsonville, via the coast, is a heavy one. I admit that it will cost a large amount of money to build and properly equip it to Watsonville, but I have my estimates carefully preserved, that will prove the fact, that a first-class standard gauge (4 feet 8½ inches) road can be built from here to the Pajaro river, for less than the average cost of a Standard gauge in the East, and over a country much more deserving of a road, than any 100 miles in any Western State.

The true policy of your people, is to build a narrow gauge (3 feet) road, and operate it for your local business, it will then be an easy matter of any time to change it, at a moderate expense—having a line of rail to work with—to the Standard size.

If the California Atlantic and Pacific Railroad is ever built, your coast line will connect with it at the Pajaro river, and feel assured, that when the day arrives, that the two roads join hands, then the day is not far beyond, when the overland travel will reach this city via the coast.

As a road for pleasure seekers and excursionists, it will have no rival out of this city, and you are aware that a traffic of that kind, assists very materially to swell the receipts of any road having the advantages of controlling the same.

Careful estimates of the cost of road, income for operating, and a liberal estimate for running expenses, including wear and tear, and renewal account, shows conclusively that a line of road 4 feet 8½ inches gauge, built from here to Watsonville, would pay one percent per month on its cost from the start. What can your people propose to subscribe, ask better?

A united effort now on the part of the coast people, to the extent of their means, to aid this line, will insure the building of it in less than 2½ years, this I am confident of.

I shall be glad to hear from you at any time.

Yours truly, E. N. Robinson.

438. *The Santa Cruz Sentinel*, September 14, 1872 (2:2)

Memorial.

To the Honorable, the Board of Supervisors of the city and county of San Francisco, and to the Honorables, the Boards of Supervisors of the Counties of San Mateo, Santa Cruz, Monterey, San Luis Obispo, Santa Barbara, Los Angeles and San Diego:

The undersigned having been appointed by the citizens of Santa Cruz as a Committee to devise ways and means for the construction of a three-foot gauge Railroad, commencing in the city of San Francisco and running thence as near as practicable on the line of survey of the Atlantic and Pacific Railroad Company, along or near the Coast, through the Counties of San Mateo and Santa Cruz, beg leave to represent that earnest efforts are now being made in this County to commence at once the construction of said road and continue the same vigorously to its completion; that it is the desire of the people of this County to co-operate with the citizens of all the other Coast Counties and with all other Railroad Companies organized or to be organized for that purpose, to construct and maintain an independent and continuous line of a three-foot gauge Railroad from San Francisco along or near the Coast to the southern line of the State; that recognizing the fact that the amount of private subscriptions obtainable for such purpose is insufficient to secure the early construction of said road, application is hereby made for such public aid as the interests of the said several Counties may demand, and that the City and County of San Francisco is hereby solicited to grant aid in the construction of such road from San Francisco to the southern line of Santa Cruz County to the amount of $1,500,00, to be paid as the said road is being constructed.

D. Tuthill, Chairman, Lucien Heath, Amasa Pray, G. B. V. DeLamater, Edward Briody, Titus Hale, F. A. Hihn, G. P. Laird, Cooper & Co., L. Schwartz, Wm. Effey. J. N. Besse, J. S. Green, John Werner, Frank Cooper, A. R. Meserve, Brownstone & Bros., Peter Warner, J. M. Cutler, L. K. Baldwin, Henry Skinner, C. Cappelmann, R. C. Kirby.

Subscription List.

We the undersigned, hereby agree to subscribe for the number of shares of One Hundred Dollars each set opposite our respective names, of the Stock of a Railroad Company to be organized for the purpose of constructing and maintaining a Railroad, to be of a three foot gauge, on the following route: Commencing on the line of the Southern Pacific Railroad, at or near the Pajaro Depot, or at a Depot near Watsonville on the line of a said Railroad which may be hereafter built on the same general route as the said Southern Pacific Railroad, and running thence as near as practicable, on or near the line of survey of the Atlantic and Pacific Railroad through the counties of Monterey, Santa Cruz, San Mateo and San Francisco, to a point at tide-water in the city of San Francisco.

Date. | Name of Subsc'r. | Residence.

Petition.

To the Honorable the Board of Supervisors of the County

of Santa Cruz, *Greeting*:

The undersigned citizens and Tax-Payers and those interested in the welfare of Santa Cruz county, recognizing the necessity of the action sought to be accomplished hereby petition your Hon. Board to submit to the qualified electors of said county, at the general election to be held on the 5th day of November, 1872, the question—Whether said county shall issue and deliver to some railroad company, now formed, or hereafter to be formed, bonds of said county, payable in twenty years, and bearing interest at the rate of seven per cent, per annum, interest payable semi-annually, to the amount of $6,000 for each and every mile of main track of a railroad, to be constructed within the limits of said county, of a gauge of not less than three feet, on the following general route, to wit: Beginning on the line of the Southern Pacific Railroad, at or near the Pajaro depot, or at a depot near Watsonville, on the line of a railroad which may hereafter be constructed on the same general route as the Southern Pacific Railroad, and running thence as near as practicable on the line of survey of the Atlantic and Pacific Railroad Company, crossing the San Lorenzo river, south of the Soquel road, and through the County of Santa Cruz to its northern boundary line near Waddell creek.

It is the understanding and request of your petitioners that the bonds hereinbefore named shall not exceed in the total the sum of $240,000; and it is further understood by your petitioners that the aid heretofore authorized to be granted for the construction of a Railroad connecting the town of Santa Cruz with the Southern Pacific Railroad shall, in the event of a favorable result, to the action now initiated and by consent of your Honorable Board and all parties in interest, be set aside. And your petitioners will ever pray, &c.

439. *San Francisco Chronicle*, September 14, 1872 (2:2)

Is it an Independent Road?

The position claimed by the friends of the Atlantic and Pacific Railroad scheme is that it is to be an independent competing railroad owned and operated by the people of San Francisco in the interest of San Francisco, so that for all future time it will be controlled by our own people. It can never enter into hostile combinations. It can never be purchased by Stanford & Co., but must always remain a competing line. And yet the articles of agreement accompanying the act of incorporation provide that it may be amalgamated and consolidated with the Atlantic and Pacific Company of Missouri with its one hundred millions of capital. In such an event it would be given to the Eastern directors. It would be operated in the interest of St. Louis discriminating against San Francisco. Our ten millions would be worse than lost; we would be liable for the $40,000,000 of debt accumulated by constructing our end of the line, and the result might be ruin to our trade or even bankruptcy to our city, while St. Louis would be built up at our expense. Let our readers carefully read the annexed article of agreement:

"Consent is hereby given that the Directors of this

company may, by a vote of a majority of their whole number, with the consent or approval of a majority of all the said Trustees, amalgamate and consolidate this company with the Atlantic and Pacific Railroad Company, or the capital stock, debts, property, assets and franchises of the one company with those of the other company; or may, by a like vote, make subscription to the capital stock of the Atlantic and Pacific Railroad Company, and make payment therefor by a transfer of the capital stock, property, assets, and franchise of this Company; or may, by the like vote, make other transfer or disposition thereof, to effectually accomplish a union with the Atlantic and Pacific Railroad Company for the construction of a through line of road from San Francisco to St. Louis."

440. *The Pajaronian*, September 19, 1872 (2:2)

Railroads.—F. A. Hihn, the great Santa Cruz Railroad bloviator, said in a communication to the *Sentinel*—and which we reproduced last week as a literary curiosities—as follows:

"The owners of the Southern Pacific Railroad Co., not complying with their promises to build a wide gauge Railroad from Santa Cruz to Watsonville, we are forced to conclude that if we want a railroad, we must build it ourselves."

And we "are forced to conclude," from what we know of Hihn and his railroad operations heretofore, that the Southern Pacific Railroad Company never promised to build a road from Santa Cruz to Watsonville.

441. *San Francisco Examiner*, September 20, 1872 (4:2)

ORDER NO. ———.— CONCERNING THE SAN Francisco, Santa Cruz and Watsonville Railroad.

Whereas, the San Francisco, Santa Cruz and Watsonville Railroad Company, a corporation formed and existing under and by virtue of the laws of the State of California, proposes to construct, stock and operate a railroad from the city and county of San Francisco to Watsonville, in the county of Santa Cruz, by the route in this Order specified, as near as may be, and has applied to the city and county of San Francisco, through the board, for aid in the construction of said Railroad, by the issuance of the bonds of said city and county, to the amount of one-half of one per cent, of the taxable property of said city and county of San Francisco, and has asked this Board to order an election, for the purpose of submitting to the qualified electors of the city and county of San Francisco, the question whether the said railroad aid shall be granted.

Therefore, in pursuance of the laws in such cases made and provided.

The people of the City and County of San Francisco do ordain as follows:

Section 1. The question of whether or not the city and county of San Francisco, by the issuance of bonds of the amount of one-half of one per cent. of the taxable property of said city and county of San Francisco, shall aid he San Francisco, Santa Cruz and Watsonville Railroad Company, in the construction of a railroad by the route and to the points specified in section 4 of this Order, shall be submitted to the qualified electors of said city and county, and for that purpose an election shall be held in said city and county, at the next general election, on the fifth day of November, 1872.

Section 2: At such election, every elector desiring to vote in favor of granting such aid, shall deposit a ballot, with the words "San Francisco, Santa Cruz and Watsonville Railroad aid—yes," thereon; and every elector desiring to vote against the granting of such aid shall deposit a ballot with the words "San Francisco, Santa Cruz and Watsonville Railroad aid—no," thereon.

Section 3. If at such election the majority of the qualified electors voting upon said question shall vote in favor of the granting such aid, the bonds of said city and county of San Francisco to the amount of said one-half of one per cent. of the taxable property of said city and county, payable within twenty years from the date of their issue, and bearing interest at the rate of six per cent. per annum, shall be issued to said railroad Company in accordance with law.

Section 4. The route of said Railroad is to be as follows, as near as may be, viz..: Commencing at the intersection of Illinois and Sixteenths streets, in the city and county of San Francisco, and running thence westerly along such streets as have already been authorized by this Board to a point at or near the intersection of Frederick street with First avenue; and thence, by the most practicable route, to the southern boundary line of said city and county; thence along the Coast Range, between the summit thereof and the ocean, to Halfmoon Bay, Spanishtown and Pescadero, in the county of San Mateo; thence by the most practicable and convenient route to the town of Santa Cruz and Watsonville, in Santa Cruz county.

Section 5. Due notice of the election herein provided for shall be given according to law.

Section 6. The amount of bonds to be issued as herein proposed shall only be in amount equal to one-half of one per cent. upon the value of the taxable property of said city and county, according to its valuation on the assessment roll prepared as required by law in the year eighteen hundred and seventy-two. Upon the construction of said railroad for the distance of five miles from its initial point, in said city and county, there shall be issued and delivered to said Company, its successors and assigns, the bonds of said city and county in an amount that shall bear the same proportion to the whole amount of bonds mentioned in this Sections, as such distance of five miles bears to the entire length of said proposed Railroad herein described, and the issuance of such bonds shall continue thereafter as fast as the construction of said Railroad progresses, but only upon completion of each five miles distance thereof at least, and only in the proportion as above specified. Upon the completion of the whole road the reminder of said bonds shall be issued. At the times and upon the happening of the contingencies herein mentioned for the issuing of said bonds and each and every parcel and amount thereof, the amount of city and county indebtedness then outstanding and incurred by granting aid in the construction of railroads shall be deducted from the amount of bonds authorized to be issued by the provisions of the act of the Legislature of the State of California, entitled "An Act to Empower the Board of Supervisors of the several Counties of this State to Aid in the Construction of a Railroad in their respective Counties," approved April 4th, 1870. And the whole amount of bonds hereby authorized to be issued, together with all the other bonds of said city and county authorized or that may hereafter be authorized to be issued in pursuance of said Act of the Legislature, and the Act amendatory and supplementary thereto shall not exceed five per cent. of the value of the taxable property of this city and county, according to its valuation on the assessment roll last preceding the time of issue of said bonds. No railroad or railroad track which shall be constructed at the time of the passage of this Order shall ever be deemed to be part of the Railroad mentioned in Section 4 hereof so as to authorize the issuance of any portion of the bonds mentioned in this Order for the construction thereof.

In Board of Supervisors, San Francisco, September 16, 1872.

Passed for printing by the following vote:

Ayes—Supervisors, Menzies, Swain, Kenney, Goodwin, King, Story, Commins, Taylor.

Noes—Supervisors McCarthy, Forbes, Shrader, Barrett.   JNO. A. BURRELL, Clerk.

442. *The Santa Cruz Sentinel*, September 21, 1872 (2:1)

Railroad Committee.

The Executive Committee of the Railroad Meeting,

The Dream of Steam, 1854–1873

held in the Court House, have held several adjourned meetings since our last report. On Monday evening, September 9th, the Secretary presented several forms of petitions and subscriptions, drawn by a sub-committee appointed for that purpose, which were adopted after amendment, and ordered printed for circulation. [*See* Article 438 above.] A communication from Dr. Goodspeed was received and filed, suggested a Railroad Convention at Pescadero or Santa Cruz, requesting this Committee to name a day.

On September 11th the full Committee met and heard the views of several capitalists and tax-payers on the subject of Railroads, etc. Forms of memorial, subscriptions and petitions ordered engrossed. On the 13th of September, it was voted that the Santa Cruz petition and lists be circulated for subscribers and signatures. The shares of stock to be $100 each.

It was moved by J. N. Besse that the Secretary suggest to the Railroad Committee of Pescadero and Half Moon Bay that a Railroad Convention be held on the 26th inst., at such time and place as may be agreeable to them.—Carried. On motion of J. S. Green, R. C. Kirby and T. W. Wright were added to the Committee.

On the 16th of September it was suggested that funds would be necessary to defray the expenses of printing, circulating petitions, etc., and on motion, T. W. Wright was appointed a Committee to collect funds for expenses of this Committee, and it was suggested that the Secretary act as *ex officio* Treasurer.

On motion of L. Heath, William Cooper, Samuel Drennan and Albert Brown were added to this Committee.

On motion of Titus Hale, B. F. Porter, C. C. Cappelmann, Chas. Brown, E. P. Kooser, George P. Laird, B. C. Nichols, A. R. Meserve, R. H. Hall and Samuel Dickens were added to the Committee.

On motion of L. Heath, Titus Hale, J. S. Green and R. C. Kirby were appointed a sub-committee to employ parties to circulate petitions. A telegram appeared, dated Half Moon Bay, September 17th, to the Secretary, stating that a delegation would attend a Railroad Convention to be held in Santa Cruz on Saturday, September 28th, if suitable to the Committee. Signed by W. H. Campbell, Secretary Half Moon Bay Committee.

In answer to W. H. Campbell's communication, the Secretary wrote under date of September 14th, 1872:

"We are circulating a Railroad Company petition list in this county, intending to co-operate with any Railroad already organized, if they will start in to build the road in good faith. If no other Company takes hold of the matter we intend to organize a Company and build the road thorough our county at any rate, with the expectation that other counties will organize and build the road through their respective counties and eventually consolidate."

A letter from Mr. J. H. Loftus to F. A. Hihn, dated August 31st, is on file, as follows:

"Upon thinking the matter over, since I left your town, in relation to Railroad: I would have given you my views the night of the meeting, but did not know then what I could do: I can now make you the following proposition: I will construct and equip a *narrow gauge* Railroad from Santa Cruz to Watsonville for the sum of one hundred and fifty thousand dollars ($150,000,) to be paid as the work is finished; it will cost about two hundred thousand dollars, ($200,000) for the necessary side tracks, depots, water tanks and turn-tables. I can furnish the balance of the money and complete the road in nine months, with a view of extending to San Francisco in a short time. Please let me know what you think of the proposition? Anything you can do to carry on the scheme will be reciprocated by me. Answer and let me know. I will come over if necessary. Very truly yours,

J. H. LOFTUS."

A telegram from Charles R. Story, dated September 16th, was received, stating that to get a vote on a subsidy at the coming election, "The Company must be incorporated, route defined, and ordinance published. Thirty days too late for the election."

On Thursday evening, Sept. 19th, Committee met and approved minutes of previous meeting.

On motion of L. Heath the Secretary was instructed to call a mass meeting at the Court House, to confer on Railroad matters, on Saturday evening, September 21st.

Moved—that a communication be sent to the Board of Supervisors of San Francisco, with a copy of the petition for subsidy, etc., with a list of the Santa Cruz subscribers; said papers to be sent by the Secretary of the meeting to be held on next Saturday night.

In the matter of a Railroad Convention. On motion of J. N. Besse a Railroad Convention was called to meet at the Court House, in Santa Cruz, on Saturday, September 28th, at 1 o'clock,

On motion B. P. Kooser was appointed a Committee

of one to arrange for the Railroad meeting next Saturday, the 21st, and the Convention, on the 28th inst.

G. B. C. DeLamater tendered his resignation as Secretary, and on motion R. Conant was elected Secretary in his stead

On motion E. S. West, James Cunningham, W. W. Waddell, Capt. J. P. Davenport, Omar Steele, Andrew Craig, D. M. Locke and R. Conant were elected members of the Committee.

On motion each member of this Committee was authorized to collect funds to defray necessary expenses. Adjourned to meet at the Court House in Mass Meeting on Saturday evening, September 21st.

443. *The Santa Cruz Sentinel*, September 21, 1872 (2:3)

Railroad Meeting.

Attention is directed to the Call for Railroad Meeting, to be held at the Courthouse in Santa Cruz, at half past seven o'clock, this evening—Saturday, September 21st. All are invited to attend and assist the ball in rolling.

444. *Daily Alta California*, September 14, via *The Santa Cruz Sentinel*, September 21, 1872 (4:1)

San Francisco to Santa Cruz.

In comparison with the immense amount of discussion upon the question of overland railroads, and railroads through this State, to Oregon, through the San Joaquin

Valley, the Santa Clara, Salinas, and elsewhere, how little has been said about the county on the western side of the Coast hills between this city and Santa Cruz. And yet there is not probably in California a stretch of territory of equal extent and capacity, of soil so rich and deep and productive, which so needs, and so much deserves, the advantages of a railroad extending through it. We have no immediate means of stating the number of acres to the south of us capable of cultivation. But one may say, that it is all thus capable, from the valley bottoms to the tops of the hills, from the redwoods to the sea. Not only is all the land thus rich, it is almost always sure of producing a crop, since the fogs which prevail through the crop-making season serve instead of rain to ensure a golden return.

All along and through this fine country are farms and ranches, and vast fields of grain. The crop has been so heavy that much of it yet lies on the earth as the reaping machine left it. There are shocks and sheafs in measureless quantities, countless and beautiful, and mountains of the gathered abundance, rich with their ripened gold, waiting for the advent of the threshing machine. We do not believe that one of ten thousand of our people have any adequate idea of the extent of ground capable of cultivation and sure of satisfactory production, which lies all along through San Mateo and Santa Cruz counties, between the line of redwoods and the sea. Scarcely a rood of it all is there which is not capable of cultivation, and sure of giving the reward in return for the farmer's toil. But the only drawback at present is the great difficulty of getting crops to market. The distance to San

Francisco is too great—and consequently costly—for hauling by team, and there are no near harbors of safe roadsteads for vessels to visit for freights.

Occasionally along the coast an open roadstead, somewhat protected from the Summer winds by a projecting point of land, may be found, where small vessels, under favorable circumstances of weather and sea, venture to anchor and await opportunity to load. This can only be done when wind and sea are favorable, and the process is attended frequently by accidents, the less of portions of the grain and other freight in loading, and not infrequently in loss of the vessel also. Thus the farmers can scarcely be said to have the benefit of a market. Their crops are frittered away in costs, or left upon their hands, of comparatively little value. And yet this is a land through which a railroad track could be constructed at limited cost, no rivers requiring trestle-work, in the way, no mountains to cross or tunnel—except, perhaps, one ridge to the north of Half-Moon Bay—and the general surface, or topography of the country very favorable to the construction and operation of a railroad.

A narrow gauge road might be constructed at comparatively small cost, which, enabling the farmers to possess the advantages of a market, would also, in consequence, aid materially in filling up that naturally fine section with hardy, industrious and prosperous settlers. For the climate is healthy, the only drawback being the fog during the Summer months, which, nevertheless, is a blessing in the form of an insurance of the crops. But it is not along upon them, and the travel, and movement of supplies that a road would have to depend for business and dividends. Just over the crests of the hills begin the redwood and other forest timber. It is abundant. It is marketable. It is wanted, is needed, and would give a railroad immediate business, more than it could perform. Before this source could be exhausted, the farming and other interests along the line would have so increased that no lack of patronage need be anticipated by the Railroad Company.

We have right valleys in California, such as San Joaquin, Santa Clara, Sacramento, Napa, the agricultural capacities of which have been considered of sufficient importance to authorize the expenditures necessary to construct costly railroads. And yet, generally, these valleys have nothing but the low, level lands for producing crops. Their borders, the hills that hem them in, are not, to any considerable degree, grain producing. But along the Pacific shore of which we have spoken, there are no barren acres, no lands worth mentioning which are not capable of producing abundant crops, the hills as well as the valleys. After a residence of almost a quarter of a century in this city, a week ago, for the first time, the writer had the privilege and pleasure of riding through this extent of natural richness, from Santa Cruz hither, and he does not hesitate to say that it impressed him as the finest agricultural portion of the State, to say nothing of its other advantages.

445. *Stockton Daily Evening Herald*, September 24, 1872 (2:2)

The meeting of the San Francisco Board of Supervisors last evening was undisturbed, notwithstanding the threatening indications during the day, though there was a large crowd congregated about and inside the City Hall. An order to submit to a vote of the people the question of a subsidy to the Colorado River Railroad was passed, and a modified order for a subsidy to the Atlantic and Pacific Railroad was rejected. A dispatch says there is little doubt of the adoption of the compromise with the Central Pacific Railroad.

446. *The Santa Cruz Sentinel,* September 28, 1872 (2:1)

Our Railroad.

By reference to the advertisement it will be seen that our Board of Supervisors, by Proclamation, have ordered "an election to be held at the next General Election (Thursday, November 5th,) to issue County Bonds, payable within twenty years, and bearing interest payable semi-annually, at the rate of 7 per cent. per annum to the amount of $6,000 per mile, but not to exceed in the aggregate the sum of $240,000 to build a Railroad, not less than three feet gauge, from Watsonville to the Northern line of our County; said road to connect with the Southern Pacific at the Pajaro depot."

We are in favor of this road, believing that at the present time it is most feasible plan to secure a road along the Coast, and that it will be the forerunner of a road clear through to San Francisco.

The Board of Supervisors of San Francisco, for the present have voted down a proposition to grant a subsidy of $1,500,000 for this coast road, therefore we must now

The Dream of Steam, 1854–1873

go to work and build the road ourselves, with the addition of such outside capital as can be induced to invest. At present writing we have neither time or room to give, in full, our reasons for advocating this measure. But will now assert, in good faith, that we believe if a reasonable amount is subscribed—5 per cent of the taxable property of the county, that the road will be built and the cars running past our doors in two years. To do this, money must be raised and properly expended. Every man should take at least one share, and every man assessed over $5,000 would find it advantageous to take five shares. It would be a good investment even if he had to borrow money to pay his 10 per cent, as each three or five miles of the road was completed. Let the road be now built and its effect will at once enliven our prospects and increase business by bringing a healthy and producing population in our midst.

We direct the attention of our readers ot the specifications of the subsidy, as given in the Proclamation. The details are carefully drawn in simple language, there can be no mistake in the matter. The directors will have to build the road, or the $6,000 per mile will be withheld. There can be no cat in the meal tub in this matter. No fox to be unearthed as the building of the road progresses. The main thing is to secure sufficient outside subscriptions, so that first mortgage bonds will not have to be given on the road. To do this, every man should take at least one share, and every tax-payer at least an amount of 5 per cent. on his assessment. Should the road not be built, no money will be required; and even if built, it will be paid in 10 per cent. Installments, as the work progresses in 5 mile sections.

We again call on our readers to think of the proposition, and remember that this is the last chance we may have for years to get a road. If we fall now, there will be an end to it, and no one will feel like again aiding the enterprise. Those who are incredulous should inquire into our resources and the effect of railroads on towns and cities. Look at Salinas City and it will there be seen what an effect even a prospective railroad has. Hollister, Modesto, and every point along the Tulare Valley road, is alive with people and commerce, brought there by a completion of the road. We can do as much for our town if we only make the sacrifice and give liberally of our means to aid the road.

447. Telegram to the *San Francisco Bulletin* via *The Santa Cruz Sentinel*, September 28, 1872 (2:1)

Railroad Matters in Santa Cruz.

Santa Cruz, September 24.—The Railroad question continues to occupy the attention of all classes in this portion of the county, and judging from present appearances will soon be solved. The following will serve to show the exact position in which the affair rests at present:

Some time ago the Board of County Supervisors ordered an election for the purposes of determining whether the people of this county should or should not grant a subsidy of one hundred thousand dollars to aid the construction of a line of railroad from this city to Watsonville, it being at that time the general impression that for the consideration of the amount stated, the Central Pacific Railroad Company would undertake the construction of the road.

The Dream of Steam, 1854–1873

The election duly transpired, and in spite of a strong opposition in the western portion of the county, the measure was carried by an overwhelming majority. The Central Pacific Railroad Company, through its President, Stanford, then refused to move in the matter, and the subsidy was lost by reason of the time allowed by the terms of the election expiring without an effort having been made towards the construction of the road:

Within the past few days the project has been imbued with new life, and the work of construction will be commenced within five weeks from the present time. The Board of County Supervisors will to-morrow order an election for the purpose of re-submitting to the people the subsidy question—the subsidy to be $120,000. The election will take place in thirty days and will, without the least possibility of a doubt, result affirmatively.

A local company has been formed and subscriptions are rapidly pouring in. As soon as the result of the election is known, this County will avail itself of the subsidy, and, with ten per cent of the incorporated capital, proceed to work at once.

The plans at present are to build and equip a first-class narrow-gauge road to Watsonville immediately, then mortgage the road and continue the work of construction up the coast as far as the county line, or as far as the proceeds of the mortgage will permit.

The promoters of this scheme are our best business men. Their plans are all arranged, the capital is all ready, and the undertaking cannot fail

448. *The Santa Cruz Sentinel*, September 28, 1872 (2:2)

Railroad Meeting.

A meeting of the citizens of Santa Cruz to consider the interests of the Coast Railroad, was held at the Court House, on Saturday evening Sept. 21st. C. Cappelmann was appointed chairman, and R. Conant Secretary of the Santa Cruz executive Railroad Committee, read the report of the committee.

On motion of Mr. Hihn, the report was received and adopted. Mr. Hihn moved that the members of the executive committee circulate the Subscription list among the persons, in order to enlarge the amount of Subscriptions to the Stock.

Eloquent speeches were made by Messrs. F. A. Hihn, F. Adams, D. Tuthill and C. Cappelmann, in favor of the motion, which was unanimously adopted.

The Subscription list was then circulated, and nearly every person in the room put his name down, and the stock was increased to 750 shares.

On motion, the Secretary was instructed to send a copy of the Subscription list to the Board of Supervisors of San Francisco, with the petition, and the Secretary stated that this was the result of the first evening's work.

On motion, the Subscription list was referred back to the committee to quadruple the amount, and circulate it up and down the coast with the petition.

On motion, the meeting then adjourned.

R. CONANT, Secretary.

Railroad convention postponed.

At a meeting of the Executive Committee held on Tuesday evening Sept. 24th, at DeLamater's Hall, in consequence of the action of the Board of Supervisors of San Francisco, it was considered best to postpone the Railroad convention to some future time.

449. *The Santa Cruz Sentinel*, September 28, 1872 (2:3)

MASS Railroad Meeting!
at the
Court House, Santa Cruz,
on
Saturday Eve at 8 o'clock.
To discuss
Railroad matters,
The Citizens of Santa Cruz and vicinity are requested to attend for the purpose of devising means to secure the early
Construction of a Railroad,
to the Town of Santa Cruz.
COME EVERYBODY!

450. *The Santa Cruz Sentinel*, September 28, 1872 (2:4)

Election Notice and Order.

County seat of the County of Santa Cruz and office of the Board of Supervisors thereof. Santa Cruz, Sept. 25, 1872.

WHEREAS, the Board of Supervisors of Santa Cruz

County, State of California, propose that said County shall aid in the construction of a railroad of not less than a three-foot gauge, and beginning at or near the Pajaro depot, on the Southern Pacific Railroad, in the County of Monterey, and running thence in the most practicably direct route through the County of Santa Cruz, crossing the Pajaro river near Watsonville, and crossing the San Lorenzo river between the county road leading to Soquel and the bay of Monterey, and thence along or near the coast to the boundary of the said county, near the south-east corner of the Point New Years' Rancho by the issue of County Bonds payable within twenty years, and bearing interest payable semi-annually, at the rate of 7 per cent, per annum, to the amount of six thousand per mile, but not exceeding in the aggregate the sum of two hundred and forty thousand dollars; such aid to be in lieu of the aid of one hundred thousand dollars heretofore authorized to be granted in the construction of a railroad connecting the town of Santa Cruz with the Southern Pacific Railroad. And whereas the Santa Cruz and Watsonville Railroad Company have agreed that the contract entered into by the said Company with the said county, dated January 18th, 1872, and entered on records of the said Board, in Vol. 3, page 184, and following shall be deemed cancelled in case the railroad aid herein proposed shall be granted.

Now, therefore, it is ordered, and notice is hereby given that at the next general election to be held on the fifth day of November 1872, there shall be submitted to the electors of Santa Cruz County, the question whether the Board of Supervisors of Santa Cruz County in lieu of the aid of one hundred thousand dollars, heretofore authorized, to be granted in the construction of a railroad connecting the town of Santa Cruz with the Southern Pacific Railroad, at or near the town of Watsonville, and upon the cancellation of the said contract of the said county, with the Santa Cruz and Watsonville Railroad Company, shall be authorized to grant upon terms which may appear to them advantageous to the County the aid of the County of Santa Cruz, in the construction of a railroad of not less than a three-foot gauge, on the route herein before described, to an amount of not exceeding in the aggregate two hundred and forty thousand dollars in the bonds of Santa Cruz County, as proposed by said Board, to be issued at a rate of not more than six thousand dollars per mile for every mile of main track actually constructed.

All Ballots cast in favor of said proposition shall contain the words—"Railroad Aid Yes,"—all ballots cast against said proposition shall contain the words—"Railroad Aid No," said election shall be held in all the election districts in said county, and in the following places, to wit: At Santa Cruz Precinct, at Hihn's Building, next DeLamater's store.

At New Years Point Precinct, at W. W. Simms House, Frog Town.

At San Lorenzo Precinct, at School House at Scotts Valley.

At Soquel Precinct, at Primary School House.

At Corralitos Precinct at School House

At Pajaro Precinct, Mansion House, Watsonville.

It is further ordered that this order shall be published in the Santa Cruz SENTINEL and the *Pajaronian*, once a

week for thirty days previous to the said fifth day of November 1872. BERNARD PEYTON, Ch'r.
FRANK PORTER, Sup.
Attest, ALBERT BROWN, Clerk.

451. *The Santa Cruz Sentinel*, September 28, 1872 (3:4)

Pescadero, September 23d.

Mr. Roger Conant, Secretary C. R. R., Santa Cruz.

Dear Sir:—At a meeting held in Pescadero on the 21st inst. I. C. Steele, Braddock Weeks, Alex. Moore and B. Hayward were appointed to attend the C. R. R. Convention to be held in Santa Cruz on the 28th inst.

The people up this way can be relied upon to do their part in a Coast Railroad. We have about $5,000 stock taken now; I think Pescadero is equal for $100,000.

Yours Respectfully,

J. R. Goodspeed, Secretary Pescadero C. R. R.

452. *San Mateo Gazette*, September 28, 1872 (2:3)

Before the road [from Watsonville to Waddell Creek] is completed to San Francisco, the San Lorenzo Railroad, a road surveyed from the town of Santa Cruz for sixteen miles up the San Lorenzo River will be completed. The San Lorenzo Co. is duly incorporated, and has a subscribed capital of $85,000, only $200,000 being necessary for the completion of the road. The San Lorenzo River and tributaries tap the largest forests of Redwood, pine, madrona and oak, and

The Dream of Steam, 1854–1873 649

the most extensive quarries of granite and lime-stone on this coast, and being within one hundred miles of San Francisco and contiguous to the trans-continental railroads likely to be constructed, must supply the proposed narrow-gauge with all the freight possible to transport over its track. The San Lorenzo road is on a line to Redwood City, and in case the coast track is not constructed may connect with the S. P. R. R. not far south of this place, or better still, in the event that the road is built too deep water-front and steamer connection established with all points on the bay, make this place its northern terminus.

453. *The Santa Cruz Sentinel,* October 5, 1872 (2:2)
Railroad Meeting.

At the last meeting of the citizens of Santa Cruz to consider the railroad question, held on Saturday evening, September 28th, at the Court House, C. Cappelmann was appointed chairman, and Dr. F. E. J. Canney Secretary. There being no written report on the table D. Tuthill gave a brief statement of success since the last meeting.

R. B. Handy advised that the County be divided into districts and responsible men appointed for each, that they may thoroughly canvass the County and raise the subscription list as much as possible.

F. A. Hihn said that there was no intention of having the Railroad stop short of Santa Cruz in coming up the Coast from Watsonville, and extend it as much further up the Coast as there may be money subscribed to complete the work. He also urged that it was necessary for everyone to subscribe to the road—if it be but one share—if they do not it will be a long time in the future before we will get a road of any kind.

F. Adams stated that the amount of shipments to and from our harbor had decreased very much in the last few years on account of so unhealthy a state of affairs; and that we might have had the I. O. O. F.'s College and Home and Branch Insane Asylum located at this place had we Railroad communications; he also stated that we would never in the future have anything of the kind if we do not have some way of communication with the outside world except by stages, although we have the best climate and facilities for manufacturing upon the Coast.

R. C. Kirby favored the raising of money as others had previously spoken.

F. A. Hihn moved and F. Adams seconded that a committee of five be appointed by the Chairman to secure the right of way, a preliminary survey, and to canvass the County thoroughly. Carried.

The following are the members of the Committee: C. Cappelmann, Chairman, F. Adams, R. B. Handy, George Otto, John Wood. R. Conant, Secretary.

D. McPherson, of the San Mateo *Gazette*, said that the people of San Mateo County were waiting for this County to build the road through this, and they were ready to extend it toward San Francisco. Over $700,000 had already been subscribed to extend the road through San Mateo county.

On motion the meeting adjourned.

Dr. F. E. J. Canney, Secretary.

454. *The Santa Cruz Sentinel,* October 5, 1872 (3:2)
Railroad Meeting.

At a meeting of the Rail Road Committee, appointed by the meeting last Saturday Evening, C. Cappelman was elected Chairman and R. Conant Secretary.

Mr. Handy moved that legal documents be drawn, for persons who lived along the proposed line of the road, to sign the right of way, and that the Secretary get one hundred copies printed, adopted. On motion Messrs. Handy, Cappelman and Otto, were appointed to act for the road on the west side of the San Lorenzo, and Messrs. Adams and Wood for the east side with power to secure such assistance as they may deem necessary.

Regular meetings of the Committee will be held at the office of the Secretary, in the Court House, every Tuesday evening at 7½ o'clock.

455. *The Pajaronian,* October 10, 1872 (2:2)

On Monday last Mr. Wm. F. White, a farmer in Pajaro Valley, sold 400 acres of his land for $33,000 cash to a Mr. Grogan of San Francisco. This is about $82 25 per acre. The last is at the base of the low hills northeast of Watsonville, and a great portion of it is rolling land, and not as desirable as the rich alluvial valley land. It is supposed that F. D. Atherton has some interest in that direction. If so it may mean railroad along the base of the mountain from the point where the Southern Pacific crosses the Pajaro, through the valley and up Corralitos Creek, crossing over Steiglemann's to the Watsonville road and thence to Santa Cruz via Aptos and Soquel.—*Santa Cruz Sentinel*, Oct. 5th.

We cannot understand how the sale of Mr. White's ranch has anything to do towards shaping the course of the proposed railroad. It has been suggested to us that the above item was intended to frighten the people here by conveying to them the impression that, unless lively exertions were made the road to Santa Cruz would leave Watsonville three or four miles out in the cold. But Watsonville don't get frightened over such trivial matters, however much the worthy citizens of the City of the Holy Cross may feel frightened for us. We think we are safe in saying that the citizens of this section do not care where the road is laid out. It seems to be exclusively a Santa Cruz enterprise, which, if constructed at all will be by Santa Cruz capital, for of course no one believes that the new subsidy will be carried. Hence we say, if capitalists of that place desire a road, invest their money and time in the furtherance of the scheme, the people of Watsonville have no right to find fault with the route of Hihn & Kirby's road, and neither will they.

456. *The Santa Cruz Sentinel,* October 12, 1872 (2:1)

Marked Appreciation in Real Estate—Our Local Railroad, &c.

It is a most encouraging and noteworthy fact that since the building of a connecting line of railroad between here and Watsonville has been agitated among us, real estate has advanced fully fifty per cent. over its value

The Dream of Steam, 1854–1873

three months since. This rise is attributable to the speculative interest taken in our county by men of sagacity, who foresee the advantage to accrue from the great influx of population which the completion of the road is sure to attract to us. Indeed, seventy-five per cent. of the real estate transfers that have been made in this county lately, were induced by the believe that we would be connected by rail to San Francisco within four months from to-day; and to tell the truth, our prospects for the consummation of our hopes in this regard were never better. In fact, one prominent public spirited citizen, possessing ample means, has it in view to begin the work of construction at once, at his own expense if necessary, of the first section of the road between Santa Cruz and Soquel. This important portion of the line can easily be built inside of two months, at a comparatively trifling cost, and will be of immense benefit to the people of both termini. Soquel, now a minor consideration, will immediately rise to the dignity of a town; and Santa Cruz, from her present lethargic condition, to one of active business importance for all future time.

This initial step in the building of the road will necessitate many abrupt changes. Sites in both places, that have been for years dreamily sustaining shanties, cottages, gardens and the like, will suddenly find themselves hustled into the noisy vortex of an overwhelming business; and consequently worth to their owners, thousands of dollars where before they were scarcely valued at as many hundreds. Instead of being cumbered with unsightly, or at best, ordinary structures, they will groan beneath the weight of handsome four-story brick or stone buildings.

Businesses that hitherto have been worth following, will of a sudden become obsolete, and be supplanted by others more lucrative, requiring greater activity and talent in their management. To illustrate, while writing we hear of two of our local stage men considering their occupation nearly gone, have decided to lay away their horses and in future use steam as a motor; and like changes will be made by many others of our people.

To the many restless spirits who are desirous to leave this lovely valley in the vain hope to better their fortunes elsewhere, we would say remain where you are; make no needless sacrifice of means or comfort, and our word for it, you will succeed better in Santa Cruz county than you can in any other on the Pacific coast. Many who unfortunately for themselves have left here, will return if they can before the year is out. Few of us living quietly here have the slightest conception of the wondrous undeveloped wealth of Santa Cruz County, which the railroad will be the primary means to lay bare and utilize.

In conclusion we would say to all, do the utmost in your power to further the immediate construction of the railroad, and in so doing you will benefit yourselves.

In view of the great demand that will at once spring up from house accommodation, we would suggest the propriety of erecting a goodly number of first-class dwellings. They will be sure to sell well and prove a profitable investment to their owners.

457. *The Santa Cruz Sentinel*, October 12, 1872 (2:1)

Letter From San Francisco.

San Francisco, Tuesday evening, Oct. 8th, 1872.

Ed. *Sentinel*:—From Santa Cruz to San Francisco gives one a view of the west side and of the east side of the mountains. The east side is 1872, and the west side is—what shall I say? About 1832! On the west side stage coaches toll through the heat and dust along roads that seem never to have known work or repair. Snail paced teams follow each other strung along the stretch of miles, pulling at little loads of lumber called for at a distance to build up more enterprising places.

On the east side how different!

It is amazing that the west has endured this behindhand condition half as long as it has. Property owners, business men—you had better give half you are worth, every one of you today, if it be necessary, to build a railroad along that beautiful tract of country, for you will be richer by half in a single year by doing even that.

A few hundreds of dollars from some and a few thousand from others is nothing to the purpose. Subscribe enough to build a railroad immediately.   W.

458. *The Santa Cruz Sentinel*, October 12, 1872 (2:2)

Railroad Committee.

The citizens of Santa Cruz can congratulate themselves on having one Committee who have gone earnestly to work to secure the right of way for the new railroad and lots for railroad buildings.

The Committee hold regular meetings to compare notes; but that is not all, they have taken off their coats and pitched into the work with a will that augurs well for the success of the enterprise. The Executive Railroad Committee might emulate their example we think, and go to work, too. They have not had a meeting for some time. If they don't propose to do anything they had better resign, and let others take their place who will work.

459. *The Santa Cruz Sentinel*, October 19, 1872 (1:9)

Favors a Narrow Gauge.

John T. Doyle, Esq., has a communication in the San Mateo *Gazette*, discussing the subject of a coast railroad. He tells the people of San Mateo county that they want additional railroad connection with San Francisco, but that they must depend upon themselves, and not upon the people of San Francisco, who have enough to do to take care of their own local wants, in order to secure that connection. After reciting the fact that the law authorizes San Mateo County to subscribe for stock in railroads, he says:

Why not avail of its provisions to build our own road? As all must contribute to the expense, let the undertaking—let our project—embrace both roads, so that as far as possible all may be equally benefited.

My proposal is to build two narrow gauge roads, intersecting the county from north to south. One around the coast, the other through the valley. A branch line should connect the two at Redwood City or San Mateo, whichever is preferable. Narrow gauge roads could be built and equipped (according to the printed reports) for $14,000 per mile, and can be operated for about half the expense of board gauge ones. The valley road would take from the Southern Pacific three-fourths of its freight and passengers and ensure cheaper and better accommodations to the remainder. The interest on the outlay involved in their construction would be saved every year in reduction of freights, and the value of the property in the county be largely increased. Let us not abandon the effort for better highways because San Francisco declines to build them for us, but rather redouble them and strive the more to help ourselves. Let us have a County Convention at an early day to consider the whole question and take practical steps toward this desirable object.

460. *The Santa Cruz Sentinel*, October 19, 1872 (2:3)

Executive Railroad Committee Meeting.

The Executive Railroad Committee held a meeting at the office of R. Conant, Secretary; present, D. Tuthill chairman, Titus Hale, John Werner, A. Pray, Sr., A. R. Meserve, G. B. V. DeLamater, Charles Brown, R. C. Kirby, J. S. Green, C. Cappelmann and R. Conant Secretary. On motion of Mr. Hale, it was resolved to hold two stated meetings a week, until the week before election, and then to hold meetings every night. Tuesday and Saturday evenings were decided upon, and the hour, 8 o'clock.

On motion, it was resolved to extend the survey, commenced by the railroad committee on right of way, through the entire length of the county, and that A. Pray, Sr., be appointed a committee of one to collect subscriptions to defray the expenses of the same.

On motion, Mr. Green was elected Treasurer.

The reports that came in were highly encouraging to the committee. Persons are coming forward and offering the right of way. The first on the list is John Leibrandt, who gives the right of way, one acre of land and sufficient frontage for wharfage purpose.

Messrs. Hale, Pray and Green were appointed a Committee to attend to the survey.

The committee then adjourned to meet at the Court House, on Saturday evening Oct. 19th, at 8 o'clock. It will also meet on Tuesday evening Oct. 22d., at the same place and hour. R. CONANT, Secretary

461. *The Santa Cruz Sentinel*, October 19, 1872 (3:2)
The Railroad.

The committee on securing the right of way for the coming railroad, are hard at work, and are meeting with much encouragement from those living along the proposed route. It is the intention of the committee to have the road commenced here, as well as at Watsonville. Mr. Spreckels, who recently purchased the Aptos Ranch, and Mr. Hihn were present at the meeting of the committee on Tuesday evening, and pledged themselves that the road should be built the entire length of the county. The different members of the committee are out every day, examining the route and securing the right of way. We trust that every citizen who has the interest of our county at heart will put his shoulder to the wheel and assist the committee in its labors. The time has come when every friend of the road must be vigilant and work for its success. We must see how large a majority we can give for the road next month, and let our friends abroad know that the people on the coast are not asleep to their intentions.

Mr. Spreckels in his remarks before the committee, showed the deep interest he took in the success of this road. We want a few more accessions of his kind to our population, men of capital and enterprise. Men who look out not only for their own interest, but for the interest of the community at large. And the only means we shall have of getting them here will be by showing some enterprise ourselves, and building a railroad. The committee have set men at work surveying out the route. And it will be pushed to completion as rapidly as possible.

462. *The Pajaronian*, October 24, 1872 (2:1)

We have received this week an excellent communication from Santa Cruz way on the railroad swindle now being strenuously pushed ahead by F. A. Hihn and a few others. The communication came too late for publication in this issue, but we will publish it next week.

463. *Daily Morning Call* via *The Pajaronian*, October 24, 1872 (2:2)

Hihn's Railroad.

A good deal of energy is being displayed by the citizens of Watsonville and Santa Cruz, respectively, for constructing the projected road between the two places. The committee to secure subscriptions are meeting with good success. Prominent men of wealth declare that the road shall be built the entire length of the county. Owners of land through which it is to pass, are exhibiting a commendable liberality in granting a right of way. Mr. John Leibrandt offers land and sufficient frontage for wharfage purposes. Others make promises equally flattering, and little doubt is now felt that the road will be built.

Watsonville has nothing whatever to do with the above railroad, and F. A. Hihn, a man whose instincts and friendship are all based upon money making, is the principal energetic mover in the swindling subsidy scheme at Santa Cruz. It is said that nearly $100,000 have been subscribed, and that it will cost $600,000 or $700,000 to complete the road. The prominent men of wealth spoken of above comprise F. A. Hihn. No promises of any account have yet been made. With these few corrections the *Call* is correct.

The *Call* probably does not fully understand the matter. F. A. Hihn, a man who was never known to do a disinteresting act in his life, owns a large amount of land between Watsonville and Santa Cruz. *He* desires to sell that land, (as the most of it is of no use to him or anyone else at this time,) and he thinks that if a railroad cuts it in twain he would make hundreds of thousands by the operation. He cares nothing for the county only in so far as his own pocket is benefited. By hard work he managed to procure numerous names to a document praying the Board of Supervisors to allow a vote to be taken at the coming election, on the proposition of granting a subsidy for a railroad between Watsonville and Santa Cruz, amounting to $240,000, which, if carried, will swell the debt of Santa Cruz county to nearly $400,000!

The Board passed the order, and Hihn is working with all his energy to carry the rascally measure. No estimates have been made by responsible persons as to the cost of the road—no surveys have been made to test its practicability—no contract has been entered into by any person or company to build the road in case the $240,000 is voted. The whole scheme is a pitiable abortion on the part of Hihn to *make money*, and the fulsome adulations of his relatives and a few hangers on puff him up with the idea that he is in reality as far up in the scale of humanity as he himself imagines. Poor men are disgusted with the whole thing, and all classes who think are amused at the game of railroad which is being played by men, not one of whom know the first principle of railroading. The citizens of this portion of the county are not opposed to a railroad to Santa Cruz. There is not a man in this section who would not rejoice to be connected with their sister town by rail, but they do not like to enter into any scheme of such magnitude blindly—led by a fellow like Hihn. A majority of the people of this section voted against granting more subsidies on principle, holding that those principles which elected Booth are good and they will not prove false to principle. They know that this small county is nearly $100,000 in debt, that taxes are now and have been very onerous, and they do not desire the debt increased $240,000 more without feeling assured that corresponding benefits will accrue. They know that Santa Cruz already has splendid transporting facilities, and feel that a narrow gauge railroad from this place there, will not work the vast change represented by that misrepresented Hihn, to Santa Cruz—and they judge from the effect of the Southern Pacific on the town of Watsonville. Our people say, however, that, *after* due examination it has been reasonably proven that a railroad will pay as an investment form this place to Santa Cruz, they will subscribe liberally, as business men, but they will not vote to give Hihn $240,000 of the peoples money.

We are actuated in this discussion only by the best motives—an earnest desire for the best welfare of the county at large. Neither would we denounce all who are working for the railroad, for there are some very worthy men who are taking active part toward carrying the subsidy. But F. A. Hihn and several others we could mention are not the men to push a scheme involving so much money. We want the *men* of Santa Cruz county to be the leaders. We want the *men* to talk with the people of all sections, instead of a few, irresponsible, selfish, spiteful blatherskites, with no souls possessing higher instincts than to rob the people for their own financial benefit.

464. *San Francisco* Examiner, October 25, 1872 (2:4)
WITHDRAWAL.

The Colorado River Railroad Company yesterday sent to the Board of Supervisors a communication, in reply to Supervisor Shrader's resolution adopted at the last meeting. The President, J. Mora Moss, encloses a copy of the resolution adopted at a meeting of the Directors on the 23rd instant, and takes occasion to state "that there is now a perverted public sentiment on the subject of subsidy, and that the people do not clearly appreciate their utter dependency upon existing monopolies, and how completely the no-subsidy dogma maintains them." The claim for subsidy, in our opinion, is withdrawn in the clearest and most formal manner, and from the high character of the Directors, we do not believe there can be any trick in the withdrawal. Next Monday night [Oct 28] the resolution will be rescinded.

465. *The Santa Cruz Sentinel*, October 26, 1872 (2:2)
Railroad Committee on Right of Way.

The Committee met at the office of the Secretary on Tuesday evening, Oct. 22d, at 7.30 o'clock, P.M.

Mr. Cappelmann reported that they had obtained right of way from Mr. Liebrandt, 100 feet in width, and two acres of land and a right of way from Third street to the land granted to be 50 feet wide.

Mr. Otto said that he had a proposition from Mr. Gharkey of about ten acres of land, right back of the Powder Magazine, between Light House street and the beach, and also four acres in addition for the benefit of the Company, and right of way through his land.

On motion the Committee accepted the same, and instructed Mr. Cappelman to prepare the necessary papers to make the contract with Mr. Gharkey.

The Committee on the west side of the river reported progress, and stated that the survey was going on. The Committee then adjourned to Tuesday evening, October 29th, at 7.30 P.M.R. CONANT, Secretary.

466. *The Santa Cruz Sentinel,* **October 26, 1872 (2:2)**

The San Lorenzo Railroad.

On the 23d of October a meeting of the officers of the above road was held in Santa Cruz, and the following Resolutions were adopted:

Resolved—That J. S. Cunningham, E. Bennett, Otis Ashley and George Evans are hereby authorized to receive subscriptions to the Stock of the San Lorenzo Valley Railroad Company, on terms equal to those granted to the present stockholders.

Resolved—That as soon as sufficient stock has been subscribed to insure the construction of the Railroad from Santa Cruz to Felton, the Company shall be re-organized by the election of new officers, and work on the road shall immediately thereafter commence.

Resolved—That if sufficient subscriptions cannot be obtained to secure the early construction of the road to Felton, this Board will recommend to the stockholders of the Company to surrender the franchise and the work done, without cost to such parties as will give sufficient assurance to procure the construction of the Railroad from Santa Cruz to Felton within two years from date.

Passed by the Board of Directors of the San Lorenzo Valley Railroad Company, Oct. 23d, 1872.

D. Tuthill, Secretary. F. A. Hihn, President.

467. *The Santa Cruz Sentinel*, October 26, 1872 (3:1)

Executive Railroad Committee.

The committee met at the office of the Secretary, on Saturday Oct. 19th, at 8 o'clock P.M. The chairman being absent, Titus Hale was elected chairman pro tem, minutes of last meeting read, and corrected so as to read "John Leibrandt gives right of way for street, leading from Third street to the land granted."

The Treasurer reported that he had received $115 from Mr. Pray, as collections.

On motion the Treasurer was instructed to pay Kooser & Littlefield $18.00 for printing.

On motion Mr. Green was instructed to see Mr. Handy and Mr. Otto about going to Watsonville and that their expenses be paid.

On motion the committee adjourned to Tuesday evening, Oct. 22d, at 8 o'clock P.M.

ROGER CONTANT, Secretary.

Executive Railroad Committee.

The committee met at the office of the Secretary, on Tuesday evening Oct. 22d, at 8 o'clock P.M.

In the absence of the chairman, A. Pray Sr. was

elected chairman pro tem. Minutes of last meeting read and approved.

On motion of Mr. Cunningham, Eben Bennett, George Evans and Adison Newell of Felton, were added to the committee.

On motion of Mr. Green, Messrs. Cunningham, Evans and Newell were constituted a sub-committee to act for the San Lorenzo Valley, and report from time to time to this committee.

On motion of Mr. Conant, it was resolved to hold a railroad meeting at Felton, on Saturday evening next, Oct. 26, and that Messrs. Kirby, Pray and Hihn, represent this committee with as many more of our citizens as they can take along.

On motion the committee then adjourned to Saturday evening Oct. 26th, at 8 o'clock P.M.

ROGER CONANT, Secretary.

468. *The Pajaronian*, October 31, 1872 (2:2)

The Subsidy.

Narrow-minded men in Santa Cruz, (and we insist that there are several there) accuse the citizens of Watsonville of selfishness and low jealousy and dog-in-the-manger feelings toward that place for the reason that the Watsonville portion of the county opposes the subsidy. We deny that such feelings exist. The people here are to be commended for adherence to principle, and not blamed by those in the county who have no principles. There is a deliberate design on the part of persons in

Santa Cruz to create a bad feeling between the two ends of the county. It has been done and is being done. The reason for this is obvious. Santa Cruz has the majority of votes, and if the two portions of the county are at swords points and vote against each other through spite, why, of course Santa Cruz will carry the subsidy, right or wrong. One of those disturbers of the public peace came to this place from Santa Cruz a few weeks since. Speaking with some gentlemen who consented to talk with him for a moment, on the railroad, the disorganizer from the Holy Cross said he didn't care a d— whether the *Pajaronian* favored the subsidy or not—"we would like nothing better than to get the paper excited." This feeling is not confined alone to the paper published here. But we think that the masses of the people are not influenced this year so much as last and if we do not greatly mistake the intelligence of the people of Santa Cruz county, the verdict regarding the subsidy of $240,000 will be "no."

Let the people think of the lamentable abortion and burlesque last year, in the subsidy line. Think of the promises then made, the money expended, the grandiloquent speeches made, by the railroad greenhorns, who succeeded in gloriously fooling you! The same thing will take place this year if you vote the subsidy.

We have received considerable abuse on account of our stand on the subsidy question in this county, and if we have ever neglected to answer back we hope our enemies will excuse us. We are proud of the course we have taken, for we have ever been conscientious. We have been actuated by principle, and entertained the opinion that the scheme was not for the benefit of the county so much as for the financial advantages of the proprietor of the Augmentation Rancho. Furthermore, we are convinced that the work is premature—that an enterprise not warranted by the resources or present requirements of Santa Cruz county, is being forced upon the people. Again, we feel that to increase the already heavy debt of the county $240,000 is an insult to the poor man—that it is wrong in principle, and calculated to materially injure the prosperity and best welfare of the county by increasing taxation, and as a consequence increasing the rent of lands, thereby keeping out men of limited means.

469. *The Santa Cruz Sentinel*, November 2, 1872 (2:3)

Railroad Meeting in Felton.

At a mass meeting held in Felton, at Glynn's Hall, October 26th, 1872, on motion, G. W. Evans was elected President, and J. F. Cunningham, Secretary. After considerable discussion and a full explanation of the position of the San Lorenzo Railroad Company, in which Messrs. Bennet, Cunningham and Evans took prominent part, the following preamble and resolution were adopted:

Whereas, The San Lorenzo Railroad Company, having met and passed resolutions to the effect that they are ready and willing to commence work on said road, as soon as sufficient stock has been subscribed to ensure its success, and having authorized a resident committee to receive subscriptions to the stock of said road; and having confidence in the practicability of the route, and relying in good faith on their pledges. Therefore:

Resolved. That we heartily endorse the action of said Company, and will lend allied in our power for the immediate construction of said road; and believing the Santa Cruz and Watsonville Railroad necessary for us to reap the full advantages of the system we endorse, and will give our support to the subsidy measure, as set forth in the proclamation of the Board of Supervisors.

G. W. Evans, Chairman.

J. F. Cunningham, Secretary.

470. *The Santa Cruz Sentinel,* November 2, 1872 (2:3)
The Coast Railroad.
San Andres, Oct. 29th, 1872.

Editor Sentinel:—If you will allow me a little room in your paper, I have a few words to say about the Railroad. The surveyors have been around here, and hunted for the last week, and have surveyed all along, from the creek up to Corralitos, and have not found the best road yet. Now I don't know much about narrow gauge railroads, but why ain't the shortest road the best? Why don't they go straight through the San Andres Rancho to Watsonville? We will all go in for it here, and give the right of way; I say go to Watsonville, though some of those storekeepers there would be served right if they would be left out in the cold. I might call names, but that would be like the *Pajaronian* man, who thinks he can pull the wool over the eyes by making a fuss about one of your Santa Cruz men. Everybody knows who *Cummings* belongs to. The fact of the matter is, we farmers want a railroad to Santa Cruz, we want to ship our hay, and buy our lumber and fencing where we please, and so do all the farmers in the Pajaro Valley, and so do all the people of Watsonville, all except one or two storekeepers and their hangers on. To hear them talk as if there ought to be but one lumber yard in the Pajaro valley,—but one man to buy ties, and but one way to shop our grain,—and that one man talks as if he wants the greatest friend Watsonville ever had; but if the truth was known, people would find out that he owns already some lots in the new town on the other side of the river, and he would be the first man to move his store and lumber yard over there just as soon as that town gets a start. It is a good thing, though, that all people are not alike. I have traded in Watsonville ever since I lived on the San Andres, and I know a good many people there; some of them may have a kind of little spite toward the Santa Cruz people, but they know well enough their town cannot do well unless the farmers do well, and they are not so blind as to see that two railroads are better than one.

But I have said already more than I meant to say; excuse my long letter. San Andres.

471. *The Santa Cruz Sentinel,* November 2, 1872 (3:1)

Railroad Sharps.

It is really amusing to listen to the harangues of some of the disconsolate few who have not fully decided to vote for granting aid to the Railroad. These testy, garrulous fogies belong to that class who never propose but always oppose any enterprise of a progressive nature; they are a hindrance to successful development of our natural resources; they can see nothing but gloom in the future. According to these short sighted moles the Railroad will not be built, even with a subsidy, unless by Stanford & Co. They seem to think that there is no available capital to be had for Railroad building, except that controlled by Stanford & Co. But, to avoid discussion, we would refer gentlemen to the subscription of stock already secured—over $100,000, with a free right of way and depot grounds have been subscribed—not by Stanford & Co., but by the solid and enterprising men of this county, whose interest is that the Railroad from and to Santa Cruz should always be an independent line. We hope voters, on next Tuesday will remember this, and act for the best interests of our whole county. Let no personal interests, political issues, or factional considerations influence a vote against aid to our Railroad.

472. *The Santa Cruz Sentinel,* November 2, 1872 (3:2)
Felton all Right.

By reference to proceedings of a railroad meeting held at Felton on last Saturday evening, it will be seen that a unanimous vote was passed to aid the railroad with the subsidy proposed by the Board of Supervisors. This settles the question. New Year's Point, San Lorenzo, Scott's Valley, Soquel and Santa Cruz will all go for the subsidy by large majorities, if we are correctly informed, and it is inferred the enterprise will get a few votes in Corralitos and Watsonville. The San Lorenzo people are earnestly at work to assist the road, well-knowing that it is but a link to connect their town, (Felton,) with the out-side world by steam. They have already subscribed, (in one evening) $7,000 in stock, and we are informed that 150 shares of $100 each will be taken in a very short time, and a larger sum can be raised if necessary. The California Powder Company is willing to take ten thousand dollars of the stock as soon as it is a certainty the road will be built. Our own citizens in Santa Cruz will also increase their subscriptions, if necessary, to make up the connection. We now feel hopeful that in a very short time the iron horse will be snorting down the San Lorenzo with lime, lumber, powder, paper, safety-fuse, granite, silver ore, stone coal, and many other productions incident to that vast section of undeveloped country. By all means give us the railroad, and vote "Yes," for railroad subsidy, and in a short time we will experience all the beneficial results that well-directed industry can give in a building up a large manufacturing and producing town and country.

473. *The Santa Cruz Sentinel,* November 2, 1872 (3:3)
Rally for the Railroad.

Every voter is expected to do his level best for the railroad. During the past few weeks we purposely avoided discussion, on the subject, believing every man true to the interests of Santa Cruz was favorable of granting aid to the road. When the vote was formerly taken for a subsidy, the subject was fully discussed, and not wishing to repeat our former arguments, fresh in the minds of all, or travel over the same ground, and reiterate reasons then given, we left the whole subject to the reflection of our property holders and tax-payers. Do you wish to double the value of your land,

and have a ready and certain market for it, and all you raise on it? Then vote "Railroad Aid: Yes." Nuff ced.

474. *The Pajaronian*, November 7, 1872 (2:1)
The Subsidy.

The two hundred and forty thousand dollar subsidy is carried in this county by a large majority, and Watsonville is the only place in Santa Cruz county that remained true to principles fought for at the last State election. The principal movers in the subsidy have, we understand, promised Felton that a branch road shall be built to that place, also promises of like nature were made to Corralitos. We feel no chagrin at the result, for all knew how the vote would be. We do feel annoyed, however, that Santa Cruz county is not ruled by men of more generous minds, a higher order of intellect, and a more decency in political matters.

475. *The Pajaronian*, November 5, 1872 (2:2)

"**Railroad Aid Yes**"—These self constituted rulers of Santa Cruz county, having in charge the election tickets, had them all printed with "Railroad Aid Yes"—not one "No" in the whole lot sent to this county, when it was known by those who ordered them that there was a large number in this section who would vote against the subsidy. Neither were the committee men here consulted in regard to the matter. The above exhibits the usual small characteristics, of certain persons in Santa Cruz who deem that they and their town stand at the head of God's glorious universe. It is a specimen of hundreds of petty insults to the people of this town and vicinity, by the would be rulers. Such small, petty maneuvers have often been practiced which, taken in connection with many of a graver nature keep this county in a constant ferment. Santa Cruz can boast of many noble and high-minded men and women, and probably has no greater proportion of shysters than can be found in other towns of like size, but, we venture to say, there is no town where the latter class is of a more pure and unadulterated quality. Our known Christian and forbearing principles will not allow us to speak with any degree of plainness, besides we might get sick some time in Santa Cruz, and then we would be sure to have twenty-seven or thirty able bodied subsidyists throw themselves upon our suffering carcass, and send our tired soul in a brilliant flight to glory. That's why we are afraid to say anything that a few persons in that town would get mad at. But, good friends, if you ever play any more little, mean, sneaking, "smart," contemptible tricks on the people here, we may get our courage up and say something severe that will aggravate you. God bless you and keep you from following the natural bent of your inclinations, is our prayer.

476. *The Pajaronian*, November 5, 1872 (5:3)

Now that the subsidy elephant has been voted, what are its friends going to do with it? We predict that it will prove of no more account than that other elephant of the same breed conceived last year.

477. *The Santa Cruz Sentinel*, November 9, 1872 (3:3)
The Railroad Vote.

On Tuesday last the general interest was taken, in Santa Cruz, on the vote for aid to the Coast Railroad. In fact, if it had not been for that vital interest, one-half the vote would not have been polled here. So far as heard from there were eight hundred and fifty-five votes polled for the aid, and 22 against it, with Corralitos and New Years' Point to hear from, which two precincts, for and against, will very nearly off-set each other; giving three hundred and thirty three majority for the road. Last year one thousand and fifteen votes were polled for the subsidy, and four hundred and seven against it... We are glad the vote carried by such a decided majority. There is nothing now left for us to do but subscribe liberally and commence to build the road. The officers, we are informed, are going ahead slowly but sure, and will make no false move, but secure all points before commencing; in the meantime our citizens should all aid with their money and friendship in starting the work of grading. Additional and new subscriptions will be required, and it is the duty of every property-holder, and all those wishing work to assist in commencing to grade this winter, so as to give employment during the dull part of the season.

478. *The Santa Cruz Sentinel,* November 16, 1872 (2:3-4)

Official Returns—Santa Cruz County, Nov. 5th, 1872.		
	Railroad	
	Yes.	No.
Santa Cruz....................................	587	36
Soquel..	133	55
Scott's Valley...............................	38	21
New Years.....................................	41	9
San Lorenzo.................................	87	16
Corralitos......................................	41	9
Pajaro..	13	395
Totals,	927	564
Majorities,	353	

479. *The Santa Cruz Sentinel,* November 16, 1872 (2:2)

Railroad Direct to San Francisco.

Santa Cruz County having voted the required aid two hundred and forty thousand dollars, to enable some company to construct a broad or narrow gauge road through the county, it now behooves those having the matter in hand, to see that the great object—a route direct to San Francisco—for which the people voted particularly, is not defeated, but pushed forward with all possible haste.

That there are many obstacles to surmount in reaching the city by the coast route is doubtless true. But are they such as will impose a perpetual barrier to the construction of a railroad, if San Mateo county would guarantee assistance to the road through that county to the extent per mile which this county has.

The people of San Mateo County are now mooting the question of aiding the construction of railroads through that county, and to this end a call is issued through the *Gazette*, signed by many of the most wealthy and prominent citizens of that city, for a mass convention to assembled in Red Wood City, the 28th inst., for the purpose of coming to some conclusion as to what is best to be done in order to ensure the speedy construction of railroads throughout that county.

This looks like business, and certain good results will speedily follow, for that county, like this, is now suffering for want of a more ready and perfect means of development.

Is not this a most favorable opportunity in which these two counties may join their energy and means to aid in constructing a railroad communication with San Francisco, and which will prove of incalculable benefit to both sections in the development of their material wealth.

There are two routes by which a road can reach San Francisco direct, and pass through San Mateo county. The first is by the coast, the other by way of the San Lorenzo river, and which, by many is considered the best and most practicable.

The latter however could not claim any portion of the aid voted, as the wording of the proclamation precludes aid to road, unless constructed up the coast. We are now satisfied that a great mistake was made in not placing the San Lorenzo route also in the way of aid, if it were possible to have done so, as more stock can be secured to build a road in this direction than another.

It rests with San Mateo to say what shall be the character of our gauge, whether broad or narrow; for, if that county will indicate a desire and intention to connect with us, and continue a line to San Francisco, our people will welcome any gauge that will the soonest effect this result. The nearer we seem to approach the possibility of railroad connection with the outside world, the more distasteful it seems to have to go around Robin Hood's barn, to get to San Francisco. Let our citizens take immediate steps to enlist our neighbors over the mountains in a direct route to the city; and let us be represented by two or three prominent citizens in their convention on the 26th inst. at Red Wood City.

They will gladly welcome us, and if we mistake not, give every assurance of a desire to connect the fortunes of the two counties by mutually aiding to construct a broad or narrow gauge railroad through the best and most valuable portions of both counties.

Our citizens will see the importance of this step when they consider that the aid now voted may possibly be given to the Southern Pacific R. R. Co., and with them the road will stop at Santa Cruz, while with any other parties it will be most likely to reach the city sooner or later. Let the people take the aid and build the road as they certainly can, and not be at the mercy of any outside party. San Mateo and Santa Cruz counties can well afford to join hands in this grand project, and own the road. A narrow gauge is all that will be required, and its cheapness will ensure its speedy construction, if San Mateo will act promptly and wisely.

480. *The Santa Cruz Sentinel*, November 16, 1872 (2:2)

The Railroad.

At a meeting of the Executive Railroad Committee, held on Friday evening Nov. 8th, 1872, F. A. Hihn, Titus Hale, R. C. Kirby, R. B. Handy, D. Tuthill and A. Pray Sr., were appointed a committee to go before the Board of Supervisors on Monday, to ascertain what assurances could be had towards securing the subsidy in case a company should be organized from the citizens and tax-payers of the county, for the purpose of constructing a three foot gauge Railroad, on the route proposed in the subsidy proclamation, and also state that it is the intention of this committee to organize said company from the tax-payers and citizens of the county. At a meeting of the Executive committee on Monday evening, the committee appointed to go before the Board made the following report:

The committee of citizens, consisting of A. Pray, R. C. Kirby, Titus Hale, R. B. Handy, D. Tuthill and F. A. Hihn, make the following proposal to the Board of Supervisors of Santa Cruz county, that if assured that the Board will grant a subsidy of $6,000 per mile, to be paid as provided by law in aid for the construction of a Railroad of a three foot gauge, from Watsonville through the county of Santa Cruz, on the general route as proposed in the subsidy proclamation, to a company having for its stock-holders, all tax-payers of the county who desire to take stock and which company will show itself able to build without delay such a Railroad from Watsonville to Santa Cruz, the committee and those who they represent will at once proceed to organize such a company.

The Board of Supervisors thereupon expressed themselves unanimously in favor of the immediate construction of the Railroad, for which the subsidy has been voted, but deemed it advisable before giving the desired assurances to postpone the consideration of the proposition for one week, so as to enable the Board to secure the best terms for the county in relation to the granting of the subsidy. On motion the report was accepted, and the Executive committee adjourned to meet at the office of the Secretary next Monday evening. ROGER CONANT, Secretary.

481. *The Santa Cruz Sentinel*, November 16, 1872 (3:2)

Personal.

Capt. Moulton, the Railroad builder is in town looking after our coast railroad interests. Capt. Moulton built the San Jose and Copperopolis roads, and is a competent, reliable and expert railroad Engineer and mechanic.

482. *The Pajaronian*, November 21, 1872 (2:2)

Railroad.

After a good deal of inquiring, we have been told that the result of Stanford's visit to Santa Cruz will be a speedy survey of the route of the proposed road, in order to determine the cost. Then he will state his terms and build the road, it said terms are complied with. Peyton, of the Santa

Cruz Powder Works, was instrumental in inducing Mr. Stanford to examine the route. We do not think that Mr. Stanford will consent to build the road for the subsidy which has just been voted—$6,000 per mile—and after the survey has been finished, and estimates made, he will undoubtedly call for $200,000 or $300,000 more. A good opportunity for Watsonville citizens to invest their surplus funds, for the benefit of their friends in Santa Cruz. Of course they will do it, for it will display such a noble, christian spirit to give to the poor and needy—cast bread upon the waters and run the risk of its coming back buttered on both sides. Of course it is not the design now to construct a narrow gauge. A few lies about narrow gauge, cheapness, home companies, peoples' enterprise, etc., etc., will do before election, but now that the subsidy is voted, the large ears of the ass can begin to be seen through the lion's skin.

483. *The Santa Cruz Sentinel*, November 23, 1872 (2:2)

Railroad Convention.

Thirty-four prominent citizens and tax-payers of San Mateo county, have signed a call to meet their fellow citizens in convention at Redwood City, on Tuesday, November 26th, 1872, to consider and take action on the construction of narrow-gauge railroads through the county. This is the proper course to pursue, and we advise that a delegation from Santa Cruz County be sent to attend the Convention. For Aptos, Claus Spreckels would be the proper delegate; Soquel, Ben. Porter; Santa Cruz, Titus Hale, D. Tuthill and

Amasa Pray; New Year's Point, W. W. Waddell; San Lorenzo, George Evans and E. Bennett; Scott's Valley, D. J. Locke. These names have been only suggested to us, and the residents of each precinct should attend to it and elect representatives at once to attend. We want two narrow-gauge roads—one down the coast, and another from the mouth of Boulder and Bear Creek, at Alcorn's place, to Santa Cruz, and possibly up Boulder Creek to the head-waters of Pescadero, Butano, Big Creek and the Gazos. Immediate action is necessary.

484. *The Santa Cruz Sentinel*, November 23, 1872 (2:3)

Prospects of a Railroad.

Our prospects for a railroad through the greater portion of Santa Cruz County are looking bright indeed. Monday morning last found two prominent Railroad men in town, one of whom was no less a personage than Ex-Governor Stanford. Their visit was with particular reference to the construction of the Railroad to which the late subsidy voted by this county is applicable. It is believed that the most advantageous terms can be had of Stanford & Co., and there seems to be a quieting down on the part of our citizens, into the idea that it is best that the great king company should take the aid and construct the road, which of course will correspond in gauge to their road throughout the State. If this is to be the ultimatum of our Railroad furor, it will be accepted as the best thing possible under the existing circumstances, and those who have been so ready and willing to subscribe to stock, can hold their assistance in readiness for the time, speedily coming, when the road can, with moderate aid, be projected to San Francisco. We notice by the *Bulletin* of the 19th inst., an article prompted no doubt by a perusal of the *Sentinel*, of Saturday last, wherein it looks upon the construction of a narrow gauge Railroad to San Francisco, from some point in this county, as a very feasible matter, and assures us that San Mateo County can, if she will, aid its progress, city ward, by an amount equally the aid granted per mile by Santa Cruz County. Our zeal for connection with San Francisco by a direct route must not cease, even though the road is certain of being constructed from Watsonville to Santa Cruz by Stanford & Co. To continue its construction on either of the lines before indicated towards the city, will require all the aid and energy this people can command, yet we feel confident that there is enough of persistent energy, somewhat dormant now, resting among us to see that the road reached the city, if San Mateo County, in her Convention of the 26th inst., determines to aid the road, if it is placed within reach of her county boundary. It is not too much to look for, or ask of our San Mateo friends that they subscribe to stock to aid the road through a part of this county, knowing as they must that the road will open up to them a trade in the wood and lumber line unequalled in palmiest days of California. It is quite necessary that this section meet and consult with San Mateo on all points involved in this Railroad question, because our interests are almost inseparably united, and when once we effect an understanding and commence acting accordingly, there is no telling to what extent our mutual efforts may advance the interests of all sections.

The day of hinderances and impossibilities is passing away, and communities feel that the life current of commerce follows in the wake of Railroads, and woe be to that town or city that fails to urge and aid forward every progressive enterprise that promises an enlarged business and growing population.

It will be a short time before we shall know what to expect at the hands of those having our Railroad affairs in charge. Supervisor Peyton is very earnest in behalf of the county, and is determined that what is done shall be done for the benefit of all classes, and to the ultimate satisfaction of his constituents; mainly through his influence have we been assisted by Railroad men from various parts of the State, all of whom pronounce the route between Watsonville and Santa Cruz as quite practicable and easy of construction.

John P. Stearns of Santa Barbara County, is in town, and urges upon our citizens the idea of forming a company for the construction of a Railroad from San Francisco to the Colorado, and assures us that he can get three millions of dollars of the necessary stock subscribed in his county alone.

We wish to give everybody's views on this great question of the age; for the small clouds seen so far away may be approaching us with more promise than we have reason to expect. It is too late in the day to smile at any proposition on any subject, for to-morrow we witness its consummation and wonder at the ease with which the miracle was wrought.

485. *The Santa Cruz Sentinel,* November 23, 1872 (3:2)

Railroad Matters.

On last Monday the citizen's Committee appeared before the Board of Supervisors to receive an answer in regard to obtaining a subsidy. Mr. Peyton stated he had seen Governor Stanford, and that the Governor had entertained the proposition to build the road, and was in town with two of his Chief Engineers; had come over the route, measured the distance, taken the elevation, &c., and had expressed a favorable opinion; and gave assurances that if a re-survey as they went back, verified their notes, and further satisfied them of its practicability, a thorough survey would be ordered, and a full report being made by the engineers, an answer would be given whether a contract would be made to build the road or not. The Committee, who were present in full number, urged the Supervisors to give them the assurances applied for at their last meeting; maintaining that the tax-payers were ready and willing to immediately organize a Company and commence operations, and would complete the road as fast as possible. After deliberation the Board of Supervisors took further time, in order that Stanford's decision might be received and if favorable acted on. Capt. Moulton, an experienced and practical railroad man, was introduced, by the Committee, to the Board, and gave some very interesting remarks and statistics about railroads, generally and more particularly about narrow gauges—which he favors above every other kind of railroad. In a few weeks, it is expected Governor Stanford will have his engineers at work, and if a favorable report is made, he will at once proceed to construct the road, early in the spring, laying aside twenty miles of railroad track for that purpose, out of the 250 miles of iron now due. Hurrah for Stanford and the Railroad.

486. *The Santa Cruz Sentinel*, November 23, 1872 (3:3)

Railroad Meeting.

At a meeting of the Executive Railroad Committee, of Santa Cruz, held on Thursday evening November 21, the following preambles and resolutions were adopted:

Whereas, we deem it the interest of the citizens of Santa Cruz county to co-operate with the citizens of San Mateo county, in their efforts to secure the construction of a three foot gauge Railroad, extending from San Francisco southerly through the counties of San Mateo and Santa Cruz.

Whereas, it is evident from the subscriptions already obtained, that with a county subsidy of $6,000 per mile, sufficient means can be obtained to secure the early construction of a three foot gauge Railroad, not only from Watsonville to Santa Cruz, but also to be continued from there to the northern line of Santa Cruz county, as soon as a similar railroad shall have been constructed extending thence through San Mateo county to San Francisco, therefore be it

Resolved, that a committee of three be appointed by the chair, to confer on this question with a similar committee which may be appointed by the citizens of San Mateo county, at the Railroad convention to be held on the 26th inst, or to attend in person at such convention.

The following committee was appointed:

Messrs. F. A. Hihn, A. Pray, Sr., and Claus Spreckles.

R. CONANT, Secretary.

487. *The Santa Cruz Sentinel*, November 23, 1872 (3:3)

Board of Supervisors.
Monday, November 18th, 1872.

Present—Supervisors B. Peyton, chairman; P. F. Dean, Frank F. Porter and the clerk....

Several Railroad propositions were presented and considered, but no action taken. On motion the Board adjourned *sine die*. The next regular meeting will be first Monday in February, 1872. A special meeting may be called at any time.

488. *The Santa Cruz Sentinel,* November 30, 1872 (2:2-3)

Railroad Convention at Redwood City.

The Railroad Convention, on Tuesday last, held in Redwood City, was largely attended by the best men in San Mateo County. From the telegraphic report in the San Francisco *Call*, we learn that Hon. T. G. Phelps was elected chairman, and T. Lemmen Meyer and Henry Toomy secretaries. The following address and resolutions were adopted:

ADDRESS

This Convention, assembled at Redwood City on Tuesday, Nov. 23, 1872, to consider the interests of San Mateo County in connection with Railroads, present to their fellow-citizens of the county the following considerations. That the development and prosperity of the County have long been retarded from the want of easy communication in its different sections and with adjacent counties. Living at the door of the first city on the Pacific coast, it is yet nearly as little known or frequented as the remote parts of the State, owing to its peculiar formation. Traversed by a mountain ridge from end to end, the larger part of it is today dependent for communication on the old-fashioned stage-coach, and sends it produce to market by coasting vessels. From Spanishtown to San Mateo direct is a distance of nine miles, and instead of being traversed in an hour, it occupies nearly half a day.

The whole of the coast county, rich in dairy and agricultural products and capable of the highest development, is practically inaccessible and unknown. The valley on the east side of the mountains is indeed traversed by a Railroad leading to the city, but one which, owing to its faulty location, ill-construction and peculiar management, operates rather to retard than advance its local prosperity. Its faulty location and severe grades serve at the same time to increase the distance and forbid rapidity of motion. The best accommodations it affords are inferior to second-class, while its rates of charge are burdensome and excessive. The result is that the surplus population of the metropolis, which ought to flow into this county, serving to increase its population and develop its resources, finds it way into Alameda County. Nor is this state of things temporary. It has endured ever since the existing road fell into the hands of its present owners, and so far from holding out any prospect of improvement, it is gradually but steadily retrograding from bad to worse, and from that to worse again. The distance from Redwood City to San Francisco which three years ago was traversed in an hour, now occupies an hour and twenty minutes. The stations on the road have thus become for all practical purposes ten mile further from the city than they were at that time, and the Superintendent of the road is the explicit authority for the statement that any improvement of the service in this respect is simply impossible. It is obvious therefore that even in the valley no change for the better is expected, until the people of the county take the matter into their own hands and build roads for themselves, to be owned by and managed in their own interest.

Such, therefore, is the course which this Convention proposes to the people of the county. Properly considered there is nothing in it that should startle any one. The highways of the country have ever among civilized people, been the property of and maintained at the charge of the public. Indeed, there construction at the expense and for the benefit of the community is one of the first peculiar characteristics of civilization. No reason exists why it should be confined to ordinary turnpike roads. The Railroad is but the improved highway of modern times, and has become, within our own days, the ordinary mode of transit, even in the streets of our cities. There is no more reason for adhering to the old-fashioned turnpike road than for continuing to use the ancient Spanish *carreta*, or refusing to adopt any of the improved labor-saving machinery or appliances of modern times.

A Railroad issuing from San Francisco, and branching so as to pass round each side of the mountain chain, would bring the whole of our produce, at the least possible cost, to the best market on the coast, and benefit all parts of the county. It would afford to the coast townships that easy access to the city of which they are so much in want, and give to the inhabitants of the valley additional accommodation, more frequent easier and better in all respects, than they now enjoy. The county has power to subscribe $500,000 to the stock of a Railroad company. This sum, with a moderate subscription from private individuals, would ensure the completion of the work. Even if the investment produced no direct reform, it would be repaid four fold in the reduction of freight on our produce, beside largely increasing our population and the value of property; but there is no reason why the stock itself should be unproductive. It is now satisfactorily shown that narrow-gauge roads can be built equipped and operated at so much less expense than those of the standard gauge, that the one may prove to be highly profitable while the other would steadily run to loss. Probably no well-informed and candid person would deny that if the question of railroad gauge were now to be determined for the first time, with the light that experience has furnished us, the narrow-gauge would be adopted with unanimity. Broad-gauge road continue to be built simply and solely to connect with others already existing, an argument which can have no weight with us, as we propose no connection with existing roads, but the commencement of another and better system, conceded by all to be specially adapted to a mountainous region such as our. Nor do we lack substantial encouragement in the undertaking from abroad.

The City of San Francisco may with confidence be relied on for aid, not indeed of such magnitude as not to be important to her, but valuable and material to us. She will doubtless give a right of way, and convenient depot grounds, and if we make a manly effort in our own behalf, will probably contribute materially to facilitate the approach to the city—an object in which she is deeply interested.

On the other side, Santa Cruz County is already in the field for a narrow-gauge road, and only awaits an assured connection with the city, to commence construction simultaneously with ourselves. It will be to the interest of Santa Clara to do the same, and our road may thus become the thoroughfare of trade and travel to the South. The time and state of the public mind are peculiarly auspicious for the proposed enterprise, and heartily undertaken, cannot fail of speedy and complete success. In view of the considerations the Convention therefore adopts the following:

RESOLUTIONS:

Resolved, That the interests of the County of San Mateo require the construction of a narrow gauge railroad, extending from the city of San Francisco to the southern boundary of the county, and connecting each side of the mountain with the metropolis.

Resolved, That for the purpose of constructing such a

road a company should be formed, whose fundamental articles should be so framed as to afford all subscribers to the stock a legal guarantee against a subsequent deviation from the routes proposed, and that the county should take stock in the company to the extent of her legal capacity.

Resolved, That an Executive Committee be appointed to prepare the necessary articles of association, and to obtain subscriptions thereto; that all the inhabitants and tax-payers of the county be invited to subscribe in large sums or small according to their means; that the company be organized as soon as the necessary subscriptions are obtained, and steps should be promptly taken to submit to the electors of the county the question of taking stock in the company.

The address and resolutions were adopted unanimously. It was then voted that an Executive Committee, consisting of four from each township, and one from the county at large, be appointed by the Chair.

The President named such Committee, and he was authorized to call them together when deemed desirable.

The Convention then adjourned.

489. *The Santa Cruz Sentinel*, December 7, 1872 (2:2-3)

Stanford and Our Railroad.

The following telegram from ex-Governor Stanford to Supervisor Peyton, speaks for itself:

"Sacramento, Nov. 26, 1872. Bernard Peyton, Esq., Will have engineer in the field as soon as they can be called off other work, which will be next week.

LELAND STANFORD."

Next week is at hand and no engineers are yet in the field.

If the Broad-gauge policy is to prevail, it will be necessary that some speedy action is taken, for every hour brings us nearer the certainty that the material interests of this county and people will be best served by the construction of a narrow-gauge road up the coast, direct to San Francisco. Our subsidy will take, or can be applied to this road, which will extend the whole length of this county, from East to West, and San Mateo bids fair to carry the project to the very gates of the city.

We believe more firmly than ever that there is a great and growing necessity for this coast road, and so great and apparent is becoming this fact, that every county and town within the counties bordering the ocean, feel and know this to be their only resource of development and growth.

It is proper that this coast road should be constructed on the Narrow-gauge principle, for the reason that it never can become tributary or consolidated with the Broad-gauge roads, and will benefit the people by keeping in operation rival facilities for transportation. It is cheap fare and the country need that the remote sections can be of some use agriculturally.

There is not that marked difference between the carrying capacity of the two roads many would have us believe. It requires but three of the freight cars of the Narrow-gauge road to carry the freight usually taken in two of the Broad-gauge cars, and the difference in speed is more than over-balanced by the cheapness of constructing and stocking a Narrow-gauge road; besides, the ease with which heights and curves are overcome brings the construction of this road possible, in and through counties that cannot for a moment entertain the idea of a Broad-gauge road.

The step then about to be taken on this question is of vital importance to Santa Cruz and our sister counties south; and we should be mindful of the general welfare of all sections, when through their growth and prosperity we hope to be prospered. It is over this coast road that our vast millions of timber will find market in the southern valleys, with which our lumber can be brought in competition. The only hope of this branch of industry becoming profitable is by securing this outlet and market; further delay is death to lumbermen, for to think of manufacturing lumber at the present prices is madness, and a sad waste of valuable timber; better let the forests live and burn the mills than dissipate your property in a vain attempt to prosper at the business.

Every other interest demands a continuous line of road extending from San Francisco to our southern border, and why not enter into the project with force, now that the time has come where the work can be accomplished.

490. *The Santa Cruz Sentinel*, December 7, 1872 (4:2-3)

Narrow Gauge Railroad.

Every day generates and brings forth some new idea, fact or thought concerning our prospects for a Railroad, and forces us to keep pace with the tide of sentiment rising about us. We had given little credence to the thought that San Mateo county could be induced to aid in constructing any line of roads that did not reach the bay towns direct, and in this thought we urged its consideration of the San Lorenzo route. We not learn through the *Gazette* that no aid can be expected to any road but that which traverses the coast, with a diverging track to hit Mayfield. If such is to be the course of the people of San Mateo county, we can safely predict, that with the assurance that a narrow gauge road would be carried city wards from the western boundary of this county, our citizens will take the matter of constructing a narrow gauge Railroad up the coast in hand, and force the work ahead with energy. It is because we saw no hope of Railroad facilities beyond Santa Cruz, that our people have manifested no great zeal in becoming personally interested in its construction. We had began to look upon that portion of our subsidy applicable to a line beyond Santa Cruz, as something mythical; but the recent interest manifested throughout San Mateo county for a continuation of the coast line through that county, and thence to San Francisco affords our citizens much gratification, and will stimulate them to aid as far as in them lies, the construction of a narrow gauge road from the most eastern boundary of this county to the most western; to which can be applied the entire aid of two hundred and forty thousand dollars. It is to be hoped, and we may say, reasonable expected, that the action of the convention held in San

Mateo county on the 26th inst., in the interest of railroads, will be productive of much good, and lead to immediate action. It will be the greatest stimulus this section has ever received, and will lead to the incorporation of a company of citizens who will form a nucleus, around which will gather all the friends, aid and means sufficient to construct the road from San Francisco to the Colorada river. Every county south of this will construct immediately, that portion of the road passing through their territory, and Santa Barbara and San Luis Obispo counties will do much more than is required to pass the road through their section. This coast line is becoming the greatest necessary of the entire Southern counties, bordering the coast; and the people are more ready to-day than ever before, to take the matter in hand and own the road. All that is now required is, for San Mateo county to do as Santa Cruz county has done, vote six thousand dollars aid per mile, and the ball that shall know no stopping until it reaches the Colorado will have been set in motion; a new era will dawn upon the State at large, and the counties south will receive that influx of population their broad plains and fertile vallies so urgently due, and to develop and ripen their great agricultural resources.

The first cost of narrow gauge roads are about sixteen thousand dollars per mile. It will be seen that with aid to the amount of six thousand dollars per mile, and a subscription to stock of about three thousand dollars more, it will be very easy to raise by first mortgage upon the road the required balance of seven thousand dollars per mile to complete the road. There are citizens in Santa Cruz who have opposed aid to railroads at all times and under all circumstances, who now say they will donate money in no inconsiderable sums to aid the construction of a narrow or broad gauge road, that shall have for its object the connecting directly of San Francisco with the Southern counties via. the coast route; this is the favor with which this project is viewed by anti Railroad men in this county, and it is to be hoped they may have the satisfaction of contributing the assistance they now so nobly offer. Let no reasonable exertions be spared to keep pace with the progress our neighboring county, San Mateo is making to the end, that our mutual efforts may result in direct railroad connection with the great mart of the Pacific coast, San Francisco.

491. *The Santa Cruz Sentinel,* December 14, 1872 (1:8-9)

The Narrow Gauge Experiment.

The San Francisco *Bulletin*, in noticing our narrow Gauge Railroad scheme, has the following. The people of Pajaro Valley should read and reflect:

"There are few topics of a practical character which interests the people more just now, than the narrow gauge railroad enterprise which have been set on foot in this State. It is the problem of cheap and substantial roads adequate to the public wants. But as cheaply as these roads may be built. they cannot be secured without the employment of home capital. In Santa Cruz county, a subsidy of $6,000 a mile was recently voted, and it was hoped that this amount, increased by private subscriptions, would insure the building of a narrow gauge road from Watsonville to Santa Cruz, twenty miles, and thence to the north line of the county to connect with a proposed road to by pushed south through San Mateo county. But this Santa Cruz project hangs fire. The subsidy was granted to no particular road; that disposition is to be made by the Board of Supervisors. In the meantime the President of the Central Pacific has visited that locality, and has placed his surveyors in the field with the view of ascertaining if the subsidy cannot be made available for a broad gauge from Watsonville to Santa Cruz. Such a road would be of great importance to the county, and particularly to those two flourishing towns. But if constructed it would completely block the narrow-gauge enterprise, as probably no more than twenty miles of broad-gauge would be constructed for many years to come.

"If there were a narrow-gauge road from Watsonville to Santa Cruz, freight might be sent out of the Pajaro Valley to Santa Cruz, and thence shipped by water to San Francisco at $1.50 a ton less than the rates now charged by railroad; the difference would probably be even greater. The shipping facilities by water of the Pajaro Valley are very poor. Sailing vessels cannot get into the slough, three or four miles below Watsonville, and small steamers can only get there in good weather, and at considerable risk. An outlet by way of Santa Cruz, where the shipping facilities have always been excellent, would give all the rich Pajaro Valley the benefit of competition and ensure a moderate freight tariff. The President of the Central Pacific sees the point and knows that it is the early bird that catches the worm. Unless a thorough organization of a narrow gauge is perfected at once and the Company go earnestly to work, this opportunity will be lost."

492. *The Santa Cruz Sentinel*, December 14, 1872 (2:1)

The Situation.

On the 26th of last month Ex-Governor Stanford, by telegraph, promised to have a corps of engineers in the field the following week to survey the route for the extension of the Railroad, from Pajaro to Santa Cruz.

Nearly three weeks have passed since the giving of this promise, and still it remains unfulfilled, and no explanation or reason tendered for thus delaying the work.

What does such a promise and consequent inaction imply? If it means anything, it is evidently equivalent saying, "hold on. I'll build your road when I've had my leisure," and not until then.

Now, unfortunately for Ex-Governor Stanford, the people of Santa Cruz County are sick of such continued trifling with their material interests, and demand nothing short of the immediate construction of a Railroad from the County seat to San Francisco. If the S.P.R. Co. cannot build the proposed branch-road for an indefinite length of time, this county cannot afford to wait for so tardy action on their part, in a matter so vital to her welfare, but must at once strike out boldly for herself and build the Narrow-gauge road to the border of San Mateo County, to connect with the line soon to be in operation, thence to San Francisco.

Our very existence, as a business community, is menaced by further delay in having easy and speedy communication by rail with the commercial metropolis of the State; and we see no reason why our local company should not immediately take the matter in hand. Let a survey be made and a contract for the construction of the first section of the road be made at once; the graders set to work, and according to the adage, the road is as well as half built!

Many who have hitherto felt indifferent about the subject, and have hung back in subscribing for the stock of the road will, when they see the company in earnest and not only meaning business, but actually in it, change their minds, and become the most liberal contributors for stock, and energetic workers for the completion of the road.

We believe that further delay on our part in the commencement of this comparatively easy, yet to us all-important undertaking is highly criminal; in fact, fatal to our reputation and prosperity as a people, and our salvation lies only in our united, prompt, vigorous construction of the Narrow-gauge road up the coast. The Supervisors should at once call on Stanford for an explanation, and if he fails to reply go on and make a contract with some other company.

493. *The Santa Cruz Sentinel,* December 21, 1872 (2:1-2)

San Mateo Railroad Convention.

A meeting of the Executive Committee of the San Mateo Railroad Convention was held at Redwood City on Saturday December 14, 1872. The Committee remained in session about four hours. An informal exchange of opinions was had on the whole subject, after which it was declared to frame articles of association to be recommended for the proposed Company and on the basis of which subscriptions should be invited. The special objects sought to be attained in these articles were:

First—To secure railroad accommodation to the inhabitants of each side of the mountain range without trammeling the directors in the location of the road, further than is necessary to attain that object.

Second—The location of the road so far as it lies within the City and County of San Francisco in such way as to encourage subscriptions and aid from the city.

Third—Safeguards against interested mismanagement by rings, contract and finance companies and the like.

Articles V., VI. and VII., were, after careful consideration, adopted to accomplish these objects. The other articles of association are in the ordinary form, complying with the requirements of the corporation law. No name for the company was decided on, nor was the number of the Directors fixed.

The names of the following gentlemen were suggested as Directors, most if not all of whom it is known will become stockholders. Amongst them a suitable Board will be selected after the preliminary subscription shall have been made: I. C. Steele, T. W. Moore, B. Hayward, Geo. H. Howard, Tiburcio Parrott, John H. Redington, Alvinza Hayward, W. C. Ralston, A. F. Green, Chas. Lux, Claus Spreckels, John T. Doyle, T. G. Phelps, Robert Sherwood, E. W. Burr, S. L. Jones, T. Lemmen

Meyer, A. N. Hamm, Henry Doble, Alexander Gordon, J. Johnston. Joseph P. Ames, M. S. Latham, Charles N. Felton, S. S. Merrill, W. W. Armstrong.

On an off-hand canvass for subscriptions, the following were promised:

I. C. Steele	$5,000
Braddock Weeks	$5,000
B. Hayward	$2,000
S. W. Preble	$1,000
J. T. Doyle	$5,000
R. E. Doyle	$2,500
Claus Spreckels	$10,000
E. W. Burr	$5,000
Gustave Mahe	$1,000
S. L. Jones	$5,000
R. E. Steele	$5,000
A. Moore	$2,000
Bartlett Weeks	$2,000
William Rayne	$5,000
T. Lemmen Meyer	$2,500
T. G. Phelps	$5,000
Charles Lux	$10,000
Robert Sherwood	$2,500
Bernard Murphy	$2,000
Alexander Gordon	$10,000

Several other prominent citizens were named who have expressed their intention to subscribe, but the amounts were not mentioned.

Members were then appointed to canvass the various

The Dream of Steam, 1854–1873

townships and report to the Secretary in a week; it being desirable to effect an organization before the 25th inst.

Articles V., VI. and VII. above referred to are to the following effect:

Article V. The place from which said proposed road is to be constructed is from a point in Mission Bay, in the city and county of San Francisco with its track extended northward therefrom to a point at North Beach, on the northern water front of said city, west of Dupont street, and thence running through the towns of San Mateo and Redwood City, to the southern boundary of San Mateo county. It shall have a branch extending from the main line to Half Moon Bay, and passing through Spanish Town and Pescadero, to the southern boundary of San Mateo County, on the west side of the Coast Range of Mountains. The counties into and through which the said proposed road is intended to pass are the city and county of San Francisco and the county of San Mateo, and its length one hundred miles.

Article VI. In order to equalize payments on subscriptions, to stock made at different dates, the payments made by the several subscribers on account of the shares subscribed for by them respectively, shall be credited with interest at ten per cent. per annum, from the date of the several payments made such credits of interest to be compensated for either by the issue of corresponding proportion of shares of stock, or by rebate of the final cash payment as the directors may determine.

Article VII. All contracts for the doing of any work or furnishing any material for the construction of any part of the said road, shall be let by advertisement and open competition. No director, engineer or officer of said company shall make any indirect gain or profit from or be interested directly in any contract let by the company, unless the same be in writing, and his interests be truly expressed thereon; otherwise all gain or profit derived therefrom shall be for the benefit of the company, and be paid over to it, and the acceptance of office in said company by any such officer shall be deemed to express his assent to and promise to fulfill this article.—S. F. *Bulletin*, Dec. 17.

The particular object in giving place to more than a brief mention of the above, is, to show to this county what San Mateo county is doing in the line of railroads; and further, to convince our folks that there is much more than talk in the idea of connecting these counties by a narrow-gauge road with San Francisco. As an impetus to the project, similar steps should be taken in this county to continue the road from Pescadero down through this county, where Monterey can take hold and carry it down to the San Louis Obispo border, and in this way the road will, with local aid and local energy be carried to the extreme southern boundary of the State.

Two hundred and forty thousand dollars aid voted by this county is the grand rallying point, and if energy was displayed among our people, as among the citizens of San Mateo county there would be no doubt of the early beginning and completion of the road to the extent to which the aid applies; delays are dangerous, and our railroad prospects may become so complicated by drawing too many plans and parties together, as to render the benefit from our aid more local than general; it certainly will be so if there is not a uniform grade and gauge secured to this coast road. With the narrow gauge road bordering the coast, there is every prospect that places of any considerable vote, more to the interior, would construct branch roads. It would be different with a broad gauge road, as the greater expense of constructing and equipping them, renders them only a thing for powerful monied corporations to handle and control.

494. *The Santa Cruz Sentinel,* December 21, 1872 (3:1)

En Route.

Stanford & Co's Surveyors are busy at work, surveying the railroad. On Wednesday they crossed the divide, between Watsonville and Santa Cruz, near the tule marshes, which they set on fire and made a tremendous conflagration, destroying numerous snakes and bullfrogs. In a few weeks we will hear their final report, when the road will no doubt be built. That is our opinion. We expect to see the cars running by the 4th of July next, at least. Hurrah for the Railroad!

495. *The Santa Cruz Sentinel,* December 28, 1872 (3:4)

The Surveyors.

We learn that the Topographical Engineers, surveying a Railroad from Watsonville to Santa Cruz, had to suspend operations on account of the heavy rains. They find the grade much better than expected. From the Pajaro depot to Sanderson's stage station there is a gradual rise of 200 feet. The rise from "Sandy's" to the sandhill divide, with a 20-foot cut is 200 feet; thence to Santa Cruz it is tide-water level, almost, excepting at Aptos where a slight incline is perceptible. The survey will be completed as soon as the storm is over.

496. *The Santa Cruz Sentinel,* January 4, 1873 (2:1)

Broad-Gauge a Finality.

Stanford, Hopkins & Co., have taken the initial steps towards securing the construction of a broad-gauge road, with deflecting branches down through the coast counties, thus checkmating the possibility of being annoyed by any competing route. This looks like the death knell of the narrow-gauge coast road.

The certificate, incorporating this branch of the Southern Pacific road, was filed with the Secretary of State on the 23d ult., and every requirement of the law compiled with in a manner that must lead the people to believe that these enterprising gentlemen intend to accomplish all they, in their certificate of incorporation, set forth.

This road down the coast is the great desire of the coast counties, and the greatest blessing that could be granted them; and if we mistake net, every assistance possible with the people, will be cheerfully accorded the company, to the end, that the road may be pushed forward to a speedy completion during the year so auspiciously begun. Don't let our neighbors stand back, or rest in their own light, but come forward with all their resources, and the population of the southern counties will more than quadruple in two years.

It is but just and proper that county aid be granted by all those counties certain to be immeasurably benefited, and in fact, whose only hope rests in the early and speedy construction of railroad facilities.

This projected continuation of the Salinas branch of the Southern Pacific road is the brightest prospect Santa Cruz county has ever had; giving promise of soon affording a profitable outlet for all the lumber manufactured from our vast forests of fir and redwood.

This section of the railroad folks should be candidly and carefully canvassed and considered by the San Mateo people, lest they commit a grievous error by hastily concluding to construct a narrow gauge road, as in their prospectus they first proposed. Should their plan be changed to suit a broad gauge road, they will be enabled to help forward the completion of a through coast road on the broad-gauge plan—a road preferable above all others—whose beginning shall be San Francisco, and terminus the Colorado river.

This prospect of a road south will have a tendency to enhance the price and value of all classes of lands, and those whose eyes have been turned southward, as a desirable place to invest and build up a pleasant home, must make haste, lest the good opportunity for securing cheap lands be lost.

There are hundreds of thousands of acres of as fine agricultural lands as embraced within the extensive valleys of the counties of San Luis Obispo, Santa Barbara, and Ventura, as can be found in either the Pajaro or Salinas vallies, and through which the road must from necessity pass.

Stanford & Co. can do no work that will so effectually dispel the prejudice the people entertain against railroad corporations and railroad monopolies, as that of pushing forward their railroad enterprises in a manner to develop the interior portion of the State; it is these parts that must depend upon such facilities to give them the benefit of good markets, and stimulate agricultural enterprises generally. Fares and freights will regulate themselves; for any road depending upon the product of a country or region for freight, would hardly be so short sighted as to place an embargo on enterprise by levying exorbitant rates. Give us the roads and we will take care of the charges.

497. *The Santa Cruz Sentinel*, January 11, 1873 (3:4)

The Surveyors.

Stanford & Co's Topographical engineers, are now operating between Soquel and Santa Cruz, and prospecting for the best route to cross the San Lorenzo and locate a depot. It is said grading will commence the middle of next month. Hurrah for the Railroad!

498. *The Pajaronian*, January 16, 1873 (3:1)

Railroad Rumors.

We understand that the Surveyors are making good headway on the proposed road between Watsonville and Santa Cruz, they being now above Soquel, and will soon

The Dream of Steam, 1854–1873

finish the survey. It is said that an estimate has been made of the cost of the road and the amount is fixed at $37,000 per mile. This is exclusive of the iron which will cost $6,000 per mile, which will make the whole cost of the road $43,000 per mile, or $860,000 for the twenty miles. Depots, rights of way, and other incidental expenses will probably amount to $40,000, making the whole cost of the road between Watsonville and Santa Cruz $900,000. This sum at first sight may seem large to many, but as the county has granted a subsidy of $6,000 per mile or $120,000 for the twenty miles, the amount which a company would be obliged to pay is reduced to $780,000. Certain wealthy and public spirited property owners of Santa Cruz, we are informed, will give liberally. Say, F. A. Hihn, $50,000; Claus Spreckles, $50,000; Mr. Green, $10,000; Lucien Heath, $20,000; R. C. Kirby, $20,000; Field & Brown, $20,000; Tuthill, of the Santa Cruz Gas Works, $20,000; E L Williams, $10,000; Hall, $10,000; and other property owners of that place, say $60,000, making the whole amount from individuals $270,000, while will only necessitate the expenditure by the Southern Pacific Railroad Co., of the comparatively small sum of $510,000, or a little over $25,000 per mile. Probably $20,000 can be obtained in the way of subscriptions outside of Santa Cruz, which will still further reduce the railroad company's expense. The route as surveyed runs through Rodriguez street in this town and follows along near the Santa Cruz and Watsonville Stage road. The right of way can be obtained here, notwithstanding former opposition on the part of citizens of this valley to the road, and we also learn that a prominent lumber firm will give ground for a depot, near the center of the town. The "Sentinel" as well as many individuals of Santa Cruz seem to think the building of the road a foregone conclusion, and we now see no difficulty in the way, if the sums above enumerated are subscribed, and we doubt not they will be, in consideration of the wealth and public spirit of the gentlemen mentions, and the benefits that will accrue from the advent of the road.

We have conscientiously opposed the road from its first inception, deeming that we were advocating the best interests of the county, by so doing. As to whether our views have changed does not come into the province of this article; suffice it to say that if the road is to be constructed in spite of former opposition from this section, continued opposition would be futile as well as a loss of time. The question of a road evidently lies with a few of the wealthy men of Santa Cruz, and from all we can ascertain they are pushing the work ahead with highly commendable zeal. As to how much would be given toward a road in this section we can make no approximation. R. C. Kirby, Esq. was in town not long ago, endeavoring to ascertain what might be expected, but as to the result of his inquiries we have received no hint—in fact he has not mentioned the subject to us. We give the above rumors as they came to us from time to time during the past few weeks, now wishing in this connection to give our own speculations to any great extent.

499. *The Santa Cruz Sentinel*, January 18, 1873 (3:2)
R. R. Survey.

The engineers have completed on survey from Watsonville to Santa Cruz, and gone back to the Pajaro Valley to run out a new line to the north of the old stage road, to find it possible an easier grade than coming through and around the hills to the south of the Lagunas. The last stake-pin near this place was set within the enclosure of Mr. Bliss, and it is quite certain the crossing will be effected from that point, through the Uhden place; this will give the Company the advantage of the Powder Companies wharf, or a fine opportunity of putting one into the bay at some point between their's and the mouth of the San Lorenzo. We shall soon know what hope to indulge for the completion of a road the coming summer; everybody is anxious and enquiring.

500. *The Santa Cruz Sentinel*, January 18, 1873 (3:2)
Straws.

A lumber dealer, of this place, while visiting Salinas City, last week, had occasion to converse with the carpenters and bridge builders of the Southern Pacific Railroad, at their boarding house in Salinas, and they informed him that orders were expected to place the full force of trestle-builders on the Santa Cruz railroad in less than two months.

501. *The Santa Cruz Sentinel*, January 18, 1873 (3:4)
Private Letter Answered.

We are in receipt of a private letter, from an old friend,

long a resident of Watsonville, and so much of the letter being devoted to prophetic expressions concerning the future result of our railroad project, we now propose to give our friend the views of one looking on the bright side of the subject: Instead of believing that the county will be sold out to any railroad company, on account of the aid this county has voted for the purpose of constructing the road between Santa Cruz and Watsonville, we think that the road will ore than pay its proportion of taxes, besides affording the people of the valley the opportunity of securing water transportation for all their produce, at at least one dollar per ton less than they have ever paid for like transportation; this item alone will annually re-emburse Watsonville and the Pajaro Valley for more than the road will cost them during the twenty years the bonds are to run. The increase of taxable property in all parts of the county, and the increase of population incident to the proper working of this road, will double the tax resources of the county and lessen immeasurably the burden of taxation now so much complained of. The cheapness with which lumber can be furnished in the Pajaro valley, will alone pay for all the inconvenience arising through taxation; lumber that now sells there, for from twenty to thirty-five dollars per thousand feet, can be furnished by rail from these parts at sixteen and twenty dollars per thousand.

It is much easier to imagine evil, as a consequence from almost any act or project, than good, but we fail to see anything but good to flow from the most thorough and complete railroad facilities throughout the State. We should not view things in the light that shone about us ten years ago, for a new and different era has dawned, even the era of universal railroads. California can never be anything without railroads, and with them she will become the most wealthy, populous and productive State in the Union. What, we ask our friend, has done so much for Watsonville of late? Is not all the good prospects of that thriving town resulted from the advent of the railroad into the Pajaro valley? Your place instead of wearing the old countryfied air, assuming, as if by magic, the life, appearance and hum of a city. We simply ask and desire to become similarly benefited.

502. *The Santa Cruz Sentinel*, January 25, 1873 (3:3)
Railroad.

The surveyors are busy at work, completing their lines. A new pass has been discovered a little north of the stage road from Aptos sand hill to Steiggleman's house, which will increase the distance a little but materially reduce the grade on this side; the soil is also better for grading and the road will be less expensive to build, and when finished not liable to be washed away or require any repairs for years.

503. *The Santa Cruz Sentinel*, February 15, 1873 (2:5)
The Railroad.

The inclement weather, preventing operations in the open field on our Railroad, we hear but little said on the subject. Information says that two companies stand ready to build the road should the Southern Pacific Railroad fail to do so. Ex-Governor Stanford has just returned from the

East, and we may soon expect to hear from him; or a report from the Engineers. We think the reported sale of the road to Tom Scott & Co., is only got up for effect, and even if the sale has been made, so much the better for us, as Stanford & Co. will connect our road with the one recently incorporated, to commence "at or near Salinas City," and thence via. the Mission of San Miguel to the Tulare Valley.

504. *The Santa Cruz Sentinel*, February 22, 1873 (3:1)
Diesing's Brewery.

As soon as the railroad is finished, it is contemplated that Santa Cruz beer will supply, in part, the whole Salinas, San Benito, Gilroy, Pajaro and other vallies, wherever railroad lines connect. At one time Mr. Diesing had agencies at Monterey, Salinas City, Castroville, Watsonville and other places, but the cost and delay in transportation compelled him to close. The railroad completed and cars running, will obviate this, and in the future, it is safe to predict, Santa Cruz will no doubt be as famous for good, pure, genuine lager beer, as is no Albany and Philadelphia in the Eastern States.

505. *The Santa Cruz Sentinel*, February 22, 1873 (3:2)
The Railroad.

We are anxiously waiting intelligence from Stanford & Co., in regard to the Santa Cruz and Pajaro Railroad. The engineers, who surveyed the route, have completed their work and reported, and are now at work south of Soledad

Mission, and to San Miguel Mission, determining the cheapest route along the Salinas river. Mr. Robinson is willing to build a narrow gauge road, for the subsidy, and a Marysville Company will also compete, if Stanford & Co. fail to take the contract. We hope that the Board of Supervisors, at their regular meeting (first Monday in April) will make a contract with some company to build the road. We care not what gauge is adopted, so that we get a railroad in the shortest possible time. Let the first offer from a reliable company be accepted.

506. *The Pajaronian*, February 27, 1873 (5:1)

The Props are Slipping.—F. A. Hihn, of Santa Cruz, seems to be losing prestige in this county. The Railroad has come to naught, the Board of Supervisors insist upon doing business without his interference, and the *Pajaronian* still lives. We would advise Hihn to have a small dark room constructed in his new house in which he can retired, and commune with his diminutive, and chagrined, soul. And yet Hihn is a good man, when he can have his own way in all matters pertaining to the county, and can have all men doing as he directs. Another thing Hihn is a brave man; no one ill deny that. He was never known to run from a cripple or sick man, and never backs down unless somebody tells him to. We are willing, and always have been to give credit even to our enemies. We are sorry that Hihn is losing his grip on the county because he must feel so worked up about it. Vale Railroad! Vale Hihn!

507. *The Santa Cruz Sentinel*, March 1, 1873 (3:4)

Narrow-Gauge.

Mr. Peyton has just returned from San Francisco, and we are now satisfied that our only plan is to build a narrow-gauge road.

508. *The Pajaronian*, March 6, 1873 (5:3)

Santa Cruz, March 3.—It is ordered that on Tuesday, April 1st, 1873, a special meeting of the Board of Supervisors of Santa Cruz County be held, to take, into consideration proposals to construct a railroad, pursuant to a vote of the voters of said county by election held under an order of said Board, dated September 25th, 1872.

509. *The Santa Cruz Sentinel*, March 8, 1873 (2:1)

A Railroad Certain.

It is an ancient and true saying, that there is no great loss without some small gain, and viewing our railroad prospects by light of surrounding circumstances, we find that the damaging effect of the investigations made by Congress into the affairs of the Credit Mobilier, an institution with headquarters at Philadelphia, and a creation of the laws of the State of Pennsylvania, have reached from one end of the continent to the other, and seriously affects every interest, the welfare of which depended in any particular, on parties connected directly or indirectly with the great trans-continental railway.

Stanford & Co. are the parties representing the western

half of this great enterprise, and by purchase, mergings and consolidations have become possessed of and control nearly every mile of broad gauge road west of Ogden.

The expose of the frauds perpetrated by the "Credit Mobilier" of the "Union Pacific Company," and the "Finance and Construction Department" of the "Central Pacific Company," have set the magnates of these two Companies, before the world in their true light, and stripped them of all the fictitious power and prestige with which they were seemingly clothed.

The consequence is, Stanford & Co., and their credit that once knew no bounds, immediately reduce to those limits, that their known private fortunes only command; and from these the people will receive no benefits in the way of newly constructed railroads; neither will they maintain others that were placed under their control.

This is the reasonable solution of the recent reports, that Tom Scott would assume control of the Southern Pacific road, and Donahue that small piece contracted of him, and others, are to take back those roads and parts of roads that, in the great eagerness of this gigantic rail road king, to control the whole network of roads of the Pacific slope, passed to the control of the Central Pacific Company.

If Tom Scott is to resume the control of the Southern Pacific road,—and there seems little doubt of it—Santa Cruz County can indulge no further hopes of Stanford & Co. constructing the branch so recently surveyed between Watsonville and Santa Cruz. The people have very generally given over the idea that it is for their greatest interest to have a broad gauge road, when there is so fine a prospect of a continuous line of narrow gauge, bordering the coast from San Diego to San Francisco, one-twelfth of which would pass through the most valuable portions of this county.

If our people will renew their zeal and render aid possible with many of them, there are parties now ready to take the aid voted, and construct a road from Watsonville to the Western boundary of the county, from which point San Mateo will complete the road to San Francisco; all this can be done in the next year and a half. Is this not, then, after all the most practicable and sensible course to be pursued? This class of roads answer every purpose, and cost so much less, and are managed and kept in repair so much easier than the sentiment of all sections of the country, east, west, north and south, are favoring the construction of narrow gauge roads.

It is better that all the roads in the State be not under the control of one company, for the chances of competition will be so small that every man is compelled to pay the tribute to the owners. We need a just and fair competition, that the people may not be burned with exorbitant rates of fare and freight. Then railroads aid to prosper individuals as well as aid in the settlement of the country.

There are several parties desirous of taking the six thousand dollars per mile, voted by the people, and constructing a narrow gauge road between Santa Cruz and Watsonville. There was a time when parties in Santa Cruz would have taken the subsidy and performed the work, but we now understand that outside parties who await opportunity are at liberty to send in their proposition, as many of those among us once intent upon investing in the project have turned their means in other directions. The Supervisors have set Tuesday, April 1st, as the day to give all propositions relating to railroad matters a hearing.

It is therefore desirable, in order to push ahead the road, if it is to be constructed this year, that all parties mature their plans and propositions and get them before the board at that time, that the Board and the people may know what is to come of all our railroad furor.

510. *The Santa Cruz Sentinel*, March 8, 1873 (3:3)
Railroad Meeting.

It is ordered by the Board of Supervisors that Tuesday, April 1st, 1873, be set apart from the purpose of considering proposals for the construction of a railroad to be constructed pursuant to a vote of the people of this county as per election, held by an order of the Board dated Sept. 25, 1872. It is expected that some action will then be taken in the premises as several parties are expected to send in proposals, some of which will doubtless find favor with the Board.

511. *The Santa Cruz Sentinel*, March 15, 1873 (3:3)
Railroad Meeting.

The Board of Supervisors of Santa Cruz county, will hold a special meeting on the first day of April next, at which they will consider all proposals that may be tendered for the construction of a Railroad, between the Pajaro and Santa Cruz, upon the basis of the subsidy of $6,000 per mile, voted by the people at the last general election. At that meeting they will award a contract for building the road, should any proposal appear to the Board, to be advantageous to the county. Notice of the special meeting has been published in the San Francisco papers. All parties desiring information on the subject, or concerning the subsidy, should attend or write to the President of the Board. The county Clerk will give any necessary information, to interested parties, required in the mean time.

512. *The Santa Cruz Sentinel,* March 22, 1873 (4:2)

Major R. P. Hammond, an able and experienced Railroad contractor was here last week, looking after Railroad interests.

513. *The Santa Cruz Sentinel,* March 29, 1873 (2:1)

Suggestion to San Francisco.

In looking out from this great city and center of commerce of the State, we see but one practicable, cheap and feasible way of approaching it by rail—from the Southeast by land.

A large and productive region, extending from San Francisco to San Diego, can be made to pour its wealth of products into the lap of that city, if some reciprocity of feeling and interest can be established and maintained between the city and the country.

There are enterprises contemplated and on foot

throughout the Southern counties, that with proper facilities for transportation will become a mere adjunct to the growth and prosperity of San Francisco. The country is rich in everything except money; and without this there can be no Railroads—the only cheap means of transportation possible—and such are the immediate necessity and demand of the whole southern country.

The Counties will aid with their bonds to the extent of about six thousand dollars per mile. The people will privately subscribe as much more, aggregating an amount sufficient to consummate one-half the work undertaken in the construction of Narrow-gauge roads. It then becomes necessary to cast about to see if other helps cannot be found and made available, the result of which may be a continuous line of road from San Francisco to San Diego.

The suggestion we offer is worthy the careful consideration of every capitalist in the State interested in the growth and prosperity of San Francisco, and is this: Whenever the people of counties adjoining San Francisco, or connected to those with Railroads leading to the city, shall have secured a sum equal to fifty per cent. of the first cost of any Railroad, that then the city or an association of capitalists organized for the purpose of aiding enterprises tending to benefit San Francisco, shall advance, on first mortgage, the remaining fifty per cent., and ensure the construction of such road.

Santa Cruz County has voted two hundred and forty thousand dollars to aid the construction of forty miles of road through this County, leading from Watsonville to Santa Cruz, thence up the coast to the boundary between

San Mateo and Santa Cruz Counties. The people will subscribe five thousand dollars per mile in addition to the six thousand given by the County, making eleven thousand dollars now available funds per mile. San Mateo, doubtless, will do as much towards securing better Railroad facilities with the city, and if San Francisco will advance, on first mortgage, the balance—nine thousand dollars per mile—the building of a Narrow-gauge road through San Mateo and Santa Cruz Counties, would be undertaken at once and hastened to completion.

There can be no doubt that the continuation of such a road would be pushed speedily through the Coast Counties, to the farthest practicable point south.

It is unnecessary, at this time, to enter into a detailed statement of the business to be done by a road constructed through the counties and country spoken of. There will be 30,000,000 feet of sawed lumber and as many million feet of split stuff taken over the road annually from Santa Cruz County alone, and a wooded country opened up in this and San Mateo County sufficient to furnish cheap fuel for San Francisco for a century to come. To these we must add the various other kinds of freight, such as leather, lime, grain, fruit, charcoal, tanbark, etc., which if increased by the productions of other counties in any reasonable ratio, will, together with the travel certain to favor a road passing through the most favored portion of the State, make up a business that must prove remunerative indeed.

We think this idea of assisting outside enterprises by San Francisco cannot fail of receiving a fair consideration, especially when it is proposed to give ample security for all assistance required, and also when the accruing benefits to said city are so apparent.

514. *The Santa Cruz Sentinel*, March 29, 1873 (3:4)
The Railroad.

Remember, that on next Monday the Board of Supervisors will hold a meeting, especially to receive proposals for building a Railroad to connect with the Central Pacific, at or near the Pajaro River, according to the specifications of the subsidy voted last year, of $6,000 per mile. We learn that our citizens propose to build a narrow track road provided no outside capitalists put in an appearance and offer to take the contract. Major R. P. Hammond has been here, looking into the proposals and attending to Stanford's interests no doubt; but whether he is prepared to build the road or make an offer to do so, we are not informed. We still think it is our policy to carry the road through, along the coast, to San Francisco, building a narrow track, up the San Lorenzo to Alarcon's [Alcorn's] place, at the junction of the Bear and Boulder creeks with the San Lorenzo. The time has now arrived for action. Talk hereafter is but idle vapor, and those who wish Railroad communication must put their own shoulders to the wheel of enterprise, and keep it moving at a gradual but sure pace, in the right direction, and soon the road will be built. Let every man give what he is able, and a company will soon offer to contract to build the road, giving ample security to complete the work and start the cars running before the year is out.

515. *The Santa Cruz Sentinel*, April 5, 1873 (2:2)

A Move in the Right Direction.

On Tuesday last, the day set by the Board of Supervisors for considering all propositions concerning the construction of our Railroad, the citizens committee appeared and were granted one month, as will be seen by our extracts from the records of that day's proceedings, in which to mature plans and determine whether they will take the six thousand dollars per mile and construct the road, or that portion of the same extending from Santa Cruz to Watsonville.

The whole matter has resolved itself into an undertaking that must be taken hold of by the whole people, and by their joint means and energy made a success, or be dropped as a thing impossible of accomplishment. There is no time to manifest or display a want of harmony. Every individual interest in the building of this road must meet every other willing or half-willing hand and unite for the common good of all. Let every man do his utmost to encourage those who are willing to take the greater burden in this project, and if every detail or minutia is not carried out as we would have it, for this, don't let us falter, so long as we are assured that the road will be constructed between the two points named, at the earliest practicable period.

The month now before us must be put in by devoting every spare moment in showing all those concerned in this project that it is for their ultimate as well as immediate benefit that the road be speedily constructed, and that it cannot be undertaken or consummated unless the people take right hold, in dead earnest, aiding to the last possible dollar. Our men of wealth will do all that can be asked of them; and if those of medium wealth will do half as much in proportion we will have the road completed in one year from the date of the first work.

There is not an individual who depends upon the thrift of Santa Cruz for a support but that can aid by a subscription of one hundred dollars; and every property owner would be better off with a Railroad if it cost him one-third part of his land. All agree that property, which a Railroad, will double in value, and the prospect of business should prompt our merchants to a liberal assistance.

Soquel will do her part in this matter, and we are assured that Watsonville has always been willing to subscribe to the stock of a Narrow Gauge road, if undertaken by the people. It is the people who are now moving in this matter, and when they move there must be some immediate necessity, and some quick and fruitful results. We believe this but the beginning of a series of narrow-gauge roads that shall—by way of the coast—connect San Francisco with all the coast counties.

Santa Barbara is moving heaven and earth to awaken an interest in behalf of that region, and will, without doubt, construct a branch of road from that place to some point to Arizona, by which Santa Barbara will be enabled to control the trade of that rich region. It is harmony and unity of purpose of energy that enables other places to accomplish every needed undertaking; and if we fail in ours it will be for want of harmony and unity of purpose. Santa Cruz has a hundred resources of wealth to Santa Barbara's nothing, and we are amazed at our neighbor's good fortune.

There is to be a citizen's meeting this (Saturday) evening, at the Court House, in Santa Cruz, where this whole subject will be thoroughly discussed and a plan of procedure arranged, in which it is desired that everybody take part.

516. *The Santa Cruz Sentinel*, April 5, 1873 (2:3)
Santa Cruz Compared with Santa Barbara.

Santa Barbara has nothing under the sun to recommend it to a people but a fine and healthful climate. That Santa Cruz has, as we believe, far surpassing Santa Barbara. Our summers are not so warm, and the variety of scenery, sports and drives have no equal on this coast; and with one-half the unity and energy displayed by the citizens of that thriving town, Santa Cruz would be the liveliest and most desirable resort on this coast. With a Railroad we would be but a few hours distant from San Francisco, an advantage that but a few places in the State enjoys, and which will go far to give us prominence over other places soon as our Railroads are completed.

517. *The Santa Cruz Sentinel*, April 5, 1873 (3:1)
Improvements.

Claus Spreckles is making considerable improvements in building and fencing on the Aptos Farm. New buildings will be erected. It is said the building of a sugar refinery, (for making beet sugar) chickory factory and a paper mill is contemplated. First we must have a railroad, and then all these enterprises will follow as a business necessity.

518. *The Santa Cruz Sentinel*, April 5, 1873 (3:2)
Citizen's Meeting.

There will be a citizen's meeting at the Court House this (Saturday) evening, for the purpose of considering the propriety of, and the manner of proceeding with, the project of constructing the Narrow-Gauge road between Watsonville and Santa Cruz. Let everybody be present, as this is the last chance for a Railroad, and we are all interested in its speedy construction.

519. *The Santa Cruz Sentinel*, April 5, 1873 (3:4)
Board of Supervisors.
Tuesday, April 1st, 1873.

Board met pursuant to adjournment: Present, B. Peyton, (chairman) F. Porter and the Clerk.

The following petition was presented to the Board:

The undersigned, in behalf of a number of citizens of Santa Cruz County, respectfully represent to their Board of Supervisors,

That they have patiently awaited the result of negotiations with Governor Stanford, in the hope that he would contract to build a broad-gauge Railroad from the Pajaro station to the town of Santa Cruz;

That it now appears that Governor Stanford will not

enter into such a contract;

That it further appears that the people of Santa Cruz County must build the road, otherwise none will be built;

And believing that the people of the County are able to build the road, and will do so, if time be allowed for the formations of a company, the survey of the route and other preliminaries, the undersigned petition the Board of Supervisors.

That they be allowed until Monday, the 5th of May next, to make surveys and other preparations, at or before the expiration of which time they may appear again before the Board to declare whether they will or will not construct a Railroad; that in the event of their electing to build a Railroad, the Board of Supervisors will then immediately contract with them, or with a company which shall have been formed under their auspices, for the construction of a Railroad from the Pajaro station to the town of Santa Cruz, which contract shall embody the following provisions:

1st, That the said Railroad shall be of not less than three-feet gauge. The rails of the T pattern, weighing not less than 30 lbs to the yard. The rail joints to be united by fish plates. The grades to be practicable for the economical transportation of heavy freight. The bridges and trellis to be of approved styles and material. The ballast to be sufficient; and, in fact, the whole work to be first-class.

2d, That the said Railroad shall extend from the town of Pajaro to and into the town of Santa Cruz, crossing the San Lorenzo River to its right or west bank.

3d. That the rolling stock of the said Railroad shall be first-class, and shall consist of a sufficient number of locomotives, freight cars and passenger cars to accommodate the trade.

4th, That the said Railroad shall be undertaken with all convenient dispatch, and shall be completed and in running order in the year 1874.

5th, That the subsidy of $6,000 per mile, in County Bonds, as voted by the people of Santa Cruz County on the 5th day of November, 1872, shall be paid for each and every mile of the main line of said Railroad, as provided by law, as completed. And further stipulations, contravening none of the above, may, on motion of the Board of Supervisors, be embodied in the contemplated contract.

6th, Guarantees, satisfactory to the Board of Supervisors, shall be given that the road shall be completed within the stipulated time, from the Pajaro station to the town of Santa Cruz, crossing the San Lorenzo river.

AMASA PRAY, TITUS HALE, LUCIEN HEATH.

The Board, on considering the above petition, granted the request.

Adjourned.

520. *The Pajaronian*, April 10, 1873 (2:1)
Santa Cruz.

We were in Santa Cruz on Sunday last, and were sorry to find the Pacific Ocean House vacant and gloomy, with no present prospects of its again being opened this season. Several whom we heard conversing about the matter of closing the house blame certain wealthy men who had claims on the furniture. They seem to think that they might have kept the house open, had they not become excited at the idea of losing a hundred dollars or such a matter. In fact the idea was conveyed that some of them who owned the furniture, were not receiving their regular three per cent. and so forced the sale in order to make their regular usury. How this is we do not know, but we cannot help thinking that the hotel might have been kept running with proper management and good feeling on the part of a few men, for we understand the hotel has not been a losing concern. On Saturday night a railroad meeting was held in the above place, something like a dozen men being present. Now our idea would be to hold a meeting regarding the re-opening of the Pacific Ocean House. We dislike to see Santa Cruz lose caste as a water place, for there is no more beautiful scenery in the State than is to be found there, and the facilities for sea bathing, picnics, etc., are not equaled anywhere. And now, just as a beautiful season is opening, the principal hotel is allowed to be shut up just on account of a difference in money matters of a few hundred dollars! While the so called financial leaders are howling railroad with their heads in the clouds of speculation, important interests that affect the people lower down are allowed to languish and die. The paper mill might have been kept running, all the material necessary being close by, but the machinery was allowed to be carted away to Stockton, while men who call themselves enterprising were figuring to carry subsidy elections that amounted to nothing so far as advancing the interest of the people was concerned. Again, Santa Cruz with its many wooden structures and a large population has no protection against fires. There are no cisterns, no engine or even hook and ladder company.

And yet the "enterprising business men" of Santa Cruz waste their time in railroad meetings and in endeavors to manage county campaigns. If our advice is good, and we believe it is in this instance, we would say, open your fine hotel building, start another paper mill and purchase a fire engine, and leave useless railroad meetings until a time more auspicious than the present. We have spoken plainly, but have told truths, and in our remarks have at heart the best interests of Santa Cruz, and consequently the whole county.

521. *The Santa Cruz Sentinel*, April 12, 1873 (2:2)
Railroad Meeting.

Pursuant to notice given in the *Sentinel*, a number of leading citizens of Santa Cruz met in the Court House, on Saturday evening, April 5th, 1873, at half-past seven o'clock, to consider Railroad matters and take action on the proposition made by the Board of Supervisors, (as published) and accepted by a committee for the citizens—Amasa Pray, Titus Hale and Lucien Heath—at a former meeting of the Railroad Executive Committee.

On motion, Mr. C. Cappelmann was elected Chairman, and B. P. Kooser, Secretary. Mr. F. A. Hihn addressed the meeting, giving in detail the result of his interviews with Ex-Governor Stanford, Major R. P. Hammond and other leading Railroad men.

Messrs. Kirby, Pray, Cappelmann and others addressed the meeting, giving their views on Railroad matters, advocating immediate action and a narrow (3 foot) gauge from the Pajaro depot to the northern line of the county; and that subscriptions be solicited and right of way secured, so as to enable a local company, aided by such outside assistance as might offer, to build the road.

In answer to a direct question the Chairman stated that about $90,000 had been offered on a former subscription; this, of course, included a free right of way through the county.

It was stated that Mr. Binney, president of the Marysville and Oroville Railroad, would be glad to build the road, and aid in the enterprise. Mr. Bishop of San Jose, also received a favorable mention, including Mr. Platt, of San Francisco.

After some debate, Mr. F. A. Hihn offered the following, seconded by Amasa Pray—chairman of the citizen's committee—which was unanimously adopted:

Resolved, That the Executive Railroad Committee be instructed to immediately proceed with the organization of a Railroad Company, having for its object the construction of a Narrow Gauge Railroad from Watsonville, thence through the town of Santa Cruz, and along or near the coast to the northern line of the county, and that canvassers be appointed to obtain sufficient subscriptions, so as to enable us to accept the county aid of $6,000 per mile, on the terms agreed upon with our Board of Supervisors, and

Resolved, Further, that the said Committee be requested to correspond with Messrs. Bishop, Platte, Binney and other railroad men, with the view to secure their co-operation in our enterprise.

On motion the Secretary was instructed to inform the

Secretary of the Railroad Executive Committee, of the results of this meeting, furnishing copies of the above Resolutions, suggesting prompt action, and calling a meeting of said Executive Committee, at the Court House, on Thursday evening, April 10th, 1873.

On motion the meeting adjourned at half-past 9 o'clock.   C. CAPPELMANN, Ch'm.

B. P. Kooser, Sec'y.

522. *The Santa Cruz Sentinel*, April 12, 1873 (3:1)

Railroad Meeting.

The Executive Committee of the friends of Railroad enterprise, will meet at the Court House, this Saturday evening, April 12th, 1873, at 8 o'clock, to consider the resolutions adopted at the recent Railroad meeting, held April 5th. A full attendance of the members of the committee is requested. Now is the time for action.

523. *The Santa Cruz Sentinel*, April 12, 1873 (3:3)

Executive Railroad Committee.

The Committee met at the Court House, on Thursday evening, April 10th, to consider the resolutions adopted at the citizen's meeting, on Saturday evening, April 5th. In the absence of the Chairman, C. Cappelmann was elected chairman, *pro tem*.

After some discussion on the resolutions the following committee, to draft a plan of subscription, was appointed: F. A. Hihn, J. S. Green, D. Tuthill, C. Cappelmann and E. H. Heacock.

The Committee then adjourned to Saturday evening, April 12th. R. CONANT, Sec'y.

524. *The Pajaronian*, April 17, 1873 (3:3)

Santa Cruz Items.

The Santa Cruz Railroad folks have determined to build the railroad be[tween] Watsonville and Santa Cruz on the Narrow Gauge plan, and are vigilantly at work getting the required $150,000 taken. Several of our citizens are doing all that can be expected. F. A. Hihn takes $25,000. August Spreckles, $55,000, George Treat, $10,000, Titus Hale, $5,000, Ben Porter, $5,000 and others all they can afford. It is believed that work will commence very soon now that the people see that they must construct the road if one is ever constructed.

525. *The Santa Cruz Sentinel*, April 19, 1873 (2:1)

The Railroad.

We are now assured that sufficient will be subscribed to construct a narrow Gauge Railroad, to the County line at the Pajaro, and, in fact, along the coast to the northern County line at New Years Point. The subscriptions already amount to some $75,000, and it is expected that in San Francisco and outside of the County nearly as much can be secured. Just as soon as the road is completed to Santa Cruz the northern track will be put under contract, then the San

Lorenzo road will commence with renewed action. The road will be some 16 miles in length, to the junction of Bear and Boulder Creeks with the San Lorenzo.

526. *The Santa Cruz Sentinel*, April 19, 1873 (3:4)

Railroad Executive Committee.

The Executive Railroad Committee met at the Court House, on Saturday evening, April 12th, at 8 o'clock P.M. C. Capplemann in the chair. Minutes of the previous meeting read and approved.

Mr. Hihn, from the committee appointed to draft a plan of subscription, made a report and offered the following prospectus for the consideration of the committee:

PROSPECTUS OF THE SANTA CRUZ RAILROAD COMPANY.

This Company is to be organized for the purpose of constructing and maintaining a Narrow Gauge Railroad, through the entire length of Santa Cruz County, from the northern to southern boundary thereof, on as direct a line, on, along or near the Coast as shall be practicable. The entire length of the road to be forty miles.

The Company shall be incorporated under the laws of the State of California, with a subscripted Capital of six hundred thousand dollars, divided into six thousand shares of one hundred dollars each; ten per cent. to be paid in cash, to Samuel A. Bartlett, who is hereby named as temporary Treasurer, the remainder as may from time to time be required.

As soon as the Subscriptions to the amount of one hundred and fifty thousand dollars of Capital Stock have been secured, and the assurance is given by the legally constituted authorities of Santa Cruz county, that all the aid within the power of the County to give, to wit: The sum of $6,000 for each mile of railroad constructed—will be extended by them in aid of the construction of the road, as the same shall be constructed, the Company shall be *organized* and the construction of the road shall be commenced at the Town of Santa Cruz, and continued thence eastwardly until completed to a point at or near the Pajaro Depot, on the line of the Southern Pacific Railroad.

The estimated cost, based upon surveys, of constructing and equipping the portion of the road between the town of Santa Cruz, and the point at or near the Pajaro Depot, is three hundred thousand dollars.

All the moneys, funds and resources of the Company, shall be first exclusively used and expended in the construction and equipment of the portion of such road extending between said town of Santa Cruz and the Pajaro Depot, so far as the same may be necessary for those purposes. The portion of the road extending between the town of Santa Cruz and the northern boundary line of the County, to be thereafter constructed and equipped, as rapidly as the funds and resources of the Company will permit.

On motion, the report was received and prospectus adopted. The following resolution was adopted;

Resolved, That the Committee immediately start in with the Prospectus, Messrs. Pray, Kirby, Capplemann and Effey were added to the Committee on subscriptions, to canvass the town and see every man. Messrs. Cunningham, Ashley and Day were appointed a special Committee to canvass Felton.

The committee then adjourned to Wednesday evening, April 16th.

April 16th, 1873.

The committee met at the Court House, at 8 o'clock P.M. Minutes of the previous meeting read and approved. The committee on canvassing for subscriptions, reported progress, and stated that they were greatly encouraged by the liberal subscriptions which had met them everywhere. The people never seemed more earnest than now, and the committee were confident that the entire amount required would soon be raised.

All who have not subscribed, are requested to be ready with their subscriptions, as they will be visited by the committee before the close of the week.

After hearing the report of the canvassing committee, the committee adjourned to meet at the Court House, on Saturday evening, April 18th, at 8 o'clock sharp. A full attendance of the committee is requested.

R. Conant. Secretary.

527. *The Pajaronian*, April 24, 1873 (2:2)

The Coast Railroad.

Strenuous endeavors are being made by prominent persons in Santa Cruz and San Francisco, and also by parties along the coast between the latter places, to construct a railroad from San Francisco via Santa Cruz to connect with the Southern Pacific at Watsonville. Should it be constructed, (and if capitalists manage the matter properly there is a probability that it will be,) there are a few ideas regarding the enterprise that are worthy of consideration.

It cannot be denied that the Coast country between Watsonville and San Francisco is of vast importance to the State, and a railroad passing through this section will open up a splendid agricultural country as well as immense forests of valuable lumber, to say nothing of several streams where there is good water power, large tracts of country suitable for dairies, besides on the route is to be found lime, coal and various minerals. A narrow gauge road would meet all the requirements of this section spoken of and after a time would undoubtedly pay a good percentage on the investment. Now here is the principal point to which we call attention. If our remarks above are correct, as to the value of the country through which the road passes, and that the investment will pay, it will be the height of folly to connect with the Southern Pacific in Monterey county, for a road from Watsonville to San Francisco, will necessarily take all the freight and travel between those two points, which will fully meet the capacity of the road, consequently there will be no need of connecting with another road. Aside from this view of the subject, there will be great danger of the Coast line being merged into the larger corporation in case a connection is made, and the people be worse off than before. Whether the road will be constructed or not, of course we can form no idea, but we offer the above for consideration in case a movement is made to construct the road.

528. *The Pajaronian*, April 24, 1873 (3:3)
Items from Santa Cruz.

The subscription to the stock for a narrow gauge road between Watsonville and Santa Cruz is progressing finely, and before the first of May the desired one hundred and fifty thousand dollar will be taken, and the building of the road this summer, ensured. There was never before a more determined feeling manifested by this people than to day, and the railroad will be constructed despite the few discouraging features. The Town is now over run with visitors, all awaiting the opening of the New Hotel, which by the way will be the most superb establishment of the kind yet stated in this delightful place.

529. *The Santa Cruz Sentinel*, April 26, 1873 (3:2)
Railroad Meeting.

The Executive R. R. Committee meets at the Court House, this Saturday evening, at 8 o'clock, sharp. A full attendance of members is requested.

530. *The Pajaronian*, May 1, 1873 (5:1)
Santa Cruz Items.

The Citizens' railroad Committee are confident that the requisite amount—$150,000—will be taken by those having faith in a Narrow Gauge road. Some $80,000, is said to have been taken, through Mr. Hihn's exertions in San Francisco. The remaining $70,000, will be easily secured here. The aim now is to secure an amount sufficient to guaranty its building through to San Mateo county, a matter that San Francisco is becoming very anxious about. An extra $100,000, in the way of valid subscription will give the project definite shape and the people a road of some intrinsic value in the county. Mr. Plat the great Narrow Gauge man of this State has been in town and says that if the people don't want to build this road, he will take the subsidy and do so. He also says that there is no possible doubt but that the road will pay handsomely, but that it is doubtful if a broad gauge could be made to pay. We have much to fear from the broad gauge folks; they will squelch all narrow gauge enterprises if possible, and more particularly this, because if the road is constructed through this county and through San Mateo county to the city, it will be but the inauguration of a narrow gauge system for the whole Southern Country, and this will run counter to the interests of King Scott and Stanford. It is to be hoped that our people will act determinedly and push this road through as it is now contemplated.

531. *The Santa Cruz Sentinel,* May 3, 1873 (2:1)
Railroad Prospects.

We are now enabled to announce that there is a fair prospect that the Railroad (Narrow-Gauge) will be built, not only entirely through the County, along the coast, but in a brief time to San Francisco. The only thing that

The Dream of Steam, 1854–1873

can prevent this, is treachery on the part of interested parties or a failure to secure the subsidy and amount already subscribed or promised. The subsidy amounts to—at 41 miles of road—$252,000, and over $120,000 have already been subscribed or promised by reliable firms, for the road. There remains to be taken, in stock, only $40,000, of which some have been promised and many small subscriptions have or will be doubled to make up the deficit.

There is a healthy showing, It should be remembered that only two subscribers—F. A. Hihn and Claus Spreckles—took heavy amounts, they subscribing $20,000 each, or 200 shares, at $100 per share. The great mass of the subscriptions are $100, each signer taking one share. Now if three-fourths of these signers will increase their subscriptions another share the road will commence immediately. Let the effort be made.

We here would say a word about the financial policy of the leading subscribers. They could go on and build the road with the amount already subscribed were they willing to issue first mortgage bonds, at 75 cents on the dollar, to complete the road. But this contingency will be avoided. They intend to go on a cash basis, and not tie up the interests of subscribers or the earnings of the road in such a manner that no profits would accrue. It would be an easy matter to make a contract with a Company to build the road; they to furnish, contract and supply all the labor and material, at their own price for it. Our leading subscribers will not permit such a contingency. They will see that for every dollar expended there will be a dollar of value received to show for it. This plan, prudently managed, will soon enable the stockholders to realize a profit or full value on the stock held.

We are informed that Major R. P. Hammond, an old and experienced Railroad man, will offer to build the road for the subsidy and $50,000 worth of additional stock subscribed. This plan is a good one, provided the stock could be secured; the result would be a wide gauge road, and for the present, only to Santa Cruz. We could then go on and build a narrow gauge, up the San Lorenzo to Boulder Creek, and along the coast to our County line, at our leisure, and as convenience or necessity dictated. The Powder Mills would send and received all their freight over a wide gauge, but will not, it is inferred, patronize a narrow gauge, on account of the expense and danger of transferring freight, and the fact that experienced engineers, conductors, brakemen, and other employees, for the first year or two, could not be secured to run the trains.

All these matters are to be taken into consideration, not only by the people, but by the Board of Supervisors who have the power to make the contract, and as the road is completed, issue the subsidy bonds, which, no doubt, can be sold at par value. We have preferred a wide-gauge road, owned by the Southern Pacific Company, if possible. But if Stanford & Co., or Major Hammond with any other company fail to secure enough means to build the road, then per force of necessity we must go on and build the narrow-gauge road—3 foot—and run it in the interest of our own county people and stockholders. There is no doubt, in this contingency, that the additional stock—about $40,000—will be taken. Every man who has taken one share can afford to take another. We have some few property-holders who hold back, and when, seeing the road is bound to be built and the venture successful in results, they will then aid the road. Some of our merchants, too, would double their stock, and thus make showing of more enterprise than their clerks, in aiding the road. We hope the Board of Supervisors will act promptly in the matter, and having full faith in their honesty and intelligence, expect favorable results.

532. *The Santa Cruz Sentinel,* May 3, 1873 (3:4)
Board of Supervisors.

The Board of Supervisors will hold their regular meeting Monday next, May 5th, 1873. All bills against the county must be sent in to-day, or they will not be considered this meeting. This rule is imperative. One of the most important duties of the session, will be consideration of the Railroad subsidy. We don't pretend to know what action may be taken. The narrow gauge project has many friends, and over one hundred thousand dollars has been subscribed, besides the $6,000 per mile subsidy, for that kind of a road. The wide gauge also has its friends, and Mr. B. Peyton, Chairman of the Board of Supervisors, is decidedly a wide gauge man. He wants no lilliputian road, (and a wide gauge should be built, in his opinion) so as not to incur the risk and expense of transferring freights and passengers on to the lines built by Stanford & Co.'s roads. We are for a railroad first, last and all the time; board gauge, if possible, if not, enough will be subscribed to build a narrow gauge, from the county line on the north, along the coast to the Pajaro depot. The road would pass through Watsonville, and give them a direct opening to San Francisco, along the coast. We hope the Board of Supervisors will promptly dispose of the mooted question, as to gauges, and receive the application deemed most favorable to the interests of the trade along the coast, and the whole people of the county.

533. *The Pajaronian*, May 8, 1873 (2:1)
The Railroad.

On Tuesday last, the Board of Supervisors of this county, pursuant to prior announcement, met the Citizens' Railroad Committee at Santa Cruz, and entered into an agreement that may eventuate in the construction of a Narrow Gauge Road between Watsonville and the Town of Santa Cruz, within two or three years. We were present during the conference above alluded to, and feel that it is the desire and intention of the people of Santa Cruz to build this road at an early day. Yet, in order to accomplish the undertaking and secure to the people the full value of their investment, it is desirable that the road be built without encumbering by mortgage or otherwise any portion of the same; and to this end, careful estimates and calculations have been made of its probable cost, showing that in addition to the $6,000 per mile by the county, $150,000 in stock taken by the people, will prove ample to complete the road between the points named,

The Dream of Steam, 1854–1873

making in the aggregate $270,000, the first cost of the road and its appendages. If the road between Watsonville and Santa Cruz, can be constructed at so small an outlay, all must admit we think, that it will be a good investment. Probably when the question of assistance, by stock subscriptions, is urged upon the people of Watsonville and this Valley, there will be found many who will accord it assistance. Of course, another road into Watsonville will be of advantage, probably making a great saving of freight. Again there is a good prospect that if the road is constructed from Santa Cruz to the Pajaro river it will be run through to San Francisco. If a responsible company is formed, and the leaders of the movement mean business, then we say, let all those who are able, do what they can to aid along the work.

Appendix

A. California Coast Railroad Company

Dated June 17th 1867, filed in Office of Secretary of State, June 20, 1867. B. B. Redding, Secretary of State, by G. C. Garrison, Clerk.

Articles of Association of the California Coast Railroad Company: dated June 15th A. D. 1867.

We, the undersigned, being subscribers to the stock of a contemplated railroad in the State of California, do hereby form ourselves into a Corporation, under and by virtue of an Act of the Legislature of the said State, entitled "An Act to provide for the Incorporation of Railroad Companies, and the Management of the affairs thereof and other matters relating thereto." Approved May 20, 1861, for the purpose of constructing, owning and maintaining the said railroad.

And we do hereby certify that stock to the amount of

one thousand dollars for each and every mile of the said railroad has been subscribed by us, and that ten per cent in cash of the said subscription has been actually and in good faith paid to Benjamin A. Barney, the Treasurer of said Company, appointed by the undersigned.

And we do further certify that the name and title of the said Corporation is the California Coast Railroad Company.

—That the said Corporation shall continue in existence fifty years.

—That the capital stock of said Corporation is four hundred thousand dollars, divided into four thousand shares of one hundred dollars each.

—That the following named persons have been duly elected Directors to manage the affairs of the Company until others are elected pursuant to the By-laws of the Company, viz: N. W. Chittenden, Charles Ford, F. A. Hihn, Benj. A. Barney, A. Mendia.

—That the said railroad is to be constructed from or near the Town of Watsonville, Count of Santa Cruz, to or near the Town of Gilroy, or to the nearest practicable point of Junction with the Southern Pacific Railroad, Count of Santa Clara, State of California; and is intended to pass onto and through the said Counties of Santa Cruz and Santa Clara, said State as aforesaid, and that the length of said railroad is twenty miles, as near as may be.

In witness whereof we have hereunto set our hands this Fifteenth (15) day of June A. D. one thousand eight hundred and sixty seven.

N. W. Chittenden	San Francisco	20 shares
Chas Ford	Watsonville	10 "
Robert Johnson	"	5 "
B A Barney	"	10 "
L Sanborn	"	10 "
T. D. Alexander	"	10 "
A. Mendia	"	15 "
Roo. Pinto	"	5 "
James W. Thrift	"	10 "
J. Ordish	"	5 "
Jas P. Sargent	Gilroy	10 "
A. W. Blair	Watsonville	10 "
R. Struve	"	10 "
Hy. Jackson	"	10 "
G. M. Bockius	"	10 "
Patrick J. Kelly	"	10 "
F. A. Hihn	"	10 "
Daniel McCusker	Watsonville	10 "
Timothy Sheehy	"	5 "
Thos Snodgras	"	5 "
James Lyman	"	5 "
James Sheehy	"	5 "

B. Santa Clara and Pajaro Valley Railroad Company

Filed in office of Secretary of State, January 2, 1868.
H. L. Nichols, Secretary, by Lew B. Harring, deputy.

Articles of Association of the Santa Clara and Pajaro Valley Rail Road Company.

Know all men by these presents, that we, the undersigned, being the subscribers to the stock of a contemplated Rail Road from a point at or near the City of San José, in the

County of Santa Clara, and State of California, to a point at or near the town of New Gilroy in the same County, said Rail Road being wholly within said County of Santa Clara, which stock subscribed by us amounts to at least one thousand dollars for each and every mile of the said proposed Rail Road, and ten per cent. in cash has been actually and in good faith paid thereon to Jos. L. Willcutt, one of our number, who has been by us appointed Treasurer; and being desirous of forming a corporation, do hereby at a regular meeting of said Stockholders, held pursuant to due notices thereof in writing, given by our said Treasurer, adopt the following:

Articles of Association

Article 1. We, the undersigned, whose names are hereto subscribed, do hereby organize, form, and become a corporation, and body politic and corporate, under and in pursuance of an Act of the Legislature of the State of California entitled "An Act to provide for the incorporation of Rail Road companies, and the management of the affairs thereof, and other matters relating thereto," Approved May 20, A D 1861, and of the several Acts supplementary to and amendatory thereof, for the purpose of constructing, owning and maintaining a Rail Road from a point at or near the City of San José, in the County of Santa Clara, connecting at such point with "'The San Francisco and San José Rail Road" and to pass to a point at or near the town of New Gilroy, in the same County, said Rail Road being wholly within the limits of said County of Santa Clara, in the State of u.

Article 2. The name of the corporation hereby formed and organized shall be the— "Santa Clara and Pajaro Valley

Rail Road Company,—and the same shall continue in existence for the term of fifty years from the date hereof.

Article 3. The length of said proposed Rail Road (as near as may be,) is thirty (30) miles.

Article 4. The Capital stock of said Corporation shall be, and is hereby fixed at one million dollars, being the actual contemplated cost of constructing said Rail Road, together with the cost of the right of way, motive power, and every other appurtenance and thing for the completion and running of said Road, as nearly as can be estimated by competent Engineers, and shall consist of, and be divided into ten thousand shares, of one hundred dollars each.

Article 5. The number of Directors to manage the affairs of said Corporation or Company, shall be five, and the names of the persons chosen to act as such Directors and hold their offices until others are duly elected, are Charles Mayne, Peter Donahue, Richard P. Hammond, Henry M. Newhall, and Miles D. Sweeny, all of whom are subscribers to these Articles of Association.

In testimony whereof we have hereunto severally subscribed our names, places of residence, and the number of said shares of stock held by each, this 31st day of December A.D. One thousand eight hundred and sixty seven. (1867)

Names	Residence	No of Shares
H. M. Newhall	San Francisco	3166 Shares
Peter Donahue	Do	3167 do
Chas. Mayne	Do	3167 do
H. Barrochut	do	100 do
Myles D. Sweeny	do	100 do
J. O. Eldridge	Do	100 do

Edward Martin	Do	50 do
Jas. O'Neill	do	50 do
R. P. Hammond	do	50 Shares
Jos. L. Willcutt	do	50 do

C. San Lorenzo Railroad Company

Filed June 20, 1867.

Articles of Subscription to the "San Lorenzo Railroad Company," in the County of Santa Cruz, and State of California.

The undersigned hereby engage with each other that they will take the number of shares, set opposite their respective names, in a Railroad Corporation proposed to be formed, under the name of the "San Lorenzo Railroad Company," to commence at a point on the Bay of Monterey, at or near the corporate limits of the Corporate body known as "The Inhabitants of the Town of Santa Cruz," in said County and State, and to run thence up the valley of the San Lorenzo River, within said County, to a point at or near the tract of land on said river, occupied by James King and known as "King's Rancho;" a distance of about fifteen miles; and pay for them as required by law and the by-laws of said corporation hereafter made; and the undersigned do hereby subscribe stock to the said corporation to the amount represented by the number of shares, set opposite their respective names; each share to be of the amount of one hundred dollars; and the capital stock to be composed of one thousand shares of the said amount; and the undersigned do hereby name and appoint Horace Gushee, of the Town of Santa

Cruz, in said County and State; the Treasurer required by law, to receive ten per cent of the amount hereto subscribed; the said corporation to be formed and conducted under the general railroad incorporation law of the State of California.

In witness whereof, the undersigned have hereunto set their hands and seals, this twentieth day of June AD, one Thousand Eight hundred and sixty seven.

Name of subscriber		Amount of Shares	[Seal]
F. W. Jones	Benicia	x Ten	[seal]
Edwin Duerpont	"	x Ten	[seal]
C. B. Houghton	"	x Ten	[seal]
James Scott	San F.	x Ten	[seal]
W. F. Peabody	Santa Cruz	x Twenty	[seal]
S. A. Bartlett	"	x Twenty	[seal]
Joseph A. Stearn	"	x Twenty	[seal]
Edmund Jones	"	x Twenty	[seal]
Sam C. Gray	San F.	x Ten	[seal]
Horace Gushee	Santa Cruz	x Twenty	[seal]

D. California Southern Railroad Company

Filed in office of the Secretary of State, January 22, 1870. N. L. Nichols, Secretary of State, by Lew B. Harris, deputy.

California Southern Railroad Co., Certificate of Incorporation, January 21, 1870

Know all men by these presents: That we the undersigned being the Subscribers to the Stock of a contemplated railroad, from a point at or near the town of Gilroy in the County of Santa Clara and State of California, to a point at or near the town Salinas City, in the County of Monterey and said State of California, which Stock Subscribed by us amounts to at least One thousand dollars for each and every mile of the said proposed Rail road; and ten per cent in Cash having been actually and in good faith paid thereon to Joseph L. Willcutt one of our number who has been by us appointed Treasurer; and being desirous of forming a Corporation do hereby at a regular meeting of said Stockholders held pursuant to due notice thereof in writing given by said Treasurer adopt the following.—

— Articles of Association. —

Article 1. We the undersigned, whose names are hereto subscribed, do hereby organize form and become a corporation, and body politic and corporate, under and in pursuance of an Act of the Legislature of the State of California, entitled "An act to provide for the incorporation of Railroad Companies and the management of the affairs thereof and other matters relating thereto"—Approved May 20th A.D. 1861 and of the several Acts supplementary to and amendatory thereof, for the purpose of constructing, owning, and maintaining a Railroad from a point at or near the town of Gilroy in the County of Santa Clara and to pass through the Counties of Santa Clara, Santa Cruz and Monterey, to a point at or near the town of Salinas City in said County of Monterey.

Article 2. The name of the Corporation hereby formed and organized shall be the "California Southern Railroad Company" and the same shall continue in existence for the term of fifty years from the date hereof.

Article 3. The length of said proposed Railroad (as near as may be) is forty five miles.

Article 4. The Capital Stock of said Corporation shall be and is hereby fixed at one million, five hundred thousand dollars—being the actual contemplated cost of constructing said Railroad, together with the cost of the right of way, motive powers and every other appurtenance and thing for the completion and running of said Road, as nearly as can be estimated by competent Engineers and shall consist of and be divided into Fifteen thousand shares of One hundred dollars each.

Article 5. The number of Directors to manage the affairs of said Corporation or Company shall be five and the names of the persons chosen to act as such Directors, and hold their offices until others are duly elected, are Charles Mayne Peter Donahue, Richard P. Hammond Henry M. Newhall and Myles D. Sweeny, all of whom are subscribers to these Articles of Association.

In testimony whereof, we have hereunto severally subscribed our names places of residence and the number of said Shares of Stock held by each, this   day of January A.D. One thousand eight hundred and seventy.

Names	Residence	No. Shares
Chas. Mayne	San Francisco	4767
Peter Donahue	--	4767
H M Newhall	do	4766
Rich P. Hammond	do	150
Edward Martin	"	100
Myles D Sweeny	San Francisco	100
J. O. Eldridge	San Francisco	100—
H Barrough	do	100—
F Palache	do	100—
J L Willcutt	do	100

E. California Southern Coast Railroad Company

Filed in office of the Secretary of State, March 23, 1870. H. L. Nichols, Secretary of State, by Lew B. Harris, deputy.

California Southern Coast Railroad Company

Know all men by these presents that we, the undersigned, being subscribers to the stock of a contemplated railroad from a point in the city and county of San Francisco, State of California, through said city and county, and through the counties of San Mateo, Santa Clara, Santa Cruz, Monterey, San Luis Obispo, Santa Barbara, Los Angeles and San Diego, by the most eligible route, to the city of San Diego, with such branch railroad, or railroads, through the counties of Los Angeles, San Bernardino, and San Diego, as may be deemed advisable, in order to connect the business centers of those counties with any overland railroad form the Atlantic to the Pacific Ocean, at an eligible point at or west of the Colorado river, and complete the connection of such overland railroad with the city and port of San Francisco; which stock subscribed by us amounts to at least one thousand dollars for each and every mile of the proposed railroad, and of which amount ten per cent, in cash has been actually and in good faith paid thereon to M. J. O'Connor, one of our number, who has been appointed by us as temporary Treasurer; and being desirous of forming a Corporation, do hereby, at a regular meeting of the stockholders, held pursuant to due notice thereof in writing, given by said Treasurer, adopt the following

Articles of Association.

ARTICLE I.—We, the undersigned, whose names are hereto subscribed, do hereby organize, form and become a Corporation and body Politic and Corporate, under and in pursuance of an Act of the Legislature, of the State of California, entitled "An Act to provide for the incorporation of Railroad Companies, and the management of the affairs thereof, and other matters relating thereto," approved May 20th, A. D. 1861, and of the several acts supplementary thereto and amendatory thereof, for the purpose of constructing, owning, and maintaining a railroad from a point in the city and county of San Francisco, passing through said city and county, and through the counties of San Mateo, Santa Clara, Santa Cruz, Monterey, San Luis Obispo, Santa Barbara, Los Angeles and San Diego, together with such branch railroad or railroads through the counties of Los Angeles, San Bernardino and San Diego, as may be deemed advisable, in order to connect the business centers of those counties with any overland railroad from the Atlantic to the Pacific Ocean, at an eligible point at or west of the Colorado river, and complete the connection of such overland railroad with the city and port of San Francisco. But this Corporation reserves the right to unite with any Southern overland railroad line, by its main line, or a branch, as may be found best, and of entering the city of San Francisco by combining with any other road or roads, should the same be found advantageous.

ART. II.—The name of the Corporation hereby formed and organized shall be "The California Southern

Coast Railroad Company," and the same shall continue in existence for the term of fifty years form the date thereof.

ART. III.—The length of said proposed railroad is as near as can be ascertained, five hundred and sixty-six miles, and of said branches fifty-four miles, making, in both, six hundred and twenty miles.

ART. IV.—The Capital stock of said Corporation shall be and is hereby fixed at twenty millions of dollars, being the actual contemplated cost of constructing said railroad and said branch railroads together with the cost of the right of way, motive power, and every other appurtenance and thing for the completion and running of said road, as nearly as can be estimated by competent engineers; and shall consist of and be divided into two hundred thousand shares of one hundred dollars each.

ART. V.—The number of Directors to manage the affairs of said Corporation shall be eleven, and the names of the persons chosen to act as such Directors, and to hold their offices until others are duly elected, are John Forster, M. J. O'Connor, Wm. H. Sharp, A. F. Hinchman, J. B. Shaw, Wm. S. Rosecrans, L. C. Gunn, C. B. Polhemus, Benjamin Dreyfus, Edward J. Pringle, and Edward Martin.

In testimony whereof we have hereunto severally subscribed our names, places of residence, and the number of said shares of stock held by each, this fourteenth day of March, A. D. 1870.

Names.	Residence.	No. of Shares.
John Forster,	San Diego,	620
M. J. O'Connor,	San Francisco,	620
Wm. H. Sharp,	San Francisco,	620

A. P. Hinchman,	San Francisco,	620
J. B. Shaw,	Santa Barbara,	620
Wm. S. Rosecrans,	San Rafael, now at	620
by Wm. Hale, his attorney in fact,	Washington, D. C.	620
L. C. Gunn,	San Francisco,	620
C. B. Polhemus,	Santa Clara,	620
Ben. Dreyfus,	Anaheim,	620
Edward J. Pringle,	San Francisco,	620
Edward Martin,	San Francisco,	620

F. San Francisco, Santa Cruz and Watsonville Railroad Company

Filed in office of the Secretary of State, March 25, 1870. H. L. Nichols, Secretary of State, by Lew B. Harris, deputy.

San Francisco, Santa Cruz and Watsonville Railroad Company, Articles of Association

Know All Men by these presents that we, the undersigned, being subscribers to the Stock of a contemplated Rail Road from a point at, or near, the City of San Francisco in the County of San Francisco, and State of California, through said County and the Counties of San Mateo and Santa Cruz to the Town of Watsonville; which Stock subscribed by us, amounts to at least One Thousand—dollars ($1,000) for each and every mile of the said proposed Rail Road, and more than ten per cent in cash, has been actually, and in good faith, paid thereon to James Regan—one of our number, who has been by us appointed temporary Treasurer. And being desirous of forming a Corporation, do hereby at a Regular meeting of said Stockholders, duly pursuant to due notice thereof in writing, given by said Treasurer, Adopt the following

Articles of Association

Article I — We the undersigned, whose names are hereto subscribed, do hereby organize, form, and become a Corporation, and body Politic and Corporate, under and in pursuance of An Act of the Legislature of the State of California, entitled 'An Act to provide for the Incorporation of Railroad Companies, and the Management of the Affairs thereof, and other matters relating thereto. Approved May 20th 1861—and of the several Acts Supplementary to, and Amendatory thereof, for the purpose of constructing, owning and maintaining a Rail Road from a Point at or near the City of San Francisco in the County of San Francisco, and to pass through the said County of San Francisco and the Counties of San Mateo and Santa Cruz, to the Town of Watsonville, all in the State of California, so that when completed there will be a continuous line of Rail Road from the City of San Francisco to the Town of Watsonville

Article II – The name of the Corporation hereby formed and organized shall be The San Francisco, Santa Cruz and Watsonville Rail Road Company and the same shall continue in existence for the term of Fifty (50) years from the date hereof

Article III – The length of said proposed Railroad as near as may be is Eighty (80) miles

Article IV – The Capital stock of said Corporation

shall be, and is hereby fixed at Three Millions dollars ($3,000,000) being the actual contemplated cost of constructing said Railroad, together with the cost of the right of way, motive power, and every other appurtenance and thing for the completion and running of said Road, as nearly as can be estimated by competent engineers; And shall consist of, and be divided into Thirty Thousand Shares (30,000) of One Hundred dollars ($100) each.

Article V – The number of Directors to manage the affairs of said Corporation or Company, shall be seven and the names of the persons chosen to act as such Directors, and hold their offices until others are duly elected, are Samuel Purdy; James Regan; Frank McCoppin; Thomas W Brennan; A. J. Bowie; C. D. O'Sullivan and Thomas W Moore—all of whom are Subscribers to these Articles of Association

In testimony whereof we have hereunto severally subscribed our names, places of residence, and the number of said shares of stock held by each. This Twenty fourth day of March A.D. 1870.

Names	Residence	No. of Shares
Samuel Purdy	– San Francisco –	855
Frank McCoppin,	San Francisco	1110
Thomas W. Brennan	San Francisco	1110
C. O'Sullivan	San Francisco	1110
J. P. Deyer	San Francisco	1110
Tho. W. Moore	do	1110
Daniel Byrne		
James Regan		1110

G. Narrow Gauge Railroad Company

Filed in office of the Secretary of State, November 15, 1870. H. L. Nichols, Secretary of State, by Lew B. Harris, deputy.

Certificate of Incorporation, Narrow Gauge RailRoad Company

The undersigned intend to form a Corporation as follows:

The name of said Corporation is "The Narrow Gauge Rail Road Company"

The Capital Stock shall be One Million of Dollars, divided into 10,000 shares of $100. each.

The affairs of the Corporation to be managed by Nine Trustees + the names of said Trustees for the first three months, and until their successors shall be duly elected, are:

L. L. Robinson

S. F. Butterworth

C. J. Bruham

Isaac Friedlander

Irving M. Scott

John Foster

Fred'k Mac Grollish

F. A. Hihn

Phineas Banning

The duration of said Corporation shall be Fifty (50) years unless sooner discontinued or disincorporated according to Law.

The objects for which said Corporation will be formed are:

First, To take contracts to construct, equip and operate Narrow Gauge Rail Roads throughout the United States and countries adjacent thereto + to receive pay therefor in Cash, Stocks, Bonds, Lands, and Properties or Securities of any kind, as to this Corporation may seem best. Also, to own, hold or sell the same as may be deemed most advisable by this Company—

Second, As such Contractors to build Narrow Gauge Rail Roads in such Territories and equip, operate and by purchase to own + operate the same as the best interests of the Company may justify.

Third, To generally transact any + all business in connection with the objects sought to be obtained by the creation of this Corporation.

Names	Residence
1. L. L. Robinson	San Francisco
2. S. F. Butterworth	"
3. Irving M. Scott	"
4. H. A. Lyons	"
5. W. B. Bourn	"
6. Wm H. Sharp	"
7. Isaac Friedlander	"
8. Benj. Flint	San Juan, Monterey Co
9. F. L. A. Pioche	San Francisco
10. T. G. Phelps	"
11. J. W. Stow	"
12. C. J. Bruham	"
13. F. A. Hihn	Santa Cruz
14. Fred'k Mac Grollish	San Francisco
15. John Foster	San Diego
16. Phineas Banning	Los Angeles

17. A. W. Macpherson   San Francisco
18. E. N. Robinson   "
19. F. R. Moseley   Stockton

H. San Lorenzo Valley Railroad Company

Filed for record at the request of Frank Cooper, March 6, 1871. Albert Brown, County Clerk.

Certificate of Incorporation of the San Lorenzo Valley Rail Road Company

This is to certify that we the undersigned do hereby agree to organize ourselves into and form a Corporation and body politic and corporate under, and in pursuance of the laws of the State of California and of an Act to provide for the Incorporation of Railroad Companies, and the management of the affairs thereof, and other matters relating thereto:– Approved May 20th 1861 and of the several acts supplementary to and amendatory thereof: for the purpose of constructing, owning and maintaining a Rail Road from the Bay of Monterey at the Town of Santa Cruz, in the County of Santa Cruz and State of California, and to pass through and entirely within the said County of Santa Cruz, up the valley of the San Lorenzo River for the length of fifteen miles, as near as can be estimated to a point on Boulder Creek near its junction with said San Lorenzo River. That the Corporate name of said Corporation shall be "The San Lorenzo Valley Rail Road Company—That the capital stock of said Corporation shall be and it is hereby fixed at Two Hundred Thousand Dollars, to be divided into Two Thousand Shares of One Hundred Dollars each. That the time of the existence of said Corporation shall be Fifty Years from the date of its incorporation. That seven Directors shall manage the concerns of said Corporation, and that the principal place of business of said Corporation shall be in the Town of Santa Cruz County of Santa Cruz State of California.

And we herewith subscribe stock to the said corporation to the amount represented by the number of shares set opposite our respective names.

And we hereby name Henry Philip as Treasurer to receive and hold for the benefit of said Corporation, Ten per cent of the amount of our subscriptions.

In Witness whereof we have hereunto set our hands and seals this sixth day of March 1871.

Number of shares.	Names.
One hundred and fifty	F A Hihn [Seal]
	Santa Cruz
(50) Fifty	Henry Philip [Seal]
	Santa Cruz
Two Hundred (200)	George Treat [Seal]
	San Francisco
(10) Ten	R C Kirby [Seal]
	Santa Cruz
(5) Five	C L Anderson [Seal]
	Santa Cruz
(5) Five	Amasa Pray [Seal]
	Santa Cruz
(10) Ten	Frank Cooper [Seal]
	Santa Cruz
(10) Ten	Mrs DeLamater [Seal]
	Santa Cruz
(5) Five	Lucien Heath [Seal]

	Santa Cruz
(5) Five	Wm Effey [Seal]
	Santa Cruz
10 (Ten)	Charles McKiernan [Seal]
	Santa Cruz
(5) Five	D. Tuthill [Seal]
	Santa Cruz
(10) Ten	J. N. Besse [Seal]
	Santa Cruz

I. San Jose and Santa Cruz Railroad Company

Filed in the Office of the Secretary of State, July 25, 1871. H. L. Nichols, Secretary of State.

Articles of Association of the San Jose + Santa Cruz R. R. Co.

Know all men by these presents that we the undersigned, being subscribers to the stock of "The San Jose and Santa Cruz Railroad Co.," a corporation formed to construct, own and operate a Railroad from the City of San Jose, in the County of Santa Clara, State of California, to the town of Santa Cruz in the County of Santa Cruz, State of California, which stock subscribed by us amounts to at least One Thousand Dollars for each and every mile of the said proposed Railroad, and more than ten per cent on each share has been actually and in good faith paid thereon to Adolph Pfister one of our number who has been by us appointed temporary treasurer, and being desirous of forming a Corporation do hereby at a regular meeting of said stockholders, held pursuant to due notice in writing given as required by law adopted the following Articles of Association.

Article 1. We the undersigned whose names are hereunto subscribed do hereby organize, form and become a corporation and body politic and corporate under and in pursuance of an act of the Legislature of the State of California entitled An Act to provide for the incorporation of Railroad Companies and the management of the affairs thereof and other matters relating thereto, Approved May 20th, A.D. 1861, and of the Several Acts Supplementary to and Amendatory thereof for the purpose of constructing, owning, maintaining and operating a Railroad from the City of San Jose in the County of Santa Clara in the State of California to the town of Santa Cruz, County of Santa Cruz, State of California.

Article 2. The name of the corporation hereby formed and organized shall be "The San Jose and Santa Cruz Railroad Company," and shall be in existence for the period of fifty years from the date hereof.

Article 3. The length of said proposed Railroad shall be as near as may be thirty eight miles.

Article 4. The Capital Stock of said Corporation shall be and is hereby fixed at Five Hundred Thousand Dollars, the same being the Actual Contemplated cost of constructing said Railroad together with the cost of the right of way, motive power and every other appurtenance and thing for the completion and running of said road, as nearly as can be estimated by competent engineers, and shall consist of and be divided into five thousand shares of one hundred dollars each.

Article 5. The number of Directors to manage the affairs of said Corporation or Company shall be five, to wit:

F. A. Hihn, A. Pfister, S. A. Bishop. D. S. Payne and S. O. Houghton

In testimony whereof we have hereunto severally subscribed our names, place of residence, and the number of shares of stock held by each:

S.O. Houghton	San Jose	Eighty (80)	Shares
F. A. Hihn	Santa Cruz	Eighty (80)	Shares
A. Pfister	San Jose	Eighty (80)	Shares
D. S. Payne	San Jose	Eighty (80)	Shares
S. A. Bishop	San Jose	Eighty,	Shares
R C Kurby	Santa Cruz	Two	Shares
John Daubenbiss	Soquel	Two	Shares
John H Moore	San Jose	Two	Shares
Tyler Beach	San Jose	Three	Shares
D. J. Porter	San Jose	Three	Shares

J. Santa Cruz and Watsonville Railroad Company

Filed in the Office of the Secretary of State, January 17, 1872. D. Melone, Secretary of State, by J. H. H. Russell, deputy.

Articles of Association of the Santa Cruz and Watsonville Rail Road Company.

Know all men by these presents that we the undersigned being subscribers to the Stock of a contemplated Rail Road from a point on the line of the Southern Pacific Rail Road in the County of Monterey at or near the Pajaro Depot on said Road, thence passing in a Westerly direction through or near the Town of Watsonville in the County of Santa Cruz, to or near the Residence of Rafael Castro on the

Aptos, thence Westerly passing through or near the town of Soquel to within the Corporate limits of the Town of Santa Cruz, the line of said Rail Road being within the Counties of Monterey and Santa Cruz in the State of California, which stock subscribed by us amounts to one Thousand Dollars for each and every mile of said proposed Rail Road and ten per cent of the said Amount has actually and in good faith been paid to Samuel A Bartlett one of our members and one of the said subscribers, who has been by us appointed temporary Treasurer and we being desirous of forming a Corporation do hereby at a regular meeting of said subscribers and Stockholders held pursuant to due and legal notice thereof given as required by law in writing by said Treasurer, for more than five days before such meeting, to each and every one of us, and waiving any other or further notice herein adopt the following Articles of Association,

Article 1. We the undersigned whose names are hereto subscribed do hereby organize, form and become a Corporation and Body politic and Corporate, under and in pursuance of the laws of the State of California, and of an Act of the Legislature of said State, Entitled an "Act to provide for the Incorporation of Rail Road and the management of the affairs thereof and other matters relating thereto," Approved May 20, 1861, and of the several Acts supplementary to and Amendatory thereof, for the purpose of Constructing, owning and maintaining a Rail Road, as near as practicable upon the following line or route, to wit: Commencing at a point on the line of the present Southern Pacific Rail Road at or near the Pajaro Depot thereon in the County of Monterey, thence passing in a Westerly direction through or near the Town of Watsonville, in the County of Santa Cruz to or near the Residence of said Rafael Castro on the Aptos Creek thence still Westerly, passing through or near the Town of Soquel to and within the Corporate limits of the Town of Santa Cruz –

Article "2" The name of the Incorporation hereby formed and organized shall be and is the "Santa Cruz and Watsonville Rail Road Company"

Article "3" The said Corporation shall Continue in existence for the period of Fifty years from the date of these presents.

Article "4" The length of said proposed Rail Road as near as may be is Twenty Miles ~

Article "5" The Capital Stock of said Corporation shall be and is hereby fixed at Five Hundred Thousand Dollars, being the actual Contemplated Cost of Constructing said Rail Road together with the Cost of the right of way, motive power and every other appurtenance and thing for the Completion and running of said Road as nearly as Can be estimated by Competent engineers, and shall Consist of and be divided into Five thousand shares of One Hundred Dollars Each ~

Article "6" The principal place of business of this Corporation shall be at the Town of Santa Cruz in said State –

Article "7" The number of Directors to manage the affairs of said Corporation or Rail Road Company shall be and is hereby fixed at five and the names of the persons Chosen to act as such Directors and to manage the affairs of said Corporation or Rail Road Company are Elihu Anthony W. F. Peabody Titus Hale F. A Hihn Samuel A Bartlett who shall hold their Offices for the period of one year and until their successors are Elected and qualified, all of whom are subscribers to these Articles of Association and to the Capital Stock of said Rail Road

In testimony whereof we have hereunto set and subscribed our names, places of residence, and the number of said shares of Stock taken by each of us in said Company or Corporation this the Eleventh day of January AD 1872 –

Names,	Places of Residence ~	No of shares.
E. Anthony	Santa Cruz	Twenty
S. A. Bartlett	Santa Cruz	Twenty
Titus Hale	Santa Cruz	Twenty
F. A Hihn	Santa Cruz	Twenty
John Werner	Santa Cruz	Twenty
Wm Effey	Santa Cruz	Twenty
L Heath	Santa Cruz	Twenty
W. F. Peabody	Santa Cruz	Twenty
[???]	Santa Cruz	Twenty
Amasa Pray	Santa Cruz	Twenty

For more books about
Santa Cruz County history,
visit ZayantePublishing.com

www.ingramcontent.com/pod-product-compliance
Lightning Source LLC
Chambersburg PA
CBHW070356230426
43665CB00012B/1142